The Great Psychologists

The Great Psychologists

A History of Psychological Thought

FIFTH EDITION

Robert I. Watson, Sr.

Late, University of New Hampshire
and The University of Florida

Rand B. Evans

East Carolina University

HarperCollins*Publishers*

Photo and Illustration Credits

Page 1, Collection of Rand B. Evans; 18, Adapted from Charles Ede, *Collecting Antiquities* (London: J. M. Dent & Sons, 1976); 50, The Mansell Collection; 68, The Mansell Collection; 92, From Henry Smith Williams, *A History of Science* (New York: Harper and Brothers, 1904), Vol. 1, fp. 280; 105, The Granger Collection; 120, The Granger Collection; 148, From Henry Smith Williams, *A History of Science* (New York: Harper and Brothers, 1904), Vol. 2, fp. 194 [Original in Louvre Museum]; 180, The Granger Collection; 204, Top: The Granger Collection and bottom: from Dagobert D. Runes, *Pictorial History of Philosophy* (New York: Philosophical Library, 1959), p. 180; 230, Top: From the Collection of Rand B. Evans and bottom: the Granger Collection; 246, The Granger Collection; 264, From Henry E. Garrett, *Great Experiments in Psychology* (New York: The Century Co. , 1930), fp. 270; 276, From Edmund Konig, *W. Wundt: Seine Philosophie und Psychologie* (Stuttgart: Fr. Frommanns Verlag, 1901), Frontis; 296, Top and bottom: From the Collection of Rand B. Evans; 316, The Granger Collection; 332, From Francis Galton, *Memories of My Life* (London: Methuen and Co., 1908), p. 243; 362, Top and bottom: From the Collection of Rand B. Evans; 412, From the Collection of Rand B. Evans; 430, Courtesy of Stoeling Co., 620 Wheat Lane, Wood Dale, IL 60191; 464, From the Collection of Rand B. Evans; 500, Courtesy of Dr. Michael Wertheimer; 552, The Granger Collection; 560, Top and bottom: The Granger Collection; 586, The Granger Collection; 608, From the Collection of Rand B. Evans.

Sponsoring Editor: Laura Pearson
Project Editor: Ellen MacElree
Art Direction/Cover Coordinator: Heather A. Ziegler
Cover Design: Edward Smith Design
Photo Research: Mira Schachne
Production: Willie Lane/Sunaina Sehwani

The Great Psychologists: A History of Psychological Thought,
Fifth Edition

Library of Congress Cataloging-in-Publication Data
Watson, Robert Irving, 1909–
    The great psychologists : a history of psychological thought /
Robert I. Watson, Sr., Rand B. Evans. — 5th ed.
        p.   cm.
    Includes bibliographical references and index.
    ISBN 0-06-041919-9
    1. Psychology—History.   2. Psychology—United States—History.
I. Evans, Rand B.   II. Title.
BF81.W35   1991   90-39371
150'.92'2—dc20   CIP

94   9 8 7 6 5 4

To the memory of
Robert I. Watson

Contents in Brief

Part Four   *The Modern Period*   *275*

Contents in Detail

Preface to the Fifth Edition

It is with great trepidation that one takes up the task of revising another's work, particularly a work as well known as Robert I. Watson's *The Great Psychologists.* There were several reasons that motivated me to take up the work.

First, Bob Watson intended his book to be revised on a regular basis and he did so. With his death in 1980 *The Great Psychologists* has gone too long without revision. Although it remains popular and is a useful text, there is much that the fourth edition cannot tell us about recent developments in psychology.

Second, *The Great Psychologists* takes an approach that is not found in other histories of psychology. Bob Watson's use of his "prescriptive theory," basically a multidimensional approach toward describing the patterns of ideas that comprise the classic psychological positions throughout history, is an important heuristic contribution to the history of psychology. I did not want to see the sole text representing that approach become unavailable for classroom use.

Although from its title *The Great Psychologists* appears to use a "Great Man" approach, it actually employs a few individuals in epitome as a way of identifying and understanding the currents of thought that circulated about them and the movements they formulated. This approach has always seemed to me to have a superior heuristic value. Frequently, histories of psychology concentrate so much on the background of the ideas and events of psychology's history that they forget the events and ideas themselves. Watson's *Great Psychologists* has tried to steer a middle course between background and foreground, and I have tried to continue that approach.

Watson wrote *The Great Psychologists* as a textbook. It is not intended to be an intellectual treatise for professionals, and it should not be judged as such. This is not to say that it is not scholarly. Watson was nothing if not scholarly, and I hope my additions and revisions continue that scholarship. It does mean, however, that the book has been designed for upper-level undergraduate and graduate courses in the history of psychology. If it has something to say of benefit to colleagues in the field or laymen interested in the history of psychology and is found on their bookshelves for reference, that will be satisfying, but its purpose is as a textbook.

I have tried to maintain the flavor and language of the fourth edition whenever possible, in many cases updating and reevaluating earlier information. Wherever possible, I have left Bob's words alone. In some cases chapters have been added—for example, Chapter 1 on different views of historical progress, Chapter 17, on American psychology before William James, and Chapter 21 on applied psychology. Many chapters have been significantly expanded or reorganized. All the chapters have been revised and updated. In some cases when new books became available after a chapter had been revised, the new work was cited for the information of the reader.

I would like to thank the reviewers of the manuscript of the fifth edition for their valuable input. They include:

Richard Alumbaugh
Central Washington University

George M. Diekhoff
Midwestern State University

Timothy D. Johnston
University of North Carolina–Greensboro

Jill Morawski
Wesleyan University

Merle J. Moskowitz
University of Pittsburgh

Fred Shima
California State University–Dominguez Hills

Wayne Viney
Colorado State University

The fifth edition of *The Great Psychologists* is put forth in the hope that it would have been acceptable to my former colleague at the University of New Hampshire, Robert I. Watson. His influence on my work has been more than either he or I ever would have expected when we worked together so many years ago. I dedicate this volume to his memory.

Rand B. Evans

Preface to the First Edition

The history of any field of study needs reappraisal from time to time. In psychology, a reevaluation is all the more necessary because a good deal of its history has long been neglected. The history of psychology from the period of the pre-Socratic Greeks through the Middle Ages has not been examined for over fifty years. Meanwhile, scholars in other fields have been hard at work, bringing to light new material and reinterpreting previous findings. The history of psychology from the Renaissance through the modern period, particularly the nineteenth and twentieth centuries, is less neglected. However, relatively few psychologists have engaged in the study of this period, and even here, relatively little has been published.

As in any science, a slow, steady advance is illuminated from time to time by a brilliant step forward. Great men—not science as a reified impersonal force—contribute to these advances. Great men in psychology live on in the work for which they are the inspiration in the field. Without these men, advances would have proceeded less rapidly. The lives; occupations; motives; families; views on fields of knowledge related to psychology; social, political, and economic circumstances of each of these men have to be considered if we are to understand them and their contributions to psychology. This detailed examination is a luxury that could not be afforded to those psychologists who have served either as links between the great psychologists or as precursors. In emphasizing the "brilliant steps forward" of a few great psychologists, therefore, I have had to neglect the work of many others who contributed to the steady advance of the field. A chapter on the work of one man in comparison to a hundred years dismissed in a few pages serves as an inevitable but necessary distortion of history.

Considering the relative size of this volume, full treatment has been given to the Greeks. I think that this is justified; the first few steps taken by an infant science are crucial, not only in deciding its future course, but as giant developmental steps. The history of a science has parallels with the life of the individual, infancy being very important developmentally.

Permission to quote material in this book is gratefully acknowledged both to the publishers and to the authors or translators. From L. H. Blum, *Psychoanalytic Theories of Personality*, Copyright 1953, by McGraw-Hill Book Company, Inc. From E. G. Boring, *A History of Experimental Psychology*, 2nd edition, Copyright 1950 by Appleton-Century-Crofts, Inc. From R. Descartes, *Discourse on the Method of Rightly Conducting the Reason*, translated by E. S. Haldane and G.R.T. Ross, Copyright 1911 by Cambridge University Press. From Theophrastus, *Characters*, translated by J. M. Edmonds, Copyright 1929 by Loeb Classical Library and Harvard University Press.

I am grateful to a number of scholars who gave generously of their time in order to read either sections of chapters, chapters, or groups of chapters in order to offer criticism and comment. My thanks go to James R. Barclay, Edwin G. Boring, Donald T. Campbell, Rudolf Dreikurs, Carl P. Duncan, Stephen E. Glickman, Richard S. Ward, James A. Weisheipl, O.P, Michael Wertheimer, and Joseph B. Wheelwright. Their contributions increased materially the accuracy and scope of this book. In most all instances I found myself accepting their criticisms, but in a few cases I demurred, perhaps thereby introducing errors that otherwise might not have been perpetrated. In any case responsibility is mine. My debt to Edwin G. Boring is the greatest of all. Out of the depth of his enthusiasm for the subject matter and his patience and attention to detail he meticulously worked over my material to improve not only its content but also its style. But my debt to him is greater even than this. It can only be met in small measure by the dedication of this volume.*

Robert I. Watson

---

*Editions one through four were dedicated as follows: "To E.G.B. my teacher, under whom I have never studied." [RBE]

The Great Psychologists

Engraving of Leopold van Ranke.

Chapter 1

History and Historical Progress

*H*istory is a troublesome word in the English language, having a number of meanings and usages. We often use the term without really considering the underlying concepts it represents. For instance, we use *history* to stand for actual events that took place in the past—"It is a fact of history." We may use the word to stand for the writings that record those events—"This book is a history of England." We also may use it to stand for the documents, memories, and artifacts on which the writings are based—"This letter is an interesting piece of history." We even use the word to stand for some presumed underlying but unseen dynamic force that ties events together, carrying some ideas along quickly and holding others back—"History was not ready for that discovery," or "History will judge the correctness of her actions."

HISTORY AND THE HISTORICAL EVENT

The most common use for the word history is in regard to knowledge of the events of the past. This poses perhaps the greatest challenge to the historian's art. The German historian Leopold van Ranke wrote once that the goal of the historian is to show the past as it *really* was.[1] It is easy to come away from a well-written biography or social history and feel that we have made contact with the past. Such feelings should be tempered by the realization of just how hard it is to know how anything *really* was.

Anyone who has dealt with the descriptions given by several people who witnessed or were involved in a minor automobile accident knows just how difficult it is to find out what happened. The two drivers often have widely differing views on who was at fault. A bystander who caught only part of the event out of the corner of his eye, but who wants very much to give a report, may think he knows what happened. Another who "saw the whole thing" from a block and a half away may think she knows what happened, too. Even two unbiased witnesses who were in a position to see everything are likely to give accounts differing significantly in details. Differences in human motivations, ability to observe events, and interpretation, as well as the tendency to fill in gaps of observation with what "must" have happened, makes it difficult to come to any judgment about what *really* happened in a simple event, even one that took place only a few minutes ago. How much more difficult it is to know what happened 50 or 500 years ago.

Historiographers, writers of history, are rarely participants or even witnesses to the events described in their writings.[2] The closest they typically get to the event is through examination of documents left by those participants or witnesses. Such documents may be written, such as letters, diaries, notebooks, and autobiographies, or they may be in oral form, such as interviews or recordings of speeches. If we assume that judgments of the individuals involved in the event we are studying differ in the same way as our witnesses to the auto accident, we will not be surprised to find conflicts in such documents. The historian's work is even more difficult, however, since only a fraction of the total observations of the event in question are ever documented. The remainder died with the observers. Of the documents created that describe the event, only a few may still exist, and of those only a few may have been collected and fewer yet are available for study. Of those that are available, the historian, because of linguistic limitations or difficulty of travel, may be able to study only part of the total.

The historian collects all the evidence available, tries to untangle the conflicting descriptions and then make the best interpretations possible as to the nature of the event. Of course, the historian is also a human being and makes interpretations that may be biased by personal motivations and background. Were historical interpretation not fallible, it would not be necessary for each generation of historians to rewrite the history of their predecessors. New documents are located, new perspectives are found, new theories espoused, the motivations of past historians questioned and so forth.

This book, like all histories, is a second-hand account of events of the past based on fragmentary and often conflicting documents that themselves may have questionable objectivity. All this is not meant to discourage the reader but should serve as a warning to carry historical "truths" lightly. Read with caution and healthy skepticism. This is about all we can do until time machines are devised that will allow us to go back and see the events of the past ourselves. Then we will be at least at the level of the observer of our auto accident.

The term *historical event* also has its difficulties. There are some clear-cut events—the assassination of Lincoln and the sinking of the *Titanic,* for example—but most of the events covered in this book are not so clearly defined. The history of psychology deals with the origin and development of ideas and so does not usually have dramatic, outwardly visible behaviors. The "event" itself may be mundane. Consider Wilhelm Wundt's "establishment" of his psychological laboratory at Leipzig, Germany, in 1879. Were we to go back to 1879 in a time machine, about all we would see would be Wundt giving his key to his graduate student, Max Friedrich. We would still know nothing about the factors that led Wundt to the view that his students should do psychological work in the laboratory or about the part the students played in prodding Wundt to let them work there—or even the various facts that led Wundt and his students alike to believe that it was possible to do laboratory research in psychology at all. The "event" of the opening of the laboratory for graduate research in psychology was only one of a long train of events, many of which are subjective processes in the thoughts of people long dead. The particular event takes its meaning from the context of a wide range of other events. One of the historian's jobs is to tie the events together and to communicate the "flow" of history—the interconnections of events. This task necessitates a great deal of interpretation on the part of the historian. As a matter of fact, the real distinction between the antiquarian, one who merely collects the documents and artifacts of the past, and the historian is the interpretive contribution.

THE DYNAMIC OF HISTORY

The view of history as a collection of events, a flow of actions and reactions, is as old as human curiosity about things that happened before their own time. The human mind has always seemed to seek consistency in things, perhaps more than is really to be found. Certainly in terms of the flow of historical events, humans have not only accepted that this flow existed, but have also attempted to explain the nature of it and the forces behind it. There is a tendency in human thought not only to tie events of the present and past together as a connected fabric, but also to find a purpose for it all.

From these attempts to understand and explain the flow of historical events at least three main views of the dynamic of historical progress have evolved: spiritualistic theory, personalistic theory, and naturalistic theory.[3]

Spiritualistic Theory

The earliest view of the progression of events revolved around the action of spirits. Animism, the view that everything contains spirits and so has a "mind" of its own, is one form of this position. In ancient times, humans explained the flooding of rivers and the damage or benefits derived from it as coming from the animosity or beneficence of the spirits of the river. The coming of the rains, important for crops, was attributed to the spirit of the rains and drought was due to its anger. A rock that fell on Uncle Harry might be surmised to have had some grudge against him.

This concept of nature spirits entering into the affairs of humans was given more definite form in later years in the pantheon of the Greek gods and other such collections of spirits who controlled the actions not only of rocks and rivers but even of human beings. These spirits, usually in human form and with the reasoning powers, emotions, and often the faults of humans, were believed to enter quite regularly into earthly events. In fact, in early times, it appears that humans did not interpret their behavior as derived through their own control at all, but through the influence of external, supernatural forces on them. The ancient poets felt the need to call on the Muses to breathe into them, literally to "inspire," their great poems. This would later become a mere poetic convention, but in early times, it seems to have been a serious belief. The creative process is still mysterious, and to credit spirits with the way in which ideas seem to "pop" into a writer's head is really no poorer a theory than any other. How better can we explain the acts of fools or madmen than that they were being controlled by spirits beyond the human realm? How better could a young man or woman explain the sudden change in attitude about the opposite sex than that some external force—the influence of Eros or the arrow of Cupid—was responsible?

If such events ruled in the present, then the past could be explained in similar fashion. In some traditions, these interventions into the affairs of humans were seen to be fairly random, as in the case of the Greek myths. Here events took place because one deity was angry with another and by way of revenge persecuted a human favorite of that other deity. If that human were the king of a great nation and the nation fell because of his death or madness, so be it. Homer's *Iliad* starts in this way. The reason for the war with Troy stemmed from the infatuation of Paris for Helen, an infatuation imposed on Paris by some jealous goddesses because of Paris's judgment in a supernatural beauty contest on Mount Olympus.

In more personal religious concepts, such as Yaweh, the God of the Hebrews, there is a more consistent plan of history. Every event in the lives of humans and in the lives of their nations is for a purpose, part of some large, cosmic plan about which the great religious leaders of the time could only guess. The Greek myths and the Bible, then, represent spiritualistic histories, dealing with the intervention of supernatural forces into human affairs.

The spiritualistic view of history is still alive today and is perhaps the most widely held view of historical progress in the general population. Anyone who believes in the efficacy of prayer believes to some degree in the intervention of forces beyond humankind into human affairs and thus believes in some sort of spiritualistic theory of history.

Personalistic Theory

The spiritualistic view has had to share the allegiance of humankind with a variety of other views. Its primary competitor has been the personalistic view, sometimes called the "great man" theory. This view is also quite ancient. As E. G. Boring tells us:

> The Great-man theory of history is as old as history, as old as the kings who caused the records of their deeds to be cut in stone in order to let posterity know how it was that they had so carved out human destiny, as old as man's belief that he himself is a free agent who chooses his acts to shape his own life and the life of those others whom his deeds affect.[4]

At least two aspects of this view must be considered. One, the "great man as emissary," blends somewhat into the spiritualistic view and states that some individuals are chosen by supernatural forces to lead or to rule in order to carry out some cosmic plan of history. The other aspect, the "great man as individual," holds that some individuals are independent of external forces, the "captains of their own fate," endowed with extraordinary abilities that allow them to exert their will on the lives of the common people. What these two aspects have in common is the belief that some individuals shape the course of history. Their plan, from wherever it comes, becomes part of the plan of history for their lifetimes and often for many lifetimes to come.

In the "great man as emissary" we find humans acting either as messengers from supernatural forces to the people of earth or as agents from a supernatural force with orders to carry out a particular task on earth. Moses and the prophets of the Hebrew Scriptures and many of the Christian saints, like Joan of Arc, can be viewed in this emissary role. Other individuals are given a specific right to rule, usually from a supernatural source. All the kings and queens of history who have claimed the "divine right to rule," a right given not to just one individual but to an entire family line, have made use of this concept. The coronation ceremony is the manifestation of this belief in a special relationship between a monarch and a supernatural force. The opposite version of this idea is the notion that supernatural forces ordained that certain races, nationalities, and classes of people should serve those endowed by a superior status. For example, the "mark of Ham" was used to rationalize the enslavement of black Africans by their lighter skinned masters.

In the "great man as individual" we find individuals acting quite independently from the influence of the gods, perhaps even in opposition to them. This position was inevitable with the rise of the concept of the individual. It is the position of the "self-made man," the individual who has reached a position of power and influence through great personal effort. The tendency in such people is not to attribute the final success to the intervention of a supernatural force or even to imagine that they are emissaries from a supernatural force, but to assume that there is some inner quality that has allowed them to do great things. *Genius* is one term used for this internalized power. The origin of the term has definite spiritualistic overtones, but the way in which it was used, particularly in the eighteenth and nineteenth centuries was completely secular. Eighteenth-century writers were vague about the precise origin of this genius, but with the coming of the theory of evolution in the nineteenth century, a secular, biological origin was touted—inheritance.

Sir Francis Galton, who had a great impact on nineteenth- and twentieth-century psychology was a proponent of this view. It was a view that fitted in with the aristocratic Englishman's view of life as well, where "good breeding" will always tell. In a number of volumes, beginning with the *Hereditary Genius* in 1869, Galton developed a rather extreme form of personalism.[5] He believed that greatness is derived from this hereditary genius, that it was completely determined biologically, and that the environment into which the individual was born had little if any influence on the expression of this genius. "Genius will out" no matter what cultural or social factors were operating, Galton thought, and fame and reputation are proper indicators for genius and greatness. Other, less extreme personalistic theorists held that there was an interaction between the genetic and environmental realms in the determination of genius and greatness.[6]

Personalistic views in one form or the other are still widely held, primarily because personalism seems so obviously correct to many individuals. Anyone asked to give the names of people who have changed the course of history can do so with no difficulty. Names like Alexander the Great, Napoleon, Darwin, Newton, Elizabeth I, Lincoln, and Hitler come to mind immediately. All these individuals left their mark on their own age and perhaps ours as well.

The most common form of historical exposition taking the personalistic view is biography. Thomas Carlyle (1795–1881), a believer in the "great man as emissary" view, is often quoted to exemplify the entire personalistic position. In his *Heroes, Hero Worship and the Heroic in History,* Carlyle makes the statement that "The history of what man has accomplished in this world, is at bottom the History of the Great Men who have worked here."[7]

Personalistic histories, then, center around the lives of particular individuals. The few great leaders, the monarchs, military leaders, and the like, are the poles around which the important events whirl, and by understanding their lives we can understand the events they determined. This position still influences our everyday way of looking at history. The personalistic view is difficult to refute and yet, the old question still lingers: Do people do great things because there is some quality of "greatness" in them, or do we merely attribute greatness to individuals who happen to be caught up in great or important events?

Naturalistic Theory

Just as the personalistic view arose out of the concept of human individuality, so the naturalistic theory developed from the notion of human society. Whereas the personalistic view depends on genius, charisma, and power in the hands of a few, the naturalistic theory depends on the mass of individuals who make up society and the lawfulness of their interpersonal relations. There are as many naturalistic theories of history as there are naturalistic historians, but the underlying basis for all naturalistic views of history is that society operates in a regular, lawful manner and, if a certain set of determinants occur, a particular social outcome will also occur. The naturalistic view requires a determinant. There are several basic forms of these determinants of which two will be discussed here—physical and psychological.

The physical form of the naturalistic view emphasizes the influences of the physical world in determining human behavior and the development of society and thus historical progress. Examples are geographical and climatic determinants. A simple version of this argument would state that societies that exist in northerly regions where the climate is severe at times during the year must develop socially and technologically to overcome the harshness of their environment. Societies that live in warmer climes where food grows wild and plentifully have not been forced to develop advanced governments, agriculture, or technology. This view would suggest climate as the main differentiation between the development of the primitive and advanced cultures and thus is a prime determinant of their different historical development.

The psychological form of naturalism depends on the lawfulness of human ideas and behavior. A given individual with a particular background, placed in a particular situation, can be expected to act in a predictable manner if all the determinants are known. Expand this idea into the social sphere, and it is possible to postulate the actions and development of a society as the sum of the actions of the individuals who make it up. The laws of society, if they are determined by the laws of human behavior, should also be predictable—if we know all the determinants. History, in this view, is merely the lawfully determined process of society over time. The view in its extreme form denies free will on the part of individuals. Individual judgments and actions are determined by the individual's past experience and present situation. In this instance free will is considered to be an artifact of the psychological process, an imaginary experience correlated with our lawful reactions.

There have been many such naturalistic views of history. The eighteenth-century view was that God invented the universe, established the laws of nature, including those of human nature, and then walked away to let the universe go its own way. Like a clockmaker, God set His clock in motion and moved on to other things.

The nineteenth century gave us a more elaborate version of this psychologically naturalistic history. Leo Tolstoy developed such a theory in his novel, *War and Peace.* In Book Nine, he sits back from his story of individuals caught up in Napoleon's war with Russia and gives a discourse on the nature of history. Tolstoy defines history as the "unconscious life of humanity in the swarm" in which a man must "inevitably follow the laws laid down for him."[8] History, in Tolstoy's view, has no plan. The flow of events that makes up history is a great stumbling accident, a convergence of countless actions and reactions, much like vectors in some complicated physical analysis of the movement of a physical body. There are no "greats" in Tolstoy's view. They are merely artifacts of the way we look at events. They do not determine the events of history. On the contrary, the events determine their behaviors and, in truth, create the "great."

> In historical events great men—so called—are but the labels that serve to give a name to an event, and like labels, they have the least possible connection with the event itself. . . . Every action of theirs that seems to them an act of their own free will, is in an historical sense not free at all but in bondage to the whole course of previous history, predestined from all eternity.[9]

In Tolstoy's novel, Napoleon's war with Russia is viewed not in terms of Napoleon's will versus the Czar's will, or even the French generals versus the Russian generals. It is in terms of events like that of a Russian artillery commander who does not hear the call to retreat and so continues to order the shelling of the French forces, holding the field for his forces. It is in terms of a multitude of random events that sum together to form a whole that is interpreted by humans as having purpose and coherence. Tolstoy's theory is a vector theory of history, where every action of every person who participates in a given event determines the final outcome of the event to some degree. In part, the behaviors of the multitudes from past generations are determinants of events going on now. Each individual exerts a small force on the progress of events, pushing them this way or that. The direction the flow of events takes is determined by the sum of all these minuscule social forces. The "great" may exert a stronger force on the flow of events than those around him or her, but his or her "choice" of those activities is determined by the pattern of vectors that make up the society in which he or she arose. In this view the existence of the "great" is only a short-hand notation for the highly complicated dynamic factors that are actually operating.

This naturalistic view is highly environmentalistic. Education, social class, patterns of belief, prejudices, fears—all these variables that make up the social inheritance of the individual and produce the antecedent conditions of human behavior—underlie the progression of history.

Perhaps the prime difficulty with the naturalistic theory is that is not possible to relate every event in the life of every person involved in some historical happening. Even if we could do so, it would be a very difficult history to read. No one has seriously attempted such a history in detail. In order to get around these difficulties, writers of naturalistic histories have devised their own short-hand concepts, larger units than individual behavioral vectors that can be more easily identified and understood. Tolstoy, for instance, went so far as to approach personification of these social vectors into an entity which he calls "History." "History makes every moment in the life of kings its own."[10]

Another makeshift term for the complex forces underlying historical events is *Zeitgeist.* The German philosopher G.W.F. Hegel used the term in the nineteenth century, and in the twentieth century E. G. Boring again popularized it. *Zeitgeist* means the "spirit of the times," and in Boring's reincarnation of the word, it had to do with the pattern of societal "forces" that push historical events along.[11] It has been a useful concept, but, as so often happens when a complicated process is summarized by a simple term, the term becomes reified into an entity that has human traits. For example, we can describe why a number of individuals within a short time of each other made the same discovery, even though none knew of the existence of the others. This description can entail all the social and cultural events that led up to a readiness for this new invention or concept. One can summarize all these influences under the term *Zeitgeist* and say that the *Zeitgeist,* that is, this pattern of past events, had prepared society to accept this new invention. The tendency to oversimplify and personify when using such concepts has cast this technique into disrepute in recent years.[12] At the extreme, the personification of the naturalistic vectors of history becomes nothing more than a secular replacement for the gods of the spiritualistic view.

Karl Marx, who developed his own form of naturalistic theory of history, was reacting against the nineteenth century to reify the historical process into something like an intellectual entity. He wrote:

> *History* does *nothing;* it "does *not* possess immense riches," it "does *not* fight battles." It is *men,* living men who do all this, who possess things and fight battles. It is not "history" which uses men as a means of achieving—as if it were an individual person—*its* own ends. History is *nothing* but the activities of men in pursuit of their own ends.[13]

For his purposes Marx chose a more limited shorthand, economics. The economic process is itself the result of the behaviors of the individuals who make up society. To Marx it was the major summation of social forces in the overall flow of history.

> In the social production of their lives men enter into definite, necessary, relations that are independent of their will, productive relations that correspond to a definite stage of development of their material productive forces. The totality of these productive relations forms the economic structure of society, the real basis on which a juridical and political superstructure arises.[14]

Marx therefore understood the historical whole in economic terms. In his view the defeat of the Confederacy in the American Civil War was determined from the beginning of the war by the region's overwhelming inferiority in the means of industrial production necessary for war and by its smaller population when compared to the Union.

Historical Analyses of Psychological Thought

The three major views of history just considered represent broad strokes in the consideration of the dynamic of history—the uniting of historical events into a meaningful flow. This list does not, of course, exhaust the differing views on the subject. There is no way to know which view is correct, if, indeed, any one perspective *can* be correct. The important point is that the approach taken, whether explicitly or implicitly, influences how events will be interpreted.

What is the point of view of this book? The title *Great Psychologists* suggests that it is a personalistic or "great man" history. To some degree it is and has to be since it would be very difficult to consider the tremendous variety of ideas and positions covered in any other way but by picking representative, major positions. Those major positions are closely identified with individuals.

The book is more than that, however. As its subtitle, "A History of Psychological Thought," indicates, it seeks to cast the individuals and ideas under consideration against other events and ideas of their times, so that the reader will understand that the "greats" were significant forces in their times but were as much a product of those times as they were determiners of them. The reader should always be aware that the creativity and influence of a "great" is only one vector or set of vectors in a sea of influences. A book of this sort can do little more than give a partial and fragmented picture.

HISTORY OF PSYCHOLOGY

The subject matter of this book is the history of psychology. Psychology has a variety of characteristics that set it apart from the older, more established sciences such as physics and biology. Thomas Kuhn, in his *Structure of Scientific Revolutions,* has pointed out that psychology, unlike physics and biology, has no paradigm.[15] That is, psychology has no conceptual, methodological, or explanatory system that is generally accepted throughout the discipline as a whole. Although behavior is dominant today as the subject matter of psychology, it is far from being the universal subject matter. Both the cognitive psychologist and the operant conditioner use the term *behavior* but mean very different things by it. There are as many methodological approaches as there are subfields in psychology and a number of competing modes and levels of explanation for psychological phenomena. Modern psychology is not even entirely a science. Unlike physics and biology, psychology has never separated its theoretical functions from its technological or applied functions. In some respects, present-day psychology has developed on the fringe of the natural and social sciences. It has linkages with physiology, biochemistry, physics, medicine, sociology, anthropology, education, and occasionally with history and linguistics. As a result, modern psychology can act as a bridge among a number of disciplines. For that very reason, however, psychologists have not reached a consensus on the basic approach to psychology or its subject matter.

Psychology is a preparadigmatic discipline. It still lacks its Isaac Newton or its Copernicus, although, as we will see in later chapters, more than one psychologist has viewed himself in that role. Whereas it can be argued that psychology in its early experimental days, before the behavioral revolution, may have come close to a paradigm—the study of consciousness—the method of study was never generally agreed on. It is not possible to analyze most eras of psychological thought under a single, universal heading in terms of subject matter or method.

PRESCRIPTIVE THEORY

For the very reason that the subject matter, method, and explanatory categories of psychology are so multifaceted, it is important to analyze the approaches of individual psychologists, the schools of thought they represent, and even the intellectual era in which they worked. Several attempts at this kind of analysis have been made, but perhaps the most succinct of these has been that taken by Robert I. Watson under the label of prescriptive theory.[16] These prescriptions are conceptual dimensions, each bounded by a pair of opposing terms. A given psychological position can be described or defined in terms of the relationship among these dimensions.

The arrangement of these prescriptions in contrasting pairs makes for clarity, since in this way we obtain a summary not only of what the attitude is, but also of what it is not. In almost all instances, at one time or another, the pairs are seen as diametrically opposed to one another. However, on other occasions interrelations within pairs and in patterns of prescriptive allegiance exist which are not bipolar. What prescriptions represent more than anything else is the approach taken to the psychological subject matter, the attitude of an individual, group, or even an age. Watson lists eighteen such prescriptions:

1. *Conscious mentalism—Unconscious mentalism.* Is the emphasis on conscious mental processes or on processes below the level of conscious awareness? For example, are our motives conscious or do we act on the basis of unconscious wishes and desires? The theory or individual who holds more to unconscious explanations is closer to the unconscious mentalism end of the dimension.

2. *Contentual objectivism—Contentual subjectivism.* Are the acceptable data (contents) for psychology considered to be behavioral, externally objectifiable acts or are they considered to be internal, subjective experiences or activities?

3. *Determinism—Indeterminism.* Are psychological events predetermined by previous events or are they independent of such conditions? The concept that humans have free will—that is, that they can make judgments independent of influences around them—is a position of indeterminism. A theory that holds there is no free will, that individuals make judgments strictly in response to influences beyond the individual, is a determinism.

4. *Empiricism–Rationalism.* Is the primary source of our knowledge through experience (empiricism) or is it already in us, to be released through the power of reason (rationalism)?

5. *Functionalism—Structuralism.* Are the relevant categories of psychology in terms of the activities of mind, what mind does for us (functional) or in terms of ideas, the contents of mind (structural)? For example, functionally oriented psychologists emphasize what mind does for us in adapting to the environment. Structurally oriented psychologists emphasize what mind is, the experiences that make it up.

6. *Inductivism—Deductivism.* Does investigation begin with observations, constructing the more complex concepts from the simpler (induction) or are there assumed truths or general principles from which specific expectancies are derived (deductive)?

7. *Mechanism—Vitalism.* Are psychological phenomena explainable in terms of mechanical or physiochemical processes (mechanism) or is there some other determinant beyond mechanical nature operating, such as a soul (vitalism)?

8. *Methodological objectivism—Methodological subjectivism.* Are the methods used so designed as to be socially verifiable or are the methods

employed used to obtain subjective and not necessarily externally verifiable results? The method of behaviorism is methodological objectivism, and that of introspection is methodological subjectivism.

9. *Molecularism–Molarism.* Are the data that make the whole of psychological phenomena describable in small units such as elements (molecularism) or in larger units (molarism)?

10. *Monism–Dualism.* Is the basic underlying principle of psychological phenomena of one kind or of two kinds? For instance, one form of psychological monism states that mind and body are not two things but only one—body. In this view mind is nothing more than the function of the brain. The dualist view would say that mind and body (experience versus brain processes) are two qualitatively different events, which may or may not be directly related in some way.

11. *Naturalism–Supernaturalism.* Can psychological phenomena be sufficiently explained in natural terms or is there a need for explanations that transcend experience, for forces beyond our direct knowledge?

12. *Nometheticism–Idiographicism.* Is the emphasis on discovering general concepts or laws or is it on explaining particular events or investigating individuals? Nomothetic approaches emphasize the average behavior of large groups, whereas the idiographic emphasizes factors that may be unique to one individual or one class of individuals.

13. *Peripheralism—Centralism.* Is the emphasis on explaining psychological events at the periphery of the organism or is it in the more central recesses of the brain? A peripheralist explanation of visual phenomena would emphasize the role of the retina, for instance, where a centralist explanation might deal with cortical currents.

14. *Purism—Utilitarianism.* Is knowledge sought for its own sake (purism) or is it to be applied toward some goal (utilitarianism)?

15. *Quantitativism—Qualitativism.* Are the descriptions or data reducible to a numerical form or to differences in kind rather than in amount?

16. *Rationalism–Irrationalism.* Is the emphasis on data supposed to follow the dictates of good sense and intellect (rational thought) or are there intrusions or domination of emotional and conative factors on the intellectual process? Are human beings ruled by their intellect (rationalism) or by their emotions (irrationalism)?

17. *Staticism—Developmentalism.* Is the emphasis on a cross-sectional view, across individuals at one age or time (staticism), or on the longitudinal view, how individuals or groups change over time (developmentalism)?

18. *Staticism—Dynamicism.* Is the emphasis on enduring aspects or on change and the factors making for change?

As can be seen, some prescriptions are primarily methodological, expressing favored ways of proceeding, such as the use of rational rather than empirical means of study. These methodological preferences are shared by later sciences and philosophers. Other prescriptions are concerned with definition and classification of psychological phenomena. For example, contentual subjectivism, the idea that psychological data are mental, dominates most of the history of psychological thought, whereas contentual objectivism, considering psychological data as behavioral, became prominent only during the twentieth century.

Prescriptions will be used throughout this book as a descriptive tool to help clarify the differences and similarities among various conceptual positions and their authors. Not all the prescriptions are relevant for a given concept or period, and some have been more actively studied than others.

SOME HISTORICAL MAXIMS

In delving into the history of a field like psychology, or the history of any other scientific field, for that matter, we should keep the following principles in mind so as not to get lost in the detail or to gloss over potentially important ideas.

1. First and foremost, remember that a written history is a mediated experience. The historian is always between you and the historical event. The historian's preconceptions, the selection of data, and a thousand other factors make it important for the reader to remember that a given history is *according to* some particular historian. This notion has already been discussed, but it bears repeating.

2. If an explanation of a complicated historical event seems to be too simple and pat, chances are that it is. Historical events are seldom neatly packaged affairs. Usually there are some loose strings here and there. Unfortunately, in historical surveys like this one, in order to cover the broad spectrum of time and events required, we must sometimes snip these strings and give more coherence to events than really exists.

3. Although it is important to understand what a particular writer had to say on a given topic, it is sometimes more important to know what those who were influenced by him thought that writer said. The history of psychological thought in particular is fraught with misreadings and misunderstandings. It is often the misunderstandings, what a seminal writer was *thought* to have said, that has a greater effect on the development of psychological thought rather than what he really said. Sir Francis Bacon, for instance, is said to have been moved to his extreme empirical view in reaction to his misunderstanding of Aristotle. The important point is the nature of the ''spark'' that ignited action leading to developments in the field.

4. Whether a given psychological theory in the past turns out, in our present perspective, to be true or false is irrelevant to our study. To start with, the correctness or falsity of a concept is always from our present context. The future may consider our context false and reverse all our value judgments about the past. What should be of importance to us is how a given school of thought or systematic position influenced the thought of its own time

and how it deflected the course of psychological thought. Phrenology, the study of "bumps on your head," is considered by modern psychology to be mere trumpery and illegitimate from beginning to end. That may be, but as we will see in later chapters, the influence of phrenology on the development of modern psychological thought was perhaps far greater than some other lines of thought contemporaneous with it which we still consider legitimate.

5. Ideas seldom, if ever, die. They may go underground for a while, but they will almost always reemerge, perhaps with a different name and in a different context. None of the basic concepts on which modern psychology is based is new to this century or even to this millennium. It would be rash to say that a given idea originated with this psychologist or that philosopher. The origination of ideas is one of the most complicated and least satisfying types of history to read and probably the least reliable. It is how an idea carries along the flow of psychological thought that should concern us and not who thought of it first.

6. Human thought, rather than being unlimited and eternally original, turns out to be surprisingly limited and repetitive. Actually, only a few basic premises underlie psychological thought throughout history. Watson's ability to analyze psychological thought in so few prescriptions illustrates this point quite clearly.

SUMMARY

The term *history* has a variety of meanings and, although these meanings are often used uncritically by historians and laypersons alike, the various uses indicate implicit assumptions about the nature of historical progress.

Considerations of the dynamic of history, the unseen "force" that moves the events along, can be classified in three broad categories, (1) spiritualistic theory, (2) personalistic theory, and (3) naturalistic theory. The spiritualistic view holds that the events of history are produced by the intervention of some intelligent force beyond humankind; the personalistic holds that some humans are "great," being superior to the common people, and make their own plan the plan of history; and the naturalistic theory maintains that there is no plan to history, that events are determined by an interaction of social and physical events—there are no "greats" in this view.

According to T. S. Kuhn, psychology has no paradigm, no descriptive, explanatory, or methodological approach that is universally held throughout the discipline. As a consequence, analysis of the various approaches to psychological thought requires a multidimensional approach. One such approach is R. I. Watson's prescriptive theory, a set of eighteen dimensions with terms at each extreme. By viewing these dimensions as vectors of human thought, we can analyze and compare the psychological position of an individual, a school, or an historical era.

NOTES

1. Ranke's intent was to encourage historians to be as close to documentary facts as possible. See Georg G. Iggers and Konrad von Molike, eds., *The Theory and Practice of History* (New York: Bobbs–Merrill Co., 1973) for a representative collection of Ranke's writings.
2. The term *historian* will be used throughout this book to denote both the student of history and the writer of history.
3. There are many such theories and varieties of theories. A good general review of the personalistic and naturalistic theories can be found in Sidney Hook, *The Hero in History* (Boston: Beacon Press, 1955 [1943]).
4. E. G. Boring, "Great Men and Scientific Progress," *Proceedings of the American Philosophical Society, 94* (1950): 339.
5. Francis Galton, *Hereditary Genius: An Inquiry into Its Laws and Consequences* (London: Macmillan Co., 1892).
6. See, for instance, the second and third chapters in Herbert Spencer, *The Study of Sociology* (London: C. K. Paul, 1873).
7. Thomas Carlyle, *On Heroes, Hero-Worship and the Heroic in History* (New York: John Wiley and Sons, 1976), p. 2.
8. Leo Tolstoy, *War and Peace,* trans. Constance Garnett (New York: Random House, n.d.), Pt. 9, I, 565.
9. *Ibid.,* 566.
10. *Ibid.,* 565.
11. E. G. Boring, *A History of Experimental Psychology,* 2nd ed., (New York: Appleton–Century–Crofts, 1950), pp. 3–5.
12. Dorothy Ross, "The 'Zeitgeist' and American Psychology," *Journal of the History of the Behavioral Sciences, 5* (1969): 256–262.
13. T. B. Bottomore and M. Robel, *Karl Marx: Selected Writings in Sociology and Social Philosophy* (New York: McGraw Hill, 1956), p. 63.
14. Marx, *Gesamte Werke,* Vol. 13, 8–9. Quoted in Helmut Fleischer, *Marxism and History,* trans. Eric Mosbacher (New York: Harper and Row, 1969), p. 144.
15. Thomas Kuhn, *Structure of Scientific Revolutions,* 2nd ed. (Chicago: University of Chicago Press, 1970).
16. Robert I. Watson, "Prescriptions as Operative in the History of Psychology," *Journal of the History of the Behavioral Sciences, 7* (1971): 311–322.

PART
ONE

The Ancient World

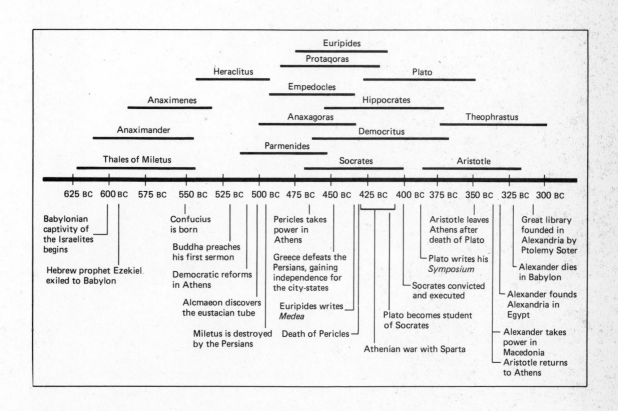

Euripides
Protagoras
Heraclitus
Plato
Empedocles
Anaximenes
Hippocrates
Anaxagoras
Theophrastus
Anaximander
Democritus
Parmenides
Thales of Miletus
Socrates
Aristotle

625 BC   600 BC   575 BC   550 BC   525 BC   500 BC   475 BC   450 BC   425 BC   400 BC   375 BC   350 BC   325 BC   300 BC

Babylonian
captivity of
the Israelites
begins

Hebrew prophet Ezekiel
exiled to Babylon

Confucius
is born

Buddha preaches
his first sermon

Democratic reforms
in Athens

Alcmaeon discovers
the eustacian tube

Miletus is destroyed
by the Persians

Pericles takes
power in
Athens

Greece defeats the
Persians, gaining
independence for
the city-states

Euripides writes
Medea

Death of Pericles

Plato becomes student
of Socrates

Athenian war with Sparta

Socrates convicted
and executed

Aristotle leaves
Athens after
death of Plato

Plato writes his
Symposium

Great library
founded in
Alexandria by
Ptolemy Soter

Alexander dies
in Babylon

Alexander founds
Alexandria in
Egypt

Alexander takes
power in
Macedonia

Aristotle returns
to Athens

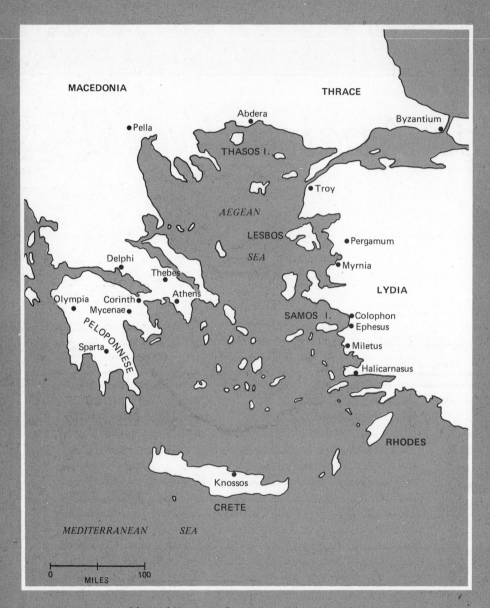

MACEDONIA

THRACE

Abdera

Byzantium

Pella

THASOS I.

Troy

AEGEAN

LESBOS

Pergamum

SEA

Myrnia

Delphi

Thebes

LYDIA

Athens

Olympia   Corinth

Samos I.   Colophon

Mycenae

Ephesus

PELOPONNESE

Miletus

Sparta

Halicarnasus

RHODES

Knossos

CRETE

MEDITERRANEAN   SEA

0   100
MILES

Map of Ancient Greece and its outposts.

Thales to Hippocrates:
Before Psychology

*B*efore we begin our study of the history of psychology, we must address two problems. The first is to define what psychology is and what it has been, historically, and the second is to decide where to begin such a history. Neither is a particularly easy question, nor will the answers be universally accepted.

A DEFINITION OF PSYCHOLOGICAL THOUGHT

Psychology as an independent, academic discipline and as a research specialty, a laboratory science, has been in existence for only a little more than a century. Psychological thought, however, is part of a number of disciplines such as philosophy, medicine, physiology, and even physics, and it has passed under a multitude of titles and used widely differing terminologies throughout the whole history of human thought. In attempting to trace the history of psychological thought, it is important to discriminate psychological thought from the other approaches and concepts in which it has been embedded. Our definition of psychological thought must hold not only for our present day but for the past as well.

Psychological thought has always centered on three fundamental questions: (1) How do I know the things I know? (2) How do I feel the things I feel? (3) How do I do the things I do? The first question deals with knowledge and its sources; it includes concepts dealing with sensory and perceptual phenomena, as well as with judgments, attitudes, learning, memory, and similar topics. The second question deals with feelings and is concerned with the nature of emotions and motivations. The third involves actions and behaviors. These three blanket concepts, knowing, feeling, and acting, constitute the core of what is called psychological thought in this book. In any given period, interest in one question or the other may have predominated to the diminution of the others.

"All men by nature desire to know."[1] So reads the first sentence of Aristotle's *Metaphysics*. A desire to know has served to motivate philosopher–scientists in their absorption not only with psychological matters, but also with all fields of knowledge. We can discern other motives, but the search for knowledge is a basic drive implicit throughout this survey. Aristotle's remark introduces his history of the earliest science–philosophy, which came into being about 600 B.C. in Ionia, on the coast of Asia Minor and spread from there to the rest of ancient Greece. To some extent, however, the study of psychological thought precedes even that distant period and includes civilizations other than ancient Greece.

ORIGINS OF PSYCHOLOGICAL THOUGHT

Aristotle speculated about the origin of the search for knowledge that includes psychological thought. "It is owing to their wonder that men both now begin and at first began to philosophize [love wisdom]."[2] It is in this seeking for wisdom, the attempt to explain the nature of things, that we find the beginning of all philosophy and science. Perhaps it is with the "wonder" about which Aristotle speaks that we should begin this history.

The point of our beginning is a time as distant and as ancient to Aristotle as Aristotle's Greece is to our own time. Aristotle explained that "a man who is puzzled and wonders thinks himself ignorant" and seeks wisdom to escape ignorance.[3] Humans throughout the ages seem to have abhorred ignorance. The reason is probably simple enough to guess. Where there is ignorance, there is fear; where there is knowledge, there is some degree of reassurance and relief from fear. Having no explanations, ancient people devised their own, based on their experiences. Many of the myths and fables that have come down to us from are quite likely explanations used to fill the void of ignorance which early people faced. Aristotle recognized this need well, saying that "even the lover of myth is in a sense a lover of wisdom, for the myth is composed of wonders."[4] We can only imagine the fear of ancient peoples who had no one to comfort them with explanations of thunder or of the invisible action of the wind.

If the objects of the outside world were a source of wonder to ancient peoples, phenomena that were closely connected with an individual's personal life must have been an even greater source of thought and concern. Consider the example of sleep. Everyone knew about sleep, had experienced it, and had seen others asleep, but what was it? In general appearance it was a state resembling death, but the sleeper could be roused back to life by a loud sound or a slap on the face. On awakening, the sleeper might report experiences that occurred while in sleep—travels, adventures, even a meeting with people known to be long dead. Those who had been with the sleeper could testify that he had not left their sight—at least not in body. What, then, was the source of these wondrous experiences?

The most mysterious event of all must have been the observation of death. A person who was alive, active and powerful only a few moments before, was now motionless, as in a sleep or a faint. In this instance, however, the person would not awaken and in time the body itself would alter and decay.

The mysteries surrounding sleep, dreams, and death required explanations, and ancient peoples supplied them. These explanations of the nature of life and death were not just flights of imagination, but were speculations based on observations of the human state in life and in death. Since these observations were based on the human body, they were shared by all people, no matter where or how they lived. It is within these explanations and descriptions that we find the seeds of psychological thought.

Consider some of the differences between the living and the dead that could have been known to ancient people without knowledge of internal anatomy. The chest is the key here, and it is not just by chance that people in ancient times almost universally located life's functions there. The chest contains an essential requirement for a life source—movement. To the ancients, objects that could move on their own were alive or filled with something that was itself alive. The most obvious bodily movement is the expansion and contraction of the chest cavity with respiration. This movement is present in the living person but stops in death. It is also connected in some way with the breath. On the relaxation of the chest an invisible substance escapes the mouth and nose. It is a substance like that which invisibly blows the leaves in the trees and, in greater force, pushes storms along. This substance, the breath, is also found only in the living.

A second movement in the chest is that of the heartbeat. The presence of the heartbeat is a distinct difference between a living person and one who is dead. This rhythmic beat speeds up in a person who is excited or is undergoing exertion and becomes subjectively louder. At rest it slows down. In battle a wound may spurt blood in a rhythm like that of the heartbeat. The blood is warm and moist in the living, but cold and dry in the dead. If too much blood is lost, the heartbeat stops and the person is dead.

So without any real knowledge of the internal organs of the human body, ancient people could well have connected respiration with breath and heartbeat with blood and associated both events with differences between life and death and between high and low emotionality in the living. These observations could easily have been made, and the literature from the most ancient times for which there are documents indicate that they were made. The chest, then, takes on the earliest locus of life and with it the locus of the psychological processes of knowing, feeling, and acting that make up so much of living activity.

In one of the most ancient texts available to us, an Egyptian stele or stone writing dating from 700 B.C. but apparently a copy of a papyrus from at least 3400 B.C., we find the chest region mentioned along with the activities of an entity, Ptah, who dwelt there:

> It happened that the heart and the tongue acquired power over all (the other) members [of the body], teaching that he (Ptah) lived as the governor in every body, and as the tongue in every mouth of all the gods, all cattle, all reptiles, and everything else—at the same time Ptah (as heart) thinks, and (as tongue) commands as he wishes. . . . The company of the gods (of Ptah) create the sight of the eyes, the hearing of the ears, the breathing of the nostrils and make announcement to the heart. (The heart) it is which maketh every information to come forth, and the tongue it is which repeats what the heart has thought out.
>
> Thus every kind of work and every handicraft, and everything done with the arms and every motion of the legs, and every action of all the limbs take place through this command, which is planned by the heart, and is brought to pass by the tongue, and giveth value to everything.[5]

Ptah, a local deity in the Memphis district of ancient Egypt, was later supplanted by Ra (Amen-Ra) of Thebes. In this document, over 5000 years old, the heart or chest region is recognized not only as the locus of life but also as the seat of intellectual functions, volition, and action, in short——knowing, feeling, and acting. This is an early form of a faculty psychology, wherein different operations or functions serve a central executive entity, a soul.

The Hebrew Scriptures also make use of a breath-soul. In the book of Genesis, God breathes the breath of life, *ruah*, into the clay, *adamah*, and makes man, Adam. This breath, once in the body, becomes a living *nephesh*, something like a soul. The word *nephesh* is related to breath in meaning and seems to have been influenced by the Babylonian term *napistu*, which is used for the entity that is in the living but not in the dead. The term is associated with the human breath and with the earthly breath, the wind.[6] In later Hebrew writings, the locus of the soul would be the heart. By then, the Hebrew breath–soul had taken on cognitive functions as well as the role of the spirit.[7] Heart and blood also take on special meaning in the Hebrew texts. The book of Deuteronomy states, for instance, "You may eat meat whenever you wish. But make sure that you do not partake of the blood; for the blood is the life, and you must not consume the life with the flesh."[8]

The Hebrew Scriptures came from a variety of sources and across a large time span. In these writings the life force and the knowing, feeling, and acting processes are located in several places. The heart is the seat of desire, thought, wisdom, and courage. The lower abdominal area, particularly the genitals and kidneys, is also a center of life and the home of the moral sentiments. Memory and emotion are located in the bowels.[9]

We have too few surviving documents to generalize, but it would appear that as thought developed from the earliest documented ideas, from around 4000 B.C. toward the eighth century B.C., the heart and blood competed with the lungs or diaphragm and breath as the locus for biological and mental life. Many of our own common-sense idioms represent some of these concepts of heart as the basis for mental events. For instance, memory ("I learned it by heart"); emotion ("I love you with all my heart"); courage, ("he had great heart").

Mixed up in all these considerations are three kinds of "psychic" entities that should be separated, although they were not always so individual to the ancient mind. Perhaps the first consideration of importance to ancient people was some concept of life force, something that separated the living from the dead—a concept that often translated as "vitality." Second was the concept of mental life, the knowing, feeling, and acting aspects of the individual. A third concept was that of the spirit double, some aspect of the human personality that exists beyond the death of the body.

The ancient Mesopotamians, Egyptians, and Hebrews as well as the Greeks gave these ideas some thought. Perhaps the most significant early document in which all these concepts are present is the *Iliad* and *Odyssey* composed if not written down by Homer. The epic was probably produced in the eighth century B.C. and was passed down orally for many generations before being written down. These tales not only epitomize the views of Homer's day, but also show some fragments of much earlier traditions.

Homer's *Iliad* contains an early reference to *psyche*. Although the term is associated with the breath, Homer used it in the sense of a spirit double, a soul, the incorporeal part that lives on after death. Only several centuries later do we find the term *psyche* used in our psychological definition of knowing, feeling, and acting. Homer represents *psyche* as a shade, an image of the dead person, without vitality, with no emotion, no motivation, and no power to act. *Psyche* is merely an empty intellect consisting of impotent knowledge. Even memory is not available to the shade. As Homer represents it, the *psyche* of the person after death goes down to Hades where it leads a shadowy life after death. Hades is not Hell; it is not a place of punishment, but it must have been fairly dull. In the *Odyssey*, Odysseus goes down to Hades to find out what has happened back home in Attica while he has been away. He has to give the shades a drink of blood before they can take on some aspect of human motivation and regain their memories of past events. Blood sacrifices were a common part of ancient Greek rituals for the dead, and the pre-Homeric Greek graves seem to have been designed for blood offerings for the dead, perhaps to give them vitality.[10] The precise role of the Homeric *psyche* during life is not easily ascertained. It may well be conscious only in human sleep, and its meanderings may be the source of dreams. Homer attributed most of the living human functions during waking hours to three other processes, *menos*, *thymos*, and *noos*.

Menos was shared by all vital, living things. It has been variously translated, though "vitality" is probably the most useful term for our purposes. It was the source of all action in humans as well as in animals. Because the ancients believed that the primary requirement for life was self-initiated movement, menos would be found in some objects which today are considered inanimate. We therefore find *menos* in the action of the sun on objects and in the action of rivers and wind. In humans, *menos* is the urge to action as well as the steadfastness of control, the restraint to prevent action. *Menos* has been associated with metabolism, the slow burning fire in living things. James M. Redfield, reviewing Homer's usage of *menos*, says:

> The life of the animal is slow-burning. In a monster like the chimera the *menos* within is breathed out in fire. . . . Less spectacularly, the vigor of a man is also the fire within him. . . . When Agamemnon filled with *menos*, his "eyes were like to shining fire . . . ; "This *menos* must be fed with food and drink . . . ; it is an organic fire, i.e., the metabolism. *Menos* comes and goes . . . ; it is diminished by pain . . . ; As long as some spark of metabolic fire persists, however, life continues.[11]

Closely related to *menos* is *thymos*, which was considered to be the locus of the feelings and emotions, of wishes, plans, hopes, and inclinations. *Thymos* was sometimes associated with the lungs, the phrenes, but not necessarily with the breath. In a variety of uses, *thymos* could as likely be associated with a fluid like the blood or with the warmth of blood and breath. *Thymos* directed the vitality of *menos* and was a practical kind of intelligence, being more akin to craft than to thought. It dealt with scheming and actions that were part of present situations rather than with long-term planning or creative thought. *Thymos*, then, is impulsive thought, thinking at a practical, concrete level, and it is more related to passion than to reason. In fact, the common translation of *thymos* is passion or the passions. *Thymos* existed in both animals and humans, but not in inanimate objects.

For creative intelligence, Homer used the concept of *noos* which he defined as understanding. *Noos* derived meanings from the perceptions of the outside world and was also the source of the imagination and the consideration of nonconcrete concepts. *Noos*, like *thymos*, was located in the chest region, in the *stethos* or diaphragm. To the ancient Greeks, it was the likely source of the movement of the lungs or perhaps it was correlated with the movement of the chest. *Noos* represented a higher level of intelligence than *thymos* and existed only in humans and specifically only in a few special men, such as Odysseus. Women did not have *noos*. This may be the source of the notion that women are ruled by emotion [*thymos*] whereas men are guided by reason [*noos*]. By the sixth century B.C. women also were said to possess *noos*. *Noos* may well have been the *psyche* in the living person. The ancient Greeks sometimes altered the names of entities with their state.

In these concepts, then, *menos, thymos, noos,* and *psyche,* we have not only a sophisticated motivational and intellectual system, but also an early differentiation between the human being and other creatures. Humans alone have *noos*, that is, abstract thought about the outside world and the future time. Human beings shared with the animals the processes of concrete thought, *thymos,* connected with reactivity and adjustment to particular situations. In addition, humans shared with both animals and all other living entities, including the sun, *menos*, the underlying source of vitality and energy. This three-level concept of life and intellect will recur in slightly altered form in the ideas of the earliest philosopher–scientists of the sixth century B.C., later in the writings of Plato and through Plato and Aristotle to the writers of the Middle Ages and, in many respects, to our own time. However we are getting ahead of the story.

Thymos and *noos* are of particular significance to a history of psychology. They represent psychological functions to the degree they were considered at that time, and as such they represent a beginning of psychological thought in ancient Greece. *Menos* represents the life force and as such is a starting point for biological science. *Psyche* as used by Homer represents an early consideration of metaphysical matters.

IONIA AND THE RISE OF NATURALISM

When Aristotle was talking about the lovers of wisdom, he was thinking about the Greeks of the sixth century B.C. who began formal consideration of the world about them, including psychological considerations. These were not mainland Greeks, however. Homer, in his *Iliad* and *Odyssey,* was writing in the eighth century B.C. about the glories of twelfth-century B.C. Mycenae, what is today the Greek mainland. Homer himself was an Ionian Greek living on the coast of Asia Minor, in what is modern-day Turkey. In many ways, Homer was recounting the story of a lost age, since the glories of the culture of Mycenae were largely destroyed when the Dorians overran mainland Greece. With the dominance of the Dorians, mainland Greece went into a dark age for several centuries. The Mycenian culture survived, however, because of the inhabitants of Attica and Peloponnesia fled to Ionia. There they founded Greek cities, safe from Dorian barbarism where they continued the development of culture and the arts. It was in these outposts of Greek culture in the sixth century B.C. that the flowering of philosophical and scientific thought took place. A main center of this cultural miracle was Miletus in southwestern Turkey. Miletus became the trade center for the Aegean Sea, with contacts southward to Egypt and throughout the European coastline to what is today Italy and even France.

What kind of world did these Greeks of the sixth century B.C., these lovers of wisdom, inhabit? Their environment was still largely pastoral, punctuated by tribal villages. Activities consisted of tilling the fields, bartering in the markets, engaging in mercantile sea voyages, and tending flocks. People worshiped in the temples of their choice, went to war, gossiped in the square, bought and sold slaves, maligned rulers (if the times permitted it), visited courtesans, and engaged in or watched athletic contests.

What set them off from other peoples to make this area the home of a new way of thinking, naturalism? Several possibilities have been offered. One has to do with their religion. Although they were as religious as the still earlier Egyptian or Oriental peoples, it was difficult to be a heretic, at least in terms of the official pantheon of gods. Their priests had little or no political power. Men worshiped the family and city divinities, and accepted or rejected other gods more or less at their own discretion. In addition, these Greek outposts were at the crossroads of many ancient civilizations. The contact with a variety of races with widely differing beliefs and cultures certainly prevented strict orthodoxy of thought which isolation might have encouraged.

The relative peacefulness associated with this commercial life also led to the accumulation of wealth. The neighboring Lydians had recently devised coinage which made possible the accumulation of surplus wealth. This economic structure, in turn, may have enabled some classes to have leisure, allowing time for creative thought. This new thought went far beyond the practical concerns of commerce and politics to the central question of the origin of things and the nature of the world itself. *Naturalism,* the belief that nature requires for its operations only principles inherent in nature without appeal to supernatural factors, found a favorable social setting in this environment.

Miletus remained in the ascendancy about 150 years, and certainly a large number of "lovers of wisdom" there would later merit the title "philosopher." Today we know only a few of the main figures who represented turning points in thought.

We have only fragments of the writings of the early Greek thinkers, but they do show both the breadth of their interests and their cheery obliviousness to incipient divisions between philosophy and science.[12] Their conception of nature was all-embracing. Science and philosophy were one. To be sure, there were a few different practitioners—physicians, lawyers, and engineers—but philosopher–scientists took as their province the whole of the universe and of the human being, speculating, observing, and thinking about the universe—every aspect of it that struck their fancy. Their "philosophy," as we would call it, would be distinguished from their "science" only by the broad sweep and vagueness of the philosophical assertions.

PURISM, NOMOTHETICISM, NATURALISM, AND QUALITATIVISM

To orient ourselves to these formal beginnings of philosophy–science, let us consult its first history as given by Aristotle. Proceeding from his statement about the desire to know, he makes it clear that the early thinkers were seeking knowledge about nature for its own sake.[13] An attitude favoring purism was advocated, as distinguished from the utilitarian attitude of seeking knowledge for its application. Aristotle also considers the relative values of science, as we would call it, and experience.[14] Science is a knowledge of universals, and experience a knowledge of individuals. Although, as we will see, he did not entirely dismiss information about individuals, knowledge and understanding, as he sees them, come from the study of universals. Many centuries later this attitude would be called nometheticism emphasizing the discovery of generalities (and general laws), rather than dealing with particular events or individuals (hereafter referred to as *idiographicism*).

A naturalistic attitude prevails in the writings of the first philosophers. Clearly, they did not share to any appreciable degree in the anthropomorphic interpretation of the gods posited by many of their Greek contemporaries. They had a tremendous confidence in their superior ability to reason, to see the fundamental order behind the varied appearances of the world. They preferred to correct the theories of their predecessors, not by empirical means (that is, by use of new observations), but by pointing out errors in reasoning. This faith in human reason as the primary, if not exclusive, source of knowledge came to be known later as *rationalism.* The belief that knowledge based on experience, or *empiricism,* did exist but only in a casual and incidental form. The use of experiment, the manipulation of the environment to test particular questions, which much later was the preferred form of empirical methodology, was used very rarely.[15]

These early thinkers were searching for the "essence" of things as Aristotle was to call it.[16] They were seeking these essences in broad terms. Theirs was a qualitative attitude based on general description rather than a quantitative attitude based on measurement. Their activities are sometimes called speculation, simply rationalizing the processes behind the appearances of the world, but this description denigrates their great pioneering feats. Both observation and reason were employed as they are still in our attempts to systematize scientific knowledge.

THALES AND MOLARISM, VITALISM, AND DEDUCTIVISM

The first philosopher–scientist, whose thinking exemplified adherence to nomotheticism, naturalism, rationalism, qualitativism, and purism, was Thales of Miletus. Virtually nothing is known of his life with any degree of certainty.

Thales was born about 636 B.C. He appears to have led an active and, to some extent, practical life. Aristotle recounts how Thales took advantage of his knowledge of the stars to foretell a great harvest of olives in the coming year.[17] He managed very cheaply to make deposits on the use of all olive presses during the time of harvest. When his fellow citizens wanted to use these presses at the same time, he rented them at a large profit. Aristotle draws the somewhat disingenuous conclusion that Thales did this to show that philosophers could easily be rich if they so desired, but that their true ambitions were not in that direction. It is also possible that Thales carried out the transaction in order to make a living. Neither he nor his successors were paid for their philosophical or scientific efforts. They either worked at something else or were supported by inherited wealth.

We owe to Thales the recognition that to solve a problem we must look for principles on which to base a solution. In this spirit he approached the problem of the nature of the world itself. Despite the multiplicity of appearances, he assumed that there must be some basic unity of substance in the universe. He reached the conclusion that water is that original substance, because from water all other things—earth, air, and living things—are derived. The reasons for his choice cannot be established with any assurance, although some of the phenomena on which he must have based his conclusions seem evident. Water is the only substance readily known to human beings in the three states of solid, liquid, and gas. Rising steam had been recognized as the same substance as the water within the kettle since that historical occasion when the first kettle boiled over. There are manifestations of water in snow, ice clouds, fog, dew, rain, hail, and in the seas and rivers. Indeed, water appears to be everywhere.

At the very dawn of philosophic-scientific thinking a molaristic attitude was advanced. The definition of a molaristic attitude—a preference for wholes rather than parts, for relatively larger rather than smaller units—seems pallid against the sheer scope of this order. The very boldness of the view that everything is water helps to show what this attitude means. Certainly, molecular units were in the various examples advanced, but they were only parts of the whole which was that which received emphasis.

The early Greeks believed that the individual is composed of the same substance as other entities and, along with all animate beings, is part and parcel of the material world. They used the characteristics of human beings to elucidate the nature of world, just as other matter was shown to help explain human nature. They saw the world as macrocosm and the individual as microcosm, each serving to give some account of the other.

Not surprisingly Thales' choice of the ultimate matter—water—was influenced by biological observations. A passage from Aristotle suggests that Thales viewed the whole world as alive and animated.[18] "All things are full of gods." It is quite likely that Thales was enunciating the common view of the time, that objects that could move on their own contained *menos* and so were alive. Aristotle tells us that Thales thought the magnetic stone must possess life because it is able to move iron, and that the soul is motivational in nature as well. Thales is said to have come to this view not only from knowledge of the properties of a magnet, but also from study of the attraction of briskly rubbed amber for straw and dried leaves. Working with both the magnet and amber and finding the same manifestation of movement, he may have concluded that all objects had the power of movement provided one could hit on the way to bring that movement about, and inanimate objects, through this power, must be alive. This line of reasoning probably led Thales to adopt a "vitalistic" position. Vitalism is a belief that living things possess some sort of life principle, since their activities are not explicable by what we would call physical-chemical constituents. (The opposite approach is commonly termed mechanism.)

Aristotle believed that Thales thought water was the ultimate substance first because all living things depend on water for nourishment and second because the sperm is moist. Considerable evidence from mythology shows that the Greeks believed water was the generative or life-giving fluid.[19]

Although the evidence is scanty, Thales seems to have used deductive logic. That is, having adopted the position that water was the universal principle of all things, he sought out particular instances that supported this view. Aristotle credits

Socrates, who came after Thales, with being the first to use the method of induction,[20] that is, proceeding from individual cases to general principals.[21] This is not to say that Thales did not use observation and thus induction. Certainly his principle had some basis in experience. To the degree that he used a formal, logical process, it was probably more deductive than inductive.

Thales propounded the problem of the nature of matter and indicated the direction for those who followed. Later thinkers offered alternatives to his premise that water was the basis of all matter. Many who came after him would dispute the nature of the primary substances. Anaximenes (c. 540 B.C.) argued that air was the primary material since, aside from its basic state, it existed in the more rarified condition of fire and in the more concentrated forms of earth and of water. Heraclitus (c. 500 B.C.) opted for fire, likely prompted by a desire to account for change, a problem that concerned him more than stability. "Ever changing" seems to have been his metaphor for change, epitomized in the best known Heraclitean fragment, "It is not possible to step twice into the same river."[22] Empedocles (c. 400 B.C.) brought together the earlier claims for a primordial substance by advancing the argument that each of the four elements—earth, air, fire, and water—was a primary substance. In the centuries to come, Empedocles' position was to have the widest following.

The nature of the soul concerned many early Greek thinkers and was often dealt with as an aspect of the problem of the constituent character of the universe. They raised a principal question: were there two fundamentally different substances, body and soul (referred to as dualism), or one substance, either body or soul (monism)?

The Greek concepts of *menos, thymos, noos,* and *psyche* have already been discussed, and the beliefs of the Greeks of the sixth century B.C. seemed to be very similar to those expressed by Homer two or more centuries before. These terms are often subsumed under one term, *soul,* but the reader should be aware that its meaning is not necessarily that of an immortal part.

What was the interest of the philosopher–scientists in this matter of the soul? Their concern was the actual construction of the soul; they sought to discover whether it was made up of one or more of the elements. As noted before, Thales held that "all things are full of gods,"[23] that is, spirits. Life properties were an integral part of his conceptions of all matter. Many philosophers also credit Thales with the idea that soul has its essence in moving and is, in itself, self-moving.[24] Those who came after him were more specific.

Anaximenes of Miletus who lived in the sixth century B.C. also followed the naturalistic explanation for the nature of things. As his element, he chose air which had a long, traditional connection with life and with the actions of the gods. In some regards, Anaximenes turned the tables on the gods. Rather than making the gods the source of the winds, Anaximenes made the air the essence of the gods. In that respect, then, even the gods fell within the natural world of Anaximenes' philosophy.

Air also possessed the necessary requirement that allowed it to be the basic essence of the things of the world: flexibility of form. Simplicius stated that Anaximenes' air "differs in its substantial nature by rarity and density. Being made finer it becomes fire, being made thicker it becomes wind, then (when thickened still more) water, then earth, then stones; and the rest come into being with these."[25] In this system, living creatures are seen as a microcosm of the world order. "The living creature is a world order in miniature. . . . As our soul, he [Anaximenes] says, being air holds us together and controls us, so does wind (or breath) and air enclose the whole world."[26] Anaximenes apparently believed that the breath–soul unifies the parts of the body into a whole. The ancient Greeks thought of the various limbs as having separate existences. Significantly, Anaximenes shows that the soul carries out the central organization of the living creature, coordinating the individual human functions into a whole.

Diogenes of Apollonia, a follower of Anaximenes in the fifth century B.C., carried this notion further, identifying not only life with the breath–soul but also intelligence. He said that "men and animals live by breathing air. And this is for them soul and intelligence, . . . and if this is taken away they die and intelligence fails."[27]

The Greek philosophers became increasingly interested in questions of knowledge and intelligence and ultimately subsumed knowledge, intelligence, and a soul concept under the term *psyche.* This new use of the term *psyche* was drastically different from that used by Homer in the eighth century B.C.

The Milesians failed in their search for a single material essence, but we can hardly fault them, since modern science has yet to fully solve the problem. The failure of the Milesians was primarily a failure of method. They appear to have come to their theoretical positions by hunch and then to have sought confirmatory examples. Once they set up their theoretical position, they apparently defended their positions against others by logical argument rather than by making further observations. This failure to decide which of the possible materials could be the essence of the universe and the failure of method it exposes may well have led to discouragement over the problem of just how much we are able to judge and know at all.

THE PROBLEM OF HUMAN KNOWLEDGE

Once knowledge or intelligence became a consideration for the new philosophers of the sixth and fifth centuries B.C., the question arose as to what was true knowledge and what was the extent of that knowledge. The Milesians seem to have been quite confident in their ability to separate the realities of the world from appearances. They were, after all, seeking the ultimates, the essences behind the appearances of things. They seemed certain that through their method they could eventually know everything.

Xenophanes of Colophon, a poet with interests in matters of nature, questioned just how complete human knowledge really was. He was born around 570 B.C. in Colophon, a settlement in Ionia about 40 miles from Miletus. In 546/545 B.C., Colophon and virtually all of Ionia fell to the invading Persians. Xenophanes was supposedly one of the group that escaped the invasion to form a new colony in what is now Sicily where he lived well into his nineties. His writings were quite varied, including such topics as rain cycles, the origin of fossils, and the matter of knowledge.

In the matter of human knowledge, Xenophanes hearkened back to the older tradition of Homer, before the Milesians, when it was believed that humans did not have true knowledge. Only the gods and other supernatural forces, such as the Muses, had true, universal knowledge. The call to the Muses for inspiration was not a mere poetic convention for Homer. He, as many of his contemporaries, believed that the gods could speak through humans by divine revelation. Homer was probably quite serious when he called out: "Tell me now, Muses that dwell in the palace of Olympus—for you are goddesses, you are at hand and know all things, But we hear only a rumor and know nothing."[28]

Xenophanes rejected the Homerian conception of the gods having human form and human characteristics, however, saying that there was but a single god, whom he regarded "in no way similar to mortals either in body or in thought."[29] Xenophanes' god was a nebulous, natural force with complete knowledge since "all of him sees, all thinks, and all hears."[30] Since human beings do not see and hear everything, their knowledge can never be complete. As much knowledge as humans are able to get, however, comes by way of experience, "by seeking."[31] Although Xenophanes expressed doubt that humans can ever have complete knowledge, he gave credence to the view that knowledge gained by experience (observation) is the only source available to humans. He also pointed out that human knowledge is relative, dependent on context. As an example he observed that "If god had not created yellow honey, they would think figs sweeter than they do."[32] Unlike human knowledge and judgment, eternal truths are not relative. Thus, whereas humans can have knowledge of a sort, only god can have true, that is, complete knowledge.

Yet another Ionian studied the nature of knowledge: Heraclitus of Ephesus who lived around 500 B.C. Heraclitus also sought to discover the essence of things. He chose fire as the basis for all material things, returning once again to the materialist explanation for the world. This cosmological view, however, is of less importance to us than his emphasis on sensory knowledge, that is, knowledge by means of observation. He wrote, "Those things of which there is sight, hearing, knowledge: these are what I honor most."[33]

Observations are at the basis of Heraclitus' human knowledge, but there is more. He said that "Evil witnesses are eyes and ears for men, if they have souls that do not understand their language."[34] To Heraclitus, sense perception is not a guarantee to knowledge, and it is only the first stage. There must be something more, Heraclitus stated; the soul must be able to interpret the information given by the senses. For genuine understanding there had to be reason, *logos,* which, he says, all people possess.[35] Not all people make use of their reasoning powers, however, for they "fail to notice what they do after they wake up just as they forget what they do when asleep."[36]

Heraclitus held that it is difficult to gain knowledge because "Nature likes to hide."[37] He also recognized the influence of emotion on knowledge: "It is hard to fight against impulse [*thymos*]; whatever it wishes, it buys at the expense of the soul."[38] Heraclitus emphasized the importance of living in moderation so as to keep the demands of impulse within the control of the intellect. Sextus Empiricus, writing in the first century A.D., gives some additional detail on Heraclitus' view of intelligence:

> According to Heraclitus we become intelligent by drawing in the divine *logos* when we breathe. We become forgetful during sleep, but on waking we regain our senses. For in sleep, the channels of perception are shut, and the intelligence in us is severed from its kinship with the environment—our only connection with it being through breathing, by which we are, as it were, rooted in it. When it is separated in this, the mind loses the power of remembering which it formerly had; but in the waking state it once more flows forth through the channels of perception as through so many openings, and making contact with the environment recovers the power of reasoning.
>
> Just as coals, when they are brought close to the fire, begin to glow, and die down when they are removed from it, so it is with thought; but when it makes contact with it through the many channels of sense, it becomes like nature to the whole.[39]

Heraclitus is important in our survey of ancient concepts of knowledge because he saw both the value of human knowledge and its limitations. To sense is not to know, but knowledge itself depends on the connection afforded by the senses to the outside world.

Another early thinker who emphasized a sensory basis for knowledge was Alcmaeon of Croton, an Ionian Greek from the region near Ephesus and Miletus. Alcmaeon, who lived in the early fifth century B.C., was a physician and, among his many studies, was his investigation of the basis for knowledge. Theophrastus tells us Alcmaeon's position on the difference between animals and humans:

> For man, he says, differs from other creatures "inasmuch as he alone has the power to understand," since to think and to perceive by sense are different processes. . . . He next speaks of the senses. Severally . . . the senses are connected in some way with the brain; consequently they are incapable of action if (the brain) is disturbed or shifts its position. For (this organ) stops up the passages through which the senses act.[40]

Here with Alcmaeon we find not only a consideration of the sensory basis of knowledge, but also the use of an organic basis for knowledge, the brain, and an attempt to explain some sensory dysfunctions and perhaps even the phenomenon of sleep. We will have more to say about Alcmaeon later in this chapter.

A rudimentary empiricism developed with Heraclitus and particularly with Alcmaeon, since they both held that human knowledge was limited to information derived from the senses. Along with that they developed a philosophical approach to the limits of the knowable. Human could not know all things; that was for the gods. Humans were able to know only what came to them by the senses, and Heraclitus adds that merely sensing the world does not allow us to understand it unless we make use of our logical processes, *logos*.

PARMENIDES: RATIONALISM AND DEDUCTIVISM

At about the same time that the beginnings of primitive empiricism were being probed, another view was developing in Elea, a Greek colony in Southern Italy. Parmenides lived in Elea around 500 B.C. and is often credited with founding the school that takes the name of the town, the Eleatic School. He is variously said to have been a student of Xenophanes and of Heraclitus, but he approached the question of knowledge in a way different from the Ionian thinkers we have considered thus far. Parmenides came to question the validity of experience in gaining understanding at all. His views have come down to us in fragments of two conjoined poems, the "Way of Truth" and the "Way of Seeming." The titles themselves indicate his perspective. There is the way of truth, and this is knowledge that comes to us from the gods. Then there is the way of seeming which is knowledge that comes to us through experience. Given a choice between the two, Parmenides would choose truth, that is, reason, rather than the appearances of the senses. In many respects, Parmenides carried on the limitations of knowledge initiated by Xenophon and Heraclitus to an extreme level. The problem Parmenides faced would recur again and again over the coming thousands of years: how much of what we know is real and how much is mere illusion?

The method Parmenides employed differs drastically from the casual rationalism of the followers of Thales and the primitive empiricism of Heraclitus and Alcmaeon. Parmenides held to an extreme rationalism, in which thought contained the only truth and this truth was implanted in humans by the gods. If something can be thought of, or conceptualized, then it has reality. It is for this reason that Parmenides denies the existence of void—of nothingness. Because a thought must be of something and we cannot think of nothing, then nothingness cannot exist. Parmenides did not deny the existence of sensory experience. He merely considered experience an unreliable source of knowledge about the truth. If experience and reason come into conflict, it is clear that Parmenides will follow reason. Reason and thought give us truth, but the senses give us only appearances.[41]

Parmenides brought deduction and rationalism to its highest point in the pre-Socratic world. What is the origin of safe knowledge? Do we gain it by the evidence of our senses, by observation and induction, or is our knowledge already present in our thought, needing only to be deduced in a well-reasoned manner? The rationalist-empiricist controversy from Plato and Aristotle to the present-day nativistic-environmentalistic arguments are derivatives of these same concerns.

Many attempts were made to combat the radical deductivism and rationalism of Parmenides and his challenge to the validity of the senses as a reliable source of knowledge. Parmenides was difficult to attack if for no other reason than that his arguments about the unreliability of the senses seemed obviously correct. We all know that our senses fool us and that our sense experiences are relative rather than absolute. After eating something sweet, for example, sour tastes much more sour. If two individuals can experience the same world and see different things, where is the truth of our senses?

DEMOCRITUS AND EMPIRICISM, DETERMINISM, AND MECHANISM

Although several thinkers opposed the rationalism of Parmenides, it was Democritus (fl. 420 B.C.) who seems finally to have succeeded in combating his position, although to do so he had largely to divide the psychological world from the physical. Democritus was a member of the school of thought called atomism, a theory that held that the things of the physical world were made up of an infinite number of absolute units called atoms. These atoms had different shapes, weights, and sizes and created all the forms viewed in the world by linking themselves together in various configurations. The inanimate objects of the world were made up not only of these atoms, but animate objects, including people, as well.

Democritus declared that some aspects of these atoms were directly perceptible as a true indicator of the outside world. Heavy and light, as well as hard and soft, are properties of the atoms themselves, because of their concentration. All other experiences gained by the senses, however, are internal to the individual and are not properties of the objects in the world itself. Theophrastus describes Democritus' view:

> Of the other objects of sense he [Democritus] says that they have no existence in nature, but that all are affects of our sense organs as they undergo the alteration which brings into being what appears to us. An indication that the aforementioned qualities do not exist in nature is that things do not appear the same to all living creatures but what is sweet to us is bitter to others, and to still others sour or pungent or astringent; and so with the rest.[42]

Nearly 2000 years later these subjective experiences would be called "the secondary qualities" and become important for Galileo, Descartes, Locke, and other moderns. We will return to the issue of the reliability of the senses after discussing Democritus' theory of atoms in greater detail.

To Democritus, the outside world was made up only of atoms and void. All the things that we perceive are due to the interaction of these atoms with the sensory receptors. The interaction of atoms was the exclusive source of all phenomena. The world of Democritus therefore ran itself. Naturalistic movement alone was sufficient; there was no necessity to postulate a prime mover such as a god, or a vitalistic principle, that the universe was alive with spirits. The service of atoms was accountable for and determined all movement and contact between atoms. There is little doubt that Democritus must be identified as an exponent of determinism, the attitude that explains events in terms of antecedents. He is a mechanist as well, since physical atoms to him are all that is necessary to account for nonliving and living things alike, without appealing to a vitalistic principle.

When applied to the problem of perception, Democritus' mechanical concept gives us what may be called the first thoroughly psychological theory of the mind. Sensation and perception involve the contact of nonbodily atoms with those of the body. Their interaction produces an impression that spreads or reverberates throughout the body. An external object is perceived because in this way its atoms pass through the organs of the body to the "mind."[43] The mind itself is made up of atoms that may be distinguished from other atoms in terms of degree only, being of a spherical shape, having greater rapidity of motion, and showing a "subtlety" of action.[44] For the atoms of the external object to make an impression on those of the body, the former must possess a certain minimum strength. Although it was not understood in this fashion at the time, in the nineteenth century A.D., G.T. Fechner conceptualized this as the sensory threshold. The mind itself rises from the senses, and there is no absolute separation of sense and thought.[45]

To Democritus the various senses reduced to the sense of touch because no matter what the sensation—vision, smell, taste, or whatever—the atoms of the object being senses were interpreted as having come into contact with the atoms of the body of the perceiver. Objects were thought to produce tastes in accordance with their shapes: a sour taste, for example, being produced by atoms that are angular, thin, small, and winding.[46] Because the source of the sensation is at a distance from the observer, vision demanded a more elaborate account. Democritus said that the seen object sends off images that mold the atoms of the air to the shape of the object; this air "figure-copy" touches the atoms of the eye from whence it is conveyed to the mind.

This is a statement of the representative theory of perception which holds that perception represents an object by being similar to it. A faint representation of the object emanates from the object and is conducted to the experiencing element of the body, the mind. Variations of this theory proved so appealing over the ages that they lingered in scientific circles until the end of the nineteenth century, despite repeated cogent objections. It may still be commonly believed that an object gives off some sort of emanation that forms a pattern of size, shape, and color, and that this pattern once impressed on the eyes is carried to the brain where this unchanged pattern is "seen."

If we assume that there is a "real world," that is, a world that somehow has an appearance we can directly experience, then Democritus' view would seem to make our experiences illusory. That is, our experiences are not like the "real world." Sextus Empiricus, for instance, said about Democritus' view that: "It is necessary to realize that by this principle man is cut off from the real. And indeed it is evident that it is impossible to know what each thing really is."[47] In order to refute Parmenides' argument of the unreliability of the senses, Democritus and the other atomists had to overthrow the faith in the reality of the sensed objects. No qualities in the outside world can be perceived directly, they said, with the exception of weight and texture, the softness or hardness of things. One ancient commentator, Aetus, tells us that "Democritus says that color does not exist in nature; for the elements—both the solids and the void—are without qualities."[48]

If this is true, then how do we come to any mutual understanding of things? Democritus tells us that "By convention are sweet and bitter, hot and cold, by convention is color; in truth are atoms and the void. . . . In reality we apprehend nothing exactly, but only as in changes according to the condition of our body and of the things that impinge on or offer resistance to it."[49] "Here by convention," as Galen explained it, means "for us," and not according to the nature of the things themselves which he calls "reality."[50]

Democritus took particular note of the relativity of sensory experience. He appears to have observed that honey appears bitter to some individuals and sweet to others, and he declared that the honey was neither sweet nor bitter in itself. Instead, he said, some condition in the makeup of the individual's bodily structure caused a constant complex of atoms to be perceived in a given way. Theophrastus tells us that Democritus believed "that men 'alter in make-up' according to age and condition—from which it is clear that man's bodily state is a cause of what appears to him."[51] So according to Democritus, nothing we experience is true. Because there are no qualities of the outside world to be perceived, there is no "true" experience. Even more, different individuals on whom the atoms of the outside world impinge will perceive different things, depending on their own composition.

Protagoras of Abdera (485–410 B.C.) extended this doctrine of the subjectivity of the senses into the areas of judgment and knowledge. Protagoras, a member of the group called Sophists in Athens, is perhaps best known for his statement, "Of all things the measure is man: of existing things that they exist; of nonexistent things, that they do not exist."[52] This concept clearly reflects the influence of Democritus' relativistic position.

With Democritus, Anaxagoras, and Protagoras we return to the mainland of Greece which in the fifth century B.C. was in the midst of a renaissance. They were all attracted to the court of Pericles in Athens, who surrounded himself with intelligent, witty people, drawn not only from Athens, but also from all over the Greek world. After the defeat of the Persians by the Athenians in 490 B.C. and its resulting peace with Persia in 448 B.C., the city-state of Athens began to take on the glory which all later ages have associated with classical Greece. Pericles was the elected General from 443 until his death in 429 B.C., the period that is often called the Age of Pericles. This was the period of the plays of Sophocles and Euripides, the construction of some of the most majestic temples of the Parthenon, and some of the greatest works of art of all time.

Owing largely to Periclean democracy in Athens, the role of the Sophists grew to great importance. A Sophist was a person who taught, among other things, proper speaking and techniques of debating and argument. They were simply professional teachers and were paid for their educational efforts. A key to the Sophist influence is the Greek concept of *areté* which may be defined as "excellence." In earlier times the *areté* of a Greek citizen was based almost entirely on family ties, a typical aristocratic view of "good breeding." Under the democratic structures of Pericles' Athens, however, *areté* became attached to those individuals who showed skill and facility in the functions of the law courts, where each contender had to argue his own case. Lawyers were not allowed. This excellence could also be demonstrated in the democratic assemblies, the membership of which were determined by lottery of all male citizens. The literary education of Athenian youth ended around the age of fourteen. The four-year period between the ages of fourteen and eighteen they spent largely in learning martial arts, wrestling, spear throwing, and the like, for at eighteen they were required to do military service. It is perhaps because of this intellectually fallow period, when the youth searched for intellectual stimulation and for *areté,* that they began to be caught up in political and legal argumentation. Law suits became a passion for Athenians. If one were to display *areté* in such settings, however, it was necessary to be able to argue well. To this purpose, the training in logic and debating offered by the Sophists was of great applicability. Protagoras was one of the most famous Sophists.

Protagoras and many of his fellow Sophists taught not only a set of skills, but also a philosophical view of knowledge. Protagoras' statement, "Of all things the measure is man," is a statement of complete subjectivism. If the wind feels cool to one person and warm to another, who is correct? There is no way to tell, Protagoras seems to say. They are both correct, because the reality is in their experiences, not in the objects. Plato records Protagoras' statements on this issue:

> [T]o the man who is sick his food seems bitter and is bitter; to the man who is well it is and seems just the opposite. Now neither of these men is to be made wiser, for that is impossible; nor should it be claimed that the sick man is ignorant because he believes what he does, or the well man because he believes otherwise. But a change must be brought about from the one condition to the other, because the other is better. So it is with education; a change must be brought about from a worse condition to a better; but whereas the physician makes this change by drugs, the sophist does it by words. . . .
>
> But I believe that one can make a man who is in a depraved condition of soul and has beliefs of a like nature good, so that he has different beliefs. These appearances some, through inexperience, call "true" but I say that some are "better" than others but not "truer." And the wise . . . when they have to do with the body I call them physicians, and when they have to do with plants, farmers. For I maintain that the latter induce in sickly plants good and healthy and true sensations instead of bad, and that wise and good orators make good things instead of wicked things appear just to their cities. For I believe that whatever seems right or wrong to each city is right or wrong for it, so long as it continues to think so. But the wise man causes the good things instead of the bad to appear and to be for them in each case.[53]

Through Protagoras' teaching, the sensory relativism of Democritus had become a moral relativism. The point Protagoras was trying to make in the above quotation was that laws of conduct are not absolute; they are determined by each city according to their view of what is best for them. Laws of conduct are determined by social convention. The result of this thinking, however, was far more individualistic than Protagoras seems to have intended.

Aristophanes, the great writer of Greek comedy, charged the Sophists with "making the worse appear the better cause." The Sophists' relativistic views and their misinterpretation among their young pupils became a source of great concern in Athens. Rather than considering personal conduct ruled by the conventional wisdom of a given community, Protagoras' view was interpreted in an individual sense. That is, if a rule of conduct does not seem appropriate to an individual, there is no need to obey it.

Conservative elements in Athens reacted to what appeared to be the collapse of morals and respect for traditional values. The reaction was against not only the Sophists but all the philosopher–scientists who had brought these new ideas to Athens. Thucydides, the author of the *History of the Peloponnesian War,* and Aristophanes were among this conservative element. Athens was not Ionia. Throughout the history of the city, an undercurrent of conservatism and orthodoxy was present. The movement was largely opposed to Pericles and the foreign intellectual element he had brought to Athens. The weapon used against these philosophers was impiety. A zealot named Diopeithes introduced a law against those "who do not acknowledge divine things or who give instructions about celestial phenomena."[54]

The first of the philosophers brought to trial was Anaxagoras who had taught that the sun was not a god but a red hot iron mass. His position fell within both counts of the law. He was tried and, even though Pericles himself defended him, was fined. Having had enough, Anaxagoras left Athens. Despite attacks against other teachers and thinkers, the popularity of the Sophists among the young continued, particularly after the beginning of the war with Sparta, the Peloponnesian War. The demoralization of Athenian society by the plague of 430 B.C. and the ravaging of Attica by the Spartans led to widespread lawlessness, loss of religious scruples, and a general decline of morality among the Athenians. The Sophists were blamed for much of this disarray, and several of Protagoras' later disciples were tried for impiety and for leading the youth astray. The greatest of the thinkers who were tried and executed was the very individual who had laid the basis for a refutation of the relativist skepticism of the Sophists—Socrates of Athens. This aspect of Greek history is mentioned here both to demonstrate the thinking of Protagoras, and to show how scientific and educational theory can have direct influence (or have such influences attributed to it) on society.

With the coming of Socrates, we can close the first major period of psychological thought in philosophy, beginning with Thales of Miletus and ending with the philosophical anarchy of the Athenian Sophists. The dominant component of psychological thought in this section has been the origin and source of knowledge. For consideration of emotion and motivation, however, we need to refer not so much to the philosophers but to playwrights and others in Athens during the Age of Pericles.

EMOTIONS AND DESIRES: IRRATIONALISM AND DETERMINISM

The Athenian Greeks were interested in the nature of human desires but did not add significantly to the view of *thymos* versus *noos* presented by Homer. Democritus held, for instance, that "Violent desires for one thing blind the soul to all others."[55]

The best documentation we have about desire and emotion in this period comes not from philosophers but from playwrights. Euripides (480–406 B.C.) is a good source for this "artistic" psychology. He was the most realistic of the Greek writers of tragedy, making less use of the religious and artistic convention of gods as being the source of the behaviors of humans than his predecessors, Aeschylus, and Sophocles. Generally, Euripides portrayed the actions of his characters as based on human motives. In his play *Medea,* performed in Athens in 431 B.C., for instance, Euripides presented a situation in which the love between Medea and her husband Jason, the argonaut, has turned to hatred. Jason had deserted Medea and their two children for another woman. The hatred leads to a compulsion for revenge, even though that revenge requires her to kill her two children and thus bring grief and suffering on herself as well as on Jason. Even though she is able to reason out why she should not commit the act and even though she knows this action will destroy her as well, the compulsion toward revenge overcomes her reason. The last line of the monologue summarizes her realization: "At last I understand the awful deed I am to do; but passion [*thymos*], that cause of direst woes to mortal man, hath triumphed o'er my sober thoughts."[56] This play is a classic representation of the battle between the rational and irrational aspects of human motivation and reflects the conflict of *thymos* versus *noos* of Homer's epic. Euripides represents the conflict as an internal one and not determined by outside forces. Although Euripides still used the gods as dramatic devices in his plays, he was far more naturalistic than most writers of his day.

Emotion and motivation are also considered in the writings of Thucydides. In his history of the Peloponnesian War, Thucydides repeats a debate between the Athenian military strongman, Cleon, and a citizen of Athens named Diodotus. The debate has to do with what Cleon would do to the people of Mytilene, who, with three other walled towns on Lesbos, had revolted against the Athenians in 428 B.C. Cleon's solution is to massacre the population, thus providing a lesson to any other cities contemplating revolt. Diodotus disagreed with the efficacy of even the death penalty to prevent such revolts.

> Now of course communities have enacted the penalty of death for many offences far lighter than this: still hope leads men to venture, and no one ever yet put himself in peril without the inward conviction that he would succeed in his design. Again, was there ever a city rebelling that did not believe that it possessed either in itself or in its alliances resources adequate to the enterprise? All states and individuals are prone to err, and there is no law that will prevent them. . . . Either than some means of terror more terrible than this [death] must be discovered, or it must be owned that this restraint is useless; and that as long as poverty gives men the courage of necessity, or plenty fills them with the ambition which belongs to insolence and pride, and the other conditions of life remain each under the thralldom of some fatal and master passion, so long will the impulse never be wanting to drive men into danger. Hope also and cupidity, the one leading and the other following, the one conceiving the attempt, the other suggesting the facility of succeeding, cause the wildest ruin, and although invisible agents, are far stronger than the dangers that are seen.[57]

So, according to Diodotus, Cleon's "example" would do nothing to discourage future revolts. Diodotus subscribed to a naturalistic determinism; that is, humans are driven by natural laws that can and do overwhelm their reason and sometimes lead them to break the laws of convention regardless of the penalties. Our behavior is determined not only by reason, but also by the influence of other factors, including needs and passion. This consideration of natural law versus human, conventional law in human affairs became an issue of great concern during the shakeup of Athenian society during the Peloponnesian War. Thinkers began to turn away from the consideration of the natural world outside of the individual and toward the inner world of human motivations and morality. Not surprisingly, the two great "psychological" thinkers from this period, Socrates and Plato, focused more on ethics than on problems of knowledge.

At the same time that philosophers were the origin of knowledge, ideas of significance to psychology were emerging from another source—medicine.

HIPPOCRATES AND THE NATURALISTIC CONTRIBUTION FROM MEDICINE AND THE BEGINNINGS OF IDIOGRAPHICISM

Medicine and psychology share an interest in the functioning of the human body and mind, and by the very nature of their art, medical practitioners must pay attention to the individual. Physicians are committed to an idiographic attitude: they must explain and treat the problems of individual patients. Treatment is to be determined by symptoms, not by some deduction from an abstract principle of the nature of the individual. This approach stands in sharp contrast to the nomothetic attitude of earlier philosophers who sought general understanding rather than knowledge of particulars. But in later ages psychology would include within its scope mind–body problems of a psychosomatic nature. On these two counts, then, medicine is relevant to the history of psychology.

It is in the *Odyssey* of Homer that we first hear of Greek medical practitioners. They made their way through the land—coming into homes to sell their services to those who had use for them—and then moved on.[58] The sign of a highly successful practitioner was the fame that preceded him wherever he went and that lingered until his return. Aesculapius, the first Greek physician of whom we have knowledge, was just such a person. His fame was so great that after his death he was deified, with over 300 temples erected in his honor. His priests jealously guarded their knowledge, passing it on only to those of the next generation whom they initiated into its mysteries.

Although instances of surgical operations were not uncommon, the percentage of cures of blindness and of lameness reported in the records that survive seems very high. This suggests that many of these maladies had a psychosomatic basis. A favorable receptivity to the suggestive influences of temple healing may have been due to the reports of wonderful cures, and the use of rituals such as the "wait to be received," the period of purification before admission to the sanctuary. There was also the wearing of special robes and the drinking of sacred waters.[59] The peak of the treatment was the incubation, a period of sleep in the sanctuary. Several characteristic phenomena were associated with the incubation. The patient, for example, might see an apparition of a god and receive from him a message specific to his illness. He might have a dream in which a priest or a god would tell him what to do (an oracle), a dream foretelling the future (a vision), or even one in which the cure itself occurred. A certain amount of rational treatment, such as the occasional use of drugs, was combined with these magical practices, but surgical treatment, bleeding, and massage were left to the layperson. As a consequence, the medical experience accumulated by the priests was almost exclusively "psychological" in nature. Faith healing, tempered by a bit of scanty scientific observation, epitomized the approach of temple medicine.

Alcmaeon of Croton

Gradually, a new and more naturalistic and rationally based medicine, relatively divorced from the supernatural and irrational aspects of temple medicine, began to emerge. One of its founders who has already been mentioned in this chapter was Alcmaeon of Croton, a physician who lived at the beginning of the fifth century B.C. Almost nothing is known of his life, and only sparse fragments of his writings remain. Many of these fragments, however, are of psychological and physiological importance. After discovering passages from the eyes to the brain, Alcmaeon concluded that the brain not only received perceptions of vision, audition, and olfaction, but was also the seat of thought.[60] Because he considered it the central organ of intellectual activity, Alcmaeon called the brain the soul. This was his way of naming the vital principle or source of life. Alcmaeon did not use the word *soul* in a theological sense and did not necessarily give it a connotation of immortality. Soul was simply a convenient name for the central psychological agency. In fact, he did accept the immortality of the soul, for he considered it to be self-moving, but his naturalistic description of it was divorced from his speculations about immortality.[61]

Alcmaeon made the advance of unifying the two entities or aspects of the soul, formerly localized in the head and lungs, into one entity centering in the head—one soul, which performed all mental functions. Alcmaeon taught that the brain, where all sensations are "somehow fitted together," contains the governing faculty of the soul.[62] This brain is also the seat of thought; it serves to store and arrange perceptions, and is responsible for memory and belief. Alcmaeon held that sensations reach the brain through the medium of channels that start with the organs of sense. These passages were not the nerves as such, but, rather, channels for breath, the pneuma.

Alcmaeon recognized thinking and perceiving as separate processes. To put it in his terminology, Alcmaeon made a distinction between intelligence and sensation, claiming that the human being alone understands, whereas other creatures have sense perception but are without understanding.[63] This distinction between perception, or what is acquired through sensory experience, and understanding, which is independent of sensory experience, was to become a major concern for the Greeks, reaching its culmination in the formulations of Plato.

Alcmaeon's work on the senses was based on observation of surgical operations. Tradition has it that he was the first to undertake the excision of a human eye.[64] His anatomical studies led him to the statement that the eye is enclosed in a membrane and is connected with the brain by "light-bearing paths" that join behind the forehead. That these paths (the optic nerves) join, he showed by dissection. He also observed that the eyes move together, not separately. The function of seeing, he stated, was made possible by the water and fire in the eye. Fire was thought to be present because when the eye is struck by a blow one sees light (intraocular light); the "water" of which he speaks is the aqueous humor. His theory attempted to combine the concept of vision as a radiation from the eye and the idea that it is an image reflected in the eye. Actually, these two notions are incompatible. The visual ray hypothesis, which concludes that seeing is an act of the eye, and the theory that the water of the eye, the aqueous humor, is a mirror that reflects objects cannot be reconciled.

In Alcmaeon's medical philosophy, health and disease are matters of equilibrium, health being a balance and disease, a rupture of that balance. This equilibrium, or lack of it, rests on paired qualities—wet and dry, cold and hot, bitter and sweet. If each pair is in balance, we have health; if one quality predominates, we have sickness. Health viewed as equilibrium was to have far-reaching influence in the centuries to come through the Hippocratic doctrine of humors.

Hippocrates

Although Hippocrates was an older contemporary of Plato—he was born about 460 B.C.—our information about his life is astonishingly meager. A few facts seem clear if we trust the account of Plato, who wrote that Hippocrates was a native of Cos and an Asclepiad, that is, a member of a family or guild that could trace its origin back to Aesculapius.[65] A number of medical schools had grown up in Greece in the course of the fifth century. The most famous one was on the island of Cos where Hippocrates had apparently studied. As he traveled from city to city practicing and teaching he became well known. Although he had been a student at an Aesculapian School, no traces of Aesculapian mysticism can be found in his works.[66] Seemingly, he never recommended the use of temple medicine, despite his firm belief in the healthful influence of the environment as exemplified in air, water, and place.

Over the centuries Hippocrates' fame grew, and a host of legends about him developed. These legends would add to his already distinguished descent from Aesculapius an ancestry going back to Hercules. One account of his clinical acumen involves his remedy for plague-ridden Athens. Because blacksmiths alone seemed immune to the disease, Hippocrates suggested that fires be lighted in all public squares. The plague disappeared and his reputation increased. By the time of Galen, Hippocrates had become the prototype of all physicians.

The Hippocratic *Writings* consist of materials that today would be called textbooks, papers, case histories, speeches, extracts, aphorisms, monographs, and manuals; they encompass the entire field of medicine.[67] The Hippocratic Oath is probably universally known. The *Aphorisms*, with adages concerning symptoms, diagnosis of disease, and the art of healing, opens with its most famous sentence, "Art is long and life is short." It includes the history of medicine; the influence of air, climate, and locale on disease; the treatment of acute disease; epidemics; injuries to the head; ulcers, and hemorrhoids.

In his history, *On Ancient Medicine*, Hippocrates states unequivocally his objection to earlier medicine: it depended on the rationalistic method of the philosophers of the past who "first laid down for themselves some hypotheses to their argument, such as hot, or cold, or moist, or dry, or whatever else they choose."[68] This dogmatic starting point is false, he asserts. Medicine has a long-established existence of its own as an art. Each physician starts by learning what others have learned and then goes on to apply the empirical procedure. Of particular relevance to the history of psychology is his paper, *On the Sacred Disease*, [69] which provides illustrations of his empirical interpretation of disease. This "sacred disease" was epilepsy, which then as now is very frightening to the beholder. The seizure of grand mal, the falling, the frothing at the mouth, and the loss of consciousness, can easily strike terror in witnesses to an attack. On regaining consciousness, the victim often complains of being buffeted by blows from an unknown source. These dramatic phenomena suggested the intervention of a spirit possessing the body of the sufferer. We must therefore admire the author who wrote sturdily and without compromise that "this disease seems to me to be no more divine than others, but it has a nature, such as other diseases have, and a cause whence it originates, . . . hereditary, like that of other diseases."[70] He indicates that epilepsy is caused in the brain. Even more specifically he relates it to a humoral congestion in the brain that makes affected individuals phlegmatic, which, in turn, brings on epileptic attacks.

The functioning of the humors just alluded to gave rise to the major theory of individual bodily function that was to dominate medical thought for many centuries to come. Polybos, who was Hippocrates' son-in-law, supposedly wrote the *Nature of Man*, the Hippocratic treatise concerning the theory of humors.[71] In propounding the theory, this Hippocratic writer implicitly accepts the view of Empedocles that the universe is composed of air, earth, fire, and water, which combine to produce all substances. These entities are unchangeable; water cannot become earth, nor earth water. By mingling, they form concrete objects. Corresponding, respectively, to these elements are the four combinations of qualities; warm-moist, cold-dry, warm-dry, and cold-moist. With these distinctions as its base, the theory postulates that these elements and qualities take bodily form in the respective humors—blood, black bile, yellow bile, and phlegm. These humors make up the constitution of the body and cause both disease and health. Deficiency or excess of one or another of the humors causes pain. Some disorders are evidenced by the appearance of liquid excretions from the body of the sick person, as from a cold in the head; or when the skin is broken and blood comes forth; or, in the case of severe injury, where other fluids of the body become visible. Relatively direct reasoning would lead to the conclusion that these fluids are of considerable importance in the economy of the body. To Hippocrates, the theory of humors was a theory of disease. Only much later did Galen relate it to personality, by adding to it in a relatively systematic fashion the theory of physical temperaments.

According to Hippocrates, therefore, a disease of an individual is a disturbance of the harmony of the elements as manifested in the humors. Hippocrates agreed with Alcmaeon that cures depend on restoration of the disturbed harmony. The humors tended toward equilibrium, a state to which they ordinarily returned because of the body's inherent tendency to recover from illness or injury. The concept of the crisis, or the critical turning point, was utilized; it was the task of the physician to assist nature by bringing his remedies to bear on the patient at these critical times.[72]

The Hippocratic School was the first to relate to the brain the conscious life in its entirety, including the emotions.[73] It discussed this relation of the emotions to the brain in specific terms. Overheating of the brain was thought to cause terror and fear, as shown by the flushed face. Conversely, when the brain is unduly cold, anxiety and grief result. Too much bile causes overheating; too much phlegm causes overcooling.

Nerves had no place in the Hippocratic *Writings,* and there was no distinct concept of the functioning of muscles; in fact, muscles and tendons were often confused.[74] The coordination of parts of the body in movement was explained by the doctrine of sympathy, or consensus, an immaterial connection between the parts of the body which brought about movement. Knowledge of the structural basis of sympathy was lacking; it did not even occur to these theorists that this structure might be sought.

SUMMARY

We began this chapter with an attempt to define psychological thought, and we came to the conclusion that it can be described in terms of three questions: How do I know what I know? How do I feel what I feel? How do I do what I do? Both in ancient times and in the present, these questions subsume most of what we would call psychological.

We considered the notions that may have begun psychological thought and the observations that the ancients could have made that would lead them to the ideas they appeared to have about life and death.

Homer described much of the processes that underlie psychological concepts in his terms *menos, thymos, noos,* and *psyche,* concepts that would influence thought for thousands of years.

The real beginning of formal psychological thought, however, came with the rise of naturalism and the philosopher–scientists and physicians of ancient Greece. They were concerned with natural rather than supernatural explanations of life and matter, and they were convinced that both the world and the individual could be understood in terms of nature. According to Aristotle, theologians had treated science as myth, whereas the philosopher–scientists set forth their theories in a demonstrable form. Life for Thales and those who came after him was not, as it was for Homer, explained by the capricious whims of the gods. The Hippocratic writers similarly rejected supernatural influences in the causes and treatment of disease. A naturalistic attitude was becoming evident.

Thales and the other Greek pioneers were the first to pursue an interest in nature for its own sake—a puristic attitude. Before them, thinkers such as the poet Hesiod, and, undoubtedly, farmers and sailors, had been interested in natural events. Their interest in nature must have been secondary, however, for it was dominated by other more important utilitarian interests. Physicians also adopted a utilitarian attitude. In psychological matters this attitude would become counter-dominant to an emphasis on purism.

The philosopher–scientists advocated a nomothetic approach in their search for the basic constituent of the universe. In some measure the idiographic attitude of the physicians served as a balance. Both attitudes had their first champions at that time, although, then as now, the nomothetic-idiographic distinction was a matter of emphasis, not an absolute distinction. As was to happen again and again, a pattern of nomotheticism accompanying purism coexisted with another pattern of idiographicism accompanying utilitarianism. Emphasis on rationalism and a deductive attitude—that is, still another pattern starting with a general principle and then finding incidents—also seemed to characterize the way of proceeding.

This early scientific and philosophical thought was thoroughly qualitative in that it took into account only similarities and differences in kinds or essences. It was not the way of thinking alone that prevented adoption of a quantitative attitude, that is, a demand that what is dealt with be countable or measurable. This modern facet of scientific thought was also prevented by the early Greeks' inability to conceive of, or to apply to scientific problems, the mathematics at their disposal, and the absence of any appreciable number of measuring instruments, aside from a few for astronomical calculations and devices. Attitudes would have to change before even the need for such instruments would be appreciated fully. At any rate, it was not until the dawn of modern science that quantitativism became an integral part of scientific investigation.

The experimental method was used very rarely. To the very limited extent that they adhered to an empirical attitude, these pioneers may be said to have depended on "nature's experiments," the phenomena of the earth, of the stars, and of the human being that occurred naturally. Observation, as yet almost unaided by instruments, was the method from which most of our first scientific knowledge was derived. After all, the function of experiment is to direct observation, not replace it. Observation may occur without experimental variations of conditions, and some of the Greeks certainly were acute observers. Hailing them as the first scientists in the modern connotation of the word would be a mistake; they did not generalize cautiously from observation and experiment. On the contrary, they proceeded by analogical reasoning to reach fantastically extensive generalizations. Sometimes there was a lucky hit, sometimes not. Democritus, for example, allowed his reason to outrun his senses, having no means of observation by which to verify his views concerning the atom. The first inquiries about scientific problems nevertheless had been made. These scientist–philosophers wanted to account for the basic nature of the world, which they interpreted as mechanical. The mechanistic theory of Democritus was the most significant for the future—atoms differing only in size and shape, their contact accounting for movement.

Only the first gropings toward a dualism involving the individual and world or the body and mind as separate entities were evident. The predominant view is exemplified by the lack of distinction between matter and what we today would call the secondary qualities of matter. To the early Greeks, "heat" had as much reality, in the sense of existing independently of the observer, as did the motion of the flames; to those who came later, heat was an experience. On the other hand, the view of Democritus that both body and mind are composed of atoms gave a rather clear expression to a monism of a mechanistic-materialistic sort.

Many problems of importance to the philosopher–scientists were, in point of fact, psychological, provided we recognize that the dominant contexts of psychological study well into the modern period were conceived as subjective. Contentual subjectivity is an attitude implicit in much of what has been discussed—in dualism of soul or mind and body and in perception, to name two obvious examples. Contentual objectivity, as expressed in the study of behavior which is so characteristic of current psychology, received some incidental mention in the symptomatology of disease but hardly anywhere else in Greek thought.

This chapter has given us the merest sampling of ideas from the earliest period of recorded psychological thought. We have come from a consideration of the thinking, feeling, and acting aspects of human life as being primarily controlled by outside forces—gods or spirits—to an examination of control by natural forces, internal to the individual, which are more or less lawful. Knowledge, as treated by the ancient Greek thinkers, progressed from a secure belief in the ability to apprehend the essences behind the appearances as espoused by the Milesians and their followers, through a position of sensation as being the basis of human knowledge, through an extreme rationalism that holds all knowledge to be inborn, through a relativistic view that maintains that the experience is the only reality, that nearly always there is nothing "out there" we can know.

All the thought contained in this chapter can be regarded as the substrate on which the magnificent constructions of Plato and Aristotle's philosophy would be built. It is with these two thinkers that the classical psychological positions become crystalized.

NOTES

1. Aristotle. *Metaphysics*, 980[a], trans. W. D. Ross, in Richard McKeon, ed., *Introduction to Aristotle* (New York: Random House, 1947).
2. Aristotle, *Metaphysics*, 982[b] 1.13. The word "philosophize" is perhaps better rendered as "to love wisdom," which seems to be what Aristotle is conveying.
3. Aristotle, *Metaphysics*, 982[b] 1.17.

4. Aristotle, *Metaphysics*, 982[b] 1.18.
5. ———, British Museum Stella #797, formerly #135, trans. E. A. Wallis Budge in *From Fetish to God in Ancient Egypt* (New York: Benjamin Blom, Inc., 1972), p. 15.
6. W. Hirsch, *Rabbinic Psychology* (London: Edward Goldston, 1947), pp. 57–58.
7. *Ibid.*, pp. 58–59.
8. Deuteronomy 13, 1. 20–24. *The Jerusalem Bible* (Garden City, N.Y.: Doubleday and Co., 1966).
9. Hirsch, *Rabbinic Psychology* pp. 58–59.
10. Erwin Rohde, *Psyche: The Cult of Soul and Belief in Immortality Among the Greeks*, trans. W. B. Hillis (London: Routledge and Kegan Paul, Ltd., 1925).
11. James M. Redfield, *Nature and Culture in the Iliad: The Tragedy of Hector* (Chicago: University of Chicago Press, 1975), p. 172.
12. The primary sources are most completely and carefully collected in H. Diels, *Fragmente der Vorsokratiker*, 7th ed., W. Krantz, ed. (Berlin: Weidmansche Verlagsbuchhandlung, 1954). An English translation of the fragments by Kathleen Freeman is available in her *Ancilla to the Pre-Socratic Philosophers* (Cambridge, Mass.: Harvard University Press, 1957). She also gives a detailed exposition of these fragments and early reports in *The Pre-Socratic Philosophers: A Companion to Diels, Fragments der Vorsokratiker*, 3rd ed. (Oxford: Basil Blackwell, 1953). Other quotations and references to pre-Socratic thought are derived from Geoffrey S. Kirk and J. E. Raven, *The Presocratic Philosophers: A Critical History with a Selection of Texts* (Cambridge: Cambridge University Press, 1962) and John Mansley Robinson, *An Introduction to Early Greek Philosophy* (Boston: Houghton Mifflin Co., 1968). The most complete and therefore the most important work on the lives of the Greek philosophers that has survived from antiquity is Diogenes Laertius' *Lives and Opinions of Eminent Philosophers*, trans R. D. Hicks (Cambridge, Mass.: Harvard University Press, 1925), III. Although frequently inaccurate, it remains our only source for many details. Most of what appears here concerning the works of Thales, Democritus, Heraclitus, Parmenides, Empedocles, and Alcmaeon is derived from these sources and from Aristotle's *Metaphysics*, cited above.
13. Aristotle, *Metaphysics*.
14. Aristotle, *Metaphysics*, 981[a] 13–982[b] 27.
15. For a discussion of this point, see W. A. Heidel, *The Heroic Age of Science* (Baltimore: Williams and Williams, 1933), and M. Clagett, *Greek Science in Antiquity* (New York: Abelard-Schuman, 1955).
16. Aristotle, *Metaphysics*, 1028[a] 10ff.
17. Aristotle, *Politics*, 1259[a] 8, trans. Benjamin Jowett, in McKeon, ed., *Introduction to Aristotle*.
18. Aristotle, *On the Soul*, 411[a] 8, trans. J. A. Smith, in McKeon, ed., *Introduction to Aristotle*.
19. B. B. Onians, *The Origins of European Thought. About the Body, the Mind, the Soul, the World, Time and Fate* (Cambridge: Harvard University Press, 1951).
20. Aristotle, *Metaphysics*, 1078[b].
21. Aristotle, *Topics*, viii, 156[a].
22. Heraclitus, in Freeman, *Companion*, No. 91.
23. Aristotle, *On the Soul*, 411[a].
24. Freeman, *Companion*.
25. Simplicius, *Physics*, 24,25, in Kirk and Raven, #143.
26. Aetus, *Epitome of Physical Opinions*, vol. 1, 1.3,4. in Kirk and Raven, #163 (DK 13 B2).
27. Simplicius, *Physics*, 152, 1.8, in Robinson, #3.25 (DK 64 B4).

28. Bruno Snell, *The Discovery of the Mind: The Greek Origins of European Thought,* tr T. G. Rosenmeyer (Cambridge, Mass.: Harvard University Press, 1953), p. 136.
29. Sextus Empiricus, *Adversus Mathematicos,* vii, 3, in Robinson, #6.3 (DK 28 B1).
30. Clement of Alexandria, *Stromateis,* v. 109, 2, in Kirk and Raven, #170.
31. John Stobaeus, *Anthologium,* I, 8,2, in Kirk and Raven, #191.
32. Sextus Empiricus, *Adversus Mathematicos,* vii, 110, in Freeman, #21.38 (DK 21 B38).
33. Hippolytus, *Refutatio ominum haeresium,* ix, 9,5, in Freeman, #22.55 (DK 22 B55).
34. Sextus Empiricus, *Adversus Mathematicos,* vii, 126, in Kirk and Raven, #201.
35. John Stobaeus, Flor. v. 6, in Freeman, #22.116 (DK 22 116).
36. Sextus Empiricus, vii, 132, in Kirk and Raven, #197 (DK 22 B1).
37. Themist, Or. 5, p. 69, in Freeman, #22.123 (DK 22 B123).
38. Plutarch, Coriol. 22, in Freeman, #22.85 (DK 22 B85).
39. Sextus Empiricus, *Adversus Mathematicos,* vii, 129, in Robinson, #5.56 (DK 22 A16).
40. Theophrastus, *De Sensu,* 25–26, trans. F. M. Stratton in *Theophrastus and the Greek Physiological Psychology Before Aristotle* (New York: Macmillan Co., 1917).
41. Simplicius, *Physics,* 146, 7, in Freeman, #28.8, 1. 34 (DK 28 B2); Clement of Alexandria, *Stromateis,* v. 15, in Freeman, #28.4 (DK 28 B4).
42. Theophrastus, *De Sensu,* 60–64, in Robinson, #10.9 (DK68 A 92).
43. Aristotle, *On the Soul,* 405^a 8–13.
44. Aristotle, *On the Soul,* 403^b 28–404^a 16.
45. Democritus, in Diels, *Vorosokratiker,* No. 125.
46. Theophrastus, *De Sensu,* Sec. 49–83.
47. Sextus Empiricus, *Adversus Mathematicos,* vii, 137, in Robinson, #10.20 (DK68 B7) and #10.19 (DK 68 B6).
48. Aetus, i. 15.8, in Robinson, 10.14 (DK 68 A 125).
49. Democritus in Sextus Empiricus, *Adversus Mathematicos,* vii, 135, in Kirk and Raven, #589 (DK 68 B9).
50. Galen, *De elem. sec. Hippocr.* i.2, in Robinson, 10.17 (DK 68 A 49).
51. Theopohrastus, *De Sensu,* 60–64 in Robinson, #10.9 (DK 68 A 135).
52. Sextus Empiricus, *Adversus Mathematicos,* vii, 60; in Robinson #12.6 (DK 80 B1); Freeman, *Companion,* p. 348.
53. Plato, *Theatetus,* 166c, in Robinson, #12.11.
54. Plutarch, *Pericles,* 32.2, quoted in C. M. Bowra, *Periclean Athens* (New York: Dial Press, 1971), p. 191.
55. Democritus, 25, in Robinson, #11.87 (DK 68 B72).
56. Euripides, *Medea,* trans. E. P. Coleridge, in W. J. Oates and Eugene O'Neill, Jr., eds., *The Complete Greek Drama,* vol. 1 (New York: Random House, 1938), p. 749.
57. Thucydides, *History of the Peloponnesian War,* iii, 45–46, trans. R. Crawley (New York: Random House, 1934).
58. Plato, *Phaedo,* trans. Jowett, in *The Philosophy of plato,* Irwin Edman, ed. (New York: Random House, 1956).
59. H. Ellenberger, "The Ancestry of Dynamic Psychotherapy," *Bulletin of the Menninger Clinic,* 20 (1956): 281–299.
60. Alcmaeon in Diels, *Vorosokratiker,* Nos. 5–11.
61. Aristotle, *On the Soul,* 405^a 29–34.
62. Alcmaeon, in Diels, *Vorosokratiker,* No. 5.
63. Alcmaeon, in Freeman, *Ancilla,* No. 1a.
64. Alcmaeon, in Diels, *Vorosokratiker,* No. 10.
65. Plato, *Protagoras,* 311; *Phaedrus* 270.
66. E. T. Withington, "The Asclepiadae and the Priests of Asclepius," in C. Singer, ed.,

Studies in the History and Method of Science (Oxford: Oxford University Press, 1921), pp. 192–205.

67. Hippocrates. *Writings of Hippocrates,* trans. F. Adams, in R. M. Hutchins, ed., Great Books of the Western World, Vol X, pp. 1–160. Unless otherwise stated, references to Hippocrates' works are from Hutchins.

68. Hippocrates, *On Ancient Medicine,* pp. 1–9.

69. Hippocrates, *On the Sacred Disease,* pp. 154–160.

70. *Ibid.,* p. 155.

71. Hippocrates, "The Nature of Man," in J. Chadwick and W. N. Mann, eds., *The Medical Works of Hippocrates* (Oxford: Basil Blackwell, 1959), pp. 202–213.

72. Hippocrates, *Of the Epidemics,* pp. 44–63.

73. Hippocrates, *On the Sacred Disease,* pp. 159–160.

74. Franklin Fearing, *Reflex Action* (New York: Hafner Press, 1930), p. 10.

Bust of Plato.

Chapter 3

Plato: Before Psychology

Plato lived during the Golden Age of Greece and saw it come to an end. His lifetime encompassed the reign and death of Pericles and Athenian acceptance of Macedonian rule.[1] During most of Plato's life, Athens was acknowledged as the intellectual center of the Greek world. His contemporaries included Sophocles, Aristophanes, Hippocrates, Thucydides, and Phidias. In short, he lived at a time when philosophy, poetry, theater, sculpture, and architecture flourished as never before. Trade and commerce were at their height as well. The quickening of the intellectual life was matched by a great deal of political and military activity. During Plato's youth, the Peloponnesian War was fought, and he himself was later involved in the struggle between democratic and oligarchic factions in Athens.

SOCRATES: RATIONALISM, CONTENTUAL SUBJECTIVITY, AND DUALISM

Plato was a disciple of Socrates, the first major philosopher produced by Athens. With Socrates, Plato, and Plato's student, Aristotle, begins the crystallization of the rationalist and empiricist prescriptions which is so significant in the history of psychology.

Socrates was born about 470 B.C. into a middle-class family; his mother was a midwife and his father may have been a sculptor. He dedicated his life to the search for knowledge, looking for it everywhere, in the gymnasium, in the marketplace, at dinner tables, wherever he could find persons willing to engage in conversation with him.

In these conversations he devised what later came to be called the Socratic method. Some general term, widely but loosely used—"friendship," "justice," or "piety"—would be advanced in the course of one of the conversations. Socrates would then ask for a definition of the idea. After his companion had given a definition, he would draw him out in such a way as to get him to admit exceptions to that particular definition. A cross-examination of questions and answers would follow until either a clear, final definition was reached on which both could agree, or, seeing the shortcomings of his particular definition, Socrates' companion would have to acknowledge that what he had accepted as true was not true at all. This procedure applies reason to the matter in hand and may be considered a classic example of the rationalistic method.

The Socratic method combined induction and deduction, as these processes of thinking are called today. Rationalist thinkers before Socrates typically had made use primarily of deduction, that is, starting with general propositions from which particular cases were derived. For instance, if the proposition were "All mortals die," and if Pericles is mortal, then we can deduce that "Pericles will die." Socrates, however, insisted on examining particular instances in order to arrive at a general statement. His formal use of that approach makes him a founder of the inductive method, that is, going from particulars to general propositions. It should be remembered, however, that deduction was his final goal, but only after the general propositions had been agreed on.

Socrates' views were opposed to those of the Sophists. As discussed in Chapter 2, Sophists were itinerant professional teachers who taught Athenian youth, generally males between the ages of fourteen and eighteen, rhetoric and other skills for attaining virtue. They taught for a fee and promised their pupils worldly success. They held to a relativistic position, not only in knowledge but also in morality. Because of their relativistic view that sensory life is entirely subjective, they believed that true knowledge, that is, knowledge of absolutes, could not be attained. The contention of Protagoras, a leader of the Sophists, that "man is the measure of all things," was what a person believes to be true determines what is true for him. There were no absolute truths. Truth was determined by convention, by mutual social agreement within a state. This position contains a strong emphasis on individualism, where truth is interpreted by the individual rather than by absolute standards, even group standards. This individualism and the Sophists' emphasis on how to achieve wordly, that is, personal success, meant that they were fostering an individualistic (idiographic) philosophy in spirit not too dissimilar from the "enlightened selfishness" in our present-day popular philosophy.

His youthful students, however, widely interpreted this view as meaning that there were no absolute morals and that they did not have to obey laws with which they did not agree.

Socrates disagreed with the Sophists in two major ways. First, he held that virtue could not be taught. Second, rather than emphasizing the relative differences of the senses, he sought absolute, universal (nomothetic), and constant moral norms. In his *Protagoras*, Plato shows Socrates and the Sophist, Protagoras, involved in a debate over whether or not men can be taught basic values.[2] Here and elsewhere, in order to debate Sophist doctrines, Socrates sought to elicit the knowledge inherent in each person. To him, knowledge was an activity of the mind. Self-knowledge resulted from the discovery of the person's own ignorance. Once this discovery is made the individual can go on to knowledge by use of the Socratic method, for truth already resides in the mind. Socrates felt that his method permitted discovery of the truth—the abiding reality that lies behind the apparent flux and relativity that the Sophists made so much of. Socrates believed that behind the world of appearances there exists a world of truth. Through rational thinking and logic one can transcend the apparent individual differences and find universals.

Socrates made rationalistic self-examination a philosophic method. "Know thyself" took on the meaning that the mind could turn to itself for knowledge. He called for methodological subjectivity precisely because if each individual would look within the self, each would find the same truths. The verification of truth was left to private experience and, indeed, could be found in no other way. This was one of the first instances of the systematic use of meditation, which was later to serve as a major psychological method, particularly in the hands of individuals such as René Descartes. Socrates did not intend to make the human mind the object of a distinct science; rather, with his interest in ethics, it served him as a tool and a means of finding the Good.

Socrates was concerned primarily with the relationship of virtue to knowledge, and this interest led him to a preoccupation with conduct. His emphasis was on ethical conduct rather than on psychological principles. Since ethics tells us how we should think, feel, and act, it does not fall within the definition of psychological thought. Socrates' notions, however, created much of the framework on which the more psychological philosophies of the future would be hung.

To Socrates the true concern of humankind was not for the body but for the *psyche*. A *psyche* using a body, a soul-like notion, was a popular formulation in ancient Greece. Socrates said that one must look to Man and tend his *psyche*. The typical Athenian of Socrates' time conceived of the *psyche* much as Homer had done—as an airy, unsubstantial double of the body that at death became either a shadow going to Hades or a breath to be dissipated in the air.[3] In the common view, human consciousness faded and disappeared with death. The body, not the *psyche*, was the concern of the ordinary Athenian, who was astonished to be told by Socrates that the *psyche* was more important.

In furthering the primacy of the *psyche,* Socrates was the first to relate consciousness of self to it. He stated that, by means of the self-knowledge of the *psyche,* we attain the insight to tell good from evil. If the *psyche* can discern what is good, it will choose what is good. The *psyche* not only allows us to see the good but also is the means whereby we choose that good. Hence, knowledge is a virtue, and no one intentionally does wrong; improper conduct is the result of ignorance.

Owing to the very nature of his quest for knowledge, Socrates never recorded his thoughts. Plato did this for him in the *Dialogues,* in which Socrates is often the major speaker.[4] Consequently, the views of the two men are mingled. It is not necessary for our purposes to differentiate further the thinking of Socrates from that of Plato.

Socrates' very style of living and his ability to puncture the weak spots of pompous and hollow men gained him many enemies. In 399 B.C., when he was seventy years old, he was caught up in the Athenian backlash against free thinking and naturalism after the death of Pericles. Socrates was accused of corrupting the youth of the city and of neglecting the city gods. He was convicted and sentenced to death. Despite an opportunity to escape, occasioned by a delay in carrying out the sentence, Socrates acknowledged that the punishment, though unjust, had been ordered by a legitimate court to which he owed obedience and he accepted its dictates. Plato recounts his last days in the *Phaedo,* a work that movingly presents Socrates' tranquil dignity and courage in the face of death.[5]

THE LIFE OF PLATO

Plato was born in 427 B.C. to Ariston and Perictione, members of old and aristocratic Athenian families. Plato shared his family's interest in politics and was assured of sponsorship in the oligarchic party with which his family was allied. His relationship with Socrates, however, caused him to become disillusioned with politics when the oligarchists tried to force Socrates to implicate himself in a particularly unsavory phase of their political machinations. This incident led Plato to give up any further thought of an active political life in Athens.

Although a matter of some dispute,[6] it seems that Plato traveled a lot during the next few years. Shortly after his return to Athens, he founded the Academy. This society of scholars and students was concerned with the study of certain branches of knowledge. Philosophical interests predominated, but some attention was paid to mathematics and a little to astronomy. Some who came to study under Plato remained at the Academy for the greater part of their lives, devoting themselves, after their probationary years, to the advancement of knowledge. Others came for relatively short periods and afterward returned to their homes. They undoubtedly paid dues of a sort but certainly not tuition. Plato, an aristocrat, was disdainful of the Sophists who taught for a fee. He probably used the Socratic method for much of his teachings. Despite recent opinions to the contrary, it is probable that Plato also gave formal lectures that revolved around the systematic and continued exposition of a particular topic. There is some indirect evidence that teaching might have been at more than one level. Advanced lectures may have been interspersed with more popular kinds of lectures. United in place and time, unlike the pre-Socratic philosophers, Plato's followers formed a definite, scholarly group. Unfortunately, however, we know very little about their interaction.

Little is known with any degree of certainty about the activities of Plato's later years. According to "The Seventh Letter,"[7] he became involved in Syracusian politics as the supporter of a former pupil who aspired to the throne. Plato died in 347 B.C. He was over eighty-one years of age and is said to be buried in the ground of the school in which he served for forty years.

THE PHILOSOPHICAL BASIS OF PLATO'S PSYCHOLOGICAL CONTENTIONS

Plato's psychological views are not systematically presented in his writings. The dialogue form, a conversation cast in a dramatic setting, was Plato's method of exposition. It is hardly conducive to systematic presentation, so that his views on ethics, religion, metaphysics, politics, social theory, and psychology are intermingled. His psychological contentions were always subordinate to other problems such as ethics.[8] Plato, like Socrates, was more of an ethical theorist than a psychologist. Still, like Socrates, he has much to say about psychological notions.

Two major themes express Plato's interest in what were to become matters of psychological concern. Plato wished to find a source of certain knowledge, that is, a knowledge of absolutes. Like Socrates, he was seeking the world of truth that lay beyond the jumble of the unreliable senses. He decided that these absolutes, called Ideas or Forms, were to be found in a reality that lay beyond the shifting phenomena of human conduct and physical processes. He was also eager to demonstrate the immortality of the *psyche*.

Plato was influenced by Socrates' admonishment to care for the *psyche* as well as by Socrates' insistence that there was a definite meaning to things that could be penetrated by using the Socratic method. Plato was also influenced by the Pythagoreans, a religious cult that taught that the soul *(psyche)* was immortal, that death was a release from the bonds of flesh, and that after repeated reincarnations a person could rise to know the Divine. The Pythagoreans attached considerable importance to number, and more or less incidentally made an important contribution to mathematical knowledge. According to Aristotle, the Pythagoreans devoted themselves to mathematics and thought its principles were the principles of all things.[9] In Pythagorean thought, all things are numerable. The relation between things can also be expressed numerically, such as the musical intervals between the notes of a lyre. Just as musical harmony is dependent on number, so also is the harmony of the world itself. And so the Pythagoreans contended that the first principle of the universe is number—that the world in a sense is based on number. Plato's absorption with mathematics based on an all-sufficient rationalism did not, however, lead to a quantitative attitude embracing a desire to measure. He was interested in the manipulation of mathematics for its own sake, glorying in the aspects of reasoning which lay within the field itself. He did not use mathematics as a tool for studying something else, except as an incidental or quasi-verifying application to astronomical problems already solved by reason.

In his reaction against the Sophists' emphases on materialism and relativism, Socrates rejected science in favor of spiritual concerns. Plato shared this view. His attitude toward science can be characterized as negative; he denied the value of experiment.[10] Plato says, for example, that those who would attempt to verify color mixtures by experiment would be ignoring the difference between human and divine nature. For Plato, only God has the knowledge and power either to combine or to resolve color mixtures. Plato warns the astronomer that knowledge of the heavens will not be gained by observation but rather from *a priori* deduction from the heavenly idea.[11] Plato's rejection of scientific observation is rendered less harsh if he is interpreted to mean that the astronomer's task should be to record the real and not merely the apparent movements of the stars. In the *Timaeus,* Plato says explicitly that an account of the material world should not be expected to be more than "likely," that is, not exact or even self-consistent.[12]

It would seem that Plato rejected quantitatively and inductively derived empirical knowledge, but this is only one side of the coin. Although he may have had a negative attitude toward what many of us today would consider crucial prescriptions of modern science—induction, quantification, and empiricism—he also did much to provide a particular theoretical background for science in his rationalistic search for the Forms that give order to the universe.

Plato laid part of the groundwork for the conceptualizations of scientists to come. When a modern biologist, physicist, or chemist takes a physical object as a subject matter—whether that may be a horse, a falling ball, or a sample of sulphur—he or she is thinking about not that object but something resembling a universal nontemporal, nonphysical version of the object, which Plato called a Form. The world of the universals, of absolutes, of which Plato speaks, would become the world of natural law for modern science. Although science begins with observation and induction, the final goal is the discovery of laws that will allow accurate and reliable deduction.

THE NATURE OF FORMS

To put it succinctly, Plato conceived of a world of substance or phenomena and a world of absolute Forms *(nomena)* or Ideas.[13] By phenomena he meant the changing and essentially unreal world of appearances, which corrupts, decays, and dies. Substance or phenomena come to us by way of the senses and, according to Plato, are unreliable. In contrast, the world of Forms is real and eternal. A tree experienced through the senses is but the appearance of a tree, a pale and imperfect representation, whereas the Form of the tree, though not perceived directly, is known through intuition and truly exists.

Plato used the words Form and Idea interchangeably. However, "idea" later came to be used in a way far different from what Plato had meant. Namely, it is used for experiences that exist in the mind only. This is not Plato's meaning, however. Plato specifically mentions that Ideas are not created by thought.[14] An

Idea to him is a reality with an independent existence, and not just a thought. (The term *Form* is capitalized in order to indicate its technical usage.)

How did Plato arrive at what common sense tells us is an extravagant and bizarre belief—that the world of appearances, of the senses, is but a shadow, masking the reality that lies beyond? One source was probably the conviction that the senses are unreliable. The sensory relativism of Democritus and the Sophists demonstrated that different individuals can look at the same object and see different things. Not accepting relativism, Plato had to conclude that it was the senses that were unreliable. Another source must have been the Socratic search through specific instances of justice, courage, and virtue for essences, the absolutes of justice, courage, and virtue. In the *Republic*, Plato assumed that whenever a number of individual qualities have a common name, they also have a corresponding Form.[15] To Plato these were not subjective concepts, as we might call them, but real essences in the qualitative sense.

A little of the meaning of Form may also be envisioned by considering the role of mathematics. Plato presented his view in much the following way.[16] Suppose a geometrician is working out a theorem to demonstrate that the sum of the interior angles of a triangle equals two right angles. Plato reasoned that the geometrician is not inventing something here but rather is making a discovery. What is discovered is not the physical triangle that the geometrician has drawn, with all its minute imperfections of surface, drawing instrument, and lack of drawing skill. The physical drawing is not a triangle but something *like* a triangle. This universal object, this nonspatial, nontemporal object of thought, which the sensed physical triangle resembles, is the Form of a triangle.

Where, then, do these absolutes, these essences called Forms exist, since they have to be somewhere? This question can perhaps be clarified by a discussion of Plato's view of the *psyche* and the origin of knowledge.

THE *PSYCHE* AND THE FORMS

The *psyche* is the means whereby we apprehend the Forms.[17] According to Plato, the *psyche* is immortal. In a previous state of existence, it had accurate knowledge of eternal truth, the absolutes, the *nomena* or Forms. At birth, the *psyche* becomes mixed with the material substance of the body. Being mixed with the flesh, the *psyche* is no longer in direct contact with eternal truth. It can experience only through the ever changing confusion of the senses. Through the senses, the body knows the changing and essentially unreal world of appearances; only the *psyche* is capable of knowing rationally the world of the Forms. The *nomena*, the Forms, the Ideas, then, are memories of the absolute truths of the universe known to the *psyche* before it entered into the body of an individual person. Only gradually and by effort will the *psyche* come to untangle itself from the confusion of the flesh and regain its knowledge of the absolute truths. Truth, then, is not in the senses but in the reason. For this reason not only was Plato's method of finding knowledge a rational one, since it used meditation and reason, but also the knowledge he sought was contentually subjective in character. It was knowledge derived from the reasoning aspect of the *psyche.* For this reason, Plato makes a fundamental division between the material world of the flesh with the unreliable representations given by the senses and the world of the *psyche* with its absolute representations of Form.

The essential character of the *psyche* is expressed in movement. Plato held the view common in Homer's time that objects that could move themselves were alive. He extended that view to say that, because the *psyche* is self-moved, it is immortal.[18] On the other hand, whatever is moved by the motion of something else, such as the body, cannot be immortal. Ceasing to move, the body also ceases to live.

Platonic Forms have a reality distinguishable from sensible objects.[19] They exist in their own right, and they are different from the things we sense. The "objects" that are sensed are impermanent; they can be the objects of opinions, but they cannot be the objects of true knowledge. Sensory experiences are always changing. Only appearances can be seen, and they are similar, as Plato put it, to shadows in a cave.[20] Human beings, as it were, live in a cave, chained in such a fashion that they cannot move but must look at a wall. Light (truth) behind and above them streams into the cave. They see only the shadows of reality projected on the walls (sensory experience).

This view does not deny the senses a role in gaining knowledge of the Forms, however. Plato made use of the senses in his concept of reminiscence. Reminiscence, he said, is the means by which the *psyche* recovers the Forms it knew before it became united with the body. Knowledge of the Forms is latent in the *psyche,* but it has been confused by its entanglement with the flesh. A sensory experience will often be similar to the Form and will generate a reminiscence in the *psyche.* Sensations, although they give us an unreliable and imperfect representation of the Form, can aid in reawakening the Form. If we look at enough trees, eventually the Form of "tree" will be reawakened.

Logic is another way to gain knowledge of the Forms. An illustration of this process is Socrates' questioning of a slave boy about a geometrical problem.[21] Faced with the problem directly, the boy had no idea of the answer; under Socrates' system of probing questions, however, the boy was able to give the answer. Plato argued that the answer had been in the boy all the time and that it simply had to be searched out. To Plato, then, knowledge of the Forms is independent of body and is present at birth. In other words, learning as we would use the term today consists to Plato of drawing out of the *psyche* what is already there. Education is the recollection of knowledge present since birth.

This doctrine is not quite the same as that of innate ideas. Innate ideas would be readily available to anyone, even to an infant without effort. This would make an infant more wise than an adult, since it would have been closer in time to the source of the absolutes. Knowledge is not ready-made; to arrive at it and to reclaim it require effort, since it is confused by the flesh and must be extracted. Reminiscence in Plato's usage is not a depository of past sensory experiences or remnants of learning in the way we might think of it today. Plato admitted that a certain amount of remembering does take place this way, but he believed it was negligible.

More specifically, reason, as an aspect of the *psyche,* makes the Forms intelligible. At long last, we come to a statement of general method that expresses Plato's desire to know. His method shows adherence to the rationalistic prescription, that the source of knowledge is to be found primarily, if not exclusively, through reason.

PSYCHOLOGICAL VIEWS OF PLATO

As we have seen, for Plato the *psyche* is independent of the flesh but is intermingled with it. Plato's psychological views then, are dualistic, a theme that runs through all the discussion to follow. A vague, implicit dualism had been latent in the pre-Socratics' studies of mind–body or soul–body functions. Plato, following the lead of Socrates, gave the problem explicitness, precision, and subtlety. Broadly speaking, the dualistic prescription in this context is based on the conviction that mind *(psyche)* and body are fundamentally different and are therefore separate entities. Moreover, since *psyche* was thought to be more important, Plato emphasized the approach labeled here as the prescription of contentual subjectivity, which holds that psychological events are mental.

MIND AND BODY

We have seen that in Plato's view the *psyche* or mental part becomes intermixed with the flesh at birth. Everyone possesses knowledge, because it is in the *psyche* from the beginning, but not everyone can have that knowledge. It is like possessing a garment that is hung in the closet but never worn. The potential for knowledge is there, but it is never realized.

To Plato, the body can become an unruly instrument and can thereby hinder the *psyche*.[22] The strong natural appetites of the body upset the functioning of reason. To be wise, to have knowledge of the Forms, a person must seek to untangle the *psyche* from the flesh. To fail in this effort is to become unwise and foolish. Individuals who lead wanton lives, ruled by strong emotions, are doomed to be cut off from true knowledge. The action of the humors of the body affects the mental part. Thus, Plato's dualism is an interactionistic dualism in which there are two parts or aspects and the material side affects the mental and the mental affects the material. Madness and ignorance are diseases of the mind brought about by the body. But excessive pain and pleasure are the greatest diseases of the mind, for people in great joy or great pain cannot reason properly. Sense perception, desire, feeling, and appetite are products of the body and are at war with the mind; in this way they interfere with the realization of the Forms.

Plato believed that the seat of (or physical link between) the three aspects of the *psyche* (reason, feeling, and appetite, as they are called later in this chapter in a discussion of the structure of the *psyche*) is the cerebrospinal marrow on which they are "strung."[23] The immortal (rational) aspect has a separate place in the brain, whereas the mortal (irrational) aspects of feeling and appetite are located in the thoracic and abdominal cavities.[24] The heart serves as an advance post of the immortal part; when wrong is committed, the heart is stimulated to anger, and this emotion is carried by the blood vessels to all parts of the body. According to Plato, the blood vessels serve as the means for conveying sensations through the body. Though more detailed, we can see the similarity of Plato's rational and irrational parts with the *noos* and the *thymos* of Homer.

The question of the independence or dependence of the body and the *psyche* may now be clarified. As an entity, the *psyche* is independent; when it is related to the body, however, the two act in unison. The *psyche* itself is immortal, but certain relations and functions it assumes when it is connected with the body are not.[25] These disappear when the *psyche* is again independent of the body. The vital principle of the *psyche* is imperishable. Hence, Plato holds to a vitalistic position—that an immortal part is involved in human affairs.

MOTIONS AND THE *PSYCHE*

In explaining sensory and other bodily processes, Plato makes use of a somewhat vague concept of motion.[26] It will be remembered that for Plato the essence of the *psyche* is movement. Nevertheless, in discussing movement he uses a concept that is to some degree disconnected from his theory of the *psyche.* This concept of movement is the nearest Plato came to a functional theory, that is, an emphasis on activities rather than on structures. The psychology of Plato always returns to the *psyche,* and this instance is no exception. He states that psychological activities are related to various inner motions. He probably arrived at this conclusion by drawing an analogy between the motion of objects in the external world and sensory experience. The instrument is the body; the function and source belong to the *psyche,* which directs the acts of the body. A sensory organ is the means whereby the motion of the external world interacts with the motion of the *psyche* so that external nature is experienced. Sensation comes about whenever some motion affects a sense organ. This outer motion is communicated to an inner motion, which is carried to the seat of consciousness in the *psyche.* Thus, sense qualities such as color emerge from the interaction of environmental motion and the internal motion of the body. Diversity in the qualities sensed is caused by the difference in the motions that the impression communicates to the psyche.

The movements of the *psyche* include motions other than those related to sensations—will, pleasure, consideration, deliberation, pain, confidence, fear, hatred, love, and other similar motions. Thinking is a functioning (motion) of the *psyche* in that it is selective, spontaneous, and self-moving.[27] Emotion and drive are also explained on the basis of motion. Thinkers before Plato conceived of sensation as being movement. Emotion was believed to be merely a more violent form of movement. Plato could not accept this relative and mechanical doctrine outright.[28] As he modified it, sensation is accompanied by emotion when the more violent degree of motion occurs, but the direction of movement—whether toward the natural or unnatural—decides whether the experience is pleasant or painful. If the violent motion conforms to nature, it is pleasant; if it does not, it is painful. When it is added that to Plato "natural" means productive of the Good and that "unnatural" means productive of the Bad, we see that here again to Plato psychology is subordinate to ethics. What we call drive today Plato also relates to motion and to the *psyche.* [29] Inner motion is spontaneous or self-active. The highest form of such movement is reserved for purposeful action directed toward a goal of some sort. Hence, purposive behavior is derived from the *psyche* and is expressed in movement.

THE STRUCTURE OF THE *PSYCHE*

Plato expressed three pertinent views regarding the structure of the *psyche.* First, in the *Phaedo* the *psyche* is conceived of as unitary and simple.[30] At one point in the *Timaeus* it is described as twofold: the rational aspect, concerned with the aspect of reasoning, or mind, and the irrational aspect, consisting of desire and appetite.[31] A little later in the *Timaeus,* [32] the *Republic,* [33] and the *Phaedrus,* [34] the *psyche* is tripartite—reasonable, spirited, and appetitive. Although some authorities find these three ways of describing the psyche contradictory, it is possible to reconcile them. The first view emphasizes the essential unity of the *psyche,* and the second and third views describe aspects—not parts—of this unitary *psyche.* Thus, the *psyche* as a vital principle is unitary, but certain aspects or modes emerge when the *psyche* is present in the body. Plato varied the classification of *psyche*— reasonable, spirited, and appetitive, or rational and irrational—as circumstances seemed to require. The emphasis that Plato placed on the unity of the *psyche* is important because it demonstrates his view of *psyche* as a consistent and integrated psychological structure.

REASONING IN THE DUAL AND TRIPARTITE *PSYCHE*

The first and highest aspect, reason, is the intellectual facet of the *psyche.* To Plato, reason is the very essence of a human; one is a person insofar as one is rational. This does not mean that rational people do not also possess the lower aspects of the *psyche,* but rather that they can be guided by reason. Reason has been discussed in connection with the theory of Forms and the theory of reminiscence. To review, reason is the means whereby we know the Forms, and reason, as reminiscence, is only indirectly dependent on the natural world or its phenomena. The senses play a role in reminiscence but are not in themselves the source of knowledge.

To go more deeply into Plato's conception of reason it is necessary to compare and contrast reason, as he sees it, with sensory experience. As we saw in discussing the pre-Socratics, this controversy over whether reason or sense is the means of securing knowledge existed before Plato. Plato denied that sensation gives knowledge. To him, reason, not sense perception, is the means by which we synthesize our experiences. We do not see with the eyes but through them. We do not hear with the ears but through them. Common characteristics of diverse objects are not perceived by the separate organs of sense but by reason. Sense perceptions give only particulars; these particulars are formed into a pattern and, by the nature of that pattern, yield some intelligibility. Reality is revealed when reason provides the interpretation of perceptual experience. Sensations supply some of the occasions for perceiving knowledge or serve as one of the tools for determining knowledge. An activity of the psyche, the faculty of reason reveals the Forms behind sense experience, and it is the *psyche* that makes us aware of the meaning of what is sensed.

SPIRIT AND APPETITE IN THE TRIPARTITE *PSYCHE*

The second aspect of the tripartite division of the *psyche* is the notion of spirit. Spirit is contentious, assertive, pugnacious, and forceful and in its drive toward action carries out the directives of reason. In so doing, spirit is the mediator between reason and appetite, the third aspect.

Both the role of spirit as a mediator and its differentiation from appetite are best shown by using Plato's own illustration.[35] A man named Leontius was present at a place of execution. He felt a desire to see the dead bodies and yet had an abhorrence and fear of them. He struggled for a time, but desire won, and Leontius "ran up to the dead bodies saying, 'Look, ye wretches, take your fill of the fair sight.' " He was angry with himself for his action, showing that spirit was on the side of reason but that nevertheless appetite won out. This situation was proof to Plato of the existence of different aspects of *psyche,* for how otherwise could Leontius in the story both want to look and yet not want to look at the bodies? The spirited element is therefore not the same as appetite because it can be used against it; since spirit and appetite are sometimes antagonists, they must be distinguished from one another.

Appetite, the third aspect, above all is undiscriminating desire. Appetite wants something, and it wants it now, without delay and without any consideration of the other aspects of the *psyche.* The goal of appetite, as Plato sees it, is attainment serving as a replenishment. Thirst, for example, arising from deprivation of water, leads to a striving for water that when satisfied results in repletion.[36]

CONFLICT AND HARMONY AND THE TRIPARTITE *PSYCHE*

That the *psyche* is unitary does not mean that it cannot have aspects that are at odds with one another.[37] Plato's awareness of the nature of the conflict is shown in the story of Leontius, but an even more dramatic illustration is given in Plato's example of the charioteer in the *Phaedrus.*[38] Plato likened the human being to a chariot team. In the team there is a powerful, unruly horse intent on having its own way at all costs (appetite). The other horse is a thoroughbred, spirited but manageable (spirit). On catching sight of his beloved, the charioteer (reason) attempts with some difficulty to direct the two horses toward the goal, which he alone (not they) can comprehend.

What Plato seems to be demonstrating in this story is a theory of conflict based on reason, emotion, and drive. A person's attitude toward his or her objective is swayed by emotional impulses and inhibitions over which reason, the charioteer, has some control. Reason acts as a check on the emotional aspect. For the ends of spirit or appetite to be met, reason must guide. Spirit or appetite need not be eliminated; instead they should be controlled. For reason to attempt to oust appetite and spirit would be as "irrational" as for appetite and spirit to banish reason. Although there is conflict among the aspects of the psyche, sometimes they agree.[39] Reason is the natural harmonizer. Balance and proportion among the three aspects is sought, with the others subordinate to reason. Order consists in harmony and this subordination.

DRIVE AND THE TRIPARTITE *PSYCHE*

Drive characterizes all three aspects of the *psyche.* Reason, spirit, and appetite— each is a drive, of and by itself, an endeavor toward a thing, a striving toward attainment of a goal.[40] The rational aspect seeks understanding and wisdom; the spirited seeks success; the appetite, the lowest form of desire, seeks bodily pleasures or the means to them—money, food, drink, sex, and the like. Reason may long for the realization of its own drives and assent to them. On other occasions reason may dissent, as it does with many of the drives of spirit or appetite. But this should not obscure the fact that reason has a characteristic drive of its own.

Plato's *Symposium* is a dialogue concerned with Eros, or love, in which each participant offers his own interpretation.[41] Plato's position seems to be that there are two kinds of love— profane and sacred. The first is concerned with the body and the second with the *psyche,* mind, and character. Physical sexual desire is interpreted not as a desire for intercourse itself, but as a masked desire for parenthood, an attempt to perpetuate oneself. This passion for physical parenthood is the most elementary or rudimentary fruition of the Good and the eternal. Only the higher love can lead to happiness. Love, as Plato conceived it, is in its highest form the love of wisdom. Whether or not we know it, what we seek is the beauty of the eternal Forms. This love is a longing for union not only with the partner through reason, but beyond this with the pure Form, or the essence of love itself. Thus, the higher or immortal *psyche* has its own enjoyment, its particular Eros. Eros is popularly translated as "love," but may often be more meaningfully called "life force." It is akin to the biological will to live, the life energy, a concept of which we will hear again.

Drives have an affective coloring of pleasure and pain. As we have seen, pain is what is contrary to nature, and pleasure is what is in accord with nature. One class of pleasures derives from the restoration of the natural state of equilibrium. At the level of the appetite, depletion causes need (lack of pleasure), which when satisfied is followed by repletion (pleasure).[42] This process whereby the organism returns to normal is one form of pleasure.[43] Excess heat or chilling causes a disturbance of equilibrium, and recovery or return to the natural state is pleasant. In this form of pleasure there is an agreeable return to a normal bodily condition.[44] The second class of pleasures is dependent on mental processes themselves (not on a balance within the organism). These are pleasures that we anticipate or remember mentally, such as anticipating recovery from a painful illness and remembering past pleasures that we look forward to enjoying again.

THE IRRATIONAL IN THE DUAL *PSYCHE*

Although Plato was not the first to recognize the irrational in human affairs, he considerably amplified, extended, and gave a basis for it. He located this lower or irrational aspect within the *psyche* itself and thought of it in terms of psychological conflict. The already familiar accounts of the passions, the tripartite division itself, and the story of Leontius all point to an appreciation of this aspect.

Emotions are related to the mortal (irrational) aspect of *psyche*, which is endowed with courage, passion, and a love of strife. The wild beast in humans may slumber or be restrained but is never tamed. Passion is irrational, liable to excess, expanding until it becomes a form of mania. Plato gives a graphic illustration of this idea when he speaks of the "unnecessary" pleasures and appetites that everyone seems to have, although some can control them by reason. With everyone, when reason

> is asleep, then the wild beast within us, gorged with meat or drink, starts up and having shaken off sleep, goes forth to satisfy his desires; and there is no conceivable folly or crime—not except incest or any other unnatural crime or parricide, or the eating of forbidden food—which at such a time, when he has parted company with all shame and sense, a man may not be ready to commit.[45]

In many ways, Plato has refined and amplified Homer's notions of *thymos* and *noos*, the passions and the reason, always doing battle. Plato's consideration of unconscious processes in his concept of *psyche* shows his use of the prescription we have called unconscious mentalism. The significance of unconscious mentalism would not be more fully appreciated until Carl Jung and Sigmund Freud in the twentieth century. Jung's conception of libido is actually closer in spirit to Plato than it is to Freud, for Jung stressed its general, nonspecialized drive character. Freud signaled his more specific debt to Plato by utilizing the very term *Eros* in his systematic formulation. To Freud personality was subject to reciprocal urging and checking forces akin to Plato's reason, emotion, and drive. Freud, in his theory of personality structure, sees personality as dependent on id, ego, and superego.

To some extent Plato, too, was advocating a dynamic prescription, an emphasis on factors making for change in humans. In a larger and much more influential sense, however, his overall conception of humans in relation to the unchanging Forms was static.

SUMMARY

Plato's rationalistic theory of Forms and his dualistic convictions determined his attitude toward science. Science deals with the physical world. By definition, the objects of its inquiry belong to what Plato saw as the shifting and relatively unintelligible world of sensation. According to him, one could never trust these phenomena to give true knowledge. His distrust of the physical world, including sensory processes, helped to turn his philosophical thought away from science, including psychology. To Plato, only an understanding of the Forms, another class of existence entirely, could give us truth. The Forms are the objects of knowledge, material things are not, and inductive, empirical, and quantitative matters belong to the material world.

It is important to note that Plato rejected science on the basis of its use of empirical and inductive methods; the rational way in which science draws conclusions was acceptable to him. In his rationalism Plato gave us the beginning of a belief in natural law—law as basic nature far removed from mere phenomena. When we understand the Forms, Plato said, we understand their natural relationship with one another. This interrelationship was later to be conceptualized as natural law. It should be evident that Plato himself did not formulate anything approaching this modern conception. He did, however, lay the groundwork from which it was to emerge.

Ironically, Plato, who glorified reason, showed keen insight into the functioning of the unconscious, irrational aspect of human nature. He gave varied and subtle consideration to the irrationalistic prescription, expressing intrusion into or domination over the intellectual processes by what we would call emotive and drive factors. His distinction between the rational and irrational aspects of living function *(psyche)*; his appreciation of the nature of conflict and, correlatively, of the nature of harmony; his primordial concept of Eros; his conception of drive as related differentially to the various aspects of living function; his realization of the perniciousness of repression and his advocacy of controlled expression—all are indicative of his deep insight into the irrational aspects of human nature. His understanding, however, was but one among a few isolated instances that occurred before the modern period and without immediate impact.

In his theory of Forms, Plato created an explicit dualism. He acknowledged a reality that could be comprehended by the senses, but he also described an immeasurably exalted realm where intelligible beings gained true knowledge by understanding the Forms. Plato established the character of the dualism that was to prevail for many centuries.

In brief, Plato was above all dualistic and rationalistic in outlook, and yet he showed keen insight into the irrational aspects of humanity. He was nonnaturalistic in that he depended on transcended guidance, though not of a religious kind. He conceived of psychological problems in a structural way, as psychological categories and contents, not as activities.

In the work of Plato, psychology still had not emerged as a separate discipline.

Plato's subordination of psychological matters to other issues is abundantly clear from his espousal of the theory of Forms, his desire to demonstrate the immortality of the *psyche,* his conviction of the subordination of the body to the *psyche,* and his distrust of the empirical evidence of the senses. He used psychology only as a means of dealing with these other, to him, more important problems.

NOTES

1. Major sources for the lives of both Socrates and Plato are Diogenes Laertius, *Lives and Opinions of Eminent Philosophers,* A.D. III, trans. R. D. Hicks (Cambridge, Mass.: Harvard University Press, 1925); G. C. Field, *Plato and His Contemporaries* (London: Methuen, 1920); A. E. Taylor, *Plato: The Man and His Work,* 6th ed. (New York: Meridian Books, 1956); and G. Boas, "Facts and Legends in the Biography of Plato," *Philosophical Review, 57* (1948): 439–457.
2. R. M. Hutchins, ed., *The Great Books of the Western World,* Vol. VII, pp. 1–799, Plato, *Dialogues,* trans. B. Jowett (Chicago: Encyclopaedia Britannica, 1952). (Citations to the various Dialogues are to this source.)
3. J. Burnet, "The Socratic Doctrine of the Soul," *Proceedings of the British Academy, 7* (1916): 235–259.
4. *Dialogues.*
5. *Phaedo.*
6. For example, Taylor, *Plato;* Boas, "Facts and Legends."
7. "The Seventh Letter."
8. *Timaeus,* 68.
9. *Works of Aristotle,* trans. W. D. Ross, in R. M. Hutchins, ed., *Great Books of the Western World,* Vols. VIII–IX (c. 340–322 B.C.). *Metaphysics,* 985b, 23–986a 3.
10. *Timaeus,* 67–68.
11. *Republic,* 530.
12. *Timaeus,* 27d 5–28a 4; 29b 3–d 3.
13. *Phaedo,* 79.
14. *Parmenides,* 132.
15. *Republic,* 596a 6–7.
16. *Ibid.,* 510.
17. *Phaedo,* 66 and passim; *Phaedrus,* 247c.
18. Plato affirmed the immortality of the psyche on several occasions, for example, *Phaedo,* 85e–86d and passim; *Phaedrus,* 245 cff; *Laws,* 893b–896d; and *Timaeus,* 69c–e.
19. Aristotle, *Metaphysics,* 987b 27.
20. *Republic,* 514–521.
21. *Meno,* 82–86.
22. *Timaeus,* 86.
23. *Ibid.,* 85–86.
24. *Ibid.,* 69d–70a.
25. *Phaedo,* 64–66.
26. *Laws,* 894–896; *Cratylus,* 400e; *Phaedrus,* 245b–c.
27. *Laws,* 896.
28. *Timaeus,* 64–65.
29. *Phaedrus,* 245c–246a.
30. *Phaedo,* 78–80.

31. *Timaeus,* 69.
32. *Ibid.,* 70–71, 77.
33. *Republic,* 439–440, 580–594.
34. *Phaedrus,* 253–254.
35. *Republic,* 439–440.
36. *Philebus,* 31.
37. *Republic,* 436, 440, 588.
38. *Phaedrus,* 253–254.
39. *Ibid.,* 237.
40. *Republic,* 580–582.
41. *Symposium.*
42. *Timaeus,* 81.
43. *Philebus,* 31.
44. *Ibid.,* 72.
45. *Republic,* 571.

Bust of Aristotle.

Chapter 4

Aristotle: The Founding of Philosophical Psychology

Only fragments of the earliest Greek thought on psychological problems exist today, and as we have seen in previous chapters, these were made primarily within the context of other discussions and subject matters. Similarly, Socrates and Plato, for all their brilliant excursions into so many different aspects of psychological thought, typically approached these ideas piecemeal, with intents other than developing a psychological system. The first to develop something approaching a systematic psychology was Aristotle, who is often regarded as the first philosophical psychologist.

Aristotle's life and works are best considered in relation to one another because of their developmental interplay. There is a literary myth that Aristotle's views were static and unchanging.[1] We now know, however, that his thinking, like that of most creative individuals, went through various stages of development. This myth was enhanced by the fact that most readers have encountered Aristotle through volumes of his collected works which were arranged many centuries after his death. The editors arranged the sometimes fragmentary manuscripts as they saw fit rather than as Aristotle himself might have intended. All works on logic or biology, for instance, were neatly grouped, to the point where even parts of different works were put together arbitrarily. One work, *Metaphysics,* got its title simply because it was grouped after *(meta)* physics. Scholars once treated contradictory views in different works or in different parts of the same work, including various ideas about the *psyche,* as though they were written at the same time. Did Aristotle or did he not accept the Platonic theory of Forms? When all his writings are treated as contemporaneous with one another, this question becomes insoluble, since affirmative and negative answers coexist. When, however, it is understood that his views show development and change with time, such questions are much more manageable.

LIFE OF ARISTOTLE

Aristotle was born in 384 B.C. in Stagira, a provincial town in northern Greece.[2] His father, who was the physician to Philip, King of Macedon, followed the Asclepiad tradition of the family and began training his son as a doctor. When his father died prematurely, Aristotle's early education was continued by a friend of the family. Aristotle visited Athens for the first time in 367 B.C. By then, Socrates had been dead thirty-two years, Plato was sixty-one years old, and the Academy had been in existence two decades. Aristotle remained in Athens for twenty years, but less is known of these years than of any other period of his life. It is even a matter of scholarly dispute as to what is meant when it is said that he "studied" under Plato. He himself makes no mention in any of his writings either of the Academy or of having studied under Plato.[3] Nevertheless, he probably entered the Academy either immediately upon his arrival in Athens or else shortly thereafter, and it is likely that at some time during these twenty years he became a "colleague" of his former teacher, Plato.

In his early years, Aristotle apparently was an enthusiastic Platonist. His first works, surviving only in fragments, were written in the popular form of the Socratic dialogue during this period at the Academy. Devotion to the Platonic theory of Forms, and all that it implies, seems to have characterized this stage of his intellectual development.

In 347 B.C. Plato died. His successor as head of the Academy was Speusippus, an inferior thinker but Plato's nephew and legal heir. Speusippus had strong mathematical and Pythagorean leanings, both of which Aristotle probably found incompatible with his already changing viewpoint.

Whatever the reason, after the death of Plato, Aristotle left Athens for Asia Minor and did not return for twelve years. He settled first in Assus, a town near Troy, and attached himself to the court of Hermias, the Tyrant of Assus. He stayed in Assus for three years, during which time he continued to study, write, and collect biological specimens. He also married Hermias' niece and adopted daughter, Pythias. After leaving Assus he went to Mitylene in Lesbos where he lived until 343–342 B.C. Here, he taught and wrote as before. He also continued with empirical research on animals. It was probably here, too, that he was joined by Theophrastus, who later succeeded him as head of the school he would in time found.

Under the influence of Hermias, whose territory was on the periphery of the Greek world, bordering on lands under Persian influence, Aristotle had become a Pan-Hellenist. This position led him to support the notion of a unified Greece rather than the cluster of individual city-states that made up the Greece of his day. The goal of Pan-Hellenism was to form a strong defense against the Persian Empire. The problem, of course, was who would rule a united Greece.

Aristotle was invited to Pella, the court of Philip of Macedon, to become tutor to Philip's son, Alexander, then a boy of twelve. The boy, Alexander, who was to become Alexander the Great was to resolve the problem of Pan-Hellenism. He would grow up to rule the known world, even though briefly. It is altogether likely that the offer of Alexander's tutorship was made not because Aristotle was a philosopher, but because he was a learned, Pan-Hellenist partisan. His tutorship ended when Alexander became regent for Philip. The assassination of Philip in 335 B.C. threw the court at Macedon into a state of turmoil. When intrigue and counterintrigue became rampant, Aristotle decided to return to Athens. Alexander apparently regarded his old tutor highly. There is a legend that during Alexander's monumental march of conquest through the East, he gave instructions to his subordinates that biological specimens were to be collected and sent to his former teacher. It also may well have been Aristotle's influence that was responsible for Alexander's passion for spreading Greek ideas throughout the world.

While he was away from Athens, Aristotle's thinking increasingly diverged from Plato's teachings. He became more and more concerned with observing the world about him using something of an empirical methodology. When his empirical conclusions contradicted Platonic or other philosophical thinking, he did not hesitate to modify the older concepts, or even to disavow what had formerly been his own convictions.

Plato's interest in science had been limited to mathematics and astronomy and was probably inspired by a Pythagorean belief in the fixed and universal character of these disciplines. His interests were in universals, Forms, not in the imperfect objects that make up the world of sense. Aristotle, on the other hand, became interested in just these imperfect and variable objects and came to direct his attention to the particulars of the world as much as the universals.[4]

Aristotle was forty-nine years old and at the height of his powers when he returned to Athens. Shortly thereafter he founded his school, the Lyceum. The name "peripatetic," which came to be attached to his point of view, arose from his habit of walking with his pupils in the school's covered walk.[5]

We know somewhat more about the organization of the Lyceum than we do about the organization of Plato's Academy. Aristotle probably devoted the mornings to lecturing on logic and metaphysics. During the afternoons he is supposed to have given public lectures on ethics, politics, and rhetoric. Along with this teaching, he and his students actively engaged in research. The school had a rudimentary organization and something of a staff, a library and specimen collections, and even special dinnerware.

The atmosphere of the Lyceum appears to have been more scientific than philosophical. Aristotle had collected zoological specimens during his years of travel, but his most extensive research took place after his return to Athens. Observational studies were made, students prepared collections, and in general the resources for research were augmented quite deliberately. The *History of Animals* shows clear traces of different authors. Apparently, the work was distributed among various persons, each having an assignment that had been schematically developed in advance. Aristotle was a powerful organizer. He was the first of a long line of individuals who, quite apart from their own direct contributions to science, were able to direct and to stimulate scientific work in their associates.

His past tutorship and his continued connection with the court of Alexander and his Pan-Hellenist leanings made Aristotle unpopular with the very strong nationalist party in Athens. In 323 B.C. the news of the death of Alexander was received in Athens while Aristotle's political protector was absent from the city. Anti-Macedonian feeling ran strong in the city. Rather than allowing the Athenians "to sin twice against philosophy" (the first sin being the execution of Socrates), Aristotle retired to his mother's former country estate in Chalcis, a stronghold of Macedonian influence.[6] There in the same year he died of some form of stomach disorder. He was sixty-two years old. His will, which is extant, shows his concern for every relative and dependent and includes provision for the emancipation of several of his slaves.

Much of Aristotle's more strictly scientific work, except some biological treatises, was completed during the years after his return to Athens. These years also saw the completion of many sections of his major philosophical work, the *Metaphysics.* His research in botany, zoology, and anatomy, through which he tried to solve many of the fundamental problems of biology, clearly established him as a great pioneer in these fields. His research on the structures and functions of living things was more exhaustive and greater in scope than that of anyone who lived before him. He was familiar with more than 500 different animal species and had dissected or investigated fifty of these with some thoroughness. In his work, then, he was often the naturalist, the field worker collecting specimens so as to classify them in some framework, more than the philosopher. In examining the extant works as a whole, we are impressed by the amount of space devoted to biological-psychological subjects. Calculation shows that 30 percent of the pages are given over to these subjects.[7] No other topics are treated so extensively.

It was also during this second stay in Athens that most of his definitive works on psychology were written or completed.[8] The predominantly psychological works include the master work, *De Anima* (On the Soul), and shorter works, known collectively (and rather misleadingly) as the *Short Physical Treatises,* including *On the Sense and Sensible, On Memory and Reminiscence, On Sleep and Sleeplessness,* and *On Dreams.*

Although one of his works on logic dates from the earlier period, the rest quite possibly were written during these middle years, as were his works on ethics.

Aristotle virtually founded the field of logic, and to this day the term *non-Aristotelian* logic is used to designate contributions to that science that did not follow his tradition. His works on logic are referred to collectively as the *Organon*, meaning "instrument" in the sense of a tool for philosophic and scientific investigation.[9] Aristotle's ethical treatises were the earliest formal works of this kind. Ethical considerations had been discussed by Plato and others before him, but these accounts had not previously been systematically organized. It was Aristotle who performed this service. Some of his biological works also date from this middle period.

DIVERGENCE FROM PLATO

Aristotle shifted from the teachings of his master, Plato, and the Platonic School in many ways. Perhaps fundamental in this change was Aristotle's contention that the universals, the Forms of Plato, did not have a separate existence from particulars, that is, matter.[10] Aristotle hearkened back to Socrates for his authority, since Socrates inferred universals from particulars and did not set them apart as a different class of existences. Plato's rationalism was in sharp contrast to Aristotle's more empirical outlook, however. Aristotle had turned to biology, with its imperfect but living and changing organisms, and away from the perfect but static and lifeless mathematics that was the science of Plato. Plato insisted on the reality of ideas apart from objects; Aristotle found form resident in physical bodies. To Aristotle, the subject matter of physics (which included psychology) is both form and matter, that is, form embodied in matter. Although substance is individual, we can treat a universal or a general type, that is, a form, as if it were a substance. We may arrive at a universal by abstracting from a class of substantial objects whatever it is they have in common.

Aristotle denied the existence of the forms apart from the particular and tangible things embodying them. A lump of wax will serve as an illustration. The shape of the lump cannot perish without the material also perishing; if form ceases, matter ceases. The lump may change its form, but form, as such, cannot disappear without matter also disappearing. Form and matter may be conceptualized separately by an act of abstraction, but we cannot imagine a substance without form or a form without substance. To Aristotle, therefore, form exists in the particular, and not apart from it. His view is that the substantial reality of things resides in the things themselves. Nothing can exist without matter, and matter cannot exist without form. The individual object as we know it is that which has separate existence—this man, this horse, this plant. Each is a man, or a horse, or a plant insofar as each has both matter and form. The substantial reality of things lies in the things themselves, not in another order apart from them.

Aristotle argued that by attributing an independent existence to his Forms, Plato made it impossible to explain the changing, moving character that objects exhibit. Platonic Forms do not contribute to the exploration of changes in the sensible world. What exists is not the perfect idea, but the imperfect drawing marked off on the ground: not the ideal of justice but the faulty justice carried out by people. The forms exist when realized in matter. To each form there corresponds, as Aristotle put it, "a special matter."[11]

This point of separation between Plato and Aristotle made possible the magnificent construction that was Aristotle's science.

ARISTOTLE'S AIM

We know of Aristotle's claim that he and other men desire knowledge above else.[12] Every kind of knowledge, he states, is to be prized.[13] There is a sheer delight in the exercise of the senses, quite apart from their usefulness[14] (a notion Plato could never have accepted). Thus, Aristotle exhibits the prescription of purism.

Aristotle held that all individuals wonder why things are as they are.[15] It was this human habit of wonder that caused the individual to seek knowledge.[16] Aristotle's very definition of *psyche* is "a substance capable of receiving knowledge."[17] More specifically, intelligence is the faculty of *psyche* that enables *psyche* to receive knowledge.[18] Since humans alone are capable of intelligence or deliberation,[19] it follows that humans are the only creatures capable of acquiring knowledge.[20] Not only did Aristotle himself seek knowledge, but he also saw humans as uniquely fitted for such a search.[21]

Although Aristotle's aim was knowledge of all kinds, he made a distinction among three kinds of knowledge. First was theoretical knowledge, which included what he called "first philosophy" and what in the Middle Ages became metaphysics. He also considered two other sciences, mathematics and physics. Psychology and biology were included under physics.[22] Theoretical knowledge seeks the universals that comprise the abstractions of the real world. Second was practical knowledge, including ethics and politics. These sciences deal with the Good and with personal conduct and are the precursors to the social sciences. Third was productive knowledge, including rhetoric and poetics, dealing with such subjects as the Beautiful.

One of Aristotle's great contributions was to combine the observation of science with the logic of philosophy to create systematic science. The system of science is made up of observations hung in a logical framework. It is in this way that general scientific principles are created which lead to the understanding of lawful relationships and to the deductions that laws of nature allow. Aristotle did not carry out this procedure in its modern form, but the outline of the process that was to come appears in much of his work. Thus, we find both induction and deduction in Aristotle's method.

KNOWLEDGE AND SCIENTIFIC METHOD

Plato, as we have seen, denied the validity of the senses. He made intuitions the basis of all true knowledge. Plato had held that the unreliability of the senses justified skepticism of all sense-knowledge. Unlike Plato who believed knowledge was in the knower already and did not depend on experience for its source, Aristotle held that without sensation thought is not possible.[23] He argued that the mind "is nothing until it has thought." He compared the mind without thought to a blank writing tablet *(tabula rasa)* "on which as yet nothing actually stands written."[24] This "blank tablet" metaphor will be important in later discussions of the empirical view of mind, although Aristotle did not make a formal doctrine of it as later writers seem to believe.

Aristotle held that it is not the senses that fool us but our incorrect interpretations of the sensory information.[25] We gain our knowledge of particulars from sensations, and through induction from those sensations we gain knowledge of universals. Aristotle agreed with Plato that science deals with universals, but he held that we gain such universals through experience.[26] This process of abstraction makes use of an intellectual agent, what was called in the Middle Ages the *agens intellectus.* In Aristotle's case this agent was a natural process that human beings and not animals possess and that acts to allow abstraction to take place, creating knowledge of universals from knowledge of particulars. It is likened to a light that illuminates parts of the experience and allows reason to carry out the abstraction. During the late Middle Ages, Thomas Aquinas would also make use of the concept of *agens intellectus* in much the same way as did Aristotle, but Aquinas would make it not a naturalistic process but the intervention of God.

Out of the welter of sense experience emerges the first of the basic or indispensable characteristics of science: principles, or basic truths. Although sense perception is concerned with particular instances, its content yields the rudimentary general principles from which we proceed inductively to higher and higher levels of principles, until the "true" principles are abstracted. Knowledge is not possible through sense perception alone, since the senses give us only particulars.[27] Nevertheless, sense perception is necessary for the acquisition of knowledge.[28] To have knowledge, we must grasp the primary or first principles. As we have seen, for Aristotle the *psyche* is a substance that receives this knowledge.[29]

Induction provides the the basic principles necessary for deductive reasoning.[30] Thereafter, sometimes we proceed from induction and at other times from deduction.[31] Without question Aristotle encouraged deduction. There is no contradiction here since the process of prediction from scientific laws *is* deductive, although the laws themselves were created inductively or through a combination of induction and deduction.

Aristotle used experience and observation as tests of his astronomical and biological theories. He carefully reported observations of hundreds of species of animals in his biological treatises. He even contrasted observation and theory. Observation, not theory, Aristotle comments, will reveal the method of generation of bees, for example, and we should accept theories only if they agree with observation.[32]

In practice, Aristotle would sometimes seize on the few available observed facts and make sweeping generalizations based on them. Naturally, he made mistakes. His driving search for knowledge often did not allow him time to confirm that he was on sure grounds before proceeding to the next question. Sometimes, too, he was not sufficiently critical of the facts he accepted. He might even believe, without any attempt at verification, old folk tales and the accounts of credulous or sensation-seeking travelers. The major source of difficulty, however, was simply that not enough facts were available to him or to anyone else of his time.

Aristotle's emphasis on classification, often considered by historians of science to be a stage of science that must precede experiment, calls attention to this sheer lack of other information. Membership of an object in a given class was of crucial importance. This knowledge determined its essential nature or essence and marks Aristotle's distinctive contribution to biology.[33]

ARISTOTLE'S PSYCHOLOGY; *DE ANIMA*

Because it deals with the functioning of the individual organism as a whole, *De Anima* must be regarded as the first book to treat psychology as a systematic philosophy. It was not Aristotle's only discussion of psychological matters, however. Psychology's emphasis on the whole organism serves to differentiate it from its biological neighbors, particularly physiology which dealt with the functions of organs. Its focus on the individual also differentiates psychology from what later became its social science neighbors.[34] With this book psychology came into existence as a discipline consciously differentiated from other fields, and in writing it Aristotle became the founder of philosophical psychology.

SCIENCE AND CAUSE

Causality plays a major role in Aristotle's treatment of scientific knowledge.[35] In fact, he considers causal knowledge to be the essence of scientific knowledge. Four causes determine everything—the material cause, the motor or efficient cause, the formal cause, and the final cause.[36] Aristotle describes their nature and interrelation in considerable detail.[37] The material cause is what a thing is made of (e.g., the bronze of a statue); the motor or efficient cause is what sets into motion the process leading to its production (e.g., the sculptor); the formal cause gives the definition of its essential character (e.g., the horse itself); and the final cause is that aim or end toward which a thing develops (e.g., serving to decorate a temple). One of Aristotle's expositions of cause appears in his criticism of Thales, Empedocles, and the other pre-Socratic philosophers' views on the *arche*. (*Arche* is their term for the basic material substance from which everything is made.) These philosophers had given inadequate answers because of their preoccupation with the material cause and their relative neglect of the other causes.[38] A major issue for Aristotle is whether the final or the efficient cause has priority over the other causes.[39] Clearly, he asserts, it is the final cause that has priority, that for the sake of which the thing is formed.

Aristotle's meaning of causality may be compared with our more or less unsophisticated view of the word today. When we speak of "cause" in an unqualified fashion, we generally have in mind what Aristotle called the efficient cause. We also occasionally refer to "final cause," but almost always in this qualified two-word fashion. These two meanings meet the contemporary requirements for cause as something both necessary and sufficient to preclude an effect. Matter and form are not considered as causes today but as static aspects or characteristics of a thing, necessary but not sufficient as a cause. To Aristotle none of the four causes alone was sufficient; all were necessary. Thus, to him cause meant conditions, none of which was individually sufficient to account for the existence of an object. It is not surprising that he would consider matter and form causes, since, without them, nothing could be or come to be.

Final cause and purpose are not synonymous; to call them so is misleading, because not all final causes have consciously foreseen ends, an implication of purpose often considered essential today. To Aristotle, human purposes do exist, people do display foresight and conscious intention, but purpose is just one aspect of final cause. No conscious purpose exists outside human actions. Natural processes are final ends but not conscious intentions.

The prominence of end gives Aristotle's views a purposive, teleological character. To say that Aristotle was a teleologist is to say that he believed there was a plan or design to the universe. Teleology views all things, including humankind, as developing and moving to an end, the final cause of their motion. Every instrument, including the human being, depends on the nature of that for which it is designed. Anaxogoras had said that people were the most intelligent animals because they had hands; Aristotle said that people had hands because they were intelligent animals.[40]

To make its meaning clear, the teleological position is often contrasted with explanation by sufficient cause. Those who accept the teleological position are said to deny efficient causes; those who accept efficient causes are said to deny final causes. In accepting both final and efficient causes (as well as formal and material causes), Aristotle was clearly more than a teleologist.

Insofar as he was a teleologist, Aristotle was also a functionally oriented thinker. A search for end is also a search for function, for what something does. For example, the eye, is designed for seeing. The explanation that Aristotle gives of its structure is based on its function. It exists for seeing. The life history of the organism as a whole seems decided from the outset by a prevision of the form which is the actual outcome. Little acorns grow into mighty oaks if nothing hinders that growth. There is no wrong turn; no beech or maple comes from the acorn. This functional approach dominates his views of biology and psychology, and in many respects he stands as the representative of a view in the ancient world of a functional psychology.

BIOLOGICAL AND PSYCHOLOGICAL FUNCTIONS

We mentioned earlier that Aristotle classed biology and psychology under the theoretical science of physics. Generally speaking, physics concerns natural things that are in motion.[41] What physical sciences tend to have in common is that they deal with things that have in themselves a principle of movement.[42]

Living things have a particular movement that arises from *psyche.* [43] Movement in this case should not be interpreted literally. *Psyche* is not self-moved; it does not transport itself in space (except incidentally as the body moves about). Its motion is more figurative, more a principle of movement than a literal movement. *Psyche* does manifest itself in movements of various sorts, however, for example, locomotion, alteration, diminution, growth, sensation, and thinking.[44] Inclusion of what we would call both biological and psychological activities is evident. *Psyche* is of primary interest to Aristotle, who wrote that all knowledge is valuable but that knowledge of the *psyche* is to be prized above all.

The word *psyche* is both more and less than "soul" for Aristotle. It means more in that *psyche* is integrated with matter, and it means less in that the term *soul* later acquired religious significance quite absent from Aristotle's thinking. Although soul is the customary translation of *psyche*, it is best to use the word without translation to avoid both the subtractions and the whole host of meanings that "soul" has acquired over the centuries since Aristotle's time.

His conception of life as *psyche* marks Aristotle as a believer in vitalism, a position that holds that there is a principle peculiar and essential to the phenomena of life. Vitalism stands in contrast to mechanism. For example, Democritus was a mechanist, since his theory of atoms encompasses living and nonliving objects alike; life was capable of mechanical expression. In contrast, Aristotle postulated the special principle, *psyche*, which is necessary for life and absent from nonanimate things.

To Aristotle, *psyche* basically meant living. In this meaning, it is again evident why in Aristotle's thinking psychology should be considered as an aspect of biology, since all psychological phenomena are included among living activities.[45] *Psyche* is operative throughout the whole scale of animate things and is not confined to humans alone. *Psyche* marks the distinction, not between thinking and unthinking beings, but between the organic and the inorganic.

Aristotle distinguished between matter and form, but in this context, body is matter; *psyche* is form.[46] The constituents of the body are matter; the form is composed of *psyche*. The living individual consists of both together: they form a unity. A dead body is only matter having no form of the person.

A recasting of the traditional four causes is thus indicated. Instead of keeping them distinct and separate, Aristotle suggests that the *psyche* functions not only as the formal, but also as the efficient and final, causes of the body.[47] *Psyche* is the efficient cause because it sets the process going in the body; it is the formal cause because the existence of the body means life; and it is the final cause because a body exists for living. His description of the final cause is Aristotle's way of saying that the body was made for *psyche*, that it exists for the sake of *psyche*. *Psyche* therefore coincides with three of the causes. The final, formal, and efficient causes all function as form and thus in an extended sense they are formal, whereas the material cause is the passive recipient of form.

It follows, then, that when a natural state of affairs prevails, *psyche* dominates the body. In a corrupt state, however, the body dominates *psyche*.[48] Although he refers to it only casually and incidentally, Aristotle goes so far as to compare movement originated by *psyche* to that which animates automatic puppets.[49] René Descartes would reestablish this idea many centuries later.

What happens then to the *psyche* when the body is gone? One interpretation is that body and *psyche* are so inextricably joined that one cannot survive without the other. *Psyche* cannot exist disembodied. Aristotle clearly states this view in Book 1 of *De Anima*.[50] Body and *psyche* are an inseparable unit, but they can be distinguished for the sake of discussion.[51]

Another view that Aristotle holds is logically discordant with this position. This view is found in the part of *De Anima* which some authorities believe was written in the earlier, Platonic phase of his thinking. Consequently, it is not representative of Aristotle's mature position. Here he seems to say that the highest element in the human being, *Nous*, which is an intellectual force not dependent on the body, is immortal in that it survives the body. This divergent view was the cause of tangled controversies, both in the Middle Ages and in modern times. Either the rejection or acceptance of the immortality of the *psyche* is a defensible interpretation of Aristotle, although the first, rejection, is adopted in discussing his psychology.

A body is composed of organs needed for the body's functions,[52] and the organs, in turn, are there to serve a function.[53] We owe the concept of something being ''organic'' to Aristotle. Even plants, he maintains, have rudimentary organs, since roots are analogous to the mouth and serve to take in nourishment.[54] In contrast to Aristotle's functional definition, today we use the distinction between organic and inorganic structure to differentiate animate from inanimate objects. For Aristotle this distinction on the basis of structure was only an incidental bit of information that helped him to differentiate life from nonlife. The different ways living and nonliving things behave was more important to him than the existence of differences in bodily structure.

Aristotle argues that *psyche* is diffused in every part of the body. This diffusion becomes less marked in higher animals; the greater the degree of organization in the animal, the greater the degree of centralization and the less the need for *psyche* in each part.[55] Despite the diffusion of *psyche* throughout the living body, a center for it in the body was sought. Aristotle found this center, the point at which *psyche* actuates the body, in the heart. He made this judgment for the following reasons: diseases of the heart are fatal; psychological experiences, such as joy or sorrow, cause a disturbance of the heart; the heart is the first organ formed in the embryo, and its palpitation shows that the embryo has life.[56] In identifying life with *psyche* and *psyche* with the heart, Aristotle rejects the Platonic doctrine of the brain as the organ of the *psyche*. As one argument for doing so, he cites his finding that the brain is insensible to direct stimulation.[57] It is ironic that Plato was correct on the basis of the ''wrong'' argument. Plato assigned reason to the brain because of several irrelevant speculations, typical of which was the fact that the brain was the part of the human being nearest the heavens. Aristotle, on the other hand, was wrong for the ''right''—that is, naturalistic—suppositions.

Aristotle referred to parts of the *psyche*, just as Plato did,[58] but neither meant ''parts'' in a literal sense. The term *aspects* should be used instead of *parts* because it better reflects the structural view of Plato. In the same way, *functions* more accurately catches the train of Aristotle's thought. *Psyche* exhibits inclusive or general functions, which in turn may be broken down into specific functions. In this way, Aristotle represents the functional prescription against Plato's structural prescription.

According to Aristotle, *psyche* may be divided into an indefinite number of general functions. In practice he most often uses two to five divisons, depending on his particular intent. He divides functions into the rational and the irrational; into growing, sensing, remembering; into desiring, reacting, and thinking; and into growing, sensing, and knowing. This last tripartite division, which Aristotle refers to in a less functional way as the nutritive, sensitive, and rational *psyche*, is the one most commonly used by later scholars to summarize Aristotle's views.[59] The more functional conception of growing, sensing, and knowing will often be used in the present account, especially when a quick, convenient way to summarize the functions of *psyche* is desired.

Living things exhibit an unbroken developmental hierarchy among levels of functioning. Each higher level incorporates the lower levels of functioning; it cannot take place without them. The lower functions potentially exist in the higher function; to use Aristotle's own illustration, they exist in the same manner as the triangle does within the quadrilateral.[60] The highest act of thinking is at the top of a chain of continuous development in which sensing is the lowest form of discrimination.[61] This hierarchy serves to demonstrate that *psyche* has a unity with several related functions. This argument for the unity of *psyche* may be seen from a slightly different perspective as a theory of development. The growth *psyche* is included in the sensing (or animal) *psyche*, and the sensing *psyche* is part of the knowing (or human) *psyche*.

ARISTOTLE'S FUNCTIONS

Although living was the fundamental activity, the master function, as it were, there were also various other expressions of *psyche*. The more specific biological-psychological functions of growing, sensing, remembering, desiring and reacting, and thinking now merit examination. It is in keeping with Aristotle's functional, active, and individually oriented point of view that they are referred to in this grammatical form rather than in the more static and passive form of "growth," "sensation," and "thought."

Growing

Progressive change of the organism is brought about by more specific activities that are included in the general function of growing. Briefly, these specific functions are persistence of the living entity, its accession of things from its surroundings, and the increase in size of every particle of it.[62] Growing is the most widely distributed general function exhibited by plants, animals, and people. Plants differ from other living things in that they possess this general function of growth, but not of sensing.[63] Because of the relation of growth to plants, the term *vegetative soul* was applied to this general function in the Middle Ages.

Sensing

The specific function of sensing is possessed by animals and people, but not by plants.[64] Indeed, the ability to sense (in what Aristotle considers to be its most primitive manifestation of touch) is the means of distinguishing an animal from a plant.[65] To Aristotle, sensing objects means in modern terminology that perceiving is involved.

Aristotle specifies that by the external senses he means the traditional five senses—sight, hearing, smell, taste, and touch—and no other. His argument for the existence of only five external senses runs somewhat as follows: If we assume that all objects in this world are known to us through these external senses, then the assumption of an additional sense would mean either that it merely duplicates an existing one or that it has no object. Both are unthinkable consequences in a world in which each thing is designed with an end in mind.

Aristotle gave each of the senses detailed consideration. He sees touch as more complex that the others, no matter how we subdivide the original five senses. Each sense organ responds to one or more sets of qualities. For example, the eye is sensitive to color, including black and white.[66]

Sensing and growing alike depend on alternation or movement from without.[67] Sensitivity is an activity aroused in the organism by the environment. This need for the dual functioning of organism and environment is based on Aristotle's basic premise of movement or change, that the senses are related to the environment. The organism's relation with the environment in sensing, however, is different from what takes place in nutrition. Through nutrition, the material object is taken in from the environment; plants and animals devour the nutritive object. A sweet fig nourishes the organism through the matter of the fig; the form, sweetness, does not enter. In sensing, not the object itself but its form is received from the environment, just as the wax receives the form of the seal without assimilating the metal of which it is composed.[68] In sensing, the body responds to the form of the external object without being acted on by the matter.[69]

Sensing is actualized by the sensible quality of the object,[70] but it is not merely the passive process of assimilating form. At this point the sensing of the organ becomes "like" the object sensed. The sense quality that is a potentiality of the object is actualized by the activity of the sense organs. The sky has the power to be seen as blue: the power of being visible to the eyes as blue. Hence, for Aristotle one does not see in the eyes but *with* the eyes.

The particular nature of sensing needs further clarification. W. K. Guthrie does this admirably in commenting on Aristotle's view of the nature of sensing. He writes: "The peculiarity of life is that when the bodily organ is materially altered by an external object, *then* another, totally different result supervenes, which we call sensation."[71] The objective stimulus is the cause of motion. A change that proceeds through a medium in the sense organ or some other part of the body becomes transformed or, to use Aristotle's term, is actualized into consciousness. The sounding in the object and the hearing of the animal are different, but when the process occurs they are merged into one.[72]

The question arises as to how sensations of qualities—white, sweet, and so on—give a perception of concrete things. Moreover, some perceptions are not peculiar to any one of the senses. Movements, rest, shape, size, number, and duration are not experienced by any one sense alone. How, then, does one experience these so-called common sensibles? They seem to belong to or to be common to all senses, but they are not peculiar to any one of them. When a person says, "I smell smoke," he means not only that the smell is experienced but also that he is aware he is smelling it. These considerations led Aristotle to postulate that a common sense carries out the functions of synthesizing the sensory elements into perceptual units, including both perception itself and consciousness that one is perceiving.

Aristotle's particular argument for a composite functioning of the special senses in sensing self-perception may be stated as follows: If I do not perceive that I perceive the stimulus in a single indivisible act, then another sense would be required in order for me to know I was sensing. But this sense would require a third to unite the previous ones. This, in turn, would require another sense to unite the three, and so on, by infinite regress. To cut this short, Aristotle asserts that the sense perceives itself. Hence, the common sense depends on the combined functioning of the various senses in order to account for what it does.

The distinction of form and matter that has been applied to the relation between *psyche* and body and between sense and sense organ may be applied to self-perception. In this instance the knower perceives the qualities of an object and is aware that she has done so. *Psyche* has form and apprehends form; the sense organ has form and apprehends form; the person has form and apprehends form.

Aristotle concerned himself with the issue of whether a common sense was a sixth sense or a composite of the single senses.[73] Despite some disagreement among authorities, Aristotle's naturalistic spirit and his argument about perceiving incline us to believe that he thought common sense was a composite and not another sense.[74] The common sense functions through the common nature of all five senses and assures us that we perceive one world, not one for each sense. It is not another or sixth sense; rather, it is a name for certain functions of the five senses collectively. The alternative interpretation that would distinguish common sense from the five external senses will be taken up in the chapter on Aquinas. The conscious being is always active. An admirable illustration may be found in Aristotle's account of sleeping, a function he related to the common sense.[75] After all, we do not sleep with some senses awake (i.e., active) and the others asleep. They function in common. Sleep is caused by fatigue of the common sense, which loses vitality. Sleep therefore has a restorative function.

In sleeping, only the growth functions are active; sleep is inhibition of conscious functioning. How, therefore, are we to account for a dream?[76] Aristotle holds that it is similar to sensation, though not the same since no object is sensed. He concludes that in dreaming the effects of sensory stimulation that occurred during the waking state persist and are carried over into sleeping.

Remembering

Memory is related to former sense perception.[77] There is a persistence of the effect of sense impressions, which allows us to make use of knowledge already acquired.[78]

Remembering, like dreaming, arises from the effects of sensing that persist after the object is removed. Sensory stimulation stamps in, as it were, an impression of the percept.[79] These traces of former movements, images, form one of the bases for remembering. There is a fainter continuation of the original movements through images. Through memory we also recognize the originally sensed object or event. Memory consists, then, of remaining aware of a perception of some event that occurred in the past. To have memory we must have awareness both of duration (time) and of a particular perception. Remembering, in the strict sense, is related to the general function of sensing and is therefore shared with animals. Memory is also a faculty in and of itself, however, for its object is distinct and separable—the past precisely as past.

Recollection (recall) is not synonymous with remembering.[80] Remembering is the spontaneous reproduction of past perceptions, that is, a retention of the effect of past experience. Recall is the active search to recover these past perceptions. Recall demands hard thinking, which in this context Aristotle called deliberation, since it involves a search in which one reasons that one has had the experience in question. Hence, unlike remembering, recollection is limited to humans, who alone have the power of deliberation.[81]

It was in connection with recall that Aristotle systematized the now famous doctrine of the laws of association—actually classifications of the principles by which memories are related. Recall occurs because we are able to call up a series of associations (although Aristotle did not use the word) in regular order,[82] that is, according to specified principles. Plato implied that similarity and contiguity are two of the means by which recollection operates, but he did not develop the idea.[83] Aristotle was the first to develop the concept systematically. He believed that three sorts of relationships serve as links in the chain of associations—similarity, contrast, and contiguity.[84] Recall occurs insofar as experiences succeed one another in memory. This is to say that the recall of one object tends to be followed by the recall of that which is like it (similar to it), contrary to it (contrasted with it), or accompanying it (contiguous with it) in the original learning. Similarity, contrast, and contiguity as sketched by Aristotle were historically to form the basis for the doctrine of association in the centuries to come.

Aristotle mentioned three other factors relevant to modern learning theory; scholarship generally overlooked these factors until the modern period. Aristotle was aware of the contention that the more often an experience is repeated, the better it will be remembered.[85] He also spoke of "some" events as better remembered after a single experience than others experienced many times. Remembering after only a single experience is a qualification of the more general norm, not specifically verbalized, that the more an experience is repeated, the better it will be remembered. Aristotle also regarded "bonds of association" as acquiring special strength from emotion. He indicates that when excited by love or by fear, the person can see a desired emotion or a feared one approaching despite there being little resemblance.[86] He goes on to state that the more one is under the influence of emotion, the less "similarity" is necessary for this to happen. Aristotle also said that things arranged in a "fixed" order were more easily recalled than items "badly" arranged.[87] Something approaching the distinction between meaningful and rote materials is suggested in this identification of order of materials as a potent factor in recall. All these factors were to be subjected to research scrutiny in the modern study of learning.

Desiring and Reacting

In some of his writings Aristotle raised desiring (appetite, conation) to a status equal with growing, sensing, and knowing and spoke of it as one of four general functions.[88] Desire is related to sensation and pleasure–pain (which gives rise to it) and has consequences in reacting.

Sensing, pleasure–pain, desire, and self-motion form a sequence. The process is as follows. Pleasure and pain follow upon sensing, although they are not a part of sensing itself. Rather, they are consequences of sensory experiences.[89] As explained earlier, sensing is the means whereby objects in the environment are perceived. Some objects are perceived as pleasurable, and others as unpleasurable. Once these feelings are experienced, desire is introduced. Where there is sensing, there is pleasure and pain; where there is pleasure and pain, there is desire.[90] Ignoring pain for the moment, we see that what the organism desires is the satisfaction that the perceived object will give. It should be noted that desire is related to sensing in a circular fashion because sensing is followed by pleasure and pain, which in turn arouse desire, and desire is a craving for the pleasant and a cringing from the painful. Thus so far, sensing, pleasure–pain, and desiring have been accounted for sequentially. Reacting (locomotion) must now be brought into this sequence.

Aristotle says that desire is the immediate and efficient cause of movement.[91] Locomotion is also related through pleasure and pain to desire since it takes us toward an object we desire or away from one we desire to avoid. As Aristotle puts it, unless moved by compulsion, an animal is moved only insofar as it seeks pleasure or avoids pain.[92] Pleasure and pain are not simple impressions following upon sensing; they incite desire, which brings about locomotion and completes the process. This sequence, however, is subject to an important qualification in that thinking is also a source of movement.

Aristotle's theory of the nature of pleasure and pain is a statement of the doctrine that pleasure is that which is according to nature and pain that which is contrary to nature.[93] Pleasure and pain are therefore the concomitants or accompaniments of activities. Aristotle holds that pleasure accompanies the free expression of activity, an unimpeded exercise of the functions of the *psyche*. If the experience is painful, it is so because it conflicts with the natural state of the functioning of the *psyche*. The realization of any natural function is pleasurable, and the pleasure is proportional to the completeness of the realization. Moreover, pleasure is related to the exercise of a function. When an activity is pleasurable, it tends to be exercised; those who delight in geometry become geometricians.[94] Instances of pathological pleasure do not contradict the claim that freedom and naturalness characterize pleasure since Aristotle held that these abnormal pleasures come about from a kind of diseased condition of the body and not from psychological activities.

In his analysis of psychological motion, or of psychological field forces, to put it in more modern terms, Aristotle appeals to the concept of an "unmoved mover."[95] Its use in connection with desire is straightforward and objective. In the relation between the desiring individual and the desired object, the desired object serves as a stimulus, or mover, as he called it. This mover, however, is not similarly affected by desire. Consequently, it is an "unmoved mover." In a sense, then, the object of desire, the unmoved mover, is outside the process of the functioning organism. Aristotle argues that every action has an unmoved mover. As a consequence, the number of unmoved movers is countless.

Scholars in later ages used the concept of the unmoved mover, in their search for God in Aristotle, and in the process a single "supreme unmoved mover" was lifted to theological heights. Aristotle's remarks lend credence to this position.[96] His "highest order" attempt at unification reduced the number of kinds of motion to either forty-seven or fifty-five kinds of unmoved movers. In this same discussion, however, he speaks of one eternal mover whose essence is actuality. It would seem that his analysis of unmoved movers took place in two different realms—one concerned with kinds of motion and the other with a theological necessity. Aristotle's use in psychology of the concept of the unmoved mover was singularly free from theological complications, however. In boldest terms he seems to mean that for every reaction there is a stimulus.

It is convenient at this point to add emotions to the discussion of desire. Aristotle's *Rhetoric*[97] and his *Nichomachean Ethics*[98] contain most of the relevant material. An illustration of how he assigns psychological implications to philosophical concerns is found in his treatment of emotions and desires as they relate to moral virtues. These virtues include courage, which necessitates a psychological discussion of fear; temperance, which requires that desire be considered in a psychological setting; and good temper, which demands consideration of the psychology of anger. He discusses other psychological matters in a similar vein. Aristotle analyzes various emotions in terms of the disposition that gives rise to the particular emotion of the person toward whom it is directed, and of the occasions that give rise to it.[99] An essentially practical description of the emotions emerges.

Aristotle's comments concerning emotion extend even into his theory of the fine arts, including the theater. In discussing the nature of tragedy, he claims that its function is to arouse pity and fear, but only in such a way and in such amounts that will allow us to purge ourselves of these emotions.[100] This is the famous doctrine of catharsis. *Catharsis*, a form of cleansing, is brought about by transferring to the tragic hero our own sufferings. In him we see ourselves, and in his fate our doom. However, since this is not the actual situation, since his particular fate is not ours, we transform our fear for ourselves into fear for him. This emotional involvement allows us to release our apprehensions and to deflect our psychic burdens onto another's shoulders. Self-pity gives way to compassion, and we are better for this emotional experience.

Thinking

A person may desire and thus act; a person may also think,[101] and thought may or may not be followed by action. In other words, not only desire but also thinking, in which calculation of the means toward an end becomes part of the sequence, may precede action.

Action by no means implies all sorts of movement. Action is a kind of movement in which an end is involved.[102] All other movements are just that and nothing more, since they do not involve an end and are therefore not complete. Again Aristotle's approach is both functional and teleological.

Some animals have the ability to sense as well as the ability to imagine, but none has the ability to think. The highest of their functions is imagination. In Aristotle's opinion the human being is the only animal that thinks.[103]

To Aristotle, thinking is a process that depends on the hierarchically lower general functions. It is not completely separable since each higher level presupposes lower ones. Those functions that bear a hierarchical relation to thought are sensation, imagination, and memory. Thought requires sensory experiences with which to work; sensation reverts to its derivative, imagination, which in turn leads to memory. The materials for thought are supplied by the imagination. In this context, images serve as perceptions.[104] Thinking depends on the retention of images, which thought molds into relations and patterns, so that there is not merely a flux of images but a meaningful organization of them.

Aristotle's insistence that images are necessary for thought is worth stressing. He leaves no doubt of his position—thinking takes place in images,[105] never without them.[106] The influence of this Aristotelian dogma of no image–no thought was to last well into the modern period—indeed, until the turn of the twentieth century and the Würzburg School of imageless thought.

By a shift of perspective from memory to thought, association becomes an integral aspect of thought. Similarity, contrast, contiguity, and the rest bring about associations that we refer to as thought.

Aristotle does not regard thought as a means of suppressing natural impulses. He considers suppression of any natural human function a distortion[107] of the natural. Fear and anger and other emotions have suitable occasions when they are appropriate. There are things we ought to fear, and there are occasions when we should be angry. Thought does not suppress emotions: it helps to determine right conduct.

It is with Aristotle that for the first time we have a reasonably complete picture of a whole psychology. He was, of course, wrong in may of his "facts," and he omitted important topics; but his overall framework of growing, sensing, remembering, desiring, reacting, and thinking, with but a few changes, bears more than a resemblance to modern psychology. Aristotle was the first philosophical psychologist. The advent of a scientific psychology was still far in the future.

SUMMARY

We have seen that Aristotle broke with Plato and Plato's followers on the nature of Platonic Forms. The form, that is, the universal, is not separate from the particular matter known. This separation was necessary to allow the study of the changing processes in the sensory world. Aristotle was interested in universals as much as Plato was, but found that the universals were not given in the *psyche* from the beginning but rather were abstracted from the particular sensory experiences by an intellectual agent. Aristotle considered the *psyche* as the knower. The *psyche* is not isolated from the thing known. This yields a functional definition of *psyche:* it is a process; *psyche* is what *psyche* does. The inner structure of *psyche* is supported and partly guided by a field of external relations. This field, the environmental world, cannot be defined unless we consider as an integral part of it what we do in response to it. Aristotle gave us the first functional view of mental processes.

The continuity of psychobiological development is another major guiding concept in the thinking of Aristotle. His account of psychological functioning from thinking, the highest level, down to growing, the lowest level, is consistent throughout. Developmentalism in reverse, as it were, was being advanced as a prescriptive attitude. The pre-Socratics had considered change but not development; Plato held to a static prescription with his Forms. Aristotle, however, conceived of development as essential to the understanding of living things. As he conceived it, the functional character of each process lends itself to a dynamic conception.

Aristotle also did much to advance an empirical point of view. Before Aristotle, some of the pre-Socratics and Sophists had taken a position of extreme sensationalism. Plato's position can be characterized as extreme rationalism. Reconciling these two points of view, Aristotle took a mediating position of empiricism and rationalism. He held that knowledge was gained from sense experience and thinking. Yet experience is still knowledge of individuals, not of universals, as such. Knowledge of universals is dependent on theory, and theory is derived from reason. Experience is therefore inferior to reason.

Aristotle stresses the process of moving from generalities to particulars, that is, deductions. However, he places as much emphasis on collecting facts, only later to be put in a theoretical framework, so that there is no doubt that he used induction in considerable measure as well.

Aristotle had a more naturalistic outlook than Plato. He tended to keep within the realm of the natural world, that is, within the natural processes of living, sensing, and thinking. When he ventured beyond physics, as all the Greeks did, his position was commendably cautious, though not without fire and conviction.

With regard to a psychological orientation, unity of body and *psyche* made

Aristotle something of a monist. In terms of epistemological knowing, Aristotle was a dualist in that he separated body and *psyche.* In the centuries to come Aristotle's theory of knowledge would be adopted by the Catholic Church, particularly through the theological doctrine provided by Thomas Aquinas.

Determinism, the theory that human events can be explained in terms of antecedent events, had been known before Aristotle. In fact, he chided the pre-Socratics for their preoccupation with material causes. It was Aristotle, however, who systematically developed the concept in terms of the four causes.

In summary, on psychological matters Aristotle was functionalistic, contentually subjectivistic, developmentalistic, rationalistic and empiricistic, deductive, deterministic (with a teleological emphasis), and monistic. It is also apparent that in the main, his outlook was naturalistic, nomothetic, and puristic. He followed the trends already established in Greek philosophy–science but sharpened them and gave them more explicit recognition than they had previously received by writing their first history.

NOTES

1. The account of Aristotle's life, works, and chronology leans heavily on information from J. H. Randall, *Aristotle* (New York: Columbia University Press, 1960) and W. Jaeger, *Aristotle: Fundamentals of the History of His Development* (Oxford: Clarendon Press, 1934). The chronology of his works given by Jaeger is followed and supplemented by that of F. J. Nuyens, "The Evolution of Aristotle's Psychology," *Proceedings of the 10th International Congress on Philosophy* (Amsterdam, 1948), pp. 1101–1104.

2. *Ibid.*

3. T. W. Organ, *An Index to Aristotle,* in English translation (Princeton, N.J.: Princeton University Press, 1949).

4. R. M. Hutchins, ed., *The Great Books of the Western World,* Vols. VIII–IX, *Works of Aristotle,* trans. W. D. Ross (Chicago: Encyclopaedia Britannica, 1952), (c. 340–322 B.C.). *Physics,* 193^b 22–194^a 18.

5. From *peri,* a prefix meaning "around," and *patos,* meaning "a path."

6. W. D. Ross, *Aristotle; A Complete Exposition of His Works and Thought,* 5th ed. (New York: Meridian Books, 1959), p. 14.

7. In the edition used, the total of his complete works are given in 1415 printed pages. The so-called Biological Treatise occupies 331 pages, whereas *De Anima* and the other psychological works occupy 98 more for a total of 429 pages or 30 percent of the works.

8. For the purposes of this presentation Jaeger's *(Aristotle)* opinion about the dating of the books of *De Anima* is followed instead of Nuyens' ("Evolution"). This means that the discussion of *Nous* in *De Anima* III, Chapters 4 and 5, is considered an earlier position in harmony with earlier ethical and metaphysical views, but is not expressive of his final thinking. The doctrine of the *Nous* as making all things and beings separate, deathless, eternal, and impersonal is questioned. This is a matter of judgment with which Nuyens would disagree—and he has some cogent arguments that this doctrine represents a final phase of Aristotle's thinking. This author is in agreement with both Nuyens and Jaeger that some of the physical treatises date from the transition period.

9. *Categories; On Interpretation; Prior Analytics; Posterior Analytics; Topics; On Sophistical Refutations.*

10. Aristotle, *Metaphysics*, 990^a 33–993^a 16, 1040^a 9, 1078^b 6–1079^b 11, 1086^a 188–1087^a 25; *On Interpretation*, 17^a 38.
11. Aristotle, *Physics*, 194^b 12.
12. Aristotle, *Metaphysics*, 980^a 1.
13. Aristotle, *De Anima*, 402^a 1–4.
14. Aristotle, *Metaphysics*, 980^a 22.
15. Aristotle, *Ibid.*, 983^b 14.
16. Aristotle, *Ibid.*, 500^a–501^a.
17. Aristotle, *Topics*, 151^b 1.
18. Aristotle, *On Dreams*, 458^b 3.
19. Aristotle, *De Anima*, 443^a 12; *On the Parts of Animals*, 642^b 18; *Politics*, 1332^b 5.
20. Aristotle, *Topics*, 130^b 8, 132^a 20, 133^a 21, 134^a 15, 140^a 36.
21. Aristotle, *Nicomachean Ethics*, 1097^b 25–1098^a 20.
22. Aristotle, *Metaphysics*, 1025^b 25–27.
23. Aristotle, *De Sensu*, VI. 445, *De Anima*, III. 8, 432.
24. Aristotle, *De Anima*, 429^b 30–430^a 1.
25. Aristotle, *Ibid.*, 428^b 19–429^a 1.
26. Aristotle, *Topics*, I.10; *Posterior Analytics*, I. 31; *History of Animals*, I, 6.
27. Aristotle, *Posterior Analytics*, 87^b 28–88^a 17.
28. Aristotle, *On Dreams*, 458^b 2.
29. Aristotle, *Prior Analytics*, 99^b 15–100^b 17.
30. Aristotle, *Nichomachean Ethics*, 1098^b 1–8.
31. Aristotle, *Ibid.*, 1139^b 18–35.
32. Aristotle, *On the Generation of Animals*, 760^b 70.
33. Aristotle, For example, *On the Parts of Animals* 639^a 1–642^b 4.
34. Aristotle, *Metaphysics*, 1040^b 5.
35. Aristotle, *Posterior Analytics*, 94^a 20.
36. Aristotle, *On the Generation of Animals*, 715^b 3–5.
37. Aristotle, *Physics*, 194^b 16–195^b 30; *De Anima*, 415^b 8–11; *Metaphysics*, 1013a 24–1014^a, 25.
38. Aristotle, *Metaphysics*, 983^b 7–985^b 22.
39. Aristotle, *On the Parts of Animals*, 639^b 12–640^a 12.
40. *Ibid.*, 687a 8.
41. Aristotle, *Physics*, 185^a 12.
42. Aristotle, *Metaphysics*, 1064^a 17.
43. Aristotle, *De Anima*, 415^b 8–28, 432^a 14–434^a 22; *On the Motion of Animals*, 700^b 4–701^a 6, 701^a 35, 702^a 35, 703^a 2.
44. Aristotle, *De Anima*, 406^a 13, 413^a 24, 415^b 19–27.
45. F. J. Nuyens, *L 'evolution de la Psychologie d' Aristotle* (Louvain: Insitut Superieur de Philosphie, 1948).
46. Aristotle, *De Anima*, 412^a 12–413^a 10.
47. *Ibid.*, 415^b 8–11; *On the Parts of Animals*, 645^b 15; *On the Generation of Animals*, 715^b 3–5; *Metaphysics*, 1044^a 37–1044^b 1.
48. Aristotle, *Politics*, 1254^a 31–1254^b 4.
49. Aristotle, *On the Motion of Animals*, 701^b 1–5.
50. Aristotle, *De Anima*, 403^a 2–403^b 19, 407^b 15–16.
51. E. Zeller, *Aristotle and the Earlier Peripatetics*, Vol. 2 (New York: Longmans, Green, 1897).
52. Aristotle, *On the Generation of Animals*, 716^a 25.
53. Aristotle, *On the Parts of Animals*, 687^a 11.

54. Aristotle, *De Anima*, 412^b 3.
55. Aristotle, *On the Motion of Animals*, 703^a 38.
56. Aristotle, *On the Parts of Animals*, 657^a 25, 656^a 30; *On the Motion of Animals*, 703^b 24; *On the Generation of Animals*, 734^b 26.
57. Aristotle, *On the Parts of Animals*, 656^a 18–28
58. Aristotle, *De Anima*, 402^b 1–8.
59. For example, *On the Generation of Animals*, 736^b 15.
60. Aristotle, *De Anima*, 414^b 29.
61. Aristotle, *Posterior Analytics*, 99^b 35.
62. *Generation and Corruption*, 321^a 19–321^b 12.
63. For example, *De Anima*, 424^a 33; *On the Parts of Animals*, 666^a 35.
64. The major discussion of the five senses occupies Chapters 5 through 12 of Book II of *De Anima*, 416^b 31–424^b 19. (Herrnstein and Boring, *A Source Book in the History of Psychology*. Cambridge: Harvard University Press, 1966), Excerpt No. 1, gives a major portion of these chapters.)
65. Aristotle, *On the Sense and Sensible*, 436^b 10.
66. Aristotle, *De Anima*, 418^a 27–29.
67. *Ibid.*, 415^b 24–416^b 32.
68. *Ibid.*, 424^a 16–24.
69. *Ibid.*, 425^b 22–24.
70. *Ibid.*, 417^a 10–418^a 6, 418^b 27–419^b 11.
71. W. K. Guthrie, *The Greek Philosophers: From Thales to Aristotle* (New York: Harper and Brothers, 1950), p. 149.
72. Aristotle, *De Anima*, 425^b 27.
73. *Ibid.*, 424^b 20–427^a 15.
74. For example, *Ibid.*, 424^b 20–22.
75. Aristotle, *On Sleep and Sleeplessness*, 953^b 12–958^a 32.
76. Aristotle, *On Dreams*, 458^b 1–464^b 18.
77. Aristotle, *On Memory and Reminiscence*, 449^b 1–453^b 11. (Herrnstein and Boring, Excerpt No. 65, gives the portion devoted to associative memory.)
78. *Ibid.*, 450^a 14, 541^a 16; *Posterior Analytics*, 99^b 36–100^a 8; *On the Sense and Sensible*, 441^b 23–24.
79. Aristotle, *On Memory and Reminiscence*, 450^a 31.
80. *Ibid.*, 451^a 21–452^b 11.
81. *Ibid.*, 453^a 13.
82. *Ibid.*, 451^b 11.
83. R. M. Hutchins, ed., *The Great Books of the Western World*, Vol. VII, Plato, *Dialogues*, trans. B. Jowett (Chicago: Encyclopaedia Britannica, 1952) (c. 390–348 B.C.) *Phaedo*, 73c.
84. Aristotle, *On Memory and Reminiscence* 451^b 19–21.
85. *Ibid.*, 451^b 11.
86. Aristotle, *On Dreams*, 460^b 2.
87. Aristotle, *On Memory and Reminiscence*, 452^a 3.
88. *De Anima*, 432^b 3.
89. *Ibid.*, 414^b 5.
90. *Ibid.*, 413^b 23.
91. *Ibid.*, 433^a 5–434^a 22; *On the Motion of Animals*, 701^a 35, 703^a 5.
92. Aristotle, *De Anima*, 432^b 17.
93. Aristotle, *Nicomachean Ethics*, 1174^b 4.
94. Ibid., 1175^a 34.
95. Aristotle, *De Anima*, 434^b 33.

96. For example, *Metaphysics*, 1071^b 3–1075^a 14, passim; *On the Motion of Animals*, 699^a, 12–700^a 26.

97. Aristotle, *Rhetoric*, 1378^a 20–1388^b 30.

98. Aristotle, *Nicomachean Ethics*, 1105^b 19–1106^a 14, 1108^a 30–1109^b 27, 1111^b 4–18.

99. Aristotle, *Rhetoric*, 1378^a 20.

100. Aristotle, *Poetics*, 1149^b 27.

101. Aristotle, *De Anima*, 433^a 5–434^a 22; *On the Motion of Animals*, 701^a 1–701^b 33.

102. Aristotle, *Metaphysics*, 1048^b 22.

103. Aristotle, *De Anima*, 433^a 12.

104. *Ibid.*, 432^b 14.

105. *Ibid.*, 431^b 2.

106. *Ibid.*, 431^a 16.

107. Aristotle, *Nicomachean Ethics*, 1103^a 14–1109^b 27.

Galen, from an old print.

Chapter 5

Theophrastus and Galen: The Hellenistic and Roman Periods

With the deaths of Aristotle and Alexander, Greek history, philosophy, and science entered a third phase known as the Hellenistic period, which extended from about 300 to 100 B.C. It followed the conquest of the Near East by Alexander, when Greek culture was carried eastward and Oriental culture spread westward. The Hellenistic period is often referred to as the twilight of Greek thinking. Although there was certainly a decline during this period, it was by no means abrupt. Progress continued to be made, but the giant shadow of Aristotle tended to dominate and thought was more derivative than original. Psychology was most advanced by Theophrastus, who was a lesser figure than Aristotle but whose views were more modern—at least in spirit—than those of his master.

THEOPHRASTUS

Theophrastus was born in 372 B.C. He first came to Athens in order to study under Plato, but he became the friend of Aristotle, whom he joined in his travels and whose interest in natural history he shared. When Aristotle was obliged to leave Athens in 323–322 B.C., he appointed Theophrastus his successor as head of the Lyceum, and though only twelve years Aristotle's junior, Theophrastus lived long enough to serve as head of the Lyceum for thirty-five years. He died in 287 B.C. complaining that life was too short; a man had to leave it just when he was beginning to understand its mysteries.

Theophrastus was particularly interested in the study of botany. His two treatises on plants have led many to call him the founder of that science. As if this were not enough of an accomplishment for one man, no fewer than 227 treatises on such varied topics as religion, politics, education, rhetoric, mathematics, astronomy, logic, natural history, meteorology, ethics, and psychology are ascribed to him![1] He showed an unflagging zeal in his scientific inquiries and continued the pattern laid down by Aristotle of systematically collecting and reviewing his material, sometimes with the aid of other experts.

In most matters he followed Aristotle faithfully, but he tended to be more consistently empirical. He sought an empirical basis for scientific theories and argued that facts should not be forced to fit into a theory.[2] He reacted against the major role assigned by Aristotle to the search for final causes, and he held that science is concerned more with efficient causes than with final causes.[3] His position anticipated an advance not actually made until the time of Galileo in the seventeenth century A.D., when it was realized that final causes are in fact scientifically irrelevant.

In expressing these objections and reservations Theophrastus shows a more naturalistic and modern spirit than Aristotle. Theophrastus went into much more detail in describing the observable processes of the mind—sensation, perception, pleasure and pain, emotion, and temperament.

Theophrastus expressed these tendencies in *On the Senses,* a treatise on physiological psychology.[4] Aristotle notwithstanding, he returned the seat of the intellect to the brain. His treatise contains not only valuable criticisms of earlier thinkers, but also a statement of his own views. His specific findings and assertions on vision, hearing, smell, taste, and touch are given in such detail as to make summarization difficult.

Throughout this work, Theophrastus shows the spirit of critical scientific thinking that characterized his general attitude. He came to the conclusion that perceptions reveal external nature and that external nature exists independently of our perception of it. Theophrastus also recognized that it was not enough to observe the stimulus alone, since the same stimulus may have different effects according to the conditions present in the sensory organs.

But how does an object act on the sense organ? He adopted Aristotle's position that sensory objects act on the senses through media and not through direct presence. He disagreed with Aristotle, however, concerning the locus of sensory qualities. Theophrastus argued that whatever the effects of the objects on the sense organs, these effects are carried to the brain before they have the quality of sensory experiences. Aristotle believed this to be true only for some sense modalities; for others he held that the sensory qualities are generated in the sense organs themselves.

According to Theophrastus, pleasure is a natural accompaniment of that which is in accord with nature. Unlike certain of his predecessors, however, he did not believe that pain is also involved in all sense impressions. He based this denial on what he called the plain facts of observation. Excessive stimulation sometimes causes pain because it disturbs the correspondence between sense organs and object, but this is not usually the case. He had no patience with the Platonic view that one's pleasures may be false. All pleasures are true in the sense that they are pleasures, Theophrastus said, no matter what our ethical or other judgments about them may be.

Today Theophrastus is best known for his *Characters,* a collection of personality sketches.[5] Before we consider this quasiliterary contribution, we should comment on the literary tradition on which he built. Centuries earlier, Homer had used the device of attributing to certain characters what might be called a master personality trait—a descriptive trait that dominates the personality of the individual. Thus, Homer referred to "crafty Ulysses" and "brave Hector." Aristotle had inserted descriptions of character types in his *Ethics* and *Rhetoric* but rather casually and unsystematically. What to his master was a passing illustration became in the hands of Theophrastus a new psychological genre—the description of character types. He was not content to use a single descriptor for a person, as Homer had done. Instead, he deduced from a particular attribute of personality the variety of consequences that would follow in the diverse circumstances in which that trait might be exhibited. He therefore demonstrated the interdependence among the behaviors described. By selection, within the limitation of a personality attribute, Theophrastus would allow neither incongruities among traits nor combinations of more than one "master" trait. In doing so, he imposed unity on the personality but missed much of the richness and inconsistencies of human personality. In this respect, at least, the Greek dramatists Aeschylus and Sophocles were immeasurably superior in giving subtlety to their portrayal of personality. Nevertheless, it would appear that this subtlety was utilized with literary aims in view. The efforts of Theophrastus, though relatively one dimensional, were carried out with some awareness of their scientific interest. He says as much in his dedicatory letter to the *Characters,* indicating that his interest in the subject was aroused when he considered that, though the whole of Greece had the same climate and all Greeks had the same upbringing, they did not all have the same character.

Each vignette emphasizes one or another major trait. Dissembling, flattery, garrulity, boorishness, penuriousness, tactlessness, and surliness are among the thirty character traits sketched.[6] Lest a misanthropic point of view be attributed to Theophrastus, there are several references in the ancient literature to a lost companion volume, devoted to "good" characters.

On the death of Theophrastus, his successor as head of the Lyceum was Strato of Lampsacus. Strato was also faithful to Aristotle's naturalistic spirit. His numerous writings, now lost, dealt with so many of the problems of natural science that he gained the title of "the Physicist." The many successors to Strato at the Lyceum over the centuries appear to have been of relatively little importance. More and more they became involved in specialized investigations in grammar, literature, and ethics; the earlier keen interest in the sciences disappeared almost completely. It was not until the sixth century A.D., after a span of 860 years, that the school finally closed its doors. However, even during Theophrastus and Strato's lifetime, the intellectual center of the Hellenistic world shifted to Alexandria, and in doing so the character of that world changed.

ALEXANDRIA AND SCIENCE

The great empire of Alexander disintegrated at his death, various parts falling into the hands of his generals. A few large monarchies replaced the empire, one of which, Ptolemaic Egypt, is of particular importance in the history of science.[7] Ptolemy I, a Macedonian general, proclaimed himself king and founded the Ptolemaic dynasty that was to last in Egypt for three centuries. The last of his line was Cleopatra, upon whose death Egypt fell to the Romans. Ptolemy's capital was Alexandria, a city founded a few years before by Alexander himself. Under the aegis of Ptolemy and of his son, Ptolemy II, both the great library—the largest in the ancient world—and the museum at Alexandria were organized. The museum, primarily a research institute, eventually comprised living accommodations for the scholars and their assistants, seminar rooms, laboratories, botanical and zoological gardens, and an observatory. The Ptolemys made still another contribution to science, indirectly but not insignificantly. The stipends they paid the museum scholars were perhaps the first financial support from the state scientists ever received. The first head of the museum was the same Strato mentioned above, before he returned to Athens to lead the Lyceum on the death of Theophrastus. In his dozen or so years in Alexandria, Strato emphasized science at the expense of philosophy, thereby assuring the future course of the institution.

During the museum's first century of existence much important scientific work was done. Alexandria became a center of specialists, for it provided an opportunity for sustained work in narrower fields. This approach survived only briefly and did not reappear on such an extensive scale until the modern period. Among the mathematicians at the museum was Euclid. Archimedes may also have visited Alexandria from Syracuse; in any event he was directly influenced by its school of mathematics. Advances in mechanics, astronomy, geography, medicine, and anatomy were also made.

These specialists were indifferent rather than actually hostile to philosophical issues. Their indifference increased in direct proportion to the success of their methods of specialization. In this respect they were perhaps the first modern scientists! These men realized that the earlier attempts at syntheses of knowledge had been premature. As scientific Candides they resolved to cultivate their own gardens, though they intended to talk with their neighbors over the fences they were erecting.

From the Alexandrian point of view, psychological matters were not scientific.

Apparently, they were considered outside the realm of naturalism, whereas anatomical and physiological concerns were not. Psychology and physiology, heretofore intermingled, were now separated. The work of Herophilus and Erasistratus, which we are now to consider, must therefore be referred to as work in anatomy and physiology. From the perspective of today, their work is relevant to psychology itself, but from the perspective of Alexandrian science it was not.

Herophilus of Chalcedon, who lived about 300 B.C., a contemporary of Euclid, was one of the founders of anatomy. In the scientifically free atmosphere of Alexandria, he not only dissected the human body, but did so publicly. He explicitly compared human anatomy to that of animals. He recognized the brain as the center of the nervous system and as the seat of intelligence. In addition, he distinguished tendons from nerves; the name he gave to nerves (neura-aisthetica) implied a recognition of their function of sensitivity.

Erasistratus, a younger contemporary of Herophilus, clearly distinguished among the arteries, veins, and nerves. He regarded the nerves as vehicles for carrying what he called the *pneuma*, the animal spirits, the carriers of sensation and motion. He thought the shortening of muscles was due to distention of the animal spirits as conveyed by the nerves. Although he distinguished motor from sensory nerves, this finding was lost to those who came after him and had to be discovered all over again.

Still another contribution deserves mention. It was made by a nameless physician, probably also from Alexandria, in a volume of lectures entitled the *Book of Medicine*. [8] He suggested that the nerves have exists from the spinal cord, that they radiate throughout the body, and that the powers of both sensation and motion are located in them. He also distinguished voluntary powers from what he called natural powers; these natural powers include attraction, growth, digestion, and expulsion, and share the ability to take place whether or not we want them to. In some slight measure, this view anticipates the concept of reflex action and marks a distinct advance over the theory of "sympathy" that was accepted at the time.

THE BACKGROUND OF THE HELLENISTIC AND ROMAN PERIODS

While these advances were being made in Alexandria, the rest of the Mediterranean world was sinking more deeply into an intellectual decline. The same process of deterioration was also at work in Alexandria itself, where a concerted interest in alchemy first became manifest. Among the causes of this decline were a growth of skepticism, a growing sense of futility, and intellectual disillusionment. Above all, there was an increased acceptance of supernaturalism in its more extreme forms. Superstition had been a part of the daily life of the earliest Greeks, but its influence had waned for a time, only to return in the wake of the political and military disasters and epidemics that later afflicted the Greeks. Oriental mystery religions began to flourish alongside the ancient Greek faiths, because the Greeks' easygoing paganism could not meet the challenge posed by these new problems. Thus, the increased appeal of the mystery cults, astrology, and magic, most of which came from the East, were related either as cause or effect to the shifting perspectives of the Hellenists.[9]

THE GRAECO-ROMAN PERIOD

It was during these years that the Roman conquest of the Hellenistic world took place. This event ushered in the fourth and final phase of ancient science, which is known as the Graeco-Roman period and which extended from about 100 B.C. to A.D. 500.

It is remarkable that the Romans are not even mentioned until this relatively late date, for they had emerged into history in the seventh century B.C. from their status as one of many city-states. Their prosperity and their military and governmental power had increased steadily through their defeat of the independent city-states, but their contributions to art, drama, philosophy, and science remained negligible. Roman culture was in fact derived from Greek sources. Changes took place nevertheless, for when Greece was incorporated into the Roman Empire, one might say that Greek thought assumed a Latin dress.

The general intellectual climate became intensely practical. The Romans had little interest in the theoretical issues that had so excited the Greeks. The engineers and architects who covered the hills of Rome with mighty buildings, roads, and aqueducts were essentially practical in outlook, relying heavily on rules of thumb.[10] The Romans also had a definite flair for law, for the maintenance of order, and for conquest. Their sense of order extended even to commenting on Greek science and adapting it, but they did little to advance it in either scope or depth. To use the words of Bertrand Russell, the period of the Roman Empire was a period of "subjection and order."[11] The doctrines from Greece and the East excited only a few Romans; the larger proportion went about their business—economic, military, and governmental—more or less unheeding. Since there was nothing that could be identified as applied psychology as yet, psychological matters would not have interested them.

Roman philosophy, as represented by the schools of Stoicism and Epicureanism, was directed toward providing a means of personal escape from the evils of the world. "Wisdom for the conduct of life," to use Wilhelm Windelband's phrase, became the fundamental philosophical quest.[12] In their search for this wisdom, however, the two schools of thought contributed continuity to psychological thinking. They maintained, for example, the representative theory of perception advanced by Epicurus[13] that had been derived from Democritus.

GALEN

The next great figure in the medical-philosophical tradition was Galen, born about A.D. 130 in Pergamon, a town in Asia Minor.[14] He was a Greek subject of the Roman Empire, and at that time his birthplace was second only to Alexandria as a center of learning in the Western world. He received as complete an education in both philosophy and medicine as the time and place could afford. At twenty he began traveling and studying abroad, and during a stay in Alexandria, he began to concentrate on anatomy. Dissection of the human body was no longer allowed in Alexandria, but he apparently studied the anatomy of apes and other large mammals which was allowed. Many of Galen's errors, perpetuated over the centuries, were based on attributing to the human organs what in fact were to be found only in nonhuman species. It was at this age that he began writing; he remained a prolific writer for the rest of his life. At twenty-eight, he returned to Pergamon and was appointed surgeon to the gladiators. This position gave him an excellent opportunity to further his knowledge of anatomy by working with both the living and the dead.

Subsequently, Galen went to Rome to practice. His fortune and his movements were bound to the court and to a whole series of emperors. Meanwhile, his eminence as a medical teacher was recognized, and he lectured to large crowds. His works on anatomy, physiology, and kindred subjects were written in these years. It seems clear that he believed knowledge of the body's structure was essential to an understanding of its working.

Galen was a skilled and astute practitioner. An anecdote[15] illustrating his clinical shrewdness anticipates by nearly 2000 years a measure now used in so-called lie detection. One day, Galen observed that one of his female patients had a quickening of the pulse when someone mentioned the name of a male dancer. On her visit the following day Galen arranged for someone to enter and tell of having seen the performance of still another dancer. A similar test was performed on the third day. Neither the second nor the third name produced a quickening of the pulse. On the fourth day when the first dancer's name was again mentioned, the pulse became rapid once more. He diagnosed her malady as the sickness of love, and he went on to comment that physicians seem to have no conception of how bodily health can be affected by the suffering of the *psyche.*

According to Galen, the basic physiological principle of life is spirit or *pneuma.* On the basis of this principle, he divides living things into the classes of plants, animals, and men—plants can grow, animals can move as well as grow, and people not only move and grow but also reason. The three grades of life had their characteristic adaptions of the *pneuma.*[16] The first adaption became natural spirit and brought about growth; the second became vital spirit and caused locomotion; the third became animal spirit and caused thought. Lest there be confusion between the second and third adaptations, "animal" spirit, possessed by the human being alone, was derived from the word *anima,* meaning soul. With regard to the seat of the soul, Galen remained faithful to Plato: the brain and nervous system were the seat of his distinctive intellectual life.

Galen integrated the existing knowledge of anatomy and physiology.[17] On cutting open the solid-looking organ that is the brain of the ape or human; Galen was struck by the four hollow intercommunicating chambers containing clear fluid.[18] Reasoning that they must serve some function, he decided that they constituted the place of generation and assembly of the animal spirits of the soul (mind). The animal spirits were thought to flow along nerves throughout the body, in accord with the now general acceptance of nerves as prerequisites for motion.[19] The belief that the animal spirits cause movement was reinforced for Galen by his observation that the living brain seemed to pulsate rhythmically. This dogma was not successfully challenged until the Renaissance. This doctrine of animal spirits was related to and expressed by the terms *sympathy* or *consent.* Communication in this manner—animal spirits flowing from one part of the body to another— accounted for the appearance of symptoms in one organ when the disease was in another.[20]

Galen completed Hippocrates' fourfold classificatory system of humors by his theory of the four temperaments.[21] It will be remembered that Hippocrates had associated Empedocles' four elements with the humors of bodily juices—blood, black bile, yellow bile, and phlegm. A vaguely formulated theory of four temperaments had been accepted more or less incidentally, particularly among the Stoics, even before Galen.

Later works have emphasized the psychological aspects of the theory of temperaments to such an extent that sometimes the theory is not recognized for what it was to Galen—a classification of medical-pathological types. It must be remembered that Galen was not deliberately developing a psychological theory; temperament was for him simply one of the three principal causes of disease, the others being climate and other external factors. To use typical medical examples of the system, he argued that foods that are naturally warmer produce more bile and that a person whose nature is warmer is more subject to biliousness than others. A distinctly secondary consideration for Galen was the explanation of individual differences in behavior and emotion. Such was his fame, however, that even to this day he is credited with taking the decisive step of systematizing the view and emerging with a full-blown theory of temperament. The story is much more complicated than that and in recent years has been told particularly well by R. Klibansky and his associates.[22] Later, Galen's classificatory scheme was extended to the common view that a person with a predominance of the blood is said to be sanguine in temperament (warmhearted, volatile); when there is an excess of black bile, a person is thought to be melancholic (sad); excess yellow bile indicates that a person is choleric (quick to anger and to action); a preponderance of phlegm leads to the phlegmatic humor (which has so little changed over the centuries that it needs no explanation). Only with these later additions to Galen's extension of the Hippocratic doctrine do we have a complete theory of temperamental humors.

The theory of the four temperaments persisted as part of the mainstream of intellectual thinking until the rebirth of medicine in the Renaissance 1400 years later, and in some aspects as late as the nineteenth century A.D. Although the doctrine of humors has now faded from the medical scene, vestiges of it in expressions such as "good humor," "humorous," and their derivatives persist. It also survives in theories of personality type, in which a person is said to be characterized by the possession of a particular temperament.

What occurred in connection with the Galenic theory of humors is indicative of Galen's influence during the centuries that followed. A variety of circumstances fostered a reliance on Galen's work after his death in A.D. 200. His strongly devout theistic attitude appealed alike to Christendom and Islam. He held that all things were determined by God and that the structure of the body was formed by God for an intelligible end, which was consonant with Christianity. He was not a Christian, although for centuries people believed that he had been. Moreover, his writings were confident and dogmatic in tone. His philosophical speculations, especially on the soul, were considerable and added to his appeal. His bulky writings, far too difficult for general study, were summarized and commented on by many lesser men. It was their works, not his, that were read. Wretched treatises not even based on his works became popular whenever they bore his name. Meanwhile, his best works were lost or fell into oblivion. This compounded the errors and further reduced the general quality of the medicine of that time.

SUMMARY

The span of time that included Theophrastus and Galen extended from about 300 B.C. to A.D. 200. Their work and that of their contemporaries made it a period of consolidation and strengthening of certain already established prescriptions. Rationalism and nomotheticism were still dominant; empiricism and idiographicism showed an increased strength and refinement and then declined. Naturalism, still strong among the individuals with whom we have been concerned, was nevertheless under increasing attack from nonphilosophical and nonscientific sources. Theophrastus and Galen were empirical and yet did not neglect the value of rationalism. They advocated idiographicism as well, despite their preference for dealing with types rather than with idiosyncratic differences among individuals. The structural prescription expressed in anatomy was seen as a prerequisite of the functional understanding of its workings.

There was increased specialization, which becomes evident when we compare the interests of the individuals of the time with those of the pre-Socratic Greeks. An increased separation of science and philosophy was also apparent. Psychology was still seen as a branch of philosophy.

Theophrastus, the successor to Aristotle, extended his master's work on science. Particularly interested in botany, Theophrastus did much work on psychology and wrote the most complete physiological psychology of the ancient Greek world. He is perhaps best known for his *Characters*, a treatment of personality.

After the death of Aristotle, the center of Greek science shifted from Athens to Alexandria, in Egypt. Little of psychological interest was produced in Alexandria, but workers such as Herophilus and Erasistratus made important advances in medicine.

The rise of Rome did not see great advances in psychological thought. One writer of significance, however, was Galen, whose influence on medicine was enormous for the next 2000 years. Galen's theory of humors along with its significance for theories of personality is discussed in the chapter.

NOTES

1. Diogenes Laertius, *Lives and Opinions of Eminent Philosophers,* trans. R. D. Hicks (Cambridge, Mass.: Harvard University Press, 1925) (III, A.D.)
2. Theophrastus, in C. J. DeVogel, *Greek Philosophy: A Collection of Texts with Notes and Explanations; Aristotle, the Early Peripatetic School and the Early Academy* (Leiden: B. J. Brill, 1953) (c. 300 B.C.), II, 230–240.
3. *Ibid.*
4. Theophrastus, in G. M. Stratton, *Theophrastus and the Greek Physiological Psychology* (New York: Macmillan Co., 1917).
5. Theophrastus, *The Characters,* trans. J. M. Edmonds (London: Heinemann, 1929), pp. 43, 45.
6. *Ibid.*
7. Sources for this account of Alexandrian science are G. Sarton, *Ancient Science and Modern Civilization* (Lincoln: University of Nebraska Press, 1947); and *A History of Science and Culture in the Last Three Centuries B.C.* (Cambridge, Mass.: Harvard University Press, 1959); B. Farrington, *Science in Antiquity* (London: Home University Library, 1936); and two more general books that nevertheless contain valuable material on this period—C. Singer, *A Short History of Medicine, Introducing Medical Principles to Students and Non-medical Readers* (New York: Oxford University Press, 1928); and W. Windelband, *A History of Philosophy: Greek, Roman and Medieval* (New York: Harper and Brothers, 1901), I.
8. *Book of Medicine,* trans. E.A.W. Budge (London: Oxford University Press, 1913) (c. 300 B.C.).
9. W. C. Dampier, *A History of Science, and Its Relations with Philosophy and Religion,* 4th ed. (Cambridge, Mass.: Cambridge University Press, 1949).
10. M. Clagett, *Greek Science in Antiquity* (New York: Abelard–Schuman, 1955)
11. B. Russell, *A History of Western Philosophy* (New York: Simon and Schuster, 1945), p. 218.
12. Windelband, *History of Philosophy,* p. 157.
13. Epicurus, Letter to Herodotus, from the original text of Diogenes Laertius, trans. C. Bailey, W. J. Oats, ed., *The Stoic and Epicurean Philosophers: Complete Extant Writings of Epicurus, Epictetus, Lucretius, and Marcus Aurelius* (New York: Random House, 1940) (c. 300 B.C.); Herrnstein and Boring, Excerpt No. 22.
14. Sources used were Singer, *A Short History of Medicine;* H. E. Sigerist, *The Great Doctors: A Biographical History of Medicine* (London: Allan and Unwin, 1933); G. Sarton, *Galen of Pergamon,* (Lawrence: University of Kansas Press, 1954); and O. Temkin, *Galenism: Rise and Decline of a Medical Philosophy* (Ithaca, N.Y.: Cornell University Press, 1973).
15. L. Thorndike, *A History of Magic and Experimental Science During the First Thirteen Centuries of Our Era* (New York: Macmillan Co., 1923), I.
16. B. Farrington, *Greek Science: Its Meanings for Us* (London: Penguin, 1953), pp. 297–298.
17. Galen, *On Anatomical Procedures: Translating the Surviving Books with Introduction and Notes,* trans. C. Single (London: Oxford University Press, 1956); *Galen, On Anatomical Procedures: The Later Books,* trans. W.L.H. Duckworth, M. C. Lyons and B. Towers, eds. (Cambridge, Mass.: Cambridge University Press, 1962).
18. C. S. Sherrington, *Man on His Nature,* 2nd ed. (London: Cambridge University Press, 1951), pp. 198–199.

19. F. Fearing, *Reflex Action: A Study in the History of Physiological Psychology* (Baltimore: Williams and Wilkins, 1930), p. 12.
20. J. F. Fulton, *Physiology of the Nervous System,* 3rd ed. rev. (London: Oxford University Press, 1949), p. 202.
21. R. M. Hutchins, ed., *The Great Books of the Western World,* Vol. X, Galen, *On the Natural Faculties,* trans. A. J. Brock (Chicago: Encyclopaedia Britannica, 1952) (A.D. 200), pp. 163–215.
22. R. Klibansky, E. Panofsky, and F. Saxl, *Saturn and Melancholy: Studies in the History of Natural Philosophy, Religion and Art* (New York: Basic Books, 1964).

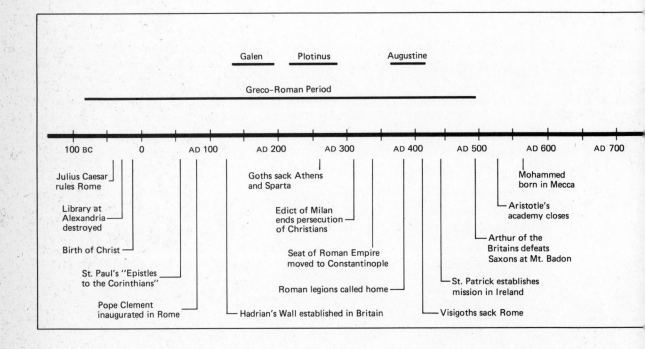

Galen   Plotinus   Augustine

Greco-Roman Period

100 BC   0   AD 100   AD 200   AD 300   AD 400   AD 500   AD 600   AD 700

Julius Caesar
rules Rome

Library at
Alexandria
destroyed

Birth of Christ

St. Paul's "Epistles
to the Corinthians"

Pope Clement
inaugurated in Rome

Goths sack Athens
and Sparta

Edict of Milan
ends persecution
of Christians

Seat of Roman Empire
moved to Constantinople

Roman legions called home

Hadrian's Wall established in Britain

Mohammed
born in Mecca

Aristotle's
academy closes

Arthur of the
Britains defeats
Saxons at Mt. Badon

St. Patrick establishes
mission in Ireland

Visigoths sack Rome

PART
TWO

The Dark and Middle Ages

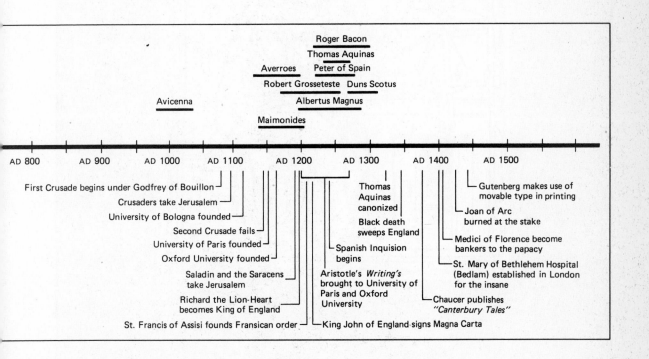

Roger Bacon

Thomas Aquinas

Averroes   Peter of Spain

Robert Grosseteste   Duns Scotus

Avicenna

Albertus Magnus

Maimonides

AD 800   AD 900   AD 1000   AD 1100   AD 1200   AD 1300   AD 1400   AD 1500

First Crusade begins under Godfrey of Bouillon

Crusaders take Jerusalem

University of Bologna founded

Second Crusade fails

University of Paris founded

Oxford University founded

Saladin and the Saracens
take Jerusalem

Richard the Lion-Heart
becomes King of England

St. Francis of Assisi founds Fransican order

Aristotle's *Writing's*
brought to University of
Paris and Oxford
University

Spanish Inquision
begins

Thomas
Aquinas
canonized

Black death
sweeps England

King John of England signs Magna Carta

Gutenberg makes use of
movable type in printing

Joan of Arc
burned at the stake

Medici of Florence become
bankers to the papacy

St. Mary of Bethlehem Hospital
(Bedlam) established in London
for the insane

Chaucer publishes
"Canterbury Tales"

Artistic representation of Augustine.

Plotinus and Augustine: The Patristic Period

*B*efore considering the work of the next two great contributors to psychology, it is necessary to turn back some two centuries from the time of Galen to the beginnings of the Christian Era. An examination of the link between philosophy and early Christianity, and the alleged influence of Christianity on the fall of science, provides a necessary introduction to Plotinus, the greatest exponent of Neoplatonism. Despite his paganism, Plotinus profoundly influenced the Christian saint Augustine, the greatest "psychologist" of the nearly thousand years to follow.

CHRISTIANITY AND THE FALL OF SCIENCE

Christianity did not lead directly to the fall of Greek scientific-philosophical endeavors; the decline had started even before the advent of Christianity. Until the end of the second century A.D., the Christians were a small, obscure, but persecuted sect with no seeming influence on the class of individuals who might be expected to study science or philosophy. They actually held science in low estate. In the centuries that followed, Christianity did nothing to promote science and in many ways discouraged its revival. The practical attitude of the Romans and the later invasions of the barbarians contributed to the fall of science; the Church maintained the situation and to some degree aggravated it. Early Christian teaching indirectly abetted the decline by diverting to theological speculation individuals of scholarly temperament who might otherwise have turned their interests to science and philosophy as it was known in the past.

PHILOSOPHY AND THE BEGINNING OF CHRISTIANITY

Once their period of comparative obscurity was over, Christians found it necessary to defend their new religion against non-Christian thinkers. Therefore, insofar as philosophy was studied, it was used for the defense of religion, for apologetics, as the written tracts were called. The second century also began the period of the Church Fathers, those writers who in later ages were used as reference sources for points of doctrinal orthodoxy. The Patristic period, as it came to be called, spanned the centuries devoted to the formation of Christian orthodoxy.

A detailed history of these early Christian views would be a history of Christian dogma, not of philosophy. Some Christian thinking of the period was antirational. Tertullian, a Church Father, not only held that his faith was unphilosophical, but was also proud of the fact.[1] He maintained that the content of revelation is not merely above reason, but in a sense contrary to reason. The Gospel was incomprehensible in terms of worldly discernment. Tertullian took an extreme position, but in varying degrees others shared this shift of focus, not to an interest in the irrational which Plato had maintained, but to an antirational stance.

Origen, born in Alexandria in A.D. 185, was one of the intellectual leaders of the Church at that time. His attitude toward science was counter to the antirationalist view. He held that all knowledge is good because it is a means toward perfection and that philosophy and science are compatible with Christianity.[2] This attitude eventually entered into the formulation of Church dogma.

Both the Edict of Milan, issued by Constantine in 313, and the recognition of the Catholic Church as the official religion of the Roman Empire, following shortly thereafter, made imperative the development of an authoritative system of theology. Christianity was no longer a small outcast sect but a state religion.

There was one paramount intellectual consequence of the official sanction of Christianity: heresy became a significant factor in human conduct. Unlike the easygoing religions of old Greece and Rome whose guardians were content to allow people to worship how and when they pleased as long as they made at least token obeisance to the gods of city or state, Christianity demanded uncompromising adherence to the one God who, through the voices of Christ and his Apostles, had made manifest the Truth. This revelation could not be disputed; to do so was heresy. One was no longer free to speculate on any and all matters. Certain truths were revealed, and no one could challenge them without being accused of heresy.

Once dogma was settled by the ecumenical councils, philosophers could no longer inquire about a given point. These councils decided by majority vote what were henceforth to be regarded as revealed Christian truths. The minorities on these votes, now faced with heresy, could either agree or, as sometimes understandably happened, break off to form heretical sects. Insofar as they drew their inspiration from the same source, these heretics were still Christian, but they denied some point of dogma. Sometimes these differences were introduced by continued adherence to one or another now-banned aspect of the old religions of the classical era, such as a belief in magic. Often differences arose over the interpretation of the Trinity, especially over the particular nature of the relation of the Son to the Father.

The effect of Christianity on psychological thought was to emphasize supernaturalism, in the sense of being concerned with that which was beyond nature. It led to a preoccupation with the world to come rather than the world as it exists. Naturalistic interests were suspect precisely because they dealt with matters of this world rather than the afterlife.[3] Since the immortal soul was elevated as a result of this emphasis, soul–body dualism became a major issue. An intense preoccupation with the problems of sin and guilt also came to prevail; this absorption was perhaps a reaction to feelings of helplessness and doom among Christian and non-Christian mystics. An attempt was made to suppress any suggestion of a relationship between human nature and the animal kingdom. The position of animals was degraded, and a sharp dichotomy was drawn between humankind and the beasts that perish. This change in attitude was demanded since animals might otherwise be thought to have reason, implying in turn that they were morally responsible beings. Psychological contributions were hereafter made only within the context of these concerns.

Plato's world view had called for the supremacy of transcendental reality and the inferior status of sense. This tendency in Plato was now even more in focus because the best known dialogue in the centuries to come would be the atypical *Timaeus* which pictured the universe as a living thing with a soul penetrating its body.

At the time of the rise of Christianity, philosophy was dominated by the Neoplatonists who stressed precisely these aspects of Plato's thinking. The adaptation of their views to Christian dogma was almost inevitable. One of these Neoplatonists was Plotinus, who would have a profound effect on Augustine, ultimately influencing the entire course of Christian philosophy.

The aspect of Platonism that most appealed to Plotinus was the antirationalism that earlier Neoplatonists had fostered. He ignored the major argument of Plato's teaching—that real knowledge could be obtained. He turned, not to skepticism, but to faith, a faith that wanted rationalism to fail. The more it failed, the more persuasive his mystic path would appear to be.

PLOTINUS

Plotinus was born in Egypt about A.D. 205 and in his youth became a disciple of Ammonius Saccas in Alexandria, with whom he remained for eleven years.[4] He and other students swore to keep secret their master's teachings, which had not been set down in writing. When he was thirty-nine years old, Plotinus left Ammonius with the intention of traveling to the East in order to learn Persian and Indian philosophy. The expedition of the Emperor Gordian, which he joined for this purpose, reached Mesopotamia but ended with the assassination of the emperor. This was the occupational hazard of emperors at the time; no fewer than eleven died in this fashion during the sixty-five years of Plotinus' life.

Plotinus arrived in Rome in 245 and remained there the rest of his life. His austere and ethical teaching soon won him influence over many of the leading Romans of his time. He functioned not only as a teacher of philosophy, but also as a counselor on ethical problems. His moral principles were high and his character unimpeachable; his advice on moral problems was eagerly sought.

During his first years in Rome Plotinus wrote nothing. It was only after repeated urgings from Porphyry, his student and biographer, that he began to write—in the last six years of his life—the major portion of his only work. After Plotinus' death in A.D. 270, Porphyry arranged the essays, according to some numerological quirk, in sets of nine works each, as a consequence of which he named them *The Six Enneads* (Six Groups of Nine).[5]

The central theme of Plotinus' teaching is mystical reunion with the world soul. Plotinus seems to have been dominated by a desire to map out the world beyond sense reality and to try to live in that world as fully as the bonds of flesh would permit. It would be easy at this point to dismiss him simply as a mystic and move on, but he was something more. His was not a crude mysticism based merely on habitual trances. In fact, according to Porphyry, Plotinus attained a state of vision only four times in the six years they worked together. In these states he felt himself to have risen to the world beyond the world of experience. At the same time, though careless of dress and hygienic considerations, he was in great demand as the executor of estates of minor children. The practical Romans would hardly have so trusted him if he had fit the stereotype of the mystic. When chided for performing this business service, which was seemingly discordant with his philosophical teaching, Plotinus is said to have remarked that the children would need the money if they did not find philosophy. It was not that he was oblivious to the world; he simply valued things other than those that the majority of people hold dear. He saw material life as a play acted out by the shadows of people, whose comings and goings were irrelevant.[6]

There is a calmness in Plotinus' writing; nowhere in evidence is there the heat so often accompanied by confusion that characterizes so many mystical excursions. Consider how he describes his mysticism:

> But there are earlier and loftier beauties than these [from sense]. In the sense-bound life we are no longer granted to know them, but the soul, taking no help from the organs, sees and proclaims them. To the vision of these we must mount, leaving sense to its own low place.[7]

Plotinus' intention was to demonstrate to those who had not had such transcendental experiences that there were realities beyond the world of sense.[8] Consequently, he appealed to experiences that were open to the understanding of the uninitiated, and in this way his thinking is relevant to the history of psychology. He adopted as his approach the analysis of the forms of mental activity. This was the rational method through which to obtain information about the soul, since, by definition, the soul is immaterial. However, such analysis was only incidental to Plotinus' major thinking and did not constitute an attempt to systematize a psychology. Nevertheless, throughout all his work he used a meditative method and thus helped to establish this approach to psychology. Despite himself, he made a modest contribution to psychology in an otherwise barren age.

Plotinus espoused a doctrine of the development of the individual toward perfection. His goal was to establish the independence of the soul from the body, or as close an approximation of this state as possible. He considered matter to be the obstacle to this goal. The Platonic doctrine of the body as the prison of the soul is central to his thinking, though he altered the relationship between the two. Plato had conceived of the soul as being within the body, but Plotinus believed that, although the body existed in space—after all, space is defined as a container for bodies—the soul could not be so contained because it is incorporeal.[9] It gives the body life but does not combine with it. Soul and body are united, he said, but never fused, mixed, or spatially connected. The soul used the body's organs of sense; motions are of the body, not of the soul. Plotinus' central point is that the soul is correlative with but independent of the body. The emotions, for example, are known to the soul, but it is the body that is perturbed.[10] The body experiences the emotion; the soul perceives it.

Plotinus states that the soul has three major classes of activity. First, it performs the functions of perceiving the world of sense. Second, it reflects. That is, there is a division of consciousness into subject and object: the soul not only thinks, but it also thinks it thinks. The first and second kinds of mental activity are characterized by a state of excitation, which is sensation; reflection is conscious perception of this excitation. Third, there is the pure activity of contemplation, without such a separation of subject and object, in which the soul transcends its immediate location in order to dwell on the eternal and changeless. This changelessness was Plotinus' goal, the ineffable state toward which he strove. It is at its highest level the experience of the "One."[11]

Psychological interest in Plotinus centers not on his goal but on the second function, reflection. His concept of this function, in which "we" (his word for self) is operating, gives us the first clear statement of self-consciousness.[12] Unlike union with the One, which is without consciousness of self, "we" become aware at this level of the object and, apart from this, of ourselves. We are self-conscious in that we distinguish the object and thinker.[13] As he puts it, "we know, and it is ourselves that we know."[14] He even used blushing as an illustration of heightened self-consciousness. To Plotinus, self-consciousness is but a means of contrast with the ineffably higher plane of contemplation of the changeless. He hit on self-consciousness as an effective means of casting this higher level into relief; once it serves its purpose, he said no more about it.

AUGUSTINE

Augustine lived in a world overwhelmed with trouble.[15] In his youth the barbarians had poured into the empire; in his middle age Rome was sacked by the Goths; and in his declining years, while all around him the whole western Roman Empire was facing its final ruin, he helped prepare for the defense of his diocese against the Vandals. Augustine did not advance science generally, and probably even impeded its development, but his subjective attitude, with its consequent attention to the self and to introspection, and his stress on the functioning of the will, make him important in the history of psychology.

Life of Augustine

Aurelius Augustine was born in 354 at Tagaste, a small town in the Roman province of Numidia in northern Africa. Many years later, he described his childhood and youth in his *Confessions*, [16] his spiritual autobiography. He tells us that at an early age he had learned something about Christianity from his mother but that her teachings had made little impression on him at the time. When he did well in his first schooling, his father aspired to make him a lawyer; so he was sent to Carthage at about the age of sixteen to study rhetoric. Again he did well in his studies, but the frivolity of student life led him into dissipation of various sorts, which he describes in detail in his *Confessions.* Since he was now sixteen, he took a mistress to whom he remained faithful for years. She bore him a son, Adeodatus, which means "Given of God." The custom of taking a concubine, sanctioned by pagan morals and Roman law, was thought to be a step above promiscuity, and his was a deeply passionate nature. "Give me chastity and continency," he cried out, "only not yet." [17] He uttered this plea many years later in Milan after his mistress had returned to Africa and before his planned but never-contracted marriage to another.

Augustine's intellectual life was also intense. His reading of *Hortensius,* a work by Cicero that is now lost, led him to a love of philosophy, and over the years he became increasingly conversant with the Roman pagan literature. Though fascinated by both Plato and the Neoplatonists, and loving Latin, he disliked Greek and never mastered it. Roman Africa at that time was also a place where many diverse Christian, heretical, and pagan religious strands intertwined. Augustine became involved with several of these factions and at age nineteen converted to Manicheanism, which basically espoused a world of opposed substances of light and darkness. The external opposition of good and evil was a battle fought on many levels. The human being on earth would strive to become part of the kingdom of light and could become part of that domain. This doctrine was submerged in a morass of esoteric teachings including, for example, dietary prescriptions. Meat belonged to darkness and was forbidden; vegetables were of light and could be eaten. Since Manes, the Persian who founded the system, claimed direct authority from Jesus Christ, his doctrine was technically a form of Christianity, but, from the orthodox Christian point of view, it was a particularly offensive form of heresy. During Augustine's time, Manicheanism had a large number of adherents and exercised considerable temporal power.

On the completion of his studies in Carthage in 373, Augustine decided to follow the career of a teacher of rhetoric rather than that of a lawyer. After a year in Rome, he accepted the municipal post of rhetoric in Milan. This post was in the control of the Manicheans and was secured for him precisely because he was one of their adherents. By this time, however, he was in the process of discarding their doctrine.

Augustine was increasingly forced to adopt a skeptical position.[18] He began to doubt whether reality could be known at all. Neoplatonism freed him from this difficulty, and through the Neoplatonists he was led to accept as legitimate an order of reality beyond the material world.

In his later writings he adapted the Neoplatonic conception of reality to a Christian context.[19] This belief was to have a profound effect on all subsequent Christian theological and philosophical thinking. Many of his ideas—about God, matter, the ascent of the soul, freedom and evil, and the relation of God to the world—show the impress of Neoplatonism, especially as expressed by Plotinus. It was this conception of reality that he inserted into Christian theology and philosophy. His views on the spiritual nature of the reality accessible to the human soul were derived from the Neoplatonists. Like them, he believed there was a supreme author of being, and like them, he desired to transcend the material world. There were, of course, differences in outlook. In contrast to the Neoplatonists, Christian thinkers insisted on a voluntary act of creation by God; existence was temporal, not eternal; and God was on a level entirely different from that of his creatures.

Augustine next came under the influence of Ambrose, the Bishop of Milan, and his relationship with Ambrose had a decisive influence on the development of his thought. Dissatisfied with what he saw as the incompleteness of Neoplatonism and philosophy, he found in Ambrose someone to fill his needs, someone to help him find peace. In his *Confessions* he says, "That man of God received me as a father, and showed me an episcopal kindness on my coming. Thenceforth, I began to love him, at first indeed not as a teacher of the truth, but as a person kind towards myself."[20] It is noteworthy that an important stride in the development of the intellectual forces of Western Christendom should have started in an interpersonal relationship that later flowered into a religious conversion.

Other influences were at work to help bring Augustine into the Church. Of foremost importance was the scene in the garden of his house in Milan, movingly described in the *Confessions.*[21] He tells us in impassioned words of his conflict of will over whether or not to renounce the joys of the flesh for the sake of God. After an intense struggle, the conflict was resolved when a voice that sounded like that of a child commanded him over and over again to "take up and read." He took up the Bible and read from Saint Paul, "Not in rioting and drunkenness, not in chambering and wantonness, not in strife and envying: but put ye on the Lord Jesus Christ, and make not provision for the flesh to fulfill the lusts thereof."[22] He proceeded to reread Paul's epistles and found in him a kindred spirit who had passed through a thousand doubts as to the Divine Word. This was not the pale abstract of the Platonic *logos* but something that was to him, as it was to Paul, much more vital, warm, and deep.[23]

After a period of intellectual and spiritual preparation, in 387 Augustine was baptized in Milan by Bishop Ambrose. Augustine had resigned his professorship of rhetoric the year before, primarily because of dissatisfaction with what he had to teach, but also partly because he was suffering from a chest ailment. Although never formally a teacher again, he did not cease teaching, though now he pursued a different goal. After his conversion, he returned home to Africa, selling his property and giving the proceeds to the poor. He and some friends organized a monastery in Tagaste, where he lived the life of an ascetic. In 389 his son, on whom he had lavished great care and affection, died. Shortly thereafter Augustine was ordained a priest in Hippo. Here, in what was to be his home for the rest of his life, he founded another monastery.

In 395 or 396 Augustine was consecrated a bishop, a post he held until his death. His quiet monastic life was now over. The successful administration of a bishopric in the fifth century in northern Africa among pagans and heretics was no light task. Practical shrewdness and forceful leadership, as well as piety, were necessary. Above all, skill in human relationships was required. Religious controversies within the Church, Church councils, combats against heresy, and even lay legal activities occupied much of his time, and he continued to be in poor health. Nevertheless, he was about to find time to engage in enormous literary activity as well as prolific correspondence with other Church leaders.

Vandals were at the gates of Hippo in 430 when Augustine died at the age of seventy-six. A few months after his death his parishioners were either slain or scattered, and less than fifty years later, in 476, the empire of the western Caesar was abolished.

Augustine's major works were written during the later part of his life, that is to say, in the first quarter of the fifth century. The two best known are his *Confessions*,[24] finished in 406, and the *City of God*,[25] completed in 426. In his *City of God* Augustine gave the classic statement of the Christian philosophy of history in the form of a contrast and comparison of the earthly and the heavenly cities. Eventually, the terrestrial city would have to yield to the heavenly city, and the course of history could be defined as the struggle between the two.

Augustine's Attitudes Toward Science

The attitude Augustine took toward faith explains both his philosophical and his scientific views. He held that it is necessary to believe in order to know, that understanding comes from faith. Nevertheless, there are many things we cannot believe unless we understand them. Supplementing the primacy of belief, therefore, is the subordinate principle that we also know in order to believe.

Knowledge of any sort is valuable to Augustine only insofar as it brings one closer to understanding God, the soul, and the human self. God is the source of all causation. Miracles are simply unusual occurrences and require no more and no less explanation than any other event.[26] If they were not rare, they would not cause surprise. Often knowledge of this fact is enough, thereby denying any need to understand miracles rationally. Eyes fastened on God have little care for the transitory mundane affairs of the world.

Augustine's views toward science were ambivalent. Deprecatory remarks abound in his works. For example, scientific knowledge, such as the ability to predict eclipses, he says, may puff a man up with pride.[27] After a short account of the work of Thales, he complains that Thales did not relate his theories to the divine mind,[28] yet Augustine also praised Thales. The apparent discrepancy is mitigated considerably when we remember that he considered science good whenever it served religious ends but irrelevant, and hence bad, whenever it did not. The positive value of scientific knowledge would be not only to understand the Bible, for example, the flora and fauna of the Holy Land, but also to be able to refute pagan arguments. When comparing profane knowledge with Scripture, he writes, "For whatever man may have learnt from other sources, if it is hurtful, it is there condemned; if it is useful, it is therein contained."[29] By and large, the effect of Augustine on science was to impede rather than to advance its progress. However, his ambivalent attitude toward science in general went hand in hand with a firm conviction in the certainty of inner experience.[30] As a consequence, Augustine is important in the history of psychology, though not in the history of the other sciences.

Philosophical and Personal Background of Augustine's Psychology

For Augustine, revelation and inner experience were the two sources of truth. His most systematic statement of the principles of sacred theology—a guide to the interpretation of Scripture—is his "On Christian Doctrine."[31] References to inner experience are repeatedly cited in developing particular aspects of the doctrine. In his dependence on subjective knowledge, his second source, he made use of a concept of self and focused on the issue of freedom of the will as an experienced phenomenon. The relation of self and freedom of the will to his philosophical views will be detailed briefly here.

Augustine wished to rise to the heavenly city by the love of God. In order to do so contempt of self was necessary.[32] This ascent of the soul to God, vividly described in his *Confessions*,[33] required various steps involving passing from body to sense, to inner sense, and ultimately to the final place of abiding with disregard of self. The direct relation of his thinking to that of Plotinus is obvious, whereas his indirect debt to Plato may also be discerned.

From Augustine's point of view, several compelling theological reasons made the problem of will a primary issue.[34] For one, Adam's fall, though in a sense brought about by Satan, would not have occurred had Adam not already had a deficient will. Moreover, the problems of the relation of absolute predestination to freedom of the will, Divine Grace, and sin all occupied central positions in Augustine's theological thought. Equally compelling were his experiences as a youth when passion overwhelmed his will—for which he later reproached himself severely. In one dramatic instance, he remembered with shame that in his youth he and some friends had stolen some pears, only to throw them away uneaten. Rather than just register his harrowing repentance, he analyzed his motives for what today we might call a typical act of juvenile vandalism.[35] In the first place he recognized that he had committed this act because he was with friends. Alone, it would not have occurred to him to steal the fruit. More important for our use of the illustration, he believed that he did it precisely because it was forbidden; he experienced a sense of power in doing what he was not supposed to do. Will, or motivation, as it may be called, is the crux of his understanding of the episode.

Augustine held a subjective view concerning these matters, but why, it may be asked, was he interested in the inner being—in psychological topics? The direction his interests took, focusing on the inner person, followed from the sort of man he was and from the experiences he had had. Augustine illustrates in an admirable fashion that we turn to reflection when we become aware of difficulties within ourselves.

What is to follow may give an impression of greater integration than is warranted by his own presentation, but it should be remembered that Augustine had no conception of psychology as a separate discipline.

Some Aspects of the Psychology of Augustine

Augustine's contentually subjectivistic approach is best illustrated by his psychological description of time.[36] Time was created when the world was created, he said, and it has no reality apart from created existence. Neither the past nor the future exists experientially when they are actually in the past or in the future. Yet time past and time future do exist. Augustine resolves the contradiction by arguing that time is thought of in the present, but the past is identified with memory and the future with expectation. There are three times, in other words: a present of things past, a present of things present, and a present of things future. Time is not of the external world but is an inner experience. Augustine's subjective emphasis led naturally to a consideration of the proof of the reality of self-existence. He argues that even to doubt one's own existence is to assert it anyway: to doubt it is to think, and to think is to exist. Under these circumstances, one cannot doubt one's existence, for to do so would be to talk nonsense. Instead of the expression spoken over a thousand years later by René Descartes, "I think, therefore I am," Augustine's formula was, "For if I am deceived, I am."[37] Of all knowledge, the existence of one's own thought is most certain. Sense perception, Augustine tells us, does not give us knowledge. The mind knows the external world only indirectly. What it does know directly is awareness of self, not from contact with the world but from contact with itself, from knowing itself. The mind produces its experiences from within the self. Life is a unity known through self-consciousness. One important consequence of this view is that the automatic functions of the body, grouped together as lower functions, are not part of this self, but are negligible and can safely be disregarded.

From this primary awareness of existence, Aristotle said, we can advance to an awareness of ideas in the mind. These ideas are universal and real concepts—goodness, being, number, and the like. Augustine followed Platonic thinking in how he expressed universals, but he differed beyond this point. The source of ideas, he asserted, is in God; we grasp these ideas by God's gift of illumination. The mind, when considering things of this world, including the body, can recognize its own superiority to them. At the same time, it realizes that it falls short of knowledge of eternal things and thereby recognizes its own shortcomings. Augustine regards the soul as an immaterial spiritual entity; the individual is a dualistic union of body and soul. Body and soul make up human nature.[38] The soul, considered immaterial and indestructible, did not preexist from eternity but was a product of creation. Since nothing was created after the six days of creation, both body and soul must have been created then also.

The soul, though immaterial, acts in and through the body, which it animates and directs. It has the form of the body but can be separated from the body after death and become immortal.[39] Both the immateriality and immortality of the soul are demonstrated by its power of grasping the eternal. Augustine's proof of the existence of the soul is an extension of what he said about self-existence: to have a thinking existence is to have a soul.

The unity of the mind does not preclude the coexistence of different functions. Augustine attributes to the mind three faculties or functions or powers of the soul: reason, memory, and will.[40] He seems to treat imagination, which mediates between memory and reason, as yet another but lesser faculty. Each of these functions is relatively independent. Augustine handles them as entities that in and of themselves explain the facts. This is especially true of will. His view is brought out clearly in the following illustration. Speaking of a youthful temptation, he wrote, "My will the enemy held, and thence made a chain for me, and bound me. For of a forward will was a lust made: and a lust served a custom; and custom not resisted became necessity."[41] The will created a habit, and habit became necessity. In so doing the will functioned as an entity in itself. The reality of the freedom of the will is affirmed in this quotation: it is the human will that makes possible a choice between good or evil.[42] On more than one occasion Augustine affirms that will is a matter of freely determined choice;[43] it concerns us because of the problems of human freedom in relation to the will of God,[44] and to sin and salvation.[45]

Augustine also considers the psychological faculties of reason and memory. A partial summary of their functioning may be offered in terms of one form of interrelationship of the three faculties. Even the simplest act of apprehension has three components: the mind is conscious of itself (memory); it is aware of the possibility of many objects potentially available to attention (reason); and it selects the one with which it becomes involved (will).

SUMMARY

As far as psychological issues are concerned, a dualism of mind and body supplied the general intellectual background for the period. More specifically, the transcendent goal of Plotinus and the religious goal of Augustine mark their dependence on supernaturalism as a prescription. The pejorative connotation which this term has assumed over time is unfortunate. Simply put, supernaturalism refers to accepting what lies beyond nature. In Augustine's time antirationalism was strong; a popularly accepted test of faith was to believe that which one could not believe because of reason, a conviction in which Plotinus shared but which Augustine did much to combat because of his personally strong faith in reason. Contentual subjectivism and purism concerning psychological matters maintained a tacit dominance over the thinking of both men without explicit discussion.

Until the rise of the scholastic Aristotelianism of Aquinas 800 years later, Augustine was the Church's chief authority on psychological matters. Saint Augustine was the most subtle contentually subjective thinker before Freud. He gave an interrelated account of unity and of conflict as expressed in the will. In this and the other faculties, he presented a functional view of human nature, all the while emphasizing a dynamic attitude. His insistence on the truth of his contentions based on the immediate certainty of inner experience did much to foster a contentually subjectivistic approach to psychological problems. Augustine's defense of the primacy of will helped to counteract too exclusive a stress on the intellectual phase of human experience. On the other side of the ledger, when combined with his negative attitude toward science, the sheer charm of his writings, his brilliantly insightful expression, and his striking metaphors probably helped delay the advance of psychology as a science.

The rise of Christianity did not lead directly to the collapse of science in the first centuries of this millennium. Science was already in a period of decline. Christianity did nothing to promote science, however, since its focus was not on the things of this world but of the things beyond it. Faith and dogma, official Church rulings on belief, even came to overrule reason as a source of truth. The chill of orthodoxy and the label of heresy did much to dampen innovative thought during the Patristic period.

Plotinus, a Neoplatonist, extended Plato's ideas but made significant changes. He adapted the rationalism of Plato, with his mistrust of the senses, to a philosophy in which faith supplies the universals. He emphasized Plato's view of soul as a prisoner in the flesh and the need for its liberation. In addition, he believed a major source of knowledge of self was by means of reflection, a form of meditation by which we can come to know our soul. Such psychology as Augustine espoused was a faculty psychology, one that dealt with the powers of the soul.

Augustine was influenced by Plato as modified by Plotinus, and much of his thought was a Christianizing of Platonism. Augustine did not write a formal philosophical psychology, but his thinking was filled with psychological conceptions. Of particular interest are his concepts of inner experience and the determination of the will. Augustine's philosophical views would dominate the Christian world until the coming of Thomas Aquinas.

NOTES

1. W. Windelband, *A History of Philosophy: Greek, Roman and Medieval* (New York: Harper and Brothers, 1901), Vol. I.
2. A. C. Crombie, *Medieval and Early Modern Science,* 2nd rev. ed. (New York: Doubleday, 1959), 2 vols.
3. G. Murphy, *Historical Introduction to Modern Psychology,* rev. ed. (New York: Harcourt, Brace, 1949).
4. Sources for the account of his life are those of his student, Porphyry, *On the Life of Plotinus and the Arrangement of His Works,* in *The Enneads,* trans. S. MacKenna (New York: Pantheon Books, n.d.) and J. Katz, *The Philosophy of Plotinus* (New York: Appleton–Century–Crofts, 1950).
5. R. M. Hutchins, ed., *The Great Books of the Western World,* Vol. XVII, Plotinus, *The Six Enneads,* trans. S. MacKenna and B. S. Page (Chicago: Encyclopaedia Britannica, 1952) (c. 270), pp. 1–130.
6. *Ibid.,* Trac. II, 15.
7. *Ibid.,* I., Trac. VI, 4, p. 23.
8. This view permeates his discussion. A good secondary discussion is to be found in Katz, *Philosophy of Plotinus.*

9. Plotinus, *Enneads*, IV, Trac. III, 20.
10. *Ibid.*, IV, Trac. IV, 28.
11. *Ibid.*, V. Trac. I, 2.
12. *Ibid.*, IV, Trac. III.
13. *Ibid.*, Trac. IX, 3.
14. *Ibid.*, p. 137.
15. Augustine, *The Confessions*, trans. E. B. Pusey, in R. M. Hutchins, ed., *Great Books of the Western World*, Vol. XVIII (c. 400), pp. 1–125. This is the major source for details about his life. It is supplemented by R. W Battenhouse, "The Life of St. Augustine," in R. W Battenhouse, ed., *A Companion to the Study of St. Augustine* (New York: Oxford University Press, 1955), pp. 15–56; V. J. Bourke, *Augustine's Quest of Wisdom* (Milwaukee: Bruce, 1945); and B. Russell, *A History of Western Philosophy* (New York: Simon and Schuster, 1945).
16. Augustine, *Confessions.*
17. *Ibid.*, VIII, 17, p. 57.
18. For example, Augustine, *The City of God*, trans. M. Dods, in R. M. Hutchins, ed., *Great Books of the Western World*, Vol. XVIII (c. 413–426), pp. 127–618, VIII.
19. M. H. Carre, *Realists and Nominalists* (London: Oxford University Press, 1946).
20. Augustine, *Confessions*, V, 23, p. 33.
21. *Ibid.*, VIII, 19–22, 30.
22. *Ibid.*, p. 61.
23. *Ibid.*, VII 27.
24. *Ibid.*
25. Augustine, *City of God.*
26. *Ibid.*, XXI, 8.
27. Augustine, *Confessions*, V, 3–5, 8.
28. Augustine, *City of God*, VIII, 2.
29. R. M. Hutchins, ed., *Great Books of the Western World*, Vol. XVIII, Augustine, *On Christian Doctrine*, trans. J. F. Shaw (c. 427), pp. 619–698.
30. Augustine, *The Trinity*, trans. S. MacKenna, in J. Deferrari, ed., *The Fathers of the Church: A New Translation* (Washington, D.C.: Catholic University of America Press, 1963), Vol. XLV (c. 416), pp. 281–282.
31. Augustine, *On Christian Doctrine.*
32. Augustine, *City of God*, XIV, 28.
33. Augustine, *Confessions*, VII, 23.
34. Augustine, *On Christian Doctrine*, II, 46.
35. Augustine, *Confessions*, II, 9–18.
36. *Ibid.*, XI, 17–40.
37. Augustine, *City of God*, XI, 26, p. 337.
38. *Ibid.*, XIV, 5.
39. *Ibid.*, XIII, 19, XIV, 2–3, 5–6.
40. Augustine, *Confessions*, X, 6, 10–11, 17, 18, 26–27, 37; *City of God*, IX, 4–5, XIV, 6–9, XIX, 18.
41. Augustine, *Confessions*, VIII, 10, p. 55.
42. Augustine, *City of God*, XIV, 6.
43. Augustine, *Confessions*, IX, 1; *City of God*, XXII, 30.
44. *Ibid.*, II, 14; *City of God*, I, 36, IV 33, V, 1, 9–10, XVIII, 2.
45. Augustine, *Confessions*, VII, 5; *City of God*, V, 9–10, XII, 21, XIV, 11–12, 15, XXII, 1, 30.

Portrait of Aquinas.

Aquinas: The Middle Ages, Rationalism, and Faith

*T*homas Aquinas, philosopher and saint, is easily the greatest philosophical psychologist of the Middle Ages. His contribution is more understandable when cast against the backdrop of his age; especially the Dark Ages, the rise and fall of Islam, and the intellectual climate of the later Middle Ages.

THE DARK AGES

The classical twilight and the Patristic period were followed by the early Middle Ages which extended from about A.D. 400 or 500 to 900 and are often referred to as the Dark Ages. Although some Fathers of the Church were still to come, some scholars[1] argue that the creative Patristic epoch closed with the death of Augustine in 430. In the fifth century the world empire of the Romans collapsed and was broken up, after which the empire in the West was divorced from that in the East. In 529 the Emperor Justinian closed the Academy of Athens, an event we may find emotionally satisfying as the date that brings to a final close both the Greek era and the early period of Christianity.

During the Dark Ages, the material preconditions for scientific advancement no longer existed. Misgovernment, top-heavy bureaucracy, civil wars, and the encroachment of neighboring barbarian peoples led to a steady decline. The uniformity of Roman law gave way to a maze of discordant local customs. When the universal monetary system of the Romans disappeared, land became the basic unit of value. Lack of order among the new kingdoms, further invasions by barbarians, and an utter lack of culture among the rulers produced chaotic systems of government and low standards of living. There was little leisure time, and illiteracy was widespread. Most of the cities were deserted; what remained were a few towns. Most of the European population lived in self-sustaining but marginally surviving villages, armed both against their neighbors and invading bands of marauders from afar.

Science and culture inevitably suffered, although in little enclaves in Ireland and at Monte Cassino some religious scholarship survived. But the Church did not decline, and the Bishops of Rome under their title of Pope successfully claimed spiritual authority over all Christendom and asserted more and more temporal authority. No psychological advance was made during this period, and insofar as there was any interest in psychology—and there *was* little—it was based on Augustinian doctrines. The works of Aristotle and Plato had, by and large, been lost to the West. Later, they would return from the East, where the Arabs, armed with the new religion of Mohammed, were already developing into a formidable cultural and political power.

ISLAM

Mohammed was born in Mecca in Arabia in 570. In middle age, he received a revelation from Allah and he began to preach. He fled to Medina in 622 to escape persecution for his teachings. Known as the Hegira, his flight marks the beginning of the Mohammedan era. He called his religion Islam, which means a surrender to God, and his followers were known as Muslims. His message is contained in the Koran.

The development of Islam was remarkably fast.[2] From the Hegira in 622 and the death of the prophet ten years later, to the conquest not only of Arabia and Syria but also of Egypt and Persia in another twenty years, an irrevocable change was wrought on the face of the Near East. Sicily and Spain soon came under the domination of Islam. One hundred years after the death of Mohammed, the Muslim Empire extended over an area larger than that of the Roman Empire at its height.

Muslims assumed positions of leadership in governmental, military, and religious affairs, but scholarship at first fell to non-Muslims. A series a historical forces had been at work making these non-Muslim scholars available in lands that fell under Muslim rule.[3] Egypt and Syria had been Hellenized and had Greek-speaking schools and strong philosophical traditions. In Persia an ancient Oriental culture came under Muslim domination. With their ties to the ancient civilization still unbroken, the scholars of these lands contributed a great deal to the cultural and scientific advances of the area. Pagan and heretical Christian scholars, especially the Syrian Nestorian Christians and the Greeks of the Byzantine Empire, fled the Christian empire in the West to take refuge in this region and helped to graft Hellenic civilization onto Muslim culture. Christian physicians, driven out of Constantinople, brought their knowledge to the Arabs.

The jostling proximity of many tongues made translation extremely important for the diffusion of knowledge. Naturally, the most important translations were from Greek sources. Material from Greek philosophy and science was available to the Arabs from the newly conquered lands. By the end of the fifth century much of Aristotle and some of Plato had been translated into Armenian and Persian. In the eighth century this non-Muslim material became a major portion of the secular intellectual provender of the Muslims. Aristotle held a particular fascination; his writings were very popular, along with Neoplatonic works which often were not attributed to their correct sources. Aristotle's writings, in going through several translations, were often, if not always, garbled. To add to the confusion, many works were falsely attributed to him. For example, the so-called *Theology of Aristotle* was actually an abridgment of the last three books of Plotinus' *Enneads*. Moreover, Aristotle was often known through the biased works of commentators rather than from first-hand study. Hippocrates and Galen were also heavily translated. Despite the confusion in the materials available to them, from the middle of the eighth century until the twelfth century, Muslim culture completely overshadowed that of the Latin West.

Having assimilated Greek and Hellenistic material, the Muslims went on to make distinctive contributions of their own. The philosophical speculation received from the Greek world had much the same effect on Islam that it was to have on Christianity. Attempts to reconcile revelation and reason became a major problem. Hotly contested arguments arose concerning the question of heresy. Mystical movements, similar in spirit to those in the Christian world, also appeared.

We have only superficial knowledge of the original contributions which Islam made to psychology. It would appear that, by and large, even the greatest of the Muslim philosophers, Alkindi, Alfarabi, and Averroes,[4] were primarily imitative of the Greeks and often showed a strong Neoplatonic strain. Insofar as they were naturalistic, they tended to follow Aristotle. Nevertheless, their contributions to psychology deserve more study than has thus far been given them.

This same neglect has befallen the Jews who lived during these centuries in the Muslim world. Generally treated by the Muslims in an enlightened fashion, they experienced one of the high points of their scholarship in these years. Between the ninth and the thirteenth centuries, especially in Spain and Egypt, several Jewish scholars presented psychological thinking of originality and power. The psychological views of the Jewish philosophers, including Abraham Ibn Daud, Solomon Ibn Gabirol, Abraham Ibn Ezra, Ibn Zaddik, Isaac Israeli, and especially Moses Maimonides, also have received far less scholarly attention than they merit.[5] Although their influence on later developments in psychology is, to say the least, obscure—their work will not be examined here—they are well worth serious study.

The Muslims also made some scientific advances in fields other than psychology and philosophy.[6] Fired with enthusiasm by Greek and Hindu sources of knowledge, they made contributions in mathematics, astronomy, chemistry, technology, and medicine. Instead of being members of the clergy, as were their contemporaries in the West, Muslim scholars were often physicians. With them the study of philosophy, medicine, and some of the rudiments of natural science went hand in hand. Advances continued even until the fifteenth century, but by the twelfth century Muslim supremacy had come to an end.

By the eleventh century in Europe, the social characteristics often associated with the Middle Ages had fairly emerged.[7] The spread of feudalism gave a measure of personal safety to individuals of all social classes and tended to stabilize social relations among them. The three major social classes of the Middle Ages were the clergy, the aristocracy, and the peasantry. The Church was influential both because of its spiritual authority and its extensive landholdings. It was beginning to have some success in its challenge of secular authority on its affairs and increasingly to free its appointments of those influences. It also wielded considerable political power. The aristocracy was, by and large, a military caste depending for its revenues on its estates. Knighthood had already emerged with its code of chivalry. The rural population worked the estates and was levied for war service, and in return received protection from their liege lords. By the eleventh century, because of a growth in population, greater political stability, more extensive trade, and increased social mobility, the towns became increasingly important. These conditions made a growth in scholarship possible.

COMMON CHARACTERISTICS OF THINKING

The thinking of the Middle Ages must be understood in context. Greek philosophy–science had been based on an attempt to see the world rationally; Christian doctrine is based on faith. One solution, the one perhaps most popularly attributed to the Middle Ages, was to deny the value of human reason and to embrace faith in the supernatural as interpreted by the authority of the Church as the Truth. Although this attitude was indeed widespread, perhaps even dominant, some churchmen did attempt to reconcile faith and reason. But the Church was unyielding in its dogma: faith was primary and fixed; reason was secondary and precarious. The dominance of one over the other was never in doubt. No matter how precise the reasoning, if the conclusion did not conform to dogma, it was not true—and errors in faith, no matter how they were introduced, were heretical. Conformity was expected and enforced.

This widespread attitude led to a considerable amount of uniformity in intellectual life during the medieval period. There was a preoccupation with death and life after death. Life on earth was regarded as a preparation for the life to come after death, either a blissful life everlasting or eternal woe. Large segments of intellectual life were guided by a contempt for earthly matters, a despising of human joy, a longing for eternity.[8]

Medieval thinking, though narrow, was not all of a piece. It did not consist of a single integrated system any more than modern philosophy does. Certainly, the uniformity of thinking was greater than it is today, but it was not all-pervasive. As Gilson has reminded us, not all Christian philosophy was either Christian or philosophy.[9] Fortunately, there were many authorities, and these authorities often disagreed with one another. The only variation and change was according to the style of the writer and the particular problem, and contrary to popular opinion the scholastic method did allow some freedom of thought.

On the whole, the spirit of the age was not conducive to psychological concerns. The union of theology and philosophy that gave us Christian philosophy in its spirit of other-worldliness was foreign to psychology. Most of its problems dealt not with the individual but with the relationship between God and humankind—a quite different proposition. Only incidentally did the question of the individual as individual occupy these thinkers. In this isolated part of the pattern, there were some matters of psychological concern.

SOURCES OF KNOWLEDGE

Most of the intellectual heritage of the West was derived from the Scriptures, from the writings of the Church Fathers, including Augustine, and from a smattering of Neoplatonism. In the early Middle Ages the largest and most important compilation of fact, and of fiction masquerading as fact, was the *Natural History* of Pliny (A.D. 23–79).[10] This work served as a textbook and encyclopedia for the medieval scholar, containing all sorts of miscellaneous information on what were thought to be facts about nature.

The Latin writer Chalcidius, who was a contemporary of Plotinus, translated a part of Plato's *Timaeus* into Latin and also wrote a commentary on it. Until the twelfth century, this was the only work of Plato known to the Latin world. Otherwise, Plato was known through Neoplatonic writers rather than from original sources. Only much later, in about 1150, were two other dialogues, the *Meno* and the *Phaedo,* made available in Latin. The remainder of Plato's works received little attention until the humanist translations of the fifteenth century.

We have encountered the *Timaeus* earlier in connection with its influence on Plotinus. A very atypical representative of Plato's writings, it is his poetic vision of the world, of the universe, and of God. Its central theme is that the world and the individual are but incidents or manifestations within the ideal patterns that reside in the mind of God. The things of the world, the visible things, are not real. They have significance only to the extent that they conform to the ideal.

The *Timaeus* is a mixture of the serious and the fanciful, which are not always easy to tell apart. The astronomical lore that it contains—each soul is said to have both a star and a numerical relation among the planets—later contributed to a lot of harmful astrological nonsense. Because of the style in which it is written, there are problems of interpretation, and the *Timaeus* probably causes more perplexity among scholars than any of Plato's other dialogues. Sarton even goes so far as to say that the influence of the *Timaeus* was largely negative.[11]

Insofar as Aristotle had been known to earlier Christian thinkers, he was seen as definitely secondary to Plato and in fundamental agreement with him. Logic was the one area in which he was acknowledged to be original. The earlier and more elementary portion of his *Organon* had come down from the early Middle Ages in the direct tradition, and it was studied along with a widely used commentary by Boethius. These works were staples of dialectic training. Together they formed one of the three subjects of the traditional curriculum of the Middle Ages, the *Trivium*; the others were grammar and rhetoric. The rest of the *Organon* was translated as early as 1150, two generations earlier than those of his works that are of more direct psychological interest. The Middle Ages was preoccupied by a search for premises about which we can be certain, and according to Schiller,[12] this search goes far to account for the relative neglect of experience during the years since Aristotle.

Ideas derived from Platonic sources dominated Christian philosophy. The fundamental theme in Platonism—the dualistic contrast between things of the senses and things of the mind, between body and spirit—was preserved. Ever the resident of two realms, the individual can choose either one or the other, either taking the tangible but temporal things of the senses or turning upward to God and eternal life. For the Christian the correct choice was clear.

SCHOLASTICISM

The Patristic period, dedicated to the formation of orthodoxy, had passed long before scholasticism made its appearance. The task of scholasticism was to elaborate a recognized and accepted orthodoxy, to build a system of principles on accepted dogma. The scholastics began with this doctrine and then traced its implications for various theological questions. Along with consciousness of a need for divine salvation, Henry O. Taylor considers two of the major characteristics of medieval thought to be a deference to authority and an all-pervasive scholasticism leading to work that was diligent and receptive rather than original.[13] Reverence for the past was a predominant attitude of the scholastic.

The scholastic method in its generic form is defined by Wilhelm Windelband as follows:

> [A] text used as the basis for discussion is broken up by division and explanation into a number of propositions; questions are attached and the possible answers brought together; finally the arguments to be adduced for establishing or refuting these answers are presented in the form of a chain of syllogistic reasoning, leading ultimately to a decision upon the subject.[14]

Naturally, the details of this method varied from writer to writer. In more general terms, oral discussion of question and answer, a form of dialectic, characterized the scholastic method. Scholasticism was especially congenial to the medieval mind because it permitted acceptance of authority and yet proceeded from that point by dialectic. It was the medieval version of eating one's cake and having it too.

The scholastic had considerable freedom within the framework of his method, whose latitude was limited by the stipulation that dogma in no way must be put to question. It should be noted that the scholastic did not merely make an appeal to authority, as is sometimes alleged. As R. McKeon indicates, an adroit scholastic could find authority for either side of a question and then proceed to find truth by examining the interplay of both sides.[15] The scholastic might know the ultimate answer on the basis of revelation and faith, but he did not necessarily, or even often, cheat to make it come out right. If his claim led to erroneous conclusions, he did not insist that it did not. Instead, he went back over his earlier arguments for the sources of his error and perhaps sometimes couldn't find them! Being human, he could delude himself that his doctrine was not contrary to dogma and proceed to argue the point. He, of course, did so at his peril because his position might eventually be judged heretical.

During the Middle Ages philosophers were almost always theologians, but, as is usually overlooked, they often considered problems that had no theological import whatever. A philosopher as philosopher, then, could depend on reason alone, limited only by his skill and the knowledge available to him.

THE UNIVERSITIES

Although some universities had been founded the century before, they did not come into real prominence until the thirteenth century.[16] They had not been important before because there was simply not enough learning to justify their existence. With the expansion of knowledge and favorable conditions for their presence, many universities came into being. Both the gathering together of people into larger communities and the increased ease of travel helped set the stage for them. The youth of the eleventh century had entered monasteries; those of the thirteenth attended universities. The universities at Bologna, Paris, and Oxford were among the most important. Paris was a truly international institution, attracting students from all over France, as well as from the Low Countries, Italy, England, and Germany. Other important universities were Cambridge in England; Padua, Naples, and the medical school at Salerno in Italy; Montpellier, Toulouse, and Orleans in France; Salamanca and Valladolid in Spain; and Lisbon in Portugal.

The university curricula consisted of an arts course and higher courses in theology, law, and medicine, each of which had separate faculties. The arts course usually involved a study of the seven liberal arts and the "three philosophies"— natural philosophy (natural science), ethics, and metaphysics. Masters and scholars were usually clergymen but not always ordained priests. Both newly founded orders of friars, the Dominicans and the Franciscans, controlled professorships and did much to further the cause of the Church. They also served to supply many of the most distinguished professors.

The universities became a potent intellectual force. They aided intellectual progress by supplying a setting that made time and resources for study possible, and they provided a less involved and more disinterested vantage point than the monasteries from which to approach fields of knowledge.

THE RECOVERY OF ARISTOTLE'S THOUGHT

It was to Spain and to Sicily, retaken by the Christian world in the twelfth and thirteenth centuries, that scholars from the West came to work on translations from the Arabic.[17] Such translations could have been done directly from the Greek sources and, as a matter of fact, some of them were, but Arabic sources were generally used. Use of these sources reflected glory on the Arabic commentaries and the original Arabic works that were translated at the same time. Along with the recovery of Galen and Hippocrates, the West acquired the medical works of Avicenna and the philosophical teachings of Averroes, and these immediately became important. In medicine the Arabic scholars had added valuable observations, and in philosophy they were responsible for a variety of distinctive new perspectives. The translations from Arabic sources included not only religious, philosophical, and medical works, but also works in the fields of science, such as optics, geology, and mathematics. Original contributions in alchemy, magic, and astrology (sometimes attributed to Aristotle) had a considerable effect for both good and ill. From the end of the twelfth century and for the next hundred years, the proportion of texts translated directly from the Greek gradually increased, and in the fourteenth century translations from the Arabic virtually ceased.

E. Renan[18] goes so far as to claim that the introduction of these texts into the West divided the Middle Ages into two distinct periods: the earlier, without knowledge of Greek, and the later, with ancient science restored. This sweeping generalization is not without merit as a summary. Certainly a major task of the scholars was to assimilate and study ancient knowledge and to express it in a fashion that would be acceptable when viewed against the imperatives of their time.

As important perhaps for the intellectual history of the West as all other works combined was the recovery of the works of Aristotle. The first medieval scholar who has been said to be familiar with Aristotelian treatises was Alexander of Hales (d. 1245). The works of Aristotle were imported into the universities of Paris and Oxford between 1200 and 1270. With this recovery the ideas of the Greek scholars began to work their influence again in Western thought. It was at this time that Aquinas came on the scene.

THOMAS AQUINAS

The task which Aquinas set for himself was the reconciliation of supernaturalism with rationalism. He carried on this effort with intricate but massive tools: the teachings of the Church and the recovered works of Aristotle.

Life and Labors of Aquinas

The life of Thomas Aquinas bears an impersonal stamp, an objectivity without many of the towering heights and dark shadows of other great men.[19] The fire was there, but it burned with a steady glow, not in a great shower of sparks and flame.

He was known to have been really angry only twice in his life. He led an intense intellectual life, and his solitary mind was always hard at work beneath a placid bulk that won for him from his fellow students at the University of Paris the nickname the "Dumb Ox." A story is told that characterizes his imperturbability and his abstractedness in the service of scholarship, regardless of circumstances. Obedient to the orders of his superiors, Aquinas had gone to a state dinner at the court of the King of France, Louis IX, later known as Saint Louis. He sat at table, a huge man in the black and white habit of the Dominicans, unheeded and unheeding, surrounded by the pomp, the colors, and the jewels of the most brilliant court of Europe. All around were people engaged in gossip, intrigue, and idle, inconsequential chatter. He said little or nothing. Suddenly a huge fist crashed down on a table, and his voice rang out clearly above the discreet hubbub, "And that will settle the Manichees!" He had been elsewhere, using his time for his intellectual task in life.

Besides being a great scholar, Aquinas was also a Christian saint. This sketch does not even pretend to illustrate this side of his nature. The omission is mentioned as a warning since some would say that Thomas the scholar cannot be understood apart from Thomas the saint.[20]

The family of Aquino was a distinguished and aristocratic one. The Castle of Roccasecca where Thomas was born in 1225 was midway between Naples and Rome. His father, Landulfo, was Count of Aquino, a town nearby, and an official in the service of Frederick II, the King of Sicily. His father had considerable influence at the Benedictine Abbey of Monte Jassono, which was only a few miles from the castle.

At about age five, Thomas entered the abbey and remained there as a student for nine years. In 1239 the monks were forced to leave the abbey because of a war between Pope Gregory II and Frederick II, whose kingdom included that portion of Italy. Thomas enrolled as a student at the University of Naples, a state institution founded only a few years before by the same Frederick whose warmaking had forced him out of the abbey. At Naples he completed his study of the liberal arts.

In 1243 his father died, and the next spring Thomas took the habit of the Dominican order. This step caused considerable consternation in his family, not because of his intention to become a priest—they had expected him to return to Monte Cassino, where in the normal course of events and with his family's influence, he would have become abbot—but because he had joined a mendicant order, one made up of begging friars. In deciding to become a beggar, he was throwing away not only wealth and power, but also ecclesiastical ambition. This decision went against the family's aristocratic grain. Aware of their anger and exasperation, John the Teuton, General of the Dominican order, took Thomas to Paris so that he might complete his philosophical and theological studies at a more comfortable distance from his family. His mother, not one to have the family wishes flaunted, boldly directed a group of relatives to abduct Thomas from the party traveling to Paris. They took him to the family castle, where he was held prisoner for about a year. He was not angry with his family at this imprisonment; indeed, he had so persuasive a tongue that he converted his oldest sister to Saint Benedict. However, one thing did make him angry during this period. His brothers, barbaric nobles of their age, conceived a scheme of trying his chastity. They slipped into his prison apartment a prostitute, presumably selected for her seductiveness. On seeing her, Thomas seized a brand from the fire, and his expression was such that she fled without saying a word. He then took the flaming log and drew a cross on the door of his prison. G. K. Chesterton says that his anger arose as much from a feeling of insult over his brothers' belief that something so cheap would tempt him as from the particular nature of the temptation.[21]

Even the Pope intervened on the side of the family, but Thomas was adamant in his resolve to be a Dominican. The Dominicans continued to appeal to both the Pope and the Emperor. Finally, in 1245, Thomas Aquinas regained his liberty and once again donned the habit of the Dominican order. He went to Paris to study under Albertus Magnus, Albert the Great.

Albertus was already known as a champion of Aristotle, whose works were coming into general use at the University. In anything more than a sketch of the greatest psychologists, Albertus would have an account of his own.[22] Though more of a scientist and an original observer than Aquinas and equally if not better versed in psychological matters, he did not have his student's gift for synthesis. The influence of Aquinas on subsequent developments was the greater, however, and so the student, not the teacher, will be discussed.

In 1248 Albertus went to Cologne to establish a Dominican House of Studies, and Thomas, his favorite pupil, accompanied him. After four years, Thomas returned to the University of Paris for still further study and to begin his career in teaching. As a teacher, he was extremely popular; as a student, he was prodigious. According to regulations, he could not receive his magistrate (doctorate) in theology until after his thirty-fourth birthday, but a papal dispensation was granted him, and he took it at thirty-one. He was also appointed to one of the two Dominican chairs at the University of Paris. As a master, he continued to teach for three additional years at Paris. For ten years after that he was a teacher of theology in various places in Italy.

Sometime between 1261 and 1264 Aquinas wrote the *Summa Contra Gentiles*.[23] Designed for use in missionary work, the "Summary Against the Gentiles" is a work addressed to those nonbelievers who are philosophically skilled and unimpressed by a call to believe—whose rationalism prevents an acceptance of revelation. This work gives not theological but philosophical arguments, proven by reason alone. Since some of his arguments concern the nature of the individual, it becomes important as a source for his views on psychology.

Late in 1268 Aquinas returned to teach at the University of Paris only to find himself in a sea of academic troubles in which he took a leading and vigorous part. Despite his active academic battles, Aquinas found time during his stay in Paris to write additional works. It was during the Italian decade that he met William of Moerbeke. At his suggestion, Moerbeke began a new translation of Aristotle directly from the Greek. Between 1260 and 1271 William translated or revised translations of nearly all of Aristotle's works. On the basis of this uncorrupted test, Thomas wrote various commentaries on the works of Aristotle, including *De Anima*.[24]

A few years earlier, around 1266, Thomas had begun the *Summa Theologica*, which was destined to become his most important work.[25] It was designed as a summary for the training of beginners in theology. The first part is concerned with God and creation. His major treatise on psychology is placed between a discussion of the six days of creation and a study of the individual in the state of original innocence. This was a scriptural order of presentation; humankind was created last and is therefore treated last. Later parts are concerned with moral life and Christ and the sacraments. This work is more obviously theological than the *Summa Contra Gentiles*, but part of *The Treatise on Man*,[26] is a detailed account of his psychology. It is supplemented in this regard by the *Treatise on Human Acts* and the *Treatise on Habits.*[27]

Certainly Aquinas was interested in psychology. In this connection he passed a test that most psychologists might fail; regardless of personal religious convictions, a psychologist could not fail to be impressed by the incident. A friend of Aquinas, one Friar Romano by name, died,[28] and Aquinas had a vision in which he saw his friend in Heaven. Out of all the questions on Heaven, Hell, the World, and Man that he might have asked, the question he put to his friend was this: "Do we retain our knowledge of this world in the next?" What more crucial projective test of the primacy of a psychologist's calling could be asked? Under similar circumstances, would even contemporary learning theorists do as well?

In 1272 Thomas left the University of Paris and returned to Italy, where he taught at the University of Naples and continued to work on the *Summa*. His career as a writer came to a sudden and dramatic end on December 6, 1273. He had been saying Mass that morning when a great change came over him. Afterward, whenever he was urged to continue writing his *Summa* he would merely say, "I can do no more; such things have been revealed to me that all I have written seems as straw, and I now await the end of my life." In January 1274, he received instructions from Pope Gregory X to attend an ecumenical council in Lyons. On the way he fell ill and was forced to break the journey at the Cistercian Abbey of Fossanova, which was not far from his place of birth. There, on March 7, 1274, he died. Less than fifty years later Thomas was canonized by Pope John XXII.

Reason and Faith in Aquinas's Thought

Before dealing with Aquinas's interpretation of Aristotle, it might be desirable to state how non-Thomistic scholars sometimes interpret certain issues today. First, we must face the problem of the inseparability of form and matter. If *psyche* is the form of the body, what happens when the body dies? The form must also be gone. The earlier chapter on Aristotle suggests that he rules out personal immortality completely. Here we get into one of the most tangled webs of modern scholarship. The very chapters of Book III of *De Anima*, described as an interpolation of his earlier views and therefore inapplicable, provide an answer that should in fairness be stated.[29] There, *Nous*, the highest intellectual manifestation of the mind, is held to be of a different order from the other functions.[30] *Nous* is regarded as imperishable.

The individual object, including the human body, perishes. Here we face another perplexing problem. In the same passage of *De Anima*[31] where Aristotle speaks of *Nous* (mind) as imperishable, he also tells us that memory and love perish because they are parts of a complex that perishes, namely, the body–*psyche* unit. Hence, personal immortality seems to be denied in the very passage that is crucial to the argument in favor of it. (Perhaps Aquinas had this very point in mind when in his dream of Friar Romano, he asked about memories of earthly existence in the life hereafter.)

In a broad perspective, we can conceive of Aristotle as being concerned not with the problem of the immortality of the human soul, but with *Nous* as a human function capable of knowing truth, of rising above our animal limitations to a direct vision of universals. He was arguing for the existence of some dominating source of intelligence outside the universe. It is hard to read religious overtones into what he has to say about movement and the unmoved mover.[32] Motion is eternal; it always has been and it always will be. We can trace movement back from one mover to another—A moves B, B moves C, and so on. Eventually we have to postulate a mover himself unmoved, a transmitter of movement not moved by an anterior movement. This unmoved mover of Aristotle is interpreted as God. The unmoved mover in Aristotle's sense, however, is not an object of worship. He is not aware of the individual, nor in any way is he concerned with the individual. Divine providence is completely absent. God in this view, is a metaphysical necessity, not an object to be loved and worshiped. What modern science disregards as irrelevant to its enterprise, the cause–uncaused, Aristotle considers necessary to investigate because he believed metaphysics cannot be divorced from physics.

This striving toward higher existence as conceived by Aristotle was seen in the Middle Ages as a striving toward God. The scholars of the Middle Ages could not have known that in his later thinking Aristotle may have discarded this theory of a higher existence. Aristotle, as he was known in the Middle Ages, appealed to the Christian thinkers precisely because they considered this postulation of a supreme intelligence an integral part, even the capstone, of his thinking. His work stressed the idea that all living creatures are subject to law, and Christian thinkers regarded this idea as demonstrating that this law was personally decreed by God. The only alternative to His guidance known to thinkers of the Middle Ages was pure chance, which to them was an abhorrent possibility. It was not until the time of Galileo and Newton that natural law was offered as yet a third alternative.

Aristotle had posited four kinds of causality—material, motor (or efficient), formal, and final—and had given weight to each of them. Those who came after him could therefore stress one or the other according to their interests. It was this teleological strain in Aristotle that Aquinas raised to a position of primacy. There in Aristotle was found an intelligent being who directs all things to their ends—and this was interpreted as God.[33] The other causes that Aristotle had used to complete the analysis were subordinated to it. Efficient causes, said Aquinas, are subordinate to final causes; this corresponds to a soldier's tactical disposition by a subordinate commander who is directed by the high command.[34]

Aquinas and others interpreted Aristotle as holding that all that exists and all that happens do so for the sake of some end. Every activity, all change, and all growth are to be understood in relation to the ends they serve. Everything is pervaded with change, and no change is meaningless. Change implies preparation, and preparation presupposes becoming. Hence, in the Middle Ages Aristotle's view was considered to be uncompromisingly teleological.

All we have just said was interpreted by Aquinas in a way that would reconcile it with Christian dogma. To his credit, he could do so in a fashion that still satisfies many contemporary thinking men and women who apply to his work their personal test of reason.

Nous in Aquinas's Thought

Nous, or active reason, minimized in the earlier naturalistic account of Aristotle, became the salient feature of Aquinas's view on the individual in general and on psychology in particular. Moreover, Aquinas did not divorce metaphysical considerations from those of psychology. Advocates of religious Aristotelianism, especially that of Aquinas, took the unmixed separable character of *Nous* to mean that *Nous* was capable of separate existence. Hence, it was considered to be the Aristotelian counterpart of the immortal soul.

Attacks on Aquinas's Thought

As a consequence of espousing Aristotle, Aquinas laid himself open to attacks on two fronts. On one side the Church conservatives saw his corroboration of Aristotle as an attack on Augustine and the other Church Fathers and the Neoplatonism with which their views had been so completely intermingled. From Aquinas's point of view the second source of attack was the crucial one; it came in the form of apparent agreement rather than opposition to him. These opponents were themselves Aristotelians. Their leader was Siger of Brabant, who followed to some extent the Averroist interpretation of Aristotle and taught that *Nous* was capable of a separate existence but was conjoined in the individual with a "material intellect." Both *Nous* and the material intellect were necessary for thinking, and since the material intellect was corruptible, this precluded personal immortality. Siger thought that matter exists from eternity, and that after the impersonal *Nous* left the matter of the body, it became part of a universal and common intelligence.

Regardless of one's own interpretation of Aristotle's views about personal immortality and the exact nature of *Nous* (and it would seem that Bertrand Russell[35] is right and that Siger may have had a case), it is possible, as stated earlier, to take the position of Aquinas and argue for the soul's immortality. The views of the Averroists concerning the eternity of matter, though definitely expounded by Aristotle, disagree with the teaching of the Church on creation. On all three counts the position of the Averroists was incompatible with Catholic doctrine. When this incompatibility was called to their attention, Siger and his followers agreed that perhaps these teachings of Aristotle did contradict the teaching of faith. Ostensibly in the interests of defending reason and faith, Siger suggested the compromise known as the doctrine of two truths: the truth of the material world and the truth of the supernatural world. When one is naturalistic, one may hold in abeyance the truth of the supernatural world; on turning to religion, one accepts this truth. Aquinas, too, followed Averroes in distinguishing faith from reason. To Aquinas, Siger said in effect, "You speak of reason and faith as both giving truth; so also do we, but with this difference, one does not need to trouble about reconciling the two. This fine distinction is all that divides us."

This doctrine, seemingly so near and yet actually so far from what he was teaching, flatly contradicted all that Aquinas stood for. To him, it was merely a subterfuge. For the second time in his life he was aroused to anger,[36] and in his reply to Siger his usually temperate style gave way to such expressions as "puffed up with false knowledge," "if he dares," and "false teaching."[37]

Aquinas's Doctrine of the One Truth

To his credit, Aquinas also opposed the opposite error, namely, that one's views about other matters are irrelevant as long as one's religious attitude is correct.[38]

What Aquinas championed was the doctrine of the one truth. He saw two paths to the same truth, not two truths. Nothing that is philosophically demonstrated, he said, will ever contradict or ever be contradicted by what is taught through revelation. This position may be made clearer if we deal more specifically with the issue of reason and faith as he saw it. Truth in reason and faith (in science and religion) are one; this concept is so important to him that Aquinas opens the *Summa* on this theme.[39] Theology is the noblest of the sciences because of the worth of its subject matter. The knowledge that we arrive at from the evidence of our senses is not enough to know the essence of God, but what we sense does come from God and this permits us to know that He exists.[40] This is not to say that there is no distinction between theology and philosophy, for there is. Theology concerns faith, that which is known immediately and without doubt; philosophy is known only after the other possible alternatives are considered.[41] Because certain truths, such as the mystery of the Trinity, cannot be known by reason, Aquinas said, they are matters of consideration for theology alone. Many other truths, however, are within the province of both reason and revelation.[42] Both the theologian and the philosopher consider the same truths but from different points of view. The theologian regards them as given, whereas the philosopher regards them as in need of demonstration. The philosopher, for example, may, through a process of reasoning, arrive at an acceptance of God as the Creator; the theologian, on the other hand, accepts God as the Creator because He has revealed Himself as such.

As far as church orthodoxy was concerned, Aquinas decisively disposed of Siger's arguments. Nevertheless, during and after his lifetime, Aquinas's teachings continued to be targets for condemnation by Church authorities.[43]

Aquinas's Philosophical Psychology

Three factors make it possible for us to be briefer in discussing the psychological views of Aquinas than those of some of the other great philosophical psychologists. The previous discussion of reason and faith is part of Thomistic psychology (as the systematic views of Thomas Aquinas are typically known). Moreover, much more complete modern statements are readily available, which is not the case for the earlier thinkers.[44] Most important of all, Aquinas followed Aristotle in much of his psychology, and Aristotle has already received rather detailed treatment. A possible misunderstanding must be disposed of in this connection. To put it succinctly, Aquinas followed Aristotle, not because of blind adherence to Aristotle as authority, but simply because much of what he had said Aquinas thought was true. Aquinas did not hesitate to disagree with Aristotle when he thought the Greek philosopher was wrong. Since Aquinas's terminology is different from Aristotle's, however, some restatement must be made even of points on which they were in agreement.

Soul and Body To Aquinas, the human being as a species has one substantial form, the rational soul.[45] The individual is neither soul alone, nor body alone, but is soul and body, a united or composite substance. There are no vegetative, sensitive, substantive forms or souls. The person is a unity; the rational soul not only has the function particular to itself, but also encompasses the vegetative and sensitive functions. The human soul thus exercises the functions of the lower forms of life, which have vegetative or sensitive souls. The rational soul as a totality is united with its body in order to carry on its natural functions. Unlike some earlier thinkers, Aquinas taught that the soul is neither imprisoned nor carrying out a sentence of punishment; it is doing what is natural and good. Its union with the body is not to the detriment of the soul but to its enrichment.[46] The soul completes human nature and also confers the incidental benefit of allowing the achievement of knowledge through the senses. It is acting according to its nature, in which matter exists for form and not vice versa.[47]

This view is not materialistic in the sense that soul or mind is made to depend on material substances (or if you prefer, cortical substances). Nor is it, to use a Thomistic term, angeletic, that is, with mind or soul interpreted as a purely immaterial entity or as an independent spiritual being.

For Aquinas there are a multiplicity of corporeal substances, that is to say, a multiplicity of substances that have matter in their nature. Four species may be distinguished—nonliving bodies, plants, animals, and humans.[48] Inanimate objects perform material activities alone; plants have material and vegetative activities; animals, these two and sensory activities; and humankind has rational activities in addition to the three lower activities.

Soul and Its Faculties In one of his most sustained and detailed psychological statements,[49] Aquinas distinguishes between the unity that is soul and its faculties or powers. He makes further divisions among these faculties or powers. The soul is not its faculties. The soul does not exercise these functions directly through its essence as such, but through powers with which it is endowed and that are distinct from its essence. These faculties exhibit an order or priority related to the corporeal substances of which they are composed. The *rational faculty* is conceived of as higher than the sensitive and, therefore, as embracing and controlling the sensitive, whereas the *sensitive faculty* is above the *nutritive* one. The nutritive faculty embraces the powers of nutrition, growth, and reproduction. The sensitive faculty encompasses the five exterior senses, the four interior senses (a description of which follows in the next paragraph), sensitive appetite, and locomotion. The rational faculty comprises the active and passive intellect, and the will. The object of the nutritive faculty is the subject's own body–soul combination. The sensitive faculty has as its object, not the body of its sentient subject alone, but every sensible body. The rational faculty has as its object not only sensible body, but being itself. The higher the faculty, the more comprehensive its scope, extending from a particular body–soul composite, to sensed bodies, to being in general.

There is no need to review the powers of the nutritive faculty or the exterior senses of the sensitive faculty since Aquinas treats them much the same as Aristotle does. This is not the case with the interior senses of the sensitive faculty. In using the expression, *interior sense*, Aquinas was referring not to additional sense modalities arising from stimulation within the organism but to operations at the level of sensitive life and, consequently, to psychological functioning not involving reason. For example, a bird goes beyond the outer senses in using vision to select twigs for nest-building because, although the exterior senses give awareness of color, they do not tell that the twig is useful for the particular task. Since the bird does not reason, he must have an interior sense by which to apprehend the utility of the twig.

Reception of sense data involves the already familiar common sense for receiving those qualities, such as softness, that cannot be perceived by one sense modality alone. Reception also includes the particular interior sense illustrated in the preceding paragraph. It becomes necessary because the data received transcend the qualities of the common sense. It is called *via aestimativa*, or estimative power. Animals are dependent on it because they are without the aid of reason. When a lamb sees a wolf and "estimates" it is to be avoided, this is done, to use a modern term, by instinct. Estimating is a power to sense what is harmful or what is useful to the organism. It is a power that does not depend on previous experience or training and as such is something like intuition. In humans, estimating is allied to mind, since there is always a background of abstract knowledge and universal principles derived from reason with which it interacts. This is analogous to instinctive estimating, but because it is carried out through reason, it must also be distinguished from it. It is given a distinctive name, *via cogitativa*, or cognitive power.

In addition to reception of sense expressed in the common sense and estimative or cognitive power, both animals and humans conserve the data of sense. Because it produces sense images, Aquinas refers to imagination as the conservation of sense data. As for the conservation of those estimative or cogitative powers that transcend sense, such as the recognition of an image as an item of personal experience in past time, this requires still another power. It is called sensory memory. Thus, the four interior senses are the common sense, the sense of estimation and cogitation, imagination, and memory.

In considering sensation, Aquinas almost echoes Aristotle, despite differences in terminology. He holds that sensed material things exist only in the sensing individual, not as material but as immaterial, and the ability to sense is the ability to receive form (species) without matter.

According to Aquinas, the power of appetite is twofold and involves sensitive appetite at the sensitive level and volition or will at the rational level. Sensitive appetite desires objects that are sensed. The two major kinds of sensitive appetites are the concupiscible, so called because they desire the objects of sensible pleasure; and the irascible, whose function is to urge a fight for the objects in question when there are difficulties in securing them. The concupiscible emotions include love, desire, joy, hatred, aversion, and sorrow, whereas the irascible embrace hope, despair, courage, fear, and anger. Aquinas calls the act of a sensitive appetite a passion.

In keeping with his teleological emphasis, Aquinas asserts that in volition or will, there must be some knowledge of purpose for the action to be called voluntary.[50] Perhaps the most typical of the arguments that Aquinas advances for freedom of the will is that it arises from freedom of the intellect; as he puts it, free choice is free judgment. Some activities forced on a person give rise to coercive necessity, but these are involuntary. Free will is evidenced in voluntary activities about which judgments are made.

Because it is an appetitive faculty, the will cannot be understood apart from its natural object. We desire happiness, which is found in the good, by our very nature, proceeding from the will in itself. This means the desire comes from the will itself and is not imposed on us from without, as by violence. We cannot help desiring because we are the creatures that we are. This naturalness of the desire for happiness does not mean we are not free to make our own individual choices. In the relation of will and intellect, will is subordinate. Intellect is dominant. "Nothing is willed unless known," is an Aquinas dictum.

We also need to consider Aquinas's views on the functioning of the rational faculty as such. The power of the so-called *agens intellectus,* the intellectual agent or active intellect, is concerned with abstraction; and the power of the possible intellect is concerned with understanding, judgment, and reasoning.

The first power is active or creative; the second is passive or receptive. Because it is material, a sensible object is only potentially intelligible. Aquinas is empirical in that he holds with Aristotle that natural knowledge begins with sensation.[51] In order to make sensory experience intelligible, however, the activity of the active intellect of the mind is necessary. With the operation of the active intellect we extract the form from the individual substance in which it is embedded and experience "color" or "horse." When the *agens intellectus* acts, the concrete nature of the datum is laid aside and what remains is something capable of being understood. It is no longer material but is intelligible, an object of intellect. The *agens intellectus* renders sensible natures intelligible by abstraction for use by the possible intellect. Sense experience provides the stimulus for setting in operation the *agens intellectus.* It makes "possible" the realization of the truth that the possible intellect potentially contains. As with Aristotle, Aquinas held that human beings alone possessed the power of abstraction and that this power resulted from the actions of an *agens intellectus.* To Aristotle this agent was a naturalistic process, but to Aquinas it was an act of God. In this way, the intellectual process resulting from abstraction becomes an aspect of revelation.

Also like Aristotle, Aquinas held that prior to sensory experience the possible intellect is like a *tabula rasa,* a blank tablet, devoid of ideas. To a certain extent the senses themselves perform this task in that through them we perceive the species to which the objects belong. That is, a green flower and a green glass have the color green, which is its species. To understand, we must penetrate sensible species to intelligible terms.

Psychology and Theology   In closing our discussion of these aspects of the psychology of Aquinas, a return to theology is particularly fitting. As far as the teachings of psychology are concerned, a reconciliation with dogma becomes imperative in connection with revealed doctrines about the resurrection of the body and its eventual reunion with the soul. This, in turn, requires the immortality of the soul. The issue at hand is how Aquinas reconciled his previously stated views on psychology with these theological imperatives. To do so Aquinas drew on previously established teachings. It will be remembered that Aquinas interprets the Aristotelian *Nous,* the active reason or active intellect, as deathless. He extended this contention of immortality to the rational soul as a unit. It will also be remembered that Aquinas himself made a distinction between the soul and its faculties. He makes use of both points in the reconciliation.

To Aquinas, some of the faculties belong to the soul as such, and these faculties transcend the power of matter. For the rational faculties, the body is not necessary as the organ of activities. The rational faculties are not intrinsically dependent on the body, even though when united with the body they draw on sense experience, which is dependent on the composite. Other lower faculties, when in the soul–body composite, do depend on the body for the way in which they are exercised in the composite and cannot be exercised in that way without the body. Relying as they do on the body, the sensitive and vegetative faculties, in the form they functioned in while part of the soul–body composite, perish with the composite. But the soul is a unity. It therefore follows that the human soul cannot be said to depend intrinsically on the body for its existence. Consequently, the whole substance of the soul shares in the deathlessness of the active intellect (the *Nous* of Aristotle). The soul, as distinguished from its faculties, is a unity, and this unity survives separation from the body.

Self-consciousness, that is, the ability of the active intellect to reflect on itself, shows the immateriality of the rational soul as contrasted with the body. So it may be added that, although the lower functions may be lost, we do not perish. Self-awareness, reason, and the will, integral aspects of the rational soul, do survive.

The Influence of Aquinas

Some would call this period the Age of Thomism.[52] Others dispute this appellation, pointing out that, although Aquinas was well known in his time, he certainly was not universally acclaimed. On the contrary, his views met with considerable opposition. His originality was recognized, but often this realization was accompanied by the suspicion that his ideas were dangerous.

The victory of Thomism did not occur overnight. Aquinas's fellow Dominicans were the first to accept him in a more or less official fashion, but opposition continued to be vigorous. As Sarton reminds us, the gradual triumph was an advantage, stirring less jealousy and opposition when it reached the stage that it was almost taken for granted.[53] Aquinas's victory, when it came, was complete, and it set the prevailing position of later Catholic philosophy to this very day.[54] The Thomist philosophy was eventually established as the official philosophy of the Roman Catholic Church.[55] The Papal Encyclical of 1897 confirmed the teachings of Saint Thomas Aquinas as the true Catholic philosophy. This does not mean, as it is sometimes mistakenly alleged, that Catholics must accept his views. Serious consideration of his teachings is required but not unthinking acceptance of them.

From the modern perspective, Aquinas's reconciliation of faith and reason still has an intellectual appeal. For those to whom it is important and relevant, he continues to provide a means of reconciling faith and reason without compromising the value or nature of either the one or the other. According to this view, experimental psychology, even psychophysical investigation, is legitimate. In no way does psychology detract from faith, and faith is neither subordinated to nor contradicted by psychology.

The work of Aquinas enhanced the stature of both rationalism and empiricism. The senses were described as the means by which the individual attained the basis of knowledge. In accepting the senses, Aquinas was accepting the human ability to use the knowledge obtained from them. He was also saying that a person's reason is sovereign while he or she is in the human state. The world may be transitory, but reason does have its own domain. Reason supplements faith; it does not deny it—and since empiricism is a useful tool, rationalism is paramount.

The appeal to reason argued so eloquently by Aquinas was highly successful, though sometimes in ways neither he nor the Church intended. In many respects the realization that human reason was of value and was not in conflict with doctrines of faith was a great contribution by Aquinas. With the belief in the value of reason would come the realization of the value of learning for its own sake. Although it would still take centuries (until the Renaissance) for the new learning to appear, we can begin to see the glimmer in the teachings of Aquinas and his immediate successors. His successors were able to draw the conclusion that reason and faith could exist side by side as two separate realms. Although this separation did occur in later philosophy, it was not intended by Aquinas. On many occasions his work was used to help justify the separation of faith and reason, or religion and philosophy. This controversy foreshadowed the separation of science and theology that was to come. Meanwhile, supernaturalism had been persuasively defended by the closely reasoned appeal of Aquinas who considered nature an important part of human earthly existence.

SCIENCE IN THE LATER MIDDLE AGES

The recovered works of Aristotle played a double and conflicting role in the scientific development of the later Middle Ages. It was as if thinkers of the time could not let him alone—they were either for Aristotle or against him; they never ignored him. In these developments his various works served different purposes.

On one hand, the works that supplied information about biology and physics formed the basis of knowledge for many scholastics. On the other, his newly recovered methodological works, with their teachings of logic, gave the opponents of the first group of Aristotelians a potent weapon. When complemented by the recovered Greek and the new Arabic mathematical works, the methodological works became a tool for the development of new ideas on induction and experiment and the use of mathematical demonstration.[56] This was especially true in the field of physical dynamics where the greatest scientific advances in these centuries were made. It was precisely Aristotle's views of motion and space that were most sharply criticized. The methodological Aristotle was used to demolish the contentual Aristotle.

In general, the great advance of the twelfth century was a dawning realization "that a particular fact was explained when it could be deduced from a more general principle."[57] A mathematical-deductive method was beginning to emerge, reinforced by the mathematical advances that took place during the thirteenth and subsequent centuries. At Oxford there was a reaction against the almost exclusive attention to theology, logic, and philosophy. Robert Grosseteste (c. 1170–1253) was the most prominent teacher and the founder of the mathematical-scientific tradition of that great institution.[58] He realized, though somewhat dimly, that a distinction could be made among the inductive, experimental, and mathematical approaches to science.

Developments within philosophy thereafter made it more possible to apply the scientific approach to nature. This was the developing gap between reason and faith as expressed in the rise of skepticism. Duns Scotus[59] and William of Ockham,[60] two Franciscan friars of Oxford at the end of the thirteenth and the beginning of the fourteenth centuries, were very important in this connection. Both contributed to the trends then emerging, which centered on a desire to separate reason from faith. Scotus and Ockham were at opposite poles in the struggle between realism and nominalism. Both probably believed they were working for the greater glory of faith, but the overall effect of their thinking was actually to facilitate the separation of faith from reason. As a consequence, skepticism toward faith went hand in hand with a greater independence of faith. It was increasingly possible thereafter for reason to go one way and faith another.

THE EXPERIMENT

In view of the grip of scholasticism on the thinkers of the later Middle Ages, it is hardly surprising that observational study of the phenomena of nature was almost nonexistent during these years. A few observations were made by some scholars. The work of Albert the Great on botany is a case in point. More significant for the future than observational excursions was the scattering of halting and imperfectly understood attempts to develop an experimental approach to the problems of nature and humankind and thus to advance empiricism.

True experiments were rare in the Middle Ages and continued to be rare even in the Renaissance.[61] Working in almost complete isolation from one another, a number of scholars tried to formulate in their writings this "new" way of studying nature. These lonely pioneers included Roger Bacon, Peter of Spain, Raymond Lull, and Arnold Villanova. Roger Bacon is by far the best known of these men today.[62] In fact, a myth of his singularity grew up among those who came after him. Bacon himself also believed that he alone in his day had a true appreciation of the scientific spirit. It is partly as a corrective for this myth that Peter of Spain, rather than Roger Bacon, is chosen for exposition here.

Peter of Spain (c. 1215–1277) was a remarkably versatile man. He was educated at Paris, became Rector of Medicine at the University of Sienna, physician to Pope Gregory X, Archbishop of Braga, and, in 1276, was elected Pope, taking the name of John the XXI. He wrote a textbook on logic,[63] which was used for centuries, and a compendium of medicine that was also very popular. But it is for two other accomplishments that he deserves to be rescued from the neglect of psychologists. Somewhere between 1245 and 1250 he wrote an original account of psychology, called *De Anima*.[64] It must be emphasized that this work was not a commentary on Aristotle (although he did write such a commentary). Instead, it was perhaps the first avowedly independent work on psychology for over a thousand years. It was concerned with psychology alone, and it even contained a chapter on the history of psychology. Peter devoted some attention to the relation between the psychological and medical aspects of the field. The "psychologist pope" has by no means received the attention he deserves.

The second of the two accomplishments that make Peter of Spain relevant to the issue at hand was his account of the experimental method. In his *Commentaries on Isaac*, a work on diets and medicines, Peter formulated his plea for something resembling an experiment.[65] He spoke of two methods by which dietary science might be investigated, *via rationis* and *via experimenti*. Both the path of reason and the way of experiment (or experience), he said, are necessary but different. The path of reason proceeds through the use of the intellect, studies causes, and uses syllogistic methods; the way of experiment proceeds through sense, studies effects, and applies induction. Reason is again a necessary further step to confirm what is found by experiment. Peter gives a series of six steps or conditions that he considers necessary to carry on medical experimentation. (1) The medicine should be free of foreign substances. (2) There should be assurance that the patient has the disease for which the medicine is intended. (3) The medicine should be given without admixture with other medicines. (4) It should be of the degree opposite to the disease. That is to say, if the disease causes an excess, the dosage should be decreased, as when a medicine cools off a heated condition. (5) It should be tested, not just once but many times. (6) The proper body should be used, the body of a man, not an ass. Through the simple and concrete language of his six steps shines a remarkable grasp of some of the implications of how an experiment is conducted today.

MEDICINE

After the classical twilight, medicine became largely overrun by folk medicine.[66] The historical situation of medicine was similar to that of ancient knowledge in general. Some medical knowledge persisted, particularly in commentaries on

Galen, and much more had come back from the Arabs. The revival of Western medicine began in the eleventh century when the medical school at Salerno, founded a century or two earlier, came into prominence. It was perhaps stimulated in its pioneering by contact with the Arabian medicine of nearby Sicily. In the twelfth and thirteenth centuries, the university medical schools of Montpellier, Bologna, Padua, and Paris gained prominence. However, the Church, in support of its abhorrence of bloodshed, prohibited its clergy from carrying out surgery. This policy, coupled with a contempt for any form of handiwork, led to the appearance of barber-surgeons as assistants to the professors. Certainly, knowledge of anatomy was in a poor state, and most university medical teaching was of a theoretical and dogmatic character.

SCIENCE AND SUPERSTITION

In the late Middle Ages superstition, the dark underside of supernaturalism, as it were, had great appeal. The history of medieval science was inextricably bound up with magical, superstitious practices. Magic was so pervasive that Lynn Thorndike, the historian of science of the Middle Ages, found it eminently fitting to include magic *and* experimental science in his work.[67]

Belief in demons and witches was widespread in the fourteenth century, though not to the terrifying extent to which it swelled in the fifteenth and sixteenth centuries. Astrology had many devotees; magic was performed everywhere, and divination by dreams was taken very seriously. These and similar superstitions were not confined to the ignorant peasant; a king might be as superstitious as his lowliest subject. Nor was the scholar–churchman exempt. The official policies of the Church toward such matters took a complicated and circuitous course, which is impossible to trace in short compass. It is sufficient to say that in earlier centuries superstition was tolerated but generally discouraged. Later, it became a matter of considerable concern, and Catholic and Protestant authorities alike carried out massive persecutions of alleged witches.

An apt illustration of the combination of science and superstition prevalent in these times is to be found in the medical teachings of Arnold of Villanova (c. 1235–1316).[68] He was simultaneously a thorough Galenist and a believer in the Devil and demons. He combined Galenic humoralism with demonology in his diagnostic and etiological considerations. For example, he believed that, because the Devil likes warmth, the presence of warm humors in the body makes an individual susceptible to seizure by the Devil. Hence, he advised, warm humors are to be avoided. Arnold likewise brought Galen into accord with astrology. Accepting the Galenic contention that epilepsy is caused by the humors, he related the particular humor bringing on an attack to the particular quarter of the moon in which it occurred. He considered the planet Mars responsible for melancholia, because the planet's color and supposed heat were said to affect the color and heat of the bile, bringing on melancholia. Although bleeding was recommended as a treatment, he argued that it must be applied in accordance with astrological portents involving consideration of the phase of the moon and constellations.

THE END OF THE MIDDLE AGES

The period of the medieval revival of learning had spent its force by the close of the first quarter of the fourteenth century.[69] Its contributions were again and again reproduced in the fourteenth through the sixteenth centuries, first in manuscript and then in printed form. Very little creative or original work was done, however, until the new period of the scientific Renaissance began.

To be sure, there were changes presaging the future. In the second half of the fourteenth century the number of scholars who were not clerics increased.[70] This statistic is indicative of changing times. In addition, books also began to be written in native tongues instead of in Latin.

The fourteenth century and the first years of the fifteenth century witnessed many stirring events, the general effect of which was to destroy the synthesis of the thirteenth century. The Black Death wiped out perhaps a fourth of the population of Europe. The One Hundred Years' War compounded the usual wastefulness of war with its incredible length. The period also saw the rise of the commercial classes, a decrease in the importance of the feudal aristocracy, a rise of strong national monarchies, and a decline in the moral prestige of the papacy.

When did this period called the Middle Ages end and a new one begin? Various dates have been advanced, but it is relatively unimportant to be precise here. With Sarton we agree that about 1450, the date when printing appeared in the West is as good a date as any.[71]

SUMMARY

The rediscovery of Greek philosophy and science during the Middle Ages brought about a great revolution in Western thought, just as it had done to the Arab world during the period we call the Dark Ages. The rediscovery of many of the writings of Plato and Aristotle was particularly significant.

Aristotle's greatest influence was probably on Thomas Aquinas, especially on Aquinas's philosophy and his psychological concepts.

The medieval educational movement called scholasticism was also influenced by both Aquinas and Aristotle. Although faith and dogma still dominated thought during this period, Aquinas revitalized the concept of human reason. Still constrained by the dictates of church and theology, Thomas Aquinas showed the beginnings of what would blossom into a new learning during the Renaissance.

NOTES

1. For example, H. O. Taylor, *The Mediaeval Mind*, 4th ed. (Cambridge, Mass.: Harvard University Press, 1959).
2. P. K. Hitti, *Arabs, A Short History* (Princeton, N.J.: Princeton University Press, 1946).
3. The influence of non-Muslim scholars and the assimilation of Greek and Hellenistic material is recounted by A. C. Crombie, *Medieval and Early Modern Science*, 2nd rev.

ed. (New York: Doubleday, 1959), 2 vols; M. Desruelles and A. Bersot, "L'assistance aux alienes chez les Arabes du VIIIe au XIIe siecle," *Annee med. psychol., 96* (1938): 689–709; and D. L. O'Leary, *How Greek Science Passed to the Arabs* (London: Broadway House, 1948).

4. Averroes is perhaps the only one of the group who has been studied from a psychological point of view. J. Bakos, *Psychologie d'Ibn Sina (Avicenne) d' apres son oeuvre as Sifa* (Prague: Editions de l'academie Tchecoslovaque des Sciences, 1956). More peripheral but still interesting is the volume by E. Renan, *Averroes et L'Averrosime* (Paris: Alcan, 1869).

5. Dimly discernible in such works as I. Husik, *A History of Mediaeval Jewish Philosophy* (New York: Meridian Books, 1958).

6. G. Sarton, *Introduction to the History of Science* (Baltimore: Williams and Wilkins, 1927–1948), 3 vols. in 5.

7. The Major sources helpful in understanding the relevant aspects of the high Middle Ages were Taylor, *Mediaeval Mind;* Sarton, *Introduction to the History of Science;* G. Leff, *Medieval Thought: St. Augustine to Ockham* (Baltimore: Penguin Books, 1958); E. Gilson, *The Spirit of Medieval Philosophy* (New York: Charles Scribner's Sons, 1936); the introductions to *Selections from Mediaeval Philosophy*, R. McKeon, ed., 2 vols. (New York: Charles Scribner's Sons, 1929); the article by the same writer, "Aristotelianism in Western Christianity," *Environmental Factors in Christian History*, J. T. McNeill et all., eds. (Chicago: University of Chicago Press, 1939), pp. 206–231; and R. Klibansky, *The Continuity of the Platonic Tradition During the Middle Ages* (London: Warburg Institute, 1939).

8. E. K. Rand, "Medieval Gloom and Medieval Uniformity," *Speculum* I (1926): 253–268.

9. Gilson, *Spirit of Medieval Philosophy.*

10. Pliny the Elder, *Natural History*, 6 vols., trans. J. Bostock and H. T. Dilly (London: Bell, 1855–1890) (A.D. 77).

11. G. Sarton, *Introduction to the History of Science.*

12. F.C.S. Schiller, *Hypotheses,* in C. Singer, ed., *Studies in the History and Methods of Science* (London: Oxford University Press, 1917), pp. 414–446.

13. Taylor, *Mediaeval Mind.*

14. W. Windelband, *A History of Philosophy, Greek, Roman and Medieval* (New York: Harper and Brothers, 1901), I, 312–313.

15. McKeon, *Selections from Medieval Philosophy.*

16. A standard source is H. Rashdall, in R. M. Powicke and A. B. Emden, eds., *The Universities of Europe in the Middle Ages,* 2nd ed. (Oxford: Clarendon Press, 1936).

17. A good succinct account may be found in O. H. Haskins, "Arabian Science in Western Europe," *Isis, 7* (1925): 478–485.

18. Renan, *Averroes et L'Averrosime.*

19. The major source for details on Aquinas and for all dates is the account of his life by V. Bourke, *Thomistic Bibliography, 1920–1940* (St. Louis: St. Louis University, 1945). Some material has also been drawn from F. C. Copleston's *Aquinas* (Baltimore: Penguin Books, 1955), G. K. Chesterton, *St. Thomas Aquinas* (Garden City, N.Y.: Doubleday and Co., 1958), and M. Grabmann, *Thomas Aquinas: His Personality and Thought,* trans. V. Michel (London: Longmans, 1929).

20. For example, Grabmann, *Thomas Aquinas.*

21. Chesterton, *St. Thomas Aquinas.*

22. Particularly relevant to psychology are his *Summa Theologiae* and *Summa de Homine* which form volumes 31–33, and 35, respectively, of *Opera Omnia,* ed. A. Bourget (Paris: Vives, 1890). A good secondary source is G. C. Reilly, "The Psychology of Saint Albert

the Great, Compared with That of St. Thomas" (*Philosophical Studies*, Catholic University of America, 1934, No. 29).

23. T. Aquinas, *Summa contra Gentiles*, 5 vols., trans. English Dominican Fathers (New York: Benziger, 1928–1929) (1258–1264).
24. *Aristotle's De Anima in the Version of William of Moerbeke and the Commentary of St. Thomas Aquinas*, trans. K. Foster and S. Humphries (New Haven, Conn.: Yale University Press, 1951) (1269–1270).
25. R. M. Hutchins, ed., *Great Books of the Western World*, Vols. XIX-XX, Thomas Aquinas, *The Summa Theologica*, trans. by Dominican Fathers and rev. by D. J. Sullivan (Chicago: Encyclopaedia Britannica, 1952) (1266–1273).
26. *Ibid.*, First Part, QQ. 75–100, Vol. 1, pp. 378–522.
27. *Ibid.*, Part 1, Second Part, QQ. 1–48, 49–89, Vol. 1, pp. 644–826, Vol. 2, pp. 1–204.
28. K. Foster, *The Life of St. Thomas Aquinas: Biographical Documents* (Baltimore: Helicon Press, 1959).
29. *Works of Aristotle*, trans. under direction of W. D. Ross, in R. M. Hutchins, ed., *Great Books of the Western World*, Vols. VIII–IX (c. 340–322 B.C.); *On the Soul*, 429^a 10–430^a 25.
30. F. Nuyens, *L'evolution de la psychologie d' Aristotle* (Louvain: Institut superieur de Philosophie, 1948).
31. Aristotle, *De Anima*, 408^b 17–32.
32. Aristotle, *Physics*, 241^b 24–245^b 2, 252^b 10–267^b 26; *On Generation and Corruption*, 334^a 8–15; *Metaphysics*, 1012^b 22–31, 1018^b 8–35, 1049^b 4–1050^b 5, 1072^a 30–3, 1074^b 14.
33. T. Aquinas, *Summa Theologica*, First Part, Q. 2, 3.
34. *Ibid.*, Part 1, Second Part, Q. 109, 6.
35. B. Russell, *A History of Western Philosophy* (New York: Simon and Schuster, 1945).
36. Chesterton, *St. Thomas Aquinas*.
37. T. Aquinas, *The Unicity of the Intellect*, in "The Trinity" and "The Unicity of the Intellect," trans. R. E. Brennan (London: Herder, 1946) (1270).
38. T. Aquinas, *Summa contra Gentiles*, Vols. 2, 3.
39. T. Aquinas, *Summa Theologica*, First Part, Q. 1, 1–3.
40. *Ibid.*, Q. 12, 12.
41. *Ibid.*, Part 2, Second Part, Q. 1, 4.
42. T. Aquinas, *Summa contra Gentiles* Vols. 1, 3.
43. F. Van Steenbergen, *The Philosophical Movement in the Thirteenth Century* (New York: Nelson, 1955).
44. J. E. Royce, *Man and Meaning* (New York: McGraw–Hill, 1969); G. P. Klubertanz, *The Philosophy of Human Nature* (New York: Appleton–Century–Crofts, 1953).
45. T. Aquinas, *Summa Theologica*, First Part, Q. 75, 1–7, Q. 76, 3; *Summa contra Gentiles*, Vol. 2, 56, 57.
46. T. Aquinas, *Commentary on Aristotle's De Anima*, 1 ad 7, 2 ad 14, (in reference 24)
47. T. Aquinas, *Summa Theologica*, First Part, Q. 76, 41.
48. T. Aquinas, *Summa contra Gentiles*, Vol. 4, 11.
49. T. Aquinas, *Summa Theologica*, First Part, QQ. 77–90. (With exceptions specified below, hereafter this is the source for discussion of his psychological views.)
50. *Ibid.*, Part 1, Second Part, Q. 6.
51. *Ibid.*, First Part, Q. 12, 12.
52. Leff, *Medieval Thought*.
53. G. Sarton, *Introduction to the History of Science*.
54. Grabmann, *Thomas Aquinas*.

55. G. Sarton, *Introduction to the History of Science.*
56. A. C. Crombie, *Medieval and Early Modern Science,* Vol. 2; *Science in the Later Middle Ages and Early Modern Times,* 2nd rev. ed. (Garden City, N.Y.: Doubleday 1959).
57. *Ibid.,* p. 3.
58. A. C. Crombie, *Robert Grosseteste and the Origins of Experimental Science, 1100–1700* (Oxford: Clarendon, 1953).
59. John Duns Scotus, *Selections from the Oxford Commentary on the Four Books of the Master of Sentences,* in R. McKeon, ed., *Selections from Medieval Philosophers* (New York: Charles Scribner's Sons, 1930) (c. 1300), II, pp. 313–350.
60. William of Ockham, *Studies and Selections,* ed. and trans. S. C. Tornay (Chicago: Open Court, 1938) (c. 1322).
61. Sarton, *Introduction to the History of Science.*
62. Roger Bacon, *Selections from the Opus Majus,* in McKeon, ed., *Selections from Medieval Philosophy,* Vol. II, pp. 7–110.
63. Petrus Hispanus, *The Summulae Logicales of Peter of Spain,* ed. and trans. J. P. Mullally (South Bend, Ind.: Notre Dame University Press, 1945) (1268).
64. Pedro Hispano, *De Anima,* P. Manuel Alonso, S. I., ed. (Consejo Superior de Investigaciones Cientificas, Instituto Filosofico "Luis Vives," Series A. Num 1, Madrid: 1941).
65. L. Thorndike, *A History of Magic and Experimental Science During the First Thirteen Centuries of Our Era,* Vol. 2 (New York: Macmillan Co., 1923).
66. A. C. Crombie, *Medieval and Early Modern Science.*
67. Thorndike, *History of Magic and Experimental Science.*
68. G. Zilboorg and G. W. Henry, *A History of Medical Psychology* (New York: W. W. Norton, 1941), p. 137.
69. Thorndike, *History of Magic and Experimental Science.*
70. Sarton, *Introduction to the History of Science.*
71. G. Sarton, *Six Wings; Men of Science in the Renaissance* (Bloomington: Indiana University Press, 1957).

PART THREE

The Renaissance and the Early Modern Period

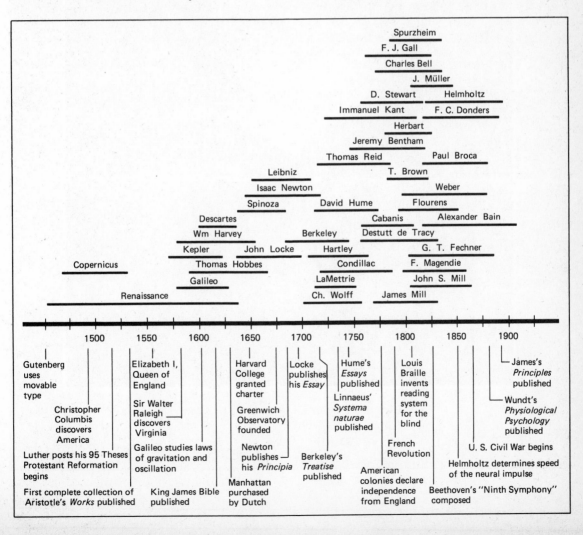

Spurzheim

F. J. Gall

Charles Bell

J. Müller

D. Stewart   Helmholtz

Immanuel Kant   F. C. Donders

Herbart

Jeremy Bentham

Thomas Reid   Paul Broca

Leibniz   T. Brown

Isaac Newton   Weber

Spinoza   David Hume   Flourens

Descartes   Cabanis   Alexander Bain

Wm Harvey   Berkeley   Destutt de Tracy

Kepler   John Locke   Hartley   G. T. Fechner

Thomas Hobbes   Condillac   F. Magendie

Galileo   LaMettrie   John S. Mill

Copernicus

Renaissance   Ch. Wolff   James Mill

1500   1550   1600   1650   1700   1750   1800   1850   1900

Gutenberg uses movable type

Christopher Columbis discovers America

Luther posts his 95 Theses Protestant Reformation begins

First complete collection of Aristotle's *Works* published

Elizabeth I, Queen of England

Sir Walter Raleigh discovers Virginia

Galileo studies laws of gravitation and oscillation

King James Bible published

Harvard College granted charter

Greenwich Observatory founded

Newton publishes his *Principia*

Manhattan purchased by Dutch

Locke publishes his *Essay*

Berkeley's *Treatise* published

Hume's *Essays* published

Linnaeus' *Systema naturae* published

American colonies declare independence from England

Louis Braille invents reading system for the blind

French Revolution

James's *Principles* published

Wundt's *Physiological Psychology* published

U. S. Civil War begins

Helmholtz determines speed of the neural impulse

Beethoven's "Ninth Symphony" composed

René Descartes from an engraving by Franz Hals.

Descartes: The Renaissance and the Beginning of the Modern Period

The one hundred and fifty years from the appearance of printing in the West in about 1450 to about 1630 has come to be called the Renaissance. Providing limiting dates for a given historical period is essentially a matter of convenience. In this case, the opening date marks the introduction of books produced through movable type printing. For the first time learning could be preserved and transmitted to the masses. It is a fitting date for our purposes, especially in regard to scientific and cultural history. The terminal date is approximately that of the appearance of Galileo's *Dialogue on the Two Chief Systems of the World.* Two years earlier, in 1628, William Harvey's crucial work on the circulation of the blood had been published. The Renaissance, which began as a cultural and humanistic revolution, became a triumph for science as well.

THE RENAISSANCE: A PERIOD OF PREPARATION

The Renaissance was a period of general and literary enrichment, not just one of specific scientific accomplishment.[1] The spirit of the age, though essentially literary, also brought differences in outlook that were to revolutionize philosophy and the sciences, including psychology.

Some anticipation of the new outlook may be found in the thinking of Petrarch, a lonely pioneer who died in 1374, only one century after Thomas Aquinas but nearly a century before the beginning of the Renaissance.[2] This dawning outlook was expressed in Petrarch's humanistic attitude—an interest in the freedom of the human spirit and freedom from the medieval traditions of scholastic theology and philosophy. Petrarch had a sense of living in a transitional period and was eager to recover and know the Latin classics. As heralded by Petrarch, the Renaissance was not a pagan movement, nor did it initially divorce itself from the Middle Ages, although it later did so. Petrarch may have loved Cicero best, but he quoted Augustine frequently. A loyal churchman, he regarded the study of the classics not as a hindrance but as an aid to Christianity. From the start, however, he was contemptuous of scholasticism. He scoffed at these interpreters of the works of others: "Like those who have no notion of architecture, they make it their profession to whitewash walls."[3]

During the Renaissance concern for the humanness of the individual assumed greater importance than had been true since the golden age of Greece. A growing number of people held that the value of the individual as an earthly being and as an integral part of the world of nature was almost as important as his or her destiny in the life beyond. This outlook was called humanism and represented a radical departure from the thinking of the Middle Ages.

Specific manifestations of this change were the discovery, preservation, and translation of ancient manuscripts; the active search for writings of the ancients; textual criticism; the writing of letters in the manner of Cicero; and concern with epigraphy, archaeology, grammar, and rhetoric. Paradoxically, at the very time of the rebirth of classical humanism, with its emphasis on Latin and Greek, there emerged simultaneously the popularization of the vernacular tongues, the "vulgate" tongues as they were called, as vehicles of the literature of the day. Rabelais and Montaigne, for example, fought for the use of French as a language of literature. The fear of novelty, which was so characteristic of the Middle Ages, gave way in the Renaissance to an actual pursuit of novelty for its own sake.

During the Renaissance another form of discovery was also taking place—the voyages of discovery of Columbus, Diaz, da Gama, and the captains of Prince Henry the Navigator. In this way the known world was enlarged. At the same time others were rediscovering ancient geography through translations of ancient manuscripts.

The New Education was one of the innovations of the Renaissance. Impatient with the Trivium and Quadrivium of the Middle Ages, and eager to transmit the newly discovered heritage to others, the scholars of the time developed a new curriculum. The Englishmen, Sir Thomas More and Roger Ascham, and the Spaniard, Vives, were leading figures in espousing this brave new curriculum. It became the "classical education" with its emphases on Latin and Greek language and the writings of the ancients, which would remain at the center of liberal education until the turn of the twentieth century. This curriculum had a heavy price, however; it proved so popular that for centuries to come it effectively precluded the widespread teaching of the sciences.[4]

The leading humanists, though well read in the ancient classics, were not concerned with working toward new developments in philosophy. This does not mean that there were no philosophers. In fact, every school of ancient philosophy had its champions during the Renaissance.

Under the patronage of Cosimo de Medici, a Platonic Academy was founded in Florence in 1462. It was dominated by Marsilio Ficino (1433–1499), who along with others of this time, attacked the Aristotelianism of the scholastics.[5] Regarding Plato equal in authority to divine law, Ficino set out to reconcile Platonic doctrine with Christian teaching.[6] In the battle of Plato versus Aristotle, it was Plato who triumphed, at least for the early Renaissance philosophers. After all, Aristotle had been the philosopher of the scholastics. Moreover, Plato's dialogues were in the process of being rediscovered, as Aristotle's works had been earlier, so that Plato's views seemed fresh and new whereas Aristotle's seemed musty and old-fashioned. Some students of the period have gone so far as to say that it was largely due to Plato's influence that the early humanists were not scientifically oriented.[7] Whatever the reason, many of the great men of the Renaissance were hostile to science. Erasmus, Rabelais, Ficino, and even Vives in one way or another had disparaging words to say about science.[8]

Neither the philosophy nor the science of that time owed anything to the Protestant Reformation, many of whose leaders detested "natural reason" and were hostile to science. Martin Luther, for example, denounced reason as the mistress of the Devil. He taught that Aristotelian metaphysics, science, and ethics were false, and even that Aristotle's logic was inconsistent with theology.[9] On a convenient pretext, John Calvin condoned the burning of Michael Servetus, the discoverer of the pulmonary circulation of the blood, because Servetus had described the Holy Land as a barren wilderness (which it was), thus contradicting the scriptural description of it as a land of "milk and honey."

With such negative attitudes, it is hardly surprising that the most important scientific work during the Renaissance appeared relatively late in the period. The year 1543 saw the appearance of both of the scientific works heralding the modern period, the *De Fabrica corporis humani* of Andreas Vesalius (1514–1564)[10] and the *De revolutionibus Orbium Coelestrium* of Nicolaus Copernicus (1473–1543).[11] Vesalius's work on anatomy had the tremendous advantage of being based on personal dissection and observation. He found that he had reason to disagree sharply with ancient authority and specifically with Galen. What had been believed for centuries about details of gross anatomy just was not so. Copernicus reported that the Ptolemaic conception of an earth-centered universe did not agree with astronomical findings and that the sun must be cast in the central role formerly ascribed to the earth. Even more importantly, Vesalius was giving a new emphasis to the use of direct observation for securing scientific data, and Copernicus was giving the world a new cosmology. Although for generations afterward the characteristic medieval scientific doctrines continued to be taught in the schools, the ideas that Vesalius and Copernicus represented steadily gained ever wider acceptance and extension.

The absence of a clearly understood scientific method placed a severe limitation on scientific work during the Renaissance.[12] It was the scientific movement of the seventeenth century, with its stress on methodology, that gave us the beginnings of the modern period of science.

THE BEGINNINGS OF THE MODERN PERIOD IN SCIENCE

The modern period in science was coming into being at the turn of the seventeenth century, just at the end of the Renaissance. A desire for the new was a prominent characteristic of the time. Whether or not they really were, a remarkable number of works published in this century claimed either in title or in preface to be new.[13]

The scientists of the seventeenth century showed a reluctance to accept rationalistic first principles, principles assumed to be correct and from which one was to deduce conclusions of what must happen. They were groping toward freedom from philosophical presuppositions. Theirs was the methodological problem of how to do the job at hand, not the metaphysical task of justifying it. They were pragmatic in that they developed working distinctions and definitions in order to handle the specific subjects with which they were concerned. A reluctance to accept first principles meant specifically that appeal to the authority of the ancients had lost its former, almost paralyzing, hold. It followed that if the authority of the ancients was to be abandoned, a new procedure must replace it. This procedure was found in mathematics.[14]

A variety of circumstances conspired to make mathematical operations characteristic of the science of the time. For one thing the Aristotelian concept of nature as a hierarchy, which was based on a qualitative prescription, had lost its strong appeal. During the early Renaissance, the influence of Aristotle and his emphasis on classification was at its lowest point in centuries. This circumstance gave mathematics an opportunity to regain its importance as a quantitative method. In addition, other, more positive factors were at work to strengthen the appeal of mathematics. The Greek mathematics of Alexandria had been rediscovered. The generality and complexity of mathematics had increased over the centuries, and the useful tool of Arabic notation for mathematical expression had been introduced, replacing the clumsy Roman numerals which were in general use up to that time in the West. A tremendous variety of practical problems in navigation and gunnery, for example, stimulated craftsmen and others to apply mathematics. More than any other one factor, the increased level of mathematical sophistication made possible the scientific advancement of the seventeenth century.

The mathematically oriented scientists of the sixteenth and seventeenth centuries followed the procedure of measuring the properties or motions of the bodies they studied.[15] These they generalized as the rules of operation in nature. The demonstration of physical relations in mathematical formulation was their contribution to physical science.

As a result, in the physical sciences (though not in psychology) quantitativism as a prescription was coming to the fore. From this time on, it was not to be seriously challenged by qualitativism.

GALILEO, QUANTITATIVISM, AND METHODOLOGICAL AND CONTENTUAL OBJECTIVISM

Galileo Galilei (1564–1642) was perhaps the most important of these early modern scientists. In his *Dialogues Concerning the Two New Sciences,* which contain some of his most important studies, he used mathematics and concerned himself with the quantitative conditions of variations in quality.[16] He reasoned that if Copernicus and others found a pattern underlying the motion of the planets, perhaps he would discover a pattern of the phases of local motion here on earth. He proceeded to search for the regularities that would manifest this pattern— uniform motion, acceleration motion, violent motion, and related phenomena.

Then and later, the reaction of many physical scientists to psychological phenomena was epitomized by Galileo's attempt to deal with the question of the separation of what we now call physics and psychology. As his focal point, Galileo seized on Democritus' distinction between the perceptual world of sensory appearances and the conceptual real world. Galileo objected to considering qualities such as heat (in the subjective sense), as well as tastes, smells, and colors, as having the same reality as shape and motion.[17] The former are names for qualities whose locus is not in the object but in the responsive body. Remove the body and these qualities would be annihilated. They are different from the primary and real. They do not exist as truly as phenomena with which a physical scientist deals. It can be seen that Galileo was in the process of excluding the human being's experience from the world of nature. Later, Robert Boyle, one of the founders of chemistry and a contemporary of Locke, would call this separation the distinction between primary and secondary qualities. It goes a long way to explain the caution and suspicion with which physicists and others view psychology, as a science, to this day. Perceptions could not be trusted as sources of information about the world because they do not correspond to anything in that world. Somehow what a psychologist deals with in terms of experience is not believed to be as "real" as what the physical scientist works with. In the service of a prescription for a methodological objectivity for the physical sciences, Galileo was tacitly reinforcing the view that psychology was contentually subjective in nature.

FRANCIS BACON AND INDUCTIVISM

Another form of rebellion against philosophical presuppositions was expressed by a contemporary of Galileo, Francis Bacon (1561–1626), who in *Novum Organum,*[18] *Advancement of Learning,*[19] and *New Atlantis*[20] sketched his views of what science should become. His was a radically different approach from that of

Galileo, however. In *Novum Organum* and the *Advancement of Learning* Bacon proposed drastic changes in scientific procedures. His target was also Aristotle, or rather the Aristotle of the *Organon*, Aristotle the logician. He missed the point that Aristotle had insisted on the admissibility of induction in reason, though by no means to the exclusion of deductive logic. Bacon eagerly espoused an inductive method. He did not hold mathematics in particularly high regard as a scientific tool, however, and in failing to stress mathematics, he was out of tune with most of the great scientists of his time.[21] He knew that mathematics was essentially deductive, and to Bacon the appropriate method was primarily inductive, based on the patient collection of instances.[22]

Bacon insisted on going beyond the simple enumeration of instances, a method that was well known long before this time. His goal was to bring into use a new and particular form of induction. He sought to draw up lists of facts with a given quality in common, lists of facts lacking the quality, as well as lists of those that possessed the quality in varying degrees. He was certain that the particular character of a given quality could emerge from a study of such lists. His was a sweeping inductive method; he held that the collection of many facts would eventually lead to a generalization about them. Bacon detested the grandiloquent theories of the Middle Ages in which some broad, rationally derived point would be declared as truth with little factual support. His reaction against rationalism was so extreme and his dependence on empiricism so intense that he did not believe that even tentative hypotheses should guide a scientist in the selection of facts to be gathered. He failed to realize, as we now do, that hypotheses are to be advanced and judgment suspended until the facts are gathered, and, then and only then, can we decide whether the hypotheses being tested are true, false, or unproved.

In his espousal of induction Bacon anticipated its success in fields where mathematics had as yet but little use. It was in biology that inductive procedure was to be most faithfully followed. To use induction properly, however, one must have preliminary hypotheses as a guide in selecting instances, something that Darwin and the other great biologists recognized. In the long run, of course, both induction and deduction were found to be essential to the scientific enterprise.

Bacon enthusiastically but uncritically endorsed the use of experiments.[23] He argued that by prodding nature to take off her mask, as he put it, experiments make her reveal her struggles and help us to decide causes. We go from experiments to the isolation of causes and, conversely, from causes to the invention of new experiments.

In service of his method, Bacon advanced his famous account of the Idols, those preconceptions that blind humankind to truth.[24] The English rendering of "idols" for Bacon's Latin *"idola"* is misleading. Bacon is not referring to graven images but to images or representations that are distortions of the truth. Bacon lists four kinds: Idols of the Tribe, Cave, Marketplace, and Theater. Idols of the Tribe have their basis in human nature. Bacon says that the "human understanding is like a false mirror, which receiving rays irregularly, distorts and discolours the nature of things by mingling its own nature with it."[25] Bacon, true to his own procedure, gives many examples of each of his idols. Some examples of the Idols of the Tribe are as follows:

> The human understanding is of its own nature prone to suppose the existence of more order and regularity in the world than it finds. And though there be many things in nature which are singular and unmatched, yet it devises for them parallels and conjugates and relatives which do not exist.[26]

This statement is a significant challenge to scientists. Is there really order in the universe, or do we create the order in our own minds so as to gain the impression of understanding? Another example of an idol of the tribe has to do with the influence of a prior opinion on observation:

> The human understanding which it has once adopted an opinion (either as being the received opinion or as being agreeable to itself) draws all things else to support and agree with it. And though there be a greater number and weight of instances to be found on the other side, yet these it either neglects and despises, or else by some distinction sets aside and rejects; in order that by this great and pernicious predetermination the authority of its former conclusions may remain inviolate.[27]

Observation is not typically made in isolation. Our preconceptions influence what we see and, perhaps more importantly, what we do not see. Bacon gives many more such examples of Idols of the Tribe, all of which are worthy of consideration by modern scientists.

Idols of the Cave are those biases and misunderstandings based on human individuality. "For every one (besides the errors common to human nature in general) has a cave or den of his own, which refracts and discolours the light of nature." This distortion may be due to one's personality, education, social identification, reading, "the authority of those he esteems and admires."[28] Because we are individuals, we see the world differently than the other individuals around us. Some individuals prefer ideas and objects of the past, whereas others thrive on novelty and reject the old. Some prefer to reduce a problem to its constituent parts, whereas others prefer to look at the problem as a whole. "Interest" seems to be the key concept here. Bacon warns his readers:

> And generally let every student of nature take this as a rule, —that whatever his mind seizes and dwells upon with peculiar satisfaction is to be held in suspicion, and that so much the more care is to be taken in dealing with such questions to keep the understanding even and clear.[29]

Idols of the Marketplace were the most troublesome of all to Bacon, "idols which have crept into the understanding through the alliances of words and names." These Idols have to do with the influence of words on thought. Bacon says that words are generally framed for common use and not for precise meanings necessary for scientific description. Just as serious is the increased appearance of reality to concepts that have a name in contrast to those that have no name. It is possible to give a name to a theoretical concept and to treat it as though it were a real entity, when it does not exist at all outside of our theories. The term may take on a reality far beyond its due. Freud's concepts of ego, id, and superego are examples of this kind of term. In a similar way, talking of "associate bonds," "increasing habit strength," and the like gives the impression that association is akin to a magnetic field, when in fact we do not know what it is at all.

The fourth of Bacon's biasing illusions are Idols of the Theater or of Systems. These idols have to do with the blind acceptance of authority and tradition. (All previous systems of philosophy seemed to him to create theatrical worlds, rather than dealing with the real one). Theories and systems of the past, though they may have been well thought out, are unlikely to represent the true universe correctly and thus tend to mislead us. By investing in such theories or systems, we blind ourselves to the truth.[30]

Clearly, Bacon was trying to find "Truth," believing that there was only one true way of looking at the world and that to attain that truth we must work our way through all the pitfalls of misunderstanding and distortion derived from the Idols. Bacon presents a daunting challenge, and modern science, although it tends to hold there are many ways of looking at the same world, can still learn much from considering Bacon's arguments.

Bacon fostered another aim that became characteristic of his age—the seeking of useful knowledge, or as we have called it, the utilitarian prescription. Power over nature in the service of humankind is the most apt way to express the Baconian spirit of the age that was to come. It was so important to Bacon that he expressed it among the first aphorisms of *Novum Organum:* effects cannot be produced without knowledge of causes; with this knowledge, power and knowledge become one.[31] This view of power as the fruit of knowledge was shared to some slight degree with others of his time, including Descartes, who in his *Discourse on the Method for Rightly Conducting the Reason*[32] spoke of a practical philosophy that masters nature.

Generally speaking, Bacon's forceful writings, his call for careful observation and induction, his enthusiasm, and his position as one of the eminent figures of his time (he was Chancellor under James I) led to a wide audience for his writings and to increased knowledge of and respect for scientific methods. Especially important in this connection was his success in pleading the usefulness of science. Henceforward, science was to be judged both by the knowledge obtained and by the usefulness of that knowledge.

BIOLOGY AND THE SCIENTIFIC REVOLUTION

The opening stages of the scientific revolution in biology lagged behind those of the physical sciences.[33] Contributions in biology in the sixteenth century were still hampered by insistence that the soul was the locus of origin of bodily action. The relative neglect of biology and psychology during these years was not entirely due to the lack of workers in these fields, but rather to the general scientific climate of the age, which was dominated by the physical sciences. Indeed, the emulation of physics by psychologists in the nineteenth century had its roots in the work of the seventeenth century.

Some noteworthy researches were carried out. As a natural extension of his interest in the primarily visual science of astronomy, Johannes Kepler (1571–1630) studied vision directly.[34] On examining the eye he found that an inverted image is cast on the retina. This observation flatly contradicted Democritus' representative theory of vision, which held that objects give off images of themselves that impinge directly on the sense organs. How could this be true if the image were inverted? Kepler was content to demonstrate the phenomenon and leave to others the reconciliation of his findings with a theory of perception.

Even more important was the demonstration of the circulation of the blood by William Harvey (1578–1657).[35] Before his time, there had been general acceptance of Galen's thousand-year-old theory, calling for pulsation of the blood, which the body consumed as nutriment. According to Galen's theory, the blood itself was not the substance we know, but included animistic and supernatural entities, "animal spirits." Harvey demonstrated conclusively not only that the blood moved, "as it were, in a circle,"[36] but also that the heart functioned as a pump in the same manner as it did for water or other nonliving things. He also measured the amount of blood passing through the heart in one-half hour and found that it would exceed the weight of the body by more than three or four times; thus, he very effectively demolished the consumption theory. However crudely, he measured a bodily function and in so doing brought a quantitative approach to physiology. He also weakened the belief in the occult qualities attributed to the blood. What made Harvey's work outstanding was his integration of scattered facts into a comprehensive generalization. His success in demonstrating, without appeal to either the soul or to any other vital force, that a bodily function could be explained solely by mechanical principles was a tremendous stimulus to later work along these lines.

At this time the biological sciences were still regarded as part of medicine, not as sciences in their own right. A. R. Hall, in his careful study of scientific developments between 1500 and 1800, concluded that the biology of today as pursued in laboratories and in field stations is essentially a creation of the nineteenth century.[37] Moreover, modern psychology's closest kin, the field of physiology, had to await further advances in the knowledge of anatomy before it could come into its own.

RENÉ DESCARTES

René Descartes was the first great psychologist of the modern age. This is not to say that he was entirely or even primarily a psychologist. His chief motivations and interests were philosophical, but his problems were often psychological. Because he still made metaphysical assumptions, his psychology was subservient to his philosophy. Nevertheless, for the first time since Aristotle a psychological system *de novo* was attempted.

Descartes fondly believed himself to be independent of past authorities. His effort to find truth from rock bottom was one of the ways he expressed the "modern" spirit of his time. It was a point of pride that he read relatively little, for he wanted to turn away from the classics to "the great book of the world."[38] Accordingly, he seldom referred to the past either to acknowledge borrowing or to criticize. Of course, no more than anyone else could he entirely escape the past, and his thinking shows its influence much more than he was prepared to acknowledge.

A remarkable amount of scientific work had been done during the early years of the century, when Descartes was growing up and attending school. Exactly what scientific knowledge was available to Descartes in 1629, the year he began publishing? Over eighty years had elapsed since the works of Vesalius and Copernicus had appeared. William Gilbert (1540–1603) had published his experiments in electricity and magnetism twenty-nine years before. Francis Bacon had died three years earlier in 1626. Bacon's form of induction had enlarged the scope of knowledge, particularly through the control of nature that it gave. Tycho Brahe (1546–1601), whose observatory Descartes had already visited, had made his meticulous astronomical observations. Kepler, who had worked with Brahe, had advanced his three basic laws of planetary motion in 1629 and was to die a year later. In 1616 the Church had secretly condemned Galileo for citing evidence supporting the heliocentric theory. If Descartes did not know of this condemnation at the time, he had only to wait until 1633, when it was made public. Harvey, born before Descartes but destined to outlive him, had published the demonstration of the circulation of the blood that very year. Of all the great scientists of that time, only the greatest of them, Isaac Newton (1642–1727), was not contemporaneous with Descartes. Newton's general theory of dynamics would embrace Descartes' laws of motion in accounting for the motions of the whole universe, the planets, their satellites, and the comets.

Descartes' Life

Descartes was born in March 1596 at La Haye in Touraine.[39] The economic circumstances of his father and mother, both of whom came from professional families, allowed him an income sufficient to assure a modest financial independence throughout life. He never occupied ecclesiastic or academic office.

In the spring of 1606, he entered the college of La Flèche, founded a year or two before by the Jesuits. Because he was physically frail, Descartes was excused from morning religious duties and allowed to stay in bed. While abed he did his lessons and developed the habit of sustained reflection and analysis. He would continue the habit of remaining in bed in the morning and working out his thinking for almost the rest of his life. The program of study he followed consisted of languages, mathematics, humane letters, physics, ethics, logic, and metaphysics. With one clear exception the subjects he studied left him "embarrassed with so many doubts and errors that it seemed to me that the effort to instruct myself had no effect other than the increasing discovery of my own ignorance."[40] Mathematics was the only exception, "because of the certainty of its demonstration and the evidence of its reasoning."[41]

Little is known about Descartes' life during the six years following his departure in 1614 from La Flèche. It would seem he went to Paris, and after his brief sampling of its pleasures palled he went into studious seclusion. Then and later, the proximity of friends proved to be too much of a distraction. It was in pursuit of even more privacy that he went to Holland in 1618.

That year he enlisted as a gentleman volunteer in the army of Prince Maurice of Nassau but apparently did not see combat. In November he met Isaac Beeckman, a mathematician and the rector of a small college. They became warm friends, and

Beeckman's influence turned Descartes toward purely theoretical problems. The following year, 1619, Descartes was ostensibly engaged in military service, and he traveled to Denmark, Hungary, Austria, and possibly Bohemia.

Descartes' winter quarters in 1619–1620 were in a small village near Ulm where he spent his time in study and speculation. The next step of his intellectual journey came during this winter: the inspiration came to him that mathematical methods could form the basis of all reasoning. He resolved to devote the rest of his life to the cultivation of reason through the method revealed to him.

In the spring of 1620 Descartes again took to traveling. Between 1628 and 1649, he lived quietly in various places in Holland and tried to avoid personal contact, but still his thinking attracted considerable attention. He was, however, a voluminous correspondent. He moved from town to town, requiring for his needs only proximity to a Catholic church and to a university.

Most of his important works were written and published in Holland; much preparation preceded their composition. During his first years of residence in Holland, Descartes wrote *Rules for the Direction of the Mind.*[42] By 1633 he had nearly completed his *Treatise on the World,* an account of the world and humankind. This work contained two heretical doctrines—a defense of the earth's rotation and an espousal of the infinity of the universe. However, he never completed the *Treatise,* and whatever he had finished of it was not published during his lifetime. Had the condemnation of Galileo intimidated him, or did he simply want to continue his work in peace? Perhaps he had resolved to reconcile both science and religion and had deferred publication until he could no more work. We simply do not know why he stopped work on it. Another factor may have been his lifelong religious orthodoxy, which may have been merely politic, but the evidence seems to point to his religious sincerity.

A portion of *The World,* called *L' Homme,* was published posthumously.[43] It has been called the first textbook on physiology and is useful for Descartes' views on physiological psychology. In 1637 he published his *Discourse on Method*[44] accompanied by three shorter pieces including "Dioptric,"[45] a study of optics, the first published statement of the law of refraction.

In order to secure criticism, Descartes circulated in manuscript form his *Meditations of the First Philosophy.*[46] When he published the book in 1641, he included his answers to the criticisms which had been submitted to him. Both the *Discourse* and the *Meditations* included accounts of his methodology of science based on his particular philosophical presuppositions.

In 1649 Descartes published the *Passions of the Soul.*[47] In accord with the times, psychological discussion early in the volume was followed by a development of the ethical significance of his psychological ideas. He held that the passions give rise to all good and evil of this life, and he wished to show how the mind might control the passions.

Meanwhile, Queen Christina of Sweden had become interested in his views, and a correspondence developed that, when reworked, became part of his *Passions of the Soul.* In the fall of 1649, at the Queen's request, Descartes took up residence at the Royal Court. This change was to prove both uncongenial and fatal. Descartes was used to spending his mornings in bed. His enthusiastic but not very competent pupil, however, set the hour for her instruction at five in the morning. It was an unusually cold winter in Stockholm that year, and before six months had passed, on February 11, 1650, he died of pneumonia.

The Rationalistic Method of Descartes

Reason had been used (and abused) as a tool since the beginning of intellectual history, but without too much explicit attention to its use as a conscious method. Descartes remedied this lack: his rational method with its deductive logic had as its ideal the treatment of all matter in the "spirit" of mathematics.

Descartes first came on the mathematical aspect of his methodology during that winter spent near Ulm. His discovery was to emerge as analytic geometry, the reciprocal application of algebra and geometry. Although Descartes was not the first to make this discovery,[48] he helped to unite and extend the relation between the two. He made it possible to express the properties of whole families of curves by means of simple algebraic equations. If these two apparently disparate fields of knowledge could be combined, he reasoned, could not all the field of knowledge be so combined? The method of analytic geometry could then be applied to all knowledge and a unity of all science might be achieved. He believed that the methodological assumptions of the physical sciences formed a unity that he was making explicit and could defend with examples. Descartes' belief in the basic unity of all the sciences was fortified still further by a conviction that it is more efficient to study them all together than to deal with them one at a time.[49]

As Descartes saw it, the particular value of the mathematical method was the possibility of "beginning with the things which were simplest and easiest to understand, and gradually and by degrees reaching toward more complex knowledge." This method may sound like induction, but to Descartes it was a deductive procedure. By "things" Descartes was not referring to simple experiences or observations but to clear and self-evident truths. Going from these fundamental ideas or truths to their consequences is a deductive procedure. He contrasted this method with the deductive logic of the syllogism. The syllogism is basically an argument laid out with a major premise, a minor premise, and a conclusion. If the major and minor premises are correct, then the conclusion should also be correct. For example, the following is a syllogism:

> Every virtue is laudable;
> Kindness is a virtue;
> Ergo kindness is laudable

Descartes recognized that the syllogism did not directly adapt itself to learning what was new but was more useful in restating, clarifying, and organizing what was already known.[50]

Descartes viewed the use of accumulated experience (empiricism) as a source of scientific knowledge, and he accepted the notion that it allows deduction. On the whole, however, he viewed the inductive, empirical method as methodologically weaker than his rational method. For if one depends on empiricism, Descartes believed that one must necessarily start with highly complex objects. Inferences may be drawn, but they may be wrong. Mathematical deductions that start with self-evident truths cannot lead to error.

How does one use this deductive method? Descartes cites several possibilities. His *Rules for the Direction of the Mind* presents twenty-one rules for applying it.[51] In the *Discourse on Method,* he considers four essential rules of procedure: (1) never accept as true anything that is not known clearly to be such; (2) divide difficulties into as many parts as possible; (3) proceed from what is simplest and easiest to understand to what is more difficult; and (4) make the connections so complete and the reviews so general as to insure that nothing is overlooked.[52] His manner, here and elsewhere, was formally clear and simple and a far cry from scholastic technicalities. (These rules are neither as self-evident nor as free from the possibility of error as Descartes thought, but to explore this aspect further would take us too far afield.)[53]

Descartes placed the problem of knowledge at the center of his inquiry. He held a rationalistic prescription of knowledge: by means of unaided reason one can know truth. At times he seems to say that people have an equal intelligence to distinguish the true from the false,[54] but he admits that individuals are born with different degrees of discernment.[55] He adds that practice can make this discernment much more expert, and he insists that all sciences should proceed from matters that are easy to understand.

Truth and falsity come from thinking alone, he said.[56] Descartes' plea for rationalism was that through thought, one can know truth. Descartes held that experience is available but is fallible.[57]

Descartes' paradigm of geometry misled him into thinking that clarity and distinctness are a guarantee of truth. The history of science is littered with self-evident truths that have had to be abandoned—the geocentric hypothesis, for example. Descartes failed to see, as Galileo saw, that principles should first be treated as hypotheses and that hypotheses, as such, are tentative and can be tested on the basis of whether or not the consequences deduced from them agree with empirical observations. In short, in his methodological account Descartes did not insist on the experimental check required by Galileo and Bacon.

Descartes' Search for Certainty

In keeping with the temper of his age and with his own distrust of knowledge, throughout his *Discourse on Method* Descartes asked himself what he could be certain of without any possibility of doubt.[58] He was not a skeptic; he merely insisted that doubt is the proper place to start constructing a system that would answer the skeptic. He wanted to doubt in order to find out what he could be certain about.

> Thus, as our senses deceive us at times, I was ready to suppose that nothing was at all the way our senses represented them to be. As there are men who make mistakes in reasoning even on the simplest topics in geometry, I judged that I was as liable to error as any other, and rejected as false all the reasoning which I had previously accepted as valid demonstration. Finally, as the same percepts which we have when

awake may come to us when asleep without their being true, I decided to suppose that nothing that had ever entered my mind was more real than the illusions of my dreams. But I soon noticed that while I thus wished to think everything false, it was necessarily true that I who thought so was something. Since this truth, I *think, therefore I am,* /or exist/, was so firm and assured that all the most extravagant suppositions of the skeptics were unable to shake it, I judged that I could safely accept it as the first principle of the philosophy I was seeking.

I then examined closely what I was, and saw that I could imagine that I had no body, and that there was no world nor any place that I occupied, but that I could not imagine for a moment that I did not exist. On the contrary, from the very fact that I doubted the truth of other things, /or had any other thought,/ it followed [very] evidently [and very certainly] that I existed.[59]

This quotation with Descartes' famous statement *"Cogito ergo sum,"* "I think, therefore I am," indicates that the central core of Descartes' solution is the certainty of his thinking and, therefore, of his existence. He found the last limits of doubt and the starting point of his system in the application of his first procedural principle, which was to accept nothing as true unless it was clearly evident. From this position, he was able to logically deduce the world which he had just destroyed by doubt.

In the *Meditations,* Descartes used a somewhat different approach to the same problem.[60] He first asked what he formerly had considered himself to be. He answered that he had believed himself to be a man—with face, hands, arms, flesh, and bones; that he had been nourished; that he had been able to walk; and that he had been able to think and to feel.

He proceeded with his argument by asking one to suppose that there was a certain powerful "genius," or demon, who was intent on deceiving him. Under these circumstances, could he, Descartes, affirm as certain these things that he had just described about the body? After thinking this matter over carefully, he realized that nothing of what he said about the body pertained to his awareness of "me." Moreover, if he had no body about which he could be certain, he could not be certain about walking or taking nourishment or perceiving. But what of thinking? Here is something, he said, about which I can be certain.

I am, I exist—that is certain; but for how long do I exist? For as long as I think; for it might perhaps happen, if I totally ceased thinking, that I would at the same time completely cease to be. I am now admitting nothing except what is necessarily true. I am therefore, to speak precisely, only a thinking being, that is to say, a mind, an understanding, or a reasoning being. . . .

I am something real and really existing, but what thing am I? I have already given the answer: a thing which thinks.[61]

For both approaches the starting point of Descartes' system is the certainty we have of our own existence. Doubt itself is a kind of thought. I doubt, but in so doing I also think. I know I exist because I perceive the fact distinctly. This doubting self is conscious. Descartes is not separating self and thought as in subject and verb; rather, he is affirming the existence of a thinking self as a unity, something whose "essence" consists of thinking. Thinking is not meant here in the abstract; it is a person he is talking about. One is reminded of Augustine's somewhat similar expression. Augustine, however, advanced the idea only incidentally, whereas Descartes used it to deduce the principles fundamental to his overall position.

Descartes' doubt was only provisional. He retrieved the world, which his doubt had denied him, by first proving to his satisfaction the existence of God, starting from his axiomatic self-certainty.[62] Because God is the most perfect of beings and would not deceive us, we may therefore examine natural reality confidently.[63]

Though not denying its existence, Descartes held that the concept of final cause should not be utilized in science.[64] This, too, was a conclusion reached by appeal to his principle of clarity. In this principle, the test of truth is in its self-evident clarity. Because we can form no clear idea of the end to which God made the world, we have no right to attribute to Him some special reason for creating it.

Comparing himself to Archimedes who said that, given a fixed point in space, he could lift the earth, Descartes claimed that he had found the bedrock on which to construct a whole system of science.[65] He built his system on what he considered to be essential philosophical certainties. However, despite the originality of his demand for basic philosophical assumptions, he resembles his philosophical predecessors rather than the great modern scientists who were his contemporaries. Now that his method has been explained, we can turn to the way he applied it to a crucial psychological question—the relation of mind and body.

Mind and Body Dualism

Descartes' major argument for mind–body dualism, that mind and body are separate entities, was related to the subjective certainty of the self that he had found after his journey of doubting. Descartes also asserted that we know mind and body are separate because if something is taken away from the body, say a foot, nothing is considered to have been lost to the mind.[66] Since we clearly perceive mind as different from body and vice versa, there is a real distinction between them, and they can exist apart from one another.[67] Fundamentally, created reality is composed of two different substances—extension and thought. Not only are they different to Descartes, but also they are subject to different laws. Mind is unrestricted: matter is subject to natural law. Moreover, this dualism implies two parallel worlds either one of which may be studied without reference to the other, although, as we will see, the two will need to interact.

The rational soul and the mind are synonymous in Descartes' treatment. Mind is the soul insofar as it thinks.[68] Descartes' notions about mind and body have become the common-sense attitude which most of Western society holds on the matter. Mind, not soul, then, will signify the central content of psychological considerations in succeeding chapters.

Descartes made several succinct statements on the nature of mind that may help us to grasp more clearly what he meant. Mind, as we have already seen, is a thing that thinks; it is a substance. This substance is unextended, however; that is, it does not exist in space or time as ordinary physical substances do.[69] This nonbodily substance has the characteristic of thought,[70] and the power by which we know things is purely mental.[71] Descartes held that the mind is outside of the physical order of matter and is in no way derived from it.[72] It does not obey natural law in the way that physical substances do. Such, then, is the Cartesian nature of mind.

There still remains one major argument for dualism.[73] What was merely a methodological distinction for Galileo became for Descartes an argument for a dualism of two worlds. In support of the immateriality of the mind, he happily enlisted the distinction between primary and secondary qualities. Odors, smells, and tastes were secondary sense qualities, "existing in . . . [one's] thought."[74] Bodies exist only in the shape and motion. He goes so far as to say that sensations represent nothing outside of our minds.[75] They are not in the objects but in our minds. Instead of sensible qualities residing in bodies, actually it is quite possible that sensible qualities and the objects are not at all similar.[76] When we approach fire and first feel heat, and then move still closer and feel pain, far from compelling us to believe that "heat" and "pain" are somehow in the fire itself, on the contrary, the experience suggests that they are not. The upshot, then, was that secondary qualities were relegated to the mind of the perceived, whereas primary qualities were the properties of nature. These primary qualities required mechanical explanation, and were, by definition, the only essential properties of the scientific concern.

Descartes insisted on a rigid separation of body and mind, contrasted and separated entities. All reality of the human being, Descartes was saying, is either spatial (body) or conscious (mind). The relationship is disjunctive; what is spatial is not conscious, what is conscious is not spatial. It follows that mind and body can be studied separately without reference to the other. The physical world, including body and its mathematically measurable relationships, is in one realm, whereas the mind with its thoughts, sensations, and free will is in another. The body's behavior is determined by mechanistic laws, but in the mind, there is purpose and freedom of will, making a person's actions subject to praise and blame. As distinguished from body, the mind then cannot be reduced to an aspect of a mechanical system because it transcends the material world and the efficient causality that governs therein.

Descartes' dualism had important implications for the sciences in general and for psychology in particular. Matter, including body, was to be described mathematically. Explanation was in mechanistic form, that is, in terms of its natural functioning processes, as though it were a machine. This dualism between mind and matter simplified physical science by means of what it excluded, while at the same time it introduced a major problem for psychology.

Mind and Its Faculties

Although it is clear that Descartes regarded the mind primarily as structural, substantial, "a thing," as he put it, he also had a subsidiary functional view of mind. Thus, the mind is a unity, but it does have functions, powers, or faculties.[77] The faculties are not parts of the mind since it is one and the same mind that employs itself in these faculties. Descartes usually speaks of thought as embracing the functioning of mind. He uses the term broadly, considering it to include all kinds of mental experience: doubting, denying, willing, imagining, and feeling.[78] In fact, as he uses the term, thought includes all that we are conscious of.[79] He usually discusses the mind in relation to thought or understanding, imagination, memory, and sense, and does not relate it to the will. Only in relating mind to will does he vary from this position.

What amounts to another classification of the modes of thought is the dual classification into will on the one hand and understanding with all its ramifications on the other.[80] Will or volition is one of the two basic powers of the mind; the other is understanding. To Descartes, one of the certain ideas we have is of freedom of will.[81] Will is related to understanding as a means of accounting for error.[82] The will is unlimited and has freedom of choice; understanding, on the other hand, is limited. This dominance of will is demonstrated by the fact that we do not always connect the same action with the same thought. Willing has intervened, causing movement in the way required by the act of will. The will then directs the action. Will gives assent or dissent to what has come into our understanding. This is a free choice.[83] One errs, not in failing to understand properly, but in willing, which is wider in compass and range than understanding. One may will improperly and may therefore fall into error. For example, if the principle of clarity is disregarded and will is allowed to precipitate a decision, error can occur. In a way this makes understanding subordinate to will.

In view of the relation of the self to will, it is plausible to consider at this point Descartes' conception of self. As was established to his satisfaction by considerations already discussed, the self is known directly; he could conceive of not having a body, but he could not conceive of not having a mind aware of itself. That the self participated in willing (as well as in discriminating and judging) is shown in the experience of having made a choice. Self is known through consciousness.

Thought gives rise to ideas, which are of two sorts: those that might be called derived and those that are innate. Derived ideas are occasioned by external stimuli. More important than these, however, are the innate ideas. A special class of ideas, they are the ones that give form to universal truths.[84] Unlike ideas arising from sensations, they are not preceded by organic impressions. Ideas are innate because they are developments of consciousness alone, and not transmitted by objects in the eternal world. It is not surprising that for Descartes, the idea of the self, the idea of God, and the axioms of geometry are among the most important innate ideas. Perfection, substance, quality, infinity, and unity are also innate to the mind and are not derived from sensory experience. To be sure, sensory experiences may remind us of these ideas, but they are not due to the sense perceptions. These ideas are innate in the sense that they are potentially capable of being developed into a form of conscious experience. They exist potentially and become actual in the presence of experience. Descartes had little occasion to consider memory or association as mental processes since for him the doctrine of innate ideas included them as well.

To Descartes understanding is the basic instrument of thought; imagination, memory, and sense are aids to understanding.[85] Understanding alone is capable of perceiving truth, but others may help when used correctly. Understanding derives directly from mental activity, uninfluenced by the body. Although imagination, memory, and sense are also purely mental in themselves, they are influenced by bodily activities and are therefore a product of the interaction of body and mind. In the section that follows, their mental nature will be considered, but discussion of the body will be deferred until we examine the interaction of body and mind.

We are exposed to error in direct experience, not through failure of the understanding but in a fashion similar to that occurring in the case of will. We fail to take into account that sense, imagination, and memory may err. Descartes' search for certainty is the setting in which he handles the problem of errors caused by the senses. He had concluded that God would not deceive us about the reality of the world of matter. In a sense Descartes proved too much. After all, errors and illusions do exist. How are we to account for them? Here he falls back on his principle of clarity. We can be sure of what we apprehend clearly; error comes when we neglect this precaution. Sensory experiences are not among the clearly thinkable ideas and are therefore among those prone to error. The same is true of imagination and memory. If we forget that these three ways of gaining knowledge may err, our conclusions may be wrong because of our failure to take their tendency to error into account. Otherwise, our understanding would have served us correctly.

Sensing, as distinguished from understanding, is the perception of qualities— colors, sounds, odors, and the like.[86] These sense experiences are convenient signs that allow us to get about in the world. Thus, the sound of horses' hooves on the roadway warns us of the approaching object, and we can step out of the way; but it has told us nothing about the true reality of matter. The image we have of the horse does not copy the natural object, as men before Descartes believed; rather, our image signifies or stands for the object. This was a considerable step forward from the naive representative theory of perception that calls our experience nothing more than a copy of a picture of the object.

What Descartes says about the specific senses needs only brief summary. He identified seven senses: the usual five, plus the internal sense by which we localize sensory happenings within the body, and the passions. Further discussion will be foregone until the consideration of body and the interaction of mind and body.

Molar Mechanistic Theory

The molecular level of mechanistic theory, traceable historically to Democritus' atomic theory, was reintroduced into seventeenth-century thinking by Pierre Gassendi (1592–1655) a priest, mathematician, and scientist. He made the theory acceptable to religious belief by arguing essentially that all phenomena—except the immortal soul—may be reduced to atoms.[87]

Although Descartes made some use of a variant of this molecular point of view, the so-called corpuscular theory, the primary thrust of his thinking was at the molar level of mechanistic theory. His was the pioneer, modern formulation of it, conceptualizing the body as the unit of study.

The body, as distinguished from the mind, Descartes said, is composed of matter and has the common characteristics of all matter. The body is extended in space and is capable of movement.[88] Fundamentally, Descartes' mechanistic princi-ple states that all natural phenomena can eventually be reduced to local motion. Action by physical contact is a special instance. Hence, the behavior of the body is determined by mechanistic laws, that is, the laws of the movement of bodies in space, and is to be studied in light of this principle.

From the point of view of movement, the human body is a machine with more parts, but it is not more alive than any manufactured *automaton* (a machine that moves itself).[89] An automaton with the outward form of a monkey and with organs resembling those of a monkey would be indistinguishable from a real monkey.[90] If a similar machine were made in the human likeness, however, we could detect that it was a machine, because the machine would not speak appropriately to the particular situation (even though a machine could be made to say words). More-over, we would soon discover "it" did not act from knowledge. It is on the basis of these two criteria that we also distinguish human from beast. Since even the deaf and dumb are able to invent signs, and since very little reason is required in order to learn to talk, brutes have no reason at all.[91] The same example demonstrates that a human being is more than body.

Descartes was especially intrigued by the flow of water in fountains, which he compared to the flow of vital spirits.[92] He uses the term *spirits* here not in the animistic or spiritual sense but as a fluid. Some of the statues in the royal gardens of his time were so arranged as to perform certain activities when someone stepped on their hidden pedals. Once set into motion, a sea monster would squirt water, or Neptune would appear to threaten the passerby with his trident. Tunnel rides in amusement parks and some of the props used at Disneyland are appropriate modern illustrations. In a description of the human body as a machine, Descartes writes of the actions of clocks, mills, and similar machines as duplicating the body's behavior.[93] He then asks the reader to compare these forms of motion with the functions of the body, such as digestion, heart action, respiration, sleeping, sensory experience, common sense, imagination, retention in memory by imprinting, the appetites, and the internal movements of the members. He concludes that these functions, which are forms of motion, follow naturally from the arrangements of the component parts. All that is necessary to set them in motion in the body, he states, is the heat of the vital spirits, which itself is in no way different from that of other fires. Again, "spirits" here is used in terms of fluid rather than in the earlier spiritual sense. The body performs functions arising from the presence of vital heat and is thus similar to that of animals in the functions it exhibits.[94]

Descartes holds that most muscular action does not depend on the mind at all.[95] Heartbeat, digestion, respiration, even walking and singing are performed without the mind attending them. A falling man who thrusts out his hands to break his fall does so merely because the sight penetrating the brain drives the animal spirits into the nerves in such a way that the motion is carried out. Mind is not involved. Descartes also uses as an illustration our inability to control the enlarging of the pupil by thinking; nature does not make this connection but instead associates its movement with looking at far or near objects.[96]

Here we have something approaching a statement of what we would later call reflex behavior. Motion follows predictably from the stimulation of nerves; there appear to be fixed channels for the behavior repertoire. This conception is akin to reflex behavior. Descartes is sometimes given too much credit in the area of reflex theory, however. True, he uses the words *undulatio reflexa* in describing the absence of voluntary action, but he was referring to the analogy between mechanical and physiological action expressed in the resemblance of the reflection or light and the reflux of water to what he thought happened in the flow of vital spirits.[97] This process involves a "rebound" of particles. Moreover, when writing in this fashion, he generally refers to activities that have a considerable degree of coordination and integration, for example, all animal behavior and in human beings, walking and talking.[98] On both counts modern neurology would disagree.

Before considering how Descartes handles the problem of the interaction of mind and body, it is worthwhile to pause and consider both the state of the knowledge of physiology of his day and some of his own research in what was to become physiological psychology. It will be remembered that Descartes came after Vesalius and was familiar with the contemporary work of Harvey. Descartes himself demonstrated, through using the excised eye of a bull, that an inverted image is actually formed by the lens in the retina at the back of the eye.[99] He also found that sensations of hearing vary in harshness or softness according to the force with which the ear is struck and that the harmony or discord of sound depends on agitations or vibrations of the air. He studied the functioning of muscles and knew that they worked in opposing pairs. He knew something about the anatomy of the brain and argued that, since the construction of the brain differs from person to person, we have individual differences among individuals in mental activities.[100] Nerves were known, but the nature of the neural impulse was not. Descartes' physiological equivalent for the neural impulse was still the vital spirits. Vital spirits were a kind of rarefied blood or subtle wind,[101] and the nervous system had a series of valves—like those affixed to water pipes—that allowed their passage. The motor force of the nerves was thought to reside in the brain.[102] Despite his limited knowledge, Descartes was the first since Theophrastus to give us a systematic attempt at a physiological psychology.[103]

Dualistic Interaction of Body and Mind

To Descartes, the human being was a mind united with a body,[104] the two interacting with each other. His position, therefore, came to be called interactionism or interactionistic dualism, a term that distinguishes it from another form of dualism, referred to as parallelism or parallelistic dualism, which will be discussed later in this chapter. Mind and body are two separate things that make the consideration dualistic. These two things or parts interact, and each affects the other. The interaction of mind and brain is merely a more specific instance of the overall interaction. The mind sometimes acts independently of the brain (as illustrated by innate ideas) and sometimes in interaction with it.[105] Thought, originating in the mind, may have consequences, such as movement. These movements are not thoughts but activities of the body.[106] In other instances the mind is present in what today might be called a sensory-motor process. In this instance, mind affects the machinery at the critical point of transmission from sensory to motor channels.[107] In both kinds of mental activity—thought as such affecting the body, and sensorially derived functioning of the mind in turn affecting the body—mind directs the vital spirits that pass from the heart through the brain to the muscles.[108]

Although each movement seems to be joined by nature to a particular thought, it may be directed "by habit." Descartes illustrates this idea by the fact that sounds are understood as words.[109] Those movements and thoughts naturally joined can also be separated, and this separation comes about from custom. Custom does not require long usage for the separation to be effected and may even be acquired by a solitary action as when we are unable to eat any food that has once made us ill. The same separation by custom may be noticed in brutes since a setter may be trained to stand still on hearing a gun, instead of fleeing, which he does naturally.

Descartes believed that a bodily locus for interactions of mind and body was necessary. He found it deep within the recesses of the brain,[110] the point of contact being the pineal gland. Since Descartes held that the mind was unitary, a unitary structure was needed. The pineal gland was the only organ in the brain that was single, that is to say, not divided into a right and a left half. Moreover, because of its strategic location it was adapted for ready accessibility to all parts of the body.

Movement of the vital spirits in the nerves produces an impression on the pineal gland as a signet seal might on wax, and from this impression the mind produces a sensation. In effect, a quantity of motion becomes a mental quality. The reverse also occurs; the mind makes an impression on the pineal gland, though in a way never made clear. At any rate, the mind affects the flow of animal spirits by changing their course in the direction of this or that muscle. To Descartes, a complete dualism still existed; the pineal gland was merely the point of contact.

The soul, Descartes affirmed, is united with the body, which it uses as an instrument.[111] The pineal gland is not the container or seat of the mind or soul; it is associated with the body, and the mind is not confined within the pineal gland at all. In order to have sensations and appetites the mind must be united with the body.[112] It is not merely lodged as would be a pilot in a vessel, but it is united with it, in fact intermingled with it, as a consequence of which pain, hunger, and the like are felt.[113] If there were only lodgement one would not feel pain, but merely perceive something external, as when a sailor knows that his ship is damaged but does not himself feel pain.

Important for understanding the interaction of body and mind, as Descartes conceived it, were what he called "the passions."[114] As Descartes uses the term, its meaning is much broader than in its modern usage and much closer to the ancient Greek notion of *thymos*. As the passions he identifies those motions from the vital spirits of the body that have effects on the perception, feelings, and emotions of the mind.[115] From the perspective of the mind, they are experiences taking place in the mind; this is their mental aspect. On the other hand, the affective aspects, feelings, or actions are in the body.[116] Although the movements of the passions are sometimes accompanied by thoughts, they need not be because they can arise in spite of a person's intentions.[117] This is additional evidence that they are of the body.

These psychological experiences, Descartes maintains, require activity of the brain prior to that of the mind. The psychological phenomena that depend, not on the activity of the mind initiated by the mind, but rather on its passivity, on its being affected from outside, are the passions. The passions include not only feelings and emotions but perceptual effects as well. Descartes also used a narrower definition of the passions when he called them feelings or emotions that are brought about by the spirits. That narrower definition is closer to the present-day meaning of "affective states."[118] In general, however, feeling and emotion are to Descartes distinguished from the other passions because they arise from considerable agitation of the animal or vital spirits but do not refer to objects outside the body.[119] The movements of the spirits nearly always create an "agitation" that remains in our thoughts until it goes down.[120]

The passions are differentiated from the will in that they are received from outside the mind and are not willed to appear. The function of a passion is to excite the will to action, although the passions should remain under the will's control.[121] The conflict is not between lower and higher levels of the soul, as it was with Plato, but between two sets of tendencies, one arising from the will and the other from the action of the vital spirits on the passions.[122] In other words, the passions arise from the mind's opposition to bodily impulses. Without a body related to a mind, there would be no passions. It is the effect of body on mind that produces passions.

A comparison of emotion in human beings and animal is enlightening. As an example, Descartes points out that because it is an *automaton*, a sheep fleeing from a wolf may not be afraid, but it behaves in a way that we interpret as terror. This is because we are afraid when our bodies are in the same condition. In the same situation, our bodies would go through the same mechanical actions, but because we have minds, those motions would cause us to feel passion as well.

Descartes discussed six primary passions: wonder, love, hatred, desire, joy, and sadness.[123] All other passions, and there are many, he said, are derivatives or combinations of these six. From wonder, an intellectual passion, are derived esteem, contempt, generosity, pride, humility, veneration, and disdain. All the other primary passions are forms of desire in a broad sense, since they incite to action. Passions of desire (in the narrower sense) arouse hope, fear, jealousy, confidence, courage, and cowardice. Joy and sadness led Descartes to advance the theory of pleasure and pain: pleasure and pain, he stated, are predecessors of the passions of joy and sadness and serve to produce them—joy is agreeableness and sadness disagreeableness. Joy and sadness are also related to secondary passions, specifically derision, envy, anger, shame, regret, and joyfulness.

Descartes' work served as a catalyst for many later trends in psychology. A summary of his psychological views should be placed within a setting of the later developments that they influenced. Especially important are the reactions to his dualism of body and mind and to his emphasis on the cognitive aspect of the human mind. Later critics also reacted against his inclusion of the human body in the mechanistic world and against his corresponding exclusion of the human mind. Despite their deep-seated differences, advocates of both the phenomenological and the mechanistic approaches owe much to Descartes. This debt will become clear after we examine the contributions of Benedict Spinoza and Gottfried W. Leibniz, who are important in their own right as well as for their reactions to Descartes' mind–body problem.

BENEDICT SPINOZA AND MONISM, RATIONALISM, DEDUCTIVISM, AND DETERMINISM

Benedict Baruch Spinoza (1632–1677) lived out his life as a lens grinder in Amsterdam, relatively obscure and uninfluential.[124] The *Ethics*, his most important work,[125] was published posthumously. The title of his work reflects his central aim: he wished to establish a way of life that was ethically correct and satisfying. In this context, psychology, he said, was a necessary step toward ethics.

Methodologically, Spinoza was both rationalistic and deductive. Sharing Descartes' enthusiasm for a geometric ideal, Spinoza began with self-evident axioms from which he proposed to deduce the nature of reality. He presented his views in geometrical form; that is, each new point was derived from preceding points. His conception of science admirably reflects his rationalistic method. The order of natural objects and the order of knowledge of them are coextensive: "The order and connection of ideas is the same as the order and connection of things."[126]

Spinoza's views are firmly rooted in his conception of God.[127] He wrote that God is infinite and is the only substance. Thought and extension are but attributes of God. To think of "things," that is, the objects of the world as we know them, is incorrect; instead of things, there are modes of substance, and whatever is, is a modification of the one substance that is God. A body is an abstraction, he stated, a finite way of regarding the infinite substance that is God. The human mind is no more than an aspect of the mind of God.[128]

Spinoza considered the human being to be a unitary individual, with the modes or forms of attributes of body (extension) and mind (thought).[129] Mind and body are not separate to Spinoza, as they are to Descartes; they are one, being two aspects of the same reality. Neither body nor mind is autonomous; a person has modes of the attributes of both extension and thought. This concept is a form of parallelism—monistic parallelism. Every bodily event coexists with and is coordinate to a mental event. Body and mind correlate, but they do not cause one another any more than the convex side of a glass causes the concave. Apparent interaction arises from ignorance on our part and shows only the coincidence of actions; it is a matter of appearance, not a reflection of reality.[130] Spinoza clearly states that it therefore follows that the body cannot determine the mind to think nor can the mind determine the body to motion or rest.

Unlike Descartes, Spinoza thought of the mind as an *automaton*, a term he explicitly applied to it.[131] Both mind and body were to be studied deterministically. Spinoza was perhaps the first modern thinker to view the world, including human beings, from a strictly deterministic standpoint. He believed both mind and body to be of equal status and to be subject to natural law.[132] Spinoza saw clearly that his deterministic view required the existence of laws of nature applicable to the individual. He mentions, for example, remembering by similarity and by contiguity as examples of the laws we should seek.[133]

Time and again Spinoza tells us that the will is not free.[134] The mind has no free will; it is determined by a cause that in turn is determined by another cause, and so on. This determinism brought Spinoza to something of a dilemma. How can the individual be ethically influenced—and ethics is after all, his main theme—if there is strict determinism? Throughout his works he offers the answer that human nature may be improved by improving the understanding and by encouraging the adherence of ethical principles that may be learned. The behavior of the ignorant is determined from without, whereas the wise can act in line with greater knowledge of nature. Acting in the light of necessity is the highest human freedom,[135] and freedom is one with necessity.

In contrast to Descartes' view of the mind as primarily cognitive, Spinoza emphasizes the conative or drive aspect of mental life. Central to Spinoza's psychology is the concept of *conatus,* an idea similar to what we would call an impulse toward self-preservation.[136] The striving for self-preservation is desire when it is conscious of itself; it is appetite when it is not.[137] In another place he speaks of the individual being led more by "blind desire" than by "reason."[138]

When unconscious desire is coupled with his emphasis on conation in general and his acceptance of determinism, it is hardly surprising that Spinoza should be seen as anticipating Freud.[139] Although this idea may be of some incidental interest, it must be pointed out that Spinoza arrived at his thinking from a perspective vastly different from that of Freud. For his part, although he was familiar with the works of Spinoza,[140] Freud shows no evidence of a direct influence.

GOTTFRIED W. LEIBNIZ AND MOLECULARISM, MONISM, CONSCIOUS AND UNCONSCIOUS MENTALISM

Gottfried Wilhelm Leibniz (1646–1716), one of the inventors of the calculus, was also a philosopher, scientist, historian, diplomat, logician, and lawyer, and, after his death, a leading intellectual force in Europe.[141] Among his many concerns, he investigated the issue of body–mind relationships.

Leibniz's unique contribution to our understanding of the nature of the mind is to be found in the theory of the *monad,* his term for the individual units of all substances, indicating that he was guided by a molecular prescription. He held that the world consists of an infinite number of monads.[142] As a unit, each monad is unextended. Leibniz's rejection of extension as an attribute of substance leaves the monads—all monads—with mind as their essential attribute. Each monad is a psychic entity. In denying substance, he also denied the reality of matter, in its place substituting an infinity of monads. Although mental, each of the monads has some of the properties of a physical point, and when collected into an aggregate, they create an appearance of extension.[143] The tree and the stones of everyday life, though appearing to the senses as objects, are actually aggregates of monads and in themselves are not phenomenal. Thus, Leibniz satisfied the need for an explanation of at least the appearance of extension in the world.

Each monad acts independently but is created by God to act in preestablished harmony with other monads.[144] The monads may appear to interact, but they do not. This takes the place of the untenable position that they influence one another.[145] There is no causality between monads, not even between those of the mind and those of the body. For our present discussion this point is most important. Noninteraction of body and mind is but a special case of the parallelism of monads.

Mind and body follow their own laws but show perfect agreement, and give the impression of interaction. Actually, however, there is a parallelism. The situation is similar to the interplay of the instruments of a symphony orchestra in which each player follows the score and yet gives the impression of one instrument responding to another. In a similar manner God composed the score, which is then played out according to preestablished harmony.

Stripped of the trappings of the monads, Leibniz's conception of parallelism was a forerunner of the doctrine of parallelistic dualism or psychophysical parallelism that was to be so important to Wilhelm Wundt and other early introspectionistic psychologists.

To Leibniz, all units of the world are endowed with life and motion and so are somewhat akin to consciousness. Even lifeless matter is only relatively unconscious; it has the least possible degree of consciousness.[146] Living organisms are composed of monads with varying degrees of consciousness.

Mental events, that is to say, the activity of monads, have degrees of clarity ranging from the totally unclear to the most definitely conscious or clearly grasped.[147] To Leibniz, this was more a matter of focal and peripheral attention than of consciousness as we would use the term.[148] Nevertheless, in view of the closeness of meaning, it was later seen as a conception of the continuum of consciousness–unconsciousness. At one extreme are mental events of which we are totally unconscious, and at the other extreme are those events that are clearly grasped or, to use the technical term, apperceived.

The degree of consciousness is a relative matter.[149] The supposedly unconscious has the possibility of becoming conscious. There are lower degrees of consciousness, or *petites perceptions*, as Leibniz called them—which, when actualized, are apperceived. Hearing the roar of the surf is apperception because it is the sum of all the drops of water we would not be conscious of if they were heard only one by one. The sound of a single drop is unconscious perception: sum up many drops at once and there is apperception.

DESCARTES' DUAL LEGACY

As a consequence of the emphasis on the cognitive part of the human mind by Descartes and those who followed him, two points of view—the phenomenological and the mechanistic—were to emerge. Although these are highly divergent movements, the very divided nature of Descartes' view of mind and body allowed him to be considered a major influence in each, as we will see in successive chapters.

SUMMARY

With the rise of the Renaissance, learning became rekindled in the West. Initially, Plato and his rationalistic and mathematical prescriptions dominated the intellectual scene. Aristotle, with his qualitative prescription, fell into disrepute for a time. Science did not reestablish itself until the seventeenth century, which was quite late in the Renaissance. The works of Harvey, Copernicus, and Galileo gave new views of the functioning of the human body and of the universe it apprehends.

Although induction as a prime method was overshadowed during the Renaissance by deductive methodology, Francis Bacon established his radical empirical view during this time in which he rejected the use of hypothesis, theory, or any other deductive methodology in favor of an unbridled inductive approach. His *idola*, his warnings of the biases of observation, however, still have much to teach us.

René Descartes, the dominant figure in psychology during the Renaissance, would greatly influence two traditions: phenomenalism and mechanism. His view of the function of mind was basically rationalistic, whereas his view of body was basically mechanistic. He reintroduced the mind–body problem and produced an interactionistic dualism that has become the common-sense view of modern Westerners. His concept of innate ideas was part of his rationalistic view of mind. His view of the body as *automaton* was part of his mechanistic view of body.

Benedict Spinoza, who also flourished in the late Renaissance, held to a monistic parallelism of mind and body. Mind and body, he said, were two aspects of the same thing. One does not cause events in the other, but as one changes the other changes with it. His method was deductive and rationalistic.

Gottfried Leibniz also held to a parallelism, but his was a dualistic parallelism. He viewed the world as being made up of units called monads, with mind and body representing different monads. He saw no causal relation between monads, including those of the mind and those of the body. Mind and body follow their own laws, but they show perfect agreement and give the impression of interaction. Actually, however, there is a parallelism. This is the commonly stated position of psychophysical parallelism that would be used in early scientific psychology.

NOTES

1. Good general sources concerning the relevant aspects of the Renaissance are the volumes by E. Cassirer et al., eds., The *Renaissance Philosophy of Man* (Chicago: University of Chicago Press, 1948); G. Sarton, *Six Wings: Men of Science in the Renaissance* (Bloomington: Indiana University Press, 1957); M. Boas, *The Scientific Renaissance 1450–1630: The Rise of Modern Science* (London: William Collins Sons, 1962); and A. R. Hall, *The Scientific Revolution; 1500–1800: The Formation of the Modern Scientific Attitude* (Boston: Beacon Press, 1956).
2. Petrarch, "On His Own Ignorance and That of Many Others," trans. H. Nachod, in E. Cassirer et al., eds. *Renaissance Philosophy of Man*, pp. 47–133 (1368).
3. *Ibid.*, p. 108.
4. J. H. Randall, *The Making of the Modern Mind*, rev. ed. (New York: Macmillan Co., 1940).
5. P. O. Kristeller, "The Platonic Academy of Florence," *Renaissance News, 14* (1961): 147–159.
6. M. Ficino, "Five Questions Concerning the Mind," trans. J. L. Barroughs, in E. Cassirer et al., eds. *Renaissance Philosophy of Man*, pp. 185–214 (1476).
7. J. D. Bernal, *Science in History*, Vol. 1 (New York: Cameron, 1954).

8. R. M. Blake et al., *Theories of Scientific Method; The Renaissance Through the Nineteenth Century* (Seattle: University of Washington Press, 1960).

9. R. McKeon, "Aristotelianism in Western Christianity," in J. T. McNeill et al., eds., *Environmental Factors in Christian History* (Chicago: University of Chicago Press, 1939), pp. 206–231.

10. Vesalius, *De humani corporis fabrica* (Basel: Oporinus, 1543); Vesalius, *The Epitome,* trans. L. R. Lind (New York: Macmillan Co., 1949) (1543).

11. N. Copernicus, "On the Revolution of the Heavenly Spheres," trans. C. G. Wallis, in R. M. Hutchins, ed. *Great Books of the Western World,* Vol. XVI, pp. 505–838 (1543).

12. Recently, it has been argued that more continuity existed between medieval and seventeenth-century science than had previously been thought. Seventeenth-century science was a cumulation of the cooperative efforts of generations of scientists, particularly at the School of Padua as J. H. Randall, Jr., demonstrates in *The School of Padua and the Emergence of Modern Science* (Padova: Editrice Atenore, 1961).

13. L. Thorndike, "Newness and Novelty in Seventeenth Century Science and Medicine," *Journal of the History of Ideas, 12* (1951): 584–598.

14. E. W. Strong, *Procedures and Metaphysics* (Berkeley: University of California Press, 1936). For an alternative view, see E. A. Burtt, *The Metaphysical Foundations of Modern Physical Science* (Garden City, N.Y.: Doubleday, 1932).

15. Strong, *Procedures and Metaphysics.*

16. G. Galileo, "Dialogues Concerning the Two New Sciences," trans. H. Crew and A. de Salvio, in R.M. Hutchins, ed., *Great Books of the Western World,* Vol. XXVII, pp. 129–260 (1638).

17. G. Galileo, *Il Saggiatore,* quoted in J. W. Reeves, *Body and Mind in Western Thought* (London: Penguin Books, 1958), pp. 106–107 (1623).

18. F. Bacon, *Novum Organum,* in R. M. Hutchins, ed., *Great Books of the Western World,* Vol. XXX, pp. 105–195 (1620).

19. F. Bacon, *Advancement of Learning,* in R. M. Hutchins, ed., *Great Books of the Western World,* Vol. XXX, pp. 1–104 (1605).

20. F. Bacon, *New Atlantis,* in R. M. Hutchins, ed., *Great Books of the Western World,* Vol. XXX, pp. 199–214 (1614–1617).

21. F. Bacon, *Advancement of Learning,* Second Book, XVII, 4.

22. *Ibid.,* Second Book, VIII, 2.

23. F. Bacon, *Advancement of Learning,* Second Book, XVII, 4.

24. F. Bacon, *Novum Organum,* First Book, Aphorisms, 39–68.

25. *Ibid.,* Aphorism 41.

26. *Ibid.,* Aphorism 45.

27. *Ibid.,* Aphorism 46.

28. *Ibid.,* Aphorism 42.

29. *Ibid.,* Aphorism 58.

30. *Ibid.,* Aphorisms 62–66.

31. *Ibid.,* Aphorism 3.

32. R. Descartes, "Discourse on the Method of Rightly Conducting the Reason," trans. Elizabeth S. Haldane and G.R.T. Ross, in R. M. Hutchins, ed., *Great Books of the Western World,* Vol. XXXI, pp. 41–67 (1637).

33. Sherrington, *Man on His Nature,* Chapter 4.

34. J. Kepler, *Ad Vitellionem paralipomena, quibus astronomiae pars optica traditur* (Frankfurt), Chapter 5, trans. A.C. Crombie, in I.B. Cohen and R. Taton, eds., *Mélanges Alexandre Koyré; L'Aventure de la science* (Paris: Hermann, 1964) (1604) (Herrnstein and Boring, Excerpt No. 23).

35. W. Harvey, *An Anatomical Disquisition on the Motion of the Heart and Blood in Animals,* trans. R. Willis, in R. M. Hutchins, ed., *Great Books of the Western World,* Vol. XXVIII, pp. 265–304 (1628).
36. *Ibid.,* Chapter 8, p. 285.
37. Hall, *The Scientific Revolution.*
38. "Discourse on Method," I, p. 44.
39. "The Discourse on the Method of Rightly Conducting the Reason" gives an autobiographical statement of some of the events of his life. A.G.A. Balz, *Descartes and the Modern Mind* (New Haven, Conn.: Yale University Press, 1952) and S. V. Keeling, *Descartes* (London: Oxford University Press, 1934) contain good secondary accounts.
40. R. Descartes, "Discourse on Method," I, p. 42.
41. *Ibid.,* p. 43.
42. R. Descartes, "Rules for the Direction of the Mind," trans. Elizabeth S. Haldane and G.R.T. Ross, in R. M. Hutchins, ed., *Great Books of the Western World,* Vol. XXI, pp. 1–40 (1629).
43. R. Descartes, "Treatise on Man," in R.M. Eaton, ed., *Selections* (New York: Charles Scribner's Sons, 1927), pp. 350–354 (1662). (Part given in another translation in Herrnstein and Boring, Excerpt No. 57.)
44. R. Descartes, "Discourse on Method."
45. R. Descartes, "Dioptric," trans. N. K. Smith, *Descartes' Philosophical Writings* (London: Macmillan Ltd., 1952), pp. 167–179 (1637) (also another translation in Herrnstein and Boring, Excerpt No. 27).
46. R. Descartes, "Meditations on First Philosophy," trans. Elizabeth S. Haldane and G.R.T. Ross, in R. M. Hutchins, eds., *Great Books of the Western World,* Vol. XXXI, pp. 69–293 (1641).
47. R. Descartes, "Passions of the Soul," *Essential Works of Descartes,* trans. L. Bair (New York: Bantam Books, 1961), pp. 108–210 (1649).
48. Keeling, *Descartes.*
49. R. Descartes, "Rules," I–II.
50. R. Descartes, "Discourse," II.
51. R. Descartes, "Rules."
52. R. Descartes, "Discourse," II.
53. A good critique is available in Keeling, *Descartes.*
54. R. Descartes, "Discourse," I.
55. R. Descartes, "Rules," IX.
56. *Ibid.,* VIII.
57. *Ibid.,* VIII, XII, XIII; "Meditations," I, VI, *Second Objection, Fifth Objection; Passions,* Part II, 3.
58. R. Descartes, "Discourse," esp. IV.
59. R. Descartes, "Meditations," IV. *Discourse on Methods and Meditations,* trans. Laurence J. Lafleur (New York: Bobbs–Merrill Co., 1960) (1637). The solidus enclosing a word or phrase indicates material found in the Latin version but not in the French, and the brackets enclose a word or phrase found in the French but not in the Latin edition.
60. *Ibid.,* "Meditations," II.
61. *Ibid.,* p. 84.
62. W. T. Jones, *A History of Western Philosophy* (New York: Harcourt, Brace, 1952).
63. R. Descartes, "Meditations," VI.
64. *Ibid.,* "Meditations," IV.
65. *Ibid.,* II.

66. *Ibid.*, VI.
67. *Ibid.*, Arguments, IV.
68. *Ibid.*, Reply to Fifth Set of Objections.
69. *Ibid.*, IV.
70. R. Descartes, *Principles of Philosophy,* trans. Elizabeth S. Haldane and G.R.T. Ross, *Philosophical Works* (Cambridge: Cambridge University Press, 1911), Vol. I, pp. 203–320 (1644), Part I, 53.
71. "Rules," XII, "Discourse," III, V.
72. *Ibid.*
73. R. I. Watson, "A Prescriptive Analysis of Descartes' Psychological Views," *Journal of the History of the Behavioral Science,* VII (1971): 238–239.
74. R. Descartes, "Meditations," Reply to Sixth Set of Objections.
75. R. Descartes, *Principles,* Part 1, LXVI–LXX.
76. R. Descartes, "Meditations," VI.
77. *Ibid.*
78. *Ibid.*, II.
79. *Ibid.*, Arguments, Definition I.
80. R. Descartes, *Principles,* Part I, XLII.
81. *Ibid.*, I.
82. R. Descartes, "Meditations," IV; Passions, XXXV.
83. R. Descartes, *Principles,* Part I, XXXVII.
84. R. Descartes, "Discourse," V, VI; "Meditations," Reply to Fifth Set of Objections.
85. R. Descartes, "Rules," XII.
86. R. Descartes, "Meditations," Reply to Fifth Set of Objections.
87. P. Gassendi, *Syntagma Philosophicum,* in F. N. Magill, ed., *Masterpieces of World Philosophy in Summary Form,* Vol. 1 (New York: Salem Press, 1961), pp. 404–410 (1658).
88. R. Descartes, "Meditations," Arguments, Definition VII.
89. R. Descartes, "Passions," VI.
90. R. Descartes, "Discourse," V.
91. R. Descartes, "Letter to Henry More," in R. M. Eaton, ed., *Selections,* pp. 358–360.
92. R. Descartes, "Treatise on Man," Part II.
93. *Ibid.*
94. R. Descartes, "Discourse," V.
95. R. Descartes, "Meditations," Reply to Fourth Set of Objections.
96. R. Descartes, "Passions," LXIV.
97. *Ibid.*, XXXVI.
98. R. Descartes, "Meditations," Reply to Fourth Set of Objections.
99. R. Descartes, "Dioptric" (Herrnstein and Boring, Excerpt No. 27).
100. R. Descartes, "Passions," XXXIX.
101. *Ibid.*, VII.
102. R. Descartes, "Rules," XII.
103. For a discussion of how he conceived the mechanism of human action, see Herrnstein and Boring, Excerpt No. 57.
104. R. Descartes, "Treatise on Man"; "Meditations," Reply to Fourth Set of Objections; "Passions," *Essential Works,* XXXIV. (Herrnstein and Boring Excerpts, No. 44, 103).
105. R. Descartes, "Meditations," Reply to Fifth Set of Objections.
106. *Ibid.*, Argument, Definition 1.
107. R. S. Peters, ed., *Brett's History of Psychology* (London: Allen and Unwin, 1953), p. 351.

108. R. Descartes, "Meditations," Reply to Fourth Set of Objections.

109. R. Descartes, "Passions," LX.

110. *Ibid.*, XXXI–XXXIV.

111. R. Descartes, "Meditations," Reply to Fourth Set of Objections.

112. R. Descartes, "Discourse," III.

113. R. Descartes, "Meditations," VI.

114. R. Descartes, "Passions."

115. *Ibid.*, XXVII.

116. *Ibid.*, II.

117. R. Descartes, "Letter to Marquis of Newcastle," in R. M. Eaton, ed., *Selections*, pp. 355–357.

118. R. Descartes, "Passions," XXVII.

119. *Ibid.*, XXVIII.

120. *Ibid.*, XLVI.

121. *Ibid.*, XLVII.

122. *Ibid.*

123. *Ibid.*, LXIX–XCVII.

124. Primary sources are mentioned later. Good secondary sources on Spinoza are those of H. A. Wolfson, *The Philosophy of Spinoza*, 2 vols. in 1 (New York: Meridian Books, 1934); R. McKeon, *The Philosophy of Spinoza: The Unity of His Thought* (New York: Longmans, Green, 1928); G.H.R. Parkinson, *Spinoza's Theory of Knowledge* (Oxford: Clarendon Press, 1954).

125. B. Spinoza, *Ethics*, trans. W. H. White, rev. A. H. Stirling, in R. M. Hutchins, ed., *Great Books of the Western World*, Vol. XXXI, 355–463 (1677).

126. *Ibid.*, Part II, prop. 7, p. 375.

127. Spinoza, "Ethics," Part III, Preface.

128. *Ibid.*, Part II, prop, 11.

129. *Ibid.*, Part II.

130. *Ibid.*, Part III, prop. 2.

131. B. Spinoza, "Treatise on the Correction of the Understanding," trans. A. Boyle, in E. Rhys, ed., *Spinoza's Ethics and de intellectus Emendatione* (New York: E. P. Dutton, 1910), pp. 228–263 (1677).

132. B. Spinoza, "Ethics," Part III, Preface.

133. B. Spinoza, "A Theologico-Political Treatise," in R.H.M. Elwes, ed., *Chief Works* (London: Bell, 1909), Vol. I, pp. 3–278 (1670), IV.

134. B. Spinoza, "Ethics," Part III, props. 4–8.

135. B. Spinoza, "Theologico-Political Treatise," Chapter II, Sec. 11.

136. B. Spinoza, "Ethics," Part III, props. 4–8.

137. *Ibid.*, Part III, prop. 8.

138. B. Spinoza, "Political Treatise," in R.H.M. Elwes, ed., *Chief Works*, Vol. 1, pp. 280–387 (1677).

139. W. Bernard, "Freud and Spinoza," *Psychiatry*, IX (1946): 99–108.

140. *Ibid.*

141. Good secondary sources include B. Russell, *A Critical Exposition of the Philosophy of Leibniz*, rev. ed. (London: Allen and Unwin, 1937); and H. W. Carr, *Leibniz* (New York: Charles Scribner's Sons, 1951), pp. 522–533 (1714).

142. G. W. Leibniz, "The Principles of Nature and Grace, Based on Reason," in P. P. Wiener, ed., *Selections*, pp. 522–533 (1714).

143. G. W. Leibniz, "The Monadology," in P. P. Wiener, ed., *Selections*, pp. 533–552 (1714).

144. G. W. Leibniz, "New Essays on the Human Understanding," in P. P. Wiener, ed., *Selections*, pp. 367–480 (1704), Preface.
145. Leibniz, "The Monadology," 61.
146. G. W. Leibniz, "Considerations on the Principle of Life and on Plastic Natures by the Author of the Preestablished Harmony," in P. P. Wiener, ed., *Selections*, pp. 190–199 (1705).
147. G. W. Leibniz, "New Essays," Preface.
148. G. W. Leibniz, "Principles of Nature and Grace," 4, 16.
149. G. W. Leibniz, "New Essays," Preface.

Portrait of Thomas Hobbes.

Chapter 9

Hobbes to Hume: British Empiricism

*T*he latter half of the seventeenth century saw important beginnings for science in general and psychological thought in particular, especially in Great Britain. In England, this period marks the age of the founding of the Royal Society; of the Newtonian synthesis; of a struggle among a line of thinkers to find the limits of human knowledge by the study of human nature; and of a general increase of interest in science. More specifically for psychology, it was the period when empiricism as a method led to association as a major contentual problem for psychology.

The Royal Society was chartered in 1662, although informal meetings of the "Invisible College," a network of scholars who corresponded and met with one another from time to time, had been taking place as early as 1645.[1] The doctrines of Francis Bacon were the central force binding the founders together. (Without entirely realizing it, however, they increasingly turned to the experimental method of Kepler and Galileo.) Their meetings were not confined to the reading of papers; public demonstrations of the most varied experiments were also carried out. The Society also served to create favorable public opinion, and its journal, *Philosophical Transactions*, fulfilled the need for a publication source. Although many of the articles were of a scientific nature, the majority were practical and dealt with such matters as shipbuilding, navigation, and mine pumping. Utilitarianism, so highly valued by Bacon, was being practiced.

As for experiment, years before the appearance of his *Opticks*, Isaac Newton had given a paper to the Royal Society on the composition of white light.[2] Using a prism and sunlight as a source, he found that the spectrum of color broke down into violet, indigo, blue, green, yellow, orange, and red. Later it was demonstrated that, instead of seven, there were an infinite number of degrees of refraction, but Newton's original findings have been the basis for all future work. He also worked out the basic principles known as the laws of color mixture still taught in introductory psychology.[3]

Newton described physical nature in terms of material particles that exist in absolute space and absolute time, propelled into motion or change of motion by force. From these descriptive categories he would derive the laws of nature.

Newton, more than anyone before him, established and promoted the four prescriptions that are basic to all science: nomotheticism, naturalism, empiricism, and quantitativism. Newton's thought was clearly in the inspiration for what would become British empiricism. The model which he established in the physical sciences would be held up as the epitome of proper science for all scientific disciplines.

The appeal to reason was still very powerful in the seventeenth and eighteenth centuries, but the term rationalism was loosely used. There were two aspects to Locke's psychological thought—one empirical and inductive, and the other rational and deductive. The question was not so much whether or not humans had reason but what was the source of their knowledge and therefore their reason.

English empiricists, methodologically speaking, relied primarily on what could be learned from cumulative sense experiences, and they tended to be skeptical of achieving absolute certainty in any field. They were seeking a more "down-to-earth" philosophy in contrast to what they considered the speculative character of the philosophy of the continent. They accepted the Baconian proposition that scientists must start from observations that are collected carefully and from which relatively cautious generalizations are made. Contentually, the psychological generalizations which they fostered centered on the laws of association—the ways in which mental events are connected. The most highly recognized psychological thinkers of this British empirical and associationist tradition are John Locke and George Berkeley, but predating their work is that of Thomas Hobbes.

THOMAS HOBBES

Thomas Hobbes (1588–1679) lived just before the period under consideration, and in many ways he stands at the headwater of mentalistic and mechanistic movements to come. He was a contemporary of and a correspondent with Descartes.

Following the careers of tutor and minor diplomat, he spent considerable time traveling on the continent. For a short time he also served as Francis Bacon's secretary and translator.

Hobbes was an implacable foe of supernatural and religious beliefs. His favorite tactic was to assert his orthodoxy and then slip in a devastating criticism. He piously asserted that one must, of course, accept divine revelation—provided one has experienced it personally—otherwise it is only a belief.[4] It is small wonder that he incurred the wrath of the orthodox majority. Hobbes is best known as a political philosopher, but he is relevant here because psychology formed the foundation for this work. His book *Leviathan*[5] and his shorter work—significantly named *Human Nature*[6]—are the most important statements of his psychological views.

Hobbes considered psychology a field to be investigated prior to making any attempt to understand the state and government.[7] Consequently, his interest in conduct was specifically in social conduct. He held a somewhat cynical view of human nature. Humankind, he believed, originally lived in a state of mutual warfare, and it was only enlightened selfishness that permitted cooperation. Without government "the life of man [is] solitary, poor, nasty, brutish, and short."[8] On the basis of self-interest and the fear of attack, people agreed to live under government. Later his doctrine that self-interest is the basis of conduct came to be referred to as "psychological hedonism."[9]

Influenced by Galileo's conception of motion, Hobbes held that everything that happens is matter in motion; mental activities are motions of the nervous system arising as reactions to motions in the external world.[10] Thinking, in this view, is nothing more than movement excited in the brain.[11] Motions account not only for cognitive processes, but also for action and emotion. Everything in nature is material. Thinking implies a thinking thing, just as walking implies a walking thing; in both instances this thing is the body. Consequently, Hobbes rejected Descartes' interactionistic dualism, one in which mind and body are separate and yet interact with one another. Instead, he chose a materialistic monism in which mind and body are one and the same. Hobbes conceived of sensation, thought, and consciousness as being due to the motion of atoms in the brain. He offered no explanation of how the connection between atomic motions and mental processes, two apparently different activities, came about. They simply did.

Hobbes was the first empiricist to reject Descartes' notion of innate ideas. In many respects, this rejection of Descartes' rationalistic position was the spark that ignited psychological empiricism. Hobbes held that the content of mind arises from sense experience, not from innate ideas.[12] This notion marks him as an empiricist since at the basis of all contentual empiricism is the position that the original source of knowledge is by means of the senses. Hobbes also held that all complex experience is derived from simple experience and that all simple experience is derived from sensation. In other words, the cognitive powers of the mind are derived from the senses and the senses alone. This also marks Hobbes as an elementist, since he holds that the complex mental states are finally reducible to simple states. In Hobbes' view cognitions are merely corruptions of the original sense elements. For example, imagination and memory are "decaying" conceptions in that they are slowly fading sensations.[13]

Hobbes argued against the common belief that the qualities of our experience—color, for example—are inherent in the object.[14] He insisted that in all instances "the subject of their inherence is not the object, but the sentient."[15] Psychological experiences, in other words, are subjective and are not counterparts of the objective stimuli that give rise to them. As such he anticipated George Berkeley's rejection of the notion of primary sense qualities. Berkeley, like Hobbes, would later hold the view that all experience is made up of "secondary" sense qualities, those pertaining to the sensations, not to the objects that produced the sensation. Hobbes goes so far as to call psychological experiences "apparitions," but adds that they come about as the result of the objects working on the brain.

Hobbes only partially outlined the notion of association, leaving its development and extension to others. However, he mentions "coherence" and repetition as the bases for the connections of "trains of thought." After several centuries of philosophical thought, Hermann Ebbinghaus (1850–1909) would establish experimentally that contiguity and repetition are, indeed, the bases for association. It is true that Hobbes introduced the notion of repetition somewhat incidentally and in a somewhat different context, but it soon became acknowledged as essential to association.[16] Hobbes identified two types of processes of association, or "trains of thought":[17] those that are unguided and without design, and those that are regulated and orderly, as when one thought introduces the one that follows or when design or desire regulate thought. This distinction contains a clear differentiation between what was later to be called free and controlled association.

Hobbes stressed the influence of the passions and desires on human action, which he saw as motions raising from within the person.[18] The basis of human action is "a perpetual and restless desire for power after power."[19] He distinguished between the appetites and aversions that one is born with and those that are acquired from experience.[20] Although he devotes a chapter to the passions, it is unsystematically presented, though he does make it clear that passions may sway reason.[21] As a consequence, the passions are regarded as human infirmities.[22] The passions serve to sustain and direct thought. Deliberation is simply a choice from among appetites and aversions.[23] Pleasure, pain, pride, and fear are prime determiners of conduct.

Notwithstanding the often incomplete nature of his views, Hobbes was prophetic of an emerging empirical, monistic, materialistic conception of mind. Many later developments followed along the lines he had marked out, for he argued that the individual is an integral part of the natural world, not just physically, as Descartes believed, but mentally as well. He held out the hope for a science of human physics, a line of thought that was to be worked out in more detail by David Hume in the next century.

JOHN LOCKE

John Locke (1632–1704) was an older contemporary of Leibniz and Newton, and although he lived most of his life in the seventeenth century, in spirit he belongs to the eighteenth.[24] Anticipated in many ways by Hobbes, Locke nevertheless usually garners the credit for launching British empiricism. In this role Locke is typically credited as the founder of psychology as the empirical science of the mind.

John Locke was born in Pensford, a village near Bristol, ten years before the outbreak of the English civil war. His father, a small landowner and a lawyer by profession, was a captain in a volunteer regiment under the Long Parliament. The unsettled conditions of the times reduced the already modest family fortunes considerably, but through the influence of his father's colonel, Locke was sent to Westminster School in 1646. After remaining at Westminster six years, he was granted a junior scholarship at Christ Church, Oxford, in 1652. Locke remained at Oxford after taking his bachelor's degree in 1656. He took a master's degree and then had academic appointments successively in Greek, rhetoric, and moral philosophy.

He was perhaps most influenced by Robert Boyle who was at Oxford during Locke's years of residence. Robert Boyle (1627–1691) was part of the group that founded the Royal Society and was one of the founders of modern chemistry, doing much to clear away the mysticism that had surrounded the field. Above all, he sought to foster the alliance between chemistry and mechanical science. His general contribution to Locke's education was to show him how to approach matters empirically; specifically, Boyle provided Locke with the conception of primary and secondary qualities. Galileo had actually made this distinction in the Renaissance, but it was Boyle who also arrived at this idea and named it. It was only later that Newton made an impression on Locke.

The founding of the Royal Society at Oxford, of which Locke became a member, led him to some studies and demonstrations in chemistry and meteorology. He also began the study of medicine. At Oxford he took an interest in political questions, particularly the relation of church and state and the importance and desirability of religious toleration. In the meantime, he had largely outgrown his Puritan upbringing. Given Cromwell's dwindling power and his repressive measures, Locke saw more hope for religious and political liberty under Charles than under the government of the Rump Parliament. So when Charles II was crowned in 1660, Locke welcomed the change in government and for some years had no reason to regret it.

During the next tumultuous decade, Locke was in and out of favor with the Crown, and for a while he was in exile in Holland. There, Locke worked on his *Essay Concerning Human Understanding.* When William of Orange ascended the English throne, Locke came back to his homeland and was given the post of Commissioner of Appeals.

Up to the time of his return to England in 1689 at the age of fifty-six, Locke had published little of importance. In the next few years a whole series of works appeared: his *Letter Concerning Toleration,* [25] which was published the year of his return; *An Essay Concerning Human Understanding,* [26] which appeared the year following; and works on government, economics, education, and Christianity, written between 1689 and 1695. His work that is of greatest interest for psychology is *An Essay Concerning Human Understanding.* [27] Aside from the posthumously published *The Conduct of the Understanding,* [28] this one work contains essentially all his psychological views. [29]

This and his other writings that followed rapidly made Locke famous both in England and on the continent, and he became the acknowledged voice of philosophical and governmental liberalism. Voltaire (1694–1778), who developed an unbounded admiration for Locke and placed him on the same exalted plane as Newton, did much to spread a favorable opinion of his views on the continent, especially in France.

Locke's Psychological Views

In proposing, as Locke did in his *Essay*, that the examination of our ability to understand ourselves is basic to later investigation in other fields, including the sciences, he was making psychology fundamental to all science. He also made explicit the limits he would set to his inquiry. In the introduction to the *Essay*, he specifically disavowed any concern with the physical aspects of understanding.[30] In a similar vein he indicated that such speculative matters as the essence of understanding would also be disregarded. He took understanding for granted and carried on his inquiry in order to see how far understanding could take him and where it would fail him, so that thereafter he would be more cautious in meddling in matters beyond comprehension.

In order to carry out his espoused intention of looking into the origin, certainty, and extent of human knowledge, Locke proposed a psychological inquiry into the ideas, "which a man observes, and is conscious to himself he has in his mind; and the ways whereby the understanding comes to be furnished with them."[31] He defined an "idea" very broadly as anything about which the mind can be employed in thinking. In other words, an idea denoted any sort of experience.

Insistence on Nonexistence of Innate Ideas   Locke immediately plunged into his task by arguing that there are no innate ideas. From the time of Plato or even Parmenides, a doctrine of innate ideas seems to have gone hand in hand with adherence to the rationalistic prescription.[32] With his rejection of innate ideas, Locke began his attack on the still dominant rationalism of his day. Although he did not mention Descartes by name, Locke's attack is often interpreted as being directed against him. In fact, Descartes' position was a moderate one involving acceptance of *potentially* innate ideas that are actualized by experience, rather than the extreme position that Locke attacked. Certainly, Locke's views were contrary to those professed by the contemporary Cambridge Platonists whose thinking dominated English academic circles. Such ideas as "what is, is" or "it is impossible for the same thing to be and not to be" are, Locke said, not imprinted on the mind. We are not born with these or any other moral, theological, logical, or mathematical principles. Locke tried to account for how the belief in these principles could have arisen. When a person once grasped some general proposition that he or she could not thereafter doubt, this person was inclined to think this now self-evident proposition must have been innate.[33] Locke held that those fostering a belief in the innate were the intellectually lazy and the dogmatically minded; they were dogmatically minded because they recognized that unquestioned propositions could be thrust on others. In his crisp way of putting the matter, acceptance stops the inquiry of the doubtful.[34]

Locke gives little credence to the argument for innate ideas based on the sheer existence of ideas commonly agreed on and universally accepted. His argument is that the universality of ideas does not demand innateness if some other way can be found to account for the presence of such ideas. If such ideas be universal, he asks, how is it that children and idiots do not have them? Moreover, he points out that children can reason long before they appreciate the truth of maxims they were given earlier as illustrations.

What children are told and retold by nurses or others, they accept.[35] When they become adults, because they are unable to remember a time when they did not accept these principles, they believe they must have held them all along. So where do generally agreed-on ideas come from? To answer this question Locke set himself the task of demonstrating that all knowledge is derived from the effects of experience, thereby declaring his allegiance to the empiricistic prescription.

Sensations, Simple Ideas, and Primary and Secondary Qualities   Like Hobbes, Locke was an empiricist and elementist. Ideas in Locke's view come from sense impressions. The mind, "the yet empty cabinet" (so-called because of what he considered the false analogy of the well-stocked cabinet filled with innate ideas), is furnished with ideas by experience.[36] Sensing takes place when the impression from the sense organs is transmitted to the mind. These sensations are simple ideas, and, in receiving them, the mind is essentially passive; it must sense when it senses and it cannot refuse impressions or blot them out.[37]

Sensible qualities are simple ideas; that is, they are not divisible into different ideas.[38] Some simple ideas are admitted through one sense, whereas others depend on combinations of the senses—for example, ideas of space and extension, rest and motion.

What we know through the senses is not known immediately but through the intervention of ideas.[39] Knowledge is real only to the extent that our ideas conform to the reality of objects. With simple ideas, there is at least a rough correspondence, for these ideas are the products of things outside ourselves operating on the mind. However, not all our ideas are exactly identical to the images, and they do not exactly resemble any object.[40]

As we have seen, sensible qualities are of two kinds in Locke's thinking: primary and secondary. Solidity, substance, figure, and mobility are primary sense qualities; they are inseparable from their objects no matter how much the objects may change in other ways. Color, sounds, and tastes are examples of secondary sense qualities; they do not really exist in the objects themselves, but they do have the capacity to produce sensations in the observer.[41] The secondary qualities exist only as modes of the primary qualities. An example is the failure of objects to have color in low illumination; the object is still visible but not its color. The most famous illustration is the experiment of the three basins of water. If, after placing one hand in a basin of cold water and the other in a basin of hot water, both hands are now placed together in a basin of tepid water, one hand will feel warm and the other will feel cold. To Locke, this example proved the subjective character of perception. The objective nature of the cause (stimulus) and the subjective character of the effect in consciousness (experience) had been established.

Although he used this and other illustrations to drive home his point about secondary qualities, Locke was no idealist. The tepid water was real enough, as were whiteness and bitterness and other secondary qualities. Locke was convinced that an external reality lies behind the ideas we have. This is the crucial issue on which his successors were to criticize Locke's position on primary sense qualities. How, they would ask, if we are aware of ideas for primary and secondary qualities alike, can we know that there is such a reality? That is, how can the senses and the senses alone tell us which experiences are like the object producing them and which are not?

Reflection, Simple and Complex Ideas   Ideas arising from sensations are supplemented by reflection, which we carry on with our minds.[42] Ideas of sensation and ideas of reflection make up all mental activity, for they are the only sources of ideas. Reflection is the operation of the mind itself, as opposed to the operation of sensations on the mind. Reflection gives rise to ideas, but these ideas are based on those already supplied from sensory experience. Ideas of reflection could not, by definition, be innate since they use the materials of sensation. The operations collectively called reflection are perceiving, thinking, doubting, believing, reasoning, knowing, and willing.

These two aspects of knowledge, sensation and reflection, also represent two aspects in the development of the individual. The infant and young child live in a world of sensations and make use of reflection only at a later stage of development. Children reflect only after time spent in examining their "floating visions."[43] Locke wrote that as experience increases, the mind has more to think about. Perception is the simplest level of reflection.[44] Children first have ideas of hunger and of warmth that exemplify perceptions. Even animals have perceptions. Perceptive reflection is the first step toward knowledge. Remembering is also present in children. When the same ideas again recur, without the operation of the object of the original sensation, we have remembering. In adults reflection may come to predominate in their judgments. Thus, Locke has two different systems of knowledge, one for children and another for adults. The one for children is primarily inductive and empirical, gradually becoming less sensationally determined as the number of sensations increase. The system for adults is more deductive and represents the origin of reason. In many respects, Locke, more than any psychological thinker of his day, was able to resolve the empiricist's dilemma of deriving all knowledge through the senses and to have a functioning mind that can reason apart from the senses.

Before mentioning the other ways in which reflection functions, it is useful to introduce another facet of Locke's psychological views, that of complex ideas. Simple ideas are received passively, but the mind can actively make ideas by putting them together in combinations.[45] Complex ideas are derived from a combination of simple ideas of sensation and simple ideas of reflection.[46] All ideas, even the most abstruse, remote, and abstract, arise from these two sources.[47] All complex ideas derive from the repetition and joining together of simple ideas from sense or reflection.

It is now appropriate to return to the question of reflection in order to consider those particular operations of the mind that involve complex as well as simple ideas. The mind contemplates both simple and complex ideas, discerns similarities and differences between them, compares and distinguishes them, and composes them in new arrangements. The process culminates when the mind begins to treat these ideas as abstractions and to use them to form general ideas.

How Locke viewed abstract ideas deserves special consideration since his successor, Berkeley, offered a very important critique of them. Locke argued that we join together ideas derived directly from sense or from reflection to form abstract ideas by considering some attributes common to several particular ideas and ignoring those aspects in which they differ. A number of objects, such as a sail, a bone, and a bowl of milk, can give us an idea of whiteness when we ignore the differences among the objects and concentrate on their similarity.

Complex ideas have their origins in the thoughts of men more than in the reality of things. Ideas are of utmost diversity as Locke himself illustrates by placing in the same list whiteness, hardness, thinking, motion, the human being, elephant, army, and drunkenness.[48] Complex ideas may be analyzed into simpler ones. Systematically analyzed complex ideas, considered in some detail by Locke, include substance; relation, including cause and effect; identity and diversity, including personal identity; and proportion. With this analysis complete, Locke proceeds to consider such issues as clarity and obscurity, distinctions and confusions, reality and fantasy, adequacy and inadequacy, and the truth and falsity of ideas.[49]

Drawing on what he had learned from Boyle and Newton, Locke extended the realm of natural law to the phenomena of the human mind. The material particles of Newton and the corpuscles of Boyle had their ideational counterpart in the ideas of the mind for which laws could be found. Without being explicit about it, to Locke ideas serve the same function for the mind that particles and corpuscles do for the physical nature. Ideas cohere as do the particles to form complex ideas. The bond that allows the ideas to cohere, of course, is association. In keeping with the Newtonian conception, Locke saw the individual as essentially static, pushed or pulled by external forces.

Feelings   Feelings play only a secondary role in Locke's psychological considerations. Pain and pleasure are simple ideas accompanying both sensation and reflection.[50] The passions, derived from the feelings, are modes or manifestations of pleasure and pain and include love, hatred, desire, joy, sorrow, hope, and anger. Basically, the passions are derivatives of good and evil in that they are identified by reference to the pleasure and the pain to which they give rise. Locke relates each passion to good and evil. Desire, for example, is the thought of some attainable good, whereas envy is the uneasiness we experience when someone obtains a good before we do.

Pleasure and pain are therefore defined by the ideas one has. Locke's views, deriving complex emotions from a base of simple pleasures and pains, were to have considerable effect on psychological theories throughout the eighteenth century.

Association of Ideas   The fame bestowed on Locke for coining the phrase "the association of ideas" is undeserved to some extent. His chapter bearing this title was not interpolated into the *Essay* until the fourth edition, published in 1700.[51]

His system of psychology was fully developed without recourse to the association of ideas. It is therefore fitting and proper that this topic be treated as an appendix to the rest of his thinking.

Earlier, Locke had stated that ideas are fixed in the memory by attention and repetition but, above all, by pleasure and pain.[52] "Hurts" and "advantages" to the body are taken notice of because of pleasure and pain. Reflection, as we have seen, is a means by which we combine a number of simple simultaneous experiences into a compound but single experience. He thus anticipated a more precise formulation of what later was called simultaneous association. He likewise referred the origin of complex ideas, even those most abstract, to the repetition and joining together of simple ideas.[53] Locke uses the changeableness of habits, as brought about by reflection, practice, application, and custom, to explain how we can change the agreeableness or disagreeableness of things.[54] Thus, Locke did not completely neglect the topic of the nature of habit and association.

Aside from the title itself, Locke uses the phrase "association of ideas" once in this relatively short chapter.[55] He makes no reference either to Aristotle or to Hobbes, and in no way does he refer to "laws of association." He approaches the topic by pointing out that there is something unreasonable in everyone, for, although each of us can readily perceive flaws in the reasoning of others, we are blinded to even much greater inadequacies in ourselves. How does this state of affairs come about? It is because of the wrong connections of ideas that occurred by chance or by custom in a particular individual. An example he gives is that of teaching children that goblins have more to do with darkness than with light and, as a consequence, finding that they are unable thereafter to separate the idea of darkness from the idea of goblins, so that now the dark brings with it these frightful ideas.

Influence

Locke's influence on later developments in psychology was varied and profound. In making understanding central to his work, Locke organized the higher mental processes into a field of psychology broader in nature than anything that could be investigated by physiological methods alone. He did much to set the limits of a psychology that was still relatively speculative and still continually subjective and dualistic, but that could later be separated more completely from philosophy.

After he denied the existence of innate ideas, Locke's strategy of starting with simple ideas that arise from experience and then trying to show that complex ideas are composed of simple ideas (with the aid of reflection) convinced many others of the validity and worth of empiricism. He may thus be said to have launched British empiricism.

Locke conceived of ideas of elements in a manner essentially similar to the particles of Newton. He held that the complex ideas of the mind were formed of these particles and were capable of analysis into units. This clearly molecular approach was to prove important; it was in vogue in the nineteenth and twentieth centuries, as epitomized in the views of Wundt and Titchener.

While disavowing an intention to consider physiological mechanisms in his account, Locke did introduce the mechanism of ideas in a manner that seemed to indicate his indebtedness to Newton's "minute particles" of matter. Like their physical counterparts, Locke conceived ideas as cohering to form aggregates in ways that have been detailed earlier. Locke was successful in establishing a basis for mental mechanisms.

To meet the difficulty of accounting for the higher intellectual processes, Locke postulated reflection as coordinate with sensation in the formation of experiences. In solving this problem, he altered his position to one that was not entirely empirical. In a sense, he substituted a native power of reflection for the innate ideas he had discarded. He made a concession to nativism that Hobbes had held was needless. Locke's concept of reflection was somewhat vague. This very vagueness was a spur to others to find a means of extending his principle of association in order to account for the origin of complex and derivative ideas.

In continuing the distinction between primary and secondary qualities and presenting them so graphically, Locke did much to draw attention to this distinction.

In a manner reminiscent of Aquinas, Locke referred to reflection as an internal sense. Locke made a distinction between being aware of an idea (reflection) and merely having an idea. The question of how the mind obtains knowledge of its own operations was thus solved; reflections were ideas about ideas. Act psychologists of the nineteenth century such as Franz Brentano made this distinction an important part of their approach, in that they distinguished between the mental act of function on one hand and mental content on the other.

In originating and illustrating the phrase "association of ideas," Locke made explicit the possibility of working out the interconnections and sequences of ideas as expressive of experiences. A reduction of the entire mental life to association would follow. As shown later, to this day association is one of the principal themes pervading psychology in an open or disguised form.

Finally, Locke's *Essay Concerning Human Understanding* (1690) initiated a continuous sequence of subsequent publications extending into our own century—from Berkeley, Locke's immediate successor, through Hume, Hartley, the Scottish School, the Mills, on to Alexander Bain.

The rest of this chapter is devoted to an account of these developments, with emphasis on the distinction, or lack of it, between primary and secondary qualities; the subjective nature of all ideas; the crucial importance of empiricism which was to become a viable alternative to rationalism; the opening up of the study of association to account for some forms of learning and to become important in perception; and encouragement of more cautious and parsimonious psychological interpretation required when trying to account for how ideas are associated with one another.

GEORGE BERKELEY

George Berkeley (1685–1753), a deeply religious man, was disturbed by the skeptical attitudes engendered by the materialistic thought that he believed was threatening to dominate the intellectual life of his time. The guiding themes of his writings were defense of religion and the refutation of skepticism. Berkeley believed that the new materialistic Newtonian science posed a danger to religion. It was not science that he wished to banish, however, but a belief in the primordial character of matter that allowed impious persons to deride immaterial (spiritual) substance, to consider the soul corruptible, and even to deny providence.[56] He held that spiritual and intellectual confusion arose from the belief in something independent of mind called matter. To Berkeley, this belief was a chimera.[57] Pursuing his theme he asked, "What sort of world does this science of matter in motion depict?" He concluded that it was the world as revealed by the senses. In an effort to combat the source of danger to religion, he turned to inquiry about mental life.

Life of Berkeley

George Berkeley was born in Ireland and was educated at Trinity College, Dublin.[58] By the time he arrived at school, his college included in its teachings the works of Descartes, Hobbes, Locke, and Newton. His academic progress was swift; he entered at fifteen, took his bachelor's degree at twenty, completed his master's degree and became a junior fellow at twenty-two, and received ordination as a deacon of the Anglican Church at twenty-four. At the same age, in the year 1709, he published the first account of his psychological-philosophical views in *An Essay Towards a New Theory of Vision.*[59] A year later he gave a more general statement in *A Treatise Concerning the Principles of Human Knowledge.* In one sense his life after the age of twenty-five is an anticlimax, since these two works are vastly more important than anything else he wrote later. Nevertheless, he had a full life—teaching at Trinity; further writing; visiting the London of Swift, Addison, and Steele, where he captivated society by his charm; traveling on the continent; and endeavoring to further educational and missionary enterprises in the American colonies. In connection with these benevolent efforts, he settled in America for nearly three years at Newport, Rhode Island. When his hopes for support from governmental grants were not realized, he returned to London, leaving his house, farm, and library to Yale University. On later occasions he also donated books to Harvard. For the last eighteen years of his life, Berkeley was Anglican Bishop of Cloyne in County Cork, Ireland.

Philosophical Position

The major arguments for Berkeley's philosophical position are psychological in nature. Before presenting them, a statement of this philosophical position is necessary, although the evidence is reserved for sections of the chapter that follow. To appreciate the full impact of his philosophical views, the psychological arguments are essential.

It is convenient to refer to Berkeley's philosophical position as "mentalism," a name given to it in later years because of his insistence that the mental aspects of life are paramount.[60]

The key to understanding Berkeley's position is found in his concept of "object." An object to Berkeley is a collection, a sum of sensations that have occurred together in experience and that habit makes it impossible to separate in our minds. The world is the sum total of our sensations. To illustrate:

> Take away the sensations of softness, moisture, redness, tartness, and you take away the cherry. Since it is not a being distinct from these sensations; a cherry, I say, is nothing but a congeries of sensible impressions or ideas perceived by various senses; which ideas are united into one thing (or have one name given them) by the mind because they are observed to attend each other.[61]

Thus, Berkeley's mentalism is the theory that our experience of objects is made up of a collection of impressions and ideas. An object comes to us not as a whole, but as a collection of impressions often from a number of senses. We think of the object as a single thing because the pattern of sensations repeats every time we come into contact with the object. The removal of any one component will alter the experience of the whole. As in Locke and Hobbes, the ideas are bonded together by that which will come to be known as association.

Berkeley was insisting on the primacy of consciousness. He declined to accept anyone else's perception, "so long as I myself am conscious of no such thing."[62] Only what one is conscious of is important, he said. One person's knowledge of another is derived only through ideas excited in oneself.[63]

Berkeley argued for direct observation of phenomena. These phenomena are real enough; their *esse is percipi*, he said.[64] Perception is his definition of reality; that is, appearances to him are real.[65] This position places him close to what we would today call a phenomenologist.[66] That perceived objects do not exist independently of perception is almost as classic a formulation of the phenomenologist's position as we have. The qualifying phrase, "close to," is necessary because Berkeley escaped the necessity of rejecting a real world. His use of the term "Infinite Perceiver" assured him of the persistence of objects even when they are not being perceived by any given individual. Anticipating much of Ernst Mach's analysis of Newtonian assumptions, Berkeley found no justification for Newton's conceptions of absolute space and time, and he argued that all motion was relative to the observer.[67] He declared unknowable not only matter but also Newtonian motion, time, and space.

Berkeley did not, however, deny the reality of matter merely because a person's own prowess allows certitude only of mental events. Based on his position on this issue, it follows that the unity of mental life cannot be explained by reference to the physical world. Berkeley raises some questions in this connection. The smell and the color of the rose are not "out there" to be experienced together. How then are they experienced together? Similarly, two people report the same sequence of events, but in explanation Berkeley could not appeal to the "stimulus objects" as we would call them. How can this come about? Furthermore, what makes a unity of the collection of experiences that belong to an individual mind? In answer, Berkeley decided that what holds experiences of this sort together is the soul, a logically necessary but supernatural substratum of our experience. Moreover, there must be an active cause for the continued experience of the "works of nature." This cause Berkeley found in God.[68] The "Permanent Perceiver"—God—guaranteed a persistence of physical objects. This phase of his thinking is captured neatly in the famous pair of limericks by Ronald Knox:[69]

> There was a young man who said, "God
> Must think it exceedingly odd
>   If he finds that this tree
>   Continues to be
> When there's no one about in the Quad."

> Dear Sir:
>   Your astonishment's odd:
> I am always about in the Quad.
>   And that's why the tree
>   Will continue to be,
>   Since observed by
>   Yours faithfully,
>   God.

Berkeley's views on these matters created a sensation, not only in scholarly circles, but throughout literate society as well. To the common-sense person he had advanced a paradox because he was misinterpreted as saying that the object itself, say a rock, was imaginary. When Boswell challenged Samuel Johnson to refute Berkeley, Johnson gave a stone a mighty kick and replied, "I refute it thus." As is sometimes the way of the world, this refutation, irrelevant to the issue at hand (because, to Berkeley, the idea of rock had among its associated ideas that of hardness), is perhaps better known than the doctrine that it was intended to demolish.

Psychological Views

In the first section of the *Principles,* Berkeley presented a short statement of the basic principles of his system of psychology.[70] He asserted that the objects of human knowledge could be reduced to ideas imprinted on the senses, perceptions obtained by attending to the passions and the operations of the mind, and ideas formed by the help of memory and imagination. To Berkeley, these are the molecular elements of mental life. The collective acts of knowing the objects of knowledge or perceiving them and exercising such operations as willing, imagining, or remembering them, Berkeley called mind, spirit, soul, or "myself." This mind is not one of these ideas but something distinct from them.

Experience and Reality   It will be remembered that Hobbes denied that psychological qualities are actually inherent in the object. Locke held that we know only through ideas, yet he made a distinction between primary and secondary qualities, with only the primary inhering in the object. Berkeley asked, then, how do we know the reality of the objects of the world?[71] If we know everything through ideas, as Locke said, how can we know by means of ideas that some qualities inhere in objects whereas others do not?[72] Berkeley wondered how Locke could know from experience that which was not derived from experience. Locke had asserted something that he could not have experienced. The same arguments that are cogent in respect to secondary qualities, Berkeley argued, apply equally to primary qualities. Berkeley insisted that all ideas are similar to what Locke had called secondary qualities. Primary as well as secondary qualities are merely sensational—or ideas, as Berkeley calls them—and an idea exists in the mind perceiving it.[73] In one bold stroke Berkeley reduced primary qualities to secondary qualities. We never know anything but our experiences. As far as Berkeley is concerned, the world is a plausible but unproved hypothesis. Moreover, he held that it is a hypothesis that can never be proved by naturalistic means, since we know only our own experience. Berkeley's answer to the question of how we can ever obtain a belief in the existence of an external world was to invert Locke's proposition that ideas enter into the mind from outside by means of the senses, since all we know are the ideas of which the mind is constituted.

Empiricism and Sensation   In spite of his divergences from Hobbes and Locke, Berkeley was still an empiricist.[74] Although he disagreed with them on the nature of the outer and inner worlds, he still agreed that knowledge could be established by verification through direct experience derived from the senses. It is sometimes said that he denied the evidence of the senses. On the contrary, he accepted the evidence of ideas but considered himself forced to find the existence of the world behind subjective phenomena on other grounds. It will also be seen that his theory of space perception is uncompromisingly empiricist in nature.

The crucial role of experience is clearly established in Berkeley's handling of the relations among sensory experiences. Ideas are classified by the separate sense departments. Hence, vision, touch, smell, taste, and hearing are five classes of sense ideas with which we are born. Berkeley insisted that ideas within each sense department are distinct, that is to say, separate and not overlapping. The smell of the rose and the color of the rose are distinct sensations, and are not innately intermingled in any way. The ideas to which they give rise are distinct from one another. No idea is common to both, and yet somehow they manage to be combined. It is evident that Berkeley had to find a combinatory factor; he found it in experience. It is only loose terminology when we refer to both seeing and hearing a coach, as if they were a single experience. One says that one "hears" a coach half a mile away. Strictly speaking, one hears only a certain sound that suggests a coach. The sound itself is no distance at all. Seeing is exactly analogous—I say that I see a coach in the distance, but what is actually seen serves merely to suggest a coach at that distance. Nevertheless, one can infer that it is the same coach because the ideas have been observed to go together constantly and are spoken of as one and the same thing. What one visualizes and what one hears are different things, but because they are united by experience, it becomes natural to treat them as one experience.

Association   Locke had doubted that a man born blind, but who by some circumstance was later able to see, would be able to distinguish by vision a cube from a triangle even though both were known to him by touch. Berkeley unequivocally agreed.[75] The blind man now having sight would have to have new experiences, wherein sight and touch would be associated, just as a man born blind would have no idea of distance by means of vision and would have need of experience before being able to see. In this and in his explicit discussion of association, he made the point that ideas are associated when they are connected in experience.

Berkeley's classification of the principles of association—although he did not use that term—was more inclusive than Locke's, and, even more important, he used it to account for normal associations.[76] He neatly summarized the nature of simultaneous association in the first paragraph of the *Principles*.[77] He states that complex ideas are formed because the ideas of sight (light and color), touch (hardness and softness), smell (odor), and so on accompany each other and come to be marked by one name. As an illustration, a certain color, taste, smell, figure, and consistency which have been observed to go together, we call apple. Elsewhere he writes:

> [M]en combine together several ideas apprehended by diverse senses or by the same sense at different times or in different circumstances, but observed, however, to have some connexion in Nature either with respect to co-existence or succession; all which they refer to one name and consider as one thing.[78]

Contiguity of sensation is the basis for a simultaneous association of ideas. Berkeley also specifies successive association and distinguishes among association by similarity, causality, and coexistence.[79]

Abstract Ideas   Because ideas arise from within separate sense departments, it is not surprising that Berkeley denied the existence of abstract ideas.[80] An abstract idea must involve material derived from several senses; otherwise, even advocates of the reality of abstract ideas would have to deny altogether that sensory content is present. For Berkeley, ideas are restricted to perceptions and images—and these come from sense and are always particular. Under such circumstances, Berkeley could not admit that abstractions were images presented to the mind. He did agree that we can form general ideas that stand for whole groups of phenomena. However, we can form no ideas from common content since there is no common content. We merely have words to denote this common element, but have no new ideas of it, strictly speaking. We can have words to connote such common features of perceived objects, but we cannot have new ideas of a strictly abstract content. We can emphasize the triangularity of a figure without attending to its other qualities, but Berkeley could not, try as he might, frame a definite idea of a triangle abstractly without any of these qualities.[81]

Mental processes, he held, are always particular.[82] A general idea is just as particular as the idea of any single object. The idea simply becomes general by standing for or representing all other particular ideas of the same sort.

Visual Perception and Space   Berkeley's first presentation of his psychological thinking was *An Essay Towards a New Theory of Vision*.[83] It is psychology's first monograph and, in many ways, his most important work. Accordingly, it will serve to integrate what has been said as well as to bring us back to his attack on materialism.

Berkeley embarked on his famous analysis of the problem of distance perception because of an objection to immaterialism that can be stated as follows. It was argued that we actually see things at a distance from ourselves, and consequently things exist independently of the mind. Most people think external objects can be seen and that direction and distance, as such, can be seen. "Out there" is a road, and beyond the road, a tree, and in the far distance there is a range of hills. Objects seem spread out before us, making us rebel against a contention that we have no knowledge of space from direct perception of it. Locke had said that perception occurs only mediately or indirectly by means of images or resemblance. Yet these images are still images of external things. To be consistent Berkeley had to go further and deny these external things if his argument of the immateriality of the external world was to gain acceptance. He did so by an analysis of visual perception.

Berkeley argued that the various properties of depth perception—shape, magnitude, distance, and the relative situation of objects—are not perceived directly by the eye but are learned after visual sensations have been associated with sensations of "touch" (in which he included movement in space, as in reaching and walking).[84] He went on to say that pictures cast on the retina are flat and give no suggestion of the distances of objects from the eye. Nor does the degree of convergence of the eyes (as visual receivers) give us a clue to distance.[85] In this work on visual perception Berkeley did not appeal to association as such, but to what he called "uniting" in experience. It is evident that he meant association. To Berkeley, distance perception was not a "given," immediately experienced, but something mediate that had to be learned. Berkeley believed he had demonstrated that sight and touch as expressed in movement have nothing intrinsically in common; "customary connexion" leads them to a common result. Space is not known directly but through this "connexion." This is essentially an experiential theory of visual perception of distance based on empiricism.

Berkeley's theory of space perception is a definite contribution to psychology since he demonstrated that distance or depth is not a sensation but an additional aspect of visual data. He reduced an apparently simple experience to the more primitive psychological experiences on which it was based. By stating that our perceptions of distance and magnitude are capable of reduction into simpler elements, he encouraged those who came after him to attempt to analyze other experiences into elements, thus perpetuating the molecular approach. Berkeley made clear that the problem of knowledge is not solely a philosophical problem, but a distinctively psychological one as well.

DAVID HUME

David Hume (1711–1776) was born in Scotland and educated at Edinburgh.[86] As a youth he gave his family some cause for misgivings about his future; his mother said of him that he was "a fine, good-natured crater but uncommon weak-minded." She was probably wrong about his intelligence; at least he later became Undersecretary of State. After several false starts he found his field in philosophical writing, but he was never satisfied with the acclaim that his writings received. Indeed, the reception of *A Treatise of Human Nature,* published anonymously before he was thirty, although it sold fairly well, fell so far below his high expectations that he was led to exclaim that it "fell dead-born from the press."[87] He recast the first part of the *Treatise* into what was later called *An Enquiry Concerning Human Understanding*, which, during his lifetime, had little more impact than its predecessor.[88] However, he did enjoy widespread popularity from other writings, particularly a history of England. While serving in various governmental posts, he was frustrated in his attempts to secure a professorship; his unorthodox religious convictions and the skepticism of his views made him suspect to the establishment.

In introducing his *Enquiry*, Hume defined his investigation as that of moral philosophy or the science of human nature.[89] A person was a natural object in a world of nature, to be studied by the methods of natural science; thus, Hume clearly affirmed his adherence to a naturalistic prescription. Moral subjects, in contrast to physical subjects, included ethics, politics, criticism, and logic conceived of as the art of reasoning.[90] He advanced this new psychological science to show that some things previously taken as inalienable features of the universe were actually characteristics of one's own psychological makeup projected onto the world.

Hume argued that we can do more than merely describe the operations of mental life; we can find the principles on which these operations are based.[91] Astronomers, he goes on to say, patiently studied the motion, order, and magnitude of the stars. Finally, a philosopher (Newton) determined the laws and the forces by which they are directed. Can we not, given equal capacity and caution, do the same with mental life? He answered in the affirmative because he thought he had found the law that corresponded to the law of gravitation in the physical world, the law of association of ideas, which seemed to him the universal principle of human nature.

Mental contents, Hume held, are of two sorts—the impressions arising from sensing, feeling, and willing, which are vivid and strong, and the ideas (images and thoughts, we might call them) that are less clear and fainter copies of impressions.[92] He specifically refused to assign any ultimate cause to impressions. He probably did not wish to deal with the source of external objects; at any rate he held that impressions are the given elements from which all else starts. Ideas are derived from impressions. As he put it, we must learn from experience that fire burns and that water is wet.

To Hume, memory and imagination are not faculties but names for the two different ways in which ideas work.[93] Memory is distinguished from imagination by its greater clarity and vivacity and by the fact that the order of memories repeats the succession of the original impressions. Imagination is not as clear as impressions nor does it follow the same order, but it is relatively free in the course its reconstructions may take. Imagination may be compounded by transposition, augmentation, or diminution, but is still dependent on material afforded by experience.[94]

Hume assigned three principles or laws of association to account for mental operations: resemblance (similarity), contiguity in place or time, and causality.[95] Among his illustrations of these principles are the following. A picture leads our thoughts to the original (resemblance), the mention of one apartment in a building leads to mention of others (contiguity), and if we think of a wound, we can scarcely avoid consideration of the pain that follows (causality).

As Hume's thinking developed, he seems to have become aware that causality was not on the same level of operation as the other two forms of association, and, without eliminating it from the list of the three principles, he reduced it to a special case of the other two. The relation of causality, he concluded, is not an ultimate law of the association of ideas but rests on the two primary relations of similarity and space–time contiguity. One phenomenon follows another, and we come to expect it to happen again.

All reasoning about factual matters, Hume said, seems to be founded on the relation of cause and effect.[96] What is the origin of our notion of cause? A billiard ball moves and knocks against another billiard ball, which also begins to move. Hume held that, despite this sequence, nothing in the motion of the first ball suggests the necessity of the movement of the second. No intuition reveals the power whereby one object produces another. All we comprehend is one phenomenon following another. The senses do not supply the ideas of a necessary connection. Are these ideas due to reflection?[97] Consider, he says, the motion of our bodies when following the command of our will. Throughout the succession of events we are completely conscious, but can we tell how this operation is affected? Hume held that we cannot, and he considered that it must forever escape our most diligent inquiry. Reflection does not supply the answer. All that we know is that the command of the will is followed by the action. We observe the succession of two phenomena—nothing more.

The mind cannot find the effect in the supposed cause, no matter how acute the scrutiny since the effect is totally different from the cause.[98] Frequent and invariable sequences make us assume that the effect must occur because the cause has occurred. Actually, there is no necessary relation of phenomena as is ordinarily implied by the concept of causality. A person cannot tell from the transparency and the fluidity of water that immersion will suffocate him.[99] Instead, we know from experience that objects are conjoined with similar ones. Hence, we can formulate another definition of cause and speak of it as "one object followed by another, the appearance of which always conveys the thought to that other."[100] To Hume, cause is recurrent concomitance. Thus, the relation of causality is reduced to similarity and succession. Causality is a habit of mind originating in experience and the association of ideas. Causal experience is nothing more than customary expectation. The consciousness of determination, which pervades our view of causality, is false. Objectively considered, causality is regularity of contiguous sequence. The necessity of cause–effect exists only in the mind, not in objects.[101] Hume is sometimes misinterpreted as denying causation. He did not. He merely shifted the locus of causality from the external world to the mind in keeping with his theme mentioned earlier.

Hume held that the principle of connection between our ideas is habit.[102] Habit, he said, is the universal law of mind, explaining not only our external perceptions, but all our experiences. As it has been put, "empiricism becomes associationism."[103] When two objects or two events are found constantly joined together, we infer one from the other. For example, flame has in the past been conjoined with heat and snow with cold, so the presentation of one part of these pairs will lead the mind to expect the other part. For this connection to take place not one experience but several experiences are necessary to establish a habit.

Hume reduced the mind to impressions and association of impressions. On introspective examination, Hume stated that he always came on particular impressions and never more than impressions.[104] What is termed the mind is essentially nothing more than a bundle of sensations.[105] This conception of mind was to have a long history, culminating in the structural psychologies of Wilhelm Wundt and Edward B. Titchener.

Hume's clear recognition of the importance of association and his formulation of the laws of association were crucial. Locke had never even considered using association as an explanation of mind and its functioning, but had relegated it to an explanation for abnormal connection between ideas. Later psychologists owe a great deal to Hume's theory that compounds of impressions and ideas give us more intricate mental phenomena.

The significance of what Hume called his "very curious discovery"—that our knowledge of causation results from experience of habitual sequences of perceptions of events—was not fully appreciated during his lifetime but has since had great influence.[106] Hereafter all individuals concerned with the problem of determinism had to take into consideration Hume's devastating criticism that we could not prove causality since experience gave us only concomitance or succession of events. Kant's reaction to it is especially noteworthy. The tendency in present-day psychology to refer to antecedent and consequent conditions rather than to cause and effect has its roots in Hume's criticism.

We can trace a clear-cut progression of thought about the nature of experience and mind from Locke through Berkeley to Hume. Locke held that experience arose directly or basically from sense impression, but he accepted the existence of objects similar to, though not identical with, our ideas. Berkeley denied the existence of objects insofar as we know them is concerned, but he held that soul or mind is necessary to make experiences cohere or hold together. Hume took the obvious next step of questioning the existence of mind, reducing it to a collection of impressions from which all else starts.

SUMMARY

Newton, the seminal figure among the major English empiricists, demonstrated that material nature may be studied successfully by considering that one is dealing with particles propelled by force into motion or changes of motion. Without being too explicit about their source, Locke applied Newtonian materialistic conceptions to mental life; Berkeley directly attacked Newton's materialistic implications by denying that matter was involved, but otherwise accepted his thinking; Hume directly and avowedly applied Newtonian materialistic conceptions to the mind.

Empiricism, a prescription to which all of these figures subscribed, became a viable alternative to rationalism. The quantitative and methodological objectivism of the physical sciences was evident to these students of human nature, and they made some beginnings in following these leads. There was a skepticism about reaching absolute certainty either avowed or expressed implicitly. The caution they displayed in the kind of evidence offered moved in the direction of a greater methodological objectivism. Despite Berkeley's spirited and brilliant appeal to supernaturalism and the Scottish realists' dogged defense of it (which we will discuss in the next chapter), naturalism was becoming more commonplace. The importance of ideas and the way they were combined resulted in the acceptance of centralism, dualism, contentual subjectivism, and molecularism. Hobbes alone raised some objections to centralism, dualism, and contentual subjectivism.

NOTES

1. An excellent authoritative source for the early history of the Royal Society is the account of Dorothy Stimson, *Scientists and Amateurs, A History* of the *Royal Society* (New York: Schuman, 1948); R. K. Merton's "Science, Technology and Society in Seventeenth Century England," *Osiris, 4* (1938): 360–362, is a detailed quantitative study that brings out clearly, among other findings, the utilitarian character of much of the science and technology of the time.
2. I. Newton, "An Hypothesis Explaining the Properties of Light Discoursed in My Several Papers," in T. Birch, ed., *History of the Royal Society of London* (London: Millar, 1757), Vol. III, pp. 262–263 (1675) (Herrnstein and Boring, Excerpt No. 2).
3. Newton, *Opticks,* Book 1, part 2, props. 5–6 (Herrnstein and Boring, Excerpt No. 3).
4. T. Hobbes, *Leviathan,* ed. Nelle Fuller, in R. M. Hutchins, ed., *The Great Books of the Western World,* Vol. XXIII, pp. 49–283 (1651), Part 1, Chapter 26.
5. *Ibid.*
6. T. Hobbes, "Human Nature," ed. W. Molesworth, in R. S. Peters, ed., *Body, Man and Citizen* (New York: Collier Books, 1962), pp. 182–244 (1650).
7. *Ibid.,* Chapter 1, Conclusion; *Leviathan,* Introduction.
8. *Ibid.,* Part I, Chapter 13, p. 85.
9. Gordon Allport, "The Historical Background of Modern Social Psychology," in Gardner Lindzey, ed., *Handbook of Social Psychology* (Reading, Mass.: Addison–Wesley, 1954), 1, 13–14.
10. T. Hobbes, *Human Nature,* Part I, Chapter 2.
11. *Ibid.,* Part I, Chapters 2, 7.
12. *Ibid.,* Part I, Chapters 1, 2, 7.
13. T. Hobbes, *Leviathan,* Part 1, Chapter 2.
14. T. Hobbes, *Human Nature,* Chapter 2, Sec. 4.
15. *Ibid.,* p. 185.
16. T. Hobbes, *Leviathan,* Part II, Chapter 30 (Herrnstein and Boring, Excerpt No. 66).
17. *Ibid.,* Part I, Chapter 3.
18. *Ibid.,* Part I, Chapter 6.
19. *Ibid.,* Part I, Chapter 11, p. 76.
20. *Ibid.,* Part I, Chapter 6.
21. *Ibid.,* Part I, Chapter 5, Part II, Chapter 19.
22. *Ibid.,* Part II, Chapter 27.
23. T. Hobbes, *Human Nature,* Chapter 12.
24. An excellent account, not only of his life, but also of his views on philosophy, psychology, ethics, education, and politics, is to be found in R. I. Aaron, *John Locke,* 3rd ed. (Oxford: Clarendon Press, 1971).
25. *Ibid.*

26. J. Locke, *An Essay Concerning Human Understanding*, 6th ed., collated and annotated by A. C. Frazer, *ibid.*, pp. 85–395 (1690).
27. J. Locke, *Essay.*
28. J. Locke, *The Conduct of the Understanding* (New York: Alden, 1883) (1706).
29. J. Locke, *Essay*, Epistle to the Reader, p. 87.
30. *Ibid.*, Introduction, 2.
31. *Ibid.*, Introduction, 3, p. 94.
32. *Ibid.*, Book I, Chapter I.
33. *Ibid.*, Book I, Chapter I, Sec. 25.
34. *Ibid.*, Book I, Chapter IV, Sec. 24.
35. *Ibid.*, Book I, Chapter II, Sec. 22.
36. *Ibid.*, Book I, Chapter I, Sec. 15, p. 98.
37. *Ibid.*, Book II, Chapter I, Sec. 25.
38. *Ibid.*, Book II, Chapter II, Sec. 1.
39. *Ibid.*, Book IV, Chapter IV.
40. *Ibid.*, Book II, Chapter II.
41. *Ibid.*, Book II, Chapter VIII (Herrnstein and Boring, Excerpt No. 5).
42. *Ibid.*, Book II, Chapter I, Secs. 1–4 (Herrnstein and Boring, Excerpt No. 104).
43. *Ibid.*, Book II, Chapter VIII, Sec. 8.
44. *Ibid.*, Book II, Chapter IX, Sec. 1.
45. *Ibid.*, Book II, Chapter XXII, Sec. 2.
46. *Ibid.*, Book II, Chapter XIII.
47. *Ibid.*, Book II, Chapter XII, Sec. 8.
48. *Ibid.*, Book II, Chapter I, Sec. 1.
49. *Ibid.*, Book II, Chapters XXIX–XLII.
50. *Ibid.*, Book II, Chapter XX.
51. *Ibid.*, Book II, Chapter XXXIII (Herrnstein and Boring, Excerpt No. 67).
52. *Ibid.*, Book II, Chapter X, Sec. 3.
53. *Ibid.*, Book II, Chapter XII, Sec. 8.
54. *Ibid.*, Book II, Chapter XXI, Sec. 71.
55. *Ibid.*, Book II, Chapter XXXIII.
56. G. Berkeley, *A Treatise Concerning the Principles of Human Knowledge*, in R. M. Hutchins, ed., *The Great Books of the Western World*, Vol. XXXV, pp. 404–444 (1710), Sec. 93.
57. *Ibid.*, Sec. 87.
58. The definitive statement of his life and works is by A. A. Luce, *The Life of George Berkeley, Bishop of Cloyne* (London: Nelson, 1949).
59. G. Berkeley, *An Essay Towards a New Theory of Vision*, A. A. Luce and T. E. Jessop, eds., *Works* (London: Nelson, 1949), Vol. I, pp. 159–239 (1709).
60. R. A. Tsanoff, *The Great Philosophers* (New York: Harper and Brothers, 1953), p. 365.
61. G. Berkeley, *Three Dialogues Between Hylas and Philonus,"* in A. A. Luce and T. E. Jessop, eds., *Works*, Vol. II, pp. 171–263 (1713). Third Dialogue, p. 249.
62. G. Berkely, *New Theory*, 12, p. 173.
63. G. Berkely, *Principles*, Sec. 145.
64. *Ibid.*, Sec. 3, p. 413.
65. *Ibid.*, Sec 35.
66. G. A. Ferguson, "A Note on George Berkeley," *Canadian Journal of Psychology*, VII (1953): 156–158.
67. G. Berkely, *Principles*, Sec. 12, 98, 117.
68. *Ibid.*, Secs. 146–147.

69. R. Knox quoted in B. Russell, *A History of Western Philosophy* (New York: Simon and Schuster, 1945), p. 648.
70. G. Berkely, *Principles*, Sec. 1.
71. *Ibid.*, Sec. 10, 14–15.
72. *Ibid.*, Secs. 9–15.
73. *Ibid.*, Sec. 1.
74. E.g., Berkely, *Principles*, Sec. 30.
75. G. Berkely, *New Theory*, 41–42, 50.
76. Another summary of his way of conceiving the connection among ideas is given in G. Berkeley, "The Theory of Vision Vindicated and Explained," in A. A. Luce and T. E. Jessop, eds., *Works*, Vol. I, pp. 251–276 (1733) (Herrnstein and Boring, Excerpt No. 68).
77. G. Berkely, *Principles*, Sec. 1.
78. G. Berkely, *Dialogues*, Third Dialogue, p. 245.
79. H. C. Warren, *A History of the Association Psychology* (New York: Charles Scribner's Sons, 1921), p. 245.
80. G. Berkely, *Principles*, Introduction, Secs. 6–25.
81. *Ibid.*, Introduction, Sec. 13.
82. *Ibid.*, Introduction, Sec. 10.
83. G. Berkely, *New Theory* (Herrnstein and Boring, Excerpts Nos. 28, 36).
84. *Ibid.*, 16–28, 52–87, 111–112, 121–159.
85. *Ibid.*, 2–15.
86. F. C. Mossner, *The Life of David Hume* (London: Nelson, 1954).
87. D. Hume, *A Treatise of Human Nature*, 2 vols., ed. A. D. Lindsay (London: Dent, 1911) (1739–1740).
88. D. Hume, *An Enquiry Concerning Human Understanding*, ed. L. A. Selby–Bigge, in R. M. Hutchins, ed., *The Great Books of the Western World*, Vol. XXXV, pp. 449–509 (1748).
89. *Ibid.*, Div. 1, p. 451.
90. D. Hume, *Treatise*, Preface.
91. D. Hume, *Enquiry*, 9.
92. *Ibid.*, 12. (Herrnstein and Boring, Excerpt No. 69, involves another edition of Div. 11–17.)
93. D. Hume, *Treatise*, Book I, Part I, Sec. III.
94. D. Hume, *Enquiry*, Div. 13.
95. *Ibid.*, Div. 19.
96. *Ibid.*, Div. 24–25.
97. *Ibid.*, Div. 48–57.
98. *Ibid.*, Div. 24.
99. *Ibid.*, Div. 23.
100. *Ibid.*, Div. 60.
101. D. Hume, *Treatise*, Book I, Part III, Sec. XIV.
102. D. Hume, *Enquiry*, Div. 36.
103. P. Janet and G. Seailles, *A History of the Problems of Philosophy*, Part I, Psychology (New York: Macmillan Co., 1902), p. 369.
104. D. Hume, *Treatise*, Book I, Part IV, Sec. VI.
105. *Ibid.*, Book I, Part IV, Sec. IV.
106. D. Hume, *An Abstract of a Treatise of Human Nature*, in A. Flew, ed., *David Hume: On Human Nature and the Understanding* (New York: Collier, 1962), pp. 287–302, p. 294 (1740).

Top: Portrait of John Stuart Mill. *Bottom:* Print of Julien La Mettrie.

Associationism and Mechanism: Two Wings of Empiricism

*A*s we have seen in Chapter 9, the essential notion that separates contentual empiricism from rationalism is the source of knowledge. Empiricists hold that the original and primary source of our knowledge comes through the senses. Rationalists, on the other hand, tend toward the view that our true knowledge is internal and usually inborn. Empiricists, then, emphasize "nurture" over "nature," the environment over instincts, and learning over innate sources of knowledge.

In the late eighteenth century and throughout the nineteenth century, several approaches to empirical psychological thought emerged. Two lines of empirical thought of particular significance to modern psychology are associationism and mechanism. They can hardly be called opposing camps since they shared basic assumptions as to the source of knowledge. Some individuals such as David Hartley and to a lesser degree Alexander Bain had a foot in each camp. Still, associationism and mechanism generally represent different forms of explanation of psychological phenomena. The associationists, like most of the British empiricists before them, excluding Hobbes, explained psychological phenomena primarily in terms of lawful relations among ideas existing quite apart from any bodily context. Once sensations came through the sense organs and became ideas, the body was of little concern. As such, the associationists were similar to many of the learning theorists of the twentieth century who model the processes of learning without any attempt to explain what nervous or brain processes are involved. The mechanists tended not only to explain mental phenomena in terms of bodily processes, but also they often dealt with the two as identical. Brain action is mind, mind is brain action, they said. Although the associationists tended to hold views of psychophysical dualism, coming closest to the mechanists with dualistic forms of psychophysical parallelism, the mechanists tended more toward psychophysical monism, the identity of mind as body.

ASSOCIATIONISM

David Hume, like Berkeley, Locke, and Hobbes before him, made use of concepts closely related to what we now call association. Locke made use of the term, although it was not as central to his views. For Hume, association became the fundamental law of human nature. Still, none of these empiricists attempted to formulate their notions of association into definite principles and doctrines. For association to be raised to the level of a doctrine and become the foundation of a formal school we have to turn to David Hartley.

David Hartley

David Hartley (1705–1759) is important to associationism not so much for his original thought but for his ability to summarize the ideas of his predecessors and to synthesize their concepts and notions of association into a definite doctrine. It is with Hartley that notions on association become the laws of association and associational theorizing becomes associationism. Clarity and comprehensiveness, rather than subtlety, mark the account of association contained in Hartley's *Observations on Man*, first published in 1749.[1] With it Hartley built the framework for associationism as a formal school of thought. He is thus best known as a promoter of associationism.

Life of Hartley   Hartley was the son of a minister in the Church of England and was himself destined to be a minister. Unlike his father, however, Hartley had unorthodox views about religion. For example, he rejected the belief in eternal damnation and thus was unable to sign the Thirty-nine Articles, a document required for membership in the Church of England. Since this stand made the idea of being a Church of England minister somewhat impractical, he decided on a career in medicine instead and spent the remainder of his life in that profession. It was the influence of Isaac Newton's writings on the vibrations of an ether-causing sensation and of John Locke's ideas on the association of ideas that seem to have been the starting point for much of Hartley's psychological thinking. Although he was a contemporary of Hume, he was probably not strongly influenced by him since Hartley began writing and publishing in a minor way on psychological matters before the appearance of Hume's *Treatise.* Hartley primarily acknowledged the influence of John Gay (1669–1745), a clergyman who wrote on association as applied to problems of moral judgments.[2] Although Hartley's work on the association of ideas is typically dated with the publication of his *Observations,* he actually published a treatise on the subject as early as 1746.[3] It was published in Latin, however, and did not have the impact of his *Observations.*

Hartley was deeply interested in morality, and he showed his religious bent in his *Observations.* Besides dealing with association and even physiology, the book also contains sections devoted to ethical and theological matters. Hartley justified the relationship between association and ethics by the argument that if we know how associations are formed, we gain the power to see to it that good associations are cherished and that sinful ones are rooted out. It is, however, the psychological and physiological rather than the social and religious aspects of Hartley's *Observations* that have been of primary influence on the line that came after him.

Part of the reason why Hartley's associationist thought was of more influence than his physiological and particularly more than his religious thought has to do with how Hartley's works were edited after his death. In 1775 Joseph Priestley arranged republication of the portion of Hartley's *Observations* that was devoted to psychology, excluding both physiology and theology.[4] It was only in 1791, fifty years after original publication, that Hartley's son issued another arrangement that was widely recognized as a clear statement of Hartley's views on morality as well as on physiology and psychology.[5] Until then the religious and moral aspect, which Hartley appears to have believed to be at least as important as the other parts, had been largely ignored.

Hartley's Psychophysical Parallelism   Locke's deliberate omission of physiology, Berkeley's idealism, and Hume's skepticism had exempted them from any need to pay attention to the relationship between physiological and mental processes. These empiricists considered mental events quite apart from the body once the sensation became an idea. It was Hartley's work that restored the body, specifically the brain and its functioning as the underlying foundation for mental events. For this reason Hartley, like Hobbes, is difficult to classify as being strictly associationistic or mechanistic.

As we can see in the very first sentence of his introduction to *Observations*— "Man Consists of Two Parts, Body and Mind"[6]—Hartley viewed human beings as having both a physical and mental aspect. Both must be studied because body and mind are related.[7] In the arrangement of the material in the 1791 edition, thereafter most widely used, Hartley presents the mental and bodily aspects in consecutive propositional form, one proposition dealing with the mind and the following one with the body. Thus, one proposition states that sensations, often repeated, leave certain vestiges that may be called simple ideas.[8] The companion proposition holds that sensory vibrations, being often repeated, leave in the brain a disposition for repetition of similar but minute vibrations.[9] Often the pairs of propositions are identical in form except that the psychological term is replaced in the second by a physiological one. What makes Hartley more of an associationist and less of a true mechanist is that he holds that mind is a separate substance from body. He declines to take the extra step that the French mechanists would take in identifying mind as bodily process. It is quite likely that he refused to take this step, even though many of his other ideas seem to direct him toward mechanism, because he feared compromising the notion of an immaterial soul. Instead, he held to a form of psychophysical parallelism that would save him from facing up to the issue.

The doctrine of vibration suggested by Newton's account of motion, Hartley tells us, is his starting point.[10] Newton had spoken of physical impulses as vibratory. Hartley held that external physical vibrations set in motion the white medullary substance of the brain with which sensations are intimately associated.[11] Changes in physical vibrations entail corresponding changes in the brain. Hartley insists that the nerves are solid, and are not tubes; this position necessitated his postulation that vibrations transmit movement from one part of the body to another.

Hartley held that cerebral vibrations and ideas run parallel to each other. One is not the cause of the other; they simply show consistent correspondence. Events in one are correlated perfectly with events in the other; that is, they are psychophysically parallel. It is sufficient for Hartley that there is a "certain connection of one kind or other between the sensations of the soul, and the motions excited in the medullary substance of the brain."[12] It would be left to others to take the next step and devise a thoroughly mechanistic view of mind.

Hartley's primary impact on the thought of his time had to do not with mind–body relationships but with the doctrine of association. Hartley agreed with Locke that the mind at birth is a blank.[13] Simple sensations are the original source of knowledge in Hartley's system. Sensations are internal states of the mind arising from impressions made by external objects; all other internal states are ideas.

Hartley's Law of Association   Hartley's best known contribution to the history of psychology was his work on association and his popularization of association as a formal school of thought. His "law of association," a principle of the growth of sensation and ideas, is that of contiguity, both synchronous (simultaneous) and successive.[14] The passage from sensation to idea or from idea to idea occurs because of associative contiguity. One is able to induce the other provided one has occurred in the past frequently, in conjunction with the other.[15] Later, the occurrence of one in sensation induces the other from ideas. By means of this "law of contiguity," Hartley explained memory, emotion, reasoning, and voluntary and involuntary action.

One or two illustrations might be given. When sensory vibrations subside, they leave their trace in fainter vibrations, the "vibratiuncles." Like Hobbes's "decaying sense," they are the sources of memory and imagination. (Seeing a tree and remembering a tree are two sets of vibrations differing only in intensity.) Vibrations are aroused by means of association. That is, when two sensations occur, either simultaneously or successively, they become connected so that when one is evoked again at a later time, the vibrations extend to the other, and we have an idea of that other. Associations are strengthened when vibration is greater. Under these circumstances, the association will be "cemented" sooner and stronger than is the case when the vibrations are less powerful.

Since association is both simultaneous and successive, for Hartley it becomes the basis for mental compounds or "clusters and combinations," as he calls them.[16] Simple ideas mix to form compounds just as letters coalesce into syllables and words. However, if the simple ideas in a particular compound are numerous, they may not be discernible in the complex because each single idea is overpowered by the sum of all the rest.

Hartley also broadened the conception of association to include motor activities: a movement may recall an idea; an idea may recall a movement. Ideas associated with movements form the basis for voluntary action. Muscular movements repeated in this same sequence become associated into automatic habits. His discussion of voluntary and involuntary action[17] attempts to relate the two, asserting that association by contiguity explains both how automatic movements come under voluntary control and how voluntary movements become automatic.

Hartley discusses the special senses in detail in a manner that distinguishes the dual roles of vibration and association.[18] Color, excited by an object, is a vibration of the rays that extend to the eye. In the eye the external vibration is changed to a backward and forward vibration of the nerve that extends to the brain, the seat of intelligence.

Hartley proceeds to apply the twin doctrines of vibrations and association to a number of other topics, ranging over sexual desires, respiration, words and associated ideas, passions or affections, memory, and imagination.[19] In so doing, he appears to be reasonably consistent.[20] He closes the portion of the volume devoted to psychological matters with a defense of determinism, although he continues to maintain that there is a difference between involuntary and voluntary motions. He argues that to state that "A" and its contrary "a" can follow from similar previous circumstances is the same as affirming that they occur without cause. If this were the case, he goes on, the foundations of all abstract reasoning would be destroyed.

Hartley was the first to explain all forms of mental life on the basis of association, in a lawful manner. Associationism as a system of psychology was thus formulated. For those who came after him, especially for James Mill, the nature and implications of association had been outlined. Because it is simultaneous (as well as successive), association was yet another step toward the mental atomism that was to come.

Hartley's physiological propositions were speculative, of course, for the state of knowledge of physiology in his day allowed little else. Although his physiology may be unconvincing to us today, his point that body and mind cooperate to function conjointly has become an integral part of much psychological thinking, even in our own century.

Through Hartley's formulation and presentation, association became a precise doctrine. It became the law of association. In seeking a name for the process, which had been called by dozens of names over the years, Hartley reached back to John Locke's book title, *On the Association of Ideas*, and chose "association" as his label. The word has stuck, and the movement of those who hold to such a notion became associationism.

The Mills

It was with James Mill (1773–1836) that association as mental compounding came to its height and at the hands of his son, John Stuart Mill (1806–1873), was overturned in favor of association as mental chemistry. The Mills are remembered primarily as social theorists, economists, and leaders of the Utilitarians. John Stuart, however, later emancipated himself considerably from Utilitarian teachings and also achieved eminence in the fields of logic and the philosophy of science. In their Utilitarianism they followed their friend, Jeremy Bentham (1748–1832). The "utility" in Bentham's Utilitarian creed may be summarized in the phrase, the "greatest good for the greatest number,"[21] which held that people are ruled by self-interest and that social, political, and legal action ought to lead to the acquisition of pleasure and the avoidance of pain for the common good.[22] It is something of an altruistic hedonism. The term *utilitarian* has heretofore been applied to an attitude reflecting an interest in practical application. It is evident, however, that Bentham and the others were using the word in an even wider context as a means of relating the motivations of people to social good. In doing so Bentham was making a considerable contribution to the psychological problem of motivation and the philosophical problem of ethics.

James Mill and Mental Compounding   James Mill began his career by being licensed to preach in the Church of Scotland but "abandoned theology after his acquaintance with Bentham."[23] He then made his living by literary journalism until 1819 when he entered the Home Service of the East India Company. He is best remembered for his *History of India* (1818), an immense and influential volume. He ended his career as Examiner, that is, head of the company's office.

James Mill's psychology is most accessible in the *Analysis of the Phenomena of the Human Mind.*[24] His is an associational view similar to that of Hartley and Hume.[25] He holds to two classes of mental elements: sensations and, when these are removed, ideas. All association, even by similarity, can be reduced to contiguity alone. Mill maintains that we get the notion of similarity through the action of contiguity. We class things alike not necessarily because they appear alike, but because they have been grouped together in our experience over and over again. Mill admitted two subdivisions of contiguity, successive and synchronous. Thus, the words of a poem are associated successively, in time, and the objects in a room are associated synchronously, in space.

Mill applied a similar reductive procedure to the causes of variation in the strength of association. The association is made through contiguity—the appearance together of the objects or events in space or time. Differences in strength of associations are explained by frequency and vividness. The more often the contiguity occurs, the stronger will be the association. The more vivid the events or objects in contiguity, the stronger will be their relationship. Strength is comprised of permanence, certainty, and assurance, or "correctness," spontaneity, and ease of formation, or "facility."[26]

Association serves to bind experiences together. James Mill held to a form of mental compounding, just as most of his British empiricist predecessors had done. According to this view, complex mental states are a cluster or compounding of two or more simpler states. Such a complex state holds within it all the original elements. In this perspective, the experience of flavor would be made up of simpler states of taste, smell, and touch. The whole is merely the sum of those simpler experiences. In this way the complex phenomena of the mind are formed out of the summation of simple ideas and sensations. The ideas of any object are the fusion of the ideas of the components, and nothing more. James Mill, then, tells us that the complex ideas of wall are made up of ideas of brick, mortar, position, and quantity. Complex ideas of plank, wall, and nail, united with ideas of position and quantity, compose an idea of floor. Similarly, glass, wood, and the like yield window, another complex idea. The even more complex idea of house comes from these ideas combined. Mill then works through furniture and merchandise and other things to the most complex idea of all, that of "everything," which is made up of these and all other ideas.

James Mill felt no need for any synthesis of ideas. Experiences sometimes appear to be simple, but indissoluble association really explains this impression. Psychological analysis shows that behind "simple" experiences a welter of elementary associations will always be found. Compounding, he stated, was an absurdity. As Boring says, the whole is less, as well as more, than the sum of its parts.[27]

For Mill, association is neither power nor cause. It is a passive process; mind has no creative function. Sensations occur in a certain way and are reproduced mechanically as ideas in that same order, one following the other. This brings association as a doctrine to its nadir as logical analysis. James Mill had gone too far beyond direct experience. He had mistaken logical analysis for a genuine analysis of experience. True, one can logically say that a brick wall is made up of bricks and mortar and number and position, but what one experiences is a brick wall, not a sum of components. With James Mill, creative thought is nothing more than a rearrangement of previous experiences or ideas. Nothing unique can emerge from this structural rearrangement. It would be John Stuart Mill who would bring associationism back from this extreme position.

John Stuart Mill and Mental Chemistry   John Stuart Mill had been a child prodigy. According to C. M. Cox and her associates his IQ in youth was 190, the highest they had obtained in their careful reconstruction of the intelligence quotients of many eminent men.[28] He was educated at home by his father, based on a plan his father and Bentham devised. At the age of three he learned Greek, and at eight he read Herodotus and Plato in the original. He had no boyhood friends, never learned to play, and was dominated by his father. This domination led to the mental crisis of John's early manhood and helped to delay the publication of his *Logic*[29] until 1843. His account of logical induction and deduction, and especially his clear explanation of the methods of agreement, difference, concomitant variation, and residues (the "Canons") is classic in scientific method, though not original with him.

The contents of the volume are broader than the main title suggests, especially in two respects.[30] An issue Mill faces squarely is whether or not there is a science of human nature. He answers in the affirmative with due consideration to the problems of exactitude and the presence of laws. It hardly approaches the ideal of exactitude, but it does have laws, the laws of association. He also suggests that alongside a general science of human nature, there should be a science to be, ethology, the science of character. This idea was ahead of its time and was fated to be almost totally disregarded by those who came after him. At the time the *Logic* was published Mill was thirty-seven, young in years, old in thought, and affected by his relationship with Harriet Taylor, whom he married after the death of her husband. After *Logic* she would influence Mill's works considerably. His output was voluminous and included works on philosophy, economics, political science, and psychology.

John Stuart Mill's more specific psychological views also appear as supplemental material to the expanded 1869 edition of his father's *Analysis*.[31] Besides editing the volume, along with Alexander Bain and others, he contributed voluminous notes. As shown in his *Logic*,[32] however, he emancipated himself from his father's rigid, compounding form of atomistic associationism. He stressed activity in mind (i.e., it was more than the vehicle for adding new experiences), and he asserted that when mental elements combine to form more complex states they give rise to something new, something not present in the original parts. In the resulting product, the parts disappear and new properties emerge that bear little or no resemblance to their constituent elements. The whole is more than the sum of the parts. This position has become known as "mental chemistry" in contrast to the "mental compounding" which James Mill and earlier associationists espoused. This notion of the whole being more than, or at least different from, the sum of its parts would be taken up in the late nineteenth and early twentieth centuries by other thinkers, notably William James and the Gestalt psychologists, though with somewhat different intent. Some may also argue that the notion of mental chemistry is also present in the psychology of Wilhelm Wundt.

Alexander Bain

For all practical purposes, philosophical associationism ends for psychology with Alexander Bain (1818–1903). Bain was born, lived, and worked for most of his life in Aberdeen, Scotland. He had brief schooling (only until his twelfth year) and like his father was trained as a weaver. Continuing his education through night school and reading, in 1836 he entered Marischal College, where he became assistant to the Professor of Moral Philosophy. As a student he wrote for the *Westminster Review* and began a lifelong friendship with John Stuart Mill, later taking the lead in revising James Mill's *Analysis of the Phenomena of the Human Mind.* This contact in London resulted in his appointment as Assistant Secretary to the (London) Metropolitan Sanitary Commission, after a brief period he spent teaching in Glasgow.[33]

Bain's major influence on psychology comes from two books, *The Senses and the Intellect* (1855)[34] and *The Emotions and the Will* (1859).[35] These works remained standard, as revised, for nearly half a century. Bain's thoroughness is evident in his coverage of previous literature, exhaustive for the British and more comprehensive than usual for the Continental. In these texts Bain linked psychological and physiological processes even more closely than Hartley had done. Bain paid particular attention to reflexes. He treated habit and instinct fully, and belief more pragmatically than others of his time did. His analysis of the origin and development of volition is penetrating.

These publications probably led to the turning point in Bain's life. He appears to have been considered something of a radical as a young man. That reputation together with his refusal to become a church member blocked him from gaining university appointments on several occasions.[36] In 1860, however, he was at last appointed Professor of Logic and Rhetoric at the University of Aberdeen owing in part to his writings. He remained there in this capacity until 1880 and in various honorary offices until his death in 1903.

Bain's *Mind and Body*,[37] *A Manual of Mental and Moral Science*,[38] and *On the Study of Character*,[39] all belong to his professorial years. The first work contains a discussion of his attempted solution to the mind–body problem which was a form of psychophysical parallelism. In his view mind and body are seen as forming a unity. They are not separate processes, suggesting the position of psychophysical monism. The dual nature of mind and matter depends on how they are viewed. Observed objectively, from the outside mind is a bodily process, matter; viewed subjectively, from the "inside," the process is mind. His *Manual* was a condensation and updating of the main works. His *Study of Character* was a pioneer work on personality, with an especially telling critique of phrenology. Bain was also the founder and the original proprietor of the journal, *Mind*, which first appeared in January 1876. This was the first journal of philosophical psychology, but the time was not yet ripe for an experimental journal. This is why Wilhelm Wundt's journal, although it appeared seven years later than *Mind*, is considered the first journal of modern psychology.

Bain's later writings (except for revisions of his major texts) are of little concern to us, for they relate mostly to rhetoric, grammar, education, and administration rather than to psychology. It is mainly as a psychologist that Bain is remembered, being commonly referred to as such.[40]

The nature of Bain's position in the history of psychology is still greatly debated. Is he the last of the old psychologists or the first of the new? He was new in his stress on physiology, and his broadening and reworking of associationism to make it serve as the basis of a psychology assimilated to that discipline. Despite his forward-looking view of mind and body as a "double-faced unit," he was old in his cautious parallelism. His views on social psychology and individual differences were more modern than is usually realized.[41] He did not assimilate evolution the way Spencer did, however, although he gave great weight to Darwin's work on emotional expression in animals as illustrating the physical side of anger.[42] He also modified an edition of *The Emotions and the Will* to include a chapter on evolution as related to the emotions,[43] but he thought "the history of the highest races does not fall in with evolution,"[44] by which he meant human beings from the Greeks onward. The main forward-looking aspect of Bain's psychology is that it rests on a genuine, thorough, and up-to-date physiology, not a hypothetical physiology like the one created by Hartley, who fit his to the psychological facts as he saw them.[45] Bain's *Autobiography* shows the care he took to read, visit with, and understand major physiologists and anatomists, in order to distinguish fact from conjecture.[46] For instance, his analysis of hunger shows how he achieved accuracy in his detailed appraisal of this area. (Perhaps Bain's dyspepsia also motivated him.)[47] Yet he cannot be considered a modern psychologist. He still regarded conscious data as primary, and he was no reductionist. He still held more to the philosophical method, and in his view the place of psychological experiment was limited.

Bain's modification of associationism had similar Januslike qualities. According to G. A. Cardno, his principal statement in all four editions of *The Senses and the Intellect* is as follows:[48] "Actions, sensations or states of feeling, occurring together or in close succession, tend to grow together or cohere in such a way that when any one of them is afterwards presented to the mind, the others are apt to be brought up."[49] This cohesion embraced contiguity as the law of association proper. Similarity was considered the second principle of association. Bain's major innovation was his somewhat more adroit assimilation of what had been called mental chemistry when discussing Mill. As already discussed, John Stuart Mill had introduced the principle into associationism. Bain's form of mental chemistry became known as constructive association or imagination. Like John Stuart Mill, Bain held that "by means of association the mind has the power to form new combinations or aggregates different from any that have been presented to it in the course of experience."[50] Although Bain did not consider it so, constructive association can also be interpreted as less than total reliance on association. This is not the only instance of this use of nonassociationist factors.

In detail, Bain is often forward looking. Thus, in constructive association-making, new combinations required something more than associations to account for novelty. Moreover, infants possess reflexes, instincts, and differences in acuteness. True, there are no innate ideas, but innate behaviors precede education. Bain accepted heredity as operative, yet his adherence to association as a general principle, especially with the vocabulary he uses, is limited. He represents a culmination rather than a radical initiation. The nature of the culmination is indicated by the fact that Bain can be suitably discussed only after considering Darwin. After Bain, association would still live on but not under its old banner. If the present-day interests of the philosopher in psychology are disregarded as not being in the mainstream of the history of psychology, then Bain was the last philosopher–psychologist in Great Britain. Probably the evaluation that his psychology is full of germinal ideas that he failed to develop is as near as we can come to a one-sentence appraisal.[51]

Bain's philosophical associationism was supplanted by the psychological associationism of the laboratory. The publication in Germany of Hermann Ebbinghaus's book *On Memory* in 1885 with its experimental approach created a new era for association theory and led away from the philosophical armchair. Although the philosophical line of association begun by Aristotle would end, for all practical purposes, with Bain, the significance of associationism continued in psychology. In the twentieth century association in one form or another would form the basis for a majority of psychological theories and systems.

MECHANISM

Another empirical movement that ran parallel to the mentalistic approach of most British empiricists and associationists was mechanism. In general, mechanism holds that mind and body, the form and matter of earlier philosophers, are not two separate things but only one entity. Since mind and body are the same thing, matter, human beings are machines, automata. Descartes had advanced a mechanistic theory of animals as automata to explicate a greater separation between the human being and the brute in support of orthodox religion. Descartes' mechanism, as we have seen, included not only animals but the human body as well. He maintained that humans were differentiated from animals by their ability to reason, and this ability required the intervention of a thinking substance, the rational soul. He contended that mind must be excluded from the mechanical sphere, that it did not obey natural law as did the body.

Many of those who came after Descartes were so convinced of his view that mechanical activity accounted for the actions of animals and the body of humans that they disagreed with his careful distinction between human mind and human body and stated that human psychology was also to be accounted for on mechanical grounds. This was done simply by considering not only animals but also humans as automata. This interpretation, abhorrent to Descartes though it would have been, places him at the headwater of influence of the modern mechanistic approach to human nature.[52] Rather than holding to the interactionistic psychophysical dualism of Descartes, a position where mind and body were different things but influenced each other, many thinkers chose another approach. This alternative view was psychophysical monism. In general, this view holds that mind and body are really the same thing—what we call mind is really only bodily action, brain, or nervous action. The significance of this position is that mind, being material, obeys natural law. No longer may it be considered to function in terms we cannot understand.

In earlier sections we have already seen approaches to mechanistic notions. Thomas Hobbes embraced a form of mechanism as, to some degree, did David Hartley. They only went part way, however. Hartley, for instance, held to a psychophysical parallelism; he believed that mind and body were two sides of the same process. The extreme position of psychophysical monism came from the French mechanists of the eighteenth century,[53] two of whom are particularly important, Julien Offray de La Mettrie and Jean George Cabanis.

Julien Offray de La Mettrie

La Mettrie (1709–1751) is usually considered the first of the modern line of thoroughgoing mechanists and was perhaps the most influential of those who sought to extend Descartes' views on animals and the human body as a machine to mental states as well.[54]

Life of La Mettrie   La Mettrie was born in France to a well-to-do family and received a good education, first in the humanities and then in rhetoric. An eloquent orator who was fond of poetry and the fine arts, he seemed destined for a career in the fine arts. His father, however, had other ideas, and the young La Mettrie was sent to become educated as a priest. It was while studying logic that he met and studied under a follower of the Jansenists, then a sect within the Roman Catholic Church, which believed that humankind is without free will and is either damned or saved at birth. This may have been La Mettrie's first introduction to a deterministic philosophy, one that teaches that our actions are predetermined and that our will is not free. He wrote a treatise on the subject which was very popular at the time. The Jansenist movement was later suppressed in the Church as a heresy, but that was only after La Mettrie had given up the idea of being a priest. Discovering that one could make more money as a medical doctor than as a cleric, he received his medical degree in 1725. His medical education was as good as could be had at the time. In addition, he went to Leyden where he worked for a number of years with the great medical luminary Booerhaave. He returned to France and, through some family connections, obtained the commission of physician of the guards to the Duke of Gramont in 1742. As part of his duties, La Mettrie followed the Duke into battle.

At the siege of Freiburg, La Mettrie fell ill with a fever that would change the course of his life. He came to the conclusion that in his fevered state his bodily illness was reflected in a mental disturbance. After recovering, he began to collect psychological and medical evidence that related to the matter. He came to believe that matter, body, is endowed not only with the attribute of motion, but also with that of consciousness. Mind and (since he did not distinguish between them) soul were to La Mettrie nothing more than the action of the body. The material substance, the body, was the only human reality.

La Mettrie originally presented his thesis in *The Natural History of the Soul*, first published in 1745.[55] There was a furor over the work, and La Mettrie was roundly attacked by the religious community. As a result he lost his commission as physician of the Guard. His works were considered heretical since he attacked the notion of the immateriality of the soul which cast doubt on its immortality. That indiscretion was serious enough, but La Mettrie added to it by shortly thereafter publishing a scathing satire on some of the foremost medical practitioners of Paris. Predictably, that led to attacks from the medical profession as well. La Mettrie's friends urged him to leave Paris to protect his physical safety. In 1746 he went to Leyden,[56] where he demonstrated how well he had learned his lesson by publishing another scathing satire on the charlatanism and ignorance of the medical profession. It was in Leyden that he wrote his best known and most significant work, *Man a Machine*, which appeared in 1748.[57] It excited much the same furor from the religious establishment in Leyden as his earlier book had done in Paris.

Frederick the Great of Prussia gave La Mettrie refuge at his court in Berlin. There La Mettrie published medical treatises on dysentery and on asthma. Unable to stay away from the philosophical sphere, he also wrote treatises advocating a hedonistic view of life.[58] There, in 1751, he suddenly died, apparently of food poisoning. Frederick, writing of La Mettrie's death, tells us: ''It seems that the disease, knowing with whom it had to deal, was clever enough to attack his brain first, so that it would more surely confound him. He had a burning fever and was violently delirious." His medical colleagues were unable to save him.[59] In death as in life, La Mettrie proved his point.

La Mettrie's Mechanism   One of La Mettrie's difficulties was that he was unable to distinguish between mind and soul. Although he rejected the notions of the scholastics, he was still locked into their system of thought. His primary thesis was that mind (which he equated with soul) is not immaterial but is material—in fact it is the bodily process itself. That is the gist of his mechanism. La Mettrie contends that all our experiences come to us through the sense organs. By means of the nerves they are connected with the brain, which he presents as the seat of sensation. La Mettrie still holds to the Cartesian notion of animal spirits that flow through the hollow tubes that are the nerves. The soul (mind) experiences only when the sense organs are stimulated, the nerves conduct the sensation, and the brain receives it. That is the only source of knowledge.[60] Although these experiences are actually in the brain, we refer them to the outside objects. Pick up a small stone, and it feels as though it is on your finger tips. In fact, the sensation is in your brain; it is merely referred to the finger tips.

In his *Natural History of the Soul* La Mettrie concludes that where there are no senses, there are no ideas; where there are no sense impressions, there are no ideas; the fewer senses, the fewer ideas; little education, few ideas.[61] In this line of thought, he shares the positions of the associationists and of the classic empiricists discussed in Chapter 9. His position is more sensationalist than that of Locke, however, since, like his contemporary, Condillac, La Mettrie makes sensation alone the source of knowledge. Reflection insofar as Locke means it as an examination of the internal processes of mind is not part of knowledge in La Mettrie's view.

La Mettrie calls on us to make experiment and observation our only guides to investigation.[62] Only by studying experience and the bodily organs can we understand human nature and action. He urges us to reject the ideas of the earlier philosophers much as Descartes had done.[63] Instead of rejecting past ideas for the method of reason, however, La Mettrie would have us reject them for our own observations, methodological empiricism.

The explanation of human action and human misbehavior, La Mettrie asserts, is to be found in bodily function and dysfunction. He believes that all "mental" ailments have at their base some damage or degeneration of the brain, or even some congestion of the brain or some minute defect. He suggests that "a mere nothing, a little fibre, some trifling thing that the most subtle anatomy cannot discover" would have made idiots out of our greatest geniuses.[64]

Although knowledge comes to us only through the senses, other influences work on our behavior. Experience can only enlighten the machine if it is properly functioning. A defective brain cannot function as a normal one. La Mettrie tells us that "everything depends on the way our machine is running."[65] In the same way, certain environmental factors may alter the way we behave. The effects of alcohol, drugs, or even the cold are treated as determinants of human behavior.[66] Still, since the the organism is whole and normal, sensation and education are what makes us wise. La Mettrie discusses the fact that education increases our ability to understand, that the organism has potential for functioning that can only be realized through education. He believed that it should be possible to educate animals as well, particularly apes and monkeys which have brains most like humans. "Why," he asks "should the education of monkeys be impossible?" "Why might not the monkey, by dint of great pains, at last imitate after the manner of deaf mutes, the motions necessary for pronunciation?" He believed that humans did not always have language and that they learned it because of a lack of other instincts. Language to La Mettrie is a significant part of the differentiation between humans and apes.

> What was man before the invention of words and the knowledge of language? An animal of his own species with much less instinct than the others. In those days, he did not consider himself king over the other animals, nor was he distinguished from the ape, and from the rest, except as the ape itself differs from the other animals, i.e., by a more intelligent face. . . .
>
>   Words, languages, laws, sciences, and the fine arts have come, and by them finally the rough diamond of our mind has been polished. Man has been trained in the same way as animals. He has become an author, as they became beasts of burden.[67]

La Mettrie tells us that he would choose a large ape as the subject of such an experiment, but he never followed through on the idea.[68] Thus, with La Mettrie, knowledge is an interaction between the mechanical structure of the brain and the experiences of the individual.

La Mettrie asserted that the separation between humans and animals that past philosophers had been so careful to establish was a fiction. For that older view he substituted an unbroken continuum from humans to the simplest animals and perhaps even to plants.[69] What distinguishes the different levels of living matter is desire or wants. Humans occupy the highest point in the animal kingdom because they have more wants. Beings without wants, he said, are also without mind.[70] La Mettrie posited his own form of hedonism, a position that holds that organisms were constructed to seek pleasure. He distinguished between debauchery and enjoyment. He defined debauchery as an act or feeling of pleasure that harms society, whereas he called enjoyment a pleasure that involves no harm to others. La Mettrie stated that organisms had a perfect right to seek enjoyment. His treatise on the subject, *L'art de jouir,* did little to endear him to the religious and philosophical establishment.[71]

In summary, then, La Mettrie believed that soul means nothing more than the part in us that thinks. "[S]ince all the faculties of the soul depend to such a degree on the proper organization of the brain and of the whole body, that apparently they are but this organization itself, the soul is clearly an enlightened machine."[72] "Let us conclude boldly," says La Mettrie, "that man is a machine and that in the whole universe there is but a single substance differently modified."[73]

Perhaps more significant than any particular part of his doctrine, La Mettrie emphasized that mental events were lawful. Unlike Descartes, he believed that mental events obey the laws of nature since they are part of material nature. La Mettrie also emphasized observation and experimentation, methodological empiricism, over the *a priori* procedures of the rationalists. His was an extreme position, but it opened the door for the line to follow: those who sought the explanation for mental life in the lawful, mechanical action of the body and finally localized those functions specifically.

With La Mettrie and particularly with Cabanis who will follow, we proceed from the traditional philosophers to medical practitioners and physiologists. Both La Mettrie and Cabanis were medical practitioners. Their training and inclinations emphasized observation and experimentation over *a priori* philosophizing. This difference caused them to view many philosophical problems from a different perspective. They were influenced in their thinking by philosophy, but that influence was only a starting point for their own ideas. Just as La Mettrie had been sparked by Descartes, Cabanis will be seen to have been influenced by John Locke, as interpreted by the sensationalist Condillac. Before we consider Cabanis, however, we should note Condillac's and Destutt de Tracy's contributions.

Condillac

Etienne Bonnot de Condillac (1715–1780) was a priest who took holy orders in 1740 but devoted his life primarily to scholarship. In 1758 after producing several of his major works, he became tutor to the son of an Italian Duke. Late in life he gained the position of Abbot of Condillac, the title by which he has been known since.[74]

Condillac may seem an unlikely source for influence on mechanistic thought; in fact, he was not inclined toward mechanistic explanations at all. His sensationalism, however, with its emphasis on sensations alone as the source of knowledge, and his rejection of the innateness of the faculties of mind, lend themselves to a mechanical view of human knowledge and actions.

Though a contemporary of La Mettrie, it is not known whether Condillac was familiar with his views. Even if he were aware of them, Condillac would hardly have admitted it since La Mettrie's books were on the list of forbidden books. Still, there are surprising similarities between La Mettrie and Condillac in their theories of knowledge in which La Mettrie has the chronological priority. The primary influence on Condillac, however, was John Locke whose work he probably knew from an early French translation. (Condillac did not read English.) In his early years Condillac was a faithful follower of Locke's theory of knowledge. In *An Essay on the Origin of Human Knowledge* published in 1746, Condillac espoused Locke's classic position of two sources of knowledge, sensation and reflection. Later, however, in his *Treatise on Sensation* published in 1754, Condillac, like La Mettrie, accepted only sensation as the source of our knowledge.[75]

In the *Treatise*, Condillac states that his chief object "is to show how all our knowledge and all our faculties are derived from the senses, or, to speak more accurately, from sensations." To Condillac, Locke's function of reflection "is in its function but sensation itself; . . . , because it is less a source of ideas than a canal through which they flow from sense."[76] The problem with Locke's system, in Condillac's view, was that he made the higher mental processes such as judging, willing, and reasoning as given, fundamental powers of mind, without attempting to trace their origins back to sensations.[77] In this way, Locke was not consistently empirical. Ideas were derived from the senses and furnished the faculties of mind with the information for knowing, yet the faculties were themselves inborn. By his famous example of the sentient statue, Condillac demonstrates that through sensation and sensation alone all the human faculties or functions that we identify with human mental life can be obtained, including judgment, reflection, emotions, and even memory.[78] They are nothing but sensations that are transformed differently. In Condillac's metaphor, he has a statue that knows the world only through information gained through the senses. At first, he reduces the statue's sensory world to only one sense or where all sensory sources but one are reduced in strength except one. That one sensation becomes attention. If another sensation arrives that is stronger than the first, *it* becomes attention.

> Our capacity for sensing is now divided between the sensation which we had [formerly] and the one we have [presently]. We perceive them both at once, but we perceive them differently; one seems past, the other seems present.
>
> ... Now, this feeling is called sensation when the impression is being presently made on the senses, and it is called memory when it is completed and no longer in process. Memory is therefore nothing but transformed sensation.
>
> As soon as there is double attention, there is comparison. . . . The acts of comparison and judgment are nothing but attention itself. In this way sensation successively becomes attention, comparison, judgement.[79]

Because Condillac rejects reflection as a primary source of knowledge, he does not reject reflection itself as an individual's awareness of his or her own mental processes.

Condillac also rejects notions of instinct as blind, innate processes, not only for humans but for animals as well. He reduces instinctive behavior to habits acquired before our awareness of them (reflection) came about or where reflection has somehow not occurred.[80] Condillac tells us that whoever "attains a thorough understanding of the system of our sensations will agree that it is no longer necessary to have recourse to the vague words instinct, mechanical movement, and the like."[81]

Like La Mettrie, Condillac argued that we may gain inferences about human mind and action from an investigation of animals. He did not allow that animals had the mental capacity of humans, but it was essential that the same laws of knowing be valid for both. After all, Condillac has made the mind passive and resultant from sensations. If so, and if human reason is produced by the transformation of sensations, then do not animals have something analogous since they also have sensations? Indeed, Condillac gave validity to a comparative psychology in his assumption that one could infer human mental events from animals. Allowing as he did a form of mental life for animals, Condillac's work represents a major movement away from the notions of Descartes and that of most traditional philosophers who gave no credence to reason or any other "higher" form of mental life in animals.

Condillac also deals with the concept of needs and develops a form of a theory of motivation:

> If a man had no reason to concern himself with his sensations, the impressions that objects make on him would pass like shadows, and leave no trace. . . . But the nature of our sensations does not permit him to remain wrapped in this lethargy. Because they

are necessarily either agreeable or disagreeable, he has an interest in seeking some and ridding himself of others. The livelier this contrast of pleasures and pains, the more will it give rise to action in the soul.

The privation of an object which we judge to be necessary for our happiness gives us malaise or uneasiness which we call need, and from which desires are born.[82]

Here again, Condillac has begun with Locke, particularly Locke's theory of uneasiness,[83] but has gone further in his analysis. To Locke, the uneasiness caused by one's deprivation of an object is the principle of action, but he makes desire the source of this uneasiness. Condillac analyzes the situation more thoroughly than Locke. He finds that this uneasiness is produced by habits derived from sensations. In effect, what Locke calls desire, the drive state in modern terms, is actually, in Condillac's analysis, a product of the uneasiness or "need state" as we might call it today, rather than the reverse as Locke would have it. This reduces the faculty of desire to stimulus situations and habits.

Condillac was not trying to write a mechanistic philosophy. He did, however, produce a thoroughgoing sensationalist psychology that removed much of the necessity for considering "faculties of the soul" as being anything more than naturalistically produced through the lawful processes of the organism. His ideas were of particular consequence to the writings of Destutt de Tracy and other writers who extended Condillac's notions into the realm of mind as matter. Condillac, though giving great emphasis to the body as mental cause, was not prepared to identify mind with body. What he did was to give respectability to the view that an analytic psychology of mind was possible, based strictly on observation and experience and excluding *a priori* metaphysical conceptions. Even though Condillac was not particularly consistent with his own admonitions, his sensationalism would draw others to a mechanical view of mind. Condillac's sensationalist philosophy was widely accepted in France and actually supplanted Descartes's teachings in French schools in the late eighteenth century.

Destutt de Tracy

Antoine Destutt de Tracy (1754–1836), for instance, projected Condillac's notions into a strictly mechanical system. Expanding on Condillac, he held that there were only four fundamental mental acts: perception, the sensation of objects; memory, the sensation of remembrances; judgment, the sensation of relations; and will, the sensation of desires. The first three, perception, memory, and judgment, are the source of our knowledge. The fourth is the source of action. In Destutt de Tracy's extension of Condillac, the first three processes are the sources of our knowledge; the fourth is our means of action. All four have their origins in reformulated sensations. The external object produces impressions on our nerves; the nerves transmit these impressions to the brain. The brain receives the impressions and converts them into

(1) a perception, if the object be present; into (2) a remembrance, if the object be absent; into (3) a relation, if several objects at once bring the image of their resemblances or their differences; into (4) a ratiocination, if there are several relations; and,

finally, if the object rouses desire, it provokes another movement to satisfy it; and this produces action, as the previous movement produced knowledge.[84]

In this way Destutt de Tracy makes knowing and willing the products of two organic processes, the one depending on the other. Psychology, which Destutt De Tracy called "L' idéologie," was, in his view, part of biology.[85]

Cabanis

Pierre Jean Georges Cabanis (1757–1808) brought the biologizing of mind to its height in the eighteenth century. He was influenced by both Condillac and La Mettrie. He drew together many of the advances in empirical philosophy and medicine in the late eighteenth century to make pronouncements on the nature of mental and physiological phenomena. His ideas would set several themes in psychological and physiological thought which would be debated well into the next century.

Cabanis, like La Mettrie, was French and born of well-to-do parents. Unlike La Mettrie, however, he was an indifferent student. He was sent to Paris while still in his teens to shift for himself. As it happens he did become well educated, though by his own reading rather than by formal schooling. He read the classics—Homer, Cicero, and Augustine—as well as the "moderns"—Locke, Descartes, Goethe, and Condillac. His original intent was to become a philosopher, but instead he decided to go into medicine.

Cabanis was politically active during the French Revolution and became physician to and finally a close associate to Mirabeau, leader of the French Revolution. In this way, Cabanis, at a relatively young age became a member of the Council of Five Hundred, the revolutionary ruling body of France. By 1795 he was appointed Professor of Hygiene at the University of Paris and by 1799 Professor of Legal Medicine and the History of Medicine. From the days of the French Republic until the rise of Napoleon, Cabanis was a powerful and influential figure.

Most of Cabanis's scholarly contributions are in the form of memoires read before the French Academy of Science in 1795 and appeared in their Proceedings in 1798–1799. They appeared with additional material in book form in 1802 as *Traité du Physique et du Moral de l'Homme.* [86]

Cabanis, an unusual mechanist, demonstrates that a person can have a mechanical view of mind without rejecting metaphysical views of soul. It is said that, early in his life, Cabanis was a vitalist and a follower of Georg Ernst Stahl (1666–1734). Stahl took the position that the chemical activities within the living organism are essentially different from those reactions in the laboratory and in nonliving matter.[87] The soul, Stahl claimed, permeates the entire organism and controls all functional manifestation. The soul is a force—a living force. To him the very fact that the body is alive proved his point. Cabanis apparently held that there *was* a substantial vital force over and above the organic forces we observe.[88] He would not have been the only physiologically oriented thinker to accept such a view, basically a vitalistic doctrine. In a less mystical form we will find such an eminent man of the nineteenth century as Johannes Müller subscribing to a form of vitalism. However, in his last article which was not published until long after his death, Cabanis shows signs of having moved to a panpsychism, a view that vital forces are present in all things.[89] These views, however, did not affect his work on the origins of mental life.

Cabanis was strongly influenced by the sensationalism of Condillac. Just as Condillac had pushed for more precise analysis from Locke, so Cabanis also pushed Condillac for more precise analysis. Condillac had sought to find the origin of the functions of mind in terms of sensations, but he did not consider what makes up the process of sensation, sensibility. Cabanis held that sensibility does not always consist just of ideas; that is, it is not always conscious experience. Many other processes are ongoing while we are sensing objects from the outside world. The intellect is judging; the will is desiring or rejecting. Cabanis said that sensibility is a part of the whole life process and is an interaction of the stimuli of the outside world and the condition and development of the organism as a whole. Cabanis tells us:

> Subject to the action of external bodies, man finds in the impressions these bodies make on his organs at once his knowledge and the causes of his continued existence; for to live is to feel; and in that admirable chain of phenomena which constitute his existence, every want depends on the development of some faculty; every faculty by its very development satisfies some want, and the faculties grow by exercise as the wants extend with the faculty of satisfying them. By the continual action of external bodies on the senses of man, results the most remarkable part of his existence. But is it true that the nervous centres only receive and combine the impressions which reach them from these bodies? Is it true that no image or idea is formed in the brain, and that no determination of the sensitive organ ever takes place, other than by virtue of these same impressions on the senses strictly so called?[90]

So Cabanis has a highly interactive view of the relationship between sensations and all the other "mental" and bodily processes. To him, ideas, instincts, and passions are developed and modified by the age, sex, temperament, maladies, and so forth of the individual organism. Ideas do not exist independently of these processes.[91]

Cabanis gives an example of the influence of external stimuli and organic conditions on what in his day would have been considered an ultimate instinct, maternal love. He tells us:

> In my province . . . when there is a deficiency of sitting hens, a singular practice is customary. We take a capon, pluck off the feathers from the abdomen, rub it with nettles and vinegar, and in this state of local irritation place the capon on the eggs. At first he remains there to soothe the pain; soon there is established with him a series of unaccustomed but agreeable impressions, which attaches him to these eggs during the whole period of incubation; and the effect is to produce in him a sort of factitious maternal love, which endures, like that of the hen, as long as the chickens have need of aid and protection.[92]

Cabanis is best known for his views on the physiological basis for mental life. We are told that his interest in the relationship between brain function and mental events began in 1795 when he was given the task of determining whether the victims of the guillotine were conscious after beheading. The question was motivated by the observation that after beheading the victims' bodies would often twitch.[93] There were also tales of beheaded bodies standing up after the fall of the guillotine blade and walking around before finally collapsing. La Mettrie had already considered this problem in his *Man a Machine*, where he described similar behavior of a chicken after being beheaded by a sword.[94] There were also reports of wild eye movements in the disembodied head and even a case where a cruel headsman picked up a disembodied head of a woman and slapped it, only to have the head blush at the insult.[95]

Cabanis decided that the bodies of decapitated people were not conscious since the brain was necessary for conscious processes.

> The movement of a part of the body does not presuppose sensation, nor does the faculty of producing these movements presuppose that of feeling. . . .
> A simple concussion of the cerebellum or of the medulla oblongata, a violent blow to the occiput or the cervical vertibrae, is enough to cause death. If the blow does no more than interrupt consciousness momentarily, the patient, when he comes to himself, has no memory of it. He did not feel it.
> . . . It follows that a man who is guillotined suffers pain neither in his limbs nor in his head; that his death is as swift as the blow which strikes it; and if certain movements, whether regular or convulsive, are noticed in the muscles of the arms, legs, and face, they prove neither pain nor sensibility. They depend solely on a residue of the vital faculty which is not instantly abolished in the muscles and the nerves by death of the individual, the destruction of the self.[96]

Cabanis, though a member of the Council of Five Hundred, did not support the excesses of the Revolution. The guillotine was originally implemented, in fact, to provide as painless a method of execution as possible. Cabanis himself tells us that he never witnessed such an execution because "My gaze could not withstand such a spectacle." In his discussion, he discounts the blushing head on the basis of eye-witness reports by medical observers.[97]

Basically, Cabanis believed there were three levels of the organization of living organisms. First, there were simple reflexes or "instincts" that did not require the brain. They can be shown in organisms completely lacking a brain. The decapitates were exhibiting this kind of reflexive action, random muscle twitches very briefly resembling coordinated actions. True coordinated behavior is semiconscious and involves the "old brain" or brain stem structures. Thought and other higher mental processes and volitional acts reside in the brain itself, he said, particularly the cerebral lobes. The same laws that govern the simple reflex, however, govern the highest level of our thought.

Cabanis refers to the brain as a "special organ, which is particularly designed to produce [thought]." He compared the function of the brain with that of other organs, "the same way that the stomach and the intestines are designed for performing digestion, the liver for filtering the bile, the partoid and maxillary and sublingual glands for producing salivary juices."[98] Unfortunately, later writers interpreted this example as meaning that thought was excreted by the brain as bile is by the liver. What Cabanis was really trying to demonstrate, however, was that brain processes are thoughts just as the process of the stomach is digestion. "Mental" events, such as thought, are not produced by the brain; they *are* the brain process.

This position leads us to list Cabanis as a mechanist. It should be obvious that his position is far more thoroughly thought out than that of La Mettrie and Destutt de Tracy. Rather than creating a hypothetical nervous system, Cabanis is making use of the current knowledge of nervous functioning. In many respects he is the most clearly identifiable physiological psychologist of the eighteenth century.

In some ways, Cabanis provided the impetus for searching out the locus of specific mental events, a task that would be a dominant theme for physiologists in the nineteenth century.

With the differentiation of biology and physiology from philosophical apron strings during the nineteenth century, we find a trend away from abstract philosophical considerations and toward a more detailed description of brain and nervous functioning.

Perhaps the most significant aspect of Cabanis's position is his emphasis on the significance of observable data for investigations into the life processes, in which "mental" events are so completely a part. The shift toward scientific measurement is clear. In the same way, Cabanis's thinking on the relationship between an intact brain and normal behavior would naturally lead later researchers to consider the effect of a deranged brain on human knowledge and action. In the hands of the somatic psychiatrists of the nineteenth century, this position would lead to a somatic theory of mental illness, one of the influences that ultimately led to more humane and medical treatment of the insane.

SUMMARY

This chapter has dealt with two very different empirical psychologies, the associationists and mechanists. The spirit of Newton was still alive in the associationists and mechanists as it was in the earlier British empiricists. The fundamental question which associational psychology dealt with was how the whole comes to be produced by a combination of simpler states, how the world as we know it may be reduced down to elemental states. The doctrine begun with Aristotle's attempt to classify the linkages among memories had led finally to a philosophical doctrine. The philosophical line ended with Alexander Bain, although the concept of association continued as the "glue" in the elementistic psychologies of the twentieth century down to our own day. They shared, then, the prescriptions of molecularism and empiricism.

The associationists, with the possible exception of Alexander Bain, also took on a mentalistic prescription, viewing mental processes apart from their physiological bases. Once a sensation became an idea, the body was largely ignored. The mechanists, particularly Cabanis, continued questioning the source and nature of ideas. The mechanists predictably took on a mechanistic prescription. Nonmechanistic empiricists such as Condillac sought the finest analysis they could, having reduced mental life to sensations. Cabanis continued this analysis and expanded on it by asking not only what constitutes sensation but also what is the process through which such events arise. With Cabanis, the search begins for the specific loci of "mental" and motor events that will occupy so many researchers in the nineteenth century.

NOTES

1. D. Hartley, *Observations on Man, His Frame, His Duty and His Expectations*, 2 vols. (London: Richardson, 1749) (Scholars' Facsimiles and Reprints, 1966).
2. John Gay, "Concerning the Fundamental Principle of Virtue or Morality," in William King, *An Essay on the Origin of Evil* (London, 1731). Part of this article is translated into English in Solomon Diamond, ed., *The Roots of Psychology: A Sourcebook in the History of Ideas* (New York: Basic Books, 1974), pp. 588–591.
3. D. Hartley, *Conjecturae quaedam de montu sensus et idearum generatione*, 1746.
4. J. Priestley, *Hartley's Theory of the Human Mind, on the Principles of Association of Ideas with Essays Relating to the Subject of It* (1749) (London: Johnson, 1775).
5. D. Hartley, *Observations on Man* (1791), 6th rev. ed., 3 vols. (London: Tegg, 1834).
6. *Ibid.*, Introduction, p. III.
7. *Ibid.*, Chapter I.
8. *Ibid.*, Chapter I, Sec. I, Prop. VIII.
9. *Ibid.*, Chapter I., Sec. I, Prop. XIX.
10. *Ibid.*, Chapter I.
11. *Ibid.*, Chapter I, Sec. I, Prop. II.
12. Hartley may well have been at heart, an occasionalist, but this point was not appreciated by those whose work he inspired.
13. D. Hartley, *Observations*, Part I, Introduction.
14. D. Hartley, *Observations*, 1749, Vol. 1, Chapter I, Sec. 2, Prop. 9, 10, 12 (Herrnstein and Boring, Excerpt no. 70).
15. *Ibid.*, excerpted in Diamond, ed., *Roots of Psychology*, p. 315.
16. *Ibid.*, p. 73.
17. *Ibid.*, Vol. 1, Chapter I, Sec 3, Prop. 18, 21 (Herrnstein and Boring, Excerpt No. 59).
18. *Ibid.*, Vol. 1, Chapter II, Sec. 105.
19. *Ibid.*, Vol. 1, Chapter II, Sec. 6–7, Chapter III.
20. *Ibid.*, Conclusion.
21. J. Bentham, *Works*, ed. J. Bowring (Edinburgh: Tait, 1838–1843), Vol. X, pp. 142.
22. J. Bentham, *Theory of Legislation* (1789) (Oxford: Clarendon Press, 1914).
23. *Concise Dictionary*, p. 875.
24. J. Mill, *Analysis of the Phenomena of the Human Mind* (London: Longmans and Dyer, 1829).
25. H. Warren, *Association*.
26. J. Mill, *Analysis* (Herrnstein and Boring, Excerpt No. 72).
27. E. G. Boring, *Sensation and Perception in the History of Experimental Psychology* (New York: Appleton–Century, 1942), p. 9.
28. C. M. Cox et al., *Genetic Studies of Genius*, Vol. II, *Regarding Mental Traits of Three Hundred Geniuses* (Stanford, Calif.: Stanford University Press, 1926).
29. J. S. Mill, *A System of Logic, Ratiocinative and Inductive, Being a Connected View of the Principles of Evidence, and the Methods of Scientific Investigation*, 8th ed. (1843) (New York: Harper and Brothers, 1874).
30. *Ibid.*, Chapters 4, 5.

31. J. S. Mill, *Analysis of the Phenomena of the Human Mind*, new ed. with notes, illustrative and critical, by A. Bain, A. Findlater, and G. Grote, ed., with additional notes by J. S. Mill (New York: Longmans, Green, Reader and Tyler, 1869).
32. J. S. Mill, *System of Logic.*
33. A. Bain, *Autobiography* (London: Longmans, Green, 1904).
34. A. Bain, *The Senses and the Intellect* (London: Parker, 1855).
35. A. Bain, *The Emotions and the Will* (London, Parker, 1859).
36. Bain, *Autobiography*, pp. 174, 196.
37. A. Bain, *Mind and Body* (London: King, 1873) (Herrnstein and Boring, Excerpt No. 108).
38. A. Bain, *A Manual of Mental and Moral Science* (London: Longmans Green, 1875) (1869).
39. A. Bain, *On the Study of Character, Including an Estimate of Phrenology* (London: Parker, 1861).
40. J. A. Cardno, "Victorian Psychology: A Biographical Approach," *Journal of the History of Behavioral Sciences, 1,* (1965):165–177.
41. J. A. Cardno, "Bain and Individual Differences," *Aberdeen University Review, 40* (1963):124–132; J. A. Cardno, "Bain as a Social Psychologist," *Australian Journal of Psychology, 8* (1955):66–75.
42. A Bain, *The Emotions and the Will*, 3rd ed. (New York: Appleton, 1875) (1859).
43. *Ibid.,* Preface.
44. *Ibid.,* p. xiii.
45. J. A. Cardno, "Bain and Physiological Psychology," *Australian Journal of Psychology,* 7 (1955):108–120.
46. A. Bain, *Autobiography.*
47. J. A. Cardno, "Bain, Lewes, and Hunger," *Psychological Reports, 2* (1956):267–278.
48. *Ibid.*
49. A. Bain, *The Senses and the Intellect*, 3rd ed. (London: Longmans, Green, 1868), p. 327.
50. *Ibid.,* "Intellect," Chapter 4, Sec. 1, p. 570.
51. L. S. Hearnshaw, *A Short History of British Psychology: 1840–1940* (New York: Barnes and Noble, 1964), p. 13.
52. L. C. Rosenfeld, *From Beast-Machine to Man-Machine: Animal Soul in French Letters from Descartes to La Mettrie* (New York: Oxford University Press, 1941), 72.
53. The notion of mechanism or materialism as it was often called has a long history. The classic treatment of the subject is Frederick A. Lange, *The History of Materialism* (1865). References in this chapter are to the English translation by E. C. Thomas (New York: Harcourt, Brace and Co., 1925), 3 vols. in one.
54. J. O. de La Mettrie, *L'homme Machine* (1748), translated as *Man a Machine*, by G. C. Bussey and Mary W. Calkins (La Salle, Ill.: Open Court, 1912, p. 142.
55. La Mettrie, *L'historie naturelle de l'ame* (The Hague, 1745). The work appears as *Traité de l'ame* in his collected works, *Oeuvres Philosophiques* (1764). Extracts appear in La Mettrie's *Man a Machine*, pp. 151–162.
56. F. Lange, *History of Materialism*, Vol. 2, pp. 55–56.
57. J. O. La Mettrie, *Man a Machine*, pp. 83–150.
58. J. O. La Mettrie, *Systeme d'Epicure* in *Oeuvres Philosophiques de Monsier de La Mettrie* (Amsterdam, 1764); *L'art de jouir* (1751).
59. Frederick the Great, "Eulogy on Julien Offray De La Mettrie," in La Mettrie, *Man a Machine*, pp. 8–9.
60. F. Lange, Vol. 2, pp. 59–61.

61. *Ibid.*, Vol. 2, p. 63.
62. J. O. La Mettrie, *Man a Machine*, pp. 88, 142.
63. *Ibid.*, p. 89.
64. *Ibid.*, p. 99.
65. *Ibid.*, p. 95.
66. *Ibid.*, p. 96.
67. *Ibid.*, p. 103.
68. *Ibid.* pp. 100–103.
69. *Ibid.*, pp. 98, 145; *L'homme Plante* (1748) in *Oeuvres Philosophiques*.
70. J. O. La Mettrie, *L'homme Plante* and *Systeme d'Epicure* in *Oeuvres Philosophiques*, Pars. 13, 32, 33, 39; *Man a Machine*, p. 121.
71. J. O. La Mettrie, *L'art de jouir* (1751) in *Oeuvres Philosophiques*. Harold Höffding, writing more than a century and a half later, still felt the need to express his disgust at La Mettrie's position on enjoyment. Höffding, *A History of Modern Philosophy* (1900), trans. B. E. Meyer (New York: Humanities Press, 1950), Vol. 1, p. 475.
72. J. O. La Mettrie, *Man a Machine*, p. 128.
73. *Ibid.*, p. 148.
74. Useful if somewhat idiosyncratic treatments of Condillac may be found in Lucien Lévy-Bruhl, *History of Modern Philosophy in France* (Chicago: Open Court Publishing Co., 1899), pp. 271–287; and George Henry Lewes, *The History of Philosophy* (London: Longmans, Green, and Co., 1880), Vol. II, pp. 348–365.
75. Condillac, *Essai sur l'origine des conaissances humaines* (1746) trans. Thomas Nugent, *An Essay on the Origin of Human Knowledge* (Gainesville, Fla.: Scholars' Facsimile Press, 1971); *Traité des sensations* (1754), trans. Geraldine Carr, *Treatise on Sensations* (Los Angeles: University of Southern California, 1930).
76. G. H. Lewes, *The History of Philosophy*, 5th ed. (London: Longmans, Green, Co, 1880), Vol. 2, p. 350.
77. Robert Weyant, "Introduction," in Condillac, *An Essay on the Origin of Human Knowledge* (Gainesville, Fla.: Scholars' Facsimile Press, 1971), viii–ix.
78. Condillac, *Traité des Sensations* (Paris, 1754). Excerpted and translated by Frederick C. de Sumichrast, in Benjamin Rand, *Modern Classical Philosophers*, 2nd ed. (New York: Houghton Mifflin Co., 1936).
79. Condillac, "Extrait raisonée du traité des sensations" [Synopsis of the treatise on sensations], *Oeuvres philosophiques de Condillac*. Ed. by G. Le Roy, Vol. I, p. 321, trans. Solomon Diamond in Diamond, ed., *The Roots of Psychology* (New York: Basic Books, 1974), pp. 376–377.
80. Condillac, *Traité des animaux* [Treatise on Animals], (Paris, 1755), excerpts translated by Solomon Diamond in Diamond, ed., *Roots of Psychology*, pp. 376–378.
81. Condillac, "Extrait raisonée du traité des sensations," in Diamond, *Roots of Psychology*, p. 416.
82. *Ibid.*
83. John Locke, *Essay Concerning Humane Understanding*, 2nd ed. (London: 1694), pp. 134–136.
84. Destutt de Tracy, *Elements d'Idéologie* (Paris, 1825), iii, p. 102; *Logique*, Chap. ii, cited in Lewes, *History of Philosophy*, pp. 384–385. See also Destutt de Tracy, *Traité de la volonté et ses effets* (1815).
85. Destutt de Tracy, cited in Lewes, *History of Philosophy*, p. 385. Actually, he used the word *zoology* for biology.
86. After 1815, editions of Cabanis's book appeared under the title *Rapports du Physique et du Moral de l'Homme*.

87. G. E. Stahl, *Theoria Medica Vera* (Halle: Orphonotrophei, 1707–1708).

88. F. Lange, *History of Materialism*, Vol. 2, p. 242 fn.

89. P. Cabanis, "Letter on First Causes," in *Rapports du Physique et du Moral de l'Homme et Lettre sur le Causes Premiéres* (Paris: L. Peisse), 8th ed., 1844; cited in Lange, *History of Materialism*, Vol. 2, p. 242 fn.

90. P. Cabanis, *Traité* (1802), Twelfth memoire, Par. ii, translated in Lewes, *History of Philosophy*, p. 389.

91. G. H. Lewes, *History of Philosophy*, Vol. 2, p. 391.

92. P. Cabanis, *Traité*, quoted in Lewes, *History of Philosophy*, pp. 391–392.

93. P. Cabanis, *Note sur le supplice de la guillotine* [A Note on Execution by the Guillotine], *Magasin encyclopédique*, 1795, *Oeurves complètes*, 1823, Vol. 2, pp. 163–183, excerpted and translated by Solomon Diamond in Diamond, ed., *Roots of Psychology*, p. 39.

94. J. O. La Mettrie, *Man a Machine*, p. 130.

95. P. Cabanis, *Note*, in Diamond, ed., *Roots of Psychology*, p. 39.

96. *Ibid.*, p. 40.

97. *Ibid.*, p. 41.

98. P. Cabanis, *Rapports*, Vol. II, Para. vii, trans Solomon Diamond in Diamond, ed., *Roots of Psychology*, p. 188.

Top: Engraving of Thomas Reid. *Bottom:* Portrait of Immanuel Kant.

The Scottish Realists and the German Idealists: Two Reactions to Hume's Skepticism

*D*avid Hume's skeptical philosophy generated vigorous reaction both in Britain and on the Continent. It would be an oversimplification to credit a reaction against Hume as the sole basis for the development of Scottish Realism or Kantian idealism. Nonetheless, his writings and those of other British empiricists certainly were significant influences.

THE SCOTTISH SCHOOL

Hume's skeptical view of the possibility of knowledge of the outside world and even of the relationship among ideas capped a period beginning with Locke that many believed, particularly in Hume's native Scotland, was leading intellectual thought in an artificial and dangerous direction. Hume had exploded the belief in human ability to know the world even more completely than Democritus had done in the ancient world. It was time, several Scottish philosophers believed, to return to basics, to a more secure grounding in the certainty of knowledge. The result was a movement called Scottish Realism or, simply, the Scottish School.

The movement became known as the Scottish School because its major leaders, Thomas Reid (1710–1792), Dugald Stewart (1753–1828), and Thomas Brown (1778–1820), were all professors at Scottish universities.[1] They were connected with the strongly Calvinist Church of Scotland, which both influenced the positions of the school and helped spread its doctrines, particularly in America. The school had a significant impact on contemporary thought in Britain. Its influence was even more long lived in America, becoming the basic academic psychology of the first two-thirds of the nineteenth century. Vestiges of its influence have extended even into the twentieth century.

The Scottish School, particularly in its early years, maintained that what we today call British empiricism had degraded human nature. The school sought to restore the individual to a dignity that would conform with Christian and particularly Calvinist dogma.

Thomas Reid and Scottish Realist Philosophy

Thomas Reid (1710–1792), who is usually acknowledged as the leader of the realist movement, was educated at Marischal College at Aberdeen. He became the college librarian there after graduation. Between 1737 and 1752 he served as a minister at New Machar at King's College, Aberdeen. In 1752 he gained the position of Professor of Philosophy at King's College, Aberdeen. Reid taught at Aberdeen until 1764 when his *Inquiry into the Human Mind on the Principles of Common Sense* appeared, and he was offered and accepted the Chair of Moral Philosophy at Glasgow. Reid held that position until his retirement in 1780, a retirement he spent writing two of his best known works, his *Essays on the Intellectual Powers of Man* published in 1785 and his *Essays on the Active Powers of the Human Mind* in 1788. The remainder of his life was spent in pursuing scientific interests.[2]

Reid's Psychological Thought   The *Inquiry*, in particular, was Reid's answer to Hume and his empirical forebears. Reid realized that Hume had not been alone in bringing philosophy to a precipice of skepticism, but had been only one of a line starting with Locke who had moved step by step to Hume's position.

How did Locke, Berkeley, Hartley, and Hume degrade the nature of the individual? Reid saw it in several forms. First was Locke's treatment of personal identity, self. To Locke and to his followers, personal identity is simply the sum of a lifetime of experiences. Each experience takes its place in memory, and each subsequent experience is associated with previous experiences now in memory. Thus, in Locke's associational theory present sensations are linked with past experiences which in turn are linked with other past experiences. This position reduces self to nothing more than a pattern of ideas and memories. Reid interpreted Locke's position to mean that "Identity consists in remembrance; and, consequently, a man must lose his personal identity with regard to everything he forgets."[3] In contrast, Reid's faculty psychology requires a "Knower," a faculty of the soul or the soul itself that stands behind our experiences and gives permanence. Clearly, the Scots' aim was to defend the doctrine of the soul against the empiricists' theory of self. To this end Reid and his followers either rejected or modified associationism. They also rejected physiological explanations of behavior, especially that of David Hartley, as derogatory to human dignity.

Another postulate of the British empiricists and Hume in particular which Reid and the Scots rejected had to do with the issue of the degree to which we can know the "real" world. Berkeley and Hume's acceptance of only secondary sense qualities effectively foreclosed the possibility of proving the existence of the outside world. To the empiricists, all our knowledge of the world is based on what the hypothesized stimuli do to our own consciousness. Although they may assume that such a world exists, they say there is no way of knowing whether it is like our experiences of it.

Reid counters that we must believe in an outside world and that we need no proof for its existence. We know such things intuitively. Reid extended the concept of "self-evident truths" from the moral realm of John Locke's theory to the intellectual realm of perception and conceptions. Such intuitions, he said, are not innate ideas, however, but are derived from innate powers of mind. Reid refers this conceptual act, this understanding that is immediate and not based on judgments, to some original instinctive principle within us. Instinct, then, some native attitude of the individual, is Reid's basis for his realism. This reduces the debate, in a somewhat oversimplified way, to the prescription of empiricism–nativism. Reid holds that our faculties are so designed as to recognize "natural signs" in our experiences that would differentiate real objects in the outside world. This argument is not particularly easy for modern psychologists to grasp, but it seems to have struck a chord in his own day, particularly since it was God who is to have established the instinct. It is a significant position, however, and provides an active alternative to the passive, almost mechanical mind of Berkeley and Hume.

Reid deals with mind as though it is a thing, an entity. This approach is typical in the faculty view and is diametrically opposed to Hume's view of mind as a collection of ideas. Reid tells us that "the mind is from its very nature a living and active being. Every thing we know of it implies life and active energy; and the reason why all its modes of thinking are called its operations, is that, in all, or in most of them, it is not merely passive, as body is, but is really and properly active."[4]

By "mind" Reid means "that in him which thinks, remembers, reasons, wills."[5] He uses the phrase "operations of the mind" to refer to "every mode of thinking of which we are conscious."[6] Every operation of mind presupposes a power in the mind. Not all the powers of mind are inborn, however. Reid distinguishes two types of powers of the mind: inborn and acquired. He uses "faculties" to stand for those powers of the mind which are original and inborn. Other powers that are acquired by "use, exercise, or study" he calls "habits." "There must be something in the constitution of the mind," Reid says, "necessary to our being able to acquire habits, and this is commonly called capacity."[7] Thus, two individuals may have equal capacities of mind, but one may fail to exercise his faculties and thus not realize his full potential.

Reid divides the powers of the mind into two classes, powers of understanding and powers of the will. The powers of understanding, the intellectual powers, are the means "by which we perceive objects; by which we conceive or remember them; by which we analyze or compound them; and by which we judge and reason concerning them."[8] Through the powers of the will, Reid says we comprehend our active powers, and all that lead to action, or influence the mind to act; such as appetites, passions, affections.[9]

Reid does not deny the function of the nerves or brain. We perceive no external objects without the function of the sensory receptors, nerves and brain. By this, however, he did not mean that the action of the nerves is perception. Reid cautions us that "We ought not to confound the organs of perception with the being that perceives. Perception must be the act of some being that perceives. The eye is not that which sees; it is only the organ by which we see. . . . When I say, I see, I hear, I feel, I remember, this implies that it is one and the same self that performs all these operations."[10]

Reid's distinction between sensation and perception has to do with the relationship between the mental act and the object of the act. In perception there is a clear distinction between the act of mind and the object; in sensation there is not. A perception refers to real objects in the outside world, not mental images or representations. Thus, when we smell a rose, the mental act is smelling and the object is the rose. For Reid smelling the rose is a perception. A sensation does not have a distinction between an act and its object. So, if I feel a pain in my leg, there is really no difference between the "feeling" and the "pain." I could just as well say, according to Reid, that I have a pain. A sensation has to do with direct experiences of what is in the mind. Perceptions refer to events and objects that exist outside the mind. To Reid, the perception of an object gives us true knowledge of the object itself. Sensations are the raw stuff of knowledge, but they contain information that allows us direct knowledge of the objects in the outside world— signs of the reality that can be decoded by the mind. As Reid says, "The senses have a double province." They furnish us with a variety of sensations, some pleasant, others painful, and other indifferent; at the same time they give us a conception, and an invincible belief of the existence of external objects. This conception and belief, which Nature produces by means of the senses, we call *perception.*"[11]

Memory differs from perception only in that the objects of memory exist in the past, whereas the objects of perception are in the present. He does not assert that memory deals with internal images or ideas. This notion leads Reid to reject the basic tenets of association espoused by the British empiricists, since they all deal with internal mental representations.

Judgments have to do with real objects and events rather than with internal mental states. He distinguishes between intuitive judgments and argumentative or propositional judgments. Not a new distinction with Reid, the position holds that intuitive judgments are clear and self-evident and do not require proof for their existence. Propositional judgments do not have qualities of self-evidence, and so we must have proof for belief in their existence. From the time of Descartes, philosophers had tried to use as few intuitive judgments as possible, but they all used them to some degree. Even Hume would have had to posit an assumption of our ability to know our conscious states of the moment. That is an assumption (intuition) presented without proof. Reid, rather than minimizing the number of such intuitive judgments, makes them central to his position. Common sense is, in fact, based on intuitive judgments. Reasoning, Reid says, is the process of passing from one judgment to another.

Reid's faculty psychology is perhaps his most significant contribution to the history of psychology.[12] Although the above discussion emphasizes his differences with Locke, it should be pointed out that Reid used Locke's nonassociational side, his notions of judgment and reason, as a starting point for some of his own thought. Reid's view also has interesting parallels to that of the German rationalist Christian von Wolff who will be considered later in this chapter.

Reid's position on the faculties of mind strongly influenced American psychological thought in the first half of the nineteenth century. It is an active view that emphasizes the functions of mind as contrasted to the passive and structural approach of the British empiricists and later associationists. Reid's emphasis on capacities and abilities would have a lasting influence on human thought, particularly in the realms of psychology and education.

To modern readers Reid is a vague and puzzling thinker, and indeed he may have been just as puzzling to his contemporaries. His followers, particularly Dugald Stewart and Thomas Brown, took great pains to explain and reformulate Reid's notions.

Thomas Brown

Dugald Stewart[13] (1753–1828) largely echoed Reid, but Thomas Brown[14] (1778–1820) was more original in his approach. While rejecting skepticism, Brown drew closer to his associationist predecessors. He was a colleague and follower of Dugald Stewart, but he was not slavishly attached to the tenets of the realist philosophy or of its insistence on innate faculties of mind. Brown sought a middle ground between the atomism and passive nature of the "minds" of the associational psychologists and the orthodoxy of the Scottish School by proposing so-called secondary laws of suggestion.[15] (He avoided the term *association* as implying mere passive sequence.) Mind was more than a combination of elements. Quite apart from association, it contained the unity of an operating, controlling self. The different kinds of possible union, the primary laws of suggestion, were resemblance, contrast, and nearness in time and space. The secondary laws of suggestion, conditional in nature, were duration, liveliness, frequency, recency, degrees of coexistence with other suggestions, constitutional differences of mind or of temperament, differing circumstances of the moment, state of health or efficiency of the body, and prior habits. The secondary laws modified the primary laws according to prevailing conditions and explained why under specified conditions a particular suggestion appeared rather than another—why, at this particular time and place, the thought of "cold" brought forth "dark" rather than "hot"; why the image of "butterfly" sometimes produced "bird" and other times "moth." This insight would lay fallow for nearly a century when the experimental attack on problems of learning began.

Brown also distinguished simple from relative suggestion.[16] He claimed that relative suggestion occurs when we experience feelings of relation as distinguished from simple connections. These feelings include resemblance, difference, and proportion. For example, we have the experience that this house is bigger than that one, that this particular class of objects has the relation of subordinate to superordinate, that there is an equality of the square of the hypotenuse of a right angle to the square of the two other sides, or that there is an incongruity between the shallowness of a posturing player and the drama of heroic proportions in which he appears. So Brown recognized a capacity for learning simple associations. This contribution was one of some originality, anticipating the day when the combination of simple mental elements would be recognized as insufficient to account for learning and perception.

Brown also spoke of a mental chemistry.[17] He used the term for the appearance of a psychological combination that is not present in the elements—the taste of lemonade is a blend, not a sum, of sweet and sour. As we have already seen, John Stuart Mill sharpened this conception somewhat later. Brown's compromises with associationism creates a problem in deciding whether or not he belongs in the Scottish School.[18]

IMMANUEL KANT AND RATIONALISM ON THE CONTINENT

Immanuel Kant was the great philosophical figure of his day on the Continent. His pronouncements on psychology and the possibility (or lack of it) of psychology as science were significant in their day. Kant attributes his intellectual awakening and his idealism to his reading of the philosophy of David Hume. The field of philosophical psychology would have to take into consideration the thinking of Immanuel Kant as it did the work of Plato, Aristotle, and Descartes. How he viewed psychology had a profound effect on both those who agreed and those who disagreed with him. A sharpening and clarification of the distinction between a rational psychology and an empirical psychology resulted. To give some context for Kant, however, before we consider his viewpoint, it is necessary to examine the views of his teacher, Christian von Wolff.

Wolff and Faculty Psychology

Implicitly or explicitly, a doctrine of faculties has often appeared in earlier theories of psychology. The soul was conceived of as carrying on its functions, such as knowing, remembering, feeling, and willing, by making use of corresponding faculties. The first important proponent of eighteenth-century German faculty psychology was Christian von Wolff (1679–1754) who for most of his academic life was a professor at Halle. To place him in temporal perspective, he was most influenced by Leibniz, his older contemporary. His view is representative of the several versions of faculty psychology that prevailed on the Continent in the period from the middle of the eighteenth century through most of the nineteenth century. In no sense is he to be counted among the greatest psychologists, but his influence on Kant would be sufficient reason to mention him. His two psychologies, rational and empirical, set the stage for Kant.

Wolff's *Empirical Psychology*[19] appeared in 1732 and was followed two years later by his *Rational Psychology.*[20] He saw the tasks of these two psychologies as interrelated. Rational psychology deduces from metaphysical conceptions and from the experience of the soul's activities; empirical psychology is concerned with the human being, the composite of body and soul. This way of formulating the distinction between rational and empirical psychology has methodological implications based on emphasis, since in Wolff's view rational psychology depends more on reason and less on experience, and empirical psychology more on experience than on reason. For him this distinction is primarily a contentual one. Soul is the concern of rational psychology; the human being (soul and matter) is the concern of empirical psychology. Both psychologies use the two methods but in varying degrees. Following similar thinking on Leibniz's part, Wolff held that rational psychology gives clear and distinct ideas, whereas empirical psychology yields only obscure, confused ideas of things. Rational psychology depends on reason and empirical psychology on sensation. At one extreme are the confused ideas of sensation and at the other are the clear ideas of reason. In short, mental activities consist of degrees of reason or clarity of ideas.

The major theme of Wolff's empirical psychology is that, though the soul is unitary[21] and lacks parts,[22] it has different powers and faculties. According to Wolff, faculties are "potencies of action" that are expressed in powers.[23] The major dual classification of groups of faculties are knowing, on the one hand, and feeling and desire, on the other.[24] Knowing is further subdivided into perception, memory, understanding, and reason. Let us take memory as an example. Asked why something is remembered, Wolff would reply that it is remembered because one has a faculty of memory. Unfortunately, to ascribe a mental activity to a faculty serves to explain it and makes further analysis unnecessary. At that time it was not apparent that the doctrine of faculties is self-defeating and circular.

Wolff's distinction between empirical and rational psychology was significant, particularly for European philosophical thought, and was prophetic of changes to come. It clarified the existence of two psychologies, even though Wolff derogated empirical psychology and defined it in such a way as to make it subordinate to rational psychology. It has been argued that it is with Wolff that the modern distinction between rationalism and empiricism begins rather than with Descartes and Locke.[25]

Kant and Transcendental Mental Activity

Immanuel Kant (1724–1804), who never traveled more than sixty miles from his birthplace in East Prussia, lived the uneventful life of a philosophy professor at the University of Königsberg. Most of the stories in his chronicles concern nothing more than interruptions of his bachelor routines—the consternation of his neighbors when one day he failed to take his walk at the usual precise hour (he had been enthralled with Rousseau's *Emile*); or the crisis brought about by fast-growing poplars that obscured his view of the church steeple he habitually gazed at while meditating (the owner of the trees obligingly cut their tops); or the trouble he had avoiding sightseers after he became famous (which led him to find a new restaurant in which to take his noonday meal).

Kant's influence on continental thought proved to be enormous. Although not without opposition (his successors, in fact, set out immediately to "correct" his views), he dominated philosophical thinking for generations. His most influential work relevant to psychology, *Critique of Pure Reason*, first appeared in 1781.[26] This publication was followed in 1788 by his *Critique of Practical Reason*[27] and in 1790 by his *Critique of Judgement.*[28] The very titles of these works, his three most important ones, show that they bear some relation to psychology. To say that his inquiry was related to psychology, however, is by no means the same as saying that his approach was psychological. On the contrary, he repeatedly insisted it was not. As he conceived it, his philosophical task was concerned with the question of the validity of knowledge. He understood psychology as an empirical search for the laws of mental functioning. His empirical psychological views are contained in his *Anthropology.*[29] Although he had taught a course with the title for many years, beginning as early as 1772, it was not until 1798 that he prepared the lectures for publication.[30] His contributions of greater moment to psychology came from his critical philosophy, not from his psychology.

Kant is usually represented in his earlier years as doing little more than critically elaborating Wolff's rationalist and faculty doctrines. He tells us that, on reading Hume, he was aroused from his dogmatic slumbers. David Leary argues, however, that the beginning of Kant's "critical period" can be dated earlier through the influence of Leibniz's posthumously published *Noveau Essais sur l'entendement humain (New Essays Concerning Human Understanding).* Leibniz had originally written the piece in reaction to John Locke's *Essay Concerning Human Understanding.*[31] In *Noveau Essais* Leibniz postulated a distinction between sensibility and understanding, sensibility being a "material" sensation received from the outside and understanding a "formal" classification of sensations by the mind. In the case of Leibniz as in Reid, the reaction to Locke's passive view of mind was an attempt to find an active alternative. Leary reports that the influence of Leibniz's distinction between sensibility and understanding was evident in Kant's *De Mundi Sensibilis atque Intelligibilis Forma et Principiis (Concerning the Form and Principles of the Sensible and Intelligible World)* published as a dissertation for his gaining the chair in philosophy at Königsberg.[32]

By Kant's own admission, however, Hume had a significant influence on his intellectual awakening. For Hume, causality was neither self-evident nor capable of logical demonstration. Kant not only was convinced by Hume's argument, but he also realized that this same lack of certainty must be true of all other principles fundamental to philosophy and science. There were two alternatives: either to accept Hume's skepticism or to find *a priori* principles, that is, principles intuitively available prior to experience. It is possible to arrive inductively at general laws only if it is also possible to establish independently *a priori* rational principles.[33] Because, as a rationalist, Kant could not accept the alternative of skepticism, his task became one of establishing that synthetic *a priori* principles are possible, despite Hume's cogent objection. He therefore set for himself the task of demonstrating the existence of these rationalistic principles.

Kant agreed with Hume that all known objects are phenomena of consciousness and not realities independent of the mind. For Kant, however, empiricism is not enough. The known object is not a mere bundle of sensations, for knowledge of it includes "unsensational" characteristics or manifestations of *a priori* principles. That is to say, in addition to sense data, phenomena would not be possible without the mind, which is inherently capable of ordering phenomena.[34]

Kant insisted that the scientist and the philosopher approach nature with certain implicit principles that underlie experience, and he understood his task to be that of finding these principles and making them explicit. He proceeded to derive them from careful rational inquiry into the logical forms of judgments that we make about the world.

These various transcendental principles, or "categories," as Kant[35] called them, are activities of the mind, and, to the extent that they are universal, necessary, and independent of sense experience, they are *a priori*. Consider the argument expressed in the following example. Events follow other events according to rules. Every event has a cause. Nature itself is a system of causal reactions. These statements have always been accepted as valid, but they cannot be verified experientially. They are *a priori* because they are conditions for the possibility of experience. That is, without causality and the other categories one would have no way to order experiences into a phenomenal world of objects. So causality was naturally one of Kant's categories. This particular illustration was chosen because it also served to answer Hume. We cannot know causality from experience, but we do know it *a priori*, intuitively.[36] Kant's twelve categories of understanding include unity, reality, totality, existence or nonexistence, and community or reciprocity.[37]

Kant reinforced the argument for his categories of understanding by claiming that intuitive forms of sensibility also exist prior to experience. Space and time are intuitively knowable, *a priori*.[38] Kant held that consciousness of time and extension in space are certainly real, and not data of the bodily senses. All objects of pure perception are located in space and time, without which objects would not be perceptible. We go on from them to perception of content through experience. They are the forms of intuition as distinguished from the contents of experience. The forms of sensibility of space and time join the transcendental principles and, together with them, become the means of structuring and understanding the world. With its concept of space as *a priori*, Kant's philosophy was a forerunner of what were to emerge as the nativistic theories of space.[39] It had definite ties with Cartesian notions of innate ideas, but it was not the same. A person is not born with ideas but with principles of ordering that provide the conditions for the possibility of experience.

Before dealing with the mind, we must mention the more general problem of Kant's view of mathematics and science. Kant was very much concerned with scientific problems. The profound impression science had made on him was strikingly demonstrated in his emphasis on space and time and causality. To him, mathematics is the source of scientific knowledge inasmuch as mathematics primarily represents *a priori*, absolute, nonempirical judgments requiring no further proof. He believed, and considered he had proved, that an empirical inquiry is as scientific as the amount of mathematics it contains.[40] To Kant, science is exact, quantitative, and mathematical; this view dominates science to this very day.

Kant dealt specifically with the problem of the mind.[41] The great modern rationalists—Descartes, Leibniz, and Spinoza—though differing among themselves, sought to know mind through mind. Kant attacked what he considered their fallacious belief that mind is a substance, that is, that it is "some thing." To state his argument in detail would be impracticable; it is enough to say he demonstrated to his own satisfaction that mind is insubstantial and a purely formal unity. Rejection of mind as substance had direct implications for psychology as a science. It followed that mental processes cannot be measured, since they have only the dimension of time and not space.[42] Psychology cannot possibly be an experimental science, he said, if it has but one dimension of time, because there is no other variable with which to relate temporal events.

This view did not mean that Kant rejected the concept of the mind. As a formal unity he lifted it to the pinnacle of his system, for he held mind to be the means whereby the categories and concepts are known. Without being spatial, the mind orders perceptual phenomena through the innate principles of time and space and supplies us with the categories that make it possible to understand experience and to make incoming sensations meaningful. In a manner reminiscent of Plato, Kant posited that the mind is an active agency that composes the raw material of the world into an order of conceptualized phenomena. But Kant was no idealist; he did not believe that the mind creates the world. The world, he stated, is made of substances that are "things in themselves" with independent existences, but they are not knowable.

Apperception was Kant's philosophical term for the mind's process of assimilating and interpreting new experiences in order to give them meaning. In this perspective he sees unity in every act of perception. In recognizing an object, we can find the bits and pieces that are the elements of the associationists, but these are meaningfully organized *a priori*, not through association. The mind has acted to form a unitary experience, to create an object within a meaningful context. The active mind organizes the experience with the help of space and time and Kantian categories. Kant viewed the mind as active apperception. This process is not passive impression, such as the British empiricists considered it, but rather an active grasping.

"Things in themselves," the causes of things, are unknowable, according to Kant. Kant agreed with Locke and Hume that knowledge comes from sensory perception; this is perception not of things as they really are, but only as they appear to us (phenomena). We perceive phenomena the way our mind makes us see them. The mind selects, according to the structures arising from the categories, from the welter of impinging sensations and imposes on them the unity inherent in their principles.

Not surprisingly, Kant was drawn to faculty psychology, which was rationalistic and thus free from appeal to empiricism, and which tended to lend itself easily to the support of religious views. From this perspective, the categories are forms, in the Platonic sense, of the mind. Kant classified mental faculties into cognitive (knowing), feeling, and desiring and subdivided the cognitive faculty into understanding, judgment, and reason.[43]

The immediate effect of Kant's philosophical pronouncements about mind and the impossibility of experiment was to cast doubt on psychology becoming a natural science, since it was "merely" empirical and so could not demonstrate the higher order lawfulness necessary for a natural science.[44] Kant's pronouncement that psychology could not be mathematical or analytical also seemed to cut it off from the natural sciences. It is always dangerous, of course, to say that something is not possible, and there are always those who will make it possible. It would be through the work of Herbart, Beneke, and finally Fechner and Wundt, that Kant's negative dictum would be overthrown.

Kant also helped to keep subjectivism alive, for he stressed the importance of mental phenomena as such. By holding that events are appearances, he helped to direct psychology toward phenomenalism. His view that ultimate principles lie outside the context of experience made Kant the great champion of nativism, which agrees that human beings have innate "given" ways of knowing that are true but not dependent on experience. This stress on unity or organization, with its nativistic base, affected German thought well into the twentieth century.

Herbart and Experience, Metaphysics, and Mathematics

Johann Friedrich Herbart (1776–1841) was a professor at Göttingen and at Königsberg; in fact, he filled the chair vacated by Kant. While a tutor in Switzerland, he became interested in problems of education, which thereafter formed a supplement to his already established philosophical and psychological interests. An account of his psychology is contained in the *Lehrbuch zur Psychologie*,[45] which appeared in 1816, and in his more extensive *Psychologie als Wissenschaft neu gegründet auf Erfahrung, Metaphysik and Mathematik*,[46] which appeared in 1824–1825. The qualifying terms in the title of this, his major book, give the clue to the nature of his psychology; it is a science based on experience, metaphysics, and mathematics. These three themes will become obvious in the account that follows.

Herbart's metaphysical starting point for psychology was his concept of being.[47] His general concept of the universe was that of independent elements called reals. To some extent he was following Leibniz, but, unlike Leibniz, he did not regard all reals as sharing the common characteristic of consciousness. Herbart's conception of mechanical interaction is the antithesis of Leibniz's conception of preestablished harmony. Despite his dependence on metaphysics, Herbart was led by his particular definition of being to define psychology as the "mechanics of the mind." In keeping with the trend of the times, which was to minimize the mind in favor of emphasizing consciousness, he explained mental states as an interaction of ideas. The mind is the stage on which the vastly more important players—the ideas—act their parts.

Herbart held that experimentation in psychology is impossible,[48] but to remain a science, psychology must at least be mathematical. He therefore prepared a series of equations that dealt with psychological matters.[49] For example, to determine how much of an idea is suppressed, he postulated that O equals the suppressed portion of the ideas in time (indicated by t), and S is the aggregate amount suppressed. Then $O = S\ (1 - e^{-t})$. He made no actual measurements; the mathematical values he assigned in any given equation were always guesses based on rational plausibility, and his mathematical formulations served only as illustrations.

Herbart's system of psychology concerned elementary bits of experiences (sensations in our terminology) which combined to form ideas. He held that ideas are the real contents of the mind. To this extent he followed the British associationists, but the mechanics of Leibniz's theory of ideas as activity gave him the means of making a substantial modification of British associationism—the concept of ideas as forces. According to British associationism, ideas combined in what he conceived to be entirely too passive a fashion. Herbart argued that associations are in reality much more complicated than the associationists had described them.[50] The associationists had assumed, implicitly or otherwise, only the attraction of ideas and had not paid particular attention to the nature of the force involved.

Herbart postulated both the attraction and repulsion of ideas, particularly when ideas clash. Ideas become forces, he said, when they resist one another.[51] Some ideas do not resist one another, and for these associations a conventional explanation is sufficient. These are the ideas that are neither opposed nor contrasted with one another such as a tone and color which unhindered form a complex.[52]

Other contrasting ideas, such as red and yellow, may become blended or fused but will never form a complex. Sometimes ideas are so resistive that they do not form even loosely affiliated complexes. One idea may be so much a hindrance to another that the second is not even available in consciousness.[53] This hindered idea, though not in consciousness, still exists. Inhibited though these ideas may be, they remain as tendencies. When the forces opposing the ideas are changed—when there is a change in the apperceptive mass—then the idea that has previously been kept out of consciousness returns.

This entering into consciousness presupposes the notion of a threshold of consciousness, a point above which an idea is conscious and below which it is not. Herbart also used the threshold concept to explain sleep. If only a few active ideas are present, we have dreaming; if all active ideas are driven below the threshold, we have the unconsciousness that is deep sleep.[54]

According to Herbart, once created an idea is never lost. The number of ideas a person is conscious of at any given moment is small in comparison with the number of ideas he or she is capable of having. A person can shift ideas that are below the threshold into consciousness.[55] Some ideas shift readily; others do not. Submerged ideas move above the threshold to the full focus of attention if they are congenial to the ideas already in consciousness, that is, if they are consonant with the apperceptive mass or dominant system of conscious ideas. Herbart derived this conception from Leibniz. An idea that comes into consciousness combines with the existing ideas, if it is congenial with those ideas. There is a unity of consciousness—attention, one might call it—so that one cannot attend to two ideas at once except insofar as they will unite into a single complex idea. When one idea is the focus of consciousness, it forces incongruous ideas into the background or out of consciousness altogether. Combined ideas form wholes, and a combination of related ideas forms an apperceptive mass, into which relevant ideas are permitted to enter while irrelevant ones are excluded.

Ideas are active and may struggle with one another for a place in consciousness. Herbart's concept of threshold and its corollary—that there are both conscious and unconscious mental processes—represent distinct advances over earlier views, as does his account of how ideas presently excluded from consciousness can reappear. Herbart gave psychology the beginning of a theory of inhibition (or interference in learning). In times to come it would be used in many forms and guises and theories, extending from Pavlov's "conditioned reflex" to Freud's "repression." However, Herbart's contribution in this area should not be overestimated. Darwinism, medical psychology, and psychiatry contributed perhaps more than Herbart did to the understanding of the dynamics of unconscious processes.

Herbart helped show that psychology was crucial to educational theory and practice, where his theory of apperception had the most direct and influential application. Since it is against the background of previous experience that a new idea is assimilated in the apperceptive mass, it follows that, if information is to be acquired as easily and as rapidly as possible, in teaching one should introduce new material by building on the apperceptive mass of already familiar ideas. This line of reasoning led educators to adopt the practice of planning lessons so that the pupil passed from already familiar to closely related but unfamiliar elements. Herbart's work was also influential in exposing the shallowness and sterility of the faculty psychology that was so prevalent during this time.[56]

SUMMARY

This chapter deals with two attempts to bring activity into the psychological process in reaction to Locke's passivity and Hume's detachment from reality. Reid responded with his faculty psychology and a reliance on intuition and instinct. In addition to the omnipresent rationalism, prescriptively speaking, conscious mentalism prevailed because psychology was concerned with experience, and a dualism of mind and body was exemplified in the thinking of von Wolff, Kant, and Herbart. Herbart, however, also emphasized unconscious mentalism by conceptualizing the threshold and related phenomena. All three philosophers explicitly and implicitly accepted nomotheticism as a concern with the general and not the particular. Kant presented what, essentially, is a static view of human nature, whereas Herbart was to some extent concerned with dynamics, as seen in his conception of attraction and repulsion of ideas.

The philosophically rooted views of Wolff, Kant, and Herbart helped to prepare the way for a psychology separate from philosophy. Wolff espoused the separation of empirical from rational psychology. Kant made quantitativeness the hallmark of a science but denied psychology a place as a science because it could not be mathematical. Herbart made psychology a mathematical science but denied it could be quantitative. The two views, different as they are, sharpened the issue of the quantitative nature of psychology without resolving it. However, each made distinctions that would help psychology emerge as a separate science—once answers to their arguments could be found.

NOTES

1. S. A. Grave, *The Scottish Philosophy of Common Sense* (Oxford: Clarendon Press, 1960). Of course, several other figures are not mentioned here. We might just as well have begun with Francis Hutcheson (1694–1746) who, though holding to many of Locke's notions, demonstrated some of the strains that would become more explicit with Reid.
2. See Baruch A. Brody's introduction in Thomas Reid, *Essays on the Intellectual Powers of Man* (Cambridge, Mass.: MIT Press, 1969), pp. vii–xxvi.
3. George H. Lewes, *The History of Philosophy*, 5th ed. (London: Longmans, Green, and Co., 1880), Vol. II, pp. 399–400.
4. T. Reid, *Essays on the Intellectual Powers of Man* (Cambridge, Mass.: MIT Press, 1969), p. 6. (1785), Essay I, Chapter 1.
5. *Ibid.*, p. 5.
6. *Ibid.*
7. *Ibid.*, p. 7.
8. *Ibid.*, p. 65.
9. *Ibid.*
10. *Ibid.*, pp. 76–77.
11. T. Reid, *Essays on the Intellectual Powers of Man* (1785), ii, Chapter xvi (quoted in Lewes, *History of Philosophy*, pp. 405–406).
12. T. Reid, *Essays.*
13. D. Stewart, *Elements of the Philosophy of the Human Mind*, 3 vols. (London: Tegg, 1867) (1793–1817).
14. T. Brown, *Lectures.*
15. *Ibid.*, (Herrnstein and Boring, Excerpt No. 71).
16. *Ibid.*
17. *Ibid.*
18. F. Copleston, *A History of Philosophy* (London: Burns, Oates, 1929), Vol. V, pp. 383–385.
19. C. von Wolff, *Psychologia empirica* (Frankfurt: Rengeriana, 1732).
20. C. von Wolff, *Psychologia rationalis* (Frankfurt: Rengeriana, 1734).
21. C. von Wolff, "Rational Psychology," sec. between 48–67, trans. E. K. Rand, in B. Rand, ed., *The Classical Psychologists* (New York: Houghton Mifflin, 1912), pp. 229–231 (1734).
22. *Ibid.*, Sec. 57.
23. *Ibid.*, Sec. 54.
24. W. B. Pillsbury, *The History of Psychology* (New York: W. W. Norton, 1929), pp. 110–111.
25. David Leary, "Kant and Modern Psychology," in William Woodward and Mitchell Asch, eds., *The Problematic Science: Psychology in Nineteenth-Century Thought* (New York: Praeger, 1982), pp. 19–21.
26. I. Kant, "The Critique of Pure Reason," trans. J.M.D. Meiklejohn, in R. M. Hutchins, ed., *The Great Books of the Western World*, Vol. XLII (Chicago: Encyclopaedia Britannica, 1952), pp. 1–252 (1781).

27. I. Kant, "The Critique of Practical Reason," trans. T. K. Abbott, in R. M. Hutchins, ed., *The Great Books of the Western World,* Vol. XLII, pp. 291–361 (1788).
28. I. Kant, "The Critique of Judgment," trans. J. C. Meredith, in R. M. Hutchins, ed., *The Great Books of the Western World,* Vol. XLII, pp. 461–613 (1790).
29. I. Kant, *Anthropology from a Pragmatic Point of View,* trans. and intro. Mary J. Gregor (The Hague: Nijhoff, 1974) (1798).
30. I. Kant, *The Classification of Mental Disorders,* trans. and ed. C. T. Sullivan (Doylestone: Doylestone Foundation, 1964) (1798).
31. D. Leary, "Immanuel Kant and the Development of Modern Psychology," pp. 18–19; G. W. Leibniz, *New Essays on Human Understanding,* trans. P. Remnant and J. Bennett (Cambridge: Cambridge University Press, 1981).
32. Immanuel Kant, *De Mundi Sensibilis atque Intelligibilis Forma et Principiis* (1770) in *Kant's Werke,* reprint of Prussian Academy edition of 1902 (Berlin: de Gruyter, 1968), 9 vols., Vol. 2, pp. 385–420.
33. "Pure Reason."
34. *Ibid.*
35. *Ibid.*
36. *Ibid.* (Hernnstein and Boring, Excerpt No. 105).
37. *Ibid.*
38. *Ibid.*
39. *Ibid.* (Herrnstein and Boring, Excerpt No. 30).
40. I. Kant, *Metaphysische Anfangsgrunde der Naturwissenschaft* (Riga: Hartknoch, 1766), Preface.
41. For example, "Pure Reason."
42. *Ibid.,* Sec. 11.
43. *Judgment,* Introduction IX.
44. David Leary in an excellent series of papers has made much of this difficult literature understandable. See Leary, "The Philosophical Development of the Conception of Psychology in Germany, 1780–1850," *Journal of the History of the Behavioral Sciences, 14* (1978):113–121; "German Idealism and the Development of Psychology in the Nineteenth Century," *Journal of the History of Philosophy, 18* (1980):299–317.
45. J. F. Herbart, *Lehrbuch der Psychologie,* 2nd ed. (Königsberg: Unzer, 1834) (1816).
46. J. F. Herbart, *Psychologie als Wissenschaft Neugegrundet auf Erfahrung, Metaphysik und Mathematik,* 2 vols. (Königsberg: Unzer, 1824–1825).
47. *Ibid.,* Chapter 2.
48. J. F. Herbart, *A Text-book in Psychology,* 2nd rev. ed., trans. M. K. Smith (New York: Appleton, 1891), Sec. 4. (1834).
49. See also David Leary, "The Historical Foundation of Herbart's Mathematization of Psychology," *Journal of the History of the Behavioral Sciences, 16* (1980):150–163.
50. Herbart, *A Text-book in Psychology,* Sec. 72.
51. *Ibid.,* Sec. 10.
52. *Ibid.,* Sec. 22.
53. *Ibid.,* Sec. 11.
54. *Ibid.,* Sec. 50.
55. *Ibid.,* Sec. 127.
56. *Ibid.,* Sec. 9, 53–125.

Hermann von Helmholtz.

Chapter 12

Helmholtz: The Physiological Substrate

Thus far the emphasis in this history has been on the origin of psychological thought in philosophy and medicine. Another significant source for psychological thought and particularly the line from which experimental psychology was to emerge was experimental physiology, the study of the functioning of the organic systems of the body.

General physiology became a separate discipline with the appointment in 1833 of Johannes Müller to the first professorship of physiology at the University of Berlin. Here, between 1834 and 1840, Müller compiled his *Handbuch der Physiologie des Menschen*, a systematic organization of comparative anatomy, chemistry, and physics as related to general physiology.[1] More pertinent to psychology at this time, however, was the study of the nervous system by physiologists. In this field the giant among pioneer neural physiologists was Hermann von Helmholtz, but, as always, others prepared the way.

PHYSIOLOGY AND ALLIED DISCIPLINES BEFORE HELMHOLTZ

During the latter half of the seventeenth century, as well as during the eighteenth century, physiology assumed many of its modern characteristics and went beyond the hypothetical science of Hartley and La Mettrie. Robert Whytt (1714–1766), for example, summarizing in 1751 the physiology of the reflex, formulated the beginnings of many modern concepts.[2] According to Whytt, Stephen Hales performed the "fundamental" experiment on the nature and existence of the reflex in about 1730. Hales made use of the already known fact that a decapitated frog responded to pinching by withdrawing its legs, and he found that it failed to continue to do so when the spinal cord was destroyed. Whytt himself repeated and extended this experiment, in the course of which he introduced the terms *stimulus* and *response.* In 1771 Johann August Unzer (1727–1799) used the word *reflex* to distinguish between this kind of action and that carried on volitionally.

The first half of the nineteenth century witnessed a variety of developments that firmly established physiology as a science. Simultaneous with these developments was the rise of phrenology, which later proved to be a scientific blind alley but which served to bring attention to the mind and its relation to the brain.

If we can point to one general theme that ties these developments together, it is the identification of nervous functions with mental and behavioral activity and the localization of such functions in the brain. We have already seen the identification of brain action with mental and behavioral events in our treatment of Hartley, La Mettrie, and Cabanis. The following investigates the search for the localization of specific brain functions. Although we can trace the origins of the search back to Cabanis's tripartite division of the nervous system, it is useful for our purposes to begin with the differentiation between sensory and motor function known as the Bell–Magendie Law.

The Bell–Magendie Law

During the years 1811–1822 Charles Bell[3] (1774–1842) in Great Britain and François Magendie[4] (1783–1855) in France, working independently, performed the research that distinguished between the sensory and motor nerves. In a general way this distinction had been known to Galen, and others had from time to time rediscovered it. By the early nineteenth century, however, the distinction between sensory and motor functions was not generally made. The nerves were conceived as if all of them more or less indiscriminately carried on both motor and sensory functions. A controversy developed over whose work came first.[5] Bell published first, but it is not entirely clear that his original paper reported what he later claimed it did; Magendie did not publish his finding until eleven years after Bell, but he stated the matter with unequivocal clarity. The important point is that their experimental work made a clearcut distinction between motor and sensory nerves.

Magendie established the distinction by cutting the nerve roots at the spinal cord and studying the functions that were lost. He found that the sensory fibers enter through the posterior (dorsal) roots of the spinal cord, whereas the anterior (ventral) roots are the path through which the motor fibers leave the spinal cord. For instance, when Magendie cut an anterior root, he found a complete paralysis, which was not present when the posterior root was cut. Since this cutting prevented movement, the anterior root must have been responsible for the movement.

One effect of this work was to separate clearly neural physiology into the studies of sensory and motor functions or, to use more obviously psychological terminology, to establish a physiological basis for a distinction between sensation and movement. This distinction between sensory and motor nerves, according to what came to be called the Bell–Magendie law, is still fundamental today in bringing order into the study of physiology and psychology. Once it was established and accepted that the nervous system was divisible into these two functions, it was only natural to push the question further. Just how many divisions does the nervous system have?

Gall and Phrenology

At about the same time Bell and Magendie made their important contributions, an attempt was already being made to attach specific mental and behavioral behaviors and traits to specific areas of the brain. This movement has become known as phrenology. The founder of this notion was Franz Joseph Gall (1758–1828). Today we think of phrenology as a fraudulent activity such as palm reading. Gall, however, and most of his followers were not charlatans but well-trained medical practitioners who knew as much about neural and cranial anatomy as anyone in their day. They believed they had discovered a new science that would allow a quantitative measure of psychological traits and abilities by reference to the development of brain matter serving different functions.[6]

Gall had been interested in correlating behaviors with physiognomy, the shape of the head or face, since his childhood. While still a boy, he believed he saw a relationship between the mental characteristics of his schoolmates and the shapes of their faces. Years later, when mapping out the location of centers for various functions on the surface of the cerebrum, the cerebral cortex, he tried to verify this impression. He reasoned that the degree to which a faculty was developed would be reflected in a proportionate increase in brain matter in the area that served that function. Since he believed that the skull conformed to the shape of the brain, which held more brain matter, there should be a characteristic bump or protrusion of the skill. Following the same logic, Gall stated that where a faculty is underdeveloped there should be less matter and thus a comparable hollow or indention in the skull. Gall collected instances of what appeared to be over- and underdevelopment of areas of the brain as reflected in the shape of the skull, and thereby formed judgments of their possessors' striking characteristics. He made these judgments by selecting individuals for supposed outstanding traits and measuring their heads. For instance, he would reason that a pickpocket, having a desire to acquire wealth, should have a bulge in the area of acquisitiveness. Since that individual was a pickpocket rather than an honest businessman, he must have a weak moral sense, so there should be an indention in the moral region.

We have represented Gall as a methodological empiricist because, although he made many assumptions, he took measurements and located his faculties following inductive procedures. He measured his pickpockets and chose for the area of acquisitiveness the region where they had a bump in common. Later, he extended his search among friends and public figures. By this means Gall constructed a system of twenty-seven faculties, duplicated on the two lobes of the brain.

From a modern perspective we are struck by the glaring inadequacy of the method Gall used. Today, any college sophomore in psychology would be able to tell him that his research called for taking an unselected sample of the population, measuring all their bumps, and, without knowledge of these measurements, estimating their standing on the psychological characteristics with which Gall was concerned. Then the two streams of data would have to be compared for the degree and nature of the relationship shown. The relationship would then be subjected to a statistical analysis to determine whether the occurrence was greater than some criterion of chance. Everyone has bumps and hollows on their heads, and everyone's skull varies in thickness regardless of the shape of the brain. Gall's data were based on chance correlations of random bumps and hollows. Of course, he did not know about statistical analyses since they were not available in his day. He used the medical model, a method involving case studies, in which one or very few individuals were selected as indicative of the whole supposed population.

Gall began lecturing on his discoveries in Vienna. It was not long before his teaching excited popular attention, and soon he had disciples and fellow practitioners, including Johann Kaspar Spurzheim (1776–1832). Spurzheim did much thereafter to extend the number of characteristics studied and to spread the phrenological doctrine. Gall held that phrenology was a specialty of medicine, and for most of the remainder of his life he would accept only trained medical practitioners as his students.

Had Gall been right, of course, he would have made one of the most significant discoveries of his day. Phrenology would have been a way to determine an individual's abilities and character by objective measurement. This is exactly what Gall and his followers believed they had succeeded in doing. When the mapping was completed, each faculty had a definite place of localization in an area of the cerebral cortex. Thus, with the aid of a chart, the phrenologist could examine the subject's skull and plot the individual's strengths and weaknesses in abilities and personality. Later, self-help books were published that taught individuals how to measure heads and make assessments of the degree of an individual's faculty developments based on standards of "small," "normal," and "large."

Phrenology was a faculty psychology to end all faculty psychologies. Spurzheim postulated thirty-seven characteristics or faculties, which he divided into affective and intellectual faculties.[7] He further subdivided these two classes into propensities and sentiments, and perceptive and reflective faculties. Some of the affective faculties were destructiveness, amativeness, self-esteem, and benevolence; the intellectual capacities included calculation, order, and causality. As in all faculty psychologies, the major task was naming and estimating the strength of the function. Once done, this made further analysis superfluous. Thus, it served as a block to further inquiry.

Phrenology was never generally accepted by scientists even when it was still possible to regard its tenets as hypothetically plausible. It was opposed by such familiar figures as Charles Bell and Thomas Brown in Great Britain and Pierre Flourens in France. The medical profession was also antagonistic, which led Gall finally to reject the notion that the phrenologist required medical training to practice. Unfortunately, this change led to the emergence of lay phrenologists who by the 1860s were trained in six weeks or less and went forth to ply their trade. Only later, after the lay phrenologists came on the scene, did phrenology gain its sideshow and charlatanistic reputation.

Spurzheim and Gall finally came to a parting over their disagreements on the nature of phrenology. Spurzheim wanted to add to the faculties originally determined by Gall. Gall resisted, believing that once the faculties were allowed to proliferate, there would be no end to the additions. In addition, Spurzheim wanted to eliminate the gaps between the circles drawn in Gall's system and replace them with contiguous blocks. The brain, after all, is not constructed like a bunch of grapes, he claimed. By the time of their break, Gall and Spurzheim were both living in Paris, having been driven out of Vienna out of fear that their doctrines would lead to the rejection of the notion of soul and thus lead individuals to atheism. Gall and Spurzheim did distinguish between mind and soul, however, and did not attack the notion of the soul as an immortal part.

Gall remained in Paris for the remainder of his life, but Spurzheim actively spread his phrenological views across Europe, Britain, and the United States. His visit to the United States in 1832 produced considerable interest even among physicians,[8] especially those who practiced in the mental hospitals.[9] Rather than necessarily accepting his views, in toto, they found that phrenology offered them general guidance in their thinking about the abnormal functioning of the mind as it relates to the condition of specific areas of the brain. To this extent phrenology was of value, and its appeal continued despite the scientific opposition and lasted even into the twentieth century. To this day, popular magazines are devoted to it, and phrenological charts with their neat demarcations superimposed on an outline of the head still appear at the booths of fortune tellers at amusement parks and fairs.

Phrenology was widely accepted in America. The notion of faculties was not new in America, having been introduced through the teachings of the Scottish faculty psychologists very early in the nineteenth century. In nineteenth-century America phrenologists served much the same role as applied psychologists have done in the twentieth century. They would, among other things, tell parents and teachers of the potential of the children under their care; they could give bankers an assessment of an employee's trustworthiness; they could tell couples planning marriage whether they had traits in common that would make them a good match. Through all the attacks by scientists and by many medical professionals, phrenology did not die out because of criticism. In many respects it disappeared primarily because it would be replaced in the early twentieth century by the psychological testing movement, a movement that shared many of the same goals as Gall's phrenology.

Phrenology served a number of other functions. It made the man in the street aware that he had a brain and that this brain was the locus of mental activity. Even more important, it stimulated physiologists to take up research on the brain to attempt a more scientific analysis of brain function. Phrenology helped to make explicit that psychological functions may be localized in the brain. It also fostered a functional approach to psychological phenomena destined to remain significant.

Flourens and Localization of Function in the Cerebrum

As noted earlier, one of Gall's sharpest critics was Pierre Flourens (1794–1867). Flourens was also engaged in investigating the function of various parts of the brain, but he did so by performing experiments, not by collecting anecdotes. His research led him to the conclusion that removal of the cerebrum, though leaving the reflexes intact, abolishes thought and volition.[10] Moreover, he concluded that the cerebrum as a whole, and not limited portions of it, is responsible for all thought and volition. He localized various functions in the other major parts of the brain—the cerebellum and the medulla oblongata, for example—but he said that each part, in its turn, functioned as a whole. This theory was directed against phrenology, of course; the phrenologists localized each of their thirty-seven faculties in definite parts of the cerebrum. Flourens's view that the cerebrum functions as a whole prevailed for years thereafter, a view that was strengthened, if anything, by being in opposition to the phrenologists' theory.

The first successful challenge to Flourens's doctrine of the unity of the cerebrum was not made until 1861. At that time Paul Broca (1824–1880), the French surgeon and physical anthropologist, showed that the loss of speech in one individual was due to a lesion centering in the third convolution of the left frontal lobe.[11] Broca had found a localization of function within a specific area of the cerebral cortex. That speech was too complicated a mechanism to be confined to one specific region, as later research showed, does not detract from the importance of this first demonstration of specific localization. Direct electrical stimulation of the brain followed in 1870, demonstrated first by G. Fritsch and E. Hitzig.[12] This milestone led to the concept of the existence of a series of motor centers and also seemed to establish (what was then accepted as fact) that a variety of brain centers existed. Needless to say, the functions that were isolated bore no resemblance to those named by the phrenologist.

Johannes Müller and the Specific Energy of Nerves

In 1833 Johannes Müller (1801–1858) was named to the newly created chair of physiology at Berlin. This chair had previously been combined with that of anatomy. Müller's appointment signaled the recognition of physiology as an independent sphere of science. His major work, *Handbuch der Physiologie des Menschen*,[13] which appeared between 1834 and 1840, systematized and exhaustively summarized the knowledge of physiology of his time in a primarily inductive fashion. (Francis Bacon would have approved.) This work served to place general physiology on a scientific footing. In it, he brought comparative chemistry and physics to bear on physiological problems. He accepted the concept that vital phenomena are fundamentally different from those of chemistry and physics, which are not concerned with living substances. His adherence to a vitalistic prescription stands in sharp contrast to the mechanistic approach, and even his students denied this concept. Müller may be said to have done for general physiology what Helmholtz in the next generation was to do for neural physiology.

Müller's most direct contribution to psychology was his doctrine of the specific energy of nerves.[14] He arrived at the conclusion that each sensory nerve, however stimulated, gives rise to only one type of sensory process, and no other.[15] The sensation that is experienced is due not to the nature of the stimulus as such, but to the sense organ, nerve, or brain center that is stimulated. For example, the optic nerve always responds by leading to the sensation of light whether it is stimulated in the usual fashion or pinched, heated, irritated by acid, or shocked by electric current. Müller was saying that every sensory nerve responds in its own characteristic way, no matter how stimulated. To paraphrase a statement of William James, if we were to interchange surgically the optic and auditory nerves, we would hear the lightning and see the thunder.[16] Müller expressed physiologically what George Berkeley had said philosophically, that we are aware not of the objects of the outside world but of the states of our sensory nerves. Müller was a Kantian, and he believed his doctrine offered unequivocal support for nativism, the belief in innate perceptual processes. What is more innate than the nervous system itself? In a moment, however, we will find Helmholtz using the same doctrine to support empiricism.

Where does the specificity arise? Müller seriously considered two possibilities: the nerves terminate either in the nerves themselves or in the centers in the brain. In an early publication he attributed specificity for vision to the portions of the brain it involved. Both views seemed to him to be defensible, but in his later *Handbuch* he decided in favor of the specific energies being in the nerves themselves. Inasmuch as Flourens's research discredited the doctrine of cortical localization, this conclusion is hardly surprising. Consequently, Müller's version of specific energies was not brought into question by the arguments concerning brain localization. Nowadays, with increased knowledge, we would assign the specificity to the brain, not the nerves.

To take Müller's doctrine in its broadest perspective is to say that we are not aware of objects directly but only through some form of intermediary—in this case, the sense organs and nerves. For example, Müller used his doctrine of specific nerve energies to answer the question of how the eye could represent whatever object it received.[17] In addition to the inverted image problem, he dealt with the question of the size of an object, especially how the eye represents large objects as such. His answer to both problems was that all the mind perceives is the state of the nerves leading to the brain. This principle of knowing only through an intermediary had been understood since Herophilus, and the British empiricists, such as Berkeley, and the associationists in their various interpretations had made much of the fact. Müller's research, however, gave a scientifically solid footing that still prevails.

Donders and Reaction Time

The speed of reaction had been a research problem since the end of the eighteenth century when N. Maskelyne, the Astronomer Royal at Greenwich, dismissed his assistant for making errors in observing the time at which stars crossed the meridian.[18] Only a moment's reflection will tell us that this is a very serious matter because astronomical findings are calibrated by these observations.

A few years later, Friedrich Wilhelm Bessel (1784–1846), the Prussian astronomer, came on an account of the incident and realized that the unlucky assistant might not be unique and that, in general, astronomers' observations of the times of stellar events might differ in accuracy. When the problem was put this way, other astronomers agreed with Bessel, and the "personal equation," as it came to be called, became a matter of widespread interest among them. A variety of methods used to compare the personal equation of one astronomer to that of another came into use. That is, relative personal equations were established—astronomer A was shown to be one-tenth of a second slower than B, but two-tenths of a second faster than C in carrying out his stellar observations. A constant correction, the personal equation of $B - A = 0.10$ second could then be used in collating their astronomical observations.

After the discovery of electric currents and electromagnets, these relative personal equations became absolute measures through the invention and perfection of the chronograph and chronoscope. In the chronograph, a key is pressed, making a mark on a drum that receives constant marks from a tuning fork vibrating 500 times a second. The first chronographs measured the time accurately to less than a tenth of a second, but technical advances continued rapidly. By 1862, the Hipp chronoscope was being used to measure the personal equation to a thousandth of a second. The measurements these instruments supplied could now be stated in absolute terms—A took 300 milliseconds to respond, whereas B took 200 milliseconds.

The astronomer's absolute personal equation, when adapted to physiological tasks, came to be called reaction time. Franciscus Cornelius Donders (1818–1889), a Dutch physiologist and a contemporary of Helmholtz, became interested in this matter.[19] First in 1865 and then more fully in 1868, he extended the study by going beyond simple reaction time or the reaction to a predetermined stimulus by a given predetermined response. A reaction already agreed on, pressing a key, for example, would be made when a light went on. The elapsed time was simple reaction time. If this reaction were to be made more complicated, Donders reasoned, the increased time taken to react could be attributed to more complicated cognitive processing. He performed experiments to study so-called discrimination and choice reaction times.

Simple reaction time had called for subjects to respond to stimulus A with response a. For discrimination time, Donders presented several stimuli—A, B, C, D—in irregular order, but his subjects were instructed to respond only to A, not to the others. Consequently, they had to discriminate A from all other stimuli before responding with a. In his new discrimination reaction, a was to be made to a red light, but the subject was to withhold his reaction if a green light, B, or a yellow light, C, was flashed. As Donders predicted, his subjects took longer to make the discrimination reaction than they did to make the simple reaction. Subtracting simple reaction time from the discrimination reaction time gave him the discrimination time. This was called the subtractive procedure. Choice was even more complicated: subjects responded to A with a, B with b, C with c, and so on. This gave a still longer reaction time; the choice time was the total time minus the discrimination and simple reaction times. From the measures, Donders obtained three reaction times—simple, discrimination, and choice. The very time taken by mental events had been brought to heel and measured. Thus, the temporal study of various mental functions—"mental chronometry," as it was called—was launched, to be followed up by Wilhelm Wundt and others later.

HERMANN VON HELMHOLTZ

The compartmentalization of knowledge is a limitation that most scientists, including psychologists, suffer gladly, human capabilities being what they are. They find one thing quite enough to do. The great abilities of Hermann von Helmholtz permitted him to disregard the convenient but artificial boundaries that had been set up between sciences. By what resembled a process of natural growth, Hermann von Helmholtz was led by his interest in research through physics (he was a co-formulator of the law of the conservation of energy); neural physiology (he measured the rate of the neural impulse); optics (he invented the ophthalmoscope and advanced the theory of color vision associated with his name); acoustics (he formulated the theory of resonance as the basis for hearing); and other important, but less relevant, work in hydrodynamics, electrodynamics, and meteorological physics. In all, he wrote more than 200 papers and books, a high proportion of which made important contributions to science.

Helmholtz conceived of psychology as a separate discipline, but as one allied to metaphysics insofar as it dealt with the laws and nature of the products of the mind.[20] He made an exception of the psychology of the senses because of its close alliance with physiology. Consequently, he had no hesitation in discussing psychological issues pertinent to his interests.

Helmholtz was empirical in the tradition of Locke and Hartley. He stated his major argument against nativism with admirable brevity: nativism might not be disprovable, but it was also not parsimonious.[21] In spite of his strong empirical tendencies, however, Helmholtz was also influenced to some extent by Kant. For example, he accepted the law of causality as *a priori* and transcendental, and not demonstrable from anything else.[22] Causality was not a law of nature but a regulative principle guiding the scientist in comprehending phenomena. Later in this chapter we will consider how he related his empirical position to space perception.

Life and General Scientific Endeavors of Helmholtz

Hermann Ludwig Ferdinand von Helmholtz (1821–1894) was born in Potsdam, Germany.[23] His father taught in the Gymnasium of that city and, because of the son's delicate health, first tutored him at home. At age nine, the boy entered the Gymnasium and advanced so rapidly that he was graduated at seventeen. Lacking the financial means to study physics, an already formed major interest, Helmholtz continued his studies at the Medico-Chirurgical Friedrich-Wilhelm Institute in Berlin where no tuition was charged to those who promised to serve as surgeons in the army upon graduation. Helmholtz was never a student at the University of Berlin, but Johannes Müller was the teacher who had the most profound effect on him during these student days. The students under Müller, who became Helmholtz's friends, included Emil DuBois-Reymond, Rudolf Virchow, and Ernst Brücke. They all admired Müller immensely, but he was of an older generation, and although he had helped to wrest physiology away from the philosophy of nature, he still held to the prevailing vitalisitic theory of biological activity. His students could not accept this theory. The spirit of their attitude is caught in a solemn oath that Brücke and DuBois-Reymond imposed on themselves during their student days. They pledged themselves to prove and to expound the mechanistic, antivitalistic principle that "no other forces than common physical chemical ones are active within the organism."[24] Such was the temper of these young scientists, all of whom were under thirty.

Shortly after graduation in 1842, Helmholtz became an army surgeon at Potsdam. While carrying on his duties with the military, he continued his studies in physics and mathematics, and wrote and published several papers.

In 1847, less than five years after his graduation, Helmholtz read before the Physical Society of Berlin his classic paper on the indestructibility of energy, giving mathematical formulation to the law of conservation. Julius Mayer (1814–1878) and J. P. Joule also shared credit for the discovery—Mayer for the theoretical formulation, Helmholtz for its mathematical statement, and Joule for its verification in research. Helmholtz's paper was in the spirit of that antivitalistic oath taken by his friends a few years before, since the theory of the conservation of energy is simultaneously a denial of the existence of biological vital force and the substitution for it of the physical and chemical analysis of energy transformation.

After serving in the army for five years and after a short stint as an instructor in anatomy at a Berlin art school, Helmholtz was called to Königsberg as Associate Professor of Physiology. Since he had a reasonably secure position, he married. He then turned to what proved to be his second major contribution, the measurement of the speed of the neural impulse, a topic to which we will return presently.

During these years Helmholtz also worked in physiological optics. In 1851 he invented the ophthalmoscope, which was a concave mirror with a small hole in the middle through which the observer looked as he reflected light into the eye of the patient. Once conceived, this relatively simple device designed to look into the eye itself was of enormous value in research and medical practice.

In 1856 the first volume of the *Handbuch der physiologischen Optik* appeared, and ten years later the last of its three volumes appeared. It was issued as a unit in 1867.[25] Nearly sixty years later, in 1924–1925, it was translated into English, not just as a classic, but as an indispensable tool for the serious student of vision.[26]

In 1855 Helmholtz went to Bonn as Professor of Anatomy and Physiology. While still at Königsberg he had become interested in acoustics. During his three years at Bonn, his first major research into hearing was carried out. In 1858, during the period in which his attention centered on acoustical problems, he moved to an even more important position in the German university system, the professorship of physiology at Heidelberg, a chair he occupied until 1871. If anything, his already tremendous productivity increased during this period. In addition to the research on audition relevant to this particular account, he showed a remarkable ability to come to grips with important and crucial problems in hydrodynamics and electro-dynamics. His interests ranged over many areas. Some of the papers he wrote between 1858 and 1871 were on such topics as afterimages, colorblindness, the Arabian-Persian musical scale, the relationship between the natural sciences and the totality of sciences, the form of the horopter, the movements of the human eye, the regulation of ice, the axioms of geometry, and hay fever. His acoustical research culminated in the appearance of *On the Sensations of Tone* in 1863.[27] Just as his book on vision did, this new book summarized his investigations, and sifted, summarized, and systematized the entire available literature. During this period, honors were showered on him, among them invitations to lecture, calls from foreign countries, and the prorectorship of the University of Heidelberg.

In 1870, when Helmholtz was fifty years old, the chair in physics at the University of Berlin became vacant, and he was asked to set his own conditions of acceptance. He asked for and received a salary of 4000 Thalers (a huge sum for that day), a promise of a new institute of physics, its directorship, and living quarters in that institute. Until his arrival in Berlin in 1871, Helmholtz had been somewhat cramped for space and limited as to apparatus. In 1887 he was made the first director of the new Physics-Technical Institute at Charlottenberg, near Berlin, while retaining his professorship at the University.

Although Helmholtz's interests in physiological problems continued, his researches during these years tended to center on problems of physics. He helped direct his pupil, Heinrich Hertz, to problems whose solution made a crucial contribution to the founding of wireless telegraphy and radio.

In 1893 Helmholtz went to the United States for the first time in order to attend the Chicago World's Fair as a delegate from Germany. While returning, he had a severe fall down the ship's stairs and he never fully recovered. He died from a cerebral hemorrhage in September 1894.

Some of the problems that influenced psychological thinking on which Helmholtz worked call for relatively detailed statements. These are the speed of the neural impulse; vision, particularly his theory of color vision; space perception; and his theory of hearing. Each problem will be taken up in turn.

The Speed of the Neural Impulse

As exemplified by Johannes Müller, before Helmholtz the prevailing view on the neural impulse was that it was instantaneous or at least so fast as to be incapable of measurement.[28] Estimates of speeds many times the velocity of light had been secured by assuming that the rate of flow of "animal spirits" would be similar for vessels of the same size and that speed varied inversely with the diameter of the conductor. Since the diameters of nerve fibers were extremely minute, indications of tremendous speeds were obtained. Helmholtz's method, which would have been entirely inadequate had the previous estimates been true, was to take a motor nerve and attached muscle from a frog's leg, the so-called nerve–muscle preparation, and arrange it so that both the moment of stimulation and the resultant movement would be recorded on a drum revolving at a known speed.[29] Helmholtz measured the time between stimulation and the muscle twitch for different lengths of nerve.

The difference in time interval between stimulation of the nerve near the muscle and its recorded reaction and stimulation far from the muscle gave him the time taken for passage. Since he knew the distance between the points of stimulation, he could now calculate its speed per second. Helmholtz found the speed to be the very modest one of about 90 feet per second.

The Bell–Magendie law, which distinguished between sensory and motor nerves, made it unsafe for Helmholtz to leave the problem as measured with motor nerves alone. Thus, he now investigated sensory-motor nerves to find out whether their speed was similar or different. He also turned to human subjects. When stimulated on the toe and on the thigh, a man can respond with his hand. The difference in the time between stimulation and reaction over the differing lengths traversed in the two instances gave Helmholtz his measure of speed of reaction— something between 50 and 100 per second. However, variability from trial to trial and subject to subject was so great that he did not follow up the original study. The individual differences, which would later become so important in themselves, were for Helmholtz nothing more than an indication of inadequate control, as indeed they turned out to be. Nevertheless, these two phases of the study gave him rough measures of the speed of sensory and motor neural impulses. In general, later and more accurate research would demonstrate that the neural impulse varies enormously. The speeds Helmholtz found proved to be too slow. Nevertheless, it was Helmholtz who carried out the pioneer study.

The fact that the nervous impulse is not instantaneous but takes appreciable lengths of time signified that mental events were definitely limited by the properties of the body and that an analysis of bodily motion was relevant to psychological phenomena. Mental events that seem instantaneous may actually be temporal events. As Boring so aptly phrases it, "it brought the soul to time."[30] This was the first "reaction–time" study as it came to be called. However, Helmholtz was interested only in the sheer speed of the neural impulse. As we have discussed earlier in this chapter, it was the work of Donders which, though published some fifteen years later than Helmholtz's study, showed a grasp of the psychological significance of the problem.

Vision

While integrating previously available research in the field of visual physiology, Helmholtz also did an enormous amount of original work in that field, as is seen in his *Handbuch der physiologischen Optik.*[31] The three volumes of this book have been characterized, respectively, as physiological, sensory, and perceptual accounts of vision.[32] Some of Helmholtz's own specific research studies show a similar affinity for psychological problems.

Helmholtz measured the optical constraints of the eye, demonstrated how the eye accommodates for different distances, and developed and supported by research a theory of visual space. Most important of all was his theory of color vision.

As early as 1802, Thomas Young (1773–1829) had published a theory of color vision in which he postulated that the retina is equipped with three kinds of color-sensitive points.[33] These three primary colors, working cooperatively, were said to furnish the range of experienced colors. The derivation of all colors from a limited number of colors was not new, as we know from Newton. Going beyond Newton, Young suggested a physiological basis of three kinds of "particles on the retina" (receptors), each kind acting independently. This suggestion lay fallow until Helmholtz espoused the theory, to be known thereafter as the Young–Helmholtz theory of color vision.

In Helmholtz's theory, three sets of fibers in the retina are said to give rise, respectively, to sensations of red, green, and violet.[34] There are supposedly three kinds of photochemically decomposable substances in the end organs, varying in degree of sensitivity to different parts of the visible spectrum. With disintegration of these substances, neural excitation occurs. The three kinds of excitation act differently on the brain only because, while playing the part of connecting wires, they are united to different functioning parts of the brain. Helmholtz then proceeded to suggest how these particulars of receptor and cerebral localization could be used to explain various psychological visual experiences. On stimulation of the red and green fibers together, yellow results. Other combinations produce other colors. When all three kinds of organs are stimulated in the right proportion, white results. Looking at a white surface after colored stimulation, we see negative afterimages because after one organ has been thoroughly fatigued by use, we see with the unfatigued organs alone. Colorblindness (red–green blindness) could result from lack of either red or green organs, or both. Critics objected to the theory as follows. Yellow, postulated as arising from stimulation of red and green organs, should not be seen by colorblind individuals, whereas actually they can see yellow. In spite of criticism, modification, elaboration, and correction, the Young–Helmholtz theory is still taken very seriously today, at least at the retinal level.

Helmholtz held that this color theory was a particular application of Müller's general law of the specific energy of nerves, with "three nerve systems."[35] Müller himself had applied the principle of the specific energy of the nerves to the differentiation of one sense from another, but not to the separate qualities within a single sense, such as sweet and sour or red and green. Helmholtz was applying the rule within a single sense modality. If we speak of Müller's theory as one of specific nerve energies, then Helmholtz was proposing a theory of specific fiber energies.[36] Although Helmholtz did much to advance this theory of fiber energies, several other investigators, including Thomas Young himself, anticipated his findings in this area. Young also anticipated Müller's more general doctrine by advancing his theory of specificity for different color qualities. Despite his citing of Müller, Helmholtz developed a theory that turned out to be more a doctrine of the specific energies of cortical areas than of nerves. As we know, Müller had raised the cortical area alternative but had not accepted it. In the location of specificity, later research was to support Helmholtz and not Müller.

Space Perception

In interpreting space perception, Helmholtz was also an empiricist. Here he saw as his opponent Ewald Hering, who held that every point on the retina was innately capable of perceiving height, breadth, and depth.[37] In part, Helmholtz defended an empirical position by use of Müller's doctrine of specific energies.[38] Helmholtz held that each of the various sense organs and nerves has characteristic qualities that are not in themselves meaningful, being bare sense impression. At this point experience enters, for recurring association gives these sense impressions meaning.[39] The doctrine of specific nerve energies as interpreted by Müller in support of Kantian nativism was now interpreted by Helmholtz as a defense of empiricism.

Helmholtz also stressed the importance of the empirical process of unconscious inference in space perception.[40] Perception of space, he said, is not inherent; instead, we "infer" space from past experience but without awareness that this process of inference is going on. Certain small cues together constitute a sign that the object is to be found at a certain distance. Without noticing the sign itself, we infer how far away the object is. To use an example—when we gaze at an object 20 feet away, intervening objects at various closer distances are actually seen as double, but we do not notice this phenomenon. (This principle can be verified by anyone who takes the trouble. Hold a pen first a few inches from the nose and then at arm's length, while looking across the room. The double image will be evident in both instances but greatest when the pen is close up.) Closer objects are seen, while one looks at the far object, with varying degrees of doubleness. A specific degree of doubleness is unconsciously interpreted, without the viewer's noticing the doubleness at a certain distance to the object. This is what Helmholtz meant by "unconscious inference."

Audition

Helmholtz made many contributions to the field of hearing.[41] Among them were his clarification of the role of timbre to round out the major harmonic components and his theory of how hearing is mediated by the ear and the relation of this theory to the doctrine of specific energy of nerves. Each of these findings must be examined in more detail. That pitch depends primarily on frequency of sound waves and intensity on the amplitude of the waves had been understood and explained in Müller's *Handbuch.* As yet timbre had received no similar explanation. The fact of timbre, that is to say, the existence of qualitative differences between tones other than pitch, was, of course, well known. Anyone hearing the same note played by different instruments realizes that something makes them sound different despite their identity of pitch. Helmholtz explained this experience of timbre by the presence, in addition to the fundamental pitch, of so-called overtones or vibration rates more rapid than the fundamental tone that fixes the pitch.[42] Most vibrating bodies vibrate not only as wholes, but also simultaneously as parts. These partial vibrations give rise to timbre. The shape of waves making up a tone from a musical instrument, if visualized, would show that the main wave is the same as that for all other instruments and gives rise to the fundamental pitch when playing that particular note. It would also show that part waves are unique to this particular instrument and result in the timbre. The more similar the tone of two instruments, the more similar are the characterizing overtones. Here again, Helmholtz was not content merely to advance a theory; he conclusively demonstrated his contention by building a series of tuning forks and resonators that permitted him to systematically vary the intensity of the overtones accompanying a fundamental tone. From these he produced synthetically the characteristic timbre of various musical instruments.

Helmholtz's theory of hearing evolved over the years, and this is not the place to trace its modifications. It was essentially a theory of pitch; he assumed that intensity was more or less explained by varying degrees of excitation of the fibers. Helmholtz marshaled evidence that a portion of the inner ear responds to an auditory wave stimulus by resonance, vibrating in tune with the frequency of the sound wave. The ear behaves like an unstruck tuning fork that begins to vibrate after another one has been struck.

Helmholtz finally reached the conclusion that the basilar membrane with its many hair cells in the cochlea of the inner ear is the resolving organ of hearing. This basilar membrane is trapezoidal in shape (narrow at one end and increasing gradually in width). He thought that the hairs on its narrower end were tuned to high pitches and the hairs on the wider portion, to the low pitches. Pitch, transmitted to the brain after analysis by resonance on the basilar membrane, is dependent on place of stimulation. The differential action of a portion of the basilar membrane is the means whereby the pitch of the heard sound is determined.

Helmholtz regarded the doctrine of specific nerve energies as an established fact, and it was natural for him to apply it to hearing. Discriminable differences in pitch qualities thus meant for Helmholtz that a separate fibre would be required for each discriminable experience. This would mean between 1,500 and 11,000 distinguishable pitches and thus separate fibers.[43] This bold position attracted attention, and the issue of the specific energies in hearing became a prominent one for research in all sense modalities.

SUMMARY

The acceptance of developments in physiological science during this period would influence the acceptance of modern psychological science. Methodological and contentual inspiration was transferred to the fledgling science.

Contentual empiricism in the form of the experimental method became the method of choice among physiologists during this period. Since it was capable of repetition by others, the use of experiment increased methodological objectivism. Nomothetic interests still prevailed. Psychologists were to claim that the contentual problems of reaction time, sensory experience, and space perception were also within their sphere of interest. Quantitativism, the use of measurement to specify results, was firmly established. Mechanism, a prescriptive allegiance to exploration in mechanical terms, had been espoused by most physiologists after the time of Müller. Determinism, the study of events explicable in terms of antecedents, was accepted as a matter of course. Appeal to events within nature, naturalism, was also now a matter of course.

The integrative work of Johannes Müller and Hermann von Helmholtz had a significance beyond that of bringing together items of a heretofore scattered research literature. So, too, did the appointment of Müller to a chair in physiology—which had become recognized as a scientific specialty. The task and the role of the physiologist had been recognized. Workers on tasks now seen as related perceived a common bond; the possibility of becoming a student in the particular subject became apparent; and making the field one's career became possible. Physiology as a field of research and teaching was to have a profound effect on Wundt, the founder in his time of a new discipline, modern psychology.

NOTES

1. J. Müller, *Handbuch der Physiologie des Menschen*, 3 vols. (Coblenz: Holscher, 1834–1840).
2. R. Whytt, *An Essay on the Vital and Other Involuntary Motions of Animals* (Edinburgh: Hamilton, Balfour and Neill, 1751) (Herrnstein and Boring, Excerpt No. 60).
3. C. Bell, *Idea of a New Anatomy of the Brain: Submitted for the Observation of His Friends* (London: Strahan and Preston, 1811) (Herrnstein and Boring, Excerpts No. 6, 8).
4. F. Magendie, "Experiences sur les fonctions des racines des nerfs rachidiens," *Journal de physiologie experimentale et pathologique*, 2 (1822):276–279; "Experiences sur les fonctions des nerfs qui naissent de la moelle epiniere," *Journal de physiologie experimentale et pathologique*, 2 (1822):366–371 (Herrnstein and Boring, Excerpt No. 7).
5. L. Carmichael, "Sir Charles Bell: A Contribution to the History of Physiological Psychology," *Psychological Review*, 33 (1926):188–217; J.M.D. Olmsted, *Francois Magendie, Pioneer in Experimental Physiology and Scientific Medicine in Nineteenth Century France* (New York: Schuman, 1944).
6. F. J. Gall, "Sur les fonctiones du cerveau et sur celles de chacune de ses parties," Vols. 4, 6, trans. W. Lewis, *Gall's Works* (Boston: Marsh, Capen and Lyon, 1835) (1825) (Herrnstein and Boring, Excerpt No. 45). For a good secondary discussion of the phrenology movement, see John D. Davies, *Phrenology, Fad and Science: A 19th-Century American Crusade* (New Haven, Conn.: Yale University Press, 1955).
7. J. K. Spurzheim, *Phrenology or the Doctrine of the Human Mind* (Philadelphia: Lippincott, 1825). Spurzheim's middle name is sometimes printed as Kaspar and sometimes as Gaspar. This is noted because his name appears as G. Spurzheim, without the first initial. It has also been printed as Christolph.
8. A. A. Walsh, "Phrenology and the Boston Medical Community in the 1830's," *Bulletin of the History of Medicine*, 50 (1976):261–273.
9. E. T. Carlson, "The Influence of Phrenology on Early American Psychiatric Thought," *American Journal of Psychiatry*, 65 (1958):535–538.
10. M.J.P. Flourens, *Recherches experimentales sur les proprietes et les fonctions du systeme nerveux dans les animaux vertebres* (Paris: Crevot, 1824) (Herrnstein and Boring, Excerpt No. 46).
11. P. Broca, "Remargues sur le siege de la faculte du langage articule, suivies de'une observation de'aphemie (parte de la parole)," *Bulletin Societe de'Anatomie*, 6 (1861):330–357 (Herrnstein and Boring, Excerpt No. 47).
12. G. Fritsch and E. Hitzig, "Ueber die elektrische Erregbarkeit des Grosshirns," *Archiv für Anatomie und Physiologie* (1870), 300–332 (Herrnstein and Boring, Excerpt No. 48).
13. Müller, *Handbuch* (Herrnstein and Boring, Excerpt No. 9).
14. Charles Bell had anticipated Müller to some extent in a privately printed paper and

many others had made use of the doctrine, but it was Müller whose authoritative publication made it an accepted and acceptable principle.

15. J. Müller, *Elements of Physiology*, trans. W. Baly (London: Taylor, 1837–1842) (1833–1840).

16. W. James, *Psychology: Briefer Course* (New York: Henry Holt, 1892), p. 12.

17. J. Müller, *Zur vergleichenden Physiologie des Gesichtssinnes* (Leipzig: Cnobloch, 1826), pp. 55–66 (Herrnstein and Boring, Excerpt No. 25).

18. E. G. Boring, *A History of Experimental Psychology*, 2nd ed. (New York: Appleton–Century–Crofts, 1950, pp. 134–142.

19. F. C. Donders, "Die Schnelligkeit psychischer Processe," *Archiv für Anatomie and Physiologie, 6* (1868):657–681.

20. H.L.F. Helmholtz, *Treatise on Physiological Optics*, 3 vols., ed. J.P.C. Southall (Rochester, N.Y.: Optical Society of America, 1925) (1856–1866).

21. *Ibid.*

22. V. F. Lenzen, "Helmholtz's Theory of Knowledge," in M.F.A. Montague, ed., *Studies and Essays in the History of Science and Learning*, Offered in Homage to George Sarton on the Occasion of His Sixtieth Birthday, 31 August 1944 (New York: Schuman, 1946), pp. 299–320.

23. The major source of details about his life was H. Margenau, Introduction, in H.L.F. Helmholtz, *On the Sensations of Tone* (New York: Dover Publications, 1954). This was supplemented by H. Gruber and Valmai Gruber, "Hermann von Helmholtz: Nineteenth Century Polymorph," *Scientific Monthly, 83* (1956):92–99.

24. Quoted in Boring, *History*, p. 708.

25. H.L.F. Helmholtz, *Handbuch der physiologischen Optik* (Leipzig: Voss, 1867) (1856–1866).

26. H.L.F. Helmholtz, *Treatise*.

27. H.L.F. Helmholtz, *On the Sensations of Tone*, trans. A. J. Ellis (New York: Dover Publications, 1954) (1863).

28. J. Müller, *Elements*.

29. H.L.F. Helmholtz, "On the Rate of Transmission of the Nerve Impulse," *Berichtn. Konig. Preussische Akadamie der Wissenschaften*, Berlin (1850):14–15, reprinted in W. Dennis, ed., *Readings in the History of Psychology* (New York: Appleton–Century–Crofts, 1948), pp. 197–198.

30. E. G. Boring, *History*, p. 42.

31. H.L.F. Helmholtz, *Optik*.

32. Boring, *History*.

33. T. Young, "On the Theory of Light and Colours," *Philosophical Transactions of the Royal Society, 92* (1892d):18–21 (Herrnstein and Boring, Excerpt No. 4).

34. H.L.F.Helmholtz,*Treatise*, Vol. 2, Sec. 20 (Herrnstein and Boring, Excerpt No. 11).

35. *Ibid.*

36. E. G. Boring, *History*.

37. E. Hering, *Beitrage zur Physiologie: Zur Lehre vom Ortsinn der Netzhaut* (Leipzig: Englemann, 1861–1864) (Herrnstein and Boring, Excerpt No. 33).

38. H.L.F. Helmholtz, *Treatise*.

39. *Ibid.*, Vol. 3, Sec. 26 (Herrnstein and Boring, Excerpt No. 34).

40. *Ibid.* (Herrnstein and Boring, Excerpt No. 40).

41. H.L.F. Helmholtz, *Sensations of Tone*.

42. *Ibid.*, Chapter 6 (Herrnstein and Boring, Excerpt No. 12).

43. E. G. Boring, *Sensation and Perception in the History of Experimental Psychology* (New York: Appleton–Century–Crofts, 1942), pp. 341–342.

G. T. Fechner.

13

Fechner: Psychophysics

*P*sychology would emerge in the 1880s as an independent scientific and academic discipline. It claimed philosophy and physiology as its progenitors, although it has been argued that psychology was born out of wedlock from a union of phrenology and science. Whatever the origins, before psychology could stand on its own as an independent scientific discipline, it had to demonstrate how the scientific method could be applied to its subject matter. Both physiology and philosophy had demonstrated their own methods for studying what we have defined as psychological thought. Kant had said that psychology could not be a natural science because it could not be mathematical; it could not analyze its data and so could never be experimental. Although Herbart had demonstrated the possibility of quantitative treatment of psychological concepts, psychology still lacked a clearly defined set of procedures such as those followed by physics and physiology that would allow it to be experimental. Without an experimental methodology, psychology would likely have remained only a subdivision of philosophy.

G. T. Fechner deserves much of the credit for laying the basis for the application of the experimental method to psychology. His establishment of psychophysics through his publication of *Elements of Psychophysics* in 1860 is a major landmark in the transition of psychology from a scattered set of subject matters found in several disciplines to a relatively coherent discipline centered on the laboratory. There is some question as to the degree that Fechner intended such an outcome, however, since his interests were not particularly in system building or discipline building.

Engrossed in philosophical and mystical interests, Fechner devoted several periods of his long life to speculation and to the investigation of what seemed to him the most fundamental problem of life—psychophysics, or the quantitative investigation of the functional interrelations of body and mind.[1] In spite of the arid quality of his psychophysical studies, his writings reveal a burning enthusiasm for grappling with the very nature of the individual.

LIFE AND CAREERS OF FECHNER

Gustav Theodor Fechner (1801–1887) was born in a small village in the Wendish country of southeastern Germany.[2] His father was a Lutheran preacher, who died when Gustav was five years old, but not before he had given his son a grounding in Latin. After attending the Gymnasium, Fechner in 1817 matriculated at the University of Leipzig, an association that was to last seventy years. He took his degree in medicine in 1822, but he decided not to go into practice.

Even early in his career there were some glimmerings of humanistic interests. Under the pseudonym of Dr. Mises, he employed the weapon of satire against views with which he disagreed. The first of these satirical pieces appeared in 1821, before his graduation; it was directed against the then current medical fad of using iodine for just about any ailment and was called *Proof That Man Is Made of Iodine.* Occasional satirical pieces continued to come from his pen. Earlier in the century, Germany had experienced a resurgence of interest in materialism or mechanism. Viewing materialism as a theory devoid of truth, Fechner devoted several of his satires to attacking the view that the universe is inert matter—the "night view," as he called it—and to a defense of the position that the universe can be regarded from the point of view of consciousness—the "day view."

This antimechanist position was to be a fixed point in what otherwise appears to be a series of shifts of interest during Fechner's life. According to E. G. Boring, between 1817, when Fechner started medical school, and his death in 1887, Fechner was successively a physiologist, a physicist, an aestheticist and, throughout most of the later years, a philosopher.[3] Following his aim steadfastly through these careers, he founded psychophysics, which in turn supplied the methodological tools necessary for the founding of laboratory-oriented experimental psychology.

After graduation in medicine, Fechner began his second career by studying physics. In 1824, after a period without official appointment, he started to lecture on this subject and to conduct laboratory investigations in electricity. In 1833 he married, and the following year, when only thirty-three years old, he became a professor of physics. His academic future seemed secure. During these years sheer economic necessity had led him into translating various French scientific works that served to add to his scientific knowledge. However, some of the jobs he took to increase his income amounted to hack work, such as editing and writing a considerable share of an encyclopedia of household knowledge in eight volumes. He broke under the strain of all this work, and he became a "nervous invalid." In general, this state could be characterized as a neurotic depression with pronounced hypochondriacal features.

In the winter of 1839–1840, a painful eye disorder developed, and Fechner resigned his chair in physics. Fechner's study of afterimages by staring into the sun had undoubtedly aggravated the condition, if it did not bring it on. Years of suffering followed. His eyes were so hypersensitive to light that he could not leave the house without bandaging them, and for the rest of his life he had to curtail his reading. Sometimes for weeks on end he could not eat at all. He eventually found that fruit, strongly spiced raw ham, and wine could be tolerated. He could not talk for long periods, and he thought of suicide. Some slight improvement occurred late in 1843, but it was thought there was no chance of his regaining his health. In 1844 he received a small pension from the university, thus officially establishing his position as an invalid. Nonetheless, hardly one of his remaining forty-four years went by without a serious contribution from his pen. There is no doubt that he really suffered, so it would be unfair to apply to him that grand phrase, "he enjoyed poor health."

Unable to use his eyes, Fechner spent many hours in contemplation, a custom that reinforced his speculative turn of mind, which came to the fore as soon as he was able to resume working. He now entered the third phase of his career and became a psychophysicist with philosophical leanings.

Fechner is included among the great psychologists because of his connection with psychophysics. Reserving details for later systematic and methodological discussion, we will simply state here that he became interested to the point of obsession in demonstrating that mind and body are aspects of a unity.[4] Since matter (body) is not to be denied any more than consciousness (mind), the two must be reconciled and made one. Fundamentally, to Fechner the difference between mind and body is nothing more than a difference in point of view concerning the psychophysical entity. The mind is related to the body as the inside of a circle is related to the outside. This makes his view a double-aspect theory, or a psychophysical monism—mind and body are but two aspects of a fundamental unity. Since the two aspects are identical, the view is also called the "identity hypothesis."

The solution, Fechner tells us, came with dramatic suddenness on the morning of October 22, 1850.[5] In bed, "before getting up," he realized that the law of the connection between body and mind is to be found in a statement of the quantitative relations between mental sensation and bodily stimulus, not in simple proportion, but such that increases in mental sensation correspond to proportional changes in bodily stimulus.

Ten years later, Fechner's *Elemente der Psychophysik* appeared. Here he discusses the functional relations of mind and body and reports his own and others' investigations of the various senses—sight, sound, and the cutaneous and muscular senses.

Some conception of Fechner's intent to measure psychological functions can be gained by turning to his next undertaking, the study of experimental aesthetics, which represents another field he founded. Fechner had a deep and longstanding interest in art. His first paper in this new career appeared in 1865 and dealt with the "golden section," the most aesthetically pleasing relation of length to breadth in an object. Here again, Fechner applied his exact method to a global goal. He rebelled against the attempt to develop an aesthetics "from above down" by formulating abstract principles of beauty by which to judge the concrete object, in the manner of the Romanticists. Instead, he believed one must start with simple figures. In order to find the linear proportions an artist used, he patiently measured the dimensions of pictures, cards, books, snuff boxes, writing paper, windows—in fact, any object that was purported to have aesthetic appeal. Thus, he sought to develop an experimental aesthetics "from below."

Fechner also became involved in a *cause célèbre* of his day concerning the authenticity of two paintings of the Madonna, each attributed to Holbein. Although the paintings were very similar, they differed in detail, and the authenticity of both was in dispute. Fechner inclined to the opinion that both were authentic. There was also a dispute over which was the more beautiful. Taking advantage of an exhibition in which they were exhibited together, he launched what may have been the first public opinion poll. He made arrangements for the public to be invited to record comments in a book placed alongside the paintings. Sparseness of returns with a disproportionate number from art critics, who had already formed opinions, made this particular venture a failure.

His major book on aesthetics, *Vorschule der Aesthetik*, appeared in 1876.[6] Its appearance also served to close his participation in aesthetics. Experimental psychology as represented by Wilhelm Wundt, now also at Leipzig, and the intense interest of many others, protagonists as well as antagonists, would not leave Fechner in peace to pursue his still strong philosophical interests. He was drawn back to a second career in psychophysics, which lasted until his death in 1887.

THE AIM OF FECHNER

The careers through which Gustav Fechner moved did not reflect a change in fundamental interest. His guiding aim was a search for an answer to an all-consuming question—the nature of the relationship between the spiritual and material worlds. He sought a unified conception of body and soul that, though based on mystical speculation, also had a scientific basis.

In the spirit of Plotinus, Fechner's spiritual ancestor of seventeen centuries before, Fechner saw the world as a system of souls that appeared to each other as bodies. His mystical strain was reflected in the very title of one of his works, *Zend-Avesta, On the Things of Heaven and the Hereafter.*[7] In this book, Fechner endowed all things with personal souls. The world is made up of external manifestations, he said, bodies that are correlated with internal animate realities, souls. This concept is known as panpsychism, a theory of the world that endows plants as well as animals with some rudimentary kind of soul. Its relation to primitive animism is direct and obvious. But Fechner was no simple throwback to primitive views; he argued these and related problems with subtlety and enthusiasm.

Consonant with the two major influences that affected him, Fechner sought precise confirmation of these speculations. His was a nature that asked for a relation between poetical and speculative world views, to be demonstrated by means of precise measurement. He made the mystical aspect his goal—to find the relationship between body and soul—and the scientific aspect his method.[8] Psychophysics, the measurement of the relationship between mind and body, was one way to approach the relationship.

Fechner found the starting point for measuring physical stimulus and mental sensation in the research of E. H. Weber, who was also at Leipzig.

THE INFLUENCE OF WEBER

Ernst Heinrich Weber (1795–1878) was appointed Dozent in physiology at the University of Leipzig in 1817, the same year Fechner arrived as a medical student.[9] The next year Weber was appointed Professor of Anatomy, and later in his career he was made Professor of Physiology. For many years Weber and Fechner moved in the same academic circles and lived in the same community.

As a physiologist, Weber was particularly interested in touch and in the muscle sense, fields of research that had hitherto been relatively neglected.[10] He wished to find the smallest discriminable difference between weights, the so-called just noticeable difference. The task he chose was simple. On each trial subjects lifted two weights, one of which was a standard weight and the other a comparison weight. On each subsequent trial the comparison weight was increased in small gradations. The subjects reported when the comparison weight felt heavier. For a standard weight of, say, 40 ounces, it would take a comparison weight of 41 ounces to be discriminated as heavier. This would produce a just noticeable difference (JND) of 1 ounce. If the standard weight were 80 ounces, however, it would take not 81 ounces to be noticed as heavier as the JND would indicate but 82, a JND of 2 ounces. Weber found that it was not the absolute difference in weight that led to the discrimination, but the ratio of the JND to the standard weight. In this case, the ratio was 1/40. Thus, if the standard weight were set to 20 ounces, one would expect a 20.5 ounce weight to be discriminated as heavier, a JND of half an ounce but still a ratio of 1/40. This was the case.

Weber found that the same phenomenon was found with passive weights, weights placed on the skin rather than being lifted as in the previous experiment. The increase required for a weight to be discriminated as different was not absolute but was in a ratio. This time it was 1/30 instead of 1/40. The ratio of the change required to be discriminated to the standard stimulus was found to differ from one sense department to another, but remained constant within a given sensory situation. Weber also tested capacity to discriminate length of lines, and he marshaled evidence on differences in the pitch of tones. He again found constant ratios which were seen to hold except for extremes. The ratios broke down for either very small standard or very intense stimuli.

Fechner reformulated Weber's ratio into the equation:

$$dR/R = K$$

in which dR is the just noticeable stimulus increment, K is a constant, and R is the standard stimulus magnitude. In other words, when divided by the magnitude of the standard stimulus, a stimulus increment required to give a just noticeable difference gives a constant value. As the standard increases, the stimulus required for a JND increases proportionately. This relationship is called Weber's law or Weber's fraction. This fraction and Weber's measurement of just noticeable differences, the JND, is arguably the first quantitatively determined measurement of a mental event.

FECHNER'S PSYCHOPHYSICS

Fechner construed Weber's results to mean that one could measure sensation as well as the sensory stimulus and state the relation between the two in the form of an equation.[11] Fechner went on to devise a more generalized formula that he also tried to give Weber's name. This more generalized final equation, given below, has since been called Fechner's law.

Fechner's law states the relationship between the growth of a physical stimulus and the psychological experience of its growth. The result of Fechner's manipulation of Weber's law was the equation $S = K \log R$ in which S is the perceived magnitude of the sensation, K is a constant, and R is the physical magnitude of the stimulus. Fechner's law infers a logarithmic relationship between the growth of physical and psychological magnitudes.

Sensation had been measured, and the identity hypothesis, his mind–body parallelism, so Fechner thought, had been demonstrated. He had found the proof for his identity hypothesis in a table of logarithms!

Fechner's work on discrimination was what psychophysicists called the difference threshold, which, along with the absolute threshold (the lowest stimulus magnitude that can be detected) and the terminal threshold (the highest level of a stimulus, such as frequency, that can be detected) are the three fundamental measures of classical psychophysics. In the course of his research, Fechner developed one and systematized two other of the three major methods of classical psychophysics: the method of limits, the method of average error, and the method of constant stimuli. The method of average error that Fechner developed along with his brother-in-law is the most fundamental and will be used as an illustration. The subject himself adjusts a variable stimulus so as to fulfill the instructions given him—for example, to make one line appear equal to the length of a standard line. Before him he sees a length of line, the standard. He is to adjust another line to be as close to the standard in length as he can make it. No matter how closely he approximates the line, however, an error, large or small, will be made. Sometimes he makes the line too long and sometimes too short, but he always makes some error. After many trials, the average of his errors is found, the so-called average error.

After publication of the *Elemente* in 1860, interest in the work was immediate, intense, and widespread. Many other researchers, seeing the value of Fechner's work, proceeded to carry out similar experiments. Various controversies raged over one aspect or the other of Fechner's formulations, but the use of psychophysical methods would be fundamental to the creation of experimental psychology. Ironically, with all the excitement his findings engendered, little attention was paid to Fechner's goal for psychophysics, that is, his attempt to find the relationship between body and soul.

Fechner was not interested in what psychophysics became. Other researchers such as Wilhelm Wundt and the students of the Leipzig laboratory, refined psychophysics to become the formal quantitative measure of changes in the physical world that could be lawfully related to changes in sensations, perceptions, and judgments.

With the introduction of Fechnerian psychophysics, sensory psychology was placed on a quantitative basis. Psychophysics gave a quantitative expression to measurement of the mind. No longer could it be argued that mind could not be measured or that mathematics could not be applied to its research study. Quantitativism and the refinement of empiricism as expressed in a positive attitude toward experiment would hereafter be characteristic of the psychologists to come.

SUMMARY

Fechner's psychophysics represented his attempt to find a scientific relationship between body and soul. Although he failed in the attempt, he devised the basic methodology that would allow mental events to be measured quantitatively. He was influenced by E. H. Weber, whose work on the discriminability of weights led to the formulation of Weber's law. This law makes use of the just noticeable difference (JND), the least change in the physical stimulus that may be detected as difference. This was perhaps the first experimentally determined, quantitative measure of a mental event. Fechner extended the idea of Weber's law into a formula concerning the relationship between the increase of a stimulus magnitude and the growth of the experience of that magnitude. That logarithmic relationship would be called Fechner's law.

Fechner's work led directly to the methodology and psychophysical theory that would allow Wilhelm Wundt and other experimental psychologists to apply the experimental method to the study of experience.

NOTES

1. G. T. Fechner, *Elemente der Psychophysik*, 2 vols. (Leipzig: Breitkopf and Hartel, 1860).

2. The major source for the details of Fechner's life was G. S. Hall, *Founders of Modern Psychology* (New York: Appleton, 1912), but the organization of the material on his life and his careers owes much to the presentation of E. G. Boring, *A History of Experimental Psychology*, 2nd ed. (New York: Appleton–Century–Crofts, 1950), pp. 275–283.

3. *Ibid.*, p. 283.

4. G. T. Fechner, *Elements of Psychophysics*, Vol. 1, trans. H. E. Adler, in E. G. Boring and D. Howes, eds. (New York: Holt, Rinehart and Winston, 1966), Chapter 1 (Herrnstein and Boring, Excerpt No. 107). Unfortunately, the more philosophical and mystical second volume has never been translated into English.

5. *Elemente*, II, p. 554. For another view on Fechner's derivation of his concepts, see Marilyn Marshall, ''Physics, Metaphysics, and Fechner's Psychophysics,'' in William R. Woodward and Mitchell G. Ash, eds., *The Problematic Science: Psychology in Nineteenth-Century Thought* (New York: Praeger, 1982), pp. 65–87.

6. G. T. Fechner, *Vorschule der Aesthetik* (Leipzig: Breitkopf and Hartel, 1876).

7. G. T. Fechner, *Zend-Avesta, On the Things of Heaven and the Hereafter* (Leipzig: Woss, 1851).

8. For a treatment of Fechner's more mystical side, see Fechner, *Das Büchlein vom Leben nach dem Tode* (1835), translated by Hugo Werneke as *On Life After Death* (Chicago: Open Court, 1906). William James, who thoroughly disliked Fechner's psychophysics, praised his mystical work. See William James, *Pluralistic Universe* (New York: Holt, 1909), pp. 133–177.

9. Lest the emphasis on Weber and Fechner give a false impression about the initiation of research in the field, one aspect, that of threshold measurement, did not wait for their work. P. P. Bouguer, *Traité de optique sur la gradation de la lumiere* (Paris: Guerin and Delatour, 1760) (Herrnstein and Boring, Excerpt No. 15) had already measured the differential threshold for brightness; and C.E.J. Delezenne, ''Sur les valeurs numeriques des notes de la gamme'' (Recueil des travaux de la Societe des Sciences, de l' Agriculture et des Arts de Lille, 1827, pp. 4–6) (Herrnstein and Boring, Excerpt No. 16) had studied the differential threshold for pitch and was cited by Weber.

10. E. H. Weber, "Der Tastsinn und das Gemeingefühl," in R. Wagner, ed., *Handworter-buch der Physiologie* (Braunschweig: Vieweg, 1846), Vol. III, pp. 481–588 (Herrnstein and Boring, Excerpt No. 10); E. H. Weber, *De pulsu, resorptione, auditu et tactu: annotationes anatomicae et physiologicae* (Leipzig: Koehler, 1834) (Herrnstein and Boring, Excerpt No. 17).

11. G. T. Fechner, "Elements of Psychophysics," trans. H. S. Langfeld, in B. Rand, ed., *The Classical Psychologists* (Boston: Houghton Mifflin, 1912), pp. 562–572 (Herrnstein and Boring, Excerpt No. 18).

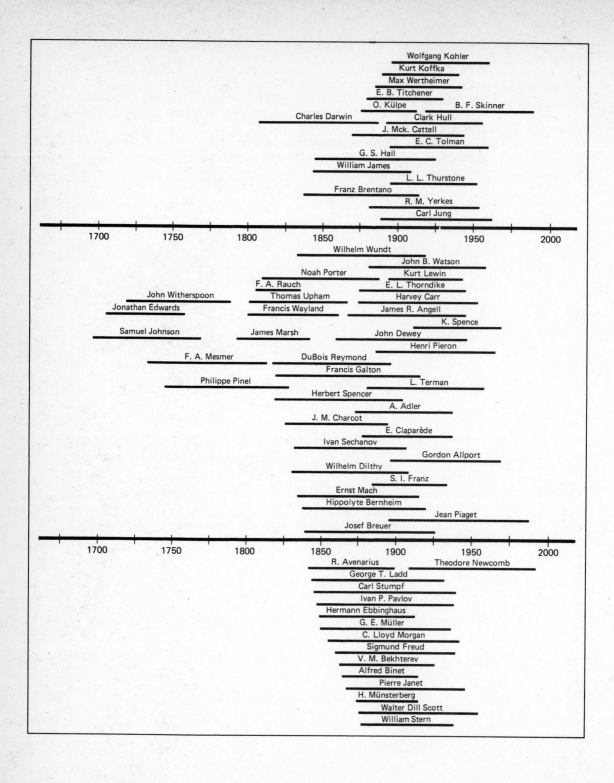

PART FOUR

The Modern Period

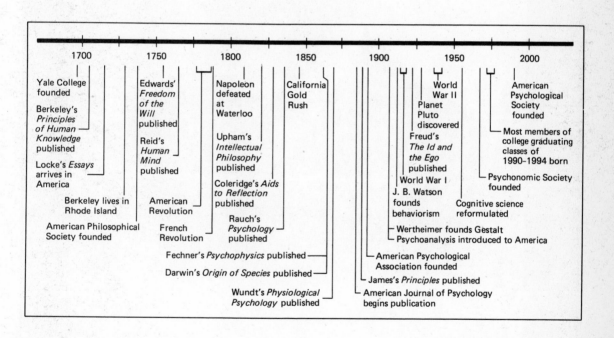

1700	1750	1800	1850	1900	1950	2000

Yale College founded

Berkeley's *Principles of Human Knowledge* published

Locke's *Essays* arrives in America

Berkeley lives in Rhode Island

American Philosophical Society founded

Edwards' *Freedom of the Will* published

Reid's *Human Mind* published

American Revolution

French Revolution

Napoleon defeated at Waterloo

Upham's *Intellectual Philosophy* published

Coleridge's *Aids to Reflection* published

Rauch's *Psychology* published

Fechner's *Psychophysics* published

Darwin's *Origin of Species* published

Wundt's *Physiological Psychology* published

California Gold Rush

World War I

J. B. Watson founds behaviorism

Wertheimer founds Gestalt

Psychoanalysis introduced to America

American Psychological Association founded

James's *Principles* published

American Journal of Psychology begins publication

World War II

Planet Pluto discovered

Freud's *The Id and the Ego* published

Cognitive science reformulated

American Psychological Society founded

Most members of college graduating classes of 1990–1994 born

Psychonomic Society founded

Wilhelm Wundt.

Chapter 14

Wilhelm Wundt: Introspection and Experiment

Wilhelm Wundt (1832–1920) is the first person who can be called a psychologist without qualifying the statement by reference to another, perhaps stronger, interest. Although he wrote four major books in philosophy, running to perhaps twenty-one editions, his primary efforts were in psychology where he published six books that appeared in about thirty-six editions. The "new psychology," the psychology of laboratory experiment, was largely his creation. He did all the things necessary to be a founder. He published the first major book in the discipline, his *Grundzüge der physiologischen Psychologie (Principles of Physiological Psychology).* [1] He arguably founded the first real, experimental laboratory in psychology and produced a large number of doctoral students whose primary interests were in experimental psychology and who consequently founded programs and laboratories of their own. His Institute of Psychology at the University of Leipzig became the prototype of psychological institutes and departments across the world. He edited the first journal devoted primarily to experimental psychology, even though it also contained philosophical works and was called *Philosophische Studien (Philosophical Studies)*.

In all these founding activities, Wundt was fully aware of what he was doing. In his preface to the first edition of his *Grundzüge,* published in 1874, he states his intent to "mark out a new domain of science."[2] Fechner is not considered the founder of psychology, even though his psychophysics provided psychology with many of the experimental methods required to make it scientific and experimental. Fechner was not interested in psychology as an independent discipline. To Wundt, psychology was both experimental and scientific; even so, he must be considered a transitional figure, since he was unable to devise a unified psychological system that was consistently experimental. Instead, he devised two psychologies—one of the lower mental processes that was experimental and one of the higher mental processes that was not. He completed the disproof of Kant by demonstrating that the lower mental processes could be studied as a natural science *(Naturwissenschaft)*. He declined to go all the way, however, and he pursued the higher mental processes as a *Geisteswissenschaft,* a mental or cultural science, a science in which the products of mind are studied rather than the mind itself.[3] Wundt states flatly, however, that as a science, psychology cannot be based on metaphysical assumptions of any sort. It is the lower mental processes and their study as a natural science that had the greatest impact on what became known as the "new psychology," the psychology of the laboratory.

Wundt's primary method in his experimental psychology was analytical introspection. This was a description of an experience broken down into its simplest terms, its elements. Wundt's approach to psychological experience was first to analyze into its simplest components, then to synthesize the components back into the whole, and finally to discover the laws of their combination. Ironically, in later years critics of Wundt and his followers would try to identify this analytical introspection with the philosophers' age-old methods of reflection and meditation. Wundt's exact and exacting method of analytical introspection supplanted the philosophers' methods and made possible the experimental investigation of mental experience. The method of the philosophers was that of "inner perception" *(innere Wahrnehmung);* what Wundt used was experimental introspection or *experimentelle Selbstbeobachtung.*[4] Wundt's method was much simpler than that used later at Würzburg by Oswald Külpe or at Cornell by E. B. Titchener, both of whom were students of Wundt. It was the nature of Wundt's form of introspection, in part, that limited the range of his psychological problems primarily to sensation, perception, and action. As Külpe and Titchener attempted to move into more elaborate subject matters, particularly the higher mental processes such as judgment and thought, their introspective methodology expanded with it. Wundt would come to disagree with many later developments of analytical or experimental introspection as it would be used by Külpe and Titchener.[5]

It would be beneficial to investigate Wundt's treatment of introspection and its relation to experiment so as to clarify the significant step Wundt was taking with his "new psychology."

INTROSPECTION AND EXPERIMENT

Wundt's reference to physiological psychology in the title of his book requires some explanation. He was not referring to the subject matter of present-day physiological psychology. In his day, physiology was the nearest experimental discipline to psychology. The careful methodology and instrumentation was a model for the discipline Wundt would like psychology to become. In this way, Wundt was using "physiological" almost synonymously with "experimental."

Wundt's use of the term *physiological psychology* might also lead the reader to assume that he was a reductionist; that he explained the phenomena of mental life with reference to physiological processes. Instead, he insisted that the psychic and the physiological processes are separate but parallel.[6] Because causality in natural science is a closed system, the phenomena that are studied by physical science cannot, in Wundt's view, affect the mind or be affected by it. Outer experience (physics) and inner experience (psychology) differ in the point of view from which the experience is observed. Outer experience is mediate, whereas inner experience is immediate. Conscious phenomena are therefore observable without reference to the body in which they occur, and "physiological" psychology does not imply an attempt to explain the phenomena of the psychical by examining the physical life.

Although he hesitated to use the term, since it smacked of the metaphysical assumptions he had promised to avoid,[7] Wundt was rejecting mind–body interaction of the sort espoused by Descartes. Instead, Wundt adopted a psychophysical dualism in which the two sides, mental and physical, are separate events and are parallel but noninteractive. This approach is called psychophysical parallelism. His parallelism was methodological; physiology follows one method to achieve knowledge, and psychology follows another. They are two bodies of knowledge. The manner of connection between elements in the subject's immediate experience is entirely different from the occurrences studied by physiology. Causality in psychology is different from causality in physiology or in any other physical science. For this reason, when Wundt discusses explanation in psychology, it is in terms of psychological laws rather than reduction to the physiological processes of the organism.

When psychology investigates the relation between the processes of physical and mental life, it is called psychophysics. On this subject Wundt explicitly acknowledges that he follows Fechner, but he denies Fechner's hope that psychophysical methods can be used for metaphysical purposes. Metaphysical implications, he admitted, may emerge from experimental research but only as an end result of research.

Although Wundt used psychophysical methods for many problems, he disagreed with Fechner on what was being measured. Wundt held that, to put the matter correctly, one must state that two sensations are of equal intensity or one sensation is just noticeably different from another sensation. Wundt was seeking to study not the relation between the body and the mind, but the relation between sensation on the one hand and psychological processes on the other. A purely psychological interpretation with no appeal to the relation of stimulus and sensation resulted. To Wundt, data obtained from psychological study were illustrative of a law of psychological relativity. The degree to which sensations differ makes judgments of their relative magnitude possible. This point of view was consistent with his conviction that psychology concerned itself with experience and not with an alleged body–mind interactionism.

Wundt firmly established the method of experimental, analytical introspection as psychology's characteristic procedure. Wundt recognized that conscious experiences, called conscious contents, are fleeting and in continual flux. He therefore laid down explicit rules for proper use of the introspective method:[8] (1) The observer, if at all possible, must be in a position to determine when the process is to be introduced; (2) the observer must be in a state of "strained attention"; (3) the observation must be capable of being repeated several times; and (4) the conditions of the experiment must be such that they are capable of variation through introduction or elimination of certain stimuli and through variation of the strength and quality of the stimuli.

The first rule is necessary so that the observer will not be caught off guard. In terms of Wundt's arrangement for introspection, the observer knows when to expect the introduction of the stimulus and is ready to observe the state of consciousness. He is therefore capable of isolating the mental processes of that moment. As for the second rule, the observer must be conscious of every nuance of that which is presented. Repetition, the third rule, allows for the uncovering of omissions and distortions of earlier trials. The fourth rule makes it possible to study the effect of variation, that is, the effect of the change resulting from addition or subtraction of various aspects of stimulating conditions as shown in variations of the experience. This last rule takes us to his conception of an experiment. Because Wundt's psychology investigates the contents of consciousness rather than the acts of mind investigated by Franz Brentano, Wundt's psychology is often called content psychology.

Wundt held that, insofar as physiological psychology draws on experiment, we can refer to it as experimental psychology. Wundt asserted that in psychology pure self-observation is insufficient.[9] Only when additional recourse to experiment is made are exact quantitative results possible. The essence of an experiment is to vary the conditions of a stimulus situation and then to observe the changes in the experiences of the observer. In advocating experimental control of conditions of introspection, Wundt was taking a giant step.

Herbart had urged using mathematics in the study of psychological problems, although he had denied the possibility of using experiment. Kant had not only denied the possibility of experiment in psychology, but had also held that the use of mathematics itself was impossible. He believed that the only dimension of consciousness was time and that with one dimension one could not carry out experiments. Consequently, psychical processes were indeterminate.[10] Since Kantians or Herbartians dominated the German philosophy of his time, it is to Wundt's credit that he overcame this formidable intellectual block and saw that both mathematics and experiment could be applied in psychology.

Wundt maintained that the elements of experience could be described in terms of two dimensions or attributes: quality and intensity.[11] Quality is what we typically call the experience, blue, sour, C#, and so forth.[12] These qualities cannot be analyzed into anything simpler. Intensity is how much of the quality there is, loudness, brightness, magnitude and the like. With the dimensions of quality and intensity, experiment becomes possible for Wundt. Experiment was impossible for Kant because he dealt with only one dimension.

Armed with intensity and quality as the two classes of variables, Wundt was prepared for the experimental study of psychological phenomena. It is true that in hearing, for example, intensity is never separable from some quality of pitch, but it is possible to change either the intensity alone (loud–soft), or the pitch alone (high–low), while maintaining the other unchanged. Moreover, we may use two notes and consequently change the quality of the sound so that it is different from that of either note alone. Intensity and quality become subjects for scientific study. On these premises Wundt was able to launch the experimental study of psychology.

LIFE AND RESEARCH OF WUNDT

Wilhelm Wundt was born at the village of Neckarau near Heidelberg in Baden in 1832; he was the son of the minister of the United Evangelical Church of the Grand Duchy of Baden.[13] He was a solitary child, sickly from his early years due to malaria. He played little with other children and thus made few friends. He was an indifferent student with a tendency to daydreaming, a trait that lasted throughout most of his public school years and even into college. His attitude led one of his teachers to suggest that he forget college and become a postman.

Wundt's father died when Wundt was in his teens, leaving him and his mother to live on a small pension. Nevertheless, he was able to matriculate to the University of Tübingen as a medical student. Apparently, he was not particularly interested in medicine, but it allowed him to live away from home and forestalled pressure to become a minister. Moreover, in those days medicine was a good alternative for the individual who had a scientific interest but was not financially set to become a university professor. In those days, in German universities, it took a number of years for a new faculty member, a Dozent, to become established and to gain a reliable salary. With a medical degree a Dozent could do scientific work on the side and be supported by his medical practice.

After a year at Tübingen, Wundt went to Heidelberg, also to study medicine. There he met the chemist Robert Bunsen (1811–1899) who had founded one of the first chemical laboratories in Germany and who used demonstrations in his scientific lectures, much as Wundt was do later in his psychological lectures. Wundt conducted his first research project with Bunsen and saw it published in 1853.[14] It was a minor study on the relation of salt ingestion to the salinity of urine.

It was at Heidelberg that Wundt seems to have awakened to his own potential. Making up his deficiencies in mathematics and some other subjects, he threw himself into his studies. In 1855 he published his first independent work in the field of physiology, a study on the effects of severing the vagus and recurrens nerves upon respiration. He did the work on his dining room table with his mother as his surgical assistant. The work received a medal from the medical faculty and was published in 1855 in Johannes Müller's prestigious journal.[15] Wundt graduated from Heidelberg with an MD degree *summa cum laude.*

During this time Wundt produced his first publication related to psychology: a study on the sensitivity to touch in hysterical patients, published in 1858.[16] He also spent the 1856 summer term at the University of Berlin where he worked in the physiological laboratories of Johannes Müller and Emil DuBois Reymond. There Wundt began his researches on muscular physiology which later resulted in his first book, *Die Lehre von der Muskelbewegung (The Doctrine of Muscular Movement),* completed and published in 1858.[17]

In 1857 Wundt was appointed Dozent at Heidelberg and began to lecture in physiology. His first announced course in physiology attracted only four students, which hardly gave him a sufficient source of income. Between 1858 and 1864, however, he became an assistant to the great German physiologist, Hermann von Helmholtz, who had just arrived from Bonn to the newly established Physiological Institute at Heidelberg. The position provided a small but reliable income that made Wundt's university career possible. His duties were primarily to conduct physiological laboratory courses for entering medical students. As such he was extremely junior to the great Helmholtz and was apparently never close to him.[18]

Wundt was extremely productive during the years of his association with Helmholtz, publishing sixty-three articles and books between 1858 and 1864. During the times students were not using the physiological laboratory, it was available for Wundt's own use, and Wundt obviously availed himself of the opportunity.

As assistant to Helmholtz, Wundt began developing his ideas on the nature of psychology. The first record we have of Wundt's lecturing on psychology was a summer course he taught in 1862 with the intriguing title, "Psychology as a Natural Science."[19] Wundt's *Beiträge zur Theorie der Sinneswahrnehmung (Contributions to a Theory of Sensory Perception)* published in 1862[20] and his *Lectures on Human and Animal Psychology* published in 1863[21] contain in broad strokes the pattern of psychology as Wundt would develop it over the remainder of his long professional life.

In the introduction of his *Beiträge* in 1862, Wundt stresses the primacy of method as a means of scientific advancement. He also cited advances in apparatus, such as the laryngoscope and the ophthalmoscope, as a means of ushering in a whole series of discoveries. Psychology, he goes on, has not yet felt the impulse of the new empirical method being used all around it. It has asked metaphysical questions first, concerning the essence, origin, and destination of the soul. These questions should be asked at a point where psychology may end but not where it should start. It must take the simplest of experiences for its point of departure; that is, psychology should crawl before it tries to walk. Wundt marshals evidence primarily from vision and secondarily from touch. This work reveals his struggle to utilize physiological methodology in dealing with psychological problems.

In 1865 Wundt, now able to support himself on the income from his books, left Helmholtz's employ. Wundt continued to teach at Heidelberg but functioned primarily as an independent scholar. It was only in 1871 that he received a regular salaried appointment at the professional level, becoming an *Ausserordenlicher Professor* ("extraordinary professor)." Helmholtz had accepted a position at the University of Berlin, and Wundt was called on to be his temporary replacement. The resulting boost in salary allowed Wundt to marry in 1872. His replacement of Helmholtz was not made permanent, however, and Wundt left Heidelberg in 1874 for a position at the University of Zürich in Switzerland.

From 1867 until he left Heidelberg, Wundt had given a course entitled "Physiological Psychology." This date establishes the formal offering of an academic course of this nature. As he "worked up" his lecture notes over the next few years, a new book, by general agreement his most important, began to take form. This was his *Grundzüge der physiologischen Psychologie (Principles of Physiological Psychology).* [22] The first half was published in 1873 and the entire volume in 1874. It was destined to go through six editions, the last in 1911, and would swell in size to three large volumes. (Most of his books would appear in new, amplified, and revised editions from time to time.) The *Grundzüge* changed in detail, sometimes very important detail. This was particularly true in the fourth edition, published in 1893 when Wundt shifted from an attempt to catalogue all current knowledge in psychology (much as Johannes Müller's *Handbuch der Physiologie* had done for physiology) to an attempt to systematize psychological knowledge. The *Grundzüge* in its many editions would establish Wundt's reputation.

Wundt's stint at Zurich in inductive philosophy lasted only a year, and in 1875 he accepted a call to the University of Leipzig, where he would spend the rest of his life and with which he would be intimately identified.

At the University of Leipzig Wundt established his laboratory of psychology. For reasons that remain uncertain, 1879 has customarily been considered the founding year of the first experimental laboratory in the world. It may have been chosen based on the mistaken belief that it was in 1879 that university authorities gave Wundt's Leipzig laboratory formal recognition. In fact, the university did not award formal recognition for a course in "experimental psychology" until the winter of 1883, when it also provided an appropriation for a laboratory. An Institute for Experimental Psychology, as such, was not listed by university authorities until 1894. Actually, before Wundt's arrival in October 1875, the Royal Ministry promised Wundt a room for his own apparatus and for demonstrations connected with his *Psychologische Ubungen* (Psychological Practicum). The promise was not fulfilled until the following year, however.[23] The most probable reason for the choice of 1879 is that even some of Wundt's earliest students mention it as the founding date because in that year the first of Wundt's students did publishable psychological research in Wundt's laboratory.[24] The date is a safe one to use for the establishment of psychology as a professional subject of graduate study. Certainly, a laboratory had to be there in the winter of 1879 for Max Friedrich to do his dissertation research, whether or not the university formally recognized it as a "laboratory."[25]

Considerable controversy has also centered on the primacy of Wundt's Leipzig laboratory. William James also established something of a laboratory at Harvard University in 1875, but it appears to have been primarily an undergraduate demonstrational laboratory rather than a research laboratory.[26] "Firsts" are always difficult to define without a long line of conditional statements. So much depends on what one considers a "laboratory" to be and on whether an officially recognized laboratory takes precedence over a laboratory in fact.

The date notwithstanding, by 1881 Wundt began to publish his journal, *Philosophische Studien,* which contained reports of experimental studies that had begun to flow from his laboratory. This was the first journal devoted as much to psychology as to philosophy. Lest the title be puzzling, Wundt thought philosophy should be psychological in nature. He did not support attempts to create a department for psychology that would be separate from that of philosophy. Moreover, between 1880 and 1901 he published four books in philosophy—a logic, an ethics, a systematic philosophy, and an introduction to the field. Wundt later published another journal called *Psychologische Studien.*

One result of the founding of the laboratory and of Wundt's spreading fame was the migration of students to Leipzig to study with him and to work in the laboratory. There gathered around him would-be psychologists who used introspection and experiment to derive the laws of the human mind. In this way Wundt became the leader of a "school" of psychology. These students, though not always united with Wundt in their systematic views, were careful to tow the party line while at Leipzig. Once away from Wundt they often diverged from the details of his systematic psychology. What they shared with Wundt, however, was an enthusiasm for experimental, laboratory psychology. The laboratory atmosphere fostered specific research studies that appeared as articles in journals. Wundt would then synthesize the results of the various studies in the successive editions of the *Grundzüge.*

The sheer availability of co-workers was important. Since a worker could hardly be the experimenter and observer at one and the same time, the experimenter of one study was available as a subject for another. Lest this point be dismissed as trivial, it is pertinent to indicate that introspection as practiced in Wundt's laboratory was not a skill acquired without a period of rigorous apprenticeship. Getting at the elements of experience required arduous training. Moreover, even if nonstudent assistants could be trained as subjects, the nature of the tasks to which they were assigned would have demanded payment.

CHARACTERISTIC RESEARCH

The work of the Leipzig laboratory may illustrate what a major segment of experimental psychology was like before and at the turn of the century. About 100 experimental studies appeared in the *Philosophische Studien* during its twenty-odd years, almost all of them carried out either in the Leipzig laboratory or conducted by Wundt's students soon after they left Leipzig. Consequently, the research bore heavily the impress of Wundt's direction, since typically he assigned the problem on which a particular student was to work.

E. G. Boring's summarizing classification may be utilized to sketch the research coming from Wundt's laboratory.[27] In quick overview the studies may be classed as those in sensation and perception, reaction, attention, feeling, and association. About half the research concerned problems in sensation and perception, particularly in vision. Papers on the psychophysics of color, peripheral vision, color contrast, negative afterimages, visual contrast, and colorblindness are typical of those concerned with visual sensation; and visual size and optical illusions are characteristic subjects of those papers on visual perception. Auditory sensation was investigated by psychophysical methods, and beats and combination tones were also studied. An attack was made on the problem of time perception by studying the ability of subjects to reproduce intervals of varying lengths in the comparison of "filled" times (time occupied with mental work or sensory stimulation) and unfilled time. Tactual sensation was investigated through the problems of the two-point threshold, by using the already familiar methods of Weber and Fechner.

About one-sixth of the workers' time and effort in the laboratory was devoted to the reaction experiment. Donders' subtractive procedure of Donders was used although his times for choice and discrimination were replaced by a more complicated classification of times for volition, perception, apperception, cognition, association, and judgment.

Hopes ran high in the Leipzig laboratory for a chronometry of the mind, since, by the additive and subtractive procedures, it appeared entirely feasible to work out the times necessary for each of these processes. These hopes were dashed, however, for as Boring notes, the times for a separate process were constant neither from person to person nor from study to study. "Later introspection showed that in a more complicated reaction the entire conscious pattern is changed and that the alternation is not merely the insertion of another link on a chain."[28] Oswald Külpe (1862–1915), the German philosopher and experimental psychologist, a student of Wundt, delivered the most telling blow against the view that the elements are additive.[29] He showed that changing the task does not merely add another unit; instead, it alters the whole process. Külpe interpreted L. Lange's results as showing that the subject's predisposition or attitude alters the perceptual-reactive process. Previously, Lange's classical research study had established characteristic differences in speed between some subjects who attend to the stimulus as compared to other subjects who attend to the response, in favor of the greater speed of the latter.[30] This finding did much to solve the problem of the personal equation. Those who attend to the response react more quickly than those who must shift attention from stimulus to the reaction to be made.

As interest in the reaction experiment waned, it was replaced first by studies of attention and then of feeling, each including about one-tenth of the laboratory's studies. Lange's study, mentioned above, helped to create the interest in attention. To Wundt, attention was clear perception of a narrow region of the content of consciousness. An example is the word or words we are reading on this page relative to the rest of the page, to the adjoining page, and to much of the surrounding environment of the room. Whatever is in the focus of attention becomes distinct and separate from the rest of the field. Research in the area of attention was performed, including the study of the range and fluctuation of attention. While a student of Wundt, J. McKeen Cattell, later a major figure in American psychology, carried out the classic study of attention span (meaning that which can be taken in at a glance). Cattell found that four, five, or six units (lines, letters, or words) can be apprehended in an exposure that is of too short duration to allow a movement of attention.[31]

In the 1890s the work of the laboratory focused on studies of feelings. These investigations involved the use of the method of expression through which feelings and correlated changes of pulse, breathing, muscular strength, and the like were analyzed. Also developed was the method of paired comparisons which requires that the subject compare each particular stimulus with every other stimulus in terms of the subjective feeling aroused. Suppose the task is to judge the pleasantness of a variety of colored paper patches: patch A is compared to B, C, D, E, F; then patch B to A, C, D, E, F, and so on. On each trial the observer is to report the most pleasing of each pair: A or B, A or C, and so on.

A survey of the research from his laboratory shows that Wundt did not occupy himself with developing new kinds of experiments; the methods he used were not particularly new. Students of the psychology and physiology of the senses owe much to the work that went before, particularly to Helmholtz. Reaction time studies again owe something, not only to Helmholtz, but also to Donders, whereas the association study can be attributed to Galton. Even the study of feeling, where Wundt was at his most original, in a theoretical sense, depended on the extension of Fechner's method of impression to paired comparisons; studies of expression were linked to the utilization of already existing methods for studying pulse, breathing, and the like. There had been antecedent studies even for attention. Wundt's experimental contribution was to reduce to quantitative terms the research areas already extant.

LATER LIFE AND STUDENTS

Wundt began sponsoring doctoral dissertations as early as 1875.[32] By 1919 the total had reached an impressive 186, of which 70 were on philosophical topics and 116 on psychological problems. Not all the students he sponsored were destined to become leading psychologists or even psychologists at all. Struck by the number of unfamiliar names, one psychologist[33] tried to trace them down; astonishingly, 86 could not be found. Apparently, a considerable number of the students who received the precious title "Herr Doktor," were content to sink back into the oblivion of the Gymnasium, the German public school.

Wundt's students came from all over Europe. Many were American, the first of whom was G. Stanley Hall, fresh from his studies at Harvard. This roving ambassador of American psychology-to-be "dropped in" for a time in the first year of the new laboratory and studied with Wundt, although he never received a degree from him. James McKeen Cattell, Wundt's first bona fide American student, studied at Leipzig on two occasions. It was on his second sojourn in 1885 that Cattell pronounced to Wundt that Wundt needed an assistant and that he, Cattell, was that assistant. Other American students were Edward W. Scripture, later director of the Yale Psychological Laboratory and a researcher in hearing; Edward A. Pace, for many years head of the Department of Psychology at Catholic University;

Lightner Witmer, the founder of the first psychological clinic at the University of Pennsylvania; and Charles H. Judd, the pioneer educational psychologist at the University of Chicago.

Even this short list shows something of the breadth of activity that these Americans managed to show on their return to the United States after the severely rigorous "pure" training they had received. Born in England where there was no suitable post for an experimental psychologist such as he, Edward Bradford Titchener, another of Wundt's students, came to America to direct the psychological work at Cornell University. None of these students in America would follow the detail of Wundt's system. What they took away from Leipzig, however, was a belief in the importance of the laboratory and psychological research. The best known continental psychologists who worked in the Leipzig laboratory, besides Oswald Külpe, already mentioned, were Hugo Münsterberg, Alfred Lehmann, Ernst Meumann, Theodor Lipps, and Felix Krueger.

According to Titchener, Wundt was a quiet, unassuming, pleasant person whose life followed a totally regulated pattern. He worked on his current book or article in the morning, and then had a consultation hour.[34] In the afternoon he paid a formal visit to the laboratory; he followed this with a walk, during which he cast his lecture into rough form; he delivered the lecture without notes and made a second, informal return to the laboratory. He was a very popular lecturer, apparently simplifying his material somewhat to suit his audience. As Hall puts it, Wundt's style of writing is as lusterless as lead—but as solid.[35] To perhaps a surprising extent, concerts and interests in current affairs occupied many of his evenings. He was a man of simple tastes who avoided public functions and virtually never traveled.

It is not surprising that from this background emerged the serious hard-working, hard-driving writer of so many books in so many editions. E. G. Boring wryly estimated that from 1853 to 1920 Wundt produced some 53,735 pages (averaging out to 2.2 pages per day for every day of that period).[36]

ATTITUDE TOWARD OTHER BRANCHES OF PSYCHOLOGY

Wundt was unalterably opposed to the application of psychology.[37] When Ernst Meumann, a gifted pupil, turned to educational psychology, Wundt treated his move as desertion in the face of the enemy. Emil Kraepelin, another student, applied psychology to psychiatry and was advised by Wundt to concentrate on psychiatry.[38] Work other than that of his own students received even more severe criticism. He was especially critical of the work of his former student Oswald Külpe, the reluctant leader of the so-called Würzburg School of Imageless Thought. In their research in the higher mental processes, the Würzburgers introduced a method called the Ausfrage method. After securing the immediate response to a stimulus situation, the experimenters at Würzburg often interrupted the experience and questioned their subjects about all that had gone on in their experience. Wundt considered this a blatant violation of the rules of introspection.[39]

Despite the admission that child (and animal) psychology were supplementary branches[40] of the field, Wundt categorically rejected the beginnings of child psychology in the work of William Preyer and J. Mark Baldwin. Wundt did not judge their work to be psychology since the conditions of study could not be adequately controlled.[41] Animal research was not conducted in Wundt's laboratory. He was also very critical of French psychology, claiming that the work done in that country was reduced to studies of suggestion and hypnotism.[42] He argued that one cannot give the name "experimental psychology" to each and every operation that brings about a change in consciousness. Those studies lacked exact introspection and so were not true psychological experiments. Lest this catalogue give the impression that he could not tolerate differences of opinion, he managed to maintain cordial relationships with a number of students such as Hugo Münsterberg, Felix Krueger, and Eduard Spranger, who disagreed with him sharply on various major theoretical points. He was, in fact, personally helpful to them.[43]

Much of Wundt's controversy with Külpe arose because of Külpe's attempt to extend experimental psychology into the "higher mental processes."[44] It may seem odd that Wundt, the promoter of experimental, laboratory psychology, would be opposed to experimentation. However, he believed that experimental methodology—which was primarily introspection—was not applicable to extremely elaborate processes such as reason, memory, thought, and the like. For this reason, as we have seen, Wundt constructed two psychologies, one for the lower mental processes—sensation, perception, attention, and the like—and one for the higher mental processes such as judgment, thought, and will. The higher mental processes could not be studied experimentally but only through studying the products of mind. These products of mind were studied in Wundt's voluminous *Völkerpsychologie.*

The *Völkerpsychologie* is sometimes translated as "social psychology," which is misleading since it has very little to do with what we call modern social psychology. It is literally translated as "folk psychology," which does not tell us much either. The meaning comes closer to an anthropological psychology and to the terms *cultural* or *ethnic* psychology.

The notion of a psychology such as the *Völkerpsychologie* had been around for a long time.[45] Wundt had taught the subject in the early 1860s while still at Heidelberg and had laid out the basic notion of such a study in his *Beiträge.* At first, Wundt saw *Völkerpsychologie* as only an auxiliary science. Not until 1893 in the fourth edition of his *Grundzüge* was he convinced that it deserved to be considered a coordinate branch along with experimental psychology. By studying the products of mind, Wundt dealt with such matters as language, myth, and custom.[46] He considered language, for example, the major key to understanding thought. In order to consider the problems of the higher mental processes, he began writing the *Völkerpsychologie,* the first volume appearing in 1900 and nine more volumes between then and 1920.[47]

Wundt's dual psychology was a source of conflict for many of his own students. Titchener and Külpe, in particular, sought to unify a psychology of mental contents into a single system. This effort necessitated, however, a shift from the idealism of Wundt to the positivistic approach of Richard Avenarius and Ernst Mach. The nature of this shift and its influences on early twentieth-century psychology, particularly in America, will be covered in Chapter 20. In terms of influence, however, the *Völkerpsychologie* was of influence primarily in Europe, whereas the Wundt best known to America was that of the *Grundzüge der physiologischen Psychologie.*[48]

As if according to plan, Wundt published his autobiographical reminiscences, *Erlebtes und Erkanntes,* in 1920.[49] He died on August 31 of that year, two weeks after his eighty-eighth birthday.

SOME SYSTEMATIC VIEWS

Wundt's claim to greatness rests more on his work as a founder of psychology than on his systematic views. His system amounted primarily to a psychological taxonomy, or a classificatory scheme and, as Boring observes, was not in itself capable of direct or indirect experimental proof or disproof.[50] This taxonomic form should not surprise us. A consideration of the history of other sciences shows a similar starting point. Chemistry, for example, began with the identification of elements into the periodic table, with investigations on how the elements combine to form more complex states. Biology's early history dealt with the classification of living things into a schema to understand how one relates to another. In the same way, Wundt sought to create a systematic structure so that every possible experience was represented and so that the "laws of combination" of elements could be understood. As new evidence appeared, Wundt revised his position on various issues. Because Wundt's thinking went through so many changes over the time between the publication of his *Beiträge* in 1862 to the sixth and final edition of his *Grundzüge* in 1911, it would be impossible to do justice to these changes in a text of this sort. A brief consideration of his later views, however, should suffice.[51]

To Wundt, psychology is the science that investigates the facts of consciousness, including sensations, feelings, ideas, volitions, and apperceptions. None of these appears in an uncompounded state; they must be abstracted from the compound by introspective analysis. In fact, all our experiences are complex and must be analyzed introspectively.

The elements of the mind, or the basic states of consciousness, are sensations and feelings. When abstracted by introspection, pure sensations are found to possess only intensity and quality and lack spatial or temporal aspects. Sensations are objective in the sense that they have reference to external things. Earlier systematists often referred to experiences directly aroused by external stimuli as sensations and those dependent on internal conditions as ideas. Wundt held this division to be an error. The sources for touch and organic sensations of our body, he said, are just as much a part of our outer world as is stimulation from external objects. Hence, these sensations, too, are external.

Feelings that accompany sensations are the subjective complements referring to states of consciousness themselves. Sensations and feelings are simultaneous aspects of immediate experience. Sometimes the aspect of feeling is apparently negligible, but it is always present. If intensity is increased, feeling becomes apparent, as when a light is increased in intensity to the point at which it becomes dazzling. Nevertheless, Wundt considered feeling an experience that was distinct from that other conscious element, sensation.

Feelings were described earlier in Wundt's system simply as a dimension of pleasantness and unpleasantness, ranging from neutral to intensely pleasant or unpleasant. After 1896, however, Wundt believed that feelings could not be described in terms of pleasantness–unpleasantness alone. Two additional dimensions, tension–relaxation and excitement–depression, must also be used to account for the range of the experiences of feeling. Wundt had found that a given feeling experience involves three dimensions but in different combinations—for example, pleasant, tense, and excited in one case or unpleasant, relaxed, and depressed in another. Feeling experience is not a matter of simultaneity alone. The dimensions in the experience change through time: at first tickling might move along the dimension of pleasantness, but then tension and excitement would become apparent, and unpleasantness would come to predominate over pleasantness.

This tridimensional theory of feeling, as it was called, stimulated a tremendous amount of research in both Wundt's own and rival laboratories, but the theory was not borne out by immediate post-Wundtian research. The results of these studies were found to be applicable in contemporary research situations, however. It is in this way that psychology, having become an experimental science, advances. A theory may stand or fall; the experiments persist, either interpreted as isolated facts or worked into a modified or different system when they are congruent with it.

The concept that the mind can be reduced to elements for purposes of study and the fashion in which these elements cohere is obviously a heritage from the empiricist–associationist tradition. Wundt, however, went beyond this level. The experiences we have, he stated, are more than the sum of their parts—there is a creative synthesis of immediate experience.[52] This point, especially in later writings, he came to stress. It has been argued that, contrary to what is often alleged, this concept was not a mental chemistry in the way John Stuart Mill had considered it. Indeed, he specifically rejected Mill's view of the matter.[53] Besides analysis there is a constructive process of psychic synthesis. Once the systematic analysis of elements had been accomplished, their manner of synthesis could be carried out. Seeing a landscape, he was aware, did not add up to thirteen specified visual sensations of variant hues and the accompanying feelings of mild excitement, high pleasure, and low tension, meaningfully perceived. This synthesis was expressed by using concepts of combination, complexes, fusion, apperception, and volition.

When sensation and feeling are combined, they form ideas and perceptions. To Wundt, the term *idea* included such complexes as memory images and perceptions.[54] Ideas, including both sensations and feelings in composite, are representative of objects either in perception or in memory.

Wundt made use of association, but it was not the association of conceptual meanings as the British empiricists had done. His association was a fusion of a kind that occurs in tones in the musical chord or in illusions.

Consciousness shows various degrees of apperception, of contexts, and of connections—the unification of the conscious contents. Children may run words together in something they recite without understanding what they are saying. Adults may parrot a difficult concept but not understand what is meant by it.

Unification requires apperception, a combination of a complex and a unity. Although this concept of apperception was not new with Wundt (Kant had developed it to a rather high degree), Wundt stressed its cognitive aspects more than his predecessors. Briefly and incompletely stated, apperception is the process by which attention takes place. To some degree it is an organizational concept where clearness of comprehension of an experience occurs through the combination of sensory experiences, previous ideas, and feelings. Feeling enters into the process; the particular quality of the experience of the feeling of a compound is dependent on apperception. Easy, smooth-flowing reactions give rise to pleasure, and conflictual discordant ones to pain.

Wundt made a distinction between the whole range of consciousness and the so-called fixation point of apperception. Only processes in the fixation point of apperception are apperceived, that is, become clear. This does not mean that apperception cannot range over the complex of ideas, referred to as the apperceptive mass, but at a given moment the experiences in the fixation point of apperception are a selection from this mass. When apperceptions refer to any given experience, Wundt calls them "states of attention."[55] Wundt preferred to discuss the phenomena in terms of apperception, but most of his followers dealt with the matter in terms of attention.

Combinations of feelings with ideational processes give rise to the emotions. In some emotions, such as joy and delight, pleasure predominates; in others, such as anger and fear, displeasure is the stronger.

Volitional processes had a central position in Wundt's system. Voluntarism was his term for psychological causality and followed from his differentiation of psychological from physical causality. Psychological causality arose from volitional processes.[56] To Wundt, feelings are the "determining factors" of volition. Sometimes feelings are not strong enough to produce volition, but volition is not operative unless they are present. Volition culminates in an action, as when an angry person strikes the object of his anger. Without the striking the process would be emotion alone.

In dealing with volition Wundt was considering action as differentiated from reception. The distinction between sensory and motor nerves that arose from the work of the physiologists carried over into Wundt's psychology at this point. Sensations are the psychological phenomena associated with sensory nerves, whereas movements, called actions, are the psychological phenomena associated with motor nerves. The natural coherence between a sensation and an action was modified through experience.

SUMMARY

The methodological prescriptive allegiances of Wilhelm Wundt are similar to those of the physiologists from whom he drew inspiration. Naturalism was accepted without question; he subscribed to methodological objectivism, in the sense that he attempted to quantify experience so that others could repeat his procedures, and to quantitativism itself. Since the combination of introspection and experiment was the method of choice, Wundt fostered empiricism. His rejection of empiricism's rival, rationalism, was equally straightforward. Psychology as a science, he held, could not be based on metaphysical, that is, rationalist assumptions. The search for general laws (nomotheticism) so dominated Wundt's priorities that he rejected attempts at studies aimed at individual differences (idiographicism) even among his own students.

Contentually, an adherence to contentual subjectivism of a conscious mentalist variety dominated. Wundt hardly conceived contentual objectivism to be possible, let alone advocated it. His methodological position of dual aspect parallelism caused him to insist that, for example, in psychophysical research one studies the relation between sensation on one hand and judgment on the other, and not the interaction of body and mind. This made systematic his conception of psychology as contentually subjective in nature. The units were the elements of mental contents and were thus molecular in that the isolation of these elements was the first task of psychology. It is important to add that Wundt advocated a principle of psychosynthesis. Thus, he also adhered to a molar view in which the sum of the elements was more than these elements. Wundt's was a structural view of the mind inasmuch as parts, not functions, were stressed. It was static in that the enduring, not the changing, facets of mind were sought. He maintained purism of an almost snobbish variety against any claims of utilitarianism.

Wundt was the first modern psychologist—the first person to conceive of experimental psychology as a science. He founded the first psychological laboratory, and he edited the first experimental journal devoted to psychology. In addition to these pioneering efforts, Wundt was the great synthesizer of research findings, both of the work that preceded him and of that carried on by his students. Wundt's *forte* was not to light up the dark corners with luminous ideas or to give us a dazzling new perspective. Rather, he refurbished the old incomplete picture, working over a thousand details, cleaning here, repairing there, filling a crack here, so that psychology as it left his hands was an improved, more coherent entity but still recognizable.

The areas of investigation worked out by Wundt—sensation and perception, reaction time, attention, feeling, association—became as fixed as the very chapter titles in the textbooks that were to come, making this work a not inconsiderable portion of psychology. Yet his treatment of other areas of psychology was either nonexistent or, at best, woefully inadequate. The problem areas of learning (as differentiated from association), motivation, emotion, intelligence, thought, and personality were to be brought systematically within the scope of psychology by men who had other points of view.

Whatever one's opinion of Wundt's narrow conception of psychology, without doubt the course he chose had the effect of solidifying an independent field of psychology. If he had struck out on uncharted paths, it is quite conceivable that the emergence of psychology as a separate discipline would have been delayed. It does not detract from his achievement to add that much of the history of psychology following Wundt consisted of rebelling against the limitations he had placed on the field. In general, forward movement is most sure when it has something to push against.

NOTES

1. W. Wundt, *Grundzüge der physiologischen Psychologie* (Leipzig: Englemann, 1874). The book went into six editions and grew to three large volumes totaling over 3600 pages. Part of the fifth edition was translated by E. B. Titchener and published as *Principles of Physiological Psychology*, 5th German ed., Vol. 1 (New York: Macmillan Co., 1904).

2. *Ibid., Principles*, author's preface to first edition (1874).

3. See David Leary, "Wundt and After: Psychology's Shifting Relations with the Natural Sciences, Social Sciences, and Philosophy," *Journal of the History of the Behavioral Sciences*, *15* (1979):231–241.

4. A. L. Blumenthal, "Wilhelm Wundt: Psychology as the Propaedeutic Science," in C. Buxton, ed., *Points of View in the Modern History of Psychology* (New York: Academic Press, 1985), p. 28. W. Wundt, "Selbstbeobachtung and innere Wahrnehmung," *Philosophische Studien*, 4 (1877–1888):292–309.

5. K. Danziger, "The History of Introspection Reconsidered," *Journal of the History of the Behavioral Sciences*, *16* (1980):241–262; "The Positivist Repudiation of Wundt," *Journal of the History of the Behavioral Sciences*, *15* (1979):205–230.

6. W. Wundt, *Lectures on Human and Animal Psychology*, 2nd German ed., trans J. E. Creighton and E. B. Titchener (New York: Macmillan Co., 1894), pp. 440–450 (1892); W. Wundt, *An Introduction to Psychology*, 2nd ed., trans R. Pintner (New York: Macmillan Co., 1912), Chapter 5 (1911); W. Wundt, *Grundriss der Psychologie* (Leipzig: Englemann, 1896), Sec. 1, Par. 2 (Herrnstein and Boring, Excerpt No. 109); W. G. Bringmann, W. Balance, and R. B. Evans, "Wilhelm Wundt 1832–1920: A Biographical Sketch," *Journal of the History of the Behavioral Sciences*, *11* (1975):287–297.

7. W. Wundt, *Principles*, Introduction.

8. W. Wundt, *Keline Schriften*, Vol. 2 (Leipzig: Engelmann, 1911).

9. W. Wundt, *Principles*, Introduction.

10. *Ibid.*

11. *Ibid.*

12. W. Wundt, *Outlines of Psychology*, 7th German ed., trans. C. H. Judd (Leipzig: Englemann, 1907) (1896).

13. Most of the biographical material in this chapter on Wundt comes from Wolfgang G. Bringmann, Norma J. Bringmann, and William D. G. Balance, "Wilhelm Maximilian Wundt 1832–1874: The Formative Years," in Wolfgang G. Bringmann and Ryan D. Tweney, *Wundt Studies* (Toronto: C. J. Hogrefe, 1980), pp. 13–32 and from Wundt's own psychological reminiscences, *Erlebtes und Erkanntes* (Stuttgart: Kroner, 1920). Another good source of Wundt's life is Solomon Diamond, "Wundt Before Leipzig," in R. W. Rieber, ed., *Wilhelm Wundt and the Making of a Scientific Psychology* (New York: Plenum Press, 1980), pp. 3–70.

14. W. Wundt, "Ueber den Kochsaltzgehalt des Harns," *Journal für practische Chemie, 59* (1853):354–363.

15. W. Wundt, "Ueber den Einfluss der Durchschneidung des Lungenmagennerven auf die Respirationsorgane," *Johannes Müllers Archiv für Anatomie, Physiologie und wissenschaftliche Medicin* (1855):269–313.

16. Bringmann, Bringmann, and Balance, "Wilhelm Maximilian Wundt," p. 23.

17. W. Wundt, *Die Lehre von der Muskelbewegung* (Braunschweig: Vieweg, 1858).

18. There is a considerable debate on Wundt's relationship with Helmholtz. A good review is given in Bringmann, Bringmann, and Balance, "Wilhelm Maximilian Wundt," p. 26.

19. E. Wundt, *Wilhelm Wundts Werk* (Munich: Beck, 1927).

20. W. Wundt, *Beiträge zur Theorie der Sinneswahrnehmung* (Leipzig: Winter, 1862).

21. W. Wundt, *Vorlesungen über die Menschen- und Tierseele* (1863, 6th ed., 1919), trans. of the second edition (1892) by J. Creighton and E. B. Titchener as *Lectures on Human and Animal Psychology* (London: Swan Sonnenschein and Co., 1894).

22. W. Wundt, *Grundzüge der physiologischen Psychologie* (Leipzig: Englemann, 1873–1874).

23. Wolfgang G. Bringmann, Norma J. Bringmann, and Gustav A. Ungerer, "The Establishment of Wundt's Laboratory: An Archival and Documentary Study," in Bringmann and Tweney, *Wundt Studies*, p. 132. This article is perhaps the best presentation of the subject.

24. J. McKeen Cattell used the date as early as 1888, less than ten years after the "event" in his "The Psychological Laboratory at Leipsic," *Mind, 13* (1888):37–51. E. B. Titchener used the dates 1878–1879 as early as 1896 in his *Outlines of Psychology* (New York: Macmillan Co., 1896), p. 32 (2nd ed., 1899). Oswald Külpe used it in 1902 in his *Die Philosophie der Gegenwart in Deutschland, (The Philosophy of the Present in Germany)*, trans. of the fifth edition (1914) by Maud Lyall Patrick and G.T.W. Patrick (London: George Allen and Co., 1913), p. 193.

25. Peter J. Behrens, "The First Dissertation in Experimental Psychology: Max Friedrich's Study of Apperception," in Bringmann and Tweney, *Wundt Studies*, pp. 193–209.

26. R. S. Harper, "The First Psychological Laboratory," *Isis, 41* (1950):158–161.

27. E. G. Boring, *A History of Experimental Psychology*, 2nd ed. (New York: Appleton–Century–Crofts, 1950), pp. 340–344. Other descriptions of early research at Wundt's Leipzig laboratory may be found in J. McKeen Cattell, "The Psychological Laboratory at Leipsic." See also E. B. Titchener, "The Leipsic School of Experimental Psychology," *Mind* (N.S. i. 1892):206–234.

28. *Ibid.*, p. 342.

29. O. Külpe, *Outlines of Psychology*, trans. E. B. Titchener (New York: MacMillan Co., 1909).

30. L. Lange, "Neue Experimente über den Vorgang der einfachen Reaktion auf Sinneseindrucke," *Philosophische Studien, 4* (1888):479–510.

31. J. M. Cattell, "The Time It Takes to See and Name Objects," *Mind, 11* (1886):63–65, reprinted in W. Dennis, ed., *Readings in the History of Psychology* (New York: Appleton–Century–Crofts, 1948), pp. 326–328.

32. M. A. Tinker, "Wundt's Doctorate Students and Their Theses (1875–1920)," *American Journal of Psychology, 44* (1932):630–637.

33. S. W. Fernberger, "Wundt's Doctorate Students," *Psychological Bulletin, 33* (1933):80–83.

34. E. B. Titchener, "Wilhelm Wundt."

35. G. S. Hall, *Founders.*

36. E. G. Boring, *History*, p. 345.

37. W. Wundt, "Ueber rein und angewandte Psychologie," *Psychologische Studien, 5* (1910):1–47.

38. G. S. Hall, *Founders.*

39. For a good summary of Wundt's criticisms, see George Humphrey, *Thinking: An Introduction to Its Experimental Psychology* (New York: John Wiley, 1951), pp. 108–119.

40. *Principles.*

41. H. Eber, "Zur Kritik der Kinderpsychologie, mit Rucksicht auf neuere Arbeiten," *Philosophische Studien, 11* (1896):586–588.

42. W. Wundt, *Principles.*

43. Bringmann et al., "Wilhelm Maximilian Wundt."
44. Kurt Danziger, "The Positivist Repudiation of Wundt," *Journal of the History of the Behavioral Sciences, 15* (1979):205–230.
45. E. B. Titchener, "Wilhelm Wundt."
46. *Ibid.*
47. W. Wundt, *Völkerpsychologie,* 10 vols. (Leipzig: Engelmann, 1900–1920). William Woodward, "Wundt's Program for the New Psychology: Vicissitudes of Experiment, Theory, and System," in William R. Woodward and Mitchell G. Ash, *The Problematic Science: Psychology in Nineteenth-Century Thought* (New York: Praeger, 1982), pp. 187–192.
48. For a view on some of the reasons for the *Völkerpsychologie*'s lack of influence in America, see Kurt Danziger, "Wundt and the Two Traditions in Psychology," and A. L. Blumenthal, "Wilhelm Wundt and Early American Psychology: A Clash of Cultures," in R. W. Rieber, *Wilhelm Wundt and the Making of a Scientific Psychology,* pp. 73–88, 117–136. See also Ryan Tweney and Stephen A. Yachanin, "Titchener's Wundt," in Bringmann and Tweney, *Wundt Studies,* pp. 380–395.
49. W. Wundt, *Erlebtes.*
50. E. G. Boring, *History,* p. 328.
51. W. Wundt, *Principles,* Introduction.
52. W. Wundt, *Gründzuge der physiologischen Psychologie,* 5th ed., Vol. 2 (Leipzig: Englemann, 1902).
53. A. L. Blumenthal, "A Reappraisal of Wilhelm Wundt," *American Psychologist, 30* (1975):1081–1088.
54. W. Wundt, *Principles,* Introduction, p. 45.
55. W. Wundt, *Principles,* p. 316.
56. For a more detailed consideration of Wundt on volition, see Kurt Danziger, "Wundt's Theory of Behavior and Volition," in Rieber, *Wilhelm Wundt and the Making of a Scientific Psychology,* pp. 89–116.

Top: Franz Brentano. *Bottom:* Hermann Ebbinghaus, G. E. Müller, and Oswald Külpe, c. 1909.

Chapter 15

Brentano and Ebbinghaus: Alternatives to Wundtian Orthodoxy

*D*espite Wilhelm Wundt's considerable dominance over German psychology, some psychologists embraced other prescriptive influences or investigated contentual areas different from those he espoused. Of Wundt's contemporaries and successors, two merit special attention: Franz Brentano (1838–1917), who advanced a view that psychology is properly concerned with mental acts rather than mental contents, and thus adhered to a functional prescription; and Hermann Ebbinghaus (1850–1909), who also dealt with mental functions and is regarded as the first psychologist to study memory and learning experimentally, thus broadening the subject matter of psychology. Two others whose contributions showed a similar but also significant broadening effect are G. E. Müller (1850–1934) who carefully followed up and expanded the work of his predecessors on psychophysics, color vision, and memory; and Oswald Külpe (1862–1915), Wundt's erstwhile assistant, who became the leader of the group of psychologists that came to be called the Würzburg School. This school extended the use of introspection to the study of the higher mental processes.

FRANZ BRENTANO

In 1874, the year that saw the complete publication of the crucial first edition of Wundt's *Grundzüge,* another significant but markedly different book appeared. This was *Psychology from an Empirical Standpoint,* written by a Catholic priest, Franz Brentano. Whereas Wundt had based his book primarily on contemporary empirical work, Brentano reached far into the past to the work of Aristotle and Aquinas, and thence to Locke and Mill. An account of Brentano's life will help put his contributions into context.

Life of Brentano

Franz Brentano was born in Marienburg on the Rhine in 1838.[1] When he was very young, his family moved to Bavaria. He lost his father early, and his mother, a devout Catholic, encouraged his early inclination toward the priesthood. In 1856 he moved on to Munich, where he worked under Ignatius Döllinger, a famous church historian. He then studied at Berlin, where he was thoroughly trained by F. A. Trendelenburg in the works of Aristotle. This training was decisive in all that he did afterward, for his psychological and philosophical thinking bear the impress of Aristotle. He also studied philosophy and theology at Munich and later at Tübingen, where he took his degree in 1862. He then entered the priesthood in 1864. Two years later he became Dozent in philosophy at Würzburg. For the next few years he busied himself with lecturing and writing papers on the philosophy of Aristotle and the history of science within the Church.

During the 1860s a controversy arose within the Catholic Church concerning the infallibility of the Pope. Ignatius Döllinger, Brentano's former teacher, was a leader of the group within the Church that opposed the doctrine. Brentano was selected to write a refutation of the doctrine, and, in doing so, he became something of a leader among the dissident clerics. When, in 1870, the Vatican Council accepted papal infallibility as dogma, he was brought face to face with a religious crisis. In 1873 he resigned the professorship to which he had been appointed as a priest and also resigned from the priesthood. To his death he remained a devout Christian of simple faith but without church affiliation.[2]

During the period that followed, without either university or clerical duties to interfere, he produced his book, *Psychology from an Empirical Standpoint.*[3] In 1874, as a layman, he was appointed professor at the University of Vienna, a post he held until 1880.

In that year a second major crisis arose when he sought to marry a Catholic woman. Marriage was illegal for a former priest in Austria. Once again he resigned his professorship, after which he took citizenship in Saxony and married. He immediately returned to the University of Vienna, not as a professor, but as a lecturer.

Over these years Brentano's lectures were very popular—so much so that his students often followed him home.[4] Among his students, at Würzburg and at Vienna, were such diverse persons as Carl Stumpf, later professor at Berlin; Edmund Husserl, the philosopher and psychologist of phenomenology; Christian von Ehrenfels, the originator of the concept of form quality and founder of the Austrian School of the Philosophy of Values; Thomas Masaryk, the founder of the Czechoslovakian Republic; and Sigmund Freud, the originator of psychoanalysis. The degree of Brentano's influence on Freud is still being debated.[5]

Brentano's students testified of their devotion to him; Carl Stumpf and Edmund Husserl were especially glowing in this respect.[6] For his part Brentano felt that he made a larger contribution through oral exchange than through the written word.

In 1894 Brentano's wife died, and his own health worsened. An eye disorder threatened his sight. In that year he resigned for the last time, never to hold an academic post again. After his resignation he devoted the remainder of his life to study, occasional writing, and informal conversational teaching among his friends and admirers. In 1895–1896 he settled in Florence, Italy.

During the years in Vienna Brentano published hardly any psychological works. Shortly before he left, he did write some papers on visual illusions. In 1907 a small but significant book on sense psychology appeared,[7] and in 1911 he published *Von der Klassifikation der psychischen Phanomene,*[8] his nearest approximation to the missing second volume of the *Psychologie* of thirty-seven years before. After Italy entered the war, Brentano, a pacifist, moved to Zurich, where he died in 1917.

Act Psychology

Because of its heavily philosophical background, Brentano's act psychology is particularly difficult for present-day psychologists to understand.

Brentano's psychology was very different from the elementism of Wundt and his followers. Brentano was much more deeply possessed by philosophy than was Wundt. This difference is understandable inasmuch as Brentano's background was heavily influenced by Aristotelian thought whereas Wundt was influenced more by the emerging natural sciences. Perhaps as a result, although he saw the promise of psychology as an experimental science, Brentano did not depend on experimental evidence for his psychological concepts. In writing his *Psychology,* he pitted one philosopher's insights on a particular question against another's, ruthlessly examining their assumptions and observations. He would then consider his own experiences and attempt to resolve the matter by coming to his own judgment.[9] That is an empirical method, but it is the method of empirical philosophy in the broadest sense of being traceable to experience and not the method of empirical science.[10] He saw the value of experimentation, but when he disagreed with the results of experiments, he tended to try to destroy them by argument, not by carrying out or suggesting research. In his studies of illusions, Brentano's character-istic method was demonstration, not experiment. Brentano reproduced the illu-sions and depended on the reader's own experience to show the phenomena he was discussing.[11] This use of demonstration was a typical method of communicating psychological information by those who made use of the phenomenological method. The Gestalt psychologists of the twentieth century also made very effec-tive use of demonstration for the exposition of their laws of perceptual organiza-tion.

Brentano was writing a philosophical psychology for the ages. His writing gives the impression that, once developed, his system was permanently fixed.[12] For Brentano there was no essential division between philosophy and psychology.[13] In this regard he was returning to the work of Locke, for whom psychology was basic to philosophy. Psychology became the means of rescuing philosophy from the morass into which it had slumped under Kant, whom Brentano considered a mystic to be classed with Plotinus. The fundamental influence on Brentano was, however, the thinking of Aristotle.

Like Aristotle, Brentano saw the mind as an active principle, not passively receiving information from the outside world, but seeking knowledge. Brentano did not break down experiences into elementary components. Instead, he viewed mind as having acts which he called ideating, judging, and loving–hating. Ideating in-cluded acts such as sensing and imagining; judging included acts such as recalling, rejecting, acknowledging, and rejecting; loving–hating includes feelings, wishing, resolving, intending, and desiring.[14] Our immediate experience is of the acts of mind, not of the objects acted on.

Quite consistently, Brentano arrived at his classification of acts by examining the various types of relationship a subject has to an object.[15] The first and most common relationship is that of having an idea of an object—real, imaginary, past, present, future, and even negative. Hence, there is ideating. In addition, the sheer diversity of kinds of objects ideated makes possible an affirmation or denial of the object. Hence, there is judging. Moreover, one may take attitudes toward objects that may be expressed as running the gamut from love (attraction) to hate (repul-sion). Hence, there is feeling. In ideating, something is ideated; in judging, some-thing is judged; in loving–hating, something is felt. Every act refers to an object or content, no matter what the kind of act. Those objects are the mental contents of Wundt's psychology. Wundt would say that we have a sensory experience, such as a sound, and could describe it in terms of its quality and intensity. Brentano would say that the sound is physical and that we are experiencing not the sound magnitude or quality but the mental act of hearing. Such mental acts can refer not only to an object (a sound, a color), but also to another act ("I remember [act] hearing [act] that sound [object]." Notice however, that at the end of the chain there is always an object.

Brentano insisted that a distinction must be made between the experience as content and the experience as a way of acting.[16] The sensation is not the unit of Brentano's psychology as it is for Wundt; Brentano's unit is the mental act. Again, this is a difficult concept for modern psychologists to understand, particularly if one thinks in terms of Newtonian science, on which Wundt and most of modern psychology is based. Brett tells us, however, that "To make sensation the beginning of a psychical activity would be absurd to a psychologist of Brentano's type; it would be like telling the anthropologist that in the beginning was the grammar, not speech."[17]

The source of all psychological experience is inner perception. Each of us has an inner perception that supplies the psychological phenomena. Calling the phenomena psychic or subsuming them under soul makes no difference. If we do so, the soul is its acts. It can be seen that in this way Brentano is neatly disposing of physiology. Psychology cannot be reduced to physiology, since psychology's field is the act.

Despite the ancient sources of Brentano's system of act psychology, it came as a revolt against established ways of thinking, especially those sponsored by Wundt. Brentano's system gained stature and point by being clearly in opposition to Wundt's psychology of content. Wundt saw mind in terms of contents. He would deny that the processes of mind were observable in themselves. Hence, the lines were drawn for a distinction between a psychology of content and a psychology of act, each to have its devoted followers.

Perhaps Brentano's thinking had its greatest effect on Edmund Husserl (1859–1938), the founder of philosophical phenomenology, and on Carl Stumpf (1848–1936), later professor at Berlin, who developed his own phenomenological psychology. Through Husserl and Stumpf, phenomenological methodology became an acceptable alternative to the elementistic analysis of Wundt and his immediate followers. Through Stumpf, the influence spread to the Gestalt psychologists whose method can best be called experimental phenomenology. That, however, is another story and will be taken up in the chapter on Gestalt psychology.

HERMANN EBBINGHAUS

In about 1876 a German student of philosophy and psychology, who was earning his way during his stay in England, chanced on a second-hand copy of Fechner's *Elements of Psychophysics*. The mathematical approach to psychological problems that it contained came as a revelation to young Hermann Ebbinghaus.[18] From his reading of this book arose a conviction that the strictly scientific measurement Fechner had carried through with psychophysics could also be applied to the higher mental processes. Wundt's recently published *Grundzüge* contained his statement that the higher mental processes were not conducive to experimental study by means of introspection. Ebbinghaus was probably familiar with this volume.[19] If so, it merely served as a challenge to him, not a deterrent.

Early Life

Hermann Ebbinghaus was born in Barman, now Wupperthal, near Bonn, in 1850. He was the son of a merchant. He studied history and philosophy at Bonn and moved first to Halle and then to Berlin. During that time his interests shifted to philosophy, perhaps through the influence of F. A. Trendelenburg, the philosopher who also influenced Brentano.[20] After serving in the army during the Franco-Prussian War, he returned to Bonn for his doctorate in philosophy in 1873, writing his dissertation on Hartmann's philosophy of the unconscious. The next seven years were spent in independent study, first in Berlin, where he followed the not unusual practice of the philosopher, spending his time in studying the sciences. After 1875, he spent three years in England and France in private study and in tutoring. It was during these years that he chanced to discover Fechner's book.

Research on Memory

Without a teacher, a university environment, or a laboratory, and without any inspiration except the general climate of the times, Ebbinghaus plunged into the study of learning and memory, subjects heretofore untouched by measurement and experimentation. Working alone, he devised the necessary methods and materials and, using himself as the only subject, carried through the research that was to eventuate in his monograph *Ueber das Gedächtnis.*[21] He perceived that his self-appointed task required careful preparation and planning. He saw that he could not take over Fechner's psychophysical methods as they stood, because they would be entirely too slow and cumbersome. However, he did want to use a method that was in the spirit of Fechner.

Associationists, particularly Brown and Mill, had attached importance to the principle of frequency as a condition of recall. Ebbinghaus saw frequency of repetition of material or number of trials until learning was complete as the essential condition for forming associations. He decided to use the number of repetitions as his measure of learning. Not only was there to be repetition of the same material to the point where it was wholly learned, but there must also be repetition of the task, each time with similar but not identical materials, until he could be confident about the accuracy of his findings. In order for variable errors from trial to trial to be canceled out, Ebbinghaus would use the same procedure again and again, as did Fechner, varying only the particular content to be learned; then he would find an average measure. In deference to the demands of experiment, he went so far as to regulate his habits, following the same rigorous pattern day after day and learning the materials always at the same time of day.

Ebbinghaus knew that some pieces of poetry or prose can be learned much more easily than others. Associations already formed with such materials facilitate learning them. Recognizing that differences owing to acquaintance with the material to be learned must be eliminated, Ebbinghaus needed homogeneous, equally unfamiliar material for the many learning sessions he was planning. Thus, although he used poetry and prose to some extent, the majority of his studies were carried out with new materials of his own invention, the so-called nonsense syllables. Two consonants with a vowel between, as in NUZ, LEF, and BUP, formed these syllables. Ebbinghaus prepared all possible combinations of German consonants and vowels, and each was put on a separate card. This gave him a reservoir of 2300 nonsense syllables from which to draw at random to form lists to be learned.

The following specific procedure is representative of what he did. He would read through cards for the twelve syllables on a particular list at a uniform rate of two-fifths of a second (controlled by the ticking of a watch). When the reading of the list was completed, there was a pause of fifteen seconds, which he used for recording the trial. Again and again he would read through the cards until he believed he could repeat them without mistake. At this point he would try to recite them without looking at the cards. If he failed, no matter how few the mistakes, he would record the errors; then he would read them again. He continued this procedure until he could give the complete list of nonsense syllables from memory without error. Then he considered the list learned. That was the method of "complete mastery," as it came to be called. He now passed on to other lists of syllables. After a given lapse of time, an hour, a day, or a week, whatever his schedule called for, he would return to the originally learned list and ascertain the number of repetitions now necessary to relearn it for complete mastery. There would be a saving in the sense that relearning did not take so many readings as learning did originally. This came to be called the "savings method." Thus, if sixteen readings were at first necessary to reach the complete mastery of one correct runthrough, and relearning the material twenty-four hours later took only eight readings, then the saving was 8/16 or 50 percent, a measure of what had been remembered for twenty-four hours.

The very first relearning trial also gave him another measure of memory. When the time came to test this first memory of a given list of nonsense syllables, Ebbinghaus would find out how many of the syllables he still knew before learning them again. The number still known divided by the total learned was this measure of memory. Suppose twelve syllables were originally learned. At the first relearning trial, say a day later, he remembered four of the nonsense syllables. That meant that 4/12 or 33 percent was retained.

From these experiments came the well-known Ebbinghaus curve of forgetting. One condition he studied experimentally was the effect of varying the length of time since learning the lists of nonsense syllables. The material would be forgotten very rapidly in the first few hours and then more and more slowly thereafter. When the results were plotted on a chart, they formed a curve that went down very sharply at first and then gradually leveled off. If the material was "overlearned" (that is to say, if Ebbinghaus went beyond bare learning by repeating the material to the point of several correct series in the original learning, instead of one), it was forgotten more slowly. Under these circumstances the plot of the curve would now show a more gradual drop and even after a considerable lapse of time would show more retention of the material than the learning to the level of merely one correct repetition. Later research confirmed these findings.[22] After carefully verifying these and many other findings by repetition, Ebbinghaus finally published his monograph in 1885.

Later Life and Research

In 1880, while still carrying on his research in memory, Ebbinghaus became Dozent at Berlin, and in 1886, a year after his research appeared, he was advanced to a rank equivalent to that of assistant professor. During this period he founded the Berlin psychological laboratory, although it was small and not well supported.

Ebbinghaus left the field for others to develop. In 1890, in collaboration with Arthur König, he founded the *Zeitschrift für Psychologie und Physiologie der Sinnesorgane*, a journal that was needed to represent psychology outside the sphere of Wundt's *Studien*.

Aside from his editorial work, Ebbinghaus's own publications were few, in relation to the norm of the German professor of his day. This may be why he failed to be advanced to a full professorship at Berlin.[23] At any rate, in 1894, when Carl Stumpf came from Munich to Berlin as professor, Ebbinghaus moved to a lesser post in the hierarchy of German universities at Breslau, where he founded another laboratory.

Here Ebbinghaus made his second major contribution, which, though not equal to the eminence of his studies of learning, deserves mention. The school officials of the city of Breslau called on him to help solve a problem of fatigue in schoolchildren, that is, to find the time of the continuous five-hour school day at which the child was least efficient. Accordingly, he devised three tests to be given in a few minutes before each class period.[24] The first and second were rapid addition and multiplication and a test of memory for digits. The third, the "completion method," which was original with Ebbinghaus, was destined to have pronounced usefulness in intelligence tests to come. Ebbinghaus argued that mental ability demands, among other capacities, the ability to combine verbal material into a significant whole. Essentially, the test consists of omitting words (or portions of words) from sentences in a story and asking the subjects to restore the appropriate words or syllables. An example in the spirit of the original ones used is, "Big things are heav__ than _____ things," with the missing syllable and word to be supplied by the child.

When the students were grouped by scholastic standing into good, average, or poor, the results from the completion test proved markedly superior in discriminating among the groups when compared with the results from the other two tests. Ebbinghaus argued that this measure showed the great importance of a combining function in intelligence. It might be added that the fatigue problem, the original purpose for the study, was largely lost sight of, with the question left open as far as the report went.

Alfred Binet, the pioneer in the development of intelligence tests, acknowledged that the success of the Ebbinghaus Completion Test had encouraged him in his conviction that he should use complex tasks to measure intelligence, rather than simpler ones, such as tapping rate or reaction time, hitherto used with little success.[25]

Ebbinghaus wrote two other very successful books. The first volume of his general text, *Die Grundzüge der Psychologie*[26] [Principles of Psychology], was published in 1902, and a shorter sketch, *Abriss der Psychologie,*[27] was issued in 1908. These became tremendous successes, resembling James's *Principles of Psychology* in their sprightliness and lucidity of style.

The first sentence of the *Abriss* is that often-quoted, beguiling half-truth, "Psychology has a long past, but only a short history."[28] Ebbinghaus was acutely aware that experimental psychology had just begun. He had seen its beginnings in the work of Fechner, Helmholtz, and Wundt, all of which had been carried out not more than fifty years before his own and most of it practically contemporaneous with his own work. Our present perspective makes it possible to see that preexperimental contributions were also necessary and that they, too, formed an essential part of the history of psychology. Experimental psychology, as we know it, has but a short history, whereas psychology has a very, very long one.

In 1905 Ebbinghaus left Breslau for Halle. Generally in good health, he contracted pneumonia and died suddenly in 1909 at age fifty-nine.

Ebbinghaus published relatively little, but what he did publish was important. He made no major systematic contributions, although his *Grundzüge* apparently laid the groundwork for a functional psychology. His work was functional because he depended more on what the mental processes did than the contents of the experiences themselves. His most important contribution, however, was in opening a new area of research for psychology. In the process of doing so, he presented a model of experimental control of factors that is still exemplary. Before Ebbinghaus, the associationists had speculated on how associations were established. Ebbinghaus started by forming these associations experimentally and then testing their resistance by later recall. It might be thought at first glance that what he did was but a small matter compared to all the sweeping claims of his predecessors. From the viewpoint of modern research, these earlier claims seem grandiose rather than great. True, they took in much more territory than those of Ebbinghaus. Their originators might be compared to monarchs who added to a statement of their holdings, "and the lands beyond the seas," without occupying these lands. Ebbinghaus not only occupied the territory, but he also tilled the soil. Perhaps even more important than his discovery of a way to do research on memory, highly original though it was, may be his determination to control factors that would eliminate sources of error and quantify his results as precisely as possible. He did such careful work in his studies of memory that to this very day contemporary textbooks quote them side by side with later studies, not just for historical interest, but as valid and accurate research findings.

GEORGE ELIAS MÜLLER

George Elias Müller, a student of Hermann Lotze, was a physiologist and philosopher with psychological interests. That Müller was not a student of Wundt meant that, free of immediate proximity to this overpowering figure, he was able to develop an independent program. In a sense he was a rival of Wundt. Müller became professor at Göttingen in 1881, succeeding Lotze, and held that post for forty years until 1921. Over the years he attracted a number of students, the more prominent of whom were Oswald Külpe (who later received his doctorate with Wundt), E. R. Jaensch, David Katz, and Edgar Rubin.

Müller undertook extensive criticism and extension of Fechner's work in psychophysics in his *Zur Grundlegung der Psychophysik*,[29] published in 1878, and in *Die Gesichtspunkte und die Tatsachen der psycho-physischen Methodik* in 1904.[30] In particular, he demonstrated that the fluctuations of the sensory threshold in the same person from day to day are not due to error but are real fluctuations in sensitivity itself. He laid down what he considered to be the fundamental psychophysical axioms of the relationship between perception and neural excitation as expressed in a parallelistic fashion. Although he also spent many years on problems of color, it is research in learning for which he is most noteworthy.

Müller was among the first psychologists to do laboratory research in the field of learning and memory opened up by Ebbinghaus. He carefully verified and extended Ebbinghaus's findings.[31] Ebbinghaus had found just how many trials it took for him to learn or relearn, but he had not recorded introspections about his mental processes while the learning was going on. Müller doubted that Ebbinghaus's account of learning as a passive and automatic process was correct as it stood. Accordingly, he added introspective report while applying the methods of Ebbinghaus and found that, instead of learning passively, the subjects were very active, using groupings and rhythms, finding meanings even in nonsense materials, and, in general, consciously organizing the material. This activity demonstrated to him that learning is not mechanical and that its study requires the combination of introspective and objective methods. He concluded that association by contiguity is not enough to account for learning. He contended that an active search for relations was also taking place. A "preparatory set" (Anlage) influences the memory processes. Müller demonstrated that judgment involves not only the expected images, sensations, and feelings, but also mental events incapable of thus being classified. For example, readiness, hesitation, and doubt seem to be present, a class of mental phenomena usually called "conscious attitudes." These findings anticipated work that followed very shortly from the Würzburg laboratory under Oswald Külpe.

Müller also worked through many other learning problems, making methodological improvements, and increased the precision of the equipment used in the study. It was he, along with a collaborator, Friedrich Schumann,[32] who introduced the familiar revolving memory drum for uniform presentation of nonsense syllables used since that time in various adaptations for countless studies of memory and learning.

OSWALD KÜLPE

Oswald Külpe already has been discussed as a student of and assistant to Wundt. After studying with G. E. Müller at Göttingen, he received his degree at Leipzig and stayed on as Dozent and assistant in Wundt's laboratory for several years before going to a position of his own at Würzburg.[33]

Külpe's most significant psychological book, his *Grundriss der Psychologie,* was published in 1893 and translated in 1895 as *Outlines of Psychology.*[34] It is significant that the book bears the subtitle, "Based upon the results of experimental investigation."[35] It is a thoroughgoing treatment of psychology as revealed by experimental research. Külpe's introduction, "Methods and Aims of Psychology," is still a classic for its time.[36]

Külpe and Mach's Positivism

As with the other figures considered in this chapter, Külpe departed significantly from the systematic positions of Wilhelm Wundt, and it was through this book that Külpe took his first important steps away from Wundt.

Külpe and his friend from Leipzig, E. B. Titchener, while still with Wundt, came under the influence of the positivistic writings of Richard Avenarius and Ernst Mach.[37] Many aspects of Mach and Avenarius ran counter to Wundt's orthodoxy, but one in particular was critical in Külpe's thought. It had to do with the nature of the psychological element and its impact on the number of simple psychological states. Wundt had held that there were only two attributes of sensations, quality and intensity. He brought space and time into his system by means of "creative synthesis," his form of unconscious inference. According to Wundt, space and time were created, psychologically, by inferences based on directly experienced qualities and intensities. On the contrary, Mach held that space and time were themselves directly observable and so should be considered elementary just as are quality and intensity.

Külpe, then, listed four attributes of sensation: quality, intensity, duration (time), and extension (space).[38] He did so because he agreed with Mach that the elementary state is not the same as an atom. That is, an elementary state may not be absolutely simple but may be the simplest state that retains its characteristic experience. Duration is directly experienced—two sensations can have the same qualities and intensities but can be discriminated on the basis of their durations. Similarly, two sensations can have the same qualities and intensities and durations but differ in their extents, the space they occupy. Külpe characterizes attributes by their inseparability from the sensation and by the fact that when such an attribute is nullified, the sensation disappears. A sensation that has no duration does not exist in our experience. A sensation that has a spatial component disappears when the space reduces to zero.[39]

By ridding himself of the need of accessory concepts such as Wundt's creative synthesis and by accepting Mach's contention that any mental state, no matter how complex, can be reduced to elementary states, Külpe was able to approach the psychological subject matter as a single unit, all under the sway of the experimental method. This was directly counter to Wundt who held that the higher mental processes could not be reduced to elementary states and so could not be studied experimentally. For this reason, Wundt held that the higher mental processes, such as memory, thought, and judgment, could only be studied by examining the products of mind, such as myths and laws.

By accepting Mach's position, Külpe and Titchener were able to unify the dual psychology of Wundt, one for higher mental processes and one for lower processes, into a single psychological system with the same basic introspectionist methodology throughout. This step, however, came later, after both had left Leipzig. It is ironic that it was their agreement on the possibility of experimentation on the higher mental processes that would set Külpe and Titchener against each other in their famous imageless thought controversy.

In 1894 Külpe became professor at Würzburg, and by 1896, with the aid of private funds, he had founded a laboratory there. Its progress was so rapid that in a few years it was referred to as the outstanding laboratory in Germany after Leipzig. Charming and friendly, Külpe attracted many students and visitors, including several Americans, among them J. R. Angell of Chicago, Karl M. Dallenbach and R. M. Ogden of Cornell, W. L. Bryan of Indiana, Robert S. Woodworth of Columbia, and W. B. Pillsbury of Cornell and Michigan.

The Würzburg School of Imageless Thought

Külpe is best known for his Würzburg School of Imageless Thought. He did not personally perform most of the Würzburg studies, but he was the professor, with all that this meant in a German university of that day. He frequently served as a subject in his students' experiments. The Würzburg School is primarily the work of doctoral students at Würzburg working under Külpe's direction. The researchers were the product of Külpe's aim to do experimental research on the higher mental processes.

The experimental methods devised for such research was called systematic experimental introspection. It was also called the *Ausfrage* method. To Külpe and the members of his school, the term meant the performance of some complex task, such as that involved in thinking, remembering, or judging, and then rendering a retrospective report of the experiences during the original operation. It was systematic in the sense that the whole experience was described methodically, time period by time period, thus fractionating it. This procedure contrasted vividly with the description of immediate experience demanded by Wundt. To use the Würzburg version of introspection, one must think, memorize, or judge and then turn around and examine how one thought, memorized, or judged. The task was not specified in advance, as it was with Wundtian introspection, so the subject at Würzburg did not know beforehand exactly what he was to observe.

Imageless Thought and Related Issues

The identification of the Würzburg School with the concept of "imageless thought" is almost absolute. Imageless thought is perhaps an unfortunate term since what Külpe's students were reporting in their researches was that there was either no experience present between the task and analysis or that the experience was vague and unclassifiable as either sensations or images.

A capsule description of two characteristic experiments is in order.[40] Karl Marbe, in a study of judgment of weights, found that, although sensations and images were present as usual, their existence told nothing about how the subjects made their judgments.[41] The subjects simply judged a weight as heavier or lighter, and they usually were right. They did not know how they arrived at their conclusions; the sensations and images they reported did not describe the process of how they reached their judgment.

H. J. Watt studied association in a variety of ways.[42] For example, his subjects were faced with finding a subordinate or superordinate for the word "bird." They reacted correctly but often without being conscious of their intention. It would seem that the conscious work had been done not after the stimulus was presented, but earlier, when the instructions were understood. Once they understood, the subjects thereafter gave the response to the stimulus without conscious effort. To account for such findings, Watt emphasized the concept of task *(Aufgabe)*. The subjects did not think of the task in terms of searching for the superordinate of bird and arriving at animal; they just thought "animal." The conscious phenomena obtained in the introspection corresponded closely to the volitional variable previously spoken of in connection with Külpe's early work. Although today similar terms are used more or less indiscriminately for any potentiality in consciousness, to Watt task meant the purpose or conscious task that precedes a later unconscious course of events. The conscious task *(Aufgabe)* brings about an unconscious set *(Einstellung)* in the subject.

Watt and Ach, in research related to the study of association, held that the organism had a set or, to use Ach's term for it, a "determining tendency" to react in the way the given instruction called for. If, in advance of exposure to material, a person has decided to subtract from a "6" and a "4," he or she will produce the response "2," not "10," which a determining tendency to add would have produced in response to the same visual stimuli. Once the task has been accepted and the set has been adopted, the actual performance runs off with remarkably little conscious content. These determining tendencies, not present consciously during performance, seemed important in volitional activities. The Würzburgers were suggesting that predispositions outside consciousness act to control consciousness.

This work on thought elements was negative in the sense that what the studies found lacked sensory content. It was not until the work of Karl Bühler in 1907 and 1908 that a new element in consciousness, the thought element, was announced.[43] His method of conducting introspections was even freer than that of systematic experimental introspection. He used very complicated problems, far removed from those of simple addition or subtraction, but always to be answered first with a "yes" or a "no." After answering, the subject gave the fullest possible account of the experiences by which he reached his decision, with questions interjected from time to time by the experimenter. For example, "Was the theorem of Pythagoras known in the Middle Ages?" "Can we with our thought comprehend the nature of thought?" or "The smaller the woman's foot, the larger the bill for shoes?"[44] The subjects (including Külpe) in their introspections used such terms as "awareness of a consciousness that" but more frequently referred simply to "thoughts." Thought was the new element that Bühler claimed must be accepted if his results were to make any sense. He went on to describe three types of thoughts—consciousness of rule, consciousness of relation, and intention. His subjects used the first type of thinking most often in solving mathematical, logical, or grammatical problems. The second occurred when several parts of a thought required a relation to be established as consequence or opposition, and the third took place when a problem was seen overall and an outcome was to be reached.

It must be emphasized that, though opposed to the Wundtian position concerning the sensory nature of certain kinds of conscious experience, Külpe and the others were still seeking new elements in thought. They remained analytical in their approach.

Their use of analytical methods did not render their interpretations acceptable to the Wundtian psychologists of content who considered what they were doing a caricature of psychology. The reports of their introspections, particularly those of Bühler, drew vigorous opposition, especially from Wundt,[45] who offered scathing criticism. He called their procedures "mock" experiments and argued that what they called experimental introspection was neither experimental nor introspective.

For his part, Külpe both then and later, showed his high admiration and regard for Wundt. Müller also attacked Külpe's methods and results, as did Titchener. For both, Külpe preserved the highest regard. The issue had been forced, however, and a rival school was consequently established. As we will see in later chapters, the controversy, particularly that between Titchener and Külpe, would ultimately weaken the hold of introspection as the primary method of psychological experimentation.

Külpe's own interpretation of the work from his laboratory is rather hard to specify. He wrote very little on the matter, and his projected description of the psychology of the thought processes was never completed.

Later Life and Work

Külpe's fifteen years at Würzburg were his most important. It was not that he lost interest later, for at Bonn, where he went next, he founded a laboratory. In 1913, when he moved to Munich, he saw to it that the laboratory allocated to his predecessor was suitably equipped. The reason, rather, was that his continuing interests in philosophical problems, particularly aesthetics, came to the fore, and they seemed to him in no way antagonistic to his interests in psychological issues. He came to reject Machian positivism[46] and to move away from his psychological career. He sought to prove that the actualities of conscious experience required independent objects. He never completed the statement of his later views. His student, Karl Bühler, published posthumously his *Vorlesungen über Psychologie* in 1920.[47] What he had covered in the *Grundriss* in 1893 constituted in this new work the content of psychology; the contribution of the Würzburg School was what he called function.

The psychological implications of these later views led him to a position much closer to that of Brentano. By now Külpe conceived of psychology as both content and act (although he called act, function), and it is regrettable that he did not live long enough to work out fully his own synthesis. To Külpe, both content and function are facts of mental life because they can be demonstrated to be different.[48] They are separable in experience: in dreams there is content but little function; in barely noticing something there is function with little content. They are independently variable: content changes without function when a person perceives objects one after the other; function changes when one object is first perceived, then recognized, and then judged. They possess characteristic differences: contents are analyzable in consciousness, observable in introspection, and relatively stable; functions are not analyzable in consciousness (analysis alters the function), are observable in retrospect only, and are relatively unstable. They obey different laws: the laws of content are association, fusion, contrast, and a relation to stimulus and sense organ; function includes the effects of the laws of determining tendency.

Külpe was actively engaged in this combined psychological and epistemological enterprise of synthesizing content and function just before the time of his death in 1915.

The work of the Würzburg School was prophetic of the development of a holistic view as separate from the elementist view of Wundt. Indeed, the Gestalt psychologists who were to come later owed a debt to Külpe for attempting to deal with both act and content.

The results of the Würzburg School were interpreted as relating to thought as such, which was their emphasis. Two other aspects of their achievement are significant today. First, there was the way they stressed volition, or motivation, as we would call it. Task, set, determining tendency, to use their key words, have a motivational connotation today. They treated motivation as a variable affecting the results of thinking, a topic that is very much a part of the modern scene in psychology. The relatively simple kinds of association of the British and of Wundt were not enough to explain the variations in volition that they found from one experiment to the next. Second, it seemed that behavior depended not only on the elements present in the subject's consciousness, but also on the way he or she adjusted to the experiment, even though the subject was not aware of this operation in conscious analysis. These directive tendencies were not evident in consciousness. They were often unconscious in nature; unconscious determinants of behavior were being demonstrated.

Members of the Würzburg School were working at the same time as Freud, but without his ruthless radicalism, they did not cut through to the bold conclusion that many of the experiences they were dealing with were unconscious. Instead, they treated the impalpable phenomena with which they were struggling as a consequence of some vague conscious element.

SUMMARY

It will be remembered that it fell to Wundt to synthesize the first modern view of a scientific psychology. The analogy was suggested that the picture of psychology that left his hands contained some, but by no means all, aspects of a modern view. His contemporaries and successors served to broaden the canvas, in terms of both methodological and contentual considerations.

In formulating act psychology Brentano was guided by a functional prescription, in contrast to the contentual prescription to which Wundt adhered. By insisting on the distinction between sensory quality and act, with psychological emphasis on sensing, he effectively committed himself to a contentually subjective position concerning the nature of psychology.

Although Wundt had declared it impossible, Ebbinghaus studied experimentally and quantitatively the higher mental process of memory and learning. At the time his approach to learning and memory received little notice except in criticism, but it was objective in the results derived. His was the first major research study, other than those in psychophysics, which would make psychology contentually objective.

G. E. Müller was cognizant of this emphasis in that he criticized Ebbinghaus for his failure to report introspections. By his own research he established what was prophetic of a modern conception of the value of introspection. It might even be called the forerunner of the "new look" in cognitive psychology. Instead of believing that learning is mechanical, as Ebbinghaus's results made it seem, he found that subjects actively searched for meaning and relations, held a preparatory set, and experienced hesitations, fleeting doubts, convictions, and the like, which the plotted curves did not reveal.

Külpe and other members of the Würzburg School broadened the scope of introspection and opened the area of the thought processes to experimental study. The essential change they made was to convert introspection into retrospection— the report of a past experience rather than a description of an immediate experience. One thought, memorized, or judged, and then turned around and examined what one experienced during the process. The lack of sensory experience during many aspects of the tasks being studied, so-called imageless thought, was one of their major contributions. Another was the discovery that various forms of directive tendencies to be adopted before performing the task gave it coherence and direction. As a consequence, toward the end of his career Külpe found it possible to conceive of psychology as both contentual and functional.

The founding of psychology, embracing as it does not only Wundt's work but also that of his contemporaries and successors, is noteworthy for certain developments, which may be referred to in prescriptive terms. Without fanfare and with remarkably little explicit discussion, certain guiding methodological attitudes common to other sciences had been accepted as characteristics of the science of experimental psychology. General agreement was reached on nomotheticism, the search for general principles, and on naturalism, that these principles are within nature and not in some transcendental realm. Also accepted were methodological objectivism, the use of methods open to other competent observers, and quantitativism, the dependence on measurement (although without the more sophisticated tools of statistics that we have today). Determinism, the belief that human events are explicable in terms of antecedents, was adhered to, as was empiricism, in the preferred form of experiment. These prescriptions are now so much a part of the psychologist's procedural approach as to be almost universally accepted. Both deviations and refinements will be encountered in later developments, but these prescriptive allegiances form a background pattern for much of what follows.

NOTES

1. O. Kraus, *Franz Brentano, zur Kenntnis seines Lebens und seiner Lehre* (Munich: Beck, 1919); Kraus, "Biographical Sketch of Franz Brentano," in Linda McAlister, ed., *The Philosophy of Brentano* (London: Duckworth, 1976), pp. 1–9; Carl Stumpf, "Reminiscences of Franz Brentano," in McAlister, ed., *The Philosophy of Brentano*, pp. 10–46; Edmund Husserl, "Reminiscences of Franz Brentano," in McAlister, ed., *The Philosophy of Brentano*, pp. 47–55; M. Puglisi, "Franz Brentano: A Biographical Sketch," *American Journal of Psychology*, 35 (1924):414–419; Antos C. Rancurello, *A Study of Franz Brentano: His Psychological Standpoint and His Significance in*

the History of Psychology (New York: Academic Press, 1968). This last-mentioned reference is probably the most authoritative current statement about Brentano and his views.

2. *Ibid.*

3. F. Brentano, *Psychology from an Empirical Standpoint*, ed. O. Kraus, English ed., ed. Linda L. McAlister (New York: Humanities Press, 1973).

4. J. R. Barclay, "Franz Brentano and Sigmund Freud," *Journal of Existentialism, 5* (1964):1–36.

5. This fascinating issue has a number of ramifications. Some of the references are J. Barclay, "Franz Brentano"; P. Merlan, "Brentano and Freud," *Journal of the History of Ideas, 6* (1945):375–377, and *ibid.*, "Brentano and Freud—a Sequel," *Journal of the History of Ideas, 10* (1949):451. John C. Brentano, the son of Franz, who had been devoting his retirement years to his father's works, assured R. I. Watson in personal conversation that Freud was relatively uninfluenced by his father and that, as far as his father was concerned, he broke not only with Freud but also with Breuer as a result of the publicity arising from the case of Frl. Anna O. This implies a closer relationship between Brentano and Freud than E. Jones (*The Life and Works of Sigmund Freud,* Vol. 1 [New York: Basic Books, 1953]), dean of the biographers of Freud, has indicated.

6. O. Kraus, "Biographical Sketch of Franz Brentano," in Linda McAlister, ed., *The Philosophy of Brentano* (London: Duckworth, 1976), pp. 1–9; Carl Stumpf, "Reminiscences of Franz Brentano," in McAlister, ed., *The Philosophy of Brentano,* pp. 10–46; Edmund Husserl, "Reminiscences of Franz Brentano," in McAlister, ed., *The Philosophy of Brentano,* pp. 47–55.

7. F. Brentano, *Untersuchungen zur Sinnespsychologie* (Leipzig: Duncker and Humbled, 1907).

8. F. Brentano, *Von der Klassifkation der psychischen Phanomene* (Leipzig: Duncker and Humbled, 1911).

9. A. Rancurello, *A Study of Franz Brentano,* pp. 30–31.

10. E. B. Titchener, *Systematic Psychology: Prolegomena* (New York: Macmillan Co., 1929), p. 8.

11. E. G. Boring, *History of Experimental Psychology,* 2nd ed. (New York: Appleton–Century–Crofts, 1950).

12. A. Rancurello, *A Study of Franz Brentano,* p. 30.

13. G. S. Brett, "Associationism and 'Act' Psychology," in C. Murchison, ed., *Psychologies of 1930* (Worchester, Mass.: Clark University Press, 1930), pp. 39–55.

14. E. G. Boring, *A History of Experimental Psychology,* 2nd ed. (New York: Appleton–Century–Crofts, 1950), p. 361.

15. F. Brentano, *Von der Klassifikation.*

16. F. Brentano, *Psychologie,* Bk. II, Chapter 1, Sec. 9 (Herrnstein and Boring, Excerpt No. 112).

17. G. Brett, "Associationism," p. 49.

18. The story that has been told since Jaenisch's obituary of Ebbinghaus (E. R. Jaenisch, *Zeitschrift der Psychologie, 51* [1909]: iii–viii) has it that Ebbinghaus found Fechner's *Elemente* in a second-hand store in Paris. Recently, however, Wolfgang Bringmann has found the original book in the library of the *Bundeswehrhochschule* (German Army University) in Munich, part of the library of Julius Ebbinghaus, a son of Hermann Ebbinghaus. The card index that includes the book, done by Hermann Ebbinghaus himself, indicates its purchase in England. Werner Traxel, "Hermann Ebbinghaus: In Memoriam," *History of Psychology Newsletter, 17* (1985):37–41. For other treatments of Ebbinghaus, see D. Shakow, "Hermann Ebbinghaus," *American Journal of Psychol-*

ogy, 42 (1930):505–518; R. S. Woodworth, "Hermann Ebbinghaus," *Journal of Philosophy,* 6 (1909):253–256.

19. E. G. Boring, *History of Experimental Psychology.*

20. W. Traxel, "Hermann Ebbinghaus," p. 38. Trendelenburg has not received a sufficient study in terms of his influence on psychology. As students he had individuals such as Franz Brentano, the American intellectual philosopher, Noah Porter, and the speculative philosopher, George Sylvester Morris. The only extended study on Trendelenburg is Gershon G. Rosenstock, *F. A. Trendelenburg: Forerunner to John Dewey* (Carbondale: Southern Illinois University Press, 1964). It is an excellent work, but there is much more to explore.

21. H. Ebbinghaus, *Ueber das Gedächtnis* (Leipzig: Duncker and Humbled, 1885) (Herrnstein and Boring Excerpt, No. 95).

22. R. S. Woodworth, *Experimental Psychology* (New York: Henry Holt and Co., 1938).

23. E. G. Boring, *History of Experimental Psychology.*

24. H. Ebbinghaus, "Ueber eine neue Methode zur Prüfung geistiger Fahigkeiten und ihre Anwendung bei Schulkinder," *Zeitschrift für Psychologie, 13* (1897):401–439 (Herrnstein and Boring, Excerpt No. 82).

25. A. Binet, "Description d'un objet," *L' Annee Psychologique,* III, 1897, pp. 296–332.

26. H. Ebbinghaus, *Die Grundzüge der Psychologie* (Leipzig: Veit, 1897–1902).

27. H. Ebbinghaus, *Abriss der Psychologie* (Leipzig: Veit, 1908).

28. *Ibid.,* p. 1.

29. G. E. Müller, *Zur Grundlegung der Psychophysik* (Berlin: Gruben, 1878).

30. G. E. Müller, *Die Gesichtspunkte und die Tatsachen der psycho-physischen Methodik* (Strassburg: Bergmann, 1903).

31. G. E. Müller and A. Pilzecker, *Experimentelle Beitrage zur Lehre vom Gedächtniss* (Leipzig: Barth, 1900).

32. G. E. Müller and F. Schumann, "Experimentelle Beitrage zur Untersuchungen des Gedächtnisses," *Zeitschrift für Psychologie, 6* (1893):81–190, 257–339.

33. R. M. Ogden, "Oswald Külpe and the Würzburg School," *American Journal of Psychology, 64,* (1951):4–19.

34. O. Külpe, *Grundriss der Psychologie* (Leipzig: Engelmann, 1893).

35. O. Külpe, *Outlines of Psychology: Based Upon the Results of Experimental Investigation,* trans. E. B. Titchener (New York: Macmillan Co., 1895).

36. O. Külpe, *Outlines of Psychology,* pp. 8–18.

37. Richard Avenarius, *Kritik der reinen Erfahrung,* 2 vols. (Leipzig: Reisland, 1888, 1890); Ernst Mach, *Beiträge zur Analyse der Empfindungen* (1886), translated as *The Analysis of Sensations and the Relation of the Physical to the Psychical,* trans. C. M. Williams and Sydney Waterlow (New York: Dover, 1959; 5th German ed., 1906). See also Kurt Danziger, "The Positivist Repudiation of Wundt," *Journal of the History of the Behavioral Sciences, 15* (1979):205–230.

38. O. Kulpe, *Outlines of Psychology,* p. 29.

39. *Ibid.*

40. For a more detailed analysis of the Würzburg researches, see George Humphrey, *Thinking: An Introduction to Its Experimental Psychology* (New York: John Wiley and Sons, 1963), pp. 30–131 (1951); and E. B. Titchener, *Experimental Psychology of the Thought Processes* (New York: Macmillan Co., 1909), pp. 79–166.

41. K. Marbe, *Experimentell-psychologische Untersuchungen über das Urteil, eine Einleitung in die Logik* (Leipzig: Englemann, 1901).

42. H. J. Watt, "Experimentelle Beitrage zu einer Theorie des Denkens," *Archiv für die gesamte Psychologie, 4* (1905):289–436.

43. K. Bühler, "Tatsachen und Problems zu einer Psychologie der Denkvorgange," *Archiv für die gesamte Psychologie*, 9 (1907):297–305; 12 (1908):1–3, 24–92.

44. K. Bühler, quoted in G. Humphrey, *Thinking: An Introduction to Its Experimental Psychology* (New York: John Wiley and Sons, 1951), p. 56.

45. W. Wundt, "Kritiche Nachlese zur Ausfragemethode," *Archiv für die gesamte Psychologie,* 11 (1908):445–459.

46. "We conclude, then, that Mach's philosophy rests upon an entirely unsafe and insecure foundation, in so far as it finds its support solely in sense-data, in immediate experience, and in that which is given in consciousness. The certainty of scientific knowledge—in particular the certainty of the uniform relations prevailing therein—can in this way neither be understood nor established. Such a limitation of science to sensations, to conscious elements, such a renunciation of realities, delivers science over to accident and caprice" (Külpe, *The Philosophy of the Present in Germany,* trans. from 5th German edition by M. L. and G.T.W. Patrick (London: George Allen and Unwin, Ltd., 1913), p. 57.

47. O. Külpe, *Vorlesungen über Psychologie,* posthumously ed. K. Bühler (Leipzig: Hirzel, 1920).

48. E. G. Boring, *History of Experimental Psychology,* pp. 451–452.

Francis Galton.

Galton and Spencer: Developmentalism, Quantitativism, and Individual Differences

*T*he single greatest intellectual revolution of the nineteenth century was certainly the rise of evolutionary theory. The fundamental idea of evolution, that living things do change with time, was not entirely novel, having been a part of intellectual history since Anaximander, a contemporary of Thales. In the centuries before Charles Darwin, the philosophers and scientists of the Enlightenment, Locke, Hume, and Diderot, for example, mentioned only the small gradations they saw as separating plants, animals, and humans. Erasmus Darwin, the grandfather of Charles, had written on evolution, and in 1809, the very year of Charles Darwin's birth, J. B. Lamarck[1] had published his theory that the great variety of animal species might be explained by the inheritance of acquired characters, possibly brought about by changes in the environment or through the use or disuse of part of the body. Moreover, Herbert Spencer was championing an evolutionary point of view prior to Darwin's publication of *The Origin of Species* in 1859. Nevertheless, the work of Darwin created a veritable scientific revolution that demanded reorganization of all previous thinking. After 1859 no well-informed thinker, unless blinded by religious or other preconceptions, could ignore the fact that a developmental view of the nature of all biological phenomena was imperative.[2]

DARWIN AND EVOLUTION

The theory of evolution advanced by Charles Darwin (1809–1882) is too well known to require more than a reminder of its most salient features.[3] Darwin demonstrated that living matter is in a plastic rather than a fixed, immutable form and that the spontaneous variability that each species demonstrates is inheritable. There is a struggle for survival, and the forms that survive have made successful adaptations to the inexorable difficulties they have had to face. The exigencies of the struggle for existence under natural conditions accomplish what every animal breeder who practices artificial selection knows—that certain strains are perpetuated by breeding. Only those forms adaptable to their particular environment survive this process of natural selection; the rest die out. Humans are no exception; they, too, are the result of this struggle. Purpose, final cause, and supernatural design do not account for evolution in this view. Darwin thus countered the teleological, that is, purposive, prescriptions that had been prominent in thought since the time of Aristotle. For Darwin change was a naturalistic process, not a purposeful one.

No summary can give more than a hint of the overwhelming mass of data that Darwin collected. Darwin organized much miscellaneous biological information, hitherto unrelated. He demonstrated the process of evolution and the range of reasons for it, but not its genetic mechanism. His theory and conclusions appeared irresistible to those who did not find them antagonistic to deep-seated convictions concerning the static nature of living things. As Thomas Huxley one of the promoters of Darwin's ideas said of himself, "How extremely stupid not to have thought of that."[4] He was by no means alone. Many saw in Darwin's evidence a means of organizing and understanding a great amount of otherwise puzzling data. In relating the Darwinian evolutionary doctrine to religious orthodoxy, fertile sources of controversy appeared. Theological disagreement was inevitable, arising from the teachings of the book of Genesis, as were arguments from others who saw the human being as separated by an impassable gulf from the "brutes." Moreover, some saw in Darwin's work contradictory scientific evidence. The stormy controversy that broke out was one from which Darwin himself held aloof—his temperament was such that even speaking sharply to someone made him unable to sleep. He found able champions, however, the greatest of whom was Thomas Huxley. The protest and acrimony died hard, stretching from 1860 and the debate of Huxley and Bishop Wilberforce of Oxford to the Scopes trial, with the antagonists, William Jennings Bryan and Clarence Darrow, in 1925.

Darwin's second major report on evolution, *The Descent of Man,* appeared in 1871.[5] It was written primarily to present the evidence that the conclusions of the

Origin also applied to humankind, a position he had held all along but that some of his contemporaries had not understood. In the *Origin* he had not tried to apply his conclusions to a species taken singly. Now he marshaled the evidence for the evolution of humankind from some lower form, along with evidence about his subsidiary theme of sexual selection.

Darwin made more specific contributions to psychology. He kept a diary of his infant son, which he began in 1840 but did not publish until 1877.[6] Along with similar work by Preyer, this record was a source for the beginnings of modern child psychology.

Darwin also studied emotional expression in animals and humans. Sir Charles Bell, the anatomist already known for his differentiation of functioning in sensory and motor nerves, held that facial movements used in the expression of emotions are primarily expressive, that is to say, their function is to express emotions.[7] Darwin espoused the alternative theory, that facial movements are originally practical, as when an angry dog bares his teeth in action preparatory to biting.[8] Expressive functions, Darwin believed, may subsequently be derived from practical functions.

In presenting his argument, Darwin developed three principles of emotional expression and gave illustrations. The first, the principle of serviceable associated habits, was that many expressive movements in emotion are vestiges of originally practical movements. A sneer was seen as a remnant of a response to a malodorous substance, clenching the fists as a vestige of preparation for combat, and being startled as a remainder of a larger flight reaction. The second, the principle of antithesis, was that opposite impulses tend to show opposed movements. When a cat shows affection by drawing up her paws, arching her tail, and pointing her ears, these are all movements the opposite of which she would make when about to attack or defend herself. Antithesis is to be found in laughter, which requires expiration of breath, while sobbing, its opposite, requires inspiration. The third principle is related to the direct action of the nervous system. There is the overflow into motor channels that we call "trembling." These expressive characteristics were acquired from prior practical functions. They then could be inherited. This assumption, of course, was more in line with Lamarckian inheritance of acquired characters than with what is often considered to be Darwinian evolutionary theory. But Darwin is quite explicit in stating that these were originally voluntary movements that turned into reflex actions through habits that are then inherited.

Darwin showed that the study of lower animals demanded consideration of their drives to action. Study seemed always to lead toward examining the causes of their activity. Even their more complicated activities often seemed unlearned. To these activities the term *instincts* had already been applied. An important chapter of the *Origin* was devoted to the instincts; Darwin compared and contrasted instinct with habit and showed that instincts are not perfect. Darwin had available to him a variety of accounts of the instincts of animals, particularly domesticated animals, for example, the shepherd dog's tendency to hunt hares, the brooding of hens, and the cell-making of bees. Such behavior can best be understood as inherited. Darwin's evidence showed that the animals did not survive if they did not have the proper instincts.

Evolutionary theory forced a recognition of the essentiality of understanding the drives to action of both human being and beast. The continuance of an instinct approach in psychology was assured.

In effect, Darwin demonstrated that all animals were related and that they all faced the common problems of adjustment and survival. In *The Descent of Man*, he likened human reasoning to what appeared to be similar processes in the lower animals. More specifically, he attempted to show that many of a person's mental capacities had rudimentary prototypes among lower animals. He also appealed to accounts of primitive humans, their susceptibility to praise and blame, for example. If the human body evolved from lower animals, does it not also follow that the human mind developed from more primitive minds? If all animals are related, does it not follow that there will be similarities in behavior and mentality among animals? It was on the basis of such questions as these that the comparative viewpoint in psychology came into being. Psychology was made ready to return to the wisdom of Aristotle, to be concerned with all living things, not with human-kind alone. After Darwin, comparative psychology became recognized as a branch of psychology.

Darwin's influence on American psychological thought is discussed separately in this text.

Evaluation

Despite his great work and his influence on psychology, Darwin is not classed as a psychologist. As was the case with Galileo and Newton, Darwin's service was to reorganize the general scientific view and to stimulate others in other sciences—psychology included. Darwin's work stimulated an interest in psychological problems. It was against a background of adherence to naturalism, empiricism, and determinism that Darwin carried out his observations. His more distinctive contributions reinforced developmentalism, functionalism, and dynamism in biological science. Darwin searched for evidence of development, for evidence of changes with time. A functional prescription was also crucial; he studied the activities of organisms, including humans and the ways they adapt to the environment. Development, activity, and adaptation go hand in hand with a dynamic stance; he was interested in change and factors causing change. Variability among members of the same species is a psychological concern, and this prepared the way for the study of psychological differences, both individual and racial. Almost incidentally, his animal behavioral studies of emotional expression suggested the contentual objectivity of the work in this field in later generations.

The man who helped to develop an almost entirely new aspect of psychology, the field of individual differences, was Francis Galton.

FRANCIS GALTON

Francis Galton (1822–1911) was the pioneer who brought about a union between psychological methods of measurement and the theory of evolution. This union came about because Galton's studies and observations initiated considerable interest in the study of individual differences among people.

Life of Galton

Francis Galton, a cousin of Charles Darwin, was born near Birmingham in 1822.[9] His large family possessed considerable wealth and among its members counted clergymen, physicians, military officers, members of Parliament, and landed gentry. This background afforded Galton connections with a large number of important persons in England at the height of the British Empire.

Following his own and his family's wishes, in 1838 Galton began to study medicine. In 1840, however, Galton changed his plans and enrolled in Trinity College, Cambridge, for the usual university program. There he specialized in mathematics.

After graduating he spent nearly a decade exploring Africa, a feat that gained him a gold medal from the Royal Geographical Society in 1854. Subsequently, he was elected a Fellow of the Royal Society for the same achievement.

Galton's book, *The Art of Travel,* a practical guide for the explorer, became a standard reference for explorers for the rest of the century. Later he turned to the serious study of meteorology. His book on the subject is said to be the first serious attempt to chart the weather on an extensive scale and to contain the first establishment of the existence of anticyclones.[10]

Mental Inheritance and Variability

During the early 1860s his cousin's *Origin of Species* stirred Galton to study anthropology and heredity, interests that resulted in the founding of the field of eugenics. Galton wished, through eugenics, to encourage the productivity of the fit while restricting the birthrate of the unfit. To do so, he undertook to demonstrate that human heredity is important and relevant. He wanted to study inherited transmissible qualities in humans and hoped that this knowledge would be used for the welfare of humankind. His first publication in this area was a magazine article on hereditary talent and character in 1865.

The first edition of *Hereditary Genius* appeared in 1869, just ten years after Darwin's *Origin.* [11] The range of human mental ability from highest to lowest was held to be enormous. Galton not only marshaled evidence about superior persons, but also referred briefly to the mentally retarded and mentioned in passing the work of Sequin with idiots and imbeciles. Once variability in ability is accepted, we come to the major issue: Is ability related to heredity?

Galton specifically acknowledged in his preface to *Hereditary Genius* that, considering his contemporaries at school and in later life, he was surprised to find how frequently ability seemed to depend on descent. Most of his book is occupied with a large quantity of biographical data about eminent men. Since, in a later edition,[12] he expressed regret at having used the word *genius* when he really meant mental ability of high order, we will use the term *eminent* hereafter. Galton hypothesized not only that there was a general tendency for eminence to run in certain families, but also that there are specific forms of eminence in the sciences, the arts, jurisprudence, and similar fields.

Galton selected his eminent men by the use of biographical sources and then found the number of eminent relations they had. The proportion of eminent relatives that he located much exceeded what might be expected by chance. There were 977 eminent men in his main sample, each judged as so outstanding as to be one man in 4000. By chance the group might have had one prominent relative. Instead, they had 332 close relatives who were about as eminent as themselves. Although upheld later in a general way, his specific results are subject to many forms of serious criticism. In his own day, his results were taken as unequivocal evidence for the biological inheritance of mental ability. Since then it has become evident that this demonstration of eminence running in families can be interpreted as due, in part at least, to similarity of education, socioeconomic status, and social proximity to other eminent (and influential) persons. This pedigree method became the favorite tool of eugenics, a social movement aimed at improving human stock, that has generated controversy to this day.

Part and parcel of Galton's relationship with the Establishment was his cavalier attitude toward the capabilities of women, and sex differences in general. In his study of eminence, the lack of representation of women is an occasion for neither surprise nor explanation. This pioneer modern student was heavily influenced by Victorian sexist attitudes.[13] He compared mental and physical traits in men and women, believing not only that women were physically weaker but also that their poorer sensory discrimination was *prima facie* evidence of intellectual inferiority.

Galton did not entirely overlook the influence of environment. In fact, for this reason he later made the first psychologically oriented research study of twins in which he endeavored to separate the influence of heredity and environment. He found that in physical characteristics at least, twins had much more in common with each other than did other nontwin children of the same parents.

Galton's essential thesis in all this was that mental characteristics are inherited in the same fashion and at the same rate as physical characteristics. He won his cousin to this view that intellectual ability is inherited; in 1869 Charles Darwin explicitly stated in a letter to him that on reading *Hereditary Genius*, he had been "made a convert since previously he had believed that excepting fools, men did not differ much in intellect, only in zeal and hard work."[14]

Statistics and Correlation

Before Galton became interested in statistics, the Belgian astronomer Jacques Quételet (1796–1874) had obtained the chest measurements of a large number of Scottish soldiers and the heights of French conscripts and found that these two sets of measures not only showed the same shape of distribution when plotted on a graph, but also that both followed the same shape of distribution as did plots of runs of luck at a gaming table and the spread of shot around a target.[15] When plotted, each measure formed a curve resembling many other common measures with a peak in the center of the distribution, whereas on each side the scores fall off symmetrically in such a fashion as to make the curve. Laplace and Gauss before him had applied mathematical principles to data on human errors; Quetelet extended their normal law of error to measures other than errors. It was Quételet's work with which Galton first became familiar. What Quételet had demonstrated was that human variation in physique follows the same statistical laws as do certain other living and nonliving phenomena.

Inspired by Quételet, Galton took the next step by extending the findings to psychological topics. He found that marks given on carefully administered and lengthy university honors examinations followed the same distribution as did the biological measures studied by Quételet.[16] Galton saw these results not only as interesting in themselves, but also as justifying the application of statistics to psychological measures.

Galton went further and developed one of the most important of all statistical measures, the correlation. In 1888 he presented a report that for the first time described what he called "co-relations," as well as the working out of several basic procedures.[17] By means of graphs he presented the fundamental properties of the correlation coefficient, as we now term it, and even developed a formula for its calculation, but that was soon superseded. Galton applied his method to variations in bodily measurements, showing that stature and head length, for example, and head length and head breadth are correlated. For instance, tall stature and long head length go together, as do short stature and short head length, as well as the various dimensions between. As stature increases, head length tends also to increase.

It was with Galton's encouragement and aid that his student, Karl Pearson (1857–1936), later improved on his work and initiated the present mathematical formula for its calculation, the so-called Pearson product–moment coefficient of correlation.[18] This formula worked out by Pearson permitted the calculation of the precise numerical degree of relationship. The values that are to be found range between nearly perfect correlations through zero to nearly perfect inverse correlations. The latter occur when an increase in one score is accompanied by a decrease in the other measure. The correlation was to prove an exceedingly useful tool because it made it possible to state results of research in quantitative terms, such as 0.30 or 0.61, instead of qualitatively and in "some, but not a great deal of relationship." This formula is now applied regularly, not in psychology alone, but in all fields where statistics are used.

Galton's Versatility

For a time after writing *Hereditary Genius*, Galton was absorbed in collecting measures of physical characteristics—height, circumference of head, and so on. According to Pearson, it was in the mid-1870s that he came to the conclusion that these static, anthropometric measures were less fruitful for an understanding of diversity among individuals than were psychometric or psychological measures that relate how individuals function.[19] Thus, Galton moved from physical anthropology to psychology.

His psychological contributions are contained in his *Inquiries into Human Faculty and Its Development*,[20] which appeared in 1883 and was based on work that had occupied him for some seven years. This collection of studies is strikingly original. Three of his contributions to psychology deserve detailed consideration: his work on mental imagery, on association, and on mental tests. As Galton saw them, these problems involved not only the evolutionary principle, but also the older traditions of associationism and empiricism.

Mental Imagery

Galton became interested in the problem of visual mental imagery because he thought demonstrations of it in varying degrees might help to establish an essential difference in the mental operations of different people.[21] After some preliminary inquiries, he devised a questionnaire that he had both students and men from various professions complete. It contained specifications for various situations in which they were to try to elicit images. The most famous of these situations was the request to recall the scene of their breakfast table that morning. His subjects were to say whether the image they had was dim or clear, the objects well or ill defined, and the colors natural or absent; they were to estimate the extent of contents of the field of view, the steadiness of maintenance of the mental picture, and the like.

To Galton's astonishment, many men of science whom he had first questioned about mental images protested they did not know what he was talking about. They strenuously denied having any imagery. In this respect they resembled colorblind persons who do not know of their disability. He accounted for this relative absence of mental imagery in scientists by their habits of highly abstract lines of thinking, considering that, if they ever possessed such imagery, they must have lost it through disuse. At the more general levels of society, and among women, boys, and girls, imagery of a clear, well-defined, distinct sort was present. In fact, when Galton feigned disbelief at certain answers, these persons were as surprised by his inability to accept their replies as obvious facts as the scientists were by his claim that such images existed. With more returns available, although similar differences persisted, he found numerous exceptions. Some scientists did have vivid imagery; some persons in the general population lacked imagery.

Frequently, Galton found distinct imagery types. His preliminary finding about the absence of imagery in scientists may have helped to bring about this belief. As a matter of fact, although he had spoken of types in his summary, Galton stressed that there was a gradation of clarity of imagery from distinct to faint. Workers who came after him popularized the notion of imagery types as if it had been his major finding. Careful later work demonstrated that Galton was right, and those who came later were wrong in their belief that imagery falls into types. It is more or less normally distributed in the population with the great majority having some, but not much, capacity for it.

Memory and Association

Another problem of even more systematic importance in psychology with which Galton concerned himself was that of association.[22] One phase of his work, the finding of diversity of association, but with repetition, has already been described. Galton did not find this study of the free play of his own associations particularly fruitful. Much more important was his work on the reaction time necessary to produce associations. Independently of Ebbinghaus, he launched this experimental study of memory and association. Words with which to associate, each written on a separate slip, were exposed to his view one at a time. When he had given two associations to each word, he recorded the time taken from a watch. This gave him an association reaction time. He followed the same procedure for each word in turn. Many of his associations were single words, but on some occasions the response took the form of a mental image that had to be described in some detail. He wished to find the probable origin of these associative reactions. Presently, it became evident that a large number of the associations came from experiences in childhood and adolescence. In fact, about 40 percent came from this period, about 45 percent from adulthood, and only 15 percent from the immediate past. This was perhaps the first demonstration by research of the importance of childhood experience for subsequent adult thinking.

Mental Tests

In addition to being the first to study abilities scientifically through estimates of those of eminent men, Galton was also the first to develop certain specific mental tests.[23] In fact, he invented mental tests (though not the term, for that came later). The first phase of his interest in tests was shown in his efforts to develop measures of intelligence based on sensory capacity, an undertaking that rested on the supposition that discrimination would be highest among the ablest individuals. He offered various anecdotes on the sensory obtuseness of idiots and imbeciles. Galton used highly contrasting groups, the able on the one hand and the mentally deficient on the other, to bring out sensory differences between them. He devised a set of weights for lifting and suggested other measures in the sensory area. Characteristically, although Galton did not collect much data, he clearly implied that intelligence can be measured and that sensory ability is correlated with intelligence. This test of weight discrimination and his measures of association can be seen as mental tests.

As early as 1882 Galton established a small laboratory in London where, for payment of a fee, a person could take a battery of tests—physical measurements, reaction time measurements, and tests of sensory acuity.[24] Each client was given the results, and another copy was kept by the laboratory. Thus Galton, in addition to inventing mental tests, started the world's first mental testing center and in the process became the first psychological practitioner. However, he had no intention of trying to do more than break even financially, and he did not succeed even in that.

Galton was knighted in 1909 and died at Haslemere in 1911. In his will he left funds for a laboratory for the study of eugenics.

Evaluation

Galton launched the measurement of individual differences in psychology. Consider the work on the Continent at this time. Helmholtz had given up the measurement of reaction time because the time varied so much from trial to trial. Wilhelm Wundt was not interested in J. McKeen Cattell's self-imposed problem of individual differences in reaction time. Galton had the insight to see that individual differences were not a nuisance to be eliminated but should be investigated for their own sake. He also forged the link between an evolutionary and a developmental outlook in psychology. He was the originator of mental tests. He made the first extensive use of the questionnaire for psychological research. For these reasons, Galton is included among the great psychologists.

Galton continued the individualistic spirit of English nineteenth-century science. He never had a specialty but ranged broadly over a wide number of fields. He was neither a eugenicist nor an anthropologist, nor was he even a psychologist; he was Galton. Like Boyle and Darwin, he never held an academic position. The brute fact was that Oxford and Cambridge were only beginning to awaken to the continental scientific spirit. They were far from ready to welcome so young an upstart as psychology, far down in the prestige order of the sciences. In Galton's case, it is fortunate that he was not confined within the mold of a professorship, where specialization would have been demanded. Yet the advantages of the university were also denied him. There was little of the followthrough in his work that a university setting might well have encouraged. His work—although Karl Pearson was a faithful follower, and an American, James McKeen Cattell, acknowledged Galton's profound influence on him—did not attract students, as did Wundt's in Germany. There was no group of enthusiastic followers to carry on his work in psychology and to clean up details and bring order generally to his thinking, although in this regard his work in eugenics and biometrics fared somewhat better.

Galton's adherence to the developmental, functional, and dynamic prescriptions that characterized the work of Darwin influenced his contributions to psychology. Far more important, however, was quantitativism, the desire to count and measure that ran as a thread throughout his diverse endeavors, psychological and nonpsychological alike. He made measurement of variability an interesting and important facet of psychological research.

Galton had worked with a profusion of psychological topics, but, once a particular study was done, there was no later integration into a larger pattern. Spencer was the contemporaneous synthesizer of psychology and evolution.

HERBERT SPENCER

Herbert Spencer (1820–1903) was born in Derby, the son of a schoolmaster. Tutored by his father, he was otherwise practically self-educated.[25] As a young man he worked as a surveyor and a railroad engineer. He then secured an appointment as a junior editor of the journal *The Economist* and was launched on his career as a writer, which was to be his means of livelihood thereafter. At this time Spencer contributed numerous articles to the *Westminster Review*, articles that sketched aspects of what was later to emerge as his philosophical doctrines. He became a friend of many of the leading scientific figures of his age—Huxley, Darwin, and others.

Psychology and Evolution

Spencer preceded Darwin in his public espousal of evolution. It was about 1840 that he read Lyell's *Principles of Geology*. Its arguments against Lamarck's theory of the inheritance of acquired characters had the effect of leading him to accept Lamarck's position. As early as 1852 Spencer had definitely disassociated himself from a belief in the immutability of species. He developed an evolutionist doctrine in the years immediately preceding the publication of Darwin's *Origin of Species*, but his publications attracted relatively little attention at that time.[26]

Before Darwin, Spencer's views were based primarily on philosophical, geological, and anthropological arguments and very little on biological data. When Darwin produced his theory and precipitated a movement, Spencer associated himself with it.[27] Once reinforced by the genius of Darwin, Spencer was caught up in the great new trend, though he preserved his independence and remained very much his own man. Darwin had supplied the detailed proof but was careful not to generalize beyond his data. In his turn, Spencer supplied a universal application, drawing out the implications of the theory so as to extend it over the range of human knowledge and endeavor.

Spencer did this through his *Synthetic Philosophy*, which was a comprehensive system in which he attempted to apply the master concept of evolution to all human knowledge. After failing to secure a state subsidy, he sent out to prospective subscribers a syllabus for his *Synthetic Philosophy*, which would eventually encompass ten volumes. Those funds along with royalties from his American publishers supplied enough money to go ahead with its preparation. Once started on the undertaking, he never wavered, working doggedly toward its completion despite frequent ill health and very little money. It was Spencer who introduced the concept of survival of the fittest into the literature and with it a purposivist, teleological setting for evolutionary theory.

Successive parts of *The System of Synthetic Philosophy* appeared from 1862 to 1893. It began with the *First Principles*[28] and proceeded through *The Principles of Biology*,[29] *The Principles of Psychology*[30] (the second edition), *The Principles of Sociology*,[31] and *The Principles of Ethics*.[32] He continued writing and reviewing through a long productive life and died in 1903.

Spencer's influence was perhaps greater in America than it was in England. His teleological presentation of evolution, particularly in the matter of survival value, set the theme that would underlie much of American functional psychology of the late nineteenth and functionalism of the early twentieth centuries. Spencer's American influence is considered in Chapter 17.

COMPARATIVE PSYCHOLOGY

In the early nineteenth century, there had been some interest in animal behavior. The concern centered primarily on the question of instinct as contrasted with reason. Meanwhile, biologists and physiologists were becoming interested in the sense organs and the motor activities of various kinds of animals. With the advent of Darwinism, research with animals accelerated rapidly. It took as its major problem the relation of forms of behavior to the phylogenetic scale of animals, particularly as expressed in the similarity and difference between humans and the lower animals, leading to the expression, "comparative psychology."

George J. Romanes

In the earliest phase, and still for some time to come, comparative psychology was conceived of as an investigation of mind. G. J. Romanes (1848–1894) saw his task as observing behavior in such a way as to be able to draw inferences about the animals' mental processes.[33] He did this work on the theoretical premise that the degree of differences between human and animal depended on the degree of evolutionary separation between them. From the evidence he collected he concluded that in varying degrees animals do possess the mental characteristics of human beings. In its earliest phase the question at issue was still seen as the contrast between instinct and reason. Naturally on the side of diminishing the gulf between human being and animal, evolutionists stressed finding evidence of "reason" in animals. At first, their major tool was to collect anecdotes about animals, that is, the accounts of casual observations of remarkable feats of animals on which they chanced or which they ferreted out by questioning farmers, animal breeders, zoo keepers, and the like. Most often the anecdotes unearthed involved behavior that could not be accounted for by instinct, such as a dog's lifting a gate latch without known previous training. Thus, it would seem that the dog had reasoned he could get out if he did what he had seen his master do, and accordingly did so.

C. Lloyd Morgan

This particular instance of the dog and the opening of the latch serves admirably to introduce one of the first crude but effective experiments that C. Lloyd Morgan (1852–1936) reported.[34] Morgan considered precisely this behavior of a dog lifting a latch. He agreed that it was not due to instinct, but rather he speculated that this behavior could be explained otherwise than by assuming that the dog had reasoned out a relation of the means employed to the end obtained. He had observed what had happened in his own dog in precisely this instance. He agreed that the person observing the behavior after the process was fixed could not be blamed for assuming that it was reasoning that brought about the solution. The surety, smoothness, and celerity with which the dog performed the necessary toss of the catch and then immediately bolted off down the road seemed to indicate reasoning. What actually had happened? Before the dog could lift the latch with his muzzle, Morgan had observed that he would run up and down, sticking his head through the vertical bars at various points, sometimes near the catch, sometimes farther away. He wanted to get out and in his excitement behaved restlessly. The dog happened to put his head beneath the latch and lifted it during the process. He looked through the gate and then noticed it was open, and bolted down the road. Thereafter Morgan waited at the gate until his dog's frequent poking, often in the wrong place, eventually lifted the latch. It was nearly three weeks and a dozen repetitions before the dog did it neatly and quickly. Morgan attributes the delay to the dog's failure to relate means and end, commenting that the dog "never had the faintest notion of how or why looking out just then came to mean walking forth into the road."[35]

In addition to such findings, Morgan carried comparative psychology further by vigorously criticizing the anecdotal work that went on before him, and he supplied more rigorously interpreted instances of observations than did his predecessors. As a means of increasing rigor, he formulated a famous interpretive dictum as a guide for the psychologist.[36] His phrasing, which has come to be called Lloyd Morgan's canon, was that in no case should a particular animal's activity be interpreted in terms of higher psychological processes if it could be interpreted in terms of processes standing lower in the scale of psychological evolution.

Morgan's work was representative of that of a small but increasing number of persons who were founding the field of comparative psychology. In fact, research studies had been performed even before those of Morgan. The British naturalist Douglas Spalding (1840–1877) had been among the first.[37] He took young swallows from the moment of hatching, confined them in cages away from other birds, and released them at an age when normally they would be able to fly. He found that they soon "learned" to fly, despite having never observed the flight of other birds.

In the United States, simultaneously with Morgan, E. L. Thorndike was carrying on his studies with the added controls of laboratory equipment. His pioneer studies on learning in cats, chicks, dogs, and monkeys began to appear in 1898.[38] More detailed discussion of his work is reserved for a later chapter.

SUMMARY

Darwin's influence on biological thought in the nineteenth century was enormous. His theory of evolution brought a naturalistic and nonteleological approach to the question of human and animal evolution. His influence on psychology was no less profound. Francis Galton, a relative of Darwin, brought biological Darwinism over into psychology. His researches were varied, but perhaps his most significant and influential work was on the inheritance of genius, a view that led to the identification of genetic determinants of intelligence. Galton's influence on correlational research and the measurement of correlations was later extended by Karl Pearson.

Herbert Spencer brought teleology back into evolutionary thought. It was he who promoted the concept of survival value and survival of the fittest into popular thought.

Evolutionary theory also promoted an increased interest in comparative psychology. Romanes and Morgan helped to develop this study which would become significant in both biology and psychology.

NOTES

1. J. B. Lamarck, *Zoological Philosophy: An Exposition with Regard to the Natural History of Animals,* trans. H. Elliot (London: Macmillan Ltd., 1914) (1809).

2. Perhaps the classic source of information on the pre-Darwinian history of evolution is Henry Fairfield Osborn, *From the Greeks to Darwin,* 2nd ed. (New York: Charles Scribner's Sons, 1929). Though a bit dated, it is still worth reading. Other sources include Ernst Mayer, *The Growth of Biological Thought* (Cambridge, Mass.: Harvard University Press, 1984) and B. Glass, O. Temkin, and W. Straus, eds., *Forerunners of Darwin: 1745–1859* (Baltimore: Johns Hopkins University Press, 1959). There is a vast literature on evolution and Darwin as any perusal of a college library card catalogue will attest.

3. C. Darwin, "The Origin of Species by Means of Natural Selection," 2nd ed., in R. M. Hutchins, ed., *The Great Books of the Western World* (Chicago: Encyclopaedia Britannica, 1952), Vol. XLIX, pp. 1–251 (1859).

4. L. Huxley, ed., *Life and Letters of T. H. Huxley,* 2 vols. (New York: Appleton, 1900), Vol. I, p. 183.

5. C. Darwin, *The Descent of Man and Selection in Relation to Sex* (New York: Appleton, 1871).

6. C. Darwin, "A Biographical Sketch of an Infant," *Mind, 2* (1877):285–294.

7. C. Bell, *Anatomy and Philosophy of Expression* (London: Longmanns, Hurst, Rees, and Orme, 1806).

8. C. Darwin, *The Expression of the Emotions in Man and Animals* (London: Murray, 1873) (1872).

9. K. Pearson, *The Life, Letters and Labors of Francis Galton* (London: Cambridge University Press, 1914–1924); F. Galton, *Memories of My Life* (London: Methuen, 1908). See also D. W. Forrest, *Francis Galton: The Life and Work of a Victorian Genius* (New York: Taplinger Publishing Co., 1974).

10. "Galton, Sir Francis," *Encyclopaedia Britannica* (Chicago: 1955), Vol. IX, p. 989.

11. F. Galton, *Hereditary Genius* (London: Macmillan Ltd., 1869) (Herrnstein and Boring, Excerpt No. 78).

12. F. Galton, *Hereditary Genius* (London: Macmillan Ltd., 1892), prefatory chapter.

13. A. R. Buss, "Galton and Sex Differences: An Historical Note," *Journal of the History of the Behavioral Sciences, 12* (1976):283–285.

14. K. Pearson, *Life, Letters and Labors of Francis Galton,* Vol. I, p. 6.

15. A. Quételet, *Physique sociale* (Brussels: Marquardt, 1869), Vol. II.

16. K. Pearson, *Life, Letters and Labors of Francis Galton,* Vol. II.

17. F. Galton, "Co-relations and Their Measurement, Chiefly from Anthropometric Data," *Proceedings, Royal Society of London, 15* (1888):135–145.

18. K. Pearson, "Regression, Heredity and Panmixia," *Philosophical Transactions, 187* (1896):253–318.

19. K. Pearson, *Life, Letters and Labors of Francis Galton,* Vol. II.

20. F. Galton, *Inquiries into Human Faculty and Its Development* (London: Macmillan Ltd., 1883) (Herrnstein and Boring, Excerpt No. 79).

21. F. Galton, *Inquiries*, 2nd ed.
22. *Ibid.*
23. *Ibid.*
24. F. Galton, "Psychometric Experiments," *Brain*, 2 (1879):149–162.
25. Sources for the details of the life of Herbert Spencer are very meager, a result of his almost complete neglect during the last fifty years or so. To be sure there is his *An Autobiography*, 2 vols. (New York: Appleton, 1904), but it is more a reworking of a diary than a full-fledged autobiography. This situation has been remedied to some extent by the publication of J.D.Y. Peel, *Herbert Spencer: The Evolution of a Sociologist* (New York: Basic Books, 1971). Other details had to be sought in secondary sources, such as E. Nordenskiold, *The History of Biology* (New York: Alfred A. Knopf, 1928); and W. C. Dampier, *A History of Conscience and Its Relations with Philosophy and Religion*, 4th ed. (Cambridge: Cambridge University Press, 1949).
26. C. Dampier, *History of Science*.
27. E. Nordenskiold, *History of Biology*.
28. H. Spencer, *First Principles* (London: Williams and Norgate, 1862).
29. H. Spencer, *The Principles of Biology* (New York: Appleton, 1872).
30. H. Spencer, *The Principles of Psychology*, 2nd ed. (London: Williams and Norgate, 1870–1872) (1855).
31. H. Spencer, *The Principles of Sociology* (New York: Appleton, 1876–1879).
32. H. Spencer, *The Principles of Ethics* (New York: Appleton, 1879–1893).
33. G. J. Romanes, *Animal Intelligence* (London: Appleton, 1882) (Herrnstein and Boring, Excerpt No. 87).
34. C. L. Morgan, *An Introduction to Comparative Psychology*, 2nd ed. (New York: Scribner's, 1904) (1894).
35. *Ibid.*, p. 293.
36. *Ibid.*, for example, pp 53, 292 (Herrnstein and Boring, Excerpt No. 88).
37. D. Spalding, *"Instinct and Acquisition,"* *Nature*, 12 (1875):507–508.
38. E. L. Thorndike, "Animal Intelligence: An Experimental Study of the Associative Processes in Animals," *Psychological Review, Monograph Supplements*, 2 (1898).

Thomas C. Upham.

American Psychology: Before William James

The attitude of many historians of psychology has been similar to that of J. McKeen Cattell when he wrote in 1929 that a history of psychology in America prior to the 1880s "would be as short as a book on snakes in Ireland since the time of St. Patrick. In so far as psychologists are concerned, America was then like Heaven, for there was not a damned soul there."[1] To Cattell and most of his generation, psychology was synonymous with scientific, experimental psychology, the psychology of Wundt's laboratory, or at least the psychology of William James. William James, as we will see in the next chapter, stands at the dividing line between the old psychology in America and the new. He is much the same transitional figure as Wundt was in Europe. Just as in pre-Wundtian Europe, in America there was a long history of psychological thought before the days of experimental psychology, the psychology of the laboratory. Much of the preexperimental psychology in America parallels developments in Europe, though usually a generation later. The resulting psychological milieu in America in the nineteenth century was quite different, however, from that which emerged in Europe at the same time.

The emergence of psychology as an independent discipline in America did not take place suddenly. It was part of several gradual developments in American thought. In America, perhaps more than anywhere else, the development of psychological thought is intimately tied with higher education, since the colleges housed most of the learned activities in the country. For this reason considerable emphasis will be given in this chapter to the development of psychological topics within the academic environment. Psychology's academic emergence in the late nineteenth and early twentieth centuries was part of an overall emergence and differentiation of the social sciences from the general matrix of philosophy that took place from the mid-eighteenth and early nineteenth centuries. That, in turn, was due to the revolution against scholasticism brought about by the triumph of the "New Learning" of Newton, Locke, and their followers.

Movements in America outside the academic halls also influenced psychological thought. As already suggested, phrenology was a significant popular psychological movement that would strongly influence popular attitudes about psychology well into the twentieth century. Both inside and outside of academics, evolutionary theory was another major development in the nineteenth century that influenced the form many psychological positions of the twentieth century would take in America.

SAMUEL JOHNSON AND THE NEW LEARNING

Although psychological thought similar to the scholasticism of the Europe of the Middle Ages existed in America from the time of the founding of Harvard in the 1630s,[2] the arrival of modern psychological thought in America can be dated at around 1714. It was in that year that the seeds of the American Enlightenment arrived on these shores, packed in nine shipping crates. Jeremiah Dummer, the colonial agent for Connecticut, had spent a good bit of his time in England collecting books to be sent to the new College of Connecticut, which later would be moved to New Haven and renamed Yale College. There were 900 volumes in the crates among which were Newton's own copy of his *Principia* and his *Optics*, Francis Bacon's *Advancement of Learning*, and most important of all, John Locke's *Essay Concerning Human Understanding*.[3] This literature had been available in Britain for almost a generation, but America's intellectual isolation from Britain had prevented their influence from being felt earlier.

Shortly after the crates were unpacked, one of the students was allowed to peruse the volumes. His name was Samuel Johnson (1696–1772), not to be mistaken for the English literary figure of the same name.[4] This literature differed radically from the scholasticism of Johnson's early education and made him desire more.[5] Dummer's crate of books provided enough food to fill that craving. Johnson had been warned against many of the books for fear that "the new philosophy would soon bring in a new divinity and corrupt the pure religion of the country."[6] In Samuel Johnson's notebook for November 11, 1714, Thanksgiving, is found the notation "And by next Thanksgiving, November 16, 1715, I was wholly changed to the New Learning."[7] The Enlightenment that had swept through England a generation before was now loosed in America.

Samuel Johnson became a tutor at Yale in 1717 when it was moved to New Haven. The influence of the "New Learning" was obvious in Johnson's curriculum for the class under his charge. L. L. Tucker tells us that "Upon becoming a tutor, he swept out much of the accumulated scholastic rubbish and began to introduce into the curriculum the empiricism of Locke, the inductive method of Bacon, and the cosmology of Kepler, Copernicus, and Newton."[8]

Johnson would leave Yale in 1719, but the new philosophy was left very much alive there. Johnson had become saturated with the New Learning, but his Puritan background made it impossible for him to take the step toward agnosticism or deism that so many others in the Enlightenment were taking. He was saved from the decision by his encounter with British empiricist George Berkeley. As an Anglican missionary in the 1720s, Berkeley lived in Newport, Rhode Island. When the project Berkeley had undertaken of educating and converting the natives of the islands of the Caribbean failed, however, he went back to Ireland in 1731. Berkeley's influence on Johnson was significant. Through Berkeley, Johnson saw how he could balance the intellectual demands of Newton and Locke with a firm belief in the direct relationship of God with the universe.[9] Johnson kept his Berkleyan ideas to himself for almost fifteen years. When he finally published his *Elementa Philosophica* in 1752, his philosophy and psychology rested solidly on Berkleyan propositions. *Elementa Philosophica* is of particular significance since it is probably the first textbook written in America on philosophy.[10]

Berkeley's impact can be seen in the differences in Johnson's conception of philosophy. Johnson had written a draft of his "General Idea of Philosophy" before he was influenced by Berkeley. In this work he followed Locke in dividing philosophy into three parts—rational, natural, and moral.[11]

By 1752, Johnson, under the influence of Berkeley, had developed beyond John Locke, and, in the edition of his *Elementa Philosophica* of that date, he divided philosophy into two subject matters, natural and moral. Natural philosophy dealt with "bodies," the things of the material world; moral philosophy dealt with "spirits," the things of the mental and theological world. He divided moral philosophy into two parts: speculative, "what relates to the Knowledge of Intellectual Things," and practical, "What relates to Life and Conduct, in our several Capacities, personal and social."

Speculative moral philosophy dealt with "Knowledge of intellectual Things" and includes pneumatology, "knowledge of the several kinds of created Intelligences" and theology, "of the DEITY . . ." The general study that allows us to understand speculative moral philosophy is logic, which Johnson called "Noetics." Noetics included in Johnson's definition "both Ontology and Dialectic of the

Conduct of the Mind in Thinking or Reasoning." Between noetics and pneumatology we have the equivalent of what would become the intellectual philosophy of
the nineteenth century. The fact that theology is listed along with pneumatology
shows how closely Johnson linked religious and intellectual matter. Ellis gives us
an excellent summary of Johnson's use of Berkeley:

> Johnson defined ideas as "immediate objects of sense." Anything and everything that
> was apprehended through the five senses was an idea. . . . The perception of the
> physical world was the first premise of the system, yet, since Berkeley and Johnson
> insisted that perception was a mental act, they called the sense-objects ideas. There
> were simple ideas, such as sounds, colors, odors; then there were complex ideas,
> combinations of the simple ideas. The complex idea of an apple, for example, con-
> sisted of the simple ideas red, juicy, round, etc. Finally, in addition to defining and
> distinguishing between different kinds of ideas, Johnson asserted that all ideas were
> passive. They did not possess a principle of self-activity. They could not cause them-
> selves to be or force a mind to perceive them. This raised a number of elementary
> philosophical problems, one of which was to explain where all these ideas originated.
>
> The answer seemed obvious. Johnson reasoned that "they [ideas] must derive
> to us from an Almighty, intelligent active cause, exhibiting them to us, impressing our
> minds with them, or producing them in us." God was the cause of all our ideas, but
> he was more than a first cause. He was the immediate cause of each and every existent
> idea. Whenever the human mind perceived an idea, that idea came directly from God
> at that instant. The human mind had "an immediate dependence upon the Deity"
> for every color, sound, and smell it received. Moreover, God was the agent responsible
> for the way in which simple ideas were combined to form complex ideas. . . .
>
> And finally, in addition to serving as the immediate cause of all ideas and
> arranging these ideas in patterns, according to his will, God was the constant source
> of all perceived objects. He was "the continual Preserver of all His creatures, and
> consequently, that the moment he should cease to will the continuance of their
> existence, they must unavoidably cease, and drop into nothing."[12]

Johnson used Berkeley's notions in which God carried out the causal functions
that matter carried out in Locke's psychology. This attempt to preserve a theological basis for philosophical and psychological ideas and to link spiritual life with
mental life would continue to permeate American psychologies until William
James finally separated the two in his *Principles of Psychology* in 1890.

Johnson later became president of the newly established College of New York,
now Columbia University. In his declining years, he would turn his back on much
of the potential of the New Learning he had seen as a youth. All his life, he had
balanced his religious convictions against the "dangerous" tendencies of the New
Learning. At last the strain was too much, and he turned to the refuge of scholarly
work on the Old Testament.

Newton and Locke's books continued to work their influence on Americans.
Johnson also assisted, successfully encouraging Berkeley to contribute to Yale his
extensive library, replete with books by Hume and other "forward-looking" philosophers of Britain.

JONATHAN EDWARDS

Jonathan Edwards (1703–1758) also encountered Newtonian science and Locke's *Essay* while a student at Yale. He was only thirteen years old when he matriculated at Yale in 1716 and was affected in much the same way as was Samuel Johnson. As with Johnson, Locke was only a starting point for Edward's ideas. Like Johnson, Edwards attempted to find a philosophical position that would fit into the new learning and yet meet the requirements of a deeply held Calvinism. In this second attempt, Edwards was more successful than Johnson and was able to use the new science to promote Calvinism. There are many parallels between Edwards' reaction to Locke's ideas and that of George Berkeley. It is possible that Edwards read some of Berkeley, but Edwards scholars believe that Edwards' thought developed largely independent of Berkeley.[13]

Although perhaps most widely known today for his "fire and brimstone" sermons, such as "Sinners in the Hands of an Angry God," Edwards was also a subtle and acute philosopher, easily the most original American philosopher of his time. Edwards' encounter with Newtonian science and Lockean philosophy would bear fruit in the form of his own idealistic philosophy.

Locke's *Essays* is the starting point for Edwards. In his "Notes on the Mind" Edwards accepts Locke's position on ideas.[14] Ideas are viewed as being the objects of mind, and simple ideas as coming to the mind through sensation. Complex ideas are made up of combinations of these simple ideas, and abstract ideas are those that subsume an entire class of ideas. Like Berkeley, however, Edwards held that Locke's primary sense qualities were not justifiable. The only true substance was God, and God was the agent of our perception and our understanding. The real world, he said, exists in the mind of God. Like Berkeley, Edwards was attempting to avoid the materialistic approach of Locke.

Edwards presaged Hume in his view on causality. Edwards tells us that: "Cause is that, after or upon the existence of which, or the existence of it after such a manner, the existence of another thing follows."[15] This, in Edwards' sometimes mind-boggling prose, is to reduce causality to invariable sequence, just as Hume did. If event A is invariably followed by event B, then A is seen as the cause of B. Edwards holds this causal relationship to be innate. He tells us, "When we therefore see anything begin to be, we intuitively know there is a cause of it, and not by ratiocination, or any kind of argument. This is an innate principle, in that sense, that the soul is born with it."[16]

Edwards makes a very significant differentiation between ideas derived from sensations and the acts of mind. Locke had differentiated between sensation and reflection as sources of ideas but both processes were passive throughout. To Edwards, the functions or acts of mind were more than the mere summation of the sensations that make up our experiences. Simple ideas and the complexes formed from them might be passive, but the acts of mind were active. "An idea is only a perception, wherein the mind is passive or rather subjective. The Acts of the mind are not merely ideas. All Acts of the mind, about its ideas, are not themselves mere ideas."[17] Again, Edwards is escaping the mechanical tendencies of Locke's psychology of ideas.

Perhaps Edwards' most significant contribution to the psychological literature is on the will. As with all other aspects of his philosophy and psychology, will was intimately tied in with religious issues. Edwards held to a deterministic view of the will. He operationally defines will as an act of choice. In talking about determination of the will, Edwards says, we are talking about something that causes one choice rather than another.[18] Whenever there is a determination there must be a cause and an effect. If the choice is the effect, then behind it there must be a cause. Edwards makes use of "motive" as the cause. Motive in Edwards' usage is "the whole of that which moves, excites or invites the mind to volition."[19] Motive is a vague concept, but Edwards identifies it with all the sensations and perceptions that the mind apprehends at the moment of choice and that move the individual to choose one way or the other. Thus, conflicting motives may be present. At the moment of choice, the stronger of these motives initiates the choice. In this way the volition, the choice, is predetermined by prior experience.

Edwards held that we have the feeling of free choice since we experience the choosing when we make it. Our will, the choice itself, he holds, is actually determined by prior experience.[20] The act resulting from the choice is freely exercised, since individuals have the freedom to do or not to do as they will. That is, individuals are free if they can do as they will.

Edwards' Puritan idealism and the idealism of George Berkeley enjoyed a period of popularity in America. The writings of both were used at Yale in the mid-eighteenth century. Locke's writings would remain the staple of psychological information in eighteenth-century America, however, until the takeover of American philosophical and psychological thought by the Scottish Realists in the early nineteenth century.

SCOTTISH THOUGHT IN AMERICA

By the close of the eighteenth century, psychological thought in America had progressed considerably beyond the vagueness of the scholastic curriculum. If the first century and a half of psychological thought in America was characteristically English in origin and influence, the second century or more was to be just as characteristically Scottish. The Scots had begun coming to America in the early eighteenth century, particularly the Scotch-Irish who had once transplanted on Ulster Plantation in Ireland. The Scots came to America in a number of waves between 1717 and 1775.[21] There was an unusually high concentration of educated people in these groups, largely Scotch Presbyterian ministers, but also medical men and teachers. These Scotch-Irish and mainland Scots brought with them their Calvinistic attitudes and ideas that deeply affected the American educational scene and with it the way psychology would be treated, particularly in the college classroom.

The first major educational "beachhead" of Scottish thought was at the College of New Jersey (now Princeton University) which had been founded in 1746. The College had been a product of the surge of fire and brimstone revivalism that took place in the 1740s, partly initiated by Jonathan Edwards, called the "Great Awakening." The Great Awakening had been prompted by a number of concerns, especially the rise of "natural religion" and other rationalistic carryovers from the New Learning. The traditional colleges such as Yale and Harvard, though in the hands of Calvinists, were considered by the evangelical wing of the Presbyterians to be too permissive and so founded their own college in New Jersey. Princeton was only the first. The New Light Presbyterians were already setting up their log colleges on the frontier (which in those days included Maine, Kentucky, and as far west as Ohio).

It was at Princeton, however, that Jonathan Edwards and, through him, George Berkeley had their greatest impact. In fact, Jonathan Edwards became president of Princeton in 1768, although he served only a few weeks before dying of a small-pox inoculation.

John Witherspoon (1723–1794) succeeded the unfortunate Edwards as president of Princeton. Witherspoon was a widely respected minister of the Church of Scotland with evangelical leanings. He arrived at Princeton straight from Scotland. He had been a student at Edinburgh between 1730 and 1736 and had closely followed the flowering of the Scottish Enlightenment. He was strongly influenced by the new Scottish Realist philosophy and held strongly to the view that empirical knowledge, the knowledge by way of the senses, is of a more accurate nature than deduction from reason. He was clearly in Thomas Reid's camp and is said to have brought a copy of Reid's *An Inquiry into the Human Mind* over with him. Witherspoon believed he was the first to introduce the Scottish philosophy to America. He was certainly espousing ideas similar to those of Thomas Reid at a very early date.[22] Witherspoon had just the antidote for Edwards' and Berkeley's idealisms.

Witherspoon was an enthusiastic supporter of learning and was responsible for the expansion of the Princeton curriculum to include practical and scientific topics, even at the expense of some of the classical topics. This curriculum change was much in line with the Scottish university reforms. Witherspoon did not alter the structure of the philosophical instruction relating to psychology so much as its contents; anything psychological at Princeton was bound to Scottish Realism. Witherspoon held that "The faculties of the mind are commonly divided into . . . the understanding, the will and the affections; though perhaps it is proper to observe, that these are not three qualities wholly distinct, but different ways of exhorting the same principle. It is the soul or mind that understands, wills, or is affected with pleasure and pain."[23]

This was very much the Scottish "party line." Witherspoon made few alterations in the Scottish authorities. He still divided the study of the faculties between courses in logic and moral philosophy as "that branch of Science which treats of the principles and laws of Duty and Morals."[24] As at Princeton, the teachings of Reid and the Scottish Realist philosophers who followed him became the standard philosophy and psychology of most of the other Calvinist colleges across the country.

It was Samuel Stanhope Smith, Witherspoon's son-in-law and successor at Princeton, who began to cast the Americanized Scottish psychology into the form that would be so common in the nineteenth-century college curriculum. Smith incorporated the psychology of knowing into the course in moral philosophy. In this way the three basic aspects of human psychology—knowing, feeling and doing—were finally put under the single rubric of moral philosophy. Samuel Stanhope Smith defined moral philosophy as "an investigation of the constitution and laws of mind." He believed that "The science of moral philosophy begins with the study of the human mind—its sensations, perception, and generally, its means of acquiring knowledge—its sentiments, dispositions and affections, and generally, its principles of action or enjoyment—its present state, and reactions to other beings—its future hopes and fears."[25]

Smith's method was inductive, based on the direct knowledge of the real world. Smith and the other Scottish writers had an argument not with Locke's empirical side, but with Locke's position that we are aware of ideas through the senses and not of the objects themselves. The Scottish Realists' reliance on senses and induction over reason and deduction is at the heart of the "Baconian" method that underlined so much of Scottish influence in American science. Samuel Stanhope Smith believed that "No law should be admitted on hypothesis but should rest solely on an induction of facts. . . . He believed that such laws that were collected "from an ample and accurate induction of facts" should be considered to be universal until invalidated by other facts.[26]

Witherspoon and Samuel Smith had great influence on the American thought of their day. During their terms at Princeton, a large number of students were imprinted with their versions of the logic and moral philosophy of the Scottish Realists. Many of these students would themselves become tutors or professors of moral philosophy. These students filled the newly created professorships in moral philosophy in the expanding college curriculum after the American Revolution. Others became the primary educated class in America, ministers, who communicated this Scottish Realist view of mind to their congregations. It was by way of the courses in moral philosophy that American psychological thought was carried into the nineteenth century.[27]

By the 1820s Scottish philosophy had already become the norm in the American college classroom. Even at Yale, John Locke's *Essays* had been supplanted in 1825 by Dugald Stewart's *Essays* as the textbook of choice in moral philosophy.[28] By 1829 James Marsh, the President of the University of Vermont, could write that "The works of Locke were formerly much read and used as text books, in our colleges; but of late have very generally given place to the Scotch writers; and Stewart, Campbell and Brown are now almost universally read as the standard authors on the subjects of which they treat."[29]

I. Woodbridge Riley has referred, perhaps unfairly, to the rise of Scottish philosophy in the 1820s as the "glacial age," "an overwhelming mass of cold orthodoxy" grinding out all opposition.[30]

THOMAS UPHAM AND THE PSYCHOLOGICAL TEXTBOOK

In the 1820s a new trend emerged in the American college, the use of textbooks surveying a subject matter rather than the use of original sources. The expansion of the colleges in the period after the Revolution also increased the number of professors who taught mental and moral philosophy. Many of these professors earned additional income by publishing textbooks, usually based on their lectures. In America, the textbook appears to have begun to define the course of study. The study of philosophy was no longer presented as "an investigation of the constitution and laws of nature . . . so far as the powers of the human mind, unaided by the light of revelation, are competent to discover them" but became, instead, the contents of a given book.[31] It is perhaps significant that in the annual reports from many American colleges in the 1820s more emphasis seems to be put on the list of texts used than on the title or the content of the courses. The Scottish Realists' texts were soon supplemented by these published lectures of American professors of moral philosophy.[32] For this reason, the history of American psychology in the nineteenth century is largely a history of the textbooks used in the courses covering those topics.

The form taken by the early textbooks and, through them, the courses offered in American colleges, was greatly influenced by Thomas Reid's *Essays on the Intellectual Powers of Man* and his *Essays on the Active Powers of the Human Mind.* Reid divided moral philosophy into intellectual powers and active powers. What is significant in Reid's organization is that the subject matter is almost entirely psychological—intellectual powers dealing with understanding, and active powers dealing with feeling and doing. Earlier, moral philosophy included a much larger group of topics that today would be referred to as political science, sociology, anthropology, and the like. These topics, now considered nonpsychological, gradually became differentiated into separate courses. Political economy was an area that separated itself quite early, with a chair devoted to the topic in some institutions.[33]

Thomas Cogswell Upham (1799–1872) of Bowdoin College is usually regarded as the author of the first American textbook in psychology, *Intellectual Philosophy* (1827). The term *psychology* was still not in current use in America. There were other competitors for the "first," but what sets Upham's series of books apart from these is the degree to which its content defined the course of psychology as it finally evolved, the degree of systemization exhibited, and the genuine spirit of eclecticism that permeated his work.

Upham issued his Bowdoin lecture notes for the period 1824–1827 under the title *Elements of Intellectual Philosophy* (1827). The title clearly derives from Reid's *Essays.* To say that Upham's book was merely a discourse on Reid, however, is to make the oversimplification that has led to the misrepresentation of the whole line of American textbook writers in the nineteenth century. As a matter of fact, Upham's 1827 volume is based more on Locke than on the Scots, although the influence of Reid and Stewart is clearly present. In analyzing the

1827 volume, J. W. Fay noted sixty-six basic sources. These ranged from Locke and the Scots to authors such as Montaigne, Descartes, Malebranche, Condillac, Helvetius, Cabanis, Pinel, Esquirol, and de Gerando, to name only a few.[34] Upham was blessed with a talent for languages and an interest in learning modern tongues, thus giving him wider access to sources than were available to most of the other early American writers on psychological matters. Upham was careful to avoid falling into the easy, uncritical approach of merely summarizing the teachings of a single school.[35]

Upham's writings show another influence which the writings of the Scots brought to America: Francis Bacon's notions of reliance on observation, description, and induction, and his abhorrence of hypotheses and *a priori* statements. Neither Upham nor those who came after him lived up to Bacon's high standards, but Upham, at least, made great effort to be inductive.

In 1832 Upham changed the title of his book, by now expanded to two volumes, to *Elements of Mental Philosophy*, judging that the term *intellectual philosophy* was too narrow to encompass the intellect and the sensibilities. Upham's choice of mental philosophy would prove quite useful, since moral philosophy connoted a variety of meanings. In 1834 Upham added a third volume, the *Philosophical and Practical Treatise on the Will*, completing his three-part system. The *Mental Philosophy* was somewhat more influenced by the Scottish Realists than had been the earlier *Intellectual Philosophy*.

In his *Mental Philosophy*, Upham also included material on abnormal psychology, under the heading of "Imperfect and Disordered Intellectual Action." At the request of the Harper Brothers publishing house, Upham wrote a separate book on abnormal psychology titled *Outline of Imperfect and Disordered Mental Action*, which appeared in 1840. This is likely the first abnormal psychology text to appear in America.[36] By 1861 Upham had come to a final form of his text in an abridgment of his three-volume *Mental Philosophy*, intended as a textbook for academies and high schools. Although the examples were somewhat briefer, there was no significant alteration in the content itself.

Upham's textbooks were widely used throughout the country well into the 1870s and did much to standardize the form of the mental philosophy and finally the psychology course.

CONSOLIDATION AND DEVELOPMENT OF AMERICAN ACADEMIC PSYCHOLOGY

As the textbooks developed in the nineteenth century, so did the curricula of American colleges. The old natural philosophy course evolved into specific courses in the natural sciences. The philosophy of the human mind was being more clearly separated in most colleges from logic on one side and the other social science aspects of the old moral philosophy course on the other. The textbooks that followed Upham's works demonstrated the clear differentiation of psychological thought from other subject matters. Francis Wayland (1799–1865),

Professor of Moral Philosophy and President of Brown, wrote both an intellectual philosophy and a moral philosophy. Wayland's *Elements of Intellectual Philosophy* covered psychology in its narrow sense of "knowing, feeling and doing," in terms of mental states. His *Elements of Moral Science* also touched on psychological matters but was more concerned with ethics and general concepts of morality—how one should behave rather than how one does behave. Wayland also wrote *Elements of Political Economy,* dealing with a variety of social science topics from the old form of the moral philosophy course. Similarly, Joseph Haven (1816–1874) wrote immensely popular books covering mental philosophy and moral philosophy as separate topics with the psychological material primarily lodged in the mental philosophy. Such attempts by one person to cover both the psychological and ethical aspects of the field lasted well into the proliferation of courses after the introduction of the elective system into colleges in the 1870s. Noah Porter (1811–1892), Professor of Moral Philosophy and Metaphysics and President of Yale, brought this model to its apex with *The Human Intellect* (1868) and *The Elements of Moral Science: Theoretical and Practical* (1885). What is important to note here is that psychological topics were clearly becoming distinguished from the other social sciences.[37]

By 1860 the recitation system of instruction had changed over to the lecture system much as that found in American colleges and universities today. Instead of merely drilling students on the assigned readings for the day, the professor often talked about the material itself or, more typically, read to the class his lecture notes on the subject. Lectures had been used in America since the time of John Witherspoon at Princeton, but the technique did not gain wide use until the 1820s. The result of this we have already seen as an increase in the number of professors turning their lecture notes into textbooks and even popular books on psychological topics.

These lecturers, as we have seen, were not content merely to paraphrase the orthodox Scots, however. Upham, for instance, while following the basic outlines of Reid and Stewart, did not agree with them in every detail. Virtually all the writers of texts of the "Scottish type" after Upham selected from ideas beyond England and Scotland. The use of exotic sources was not highly publicized in most cases. There were still more rewards for appearing orthodox and safe than being labeled as controversial. The Baconian vogue of being descriptive and inductive rather than explanatory allowed some degree of protection from criticism, as did the rather sparse referencing of sources that was common in most textbooks of all kinds in the early nineteenth century.

The phrase "orthodox Scottish philosophy" itself must be used with care and should perhaps be restricted to the ideas of Reid and Stewart. Thomas Brown, whose books were exceptionally popular in America after their appearance in the 1820s, was attempting to go beyond Reid and Stewart and make a tie-in with the concepts of the psychology of association. Sir William Hamilton, whose books appeared somewhat later, attempted to find rapport between Scottish and Kantian thought. All these individuals are often lumped together as though their views were the same, but Hamilton and Brown were very different from Reid and Stewart. In short, by the 1830s not even the Scottish School was orthodox. As Stewart had replaced Locke in American colleges, so Brown replaced Stewart, and finally, just before the American Civil War, Hamilton began to replace Brown as the standard source for Scottish philosophy.

THE ENTRY OF GERMAN IDEALISM INTO AMERICAN PSYCHOLOGICAL THOUGHT

Despite all the efforts in American colleges to hold back the tide of the continental philosophers, the influence of Kant and the post-Kantians such as Schelling, Fichte, and Hegel was still felt among the Americans, largely through interpretations of the French eclectics such as Victor Cousin and the English poet and philosopher, Samuel Taylor Coleridge.

The Kantian philosophies had slipped into the country before the door of orthodoxy could be slammed shut in the colleges. It was James Marsh (1794–1842), a classmate of Upham while at Andover Theological Seminary, who was largely responsible for leaving the door ajar. Marsh was Professor of Moral Philosophy and President of the University of Vermont. In the late 1820s, he came across a copy of Samuel Taylor Coleridge's *Aids to Reflection*, an explication of Coleridge's idealism with sources in Berkeley but primarily in Kant and the post-Kantians. Being surprised to find that his ideas were similar to those of Coleridge, Marsh gained permission to put out an American edition of the work, which appeared in 1829.[38]

Up to that time what little Americans knew about Kant had been through Dugald Stewart's rather negative review of the German philosophy in his *History of Philosophy*.[39]

Marsh's course at Vermont appears to be the first point of direct contact between German philosophy and the American college classroom. Marsh used the term *psychology* in his classes, although it was only part of the subject matter of his course of philosophy.[40] Marsh's lectures on psychology have the flavor of Sir William Hamilton's thought in many respects which should not be surprising, since both were attempting a similar synthesis. Marsh died before publishing his own lectures, and much of the potential of his own thought was never realized in the wider American intellectual sphere.[41]

Frederick Augustus Rauch (1806–1841) was another source of German philosophical ideas in America. Rauch was educated in Giessen and Heidelberg. He earned his Ph.D. in 1827 and reached the rank of *Professor Extraordinarius* before political problems caused him to come to America in 1831. Rauch was ordained a minister in the German Reformed Church, and in 1836 he became the first President of Marshall College (later combined with Franklin College to form the present Franklin and Marshall College).[42] Rauch's textbook, *Psychology: or A View of the Human Soul, Including Anthropology*, was published in 1840. The book appears to be the first American text to make use of the term *psychology* in its title. It was not an uncommon term in German books, but American and British writers still preferred ''mental philosophy'' or ''pneumatology'' to name the topic.

The word only became common after the appearance of Herbert Spencer's *Principles of Psychology* in 1855.

"Psychology" in Rauch's usage dealt with the relation of internal mental functions. Psychology was divided into two major sections, reason and will. Reason was divided into three sections: (1) sensation, (2) conception, fancy, and imagination, and (3) pure thinking. Will was also divided into three sections: (1) desires, (2) inclinations and passions, and (3) emotions. Rauch's psychology emphasized mind as a process rather than in terms of independent faculties. Reason and will were considered to be inseparable functions of a unitary mind.[43] Rauch wrote that reason and will were "two sides of the same coin. Reason is nothing else than will with prevailing consciousness, and will is reason with a prevailing practical tendency."[44]

Rauch emphasized the growth of the mind as a continuing process. His objective was to merge German with American philosophy, all to be done with careful consideration of the religious predilection of his American audience. The book was quite popular. The first edition was sold out in a matter of a few weeks.[45] In 1840 Rauch changed the title of his course to "Psychology," making it perhaps the first course to bear that name in an American college.[46] Rauch died the year following the publication of his *Psychology*, which may explain his lack of lasting influence.

Another source of German idealistic thought in America was the French writer, Victor Cousin (1792–1867). Cousin's eclectic psychology was a composite of post-Kantian German romantic philosophy and British views. There were some French editions of Cousin's writings in the United States by the 1830s. However, it was Caleb Sprague Henry, Professor of Philosophy at New York University, who translated and edited Cousin's writings and issued English editions. In 1834 he published Cousin's *Elements of Psychology: Included in a Critical Examination of Locke's Essay.* At first Cousin had greater impact on the nonacademic transcendentalists than on the academicians, but in years to come he would be found commonly in the college library and classroom.

Perhaps the most widely read early American textbook writer of the German idealist persuasion was Laurens Perseus Hickok (1798–1888). Herbert Schneider calls Hickok "the first American theologian and professor to become a systematic expositor of German idealism."[47] Although Rauch might better deserve this credit, Hickok was certainly more widely read and was influential in the shift of American academic thought toward German idealism as the century progressed. Hickok's best known psychological works are his *Rational Psychology* (1848) and his *Empirical Psychology* (1854). Hickok defined psychology as the "Science of Mind":

> Empirical Psychology attains the facts of mind and arranges them as a system. The elements are solely the facts given in experience, and the criterion of their reality is the clear testimony of consciousness . . .
>
> Rational Psychology is a very different process for attaining a science of Mind. . . . It is truly a transcendental philosophy inasmuch as it transcends experience and goes up to those necessary sources from which all possible experience must originate. . . . It enters into the very essence of Rational Psychology to make this *a priori* investigation of the human intellect; to attain the idea of intelligence, from the *a priori* conditions which make an intellectual agency possible, and thereby determine how,

if there be intelligence, it must be both in function and operation; and then find the facts which shall evince that such intellectual agency is not only possible in void thought, but is also actual being in reality.[48]

Hickok, though clearly influenced by Kantian thought, was still eclectic. He perhaps did more than any American textbook writer to open the door left ajar by James Marsh and let in Kantian and post-Kantian idealism. Although some conservative elements criticized the early editions of Hickok's books, particularly the *Rational Psychology*, for its emphasis on German idealism, Hickok was careful to demonstrate that there was no conflict between Kantian thought and religion. He seems to have satisfied enough academicians, since his texts, particularly the *Empirical Psychology*, were widely used both in their original editions and in their revisions by Seelye as late as the 1880s.[49]

By the 1850s, Cousin's eclectic psychology became widely used in the antebellum college classroom. That along with the eclectic nature of Sir William Hamilton's "Scottish" philosophy helped reduce the fear of German idealism in all except the most conservative institutions.

Outside of academics from the 1830s on, particularly in New England, receptiveness to European idealism was increasing. Even in the colleges, although severe limitations were placed on the books available in classrooms, student literary societies were independent of the colleges and were often much larger than the college libraries as well as far more varied. Literary societies met to read and discuss works that would have sent shivers up the spines of the college trustees. Once out of the college atmosphere, the appetite for the new ideas was quickly fed by American editors and publishers.

In 1838 George Ripley initiated his publication of a series of fourteen volumes under the general title "Specimens of Foreign Standard Literature." Early in the series were works by Cousin, Jouffroy, and Constant in English translation.[50]

In the midwestern United States, the German philosopher, Hegel, developed a strong following in the form of the St. Louis Movement. The *Journal of Speculative Philosophy*, the organ of the school, contained translations of both "classic" and new German philosophy as well as commentaries by American authors. A psychologist who was strongly influenced by this school was John Dewey, whose first edition of his *Psychology* (1887) shows the influence of Hegel.

It was after the Civil War that the neo-Humean idealism of John Stuart Mill and the evolutionary writings of Charles Darwin and the psychology of Herbert Spencer burst on the American scene. Their influence would open up the wide range of attitudes and approaches that have characterized American philosophy and psychology ever since.

EVOLUTION

Darwin, Spencer, and Galton have been considered in earlier chapters, but we have not yet seen their impact on American thought. Darwin's *Origin of Species* appeared in England in 1859 to a roar of controversy. It appeared that same year in

America, published by D. Appleton and Company. Appleton would be the primary publisher of evolutionary writers in America in the nineteenth century. Although many American scientists were enthusiastic, most were not. There was a storm of protest from the religious press and clergy. Appleton's editorial offices received hundreds of threatening letters. One noted American clergyman of the day wrote Mr. Appleton that he would be punished in this world and in the world to come for publishing Darwin's book.[51]

The evolutionary debate in America did not begin with Darwin, however. Lamarck's ideas of the inheritance of acquired characteristics had been known in America since about 1802, although not much attention seems to have been paid to them. Much of the controversy, however, had to do with geology. James Hutton's *Theory of the Earth* had been published in 1788, opening up the new discipline of geology and questions about the origin of the world. Charles Lyell published his *Principles of Geology* in 1830, which also argued for a nontraditional view of the origin of the earth. Both views met with great opposition by noted naturalists of the day, who held to the creationist view. Louis Agassiz (1807–1873), Professor of Zoology and Geology at Harvard, was director of the Harvard Museum and had been a student of the naturalist Cuvier. He supported more traditional views of the origins of the earth and the development of species.

Darwin's *Origin of Species* was thus introduced into an already excited atmosphere. Darwin's marshaling of evidence to back up his hypothesis gradually won the day, however. By 1871, when Darwin's potentially more threatening work, *Descent of Man,* appeared, the scientific debate was largely settled in support of Darwin. Even Agassiz's students had all gone over to the "other side" by that time. The general public's acceptance was slower to develop, but the notion of natural selection, which any farmer of the time who bred livestock could translate into his own experience, was widely held, although often in a form that would probably have been unrecognizable to Darwin. In fact, however, the typical American learned about Darwin's evolution theories not by reading Darwin but by reading his popularizers.[52]

The most notable popularizer of Darwinian ideas in America was Herbert Spencer who has already been discussed in Chapter 16. His writings on evolutionary topics actually predated those of Darwin. Spencer's *Social Statics* had been published in 1850 and contained aspects of a philosophy of life that would become known as Social Darwinism. He emphasized natural selection, introducing the phrase often incorrectly credited to Darwin, "survival of the fittest."

Much of Spencer's success in America can be attributed to Edward L. Youmans (1821–1887), one of D. Appleton and Company's editors and an avid follower of Spencer. In 1860 Youmans persuaded Appleton to publish Spencer's books in the United States. Up to that time, Spencer's books had made no impact in America and were but little known, even in England. In 1862, over ten years after the first appearance of *Social Statics,* Spencer had not yet sold out the first English edition of 750 copies. By 1862 his *Principles of Psychology* had sold only 200 copies. Appleton published *Social Statics* in 1864 and eventually produced all of Spencer's American editions. Appleton royalties and Youman's encouragement allowed Spencer to complete his *Synthetic Philosophy.*[53]

Spencer's writings were phenomenally successful in the United States. Spencer was seen as bringing Darwin's scientific doctrines into perspective with everyday life and morality. To the businessman and farmer alike his writings appeared to make rugged common sense. In fact, much of what goes under the rubric of "rugged individualism," and even "rugged republicanism" with its laissez-faire economics and rejection of governmental intervention into the affairs of individual citizens, can be attributed to the notions of Herbert Spencer and his American followers.

Youmans continued to promote Spencer through his editorial work in *Appleton's Journal* and the *Popular Science Monthly*.[54] Under his guidance, those journals became a pipeline for evolutionary ideas, particularly Spencerian doctrines, for the remainder of the nineteenth century.

Youmans and Appleton also promoted the other followers of Darwin and Spencer. The books of Thomas Huxley and John Tyndall were introduced to the American public through their efforts.

CHAUNCEY WRIGHT

Although perhaps better known today as an early contributor to the philosophical views that would later be called pragmatism, Wright was a follower of John Stuart Mill and Charles Darwin.[55] He was considered one of evolution's most able defenders in America in the 1860s and 1870s.[56]

Chauncey Wright (1830–1875) was born in Northampton, Massachusetts—the stamping ground a century earlier of Jonathan Edwards. However, Wright was the son of a Unitarian minister—a position about as far away from Edwards' Calvinism as possible. Later, Wright became an agnostic. While in high school, Wright found Robert Chambers' book, *Vestiges of Creation,* although the identity of its author, a Scottish encyclopedist and anthologist, was not known at the time. The book expressed a mildly evolutionary point of view, and it impressed the young Chauncey Wright.[57] Wright attended Harvard and showed a talent for mathematics and philosophy. He graduated from Harvard in 1852, gaining employment as a computer for the *Nautical Almanac,* a position his ability in mathematics made an easy one. He was not tied down to particular hours in his position, which gave him a freedom rarely found outside of academic positions.

In 1860 Wright first read Darwin's *Origin of Species.* He accepted Darwin's evolutionary position and his theory of natural selection. Throughout the 1860s Wright fairly regularly contributed scientific and philosophical articles and reviews to the pages of the *Nation* and the *North American Review.* He was a strong supporter of Darwinism and the concept of natural selection, even though he continued to hold to a version of Lamarck's theory of the transmission of acquired characteristics.

Wright was a close associate and perhaps even something of a mentor to William James, Charles Peirce, and others in the Boston circle called the Metaphysics Club. Besides these individuals the club included such luminaries as Oliver Wendell Holmes, Jr., and John Fiske. Wright also taught a course in psychology at Harvard in 1870.[58]

Wright was an acute thinker and had remarkable insights on a number of scientific and philosophical problems. Darwin himself recognized his writings as significant. Wright was highly critical of much of Spencer, particularly of Spencer's views on the nature and method of science.[59] Like Darwin, Wright did not make teleological arguments concerning the "purpose" of evolution. In this way as well, he opposed Spencer who did much to give American functional psychology its teleological thrust.

Wright made several positive contributions to the technical debate on evolution, but perhaps his most significant contribution to the development of American psychological thought is found in his article, "The Evolution of Self-Consciousness," published in 1873.[60]

There is a great deal to the article,[61] but a few aspects are of particular relevance to this discussion and to the American psychology that would emerge after Wright's death. First, he spoke about the variables to be considered in psychology. As Madden tells us:

> The classical British associationists (Mill and Bain) dealt with only one type of variable, the traditional "impressions" and "ideas" that become fused into complex perceptions as a result of association by contiguity, similarity, and so on. Likewise the experimental Wundtians were engaged in building their psychological system out of a single variable, namely, mental contents like sensations, feelings and ideas. Wright was unique in dealing with two variables which can best be described as stimulus and response variables. . . . The psychologists who came after Wright in the United States (with the exception of the structuralists)—most notably James, Baldwin, Cattell, and the functionalists Angell, Mead, and Dewey—followed Wright in a stimulus–response orientation.[62]

As stated above, however, there was a significant difference between Wright and functional psychologists in that Wright did not make teleological assumptions or relationships between the variables, whereas the functionally oriented psychologists did.

Another link with Wright and the functional psychologies of William James, John Dewey, and James Rowland Angell has to do with the relationship among instincts, habits, and volitions. Rather than considering these as three separate mental states, Wright takes what he calls the "naturalist's point of view" and looks at them as indistinctly separated points along a single series or continuum.[63] Along this series, Wright differentiates a number of intermediary points. First there are "consequent actions." These are strictly instinctive and generally cannot be modified by habit or through the will. They have several forms, but, to simplify, they generally correspond to the current term *reflexes*. Further along the series Wright differentiates *dispositions*, which he describes as inherited effects of habits. This is Wright's expression of Lamarck's notion of inheritance of behavioral traits. A habit, strongly established in one generation, could be transferred to future generations as dispositions to act in certain ways. Wright calls the next clear differentiation in the series "habits"—"effects produced by higher voluntary action of the individual." That is, consciously willed acts that are repeatedly carried out eventually become habitual and are no longer separate operations. Wright holds that habits and dispositions cannot be differentiated in their practical character or modes of actions from true instincts, except that their origins are different and they are capable of alteration through volition, where instincts are not. Volitions, the next point along the continuum, are connections between the stimulus situation (what Wright calls the occasions or external means and conditions of an action) and the production of the action itself. This connection between the stimulus situation and the response or action is not carried out by means of emotion or any instinctive ties (which would include dispositional or habitual ties). The connection is through what Wright calls "the motive of the end." The motive of the end is an "ulterior motive" in Wright's vocabulary, a conscious image of the result or act, an image of the "end or good to be effected by an action." As Wright tells us: "The desirableness of what is effected by an action connects its occasions, or present means and conditions, with the action itself, and causes its production through the end felt in imagination."[64]

So, Wright presents a continuum with instinct at one extreme and intelligence at the other. They are not different classes of events but different discriminable points within the same class. The terms *instinct, habit,* and *volitions* are only points of definition. They blend gradually one into another across this whole expressed as a series or continuum.

Will may be considered free and unconstrained when the relationship between the situation and action is in consciousness. Wright calls the relationship one in which the ulterior motives are within the will. When the ulterior motives are outside the will, that is, when the relationship is mediated by instinctive or habitual tendencies, the will is said to "consent" or "yield" to such tendencies or to be opposed to such tendencies. Wright defines an individual's "character" as the motives within the will, either distinctly or vaguely operative, or completely superseded by forces of habit.

Chauncey Wright did not have the remarkable expressive skills that William James would demonstrate, but Wright's treatment of intelligence, when teleologically reinterpreted by James and others, became two of the fundamental principles underlying American functionalism: the view of the stimulus–response relationship as a continuous whole and what would come to be known as the "lapsed intelligence theory of instincts," by which consciousness became a problem solver and thus demonstrated survival value.

Chauncey Wright died of an apparent stroke in 1875 at the age of forty-five, but his influence on his associates would continue to work its way in American philosophical and psychological thought.

Evolutionary theory brought a new dimension into the consideration of psychological thought in America: the problem of adjustment to the environment and the notion of the mind having survival value. The notion of mind having survival value and the transmission of acquired mental characteristics from one generation to another would continue to be part of American psychological thought well into the twentieth century, being expressed not only in the psychology of William James but also in the fundamental principles underlying James Rowland Angell's Chicago Functionalism.

PHRENOLOGY

Phrenology was another major influence in psychological thought in America adapted from European ideas. Its influence was particularly strong among average Americans, but it was also espoused by many scientific and civic leaders. Since it emphasized the concept of faculties, phrenology seemed to fit well with the orthodox Scottish psychologies. Although much opposition to phrenology had arisen in Europe among groups fearing its mechanistic view of mind, it seems to have been well accepted in the United States.[65]

Phrenological doctrines were first made available in America in 1822 when George Combe's *Essays on Phrenology, Or An Inquiry into the Principles and Utility of the System of Drs. Gall and Spurzheim, and into the Objections Made Against It* was published in Philadelphia.[66] Combe was a Scottish writer and an avid follower of Spurzheim's form of phrenology. His books were very successful in America. His work, *The Constitution of Man Considered in Relation to External Objects*, first published in 1828, was something of a synthesis of Scottish Realism and phrenology. It was immensely popular and ran to over twenty printings in its American edition alone by 1891.

Phrenology had been the subject of medical lectures as early as 1820, however.[67] As far back as 1806 Nicholas Biddle had brought to America a skull marked by Spurzheim himself.[68] Charles Caldwell of the Medical Department of Transylvania College toured the United States in the 1820s spreading the word of the new mental science. He was apparently the first American to publish a book on phrenology, *Elements of Phrenology* (1824).[69] He also founded the *American Phrenological Journal.* George Combe's *The Phrenological Journal and Miscellany* began publication in 1823 and was doubtlessly available in the United States soon thereafter. The major impetus to the development of phrenology as a movement in the United States, however, was the lecture tour of Johann Cristolph Spurzheim in 1832. That movement would be influential throughout the remainder of the nineteenth century.

Spurzheim arrived in New York for a lecture tour in August 1832. American editions of his books were just becoming available through the Boston publishers, Marsh, Capen, and Lyon. They ranged from the technical, two-volume *Phrenology, or the Doctrine of the Mental Phenomena* to his *Philosophical Catechism of the Natural Laws of Man*, written, as the title indicates, in the simple question and answer style of the catechism.

Spurzheim had the same charismatic effect on his American audiences as he had on the Europeans. His tour took him to New York, New Haven, and Boston. He conducted very successful public lectures in Boston and before the intellectual elite at Harvard. Before the course of his lectures could be completed in Boston, Spurzheim became ill and died.[70] His impact had been so great that for ten years after his death memorial ceremonies were held on the date of his birth in Boston.[71] Both Spurzheim and Combe were extremely influential on psychological thought, particularly in the Eastern United States in the 1830s and 1840s. Combe made his own visits to America during that period and had remarkable success wherever he went.

THE FOWLER BROTHERS AND APPLIED PHRENOLOGY

The continued growth in the popularity of phrenology in America in the 1840s and later was due in large part to the applications of phrenology and its promotion by the Fowler Brothers. Orson Squire Fowler was first introduced to phrenology in 1833. He and his classmate, Henry Ward Beecher, were students at Amherst College in Massachusetts. Beecher, later a famous minister and the father of Harriet Beecher Stowe, had been given the topic for a student debate. He had the negative side and won the debate but after the debate declared his belief in phrenology. He and Fowler began lecturing on the subject at the local Society of Natural History. Fowler began giving character readings to his fellow students. Beecher, who retained his belief in phrenology throughout his lifetime, decided to go into the ministry on graduation but Fowler decided to go into phrenology. He teamed up with his brother, Lorenzo Niles Fowler, and they began their tours of the United States, lecturing and giving character readings.[72] Through their publishing house, Fowler and Wells, in Boston, a complete library was available on phrenology. Their books ranged from the classics of Gall, Spurzheim, and Combe to popular manuals—often very similar to psychological "self-help" books published today.

Stimulated by Fowler's lectures and by the popular books and training classes of the American Institute of Phrenology in Philadelphia, a large number of individuals devoted themselves to the practice of phrenology. Throughout the remainder of the nineteenth century practicing phrenologists could be found in every part of the United States. A city would have at least one and perhaps many of them. Traveling phrenologists would visit small towns and villages several times a year. Although many of the traveling phrenologists were charlatans, particularly later in the century, most of the early practicing phrenologists seem to have been real believers in the scientific basis of the discipline.

In the nineteenth century phrenologists were performing many of the characteristic activities of applied psychology in the twentieth century. They functioned as psychological testers, measuring the character of children and instructing parents as to how their child-rearing practices should be adjusted to deal with their child. A child, for instance, who showed a smaller than normal "moral" faculty should be instructed in moral matters with great care. In this way, the child's limited moral faculty would be developed to its highest level. The upper limit of a faculty was determined by the amount of brain matter, but the environment determined how much of that limit was realized. The phrenologist was safe in giving such advice. If the parents did as instructed and the child demonstrated moral behavior, the instruction overcame the child's limitations. If, later, the child demonstrated immoral behavior, the limit of the moral faculty was just too low for any amount of instruction to counteract.

Phrenologists also carried out reading of couples considering marriage. By measuring their faculties and relating them on a chart, the phrenologist could counsel the couple on their compatibility. Phrenologists, such as Nelson Sizer, later President of the American Institute of Phrenology, even did work with the insane using phrenological methods.[73] The phrenologists held that insanity was a product of improper brain action or, perhaps more correctly, improper action of some portion of the brain that controls a given activity. In 1844 the *American Journal of*

Insanity was founded, which would later become an organ of the American Psychiatric Association. In the second number of the journal the editors stated their belief that the "brain is not a single organ, but a congeries of organs, as maintained by the illustrious Gall and his celebrated successors Spurzheim and Combe. Thus each mental faculty has a special organ, and therefore certain faculties may be disordered by disease of the brain, while others are not affected; a fact every day observed in Lunatic Asylums, but which we know not how to explain if we believe the brain to be a single organ."[74] Davies tells us that the *American Journal of Insanity* published many articles on phrenology and its applications to "cerebral pathology."[75] Even Isaac Ray, one of the pioneering "alienists" in the United States, cited numerous examples from Gall, Spurzheim, and Combe in his classic *The Medical Jurisprudence of Insanity* (1839).[76]

Although the location of the phrenological faculties had nothing to do with the actual functions of the brain, the acceptance in America of the notion of insanity as brain dysfunction owes much to the influence of phrenology.

THE ADVENT OF THE NEW PSYCHOLOGY

After the upheaval of the American Civil War, the intellectual climate in the United States began to liberalize. The passing of the Morrill Land Grant Act in 1862, which established land grant colleges across the country, perhaps did more than anything else to secularize higher education. For whatever the cause, the thaw of orthodoxy was evident in the increased breadth of education and in the heterogeny of psychological thought in the college classroom.

Charles W. Eliot's implementation of an elective system at Harvard in 1874 and its gradual acceptance across the country during the following decade further encouraged a broadening of the curriculum. The effect of the reform was to allow the student to go beyond the general course in a given topic and begin explorations of the subject matter in depth. This, in turn, encouraged the development of specialty courses by professors on specific topics beyond the traditional general surveys.

By the 1870s courses titled "Psychology" were common in the philosophical curriculum. The term *moral philosophy* and *mental philosophy* faded away in the 1870s. With the development of many of the subject matters once included under the rubrics of economics, political science, sociology, and anthropology into independent social sciences, the older titles lost their meaning. Psychology, for the time, still resided in philosophy.

It was during this period from the Civil War to 1890 that the last of the psychologies written as philosophy were published. Noah Porter of Yale was one of these authors. Porter was, in some ways, a transitional figure in American philosophical psychology. He had been one of that first generation of philosophers to go to Europe to discover the new philosophies at first hand. Porter's *The Human Intellect* shows how the tenor of higher education had changed in terms of the freedom of ideas. Porter had his book published with different type faces. The basic definitions and propositions were printed in the largest type. Explanatory material and illustrations of the major lines of thought were in a smaller type, and Porter's own criticisms and other "controversial material" were printed in the smallest type. Porter's *Human Intellect* was called "a 'thesaurus' on its subject, containing in outline the results of the best thinking which had been done in all ages on the human mind."[77] Porter's book was genuinely eclectic, drawing on different lines of thought as they served the topic at hand. Although a genuine conservative in philosophical matters, Porter sought to present all sides of the question at hand and to let the student decide the truth of the matter.

George Trumbull Ladd (1842–1921) was appointed Instructor in Psychology at Yale in 1881.[78] Ladd, a Congregationalist minister, was conservative in much the same way as was Porter, which may explain his selection to the post. Ladd was open minded, and as the new German psychology of Wundt became known, he steeped himself in the new experimentalism. In 1887 Ladd published his *Elements of Physiological Psychology,* based heavily on the 1880 edition of Wundt's *Grundzüge der physiologischen Psychologie.*[79] The content of Ladd's *Elements* was different from that of Wundt's *Grundzüge,* however. The subtitle of Ladd's book demonstrates this: *A Treatise on the Activities and Nature of the Mind.* Ladd, as did nearly all the writers of American psychologies, viewed mind as a set of activities and believed these activities had behind them a real unit-being, a soul. Although Ladd was dealing with the functions of mind, he was still working in the traditions of mental faculties of the soul. For a number of years, however, Ladd's book would provide the initial introduction of most American students to Wundt and experimental psychology.

In the late 1880s Ladd became Chair of Philosophy at Yale and continued to forward the new experimental psychology. In 1892 he hired Edward Scripture (1864–1943), fresh from Wundt's laboratory. Scripture then founded Yale's experimental psychology laboratory and the *Studies from the Yale Psychological Laboratory,* a house organ for the results of Yale researches. For more than a decade to follow, Yale would be a leader in the new experimental psychology in America.[80]

James McCosh of Princeton also helped usher in the epoch of the new psychology of experimentation.[81] The fact that he played this role is ironic in many ways since, more than anyone else in the late nineteenth century, he represented the old Scottish Realist philosophy. McCosh was a native Scot and was deeply committed to the Scottish School. He had been a student of Sir William Hamilton. Although a conservative in religious matters, McCosh had an open mind to matters of science and learning. He was elected President of Princeton in 1868. Although McCosh disagreed with the wide-open system of electives available at Harvard, he provided a reform of his own, similar to the "concentration and distribution" system of today.

In his own teaching on philosophical and psychological topics, McCosh held fast to the Scottish view, calling for a return to Reid's pristine view. In his *Psychology,* published in two volumes in 1886 and 1887, two years before he retired as President of Princeton, McCosh gives the last gasp of psychology as the study of soul.[82] McCosh's attempt to revive Scottish Realism simply came too late.

McCosh was open to new ideas, however, although he seems to have found it necessary to justify each new idea as really being an extension of the Scottish philosophy. He was particularly interested in the new experimental psychology. In 1882 he wrote:

Last winter in Princeton College half a dozen of the younger officers formed a club to study Wundt's work on physiological psychology, and his anatomical experiments were repeated by skillful anatomists with a well-prepared apparatus. I have sought in correspondence with one of our young professors, Dr. Osborn, to make all my students take an interest in the curious investigations which have been made by Dr. Galton of London, as to the Visualizing Faculty, as he calls it . . . and we have sent the answers to queries on to Dr. Galton.

The tendency of the day is certainly towards physiology. This should not be discouraged, but rather furthered. Physiology has already made many interesting discoveries bearing on mental action.[83]

Laboratory psychology was on its way at Princeton.

Harvard was also developing its curriculum in psychology. Francis Bowen (1811–1890) was Alford Professor of Philosophy at Harvard and was head of the Department of Philosophy in the 1870s. Bowen was a strong supporter of the views of Sir William Hamilton. Still, in the opening spirit of the era, when John Stuart Mill published his *Examination of the Philosophy of Sir William Hamilton*, a scathing analysis and attack on Hamilton, Bowen offered an elective course using Mill's book as a text.[84] Although Bowen doubtlessly used Mill's book as a foil to defend Hamilton, students had the opportunity to read the controversial work in the original and to make their own decisions.

In 1870 Chauncey Wright was able to offer a course at Harvard on the topic of psychology, although it was rather unsuccessful. Bowen's Philosophy I course was itself almost entirely psychological. In 1872 Bowen changed the title to "Psychology" and required readings in Locke's *Essay,* Cousin's *Philosophie sensualiste* and *Philosophie de Locke,* as well as Mill's *Examination of the Philosophy of Sir William Hamilton.* [85] In 1877, however, Bowen opposed William James's introduction of an elective also titled "Psychology."[86] The reason might have been that James had previously used Spencer's *Principles of Psychology* in his Natural History 2 course, "Physiological Psychology," and was viewed as a supporter of evolution. It is more likely, however, that Bowen's opposition was based on the fact that James had no formal training in philosophy but had done his undergraduate work at the Lawrence School of Science and was a medical doctor.

Whatever the basis of Bowen's objections, President Eliot overruled them, and the course was instituted in the Department of Philosophy.[87] G. Stanley Hall, who was a student at Harvard at the time, reported these developments a couple of years later. He noted that the course

was admitted not without some opposition into the department of philosophy, and is up to the present time the only course in the country where students can be made familiar with the methods and results of recent German researches in physiological psychology: the philosophical standpoint of Dr. James is essentially that of the modified new-Kantianism of Renouvier.[88]

Chapter 18 will consider William James in detail, but he is mentioned here since it is customary to date the beginning of modern psychology in America with the publication of his *Principles of Psychology* in 1890.

One other institution, Johns Hopkins University, might be mentioned here because of the activities carried out there concerning the new psychology.

G. Stanley Hall had given a series of lectures on psychology at Johns Hopkins in the fall of 1881 and was offered the position of Lecturer of Psychology and Pedagogy there. In April 1884 Hall was officially appointed to the full professorship.[89] He had spent the time after graduation from Harvard studying in Europe with Wilhelm Wundt, Ludwig, and Helmholtz. He established a laboratory at Hopkins where he reported being given a budget of $1000 a year for laboratory equipment.[90] In Hall's time at Hopkins he had students including J. McKeen Cattell, John Dewey, J. H. Donaldson, Joseph Jastrow, and E. C. Sanford.[91] Between 1882 and 1888, the spirit of the new experimental psychology was very much alive at Hopkins. In 1887 Hall began publication of the *American Journal of Psychology,* the first journal in English to be devoted to research in psychology.

The psychology course Hall taught at Hopkins "was almost entirely experimental and covered for the most part the material that Wundt had set forth in the later and larger edition of his Physiological Psychology."[92] Not all of this was Wundtian, of course. Hall, like the preexperimental psychologists before him, was eclectic, selecting the aspects of the new experimental psychology of Wundt that appealed to him and selecting, from whatever sources were at hand, other topics— such as "morbid psychology"—that were of interest to him. In many respects, Hall's course at Johns Hopkins was the experimental realization of Thomas Upham's program of 1831 at Bowdoin.

During the 1870s and 1889s the course in psychology, now most commonly offered under the name "Psychology," became standard in the curriculum of even the smallest college. In the larger colleges, entire departments were being created for philosophy, and in the 1890s the curriculum would expand sufficiently for the creation of departments of psychology. The trek to Germany for advanced training in psychology had become almost obligatory for those who could afford it.[93]

A new day was dawning for American psychology, but the psychological thought that had developed, particularly since the early eighteenth century gave a particular slant to American psychological thought. Americans showed a particular interest in the functions of mind, what mind does for us, how it helps us adapt. It was, at root, a thoroughgoing functional psychology with a tendency toward teleological explanations.

Those American students who studied in Germany in the 1880s and 1890s, particularly those with Wundt, would bring back with them the new experimental psychology. The market for these new experimental psychologists expanded in America, as did the psychology curricula in American colleges and universities. A peculiar thing happened to these experimentalists from Wundt's laboratory, however. When they left Wundt, they were often fired up with the promise of mind-as-contents, but after coming back to America they soon found themselves talking in the American terms of mind-in-use. The veneer of Wundt's content psychology was not thick enough to survive a thorough immersion in the intellectual atmosphere of America. Hardly a single American student remained faithful to the precepts of Wundtian content psychology for more than a few years. The courses they offered in their classes sounded remarkably like the subject matter of *Upham's Mental Philosophy* or Porter's *Intellectual Philosophy.* What survived the trip from Germany was the experimental methodology, not the content of Wundt's system.

The new experimental psychology was responsible for a major shift in the academic philosophy and psychology curriculum in America, but it must be emphasized that it was just a shift and not a new creation. The arrival of laboratory psychology brought about as great a change in American psychological thought as had the arrival of Locke's philosophy in the eighteenth century and Darwinian evolution in the nineteenth, but the problems of psychological investigation continued to be the same with only another switch of terms and method. The result of the merger of the experimental method of the new psychology and the functional view of mind-in-use that underlies all American psychological thought led to a characteristically American psychology in the twentieth century. This amalgam of experimental, functional psychology has continued to work its way in American psychology to the present time, adapting each new movement as it comes along, but continuing to emphasize mind-in-use (under whatever guise or rubric is acceptable at a given time) as central to psychological consideration. The next few chapters outline this process.

SUMMARY

The nearly 300 years from the founding of Harvard to the publication of William James's *Principles of Psychology* was a period of great intellectual change in America. This era of psychology in philosophy in America shared some dominant prescriptions, however. There was a domination of supernaturalism in the treatment of mind, owing largely to the concentration of ministers in the educated class and particularly as professors in the colleges and writers of books. This supernaturalism was accompanied by a strong tendency toward vitalism over mechanism. Phrenology might seem a negative example, but it was presented in America in such a way as to make it compatible with the notion of the soul. It was only at the very end of the era that naturalism and a more mechanical view gained the upper hand.

Another dominant prescription was functionalism. Americans have always been more interested in what mind does than in what mind is.

This chapter has dealt with the major movements of philosophical psychology that were either imported into America or were created there. The early influences were entirely European. In the seventeenth and well into the eighteenth centuries, American psychological thought was that of medieval European scholasticism. It was with the coming of John Locke's writings that we can date the beginning of modern psychological thought in America, although it came a generation later than in Europe. Psychological thought in the eighteenth century through the 1820s was largely imitative of European developments, with Locke and Berkeley wielding strong influence. It was in the late eighteenth and early nineteenth centuries that the Scottish philosophies came to dominate American psychological thought. At the same time, American writers began developing their own psychological thought, first as summaries of British and European thinkers, but gradually devising a genuinely eclectic philosophical psychology. By the time of the American Civil War there were many competing views of psychological thought, both home grown and imported. Perhaps the most significant influence of the latter portion of the nineteenth century was that of evolutionary theory. Gradually, by the end of the nineteenth century, the "new psychology" was introduced to America with its innovation of experimentation. All these influences led to the line of thought that would be crystalized by writers such as William James and John Dewey in the creation of American functional psychology.

NOTES

1. J. McKeen Cattell, "Psychology in America" in *Proceedings and Papers: Ninth International Congress of Psychology* (Princeton, N.J.: Psychological Review Co., 1929), p. 12.
   There are several excellent sources on early American philosophy which include much of psychological interest. See J. W. Fay, *American Psychology Before William James* (New Brunswick, N.J.: Rutgers University Press, 1939); Elizabeth Flower and Murray G. Murphey, *A History of Philosophy in America* (New York: G. P Putnam's Sons, 1977), 2 vols.; I. Woodbridge Riley, *American Philosophy: The Early Schools* (New York: Dodd, Mead and Co., 1907); and Herbert Schneider, *A History of American Philosophy* (New York: Columbia University Press, 1946; 2nd. ed., 1963). This chapter is based in part on a chapter by Rand Evans in Josef Brozek, ed., "The Origins of American Academic Psychology," *Explorations in the History of Psychology in the United States* (Lewisburg, Pa.: Bucknell University Press, 1983), pp. 17–60.
2. George P. Schmidt, *The Liberal Arts College* (New Brunswick, N.J.: Rutgers University Press, 1957), p. 4; Anonymous, *New England's First Fruits* (London: Henry Overton, 1643), reprinted in Samuel Eliot Morison, *The Founding of Harvard College* (Cambridge, Mass.: Harvard University Press, 1935), p. 432. An excellent source on scientific education in early America may be found in Theodore Hornberger, *Scientific Thought in the American Colleges: 1636–1800* (Austin: University of Texas Press, 1946), p. 23; Louis Franklin Snow, *The College Curriculum in the United States* (New York: Teachers College, Columbia University, 1907), pp. 32–34.
3. Edwin Oviatt, *The Beginnings of Yale, 1701–1726* (New Haven, Conn.: Yale University Press, 1916), pp. 298–300.
4. For a detailed treatment of Johnson's life and thought, see Joseph J. Ellis, *The New England Mind in Transition: Samuel Johnson of Connecticut, 1696–1772* (New Haven, Conn.: Yale University Press, 1973).
5. E. Flower and M. G. Murphey, *History of Philosophy in America*, Vol. 1, p. 82.
6. I. W. Riley, *American Philosophy*, p. 210.
7. J. W. Fay, *American Psychology Before William James*, p. 13.
8. L. L. Tucker, *Puritan Protagonist: President Clap of Yale College* (Raleigh: University of North Carolina Press, 1962) p. 24.
9. J. Ellis, *The New England Mind in Transition*, pp. 152–168.
10. Samuel Johnson, *Elementa Philosophica: Containing Chiefly Noetica Or Things Relating to the Mind or Understanding and Ethica or Things Relating to the Moral Behaviour* (Philadelphia: B. Franklin and D. Hall, 1752).
11. *Ibid.*, p. 66.
12. J. Ellis, *The New England Mind in Transition*, pp. 154–155.
13. For a discussion of the relationship between Edwards and Berkeley, see Flower and Murphy, *History of Philosophy in America*, p. 189.
14. Leon Howard, *"The Mind" of Jonathan Edwards: A Reconstructed Text* (Berkeley: University of California Press, 1963).
15. *Ibid.*, p. 53.

16. *Ibid.,* p. 77.
17. *Ibid.,* p. 57.
18. J. Edwards, *Will,* p. 141.
19. *Ibid.*
20. There is much more to this matter of will than this discussion would indicate. See Flower and Murphey, *History of Philosophy in America,* pp. 167–183, from which this section is drawn.
21. James G. Leyburn, *The Scotch-Irish* (Chapel Hill: University of North Carolina Press, 1962), p. 169.
22. Douglas Sloan, *The Scottish Enlightenment and the American College Ideal* (New York: Teachers College, Columbia University, 1971), pp. 129–131.
23. John Witherspoon, quoted in Fay, *American Psychology,* p. 60.
24. J. Witherspoon, quoted in Fay, *American Psychology,* p. 59.
25. Samuel Stanhope Smith, *The Lectures, Corrected and Improved, Which Have Been Delivered for a Series of Years, in the College of New Jersey; On the Subjects of Moral and Political Philosophy* (Trenton, N.J.: Daniel Fenton, 1812), p. 13.
26. Samuel Stanhope Smith, quoted in Fay, *American Psychology,* p. 62.
27. D. Sloan, *Scottish Enlightenment,* pp. 182–183.
28. Noah Porter, "Mental and Moral Science in Yale College," in William L. Kingsley, ed., *Yale College: A Sketch of Its History* (New York: Henry Holt and Co., 1879), Vol. 1, p. 389.
29. James Marsh, Letter to Samuel Taylor Coleridge, March 23, 1829, quoted in Joseph Torrey, ed., *The Remains of the Rev. James Marsh D.D.* (1843), reprinted (Port Washington, N.Y.: Kennikat Press, 1971), p. 136.
30. I. Woodbridge Riley, *American Thought* (New York: Henry Holt and Co., 1915), p. 121.
31. The quotation is from the Samuel Stanhope Smith lectures in the 1790s, quoted in Schmidt, *Old Time College President* (New York: Columbia University Press, 1930), p. 117.
32. L. Snow, *College Curriculum in the United States,* p. 125.
33. Gladys Bryson, "The Comparable Interests of the Old Moral Philosophy and the Modern Social Sciences," *Social Forces 10* (1932):20–21; "The Emergence of the Social Sciences from Moral Philosophy," *International Journal of Ethics, 42* (1932):304–323.
34. J. W. Fay, *American Psychology,* p. 196.
35. T. Upham, quoted in *ibid.,* p. 92.
36. Jacques Quen gives credit for the first abnormal text to Isaac Ray, whose *A Treatise on the Judicial Jurisprudence of Insanity* appeared in 1838. See Quen, "Isaac Ray and His 'Remarks on Pathological Anatomy,'" *Bulletin of the History of Medicine, 38* (1964):113.
37. Mark Hopkins, *Lectures on Moral Science* (Boston: Gould and Lincoln, 1870), pp. 79–80.
38. J. Torrey, *The Remains of the Rev. James Marsh,* pp. 91–92, 103.
39. Letter, Marsh to Coleridge, in Torrey, *Remains,* p. 137.
40. See Torrey, *Remains,* pp. 239–367 for Marsh's lectures on psychology.
41. John Dewey, "James Marsh and American Philosophy," *Journal of the History of Ideas, 2* (1941):131–150.
42. H.J.B. Zigler, *Friedrich Augustus Rauch: American Hegelian* (Lancaster, Pa.: Franklin and Marshall, 1953). The author thanks Mr. David Lewis, Reference Librarian at Franklin and Marshall College, for materials on Rauch.
43. R. C. Davis, "American Psychology, 1800–1885," *Psychological Review, 43*

(1936):479–480. Gabriel Darrow Ofiesh, "The History, Development, Present Status, and Purpose of the First (Introductory) Course in Psychology in American Undergraduate Education," Ed.D. Dissertation, University of Denver, 1959, pp. 124–125.

44. Friedrich Augustus Rauch, *Psychology; or, a View of the Human Soul; Including Anthropology* (New York: M. W. Dodd, 1840).

45. J. W. Fay, *American Psychology*, p. 114.

46. *Catalogue of the Officers and Students in Marshall College*, 1839–1840, p. 13; 1840–1841, p. 19.

47. Herbert W. Schneider, *A History of American Philosophy*, 2nd ed. (New York: Columbia University Press, 1969), p. 379.

48. Laurens P. Hickok, quoted in Fay, *American Psychology*, p. 121.

49. H. Schneider, *History of American Philosophy*, p. 384.

50. Octavius Brooks Frothingham, *Transcendentalism in New England* (New York: G. P. Putnam's Sons, 1876), pp. 116–117.

51. Grant Overton, *Portrait of a Publisher and the First Hundred Years of the House of Appleton: 1825–1925* (New York: D. Appleton and Co., 1925), p. 46.

52. Flower and Murphey, *History of Philosophy in America*, pp. 517–528; see also Edward Lurie, *Louis Agassiz: A Life in Science* (Chicago: University of Chicago Press, 1960).

53. G. Overton, *Portrait of a Publisher*, pp. 48–51; Donald Fleming, "Social Darwinism," in Arthur Schlesinger, Jr., and Morton White, eds., *Paths of American Thought* (Boston: Houghton Mifflin Co., 1963), pp. 123–146.

54. E. Flower and M. G. Murphey, *History of Philosophy in America*, p. 534.

55. Herbert Schneider, *A History of American Philosophy*, 2nd ed. (New York: Columbia University Press, 1963), pp. 293–294.

56. Edward H. Madden, *Chauncey Wright and the Foundations of Pragmatism* (Seattle: University of Washington Press, 1963).

57. *Ibid.*, p. 5. The remainder of this biographical section on Wright is drawn largely from Madden.

58. *Ibid.*, pp. 25–26.

59. *Ibid.*, p. 74.

60. Chauncey Wright, "The Evolution of Self-Consciousness," *North American Review* (April 1873), republished in Charles Eliot Norton, ed., *Philosophical Discussions by Chauncey Wright* (New York: Henry Holt and Co., 1877), pp. 199–266.

61. Other aspects of Wright's article are ably summarized by Madden in "Chauncey Wright's Functionalism," *Journal of the History of the Behavioral Sciences*, *10* (1974):281–290.

62. *Ibid.*, p. 284.

63. C. Wright, "Evolution of Self-Consciousness," *Philosophical Discussions*, p. 218.

64. *Ibid.*, p. 221.

65. For an excellent survey of phrenology in America, see John D. Davies, *Phrenology, Fad and Science: A 19th-Century American Crusade* (New Haven, Conn.: Yale University Press, 1955).

66. Anthony A. Walsh, "The American Tour of Dr. Spurzheim," *Journal of the History of Medicine and Allied Sciences*, *27* (1972):188.

67. *Ibid.*

68. George Combe, *Notes on the United States of North America During a Phrenological visit in 1838–1840.* (Philadelphia, 1841), Vol. 1, p. 188. Cited in Walsh, "American Tour."

69. Charles Caldwell, *Elements of Phrenology* (Lexington, Ky., 1824).

70. For a detailed description of Spurzheim's last days in Boston, see Nahum Capen, *Remi-*

niscences of Dr. Spurzheim and George Combe. . . . (New York: Fowler and Wells Co., 1881).

71. N. Capen, *Reminiscences,* p. 122.

72. J. Davies, *Phrenology, Fad and Science,* p. 32.

73. Nelson Sizer and H. S. Drayton, *Heads and Faces: How to Study Them* (New York: Fowler and Wells Co., 1887), p. 16.

74. *American Journal of Insanity,* 1, 1844–1845, p. 105, cited in Davies, *Phrenology,* p. 93.

75. Davies, *Phrenology,* p. 93.

76. *Ibid.,* p. 95.

77. George M. Duncan, "Dr. Porter as a Philosopher," in George S. Merriam, *Noah Porter: A Memorial by Friends* (New York: Charles Scribner's Sons, 1893), pp. 94–98.

78. An excellent source for information on Ladd is Eugene S. Mills, *George Trumbull Ladd: Pioneer American Psychologist* (Cleveland: Case Western Reserve, 1969).

79. George Trumbull Ladd, *Elements of Physiological Psychology: A Treatise on the Activities and Nature of the Mind* (New York: Charles Scribner's Sons, 1887).

80. George Wilson Pierson, *Yale College: An Educational History 1871–1921* (New Haven, Conn.: Yale University Press, 1952 pp. 147–149.

81. See William Milligan Sloane, *The Life of James McCosh* (New York: Charles Scribner's Sons, 1896) for more details on McCosh's life and work.

82. J. McCosh, *Psychology, The Cognitive Powers* (New York: Scribner, 1886); *Psychology, The Motive Powers* (New York: Scribner, 1887). McCosh had an extensive bibliography including many books on psychological matters not mentioned here. See Sloane, *Life of James McCosh,* pp. 269–282.

83. J. McCosh, "The Scottish Philosophy as Contrasted with the German," *Princeton Review, 10* (1882):334.

84. Bruce Kuklick, *The Rise of American Philosophy: Cambridge, Massachusetts 1860–1930* (New Haven, Conn.: Yale University Press, 1977), p. 120.

85. Robert S. Harper, "The Laboratory of William James," *Harvard Alumni Bulletin, 52* (1949):169.

86. This was not the first of James's courses on psychological topics at Harvard, however. James first offered his course on physiological psychology in the graduate curriculum in 1875, titled "The Relations Between Physiology and Psychology" and included a demonstrational laboratory. In 1876 the course was offered for undergraduates under the title "Physiological Psychology." All this was in the Department of Natural History, however. The "Psychology" of 1877 was the first of James's offerings in the philosophy curriculum.

87. B. Kuklick, *Rise of American Philosphy,* p. 135. Kuklick incorrectly states that James used Spencer's *Principles of Psychology* as the text in his Philosophy 4 course, "Psychology." He used Taine's *On Intelligence.* This is a commonly stated error, most likely derived from a misreading of Ralph Barton Perry, *The Thought and Character of William James* (Boston: Little, Brown and Co., 1935) Vol. 1, pp. 475–476.

88. G. Stanley Hall, "Philosophy in the United States," *Mind 6* (1879):97.

89. Dorothy Ross, G. *Stanley Hall: The Psychologist as Prophet* (Chicago: University of Chicago Press, 1972), p. 136.

90. Hall, *Life and Confessions,* p. 227.

91. Ibid., p. 232.

92. Ibid., p. 234.

93. Hall, "Philosophy in the United States," p. 104.

Top: William James. *Bottom:* G. Stanley Hall.

Chapter 18

William James and G. Stanley Hall: The Founding of Scientific Psychology in the United States

*I*t is always dangerous to talk of founders. It is the oversimplification of the great man theory of history. American scientific psychology came about in the way it did through the actions of numerous people in their individual and institutional capacities. Still, it is worthwhile to consider in some detail a few of the major figures about whom much of this activity centered. William James (1842–1910) and Granville Stanley Hall (1844–1924) were two such figures.

One could hardly find two more different individuals. William James was a mercurial individual, defying labels. He was as organizationally naive as he was interpersonally magnetic. He was constantly looking for the possibilities in things and constantly being disappointed at the realities behind those possibilities. He was a man of great ideas, though often uninterested as to how those ideas related one to another. James founded no system of psychology, although his ideas influenced the systems that were established during his lifetime. He drew his inspiration not from one individual or even from one movement, but from a combination of sources and in a fashion that made it self-initiated. He knew of the developments in German experimental psychology; he assimilated some aspects, rejected others, but was guided by none. He showed similar independence regarding British associationism and French psychopathology. Nevertheless, William James was and is considered the first great psychologist in the United States and father of scientific psychology here.

G. Stanley Hall was predictably unpredictable. He was given to great enthusiasms and could easily be labeled in any one of them. He was an excellent organizer but fell into serious interpersonal blunders that would often negate all his careful organizing. He was very interested in the ways his ideas fit in the scheme of things but rarely carried his ideas and innovations beyond their initial stages. Hall consciously wanted to be the leader of American scientific psychology and felt great competitiveness with James for that position. He gave great support to the laboratory and the new scientific psychology, and he did everything a founder would be expected to do. He founded the major journal in the field, as well as the national professional organization, and directed a major laboratory-oriented graduate program, just to name a few. Still, he is rarely discussed today and almost never as the founder of American scientific psychology. The reason why says a great deal about the early days of scientific psychology in America and will be considered later in this chapter. First, however, we need to consider the changes in American higher education that made much of what James and Hall were to do possible.

INFLUENCE OF THE GERMAN UNIVERSITY SYSTEM

In the United States between 1880 and 1895, psychology was transformed in a dramatic fashion.[1] By 1895 there were twenty-four psychology laboratories, three journals, and a flourishing scientific society, many of whose members were full-time psychologists. Only fifteen years before, none of this had existed. The new psychology had obviously arrived. The antecedents for these sweeping changes were to be found largely in the American system of higher education as was discussed in the last chapter. Another significant change had to do with the development of graduate education in the American university system. This development was greatly influenced by German graduate education.

Before the 1870s there was virtually no graduate education in the American college with the exceptions of medicine and law. The establishment of scientific schools, beginning with those at Rensselaer, Yale, and Harvard, helped to break this exclusion, although these schools were isolated within their colleges. From well before the American Civil War, students had begun going to Europe and particularly Germany for their graduate training.[2] Even in 1880 there were about as many American graduate students abroad as there were in all the graduate programs in the United States.

The German universities were dominated by the idea of research. The professor had a considerable amount of freedom to work on problems of his own choosing. Within the limits of his field, he could choose to teach what he wished. The student was also free to study what and when he chose. Largely because of the effectiveness of their research, the German universities were the scientific centers of the world.

After the Civil War, a strong movement sprang up to extend the scope and improve the quality of university education in America. Three college presidents in the forefront of this movement were Charles Eliot of Harvard (despite his bias against research), Andrew White of Cornell, and Daniel C. Gilman of Johns Hopkins; all were influenced by the German university system in the changes they introduced at their respective institutions. These three schools will figure prominently in the account that follows. In addition, Clark University, whose first president was G. Stanley Hall, was initially founded as a graduate-only institution and was avowedly modeled on European graduate schools. Stanford University and the University of Chicago were also to come into prominence as examples of the new trend. Meanwhile, a gradual reform and reorganization of the so-called graduate schools already in operation was taking place at such universities as Harvard, Yale, and Princeton. These older schools had suffered losses of students, prestige, and the services of some of their able professors to the new graduate schools.

As we saw in the last chapter, reform began by replacing the fixed curriculum with an elective system. This resulted in an increase not only in the number of courses, but also in the number of departments. Most important of all was the establishment of graduate schools to take the place of the fifth year in residence that had previously led to the M.A. degree. Johns Hopkins, which began as a graduate school in 1876, was the leader in this field; it required an independent research project from each student.

In these changes psychology occupied a favored and strategic position. It was one of the new subjects introduced into colleges and universities from the German system.

As F. M. Albrecht reminds us, the last decade of the nineteenth century was a time of preparation; actual scientific advances came later.[3] Two individuals who helped psychology in America take its initial steps as a scientific rather than a philosophical enterprise were William James and Granville Stanley Hall. Both were transitional figures, moving psychology from what it once was, but not far enough to join what the field became, even in their own lifetimes.

WILLIAM JAMES

William James is certainly the most famous of America's philosopher–psychologists. His most famous work, *The Principles of Psychology*, wrought a fundamental change in the way psychology was approached in America, a transition between the mind-as-soul psychologies of the nineteenth century and the naturalistic, mind-as-experience psychologies of the early twentieth century.

Life and Interests

William James was born into wealth and privilege in New York City in January 1842.[4] Fourteen months later, his brother Henry was born, also in New York City. Their father Henry, Sr., devoted himself enthusiastically to their education. He alternated between rushing them off to Europe because of his conviction about the "narrowness" of American schools and bringing them home because of an equally strong feeling that his children should be with their own kind. Extensive travel and sporadic schooling in the United States, England, France, Switzerland, and Germany followed for William and Henry and their younger brothers and sisters. They studied with tutors and in various kinds of schools, learning even more from the galleries, museums, and theaters they visited. Unlike the rigors that faced John Stuart Mill in having his education supervised by his father, they had a delightful, unsettling time with their kindly and enthusiastic father.

As befitted their very different personalities, Henry and William later disagreed flatly on the value of their schooling. William regretted its lack of discipline; he believed it had prevented him from developing an ability for orderly reasoning. Henry found it invaluable in stirring the free play of curiosity.

Following the advice of his father who insisted that a hasty decision of one's life work would be wrong and "narrowing," William took years to decide on the work for which he was most fitted. He tried painting; after six months at the studio of William Morris Hunt in Newport, Rhode Island, he quickly realized his lack of professional promise.

In the autumn of 1861, at the age of nineteen, William enrolled at the Lawrence Scientific School of Harvard University. By now his choice of a career had been narrowed down to the sciences and philosophy. Despite his interest in chemistry, on which he concentrated first, William's teachers observed an impatience that drove him away from accurate and painstaking laboratory determination. This was prophetic of his distaste for such work throughout his life. He soon left chemistry for physiology, anatomy, and biology and enrolled in the medical school, even though he was already convinced that medical practice held no attraction for him.

In 1865 James accompanied Louis Agassiz, that staunch opponent of Darwinism, to the Amazon as the start of a possible career in biology, but he soon found that he hated collecting. On his return he resumed his medical studies, interrupting them again to go abroad for two years, because he felt he did not have the stamina to continue the arduous work. Indecision about a career was now complicated by a neurotic depression with insomnia, eye trouble, digestive disorders, very severe back pain, and other symptoms. These symptoms lasted nearly five years. There was even some preoccupation with thoughts of suicide, but he managed to put them aside. He wrote home to his father in a carefully restrained fashion that "thoughts of the pistol, the dagger, and the bowl began to usurp an unduly large part of my attention; and I began to think that some change . . . was necessary."[5] During this trip abroad he mentioned in a letter to a friend that he considered the time had come for psychology to be a science and that he had decided to do some work in it.[6] He also mentioned plans to go to Heidelberg to work with Helmholtz and Wundt, but, whatever the reason, he was to catch only a glimpse of them. His knowledge of their work attests to his general alertness to contemporary developments in psychology. This was in 1868, only eight years after Fechner's *Elements* had appeared.

In 1869 he returned to the United States to take his medical degree. It was obvious to William, to his friends, and to his family that he could not practice, since his back pain precluded standing for long hours. Laboratory work also was out of the question. That summer he resolved to continue to work in "psychological subjects."[7]

A philosophical crisis preceded the beginning of a partial recovery from his various ills. Feeling lost and alone, on occasion becoming panic-stricken in a world that seemed filled with evil, James read the evolutionary philosophy of Renouvier's *Second Essay*,[8] which persuaded him that there was freedom of the will and that spontaneity is available to him who makes it so. James resolved that his "first act of free will shall be to believe in free will."[9] This apparently delivered him from the clutches of the strict determinism of Mill, Spencer, and Bain and opened up the way to his becoming a philosophical psychologist. Perhaps next to his father, Renouvier was the single most significant influence on James's philosophical thought. Gerald Myers tells us that "James discovered in Renouvier a systematic outlook which contained practical guidelines for conduct—exactly what he wanted and needed in his own philosophy. Renouvier connected elements of pluralism, moralism, phenomenalism, fideism, and theism in a way that appealed to James."[10]

In 1872 James accepted an offer from President Eliot to teach physiology at Harvard. By this time a gradual recovery of his health was taking place. In 1875 James gave his first course in psychology—on the relation between physiology and psychology. He thus moved closer to his now established goal. James never had instruction in psychology. As he put it, the first lecture he ever heard, he gave himself.

James founded a psychological laboratory of sorts at Harvard in 1875. In retrospect, he himself was not sure whether it was 1874, 1875, or 1876, but the evidence found by R. S. Harper in the references cited[11] shows it was in 1875. One especially compelling item that Harper mentions is the report of the Harvard treasurer of that year, which cites an appropriation to James of $300, for use in physiology. Other evidence, including the nature of the 1875 course mentioned earlier, shows that the appropriation was for equipment for physiological psychology. The laboratory was located at Lawrence Hall. In 1876 James was advanced to Assistant Professor of Physiology. G. Stanley Hall, about whom we will be hearing presently, arrived as a student in that same year and took his degree in 1878, although he did his work not in James's laboratory but in Henry Bowditch's physiological laboratory.

The year 1878 was notable for two events. First, James married Alice Gibbens, a Boston schoolteacher. She shared his interests and watched over him with untiring devotion. She, and marriage itself, introduced a certain amount of organization into his life that had not been present before. Sensitive and nervous as he was, however, it is hardly surprising that the five children that were born over the next several years occasionally got on his nerves. Moreover, the financial strain of a growing family led James to write a considerable number of popular articles and to give many lectures for the sake of the financial return they brought. The second event of 1878 was his signing of a contract with the publisher Henry Holt for a volume on psychology. John Fiske (1842–1901), a follower of Spencer and a member, along with James, of the Metaphysics Club, had originally been approached to do the book but suggested James instead.[12] At the time James apologized to his publisher that he would have to take two years in which to write it.[13] He actually took twelve! The volume would become James's *Principles of Psychology* about which we will have more to say later.

In 1880 James was made Assistant Professor of Philosophy at Harvard, a department where psychology more properly belonged. He was admitted to the department but "not without opposition."[14] The thought of a physiologist teaching psychology infuriated some members of the department, who were quite content with the accustomed traditional philosophical treatment of that subject. Despite the lack of a major publication, James was advanced to Professor of Philosophy in 1885, and in 1889 his title was changed to Professor of Psychology.

James's book was growing in connection with his classroom teaching. In the classroom, as in his writing and conversation with friends, James was charming; his presentation of his material was without obvious order. He was vivacious, so full of humor that one of his students interrupted him one day with the remark, "To be serious for a moment."[15] His picturesque language and vivid imagery were such that his students remembered them long after the more methodical lectures of others had been forgotten.

Although it took twelve years for the *Principles* to appear as a whole, numerous chapters were published earlier as articles in journals and magazines of the day, which only increased the anticipation of his readers for the big book. In 1890 *The Principles of Psychology* finally appeared. James was scarcely original throughout, but the brilliance of his writing gave new life to old themes. The reviews hailed the book as an important contribution; it was a pronounced success. An observation made some years ago remains true; it is still read by persons who have no obligation to do so.[16] The criticisms offered tended to center on its "unsystematic" or "impressionistic" character. To call the *Principles* unsystematic does not mean that it is disorganized. In fact, it would sometimes appear that what was meant by this charge is that James did not follow the conventional ordering of topics. James believed that the proper starting point is experience as immediately given and as it flows in perception. Hence, unlike others before and after him, he did not start with sensations, for he believed that is not the way in which we experience.

Two years after *Principles*, James published *Psychology: Briefer Course*,[17] a condensation explicitly designed to serve as a textbook and to make both him and his publisher money.[18] For many years "Jimmy"—as the book became known in order to distinguish it from its parent—was used as a textbook, for it eliminated many of the digressions of the portlier "James."

Laboratory work was more of a symbol and never a habit with James, despite the rooms used for equipment when he was in the Department of Physiology and his mention of spending two hours a day in the psychophysics laboratory that he started in 1885.[19] Both in the *Principles* and in other writings James took a disparaging view of laboratory psychology. In 1894 he commented that the United States was overstocked with laboratories.[20] In the *Principles* James offered the opinion that the results of laboratory investigation were not yet commensurate with the labor involved. In another well-known passage, he remarked that the psychophysical methods "could hardly have arisen in a country where natives could be bored."[21] Elsewhere he said that "brass-instrument and algebraic-formula psychology fills me with horror."[22] In view of his attitude, it is not surprising that, except for a study on the transfer of training, he did not contribute experimental results of any importance.

James recognized that laboratory work was useful for psychology, but he wanted to be relieved of responsibility for it. In 1890 he succeeded in raising $4000 for a psychology laboratory.[23] The laboratory opened up the following year in Dane Hall. Herbert Nichols (1852–1936), who had recently received his doctorate from G. Stanley Hall, was hired to run the laboratory, at least until a permanent director could be found. James, impressed by the work of Hugo Münsterberg at the University of Freiburg, recommended that Münsterberg be offered the directorship of the new Harvard laboratory. The offer was made, Münsterberg accepted it, and the German assumed his new post in 1892. Unfortunately, Münsterberg never became for Harvard the leader in experimental psychology that James had hoped he would be.

James trained a surprisingly small number of psychologists and supervised the completion of few doctoral dissertations in psychology. Hall had worked with him in 1876–1878. From about 1890 onward he had some students who became psychologists, including James R. Angell, Mary W. Calkins, William Healy, Edward L. Thorndike, and Robert S. Woodworth. Their number may have been small, but all of them went on to achieve considerable prominence.

James's interests wandered far beyond the confines of laboratory psychology, or even most philosophical psychologies. He grew up in an atmosphere of liberalism; topics such as abolition, homeopathy, and women's rights were freely and eagerly discussed, and often championed. With the combination of his liberal upbringing and his father's devotion to the teachings of Swedenborg, which formed part of his son's experience, it is no wonder that James expressed a kindred interest in spiritualism. He approached with an open mind such matters as mediumship, clairvoyance, and so-called automatic writing carried on without the conscious cooperation of the subject. In the same spirit, he came to the defense of the mental healers who were being attacked by the medical profession. In 1882–1883 James met the Englishmen who were the founders of the new Society for Psychical Research, and when their friendship ripened, their cause became his. He was an eager student; he attended many seances, carried on an extensive correspondence, and published his findings. As usual, facts were what he wanted. He was interested not only in the problem of survival after death, but also in psychic phenomena and the continuity they formed with those of hypnotism, hysteria, and multiple personality.

In the 1890s James came to be recognized as America's leading philosopher. His later work, after the turn of the century, on pragmatism and radical empiricism represented his major philosophical contribution. The central theme of pragmatism is that the value of ideas must be tested by their practical consequences. Contrary to what was generally supposed, beliefs do not work because they are true; they are true because they work. This ambiguous usage of "work" was open to various criticisms that were not long in coming. Despite them, pragmatism was a popular success. These developments after 1900, however, had less of an impact on the development of psychology than did the James of the *Principles of Psychology*.

In 1909 G. Stanley Hall, President of Clark University, invited Sigmund Freud as one of many distinguished figures to a celebration in Worchester. James attended and naturally met Freud. James already believed, of course, in the existence of a mental life of which the individual himself is not fully aware. Earlier, he had praised F.W.H. Myer's view of extramarginal consciousness as the most important advance since he (James) had begun the study of psychology.[24] The existence of mental events outside of awareness was a very intriguing fact to James, since it seemed to be such an unexpected peculiarity of human nature. There is, however, a tremendous gulf between Myer's subliminal consciousness and Freud's unconscious. Myer and others of similar interests were looking for subconscious feats; Freud was searching for unconscious motives. In keeping with his openmindedness and his desire to give everyone a hearing, James expressed the hope that Freud would push his ideas to their utmost limit, though he added that Freud impressed him as a man with fixed ideas and that he could make nothing of his dream symbolism.[25]

After talking about retiring for years, James finally did so in 1907. While intellectually vital and active, his health continued to decline. For the sake of his health, James went to Europe in the spring of 1910, but he did not slow down his pace sufficiently to reap any benefit. Despairing of any relief, he turned homeward to die two days after his return, late in August 1910, at his country home near Mount Chocorua, New Hampshire.

William James is not remembered because of any organizational skill for psychology, for his founding of anything (with the possible exception of his informal laboratory at Harvard), or for his promotion of the field of psychology. Rather, his great fame rests on his ideas and on the possibilities they presented and for the magnificent way he expressed them. Those ideas, communicated through his *Principles of Psychology*, had he done nothing else, would have given James a major place in the history of American psychology.

James's Principles of Psychology

James's *Principles* with all its ideas and beautiful prose is often a source of frustration to present-day readers, particularly if they pick a chapter here and there to read without seeing the individual chapters in the context of the whole work. Even so, one hears the complaint that James seems to contradict himself. To some degree this is true. James wrote his book over twelve years and sometimes changed his mind on some issues later in the book without bothering to revise some positions at the beginning. However, what often seems to be contradiction is not so at all, but is the result of reading a fragment of James's writing out of context. When we read the chapters in order, we can see more clearly what James was doing.

First, it is important to understand that James was writing a nonmetaphysical psychology. This "naturalizing" of psychology was a bold move on James's part. James wrote of his decision to take the naturalistic approach in the *Principles:*

> I thought that by frankly putting psychology in the position of a natural science, eliminating certain metaphysical questions from its scope altogether, and confining myself to what could be immediately verified by everyone's own consciousness, a central mass of experience could be described which everyone might accept as certain no matter what the differing ulterior philosophic interpretations of it might be.[26]

James was attempting to eliminate several "metaphysical questions," but two in particular are of importance to the present discussion.[27] The first was faculty psychology, which was still dominant in American popular thought. It dealt with the mind as though it were a real unit-being, a soul, whose actions were its faculties. For the average American faculty psychology was perhaps still the dominant view of mind. James produced the first successful secular psychology in America, a psychology in which the thought itself becomes the thinker.

The second position James termed "metaphysical" was that of the atomistic and associationistic psychologies, represented by the British empiricists from John Locke to the Mills and by the followers of Herbart on the Continent. Also included were those who followed the experimental psychology of Wilhelm Wundt. To James, the elemental "ideas" of the associationists and the elementary sensations of Wundt's psychology, along with their concepts of productive synthesis, were no less metaphysical than the "mythological" faculties of the Scottish faculty psychologists or of Descartes' soul. James criticized the current elementistic psychologies as follows:

> Most books start with sensations, as the simplest mental facts, and proceed synthetically, constructing each higher stage from those below it. But this is abandoning the empirical method of investigation. No one ever had a simple sensation by itself. Consciousness from our natal day, is of a teeming multiplicity of objects and relations, and what we call simple sensations are results of discriminative attention, pushed often to a very high degree.[28]

James carried out his plan in the first ten chapters of the *Principles.* He took what he called a positivistic stand, although it should not be identified with the views of either Comte or Mach. He appears to be using the term more generically as dealing with direct experience rather than with interpretation.

James's attacks in those first chapters were much bolder against the elementistic psychologies than the faculty psychologies. Throughout he appealed to his readers' own experiences. He comes to the position that the most basic experience is not sensation but thinking itself:

> All people unhesitatingly believe that they feel themselves thinking, and that they distinguish the mental state as an inward activity or passion, from all the objects with which it may cognitively deal. I regard this belief as the most fundamental of all the postulates of psychology.[29]

He concluded that "the universal conscious fact is not 'feelings and thoughts exist,' but 'I think' and 'I feel.' No psychology . . . can question the existence of personal selves." It is through this reliance on universal experience that James comes to the "cogito" of Descartes' famous dictum. Each person's own thought is the most basic fact of his or her mental life. James adds to these universal facts another: that consciousness does not present itself to us as elementary components but as a unitary flow. James concludes: "Consciousness . . . does not appear to itself chopped up in bits. Such words as 'chain' or 'train' do not describe it fitly as it presents itself in the first instance. It is nothing jointed; it flows."[30]

Thought, then, as it presents itself to us, is the starting point for James's psychology. He urged psychologists to accept this irreducible, unitary, and personal thought as "their ultimate datum on the mental side." James came this far with no metaphysical assumptions and no concepts but those directly observable in experience. He avoided all the problems surrounding the origin of thought. The associationists' theory of ideas as well as the constructionists' (such as J. S. Mill and Wilhelm Wundt) productive consciousness or creative synthesis became irrelevant for James's psychology.

The concept of the unitary nature of thought, once accepted, leads to another, the "stream of thought." Acceptance of the stream of thought, the correlation between brain action and thought, and the personal nature of thought all lead to James's presentation of the self and to the conclusion he had been working toward all along: that the thought itself is the thinker and that accessory concepts such as soul or faculties of soul are unnecessary for psychology.

The Stream of Thought

James demonstrated early in the *Principles* that thought is not a sensation, a collection of sensations, or an integration of ideas. Thought is an "undecomposable" whole, he claims, and no matter how complex the object of that thought may be, the thought is "one undivided state of consciousness."[31] These two aspects of thought, its personal nature and its undivided state, are of great importance to his psychology and are major bases on which rest the remainder of his psychological views in the *Principles*.

James's method led him to assume a dualism of thought and object in the *Principles*, although he later deserted this position in his pragmatism.[32] In his dualism, thoughts, according to James, deal with objects—which may be of external origin or which may be other thoughts. He relegates the question of the genesis and constitution of thoughts to metaphysics, with one exception. Thoughts, however they come, are related to brain action. James, in typical style, cuts through the details of the mind–body problem and states in simple terms: "[The] bald fact is that when the brain acts, a thought occurs."[33] He had prepared his readers for the intimacy of brain and thought in the first pages of the *Principles*. If thought is the starting point on the mental side of existence, then "definitely to ascertain the correlations of these with brain-processes is as much as psychology can empirically do."[34] The empirical connection of the processes of brain action with thought is, to James, the "ultimate known law." James uses the continuous nature of brain changes to support his contention of the unity and continuity of thought processes: "As the brain-changes are continuous, so do all these consciousness melt into each other like dissolving views. Properly they are but one protracted consciousness, one unbroken stream."[35]

James describes the nature of thought as having five characteristics:

> 1) Every thought tends to be part of a personal consciousness. 2) Within each personal consciousness thought is always changing. 3) Within each personal consciousness thought is sensibly continuous. 4) It always appears to deal with objects independent of itself. 5) It is interested in some parts of these objects to the exclusion of other, and welcomes or rejects—chooses from among them, in a word—all the while.[36]

His emphasis on the personal nature of thought is clear, since "personal consciousness" is repeated in the first three of the five characteristics.

The second and third characteristics summarize aspects of James's unitary conception of thought. James portrayed the process of thought as a flow: "A 'river' or a 'stream' are the metaphors by which it is most naturally described. In talking of it hereafter, let us call it the stream of thought, of consciousness, or of subjective life."[37] James uses the terms *thought, consciousness,* and *subjective life* interchangeably.

Although he once denied it, the stream of thought metaphor is at the heart of the psychology of James's *Principles.* [38] He even defined psychology as "an account of particular finite streams of thought, coexisting and succeeding in time."

It is within the context of the stream of thought that James differentiates between bare experience and its meaning, "acquaintance-with" and "knowledge-about." It is also in the stream metaphor that James describes the process by which thoughts come into being, rise, and pass away. Thoughts "pass," that is, they have a definite lifetime. As one thought "pulse" dies out, it is appropriated by a new one on the rise, becoming "known" by the new thought pulse. Thought is a continuously renewing process—a necessity, if mental life is to be sensibly continuous—and an essential concept as well for a naturalistic consideration of self as a process of thought rather than as an attribute of spiritual faculty.

The fourth characteristic, that thought appears to deal with objects independent of itself, is also important for a naturalistic self. James postulates a dualistic position, supposing two aspects, "mind knowing and the thing known and treats them as irreducible."[39] Within this dualism, however, the dividing line between object and subject is not always clear. According to James, "thought may but need not, in knowing, discriminate between its object and itself."[40] The confusion between the object of the thought and the thought itself leads at times to the inclusion of external objects as part of one's thought and thus of one's self. This we will see again below in the section on self.

Self

The fifth characteristic of thought, that thought is interested in some objects of experience more than in others and selects among them, is at the basis of James's views on attention, reasoning, will, and ultimately on self. Interest determines which parts of experience are noticed. According to James, "A man's empirical thought depends on the things he has experienced, but what these shall be is to a large extent determined by his habits of attention. . . . A thing may be present to him a thousand times, but if he persistenly fails to notice it, it cannot be said to enter into his experience.'' The stream of thought is neither entirely free nor consistently flowing. Its tributaries are controlled by the nature of interest, which is another essential process for James's naturalistic view of self. James wrote about this great division of our personal worlds into ''me'' and ''not me.''

> The altogether unique kind of interest which each human mind feels in those parts of creation which it can call me or mine may be a moral riddle, but it is a fundamental psychological fact. No man can take the same interest in his neighbor's me as in his own. The neighbor's me falls together with all the rest of things in one foreign mass, against which his own me stands out in startling relief.[41]

In the tenth chapter of the *Principles,* ''The Consciousness of Self,'' James brings together the various conceptions he has built up in the earlier chapters, in particular those relating to the stream of thought. He begins with a definition of the ''Empirical Self or Me,'' a definition clearly derived from his conclusions concerning the dividing line between object and subject. James tells us that: ''In its widest possible sense . . . a man's Self is the sum total of all that he CAN call his, not only his body and his psychic powers, but his clothes and his house, his wife and children, his ancestors and friends, his reputation and works, his lands and horses, and yacht and bank account. All these things give him the same emotions.''[42] Self is a process of thought developed in the context of the stream of thought.

The Soul

James then moves to the question that he has been leading to through the previous nine chapters, but that he had ''always shied from and treated as a difficulty to be postponed.''[43] That question pertains to the ''pure Ego,'' the substantial soul, its nature and role in psychological processes. James considers three theories of the ego in detail—the spiritualist theory, the associationist theory, and the transcendental-ist theory. He concludes that the substantial soul is unnecessary for ''expressing the actual subjective phenomena of consciousness as they appear.''[44]

James's reader has been prepared for this position in the earlier chapter. The replacement for the soul in this case has been the ''supposition of a stream of thoughts, each substantially different from the rest, but cognitive of the rest and 'appropriative' of each other's content.''[45]

At this point James admits that if his reader does not accept his point of view by now, his arguments will never carry conviction. He charges that the substantial soul is a metaphysical concept unnecessary in psychological considerations: ''As psychologists, we need not be metaphysical at all. The phenomena are enough, the passing Thought itself is the only verifiable thinker, and its empirical connection with the brain-process is the ultimate known law.''[46] James tells his readers, ''I therefore feel entirely free to discard the word Soul from the rest of this book. If I ever use it, it will be in the vaguest and most popular way.''[47]

It should be noted that James does not attempt to undermine the ideas of readers who wish to hold on to some aspect of soul-theory outside of scientific psychology. "The reader who finds any comfort in the idea of the Soul, is . . . perfectly free to continue to believe in it; for our reasonings have not established the non-existence of the Soul; they have only provided its superfluity for scientific purposes."[48]

If James's reader is in substantial agreement with his position, then he or she is open to James's ideas for the remainder of the book. With such an acceptance James may now present the wide vista of mental life that earlier textbooks would have treated either in terms of the faculties of a substantial soul or in associationistic or transcendental terms. Through James's eyes, however, the topics take on an entirely different appearance. Faculty classifications such as attention, conception, comparison, memory, imagination, and the like are now treated objectively as derived from the stream of thought.

For all practical purposes, James's *Principles* called an end to the era of faculty psychologies and of psychologies that rest on the assumption of the substantial soul. No major psychological work that followed James made use of the substantial soul as a psychological concept.

James's naturalistic view of mind was, as E. L. Thorndike recalled, "news, and good news, to young students of psychology in the nineties and attracted to the further study of psychology some who would have avoided it like the plague if they had been introduced to it by Porter or McCosh or even by Ladd or Baldwin."[49]

James established a naturalistic psychology but one that did not require the analysis of the mental states into atomistic units such as elements. His holistic and phenomenalistic approach was the fundamental base on which American functionalism would be built.

Methods of Investigation

In terms of methodology, James expressed the belief that introspective observation must be relied on "first and foremost and always." James's meaning of "introspection" should not be confused with the analytical introspection of Wundt, which was later brought to such a high state of development by E. B. Titchener at Cornell. James's introspection was "the looking into our own minds and reporting what we there discover."[50] Introspection to James was the description of common universal experience. What Wundt and particularly Titchener did was to analyze this complex common experience into microscopic parts. James considered this kind of analytical introspection to be based on abstractions, the result of discriminative attention. James's introspective method was a form of phenomenological description. It did not involve analysis but described experience as it appeared, phenomenally, in all its complexity and without theoretical presuppositions. In addition, James's introspection was not necessarily the introspection of the laboratory. It was the empirical introspection of the philosopher, what later laboratory psychologists would call "armchair psychology."

Although James appreciated the primacy of introspection in his psychology, he understood its fallibility. He concluded that "introspection is difficult and fallible;

and that the difficulty is simply that of all observation of whatever kind."[51] The errors encountered through the introspective procedure are corrected by replication. Through generations of such introspection, later views correct earlier ones "until at last the harmony of a consistent system is reached."[52] This is the classic mode of system building exemplified by the British empiricists. "Such a system, gradually worked out, is the best guarantee the psychologist can give for the soundness of any particular psychologic observation which he may report."[53] James recognized, however, that in itself such unrestricted, natural observation was becoming a thing of the past—"the last monument of the youth of our science, still untechnical and generally intelligible, like the Chemistry of Lavoisier, or Anatomy before the microscope was used."[54]

James recognized the legitimacy of the experimental method, but he saw it as a supplement to the traditional introspective method of empirical philosophy. He gave rather grudging support to the experimental method but roundly criticized proponents.

James also recognized the comparative method. The comparative method, he said, involves observing the behavior of animals, insects, children, and savages and gaining from those observations information relevant to civilized adult humans. Although he was no more sympathetic to it than to the experimental method, James saw the comparative method as a supplement to the introspective and experimental methods. He also included in the comparative method the results of questionnaires and similar anthropometric procedures, a method he predicted would become one of the "common pests of life."[55]

Within a decade after the publication of the *Principles*, James's type of introspection, description of experience in a natural and uncontrolled way, was replaced by the analytical introspection of the laboratory. The "laboratory blackgards," as James called them, were taking psychology in a direction he was unwilling to follow.[56]

Mind as Problem Solver

James insisted, as did Spencer before him, that the mind did more than passively adapt to the external environment.[57] The mind has a spontaneity, a selectivity of its own. Consciousness in the mind is causative, he stated; it intervenes in cause–effect sequences. James advanced the argument that the reality of the intervention of consciousness as causative is demonstrated by our more intense awareness of the functioning of consciousness when obstacles are encountered. When there are no obstacles and things run smoothly, consciousness tends to lapse and habit takes over. Moreover, consciousness, shows interest or attention. It is volitional as well as sensory. It selects and dwells on some aspects of the experience to which it is open and rejects others. What is selected becomes vital and real; what is rejected becomes unimportant and unreal. Mind is an instrument drawing from the world whatever interests it. Persons differ in that they introspect identical situations in different ways according to their interests. This selectivity of consciousness, presumably resulting from the action of selective natural evolution, runs as a theme through the chapters of the *Principles* devoted to attention, conception, and discrimination and comparison. It is most explicitly stated in Chapter 5 when James argues against the conception of the individual as an automaton.

In this concept James follows Spencer by inserting a teleologial thrust into mental events. In giving his support to this notion, James made consciousness, the mental events of the present moment, a problem solver, a purposivistic function that James Rowland Angell would take as the fundamental principle underlying Chicago Functionalism. Angell would meld James's teleological principle of consciousness as problem solver with Chauncey Wright's process by which consciously willed processes reduce through repetition to habit and finally pass to future generations as dispositions. For Angell this concept would become the Lapsed Intelligence Theory of Instincts.

Habit

James treated habit, "the enormous fly-wheel of society, its most precious conservative agent,"[58] as a matter of the functioning of the nervous system. He viewed habit as originating from the increased plasticity of neural matter, which makes it easier for repeated actions to be carried out. At the same time, habit lessens the need for attention to the activity in question. Moreover, it has enormous social implications. James's account of habit, perhaps the most famous chapter in his book, received separate publication many years later.

Emotion

James would have had us reverse the usual way of thinking about the emotions. The common-sense view of emotions holds that perception gives rise to emotion. The emotion, then, brings about bodily expression. James, however, said that the bodily expression directly follows the perception of the emotion-provoking events. The feeling engendered is the emotion.

> Common-sense says, we lose our fortune, are sorry and weep; we meet a bear, are frightened and run; we are insulted by a rival, are angry and strike. The hypothesis here to be defended says that this order of sequence is incorrect, that the one mental state is not immediately induced by the other, that the bodily manifestations must first be interposed between, and that the more rational statement is that we feel sorry because we cry, angry because we strike, afraid because we tremble, and not that we cry, strike, or tremble, because we are sorry, angry, or fearful, as the case may be.[59]

For evidence James appealed to introspection; if all experiences of bodily symptoms, such as the heartbeat, the tensions in the muscles, and so on, are abstracted, there is nothing left to the emotion. Independently and almost simultaneously, Carl Lange,[60] in studying the circulatory system, reached the conclusion that feelings of vascular change are the essentials of emotion.

Evidence has been brought to bear against the so-called James–Lange theory in the research that was almost immediately stimulated by their work. James's felicitous expression could and did lead to misunderstanding. When he said, "we feel sorry because we cry, . . . afraid because we tremble," he disregarded the fact that we can be sorry without crying and afraid without trembling. This does not alter the fact that some bodily process precedes and is the sensory source of the emotion; that, after all, is the essence of his theory. No one denies that emotions have physical causes, but modern research shows that they are caused by processes in the thalamic region of the brain, mediated through the autonomic nervous system. Nevertheless, James's theory did much to stimulate the research that established the organic basis of emotion.

Instincts

James endowed the human organism with a generous number of instincts—more, in fact, than those of the lower animals. For the beginnings of his catalogue, he drew on observations of children by Preyer, an embryologist and a pioneer child psychologist. But he went considerably beyond Preyer. He listed sucking, biting, crying, locomotion, and vocalization among the human instincts. They were the more specific forms of instinct, reflexlike in character; they stood in contrast to the broad generalizations sometimes offered as instincts, as when the instinct of self-preservation is postulated. This is not meant to imply that James did not list more complicated instincts than those just mentioned; he went on to include imitation, emulation, pugnacity, hunting, fear, acquisitiveness, play, curiosity, shyness, cleanliness, modesty, love, and jealousy.

According to James, we follow the dictates of instincts because at the time it seems the natural and appropriate thing to do. Every instinct is an impulse to action of some sort, but not all instincts are blind or invariable. The sheer possession of many and contrary instincts means that with slight alterations of conditions, now this, then another impulse may be in the ascendant. Pugnacity and timidity, bashfulness and vanity, sociability and pugnacity are paired antithetical instincts that permit variability in behavior since they mutually conflict with one another, and at a given moment only one or the other can be manifested. An additional factor making for nonuniformity of expression of instincts is that instincts may be inhibited by habits.

After the work of James, preparing catalogues of instincts became a popular pastime of psychologists, and considerable ingenuity was exercised in getting a complete and logically consistent classification. In today's perspective we consider this a self-defeating form of armchair theorizing because the concept of instinct lends itself to an explanation of behavior akin to that of faculty psychology—we fight because we have a fighting instinct. In James's time, however, appeal to instinct in the human species was a way of calling attention to the human biological heritage, a view that then needed defense. The individual as an organism in a world of nature was being defended by an appeal to instinct.

Significance of James to Psychology

E. L. Thorndike, who was a student at Harvard in the 1890s, believed that the "influence of James on psychology means, essentially, the influence of *The Principles of Psychology.*"[61] Often that influence was direct and immediate. John Dewey admitted that the major shift in standpoint among the editions of his own *Psychology* resulted at least partly from James's treatment of sensation in terms of the stream-of-thought metaphor. The influence of James's thought is most immediately demonstrated in the development of American functionalism. Both Dewey and James Rowland Angell, founders of Chicago Functionalism, acknowledged the influence of James's psychological thought. Through Angell in particular, and his successor at Chicago, Harvey Carr, the psychological idea of James became a force in American laboratory psychology during the prebehavioristic period.

GRANVILLE STANLEY HALL

G. Stanley Hall (1844–1924) was much more important in his role as the first organizer and administrator in American psychology than as a contributor to psychological research or theory.[62] This is not to say that Hall's research was unimportant, since many credit him with the beginnings of several important lines of investigation in psychology, including child study. On balance, however, his genius as an organizer has had the greatest impact.

Early Life

Granville Stanley Hall was born of English ancestry in 1844 at Ashfield, a rural hamlet in Massachusetts, the son of substantial, hard-working, pious farmers. His parents were unusual only in the extent of their education. His mother had attended the Albany Female Seminary, then one of the very few institutions in the East for higher education of women; and his father had saved his money from some years of farm labor to return to school. Both parents then taught school for several years.

After doing well in the local rural school, Hall "kept school" for a while himself. His mother had always wanted him to go to college, however, and he enrolled in Williams College in 1863.

At Williams, Hall studied philosophy with Mark Hopkins and found diversified interests such as associationism, the Scottish school, John Stuart Mill, and the theory of evolution. Without too much in the way of a call, he prepared for the ministry. Consequently, on graduation in 1867, he enrolled in the Union Theological Seminary in New York City. During his year in New York, he explored the city with zest, roaming the streets, visiting police courts, and attending churches of all denominations. He joined a discussion club interested in the study of positivism, visited theaters for plays and musicals, tutored young ladies from the elite of New York, visited a phrenologist, and generally had an exciting year.

One member of the faculty, a foreign-trained scholar who tutored him in philosophy, advised him to seek foreign study. Through the intercession of Henry Ward Beecher, the famous preacher, he received a loan of $500 for this purpose.

In the early summer of 1868 Hall sailed for Europe and made his way to Bonn. After studying theology and philosophy there, he moved to Berlin, where he continued his theological and philosophical studies. In particular he studied Aristotle which led him, like Noah Porter, George Sylvester Morris, and Franz Brentano before him, to F. A. Trendelenburg's seminar in Berlin. Trendelenburg led Hall to an acceptance of all he could understand of Hegel's logic and was perhaps instrumental in Hall's decision to become a philosopher. Trendelenburg and Hegel also influenced Hall by strengthening his interest in historical progress and by emphasizing developmental conditioning in ideas and institutions. Dorothy Ross tells us that Trendelenburg's ideas would gradually enter into Hall's mind as the next decade progressed.[63] Hall also worked under DuBois-Reymond in physiology; he studied physics, attended a clinic for mental diseases, and satisfied a wide array of other interests. Beer gardens, theaters, and some lighthearted romantic episodes helped to round out his German education.

It was not until 1871 that he returned home, heavily in debt and without a degree. At this point he returned to Union Theological Seminary to complete his work for the ministry, where he felt stifled by the orthodoxy. Although he was not noted for his religious orthodoxy, he did manage to get his degree. He decided not to preach, however, a decision that may have been influenced by the reception of his trial sermon before the faculty and students. After the sermon he went to the office of the president for criticism. Instead of discussing his sermon, the president knelt and prayed that Hall would be shown the errors of his ways![64] While looking about for a position, George Sylvester Morris helped him obtain a position as a tutor to the children of a New York banker. Hall spent two years in that occupation. While in New York, Hall became involved with a group of positivistic followers of Comte. The group was also interested in Herbert Spencer's thought. During that time, as Hall tells us, he was "profoundly influenced" by Darwin, Spencer, and the English physicist and naturalist, John Tyndall.[65] All of this radical thought led Hall to the belief that "Comte and the Positivists had pretty much made out their case and that the theological if not the metaphysical, stage of thought should be transcended."[66]

Hall's lack of orthodoxy made a college appointment difficult. Finally, however, Antioch College in Ohio, a western outpost of Unitarianism, gave him a post teaching English literature. Later he shifted to French and German and finally to philosophy. As was not unusual in small colleges, he was assigned many extracurricular duties—he served as librarian, led the choir, and took his turn at preaching. In his second and third years he managed to spend most of his time teaching philosophical subjects. After he read the first volume of Wundt's *Physiological Psychology* immediately after its publication, he decided to return to Germany to study psychology. He started out in the spring of 1876, but he got only as far as Cambridge, Massachusetts, where he was offered an instructorship in English at Harvard. He took it, hoping for a chance to transfer to philosophy and psychology. His work in required sophomore English was monotonous and time consuming, but he found time to work with H. P. Bowditch at the Harvard Medical School and to carry out in Bowditch's laboratory a study on "the Muscular Perception of Space," which he presented as a thesis for the doctorate in philosophy at Harvard in 1878. He also did work with William James, whom he got to know quite well. Hall received his degree in psychology upon the recommendation of the Department of Philosophy. After his degree he immediately left for Europe.

Hall first studied at Berlin, where he did a considerable amount of work in physiology. In his second year he moved to Leipzig and became Wundt's first American student. Despite the enthusiasm with which he had looked forward to working with Wundt, the reality does not seem to have been to his liking. Hall attended Wundt's lectures and served as a subject in experiments, but he seems to have performed no research of his own in the laboratory. Instead, he undertook a considerable amount of work in physiology, particularly in the physiology of muscles. He then went to Berlin to work with Helmholtz, only to find him immersed in physics. Nevertheless, he wrote James that he was disappointed in Wundt and had gotten much more out of Helmholtz.[67] Travel to educational centers followed. He had decided that they way to make a living was to apply psychology to education, though when he returned to the United States, he was without a job and had no prospects of getting one.

Meanwhile, Hall married a girl he had known from his days at Antioch whom he met again in Berlin, where she was studying art. They took a small flat in a suburb of Boston in September 1880. Things appeared bleak until a good fairy in the unlikely guise of President Eliot of Harvard appeared at their house with the request that Hall give a series of Saturday talks on education in Boston under the auspices of Harvard University. These talks, which were well attended, brought him considerable favorable publicity.

The Johns Hopkins Years

On the strength of reports of his Saturday morning lectures, President Gilman of Johns Hopkins University invited Hall to Baltimore for a series of public lectures. In 1882 Hall arrived at Johns Hopkins, a school already celebrated in 1876 for the beginning of its bold experiment in higher education on the German plan. President Gilman had been having trouble finding just the right philosopher for his school; he wanted someone who would be both "modern" and favorably disposed toward science, but who would not offend orthodox religious sensibility. For a while there was considerable academic "infighting" involving Hall and the two other part-time appointments in a department for which only one professorship was planned. Both of the other contestants, Charles S. Peirce and George Morris, were very eminent men in philosophy. The scales tipped more in Hall's favor not only because he was a scientist, but also because of his accommodating attitude toward religious orthodoxy. Although he wanted to dissociate psychology from religion, he held no animosity toward his former field. He remained discreetly silent, and in 1884 he was appointed Professor of Psychology and Pedagogics.

After his professorial appointment, Hall immediately proceeded to separate his work from that in philosophy. He arranged it in such a way that the Metaphysics Club, which had flourished before his time, died for lack of appropriate material for presentation.

In 1883, while still a lecturer, Hall set up laboratory equipment in a private house adjacent to the campus.[68] The next year he was given rooms on the campus. Hall's laboratory at Johns Hopkins opened in 1884 and is often said to be the first formally accepted psychological laboratory in the United States. This claim is somewhat obscured because the university did not officially list it as a laboratory. In fact, the university specifically refused to call it a laboratory, and its equipment was treated as private property. That was to Hall's later benefit, since he later took it with him to Clark University.[69]

Among Hall's students were James McKeen Cattell, John Dewey, Joseph Jastrow, William H. Burnham, and Edmund C. Sanford—all of whom were destined to become prominent psychologists. Cattell and Dewey, however, were only incidentally his students. Cattell was at Hopkins when Hall arrived and left shortly thereafter for Leipzig. Dewey's degree, though taken during Hall's professorship, was for work done under Morris. But Dewey did work in the laboratory and appreciated the significance of the "new psychology." The first Ph.D. in psychology at Hopkins went to Joseph Jastrow. Hall's own degree at Harvard had been awarded in psychology, but this was in one sense the Philosophy Department's afterthought at the time of completion of the work. Jastrow had actually enrolled for a degree in psychology, and so his was the first Ph.D. in psychology in the United States.

In 1887, while still at Hopkins, Hall established the *American Journal of Psychology*.[70] Its founding was entirely unexpected, though he had hoped to found a journal some day. A total stranger walked into his office, suggested he found a journal, and, then and there gave him a check for $500. It later turned out that his benefactor had confused experimental psychology with psychical research, and he canceled his subscription in the second year of publication. This mistake is by no means as foolish as it sounds. Psychical research organizations used the designation "committee on experimental psychology" as the name for their investigatory bodies. The *American Journal of Psychology* was the first English-language journal to be devoted primarily to psychology. When Hall went to Clark University, he took the *American Journal.* He would remain its editor until 1921 when it went to Cornell University under E. B. Titchener's editorship.

Hall used his opportunity as editor and primary book reviewer to strike blows against the traditional American philosophical psychologies. He viciously attacked James McCosh's *Psychology: The Cognitive Powers* and Borden P. Bowne's *Introduction to Psychological Theory.* McCosh represented the last gasp of Scottish Realist faculty psychology, whereas Bowne was the Christian interpreter of Kant and idealism. Hall intended his new journal to be the standardbearer of the new psychology in America and to set itself against the philosophical psychology of the past.

Clark University

Hall was named to the presidency of the soon to be established Clark University in Worcester, Massachusetts. A wealthy merchant, Jonas Gilman Clark, had decided to endow an institution of higher learning in his hometown. Even before the school actually opened, Hall had high aspirations for it, higher than could actually be realized. He embarked on a tour of the European educational centers. Hall's letters[71] from Europe addressed to Clark are filled with the ideas which these encounters suggested to him, discussion of the chance of persuading a distinguished scholar to come to Worcester, and the like. He planned to make Clark University a graduate scientific institute, modeled after the German universities and surpassing Johns Hopkins. Research was to be its task, with education a necessary accompaniment.

Fortunately for psychology, President Hall had also made himself professor of psychology and continued to teach in the graduate school throughout his tenure at Clark. He had also brought along Edmund C. Sanford from Baltimore to head the laboratory. William H. Burnham, another Hopkins student, was put in charge of pedagogics, which in this setting meant educational psychology and mental hygiene. Adolph Meyer, later the leading psychiatrist of his time, who was then at Worcester State Hospital, also gave lectures.

Hall's last publication within the conventional limits of experimental psychology (on touch sensitivity) appeared in 1887. His own work thereafter was nonexperimental, but this limitation does not reflect his attitude toward the field and his faith in the advantage of scientific method. He eloquently and unequivocally defended laboratory work. His students saw him as the leader of the forces that would make psychology a science. There are many indications, however, that the laboratory was too far removed from life to meet his own personal interests. He was impatient with the slow, plodding nature of laboratory work. Nevertheless, experimental psychology was still his vision of psychology, even though he realized that others would have to carry on the work.

Founding of the American Psychological Association

It was Hall's idea to institute the first scientific organization of psychologists, the American Psychological Association, which was founded in July 1892.[72] He issued the invitations, arranged for a meeting in Worcester, and in general dominated the proceedings. Almost as a matter of course, he was elected the first president. The scientific character of the organization was established at this very first meeting. After all these years it is impossible to determine just who was present, but apparently ten to eighteen psychologists were there.[73] Although James was in Switzerland, he was included in the twenty-six charter members who received invitations. The first annual meeting was held later the same year. After considerable controversy over the years, it has broadened its functions to include the application of psychology and the advancement of its professional status while maintaining its original scientific goal.

Hall's Competition with James

In the 1880s and 1890s Hall vied with William James for the leadership of American psychology. In the late 1880s he seemed destined to be the "founder of American experimental psychology." First, his productive laboratories at Hopkins and Clark Universities were far ahead of most others of the time. Second, his founding of the *American Journal of Psychology* and of the American Psychological Association were both acts of the leader of a new discipline. With the publication of James's *Principles of Psychology,* however, the tide appears to have gone against Hall. Perhaps because James did not threaten his junior colleagues in American psychology by trying to be the leader, they gathered around him to use his position and reputation for their own purposes. Hall would find that the American Psychological Association (APA) would be taken away from him within two or three years and put in the control of James's followers. Hall would lose interest in the APA and seldom attended meetings thereafter. Some of James's followers attempted to tell Hall how he should run the *American Journal of Psychology* and, even though Hall tried to accommodate them, they founded the rival journal, the *Psychological Review.* In many respects, even past the first decade of the twentieth century American psychology was split between Hall's and James's followers.[74]

Child Study and Developmentalism

Developmentalism as expressed in evolutionary theory, served as a guiding prescription for Hall. The subject had interested him since his student days at Williams and was only strengthened during his European travels. Hall's thinking concerning a whole host of psychological topics was guided by the conviction that the normal growth of the mind occurs as a series of evolutionary stages. Pursuing this aim, he turned to the psychological study of the child through the use of questionnaires, a procedure he had learned in Germany. In fact, in 1881, before leaving Boston for Baltimore, Hall had an opportunity for research in the Boston school system. In this study, entitled "The Contents of Children's Minds," and in subsequent studies, he unearthed a considerable body of miscellaneous information about children's thinking on a variety of subjects.[75] By the end of 1915, Hall and his students had developed and applied 194 questionnaires. The topics included anger, dolls, crying, the early sense of self, fears, foods, religious experience, death conventionality, mathematics, superstitions, and dreams.

These studies created great public enthusiasm at the time and led to the founding of the so-called child-study movement. Large numbers of parents and teachers turned to the task of applying and interpreting questionnaires. All over the world they uncritically and dogmatically reported their superficial excursions into child development. The sentimentality and general wooliness of the movement led to a reaction against it, both within psychology and from various sectors of the public, and in a few years it disappeared. Nonetheless, the concept of psychological development had been firmly established through this work. The child-study movement served to bring home forcefully the importance of the empirical study of the child, while through its very excesses it made for an increased critical evaluation of research.[76]

In 1893 Hall founded, at his own expense, the *Pedagogical Seminary* (now the *Journal of Genetic Psychology*), to which he and his students contributed a large share of the articles. For some years this journal was the chief outlet for research in child study and educational psychology.

It was in his huge work entitled *Adolescence* that Hall stated most completely his particular recapitulation theory of development.[77] He offered the conjecture that in his individual development, the child repeats the life history of the race. For instance, the level of the primitive in an individual is repeated when the child plays at cowboys and Indians.

Attitude Toward Psychoanalysis

Hall was one of the first Americans to become interested in psychoanalysis. The twentieth anniversary of Clark University in 1909 was celebrated with a series of conferences, including the famous visit of Freud and Jung to the United States at Hall's invitation. This invitation was a courageous step in view of the suspicion and dislike that Hall knew was being directed at the whole psychoanalytic movement.[78] Even so, Hall cannot be called a Freudian. He was an eclectic, cheerfully borrowing from Freud what he saw as useful and equally without malice accepting whatever contradicted Freud.[79] He could admire Freud, but he wanted to go beyond the "psychology of sex." As his letters show, he could never understand why Freud was so intolerant of eclectic borrowing.[80] Freud, of course, saw this behavior as unforgivably inconsistent. Hall maintained his interest in psychoanalysis throughout his life, although in his later years he was much more negative about it. In Cattell's last conversation with him, Hall expressed puzzlement over academic psychology's vehement rejection of psychoanalysis.[81]

G. Stanley Hall was primarily a source of stimulation for others, opening up for them areas of study and research. As Titchener stated at about the same time, "He sought to inspire and I tried to train."[82] They shared the goal of research; their difference was in the means used, not in the end sought. A psychologist who worked with Hall at Clark spoke of Hall's conviction that psychology should not set limits for itself and of his desire, "to build the top of the mountain first."[83]

Throughout his life Hall remained an intensely agile thinker with boundless enthusiasm for often contradictory views on practically everything. He was a founder so intent on his pioneering that he almost always moved immediately to his next adventure, leaving for others the task of tidying up. He himself wondered if his life had not been a series of fads or crazes.[84] He said that Wundt would rather have been commonplace than brilliantly wrong;[85] one suspects that Hall would have reversed the statement for himself.

G. Stanley Hall was versatile and broad in his interests, a pioneer in many areas of psychological endeavor. A considerable number of the psychologists polled considered him a pioneer in studies of childhood, adolescence, senescence, and human genetics. Of these, the stimulation he gave to child psychology is the most important. In a sense Hall made a gospel of childhood, lifting it to a new plane of importance, focusing on the child as a child, and studying the child for his or her own sake.

An all-pervasive developmental allegiance characterized Hall's work. His adherence to a dynamic rather than a static attitude and some appreciation of unconscious mentalism were apparent, but neither was integrated into an overall view in any systematic fashion.

SUMMARY

William James and G. Stanley Hall greatly influenced scientific psychology in the United States at its beginnings in the late nineteenth century. James's influence was primarily one of ideas, particularly those expressed in his *Principles of Psychology*. Perhaps his greatest contribution to American psychology was his clear separation of mind from soul and the resulting secularization of psychological concepts of mind. Hall's contribution was primarily organizational, reflected in his founding of the American Psychological Association and the *American Journal of Psychology*. James remained chiefly a philosopher, preferring the contemplative model of traditional philosophy to the methods of the research laboratory. Hall, although he did little direct experimentation himself, emphasized laboratory work whenever possible. Both figures were finally left behind amid the fast-moving changes that were revolutionizing the psychologies of the twentieth century, yet both played major roles in directing those changes in their early phases.

NOTES

1. F. M. Albrecht, "The New Psychology in America: 1880–1895," Unpublished Ph.D. dissertation, Johns Hopkins University, 1960.
2. *Ibid.*
3. *Ibid.*
4. There are several excellent resource works on William James's life and thought. The classic work is Ralph Barton Perry's *The Thought and Character of William James*. It is primarily a collection of James's letters with connecting commentary. Another excellent set of letters is Henry James's *The Letters of William James*. A more traditional biography is Gay Wilson Allen's *William James* (New York: Viking Press, 1967). An excellent new work on James's thought is Gerald E. Meyers's *William James: His Life and Thought* (New Haven, Conn.: Yale University Press, 1986). All of James's writings are in print; Harvard University Press has published all of his books with scholarly introductions and excellent annotations. The series, under the general editorship of Frederick Burnkardt, is the ultimate resource for any detailed study of James's writings. This only scrapes the surface on James. Any college library has dozens of books on special aspects of James's thought.
5. H. James, *Letters*, Vol. 1, p. 96.
6. *Ibid.*, pp. 118–119.
7. *Ibid.*, p. 154.
8. Charles Renouvier, *Essais de critique génerale*, 3 vols. (Paris, 1854–1864); translated in part as "Second Essay: Man—Certitude," in Benjamin Rand, ed., *Modern Classical Philosophers*, 2nd ed. (New York: Houghton Mifflin Co., 1936), pp. 772–787.
9. H. James, *The Letters of William James*, Vol. 1, p. 147.
10. Meyers, *William James: His Life and Thought*, pp. 46–47.
11. R. S. Harper, "The Laboratory of William James," *Harvard Alumni Bulletin*, 52 (1949):169–173; R. S. Harper, "The First Psychological Laboratory," *Isis*, 41 (1950):158–161.
12. Ethel F. Fisk, ed., *The Letters of John Fiske* (New York: Macmillan Co., 1940), p. 371.

13. William James to Henry Holt, James Papers, Houghton Library, Harvard, bMS Am 1092.1 (undated; early June 1878).
14. G. S. Hall, "Philosophy in the United States," *Mind, 4* (1879):89–105.
15. E. Boutroux, *The Life and Work of William James* (New York: Longmans, Green, n.d.).
16. R. B. Perry, *Thought and Character.*
17. W. James, *Psychology: Briefer Course* (New York: Henry Holt, 1892).
18. W. James, *Letters,* Vol. I, p. 314.
19. R. B. Perry, *Thought and Character.*
20. *Ibid.*
21. W. James, *Principles,* Vol. 1, p. 192.
22. R. B. Perry, *Thought and Character,* Vol. II, 195.
23. *Ibid.,* I, 415.
24. W. James, *Varieties,* p. 233.
25. H. James, *Letters,* Vol. 2, p. 328.
26. W. James, from the English original of the Preface to W. James, *Principii di psicologia,* ed. G. C. Ferrari, (Milan, 1901), quoted in Perry, *Thought and Character,* Vol. 2, p. 53.
27. This discussion of the *Principles* is drawn, in part, from Rand B. Evans, "Introduction: The Historical Context" in William James, *The Principles of Psychology* (Cambridge Mass.: Harvard University Press, 1981), Vol. 1, pp. xlvii–lvix.
28. W. James, *The Principles of Psychology* (New York: Henry Holt and Co., 1890), Vol. 1, p. 224.
29. *Ibid.,* p. 185.
30. *Ibid.* p. 239.
31. *Ibid.,* p. 276.
32. James would desert this position in his later philosophical writing for a pluralism, effectively rejecting the differentiation between object and subject.
33. James, *Principles,* Vol. 1, p. 345.
34. *Ibid.,* p. 350.
35. *Ibid.,* p. 248.
36. *Ibid.,* p. 225.
37. *Ibid.,* p. 239.
38. R. B. Perry, *Thought and Character,* Vol. 2, p. 103.
39. W. James, *Principles,* Vol. 1, p. 218.
40. *Ibid.,* p. 275.
41. *Ibid.,* p. 289.
42. *Ibid.,* p. 291.
43. *Ibid.,* p. 330.
44. *Ibid.,* p. 344.
45. *Ibid.*
46. *Ibid.,* p. 346.
47. *Ibid.,* p. 350.
48. *Ibid.*
49. E. L. Thorndike, "James' Influence on the Psychology of Perception and Thought," *Psychological Review, 50* (1943):90.
50. James, *Principles,* Vol. 1, p. 185.
51. *Ibid.,* p. 191.
52. *Ibid.,* p. 192.
53. *Ibid.*

54. *Ibid.*

55. *Ibid.*, p. 194.

56. R. B. Perry, *Thought and Character*, Vol. 2, p. 17.

57. W. James, *Principles*, Vol. 1, pp. 138–139.

58. *Ibid.*, p. 121.

59. *Ibid.*, Vol. 2, pp. 449–450.

60. C. G. Lange and W. James, *The Emotions*, Knight Dunlap, ed. (Baltimore: Williams and Wilkins, 1922).

61. E. L. Thorndike, "Psychology of Perception and Thought," p. 87.

62. L. N. Wilson, "Biographical Sketch, Granville Stanley Hall, Feb. 1, 1844—April 24, 1924," *Publication of Clark University Library*, 7 (1925):3–33; G. S. Hall, *Life and Confessions of a Psychologist* (New York: Appleton, 1923). The most complete biographical assessment of Hall is Dorothy G. Ross, *G. Stanley Hall: The Psychologist as Prophet* (Chicago: University of Chicago Press, 1972).

63. D. Ross, *G. Stanley Hall*, p. 39.

64. G. S. Hall, *Life and Confessions of a Psychologist* (New York: D. Appleton and Co., 1923), p. 178.

65. *Ibid.*, pp. 184–185, 222.

66. *Ibid.*, p. 222.

67. H. James, *Letters*, Vol. 2, pp. 17–18.

68. J. M. Cattell, "The Founding of the Association and of the Hopkins and Clark Laboratories," *Psychological Review*, 50 (1943):61–64.

69. Albrecht, *The New Psychology in America.*

70. For a detailed discussion of the founding of the *American Journal of Psychology* and Hall's years as editor, see Rand B. Evans and Jozef B. Cohen, "The American Journal of Psychology: A Retrospective," *American Journal of Psychology*, 100 (1987):322–340.

71. N. O. Rush, ed., *Letters of G. Stanley Hall to Jonas Gilman Clark* (Worcester, Mass.: Clark University Library, 1948).

72. W. Dennis and E. G. Boring, "The Founding of APA," *American Psychologist*, 7 (1952):95–97.

73. *Ibid.*

74. R. Evans and J. Cohen, "American Journal of Psychology," pp. 328–332, Ross, *G. Stanley Hall*, p. 232. For some of the long-term consequences of the competition of the two factions, see R. Evans and Frederick J. Down Scott, "The 1913 International Congress of Psychology: The American Congress That Wasn't," *American Psychologist*, 33 (1978):711–723.

75. G. S. Hall, "Contents of Children's Minds," *Princeton Review*, 11 (1883):272–294.

76. D. E. Bradbury, "The Contribution of the Child Study Movement to Child Psychology," *Psychological Bulletin*, 34 (1937):21–38.

77. G. S. Hall, *Adolescence: Its Psychology and Its Relations to Physiology, Anthropology, Sociology, Sex, Crime, Religion and Education* (New York: Appleton, 1904).

78. For more detail on the conference, see Rand B. Evans and William A. Koelsch, "Psychoanalysis Arrives in America: The 1909 Psychology Conference at Clark University," *American Psychologist*, 40 (1985):942–948.

79. J. C. Burnham, "Sigmund Freud and G. Stanley Hall: Exchange of Letters," *Psychoanalytic Quarterly*, 29 (1960):307–316.

80. *Ibid.*

81. J. McK. Cattell, "Founding."

82. E. B. Titchener, "Letters in Memory of G. Stanley Hall," G. S. Hall, Feb. 1, 1844–April 24, 1924, *Publication of Clark University Library*, 7 no. 6 (1925):1–92.

83. E. D. Starbuck, "G. Stanley Hall, as a Psychologist, *"Psychological Review 32* (1925):117.

84. M. L. Reymert, "Letters in Memory of G. Stanley Hall," Granville Stanley Hall, Feb. 1, 1844–April 24, 1924, *Publication of Clark University Library*, 7 (1925:81–84; G. S. Hall, *Founders of Modern Psychology* (New York: Appleton, 1912).

85. *Ibid.*

E. B. Titchener.

Titchener and Structuralism: The Beginning of Experimental Psychology in America

*T*he precise beginning of professionalism in American psychology can be documented. On July 8, 1892, G. Stanley Hall convened a meeting of academic and professional men in the parlor of his home in Worcester, Massachusetts, to discuss the organization of a society for the promotion of the "new psychology."[1] The group quickly decided that it was time for such an organization, and with that decision the American Psychological Association was born. Of the charter members, twenty-six individuals were originally listed; five were added at the last minute to make up a total of thirty-one original members. The American Psychological Association would become the primary vehicle for the professionalization of psychology in America.[2]

The new psychology had as its "new" aspect, experimentation, but at the time of Hall's meeting, most of those who identified themselves as psychologists gave only lip-service to experimentation. Some, like William James, were actually hostile to it.

The move to the laboratory as the primary source of psychological information and the systemization of the data from the laboratory did not come from William James or G. Stanley Hall or even the nineteenth-century American milieu. It was the next generation, particularly the psychologists returning with their degrees from German universities, who would initiate the epoch of experimental psychology. One of these second-generation psychologists who would unfurl the banner for a nonteleological and nonfunctional psychology and who would act as a catalyst for the reformation of American psychology was Edward Bradford Titchener (1867–1927). Others of the second generation, particularly James Rowland Angell (1867–1949) and J. McKeen Cattell (1860–1944), who will be discussed in the next chapter, developed functionally oriented experimental psychologies, typically called Chicago Functionalism and Columbia Functionalism, respectively.

EDWARD BRADFORD TITCHENER AND STRUCTURALISM

For over thirty years, well into the second decade of this century, an academic ceremony took place at Cornell University each day the professor of psychology lectured on introductory psychology. Shortly before the class hour the professor would inspect the demonstrational material that had been laid out; the staff and assistants would gather in his office, which adjoined the lecture room; the professor would don his Oxford master's gown, which, as he put it, "gives me the right to be dogmatic"; the staff would file through one door to take front-row seats, and the professor would emerge through another door directly onto the lecture platform. Then the lecture would begin.

Such was the grand manner in which lectures were offered by Edward Bradford Titchener, the representative in America and, in his view, the perfecter of the analytical, introspective psychology originated by Wundt in Leipzig.[3] Trenchant and powerful lectures, they were often the occasion for pronouncements about his system of psychology. To Titchener's audience of staff, graduate students, and sophomore college students, Titchener's system *was* psychology.

Titchener was not the first of Wundt's students to come to America; there had been several American students before him. After these American students returned home from their one or two years with Wundt, however, they modified his views according to their particular temperaments and almost always in the direction of the functionally oriented and teleologically tinged concepts that permeated the American scene. Titchener was not American, however, but English. Perhaps because of the difference between his early education and that of his American contemporaries, he was less disposed toward functional and teleological views. This is not to say that Titchener was an uncritical follower of Wundt. As we will see, he fundamentally disagreed with much of his master's idealism and developed a positivistic psychology to "correct" Wundt's shortcomings. Titchener did not feel that he was opposing Wundt, however, but was merely expanding and perfecting what Wundt had begun. In general, Titchener's version of Wundt's psychology was more consistent and systematically more explicit than was Wundt's. Titchener also went beyond his master in his devotion to and dependence on the laboratory and its experimental method as the primary source of psychological data. As we will see, this was perhaps Titchener's major contribution to American psychology.

Life of Titchener

E. B. Titchener was born in 1867 in the old Roman town of Chichester, England. His father died while Titchener was still a boy. Even before the father's death, however, Titchener was sent to live with his namesake paternal grandfather, Edward Titchener, who was an attorney. Titchener was reared with all the trappings and notions of an English gentleman. His early education was begun by a tutor, but he later went to the local Anglican cathedral school. By the time Titchener was in his early teens, his grandfather lost much of the family wealth during an economic downturn. The grandfather died soon thereafter, leaving young Titchener with little monetary security. At fourteen, Titchener went to Malvern College on a scholarship, a new but already recognized public school. He was very successful there and grew from a withdrawn, bookish boy to a skilled debater and confident young man. He continued his studies at Oxford, also on scholarship, where for four years he concentrated on philosophy and the classics.

At one time Titchener considered himself a follower of Herbert Spencer. Although he later rejected most Spencerian notions, Spencer's positivistic aspect appears to have remained an influence. It was perhaps due to his contact with Spencer's teachings that Titchener came in contact with the "new biology" of Darwin. He came to know personally Darwin's son, George, Thomas Huxley, Francis Galton, E. B. Tylor, and several other leaders of the Darwinian revolution. Titchener's interests turned to comparative animal psychology, and he published several articles on the subject while still a student at Oxford. He also knew John George Romanes, one of the early writers on comparative psychology, but Titchener was disappointed in Romanes and the comparative psychology of his day because the research was almost entirely anecdotal. Even in those days, Titchener was searching for a systematic and experimental approach to mental life. He was also dissatisfied with what he called the "logical construction of the English school."[4] It was in the psychology of Wilhelm Wundt that he found the approach he was looking for. As he later put it, he heard about psychology at Oxford; he studied it at Leipzig.[5]

Because his background was almost entirely in philosophy, Titchener had very little formal training in science. For this reason Wundt felt it would be better for him to stay at Oxford for an additional year beyond his bachelor's degree and gain direct experience in laboratory work. Titchener therefore spent a year as research student to John Scott Burdon Sanderson, the premier experimental physiologist in England. The year was a revelation to Titchener. He would identify with the careful experimental procedures and systematic care he saw in Burdon Sanderson's laboratory for the remainder of his life.

Titchener arrived in Leipzig in the fall of 1890. He found himself a part of an active, enthusiastic group of future psychologists, including a half-dozen from the

United States. Ernst Meumann, mentioned earlier, was his roommate, and Oswald Külpe was Dozent and Wundt's laboratory assistant. Even though Titchener's stay at Leipzig lasted only two years, Wundt made a lifelong impression on him.[6] Titchener could not have been with Wundt at a better time, for in the early 1890s Wundt was making the transition from his attempt to catalogue every psychological experience to a more organized systemization. Although Titchener would later move away from many of Wundt's ideas and approaches, he would always hold to the values of the laboratory and of system building which he learned from Wundt. Still, Titchener's saturation in English psychology and particularly the influence of the positivistic views of Hume, Spencer, and John Stewart Mill caused Titchener to question Wundt's idealistic view. As we saw in Chapter 16, Külpe and Titchener were greatly influenced by their reading of Richard Avenarius and particularly Ernst Mach. That influence would give Titchener the conceptual tools he needed to ''perfect'' Wundtian psychology. That influence will be discussed below.

After receiving his degree from Leipzig in 1892, Titchener returned to Oxford, where for a summer he served as an extension lecturer in biology. To stay on at Oxford would have been his ambition, but neither Oxford nor England was ready for psychology. In any event, he had agreed to accept a position at Cornell University, replacing a friend from Leipzig, Frank Angell, who was leaving for Stanford University. Titchener intended to stay at Cornell only two or three years until something turned up at Oxford or Cambridge; instead, he spent the remaining thirty-five years of his life at Cornell.

In 1892 Titchener arrived in Ithaca, New York, on the relatively new campus of Cornell University. He was Assistant Professor of Psychology, but, more importantly, he was in charge of the laboratory that his friend Frank Angell had begun the year before. In 1892 psychology at Cornell was still part of the philosophy program. In 1895, when psychology separated from philosophy, Titchener became the head of the new program and gained a full professorship.

For the next few years, Titchener was busy organizing the laboratory, buying and building equipment, carrying out research, writing articles (sixty-two between 1893 and 1900), and gradually attracting more and more students. At first he personally participated in every study in his laboratory, but he discontinued this arduous practice in later years.[7] His research then came almost entirely through his students; he himself published nothing from the laboratory under his own name alone. Consequently, his own published research gives no indication of his productivity; it was through his direction of student investigations that the basis for his systematic statements was developed. Under his direction, fifty-eight doctorates and many minor studies were conducted. Of the forty-six studies published in the first thirty volumes of the *American Journal of Psychology*, fifteen were on sensation, eight on perception, six each on memory and attention, and the rest were scattered over related fields.

When Titchener arrived at Cornell, he was surprised by the primitive state of American psychology. He considered the functionally oriented American psychology little more than a watered-down Cartesianism, where mind was still identified with soul and its activities were the functions studied. Titchener, like Wundt and

James, considered mind in a naturalistic way. To Titchener, consciousness was the sum total of an individual's experiences at any given moment. Mind was defined as the sum total of these conscious moments from birth to the present moment. Mind, then, was nothing more than experiences and was not a substantial entity or some permanent being that stood behind the experiences.

Titchener found that his undergraduate students maintained the earlier faculty concepts of mind. He also found that his students were largely monolingual and, as a result, were cut off from the German psychological classics of the new psychology. In 1892 there were only a handful of books of any consequence in English, and none of those took the position of the new German psychology.

Titchener sought to introduce his American students to the German literature of the Wundtian strain. This he did by a program of translation of Wundt's *Human and Animal Psychology* in 1894, Oswald Külpe's *Outlines of Psychology* in 1895, and, eventually, the first volume of Wundt's *Grundzüge der physiologischen Psychologie,* just to name a few. Titchener also influenced others to translate still more of the German literature, while he developed his own version of the new experimental psychology in his *Outline of Psychology* in 1896 and his *Primer of Psychology* in 1898. After the turn of the century, he would publish the four important volumes of his *Experimental Psychology* (1901–1905), often called "Titchener's Manuals." His *Experimental Psychology* bears the significant and relevant subtitle, *A Manual of Laboratory Practice;* it was designed to be used in laboratory courses for training in the methods of psychology.[8] It is divided into four parts, two instructor's manuals and two student's manuals, one of each devoted to qualitative experiments—sensations, affective qualities, attention, action, perception, and association of ideas—and the other devoted to *quantitative experiments*—thresholds for pressure, tone and sound, Weber's law, the various psychophysical methods, the reaction study of simple discrimination, cognition and choice times, and the reproduction of a time interval. *Qualitative experiments,* as he saw them, were essentially descriptions of conscious experiences by means of introspection, in which questions of "what" or "how" are asked. Quantitative experiments assume that the mental process as such is already familiar from prior examination, and the task is to gather a long series of rather simple observations, which are then expressed through mathematical shorthand in which questions of "how much" are asked.

Titchener wrote the larger two of these four volumes for instructors because at the time, most instructors in the laboratory course had not had laboratory experience themselves. Most experimental psychologists trained between the early 1900s and the 1930s learned their experimental methodology from Titchener's manuals, even though their theoretical positions and areas of research were far different from those of Titchener and his group. For instance, John B. Watson, founder of behaviorism and arch opponent to Titchener's introspective psychology once wrote to Titchener that "[J. R.] Angell and [H. H.] Donaldson have been like parents to me and I am sure that they will live in my memory as long as I live. It is an intellectual, social and moral debt. . . . I am not so sure that I do not owe you as much as I owe them. I think if I had to say where the stimulus for hard persistent research came from I should have to point to you."[9] These volumes are probably the most erudite and encyclopedic works on experimental psychology written in English.

Titchener later updated his *Outline* in the form of his *A Textbook of Psychology* published in 1910 and recast his *Primer* under the title *A Beginner's Psychology.* He was never able to write his "big psychology," however. By the time of his death in 1927, the large systematic psychology consisted of only a few introductory chapters which were published posthumously as *Systematic Psychology: Prolegomena* (1929). One often hears great praise for James's writing skills, but Titchener's books are equally and deceptively easy and interesting to read.

A second of Titchener's activities was to produce experimental psychological research using laboratory methods and concepts and to gain a reliable source for their publication, both for himself and his students.[10] In 1894 Titchener joined G. Stanley Hall on the editorial board of the *American Journal of Psychology.* He soon gained editorial control over a third of every issue, and, at last, in 1921, he gained sole editorship. Titchener filled the *American Journal of Psychology* with the experimental work from the Cornell laboratory and from the work of researchers elsewhere working in the Titchenerian mold.

A third activity was to produce high-quality students, saturated with Titchener's psychology and to spread this psychological view across the country. Titchener had a genuinely missionary zeal about the new psychology. He produced a large number of excellent students and placed them with military care in positions around the country where they could come to prominence. As psychology departments separated from philosophy, Titchener assumed that his students would become the head of the department. In those days, the head determined the type of psychology presented in the department. If those psychologists were Titchenerian, then his view would eventually gain the upper hand. If this was Titchener's plan, it did not work out. Titchener's students were of extremely high quality and often rose to the top in their departments and became department heads. However, just as in the case of Wundt, Titchener's students did not always remain faithful to the precepts of his psychology, particularly after the rise of behaviorism. Like Wundt's students, however, the imprint of the laboratory as central to the psychological enterprise did remain with Titchener's students, along with a belief in the significance of theory building.

Here in a discussion of Titchener's students it should be pointed out that Titchener has erroneously been called a misogynist. First, let us say that it is unfair to hold up a nineteenth-century man to late twentieth-century standards. Second, he was, in fact, a strong promoter of women in psychology. Most of Titchener's negative reputation concerning women stems from his exclusion of women from the Experimentalists Society, his informal group of research psychologists. Titchener designed the club to be like an Englishman's smoker. It was an unfortunate decision and one that Titchener later regretted. In every other aspect of his professional life, however, he was a supporter of women in psychology. Almost half of his students were women. Both in percentage and absolute numbers, no male psychologist in a coeducational institution in Titchener's day produced as many. He actively promoted women for positions and lamented that so many married and ceased being academic psychologists. He also appointed Cornell's first female instructor over the objections of his dean. In his day and time, when many psychologists would not even accept women as students at all, he was far advanced.

Perhaps the most significant professional activity in Titchener's own mind was his establishment of a systematic psychology in America that was consistently structural in form and dealt entirely with the contents of experience. This was his structuralist system, which will be discussed in more detail later in this chapter.

At first Titchener participated in Cornell's social life, but as he grew older, he withdrew more and more from the usual social and university contracts. He became a living legend to some members of the Cornell faculty, who had heard of him for years but had never met him. Punctilious and somehow formidable, he gave deference where he thought it due and he expected it in turn from those he thought owed it to him.

Cornell is somewhat isolated in its location in relation to the other major universities of the eastern United States. Travel was still difficult in Titchener's day, with the exception of the train, and communications were mainly by letter. The telephone, though available, was used primarily for emergencies. To a degree, then, Titchener was isolated from his colleagues elsewhere. He was often seen as withdrawn. There were the meetings of the American Psychological Association, of course, but Titchener soon felt that it was not a serious, experimental organization and that it was more a place to be seen than a place for serious discussion of scientific issues. After the Association had been wrested from G. Stanley Hall's control by William James's followers, Titchener rarely went to its meetings. He broke with the Association in the 1890s because it would not censure a member whom Titchener believed, with good evidence, had plagiarized his translation of Wundt's *Human and Animal Psychology*.[11] He rejoined the Association on two other occasions only to resign again.

This severance further isolated Titchener, although his Cornell colleagues and students continued to be active in American Psychological Association meetings and affairs. Perhaps to allay his isolation, in 1904, Titchener organized his own group, the Experimentalists.[12] It was not an organization in the strict sense; annual meetings were arranged by the director of the laboratory where the group was to meet. Needless to say, Titchener dominated the meetings and had much to do with selecting those invited and the topics included. To this day, the group, now somewhat more formally organized, carries on as a worthy representative of experimental psychology of the purest variety.

The Development of Structuralism

In the 1890s when Titchener arrived at Cornell, functional psychology had not yet become functionalism. The functional psychology was that of James, George T. Ladd, and the early John Dewey. It was unsystematic and not yet particularly experimental. Titchener sought to draw a sharp contrast between his positions and that of American functional psychology.

By 1896 Titchener was ready to draw the battle lines with functional psychology. His *Outline of Psychology* presented the new psychology in his structural form. That book, along with his articles "Postulates of a Structural Psychology" and "Structural and Functional Psychology,"[13] formed a challenge to American functional psychology. Titchener was never very happy with the term *structuralism,* but at the time it was a useful term to contrast it with the functional psychologies. Titchener sought to identify functional psychology or "descriptive psychology," as he called it, with the "armchair" or philosophical psychologies of the past and structuralism with the psychology of the laboratory. As we will see, much of the impetus to the development of functionalism, particularly Chicago Functionalism was in reaction to Titchener's "threat" to functional psychology.

In his "Postulates of a Structural Psychology" Titchener had differentiated several systematic approaches to psychology, each roughly analogous to divisions in the biological sciences.[14] First was a structural psychology which Titchener saw as a parallel to morphology. Structural psychology was "experimental psychology." Titchener tells us that:

> The primary aim of the experimental psychologist has been to analyze the structure of mind; to ravel out the elemental processes from the tangle of consciousness, or (if we may change the metaphor) to isolate the constituents in the given conscious formation. His task is a vivisection but a vivisection which shall yield structural, not functional results. He tries to discover, first of all, what is there and in what quantity, not what it is there for.

This was the position which Titchener took as his own and which he held as prior to the other systematic approaches.

The second systematic approach was that of functional psychology. Rather than dealing with the analysis of experience into its constituent parts, he said functional psychology was "the collective name for a system of functions of the psychophysical organism." Titchener identified this functional psychology with the older, "descriptive psychology." The same objects of study may be dealt with differently in the structural and functional systems, but the result is quite different.

Titchener believed that just as experimental psychology was largely concerned with problems of structure, so was "descriptive" psychology, ancient and modern, chiefly occupied with problems of function.

Titchener listed many other types of psychology, including developmental and social psychologies. It was the distinction between experimental, structural psychology and descriptive, functional psychology that most concerned Titchener, however, since the psychologies of William James, John Dewey, and James Rowland Angell fell into the functional category and were Titchener's major competition in the American psychological arena. By the second edition of his *An Outline of Psychology,* published in 1899, Titchener formally distinguished between "structural psychology" and "functional psychology," reserving the proper use of the term *psychology* for the structural approach.

By 1910, when Titchener's *Textbook* was released, he was considered the leader of experimental psychology in America. He was even called the "dean" of American psychology, even though he was only forty-three at the time and not an American.

During the teens of this century, Titchener's structuralism was threatened on several sides, but primarily by the attacks of John B. Watson. In his behaviorist manifesto, "Psychology as the Behaviorist Views It," and his "Image and Affection in Behavior,"[15] both published in 1913, Watson attacked all orthodox introspectionist psychology but drew a particular bead on the concepts used in Titchener's structural system. We should emphasize that Watson attacked Titchener's mentalistic concepts, not the elementistic structure of the system itself. This is important, for, as we will see in Chapter 22, Watson would make use of the logic of Titchener's structural system and replace his mentalistic elements with behavioral elements. The attack was real and serious. Titchener responded to Watson in an article entitled "On Psychology as the Behaviorist Views It,"[16] but Titchener's students were surprised by the apparent mildness of Titchener's response. Titchener's response will be treated in detail in Chapter 22, in the section on Watson's behaviorism. Let us point out briefly here, however, that Titchener made a measured response to Watson's manifesto, basically taking the position that Watson's behaviorism was not new, was not psychology, and was not science. Titchener simply did not believe that psychologists, even American psychologists, could be so naive as to accept the premises of Watson's behaviorism. He simply underestimated the appeal of behaviorism. Titchener sensed a much greater threat to scientific psychology coming from applied psychology and from the followers of Freud. He saw a looming conflict between the forces of science and those of application and teleology. When, in fact, the fear became the reality, as it did in the late 1920s, Titchener was not there to attempt to stem the tide.

Titchener's productivity dropped somewhat during the last decade of his life. Many suggestions have been given for that decline, ranging from his having gained too much early recognition, which left no new fields to conquer, to having run out of ideas.[17] First, Titchener's "lack of productivity" during the last decade or so of his life is a relative matter. Between 1917 and 1927, he published fifty-five notes and articles, which can hardly be called unproductive. It is true, however, that more of his later production was in the form of short notes than previously. If one adds the theses and minor studies conducted under Titchener's direction during those years, each carefully molded by Titchener, the total is much larger.[18] To the degree that there *was* a reduction, it can be attributed to two factors. First, the First World War led to a decimation of the small psychology faculty at Cornell. Most of the young instructors and graduate assistants went to the military. Although Titchener was able to replace some, his workload more than doubled during the 1917–1919 school years. Shortly after the war, Titchener became the sole editor of the *American Journal of Psychology.* Although he had cooperating editors, Titchener still did virtually all the editing between 1921 and late 1925. There is also evidence that the brain tumor that killed him in 1927 had been developing for a number of years and had probably drained him of much of his energy for several years, and certainly in 1926 and 1927. Another matter that occupied Titchener during these years was the revision of his psychological system and the preparation of his "big psychology." After he signed the contract with Macmillan to publish the work in the early 1920s, he agreed not to publish elsewhere on systematic matters until the appearance of the book. The book, of course, never appeared.

Titchener's formal system did not long outlive him. He had taken structuralism well into the era of behaviorism and Gestalt. He had held fast against the tide of teleological thinking and had held his followers together almost entirely by the power of his own personality. As we will see, he had made major changes in his psychological system in his last few years, but they were unpublished at the time of his death except for their obvious impact on theses carried out at Cornell during those last years. The students who carried on many of Titchener's ideas quickly amalgamated them with functional and even behavioral lines. Edna Heidbreder, writing only a few years after Titchener's death, called structuralism "not only a distinct and lasting achievement, but also . . . a gallant and enlightening failure."[19]

Titchener's Views

Positivism   To understand Titchener's psychology and his differences with the views of Wilhelm Wundt, the influence on him of positive science and particularly the positivism of Ernst Mach must be considered. Titchener was trained in the "English school" of philosophy and was particularly attracted by the ideas of David Hume. Hume and many others in England who followed his ideas held to a positivistic view of knowledge. In its basic form, this type of positivism is merely antimetaphysical. That is, only events that may be directly experienced are considered for discussion. Because one cannot experience some permanent being standing behind the experiences, then psychology is made of the experiences themselves, the sensations and perceptions that make up our experiential world. Titchener was greatly influenced by this antimetaphysical view. He was also influenced by Darwin's nonteleological view. This led Titchener to consider experiences for what they were, not for what they did for us. Mental events, then, were to be considered structurally, in analyzing them to discover their nature rather than their purpose.

The most significant influences on Titchener's thinking, after that of Wundt and Hume, were Ernst Mach and to a lesser degree Richard Avenarius. Nonetheless, Titchener did not accept all of Mach or Avenarius—particularly not their views on science which were interpreted teleologically or their acceptance of not only sensations but also relations as elements. In later years, Titchener strongly attacked these aspects of Machian positivism. Where there was influence, however, it was profound.[20]

Mach had two primary influences on Titchener. One was the matter of the nature of the psychological element, which we have already seen influencing Külpe. As we will see when the structure of Titchener's system is described, Titchener followed Mach and Külpe's lead in his treatment of sensations and attributes of sensation.

The second and perhaps more significant influence on Titchener was Mach's relativism. Mach held that the differentiation among physical, physiological, and psychological dimensions and their associated sciences, physics, biology, and psychology is due to the fact that they view experience in different ways.[21] Titchener expanded these aspects of Mach's views and made them fundamental to Titchenerian structuralism.

Point of View   If a single term can be said to epitomize Titchener's approach and to demonstrate his extension of Mach's relativism, not only to psychology but also to science and knowledge in general, it is "point of view."[22] It is the particular observational or attitudinal perspective an individual takes concerning the world of his or her experience. Extending Mach's notion, Titchener believed that there is only one existential, that is, observable universe but that it may be observed in a multitude of ways, making it appear differently, depending on the point of view taken by the observer. No one of these points of view is necessarily truer than another, but they are different. For correct understanding of the existential universe, the universe that is observable to us, Titchener believed it was essential that the observer specify the particular point of view being taken and that it be followed consistently. Through a description of the existential universe from a consistent point of view, Titchener believed that the subject matter of a discipline is produced. To mix the points of view within a given observation would produce subject matters made up of incompatible or at best inconsistent contents. The result of such an uncritical mix he called "muddle," which he believed to be perhaps the greatest threat of all to systematic understanding.

An example can be found in the different ways physics, biology, and psychology look at the same universe. To the old problem: "A tree falls in the forest but there is no one there to hear it. Is there a sound?", Titchener would answer that it depends on the point of view taken. From the point of view of physics, which looks at the universe and describes it in terms of radiations, vibrations, and material elements and compounds, there would be a sound whether or not anyone was there to hear it. The world described by classical physics and chemistry exists independently of organisms. To physics, sound is a cyclical rarefaction and compression of air molecules. Biology would say no sound was present unless it excited the nervous system of an organism. Classical biology studied the functions of organismic systems, in this case the nervous system, and how the organism adjusts to environmental changes. A stimulus exists for biology if an organismic system is altered by it, in this case the auditory nerve of an organism. Sound for biology, then, is a nervous impulse. Titchener's psychology would say there was no sound unless an individual was there who heard it. Even if the auditory nerve were stimulated by the sound, should the individual be asleep, psychologically there would be no sound since it had no conscious representation. Classical psychology studied only conscious experience. Psychologically, sound is an experience. Thus, depending on whether you are speaking as a physicist, biologist, or psychologist, the answer to "Is there a sound" will differ markedly. According to Titchener, the subject matters that make up these three disciplines were created by their observing the universe from three consistent but different points of view.

The Fundamental Sciences   This representation of three points of view does not exhaust all the sciences possible, but for Titchener, these three were the three fundamental sciences: physics (which included chemistry), biology, and psychology. One of Titchener's major ambitions was to have psychology accepted as one of these three fundamental sciences. His opposition to Watson's behaviorism can be understood in part because he believed that if behaviorism became part of psychology, psychology would lose its independent status as the science of mind and would be reduced to a subset of biology. Titchener wanted psychology to remain independent both of biology and philosophy.

Scientific Explanation   Science is not just description, of course, but includes explanation. To Titchener, explanation was a one-step reductive process relative to the three fundamental sciences. Psychology describes in terms of conscious experience—sensations, images, and feelings—and explains these experiential processes by means of the functioning of the nervous system, that is, biologically. Biology describes in terms of organismic systems including the nervous system but explains in terms of the physical elements that make up living systems. Physics describes in terms of physical elements, but explains in terms of the relation of space, time, and mass. The psychologist may explain at the biological level and still remain a psychologist. In Titchener's view to go beyond that and to seek explanation at the physical level makes the individual a biologist, not a psychologist. In this way, Titchener escaped infinite regression, the bugaboo of reductionism.

Scientific Versus Applied Psychology   Using the same logic, Titchener held that scientific psychology and applied psychology have fundamentally different points of view. Scientific psychology, Titchener believed, seeks to understand the facts of psychological experience from a disinterested point of view. Scientific psychology attempts to understand the nature of things. The potential utility of the understanding does not enter into the scientific motive. Titchener believed that, once understanding occurs, the applications will follow of themselves. Applied psychology, or "psychotechnics" as Titchener sometimes called it, does not share this point of view. Technologies seek not to understand but to utilize. It is sufficient for technology to be able to predict an outcome of an environmental manipulation without understanding how the two events are related. That is not sufficient for science. Science seeks to maintain a distance from the subject matter it treats—to view the event or fact in a disinterested or objective way. Technology is interested in obtaining value and thus, in Titchener's view, loses the objectivity of the pure scientist. Because of this position, for instance, when Watson declared behaviorism to deal with the prediction and control of behavior, Titchener was able to reject it as a scientific enterprise. Prediction and control are utilitarian and thus technological attitudes, he said, not scientific ones.

Subdisciplines   Continuing to follow the logic of his concept of point of view, Titchener divided each of the fundamental sciences into a large number of subdisciplines, each of which was determined by its particular point of view. Titchener distinguished several such subdisciplines within what was generally called psychology. They included physiological psychology, psychophysics, experimental introspective psychology, and anthropological psychology. Each looks at the same existential universe but describes it differently, thus creating different subject matters. Titchener held that each discipline and subdiscipline must state explicitly its particular point of view and must stick to that point of view throughout. Inconsistency in this matter would lead, he warned, to a confused and muddled subject matter.

Experimental Versus "Other" Psychologies   Titchener's own special area of study was experimental psychology, which he defined as the study of the mental processes of normal, adult, human individuals as obtained through introspective analysis under experimental control. He made it very clear that his textbooks were a survey of that particular subdiscipline, experimental introspective psychology. Although he mentioned other subdisciplines, he urged the student who was interested in them to find published treatments elsewhere.

It had been easy enough in the 1890s for Titchener to contrast his introspectionist experimental psychology as *the* experimental psychology. Neither comparative psychology, developmental psychology, nor abnormal psychology made much use of experimental techniques in those days. Even functional psychology, the psychology of William James and George Trumbull Ladd, had been easily dismissed because their data were not derived experimentally. The transition from functional psychology to functionalism, particularly that wrought by James Rowland Angell at Chicago during the first decade of the twentieth century, made matters more difficult for Titchener. Chicago Functionalism was also experimental and so was able to compete with Titchener's structuralism in a way that the older functional psychologies could not.

Stimulus Error   In psychological observation, one result of the uncritical mixture of physical and psychological points of view is what Titchener called the stimulus error. Stimulus error is encountered when a psychologist mixes his knowledge about the physical stimulus (a physical point of view) with his experience of that stimulus (psychological point of view). An example Titchener liked to use was that of the Müller–Lyer Illusion. Shown the two lines in Figure 19-1, how should we describe them? To Titchener, the psychological description would be "two visual extents with *a* longer than *b.*" The observer who knows something about the physics of the Müller–Lyer illusion, however, might describe it as "two lines that look unequal but which are really equal." To Titchener, physically the lines are equal, but psychologically they are not. By mixing the physical with the psychological standpoints, the result is muddle, neither consistently physical nor psychological.[23]

(a)   (b)

Figure 19.1 The Müller-Lyer illusion. (*Source*: Adapted from E. B. Titchener, *A Textbook of Psychology* (New York: Macmillan, 1909), p. 14.

Psychophysical Parallelism Another significant aspect derived from Titchener's concept of point of view is found in his version of psychophysical parallelism. Throughout most of his career Titchener adhered to the doctrine of psychophysical parallelism instead of the common-sense view of mind–body interactionism. He wrote:

> Our own position has been that mind and body, the subject-matter of psychology and the subject-matter of physiology, are simply two aspects of the same world of experience. They cannot influence each other, because they are not separate and independent things. For the same reason, however, wherever the two aspects appear, any change that occurs in the one will be accompanied by a corresponding change in the other.[24]

Following Avenarius, he handled the matter of mind–body relationship in terms of dependent versus independent experience.[25]

> If we look at the whole experience under its independent aspect, we find that certain physical events, certain stimuli, affect the body; they set up in the body, and especially in the nervous system, certain physical changes; these changes cause the secretion of tears. This is an exhaustive account of the experience, considered as independent of the experiencing person. If we look at the experience under its dependent aspect, we find that our consciousness has been invaded by grief or remorse or some kindred emotion. The two sets of events, physical and mental, are parallel, but they do not interfere with each other.[26]

These points of view make up the relational equation in Titchener's psychological science, one physical or biological and the other psychological.

Meaning It was Titchener's determination to keep the observational point of view consistent, avoiding a mixture of perspectives, that led him to exclude meanings from psychological description.[27] In this respect, he diverged from much of his English empirical and associational background, and from Mach and Avenarius as well. To Titchener, psychological description involves that which is directly observed—sensations, images, and feelings—and not inferences or logical abstractions made from them, which he believed ordinary meanings to be.[28]

Titchener exhorted the psychological observer to describe what the experience is and not the meanings derived from it. For instance, if the observer placed a finger in a glass of water, a Titchenerian would describe the sensations directly as pressure and coolness. Those are the sensations produced in that experimental condition, although images may be called up as well as feelings of pleasantness or unpleasantness accruing to the sensations and images. The observer who reports "wetness," however, is not describing the experience, the content–process, but only the "meaning" of the experience. Titchener accepts, however, that it is possible to do a psychological study of the psychological constituents of meanings. Meaning can be studied psychologically, he said, by studying the content–processes that carry the meaning, usually kinaesthetic or verbal images. To Titchener, meaning as content–processes is produced by a pattern of experiences that form a context for another experience. Titchener's position was that the meaning of an experience should not be confused with the experience itself, nor should the two be mixed together uncritically.

Titchener's view of meaning is perhaps his most original contribution to psychology. We might do well to consider in some detail just precisely what he defined as meaning. In his *Textbook* Titchener tells us:

> No sensation means; a sensation simply goes on in various attributive ways, intensively, clearly, spatially, and so forth. All perceptions mean; they go on, also, in various attributive ways; but they go on meaningly. What then, psychologically, is meaning?
>
> Meaning, psychologically, is always context; one mental process is the meaning of another mental process if it is that other's context. And context, in this sense, is simply the mental process which accrues to the given process through the situation in which the organism finds itself.[29]

The situation, then, is the context, the fringe or background that gives meaning to the experience at the focus or foreground. It can be a transitory collection of sensations, or it can be what Gestalt psychology later called "set." As the context changes, so does the meaning that accrues to the foreground. A Swastika will have a very different meaning to someone who has just been reading a history of Nazi Germany than it will to someone who has just read an article on Hindu symbolism. The content–process, the "object," remains the same, but its context has changed and, with it, the meaning it carries.

How, then, does the context mean? Titchener can be interpreted to say that the context does not mean as long as it remains context. If we shift our attention from the foreground to the context, what was previously context now becomes foreground. It can then mean if it is brought together with another context. As context it does not mean. Is this infinite regress? Titchener would think not. Meaning is produced through the relationship of an experience at the focus of attention (foreground) with an experience at the margin of attention (context). One does not go farther back than context. If one shifts attention to the context, one is dealing with a different equation, even if the previous foreground becomes the new context.

As we have said, Titchener held that one may study meaning psychologically, but only in terms of content–processes. What he opposed is mistaking meanings for content–processes and then uncritically mixing them as though they were equivalent experiences.

This distinction between the description of content–processes and meanings was at the heart of the long, unresolved imageless thought controversy between Titchener and Oswald Külpe. Külpe's *Bewusstseinslage*, the vague experience unanalyzable as image or sensation, was, to Titchener, a product of meaning experiences uncritically mixed with the experiences of thought.[30]

Titchener's Psychology

Description of Titchener's system of psychology is sometimes oversimplified. Critics say that Titchener's structuralism was concerned only with the static elements of experience, not with the study of the process of experience, as James and others had been. This is simply not true. To Titchener the "elements" were not fixed "things" but were processes. He shared William James's view that mental life is a constant flux. Titchener believed, however, that lawful aspects of this flux could be abstracted out by means of analytical introspection. If, in James's terms, the cross-section of the stream of thought were made, that section would be unique. In contrast, Titchener would say that the aspects that make up that unique cross-section have typical patterns. Thus, sensations, images, feelings, and the like can be abstracted out of the whole and their relationships understood. Titchener's structuralism was a system of arranging these typical existences.

Titchener begins his system with the same problem Wundt did: analysis. The observer's first task is to analyze this conscious moment into its simplest parts: elements. Titchener, following Külpe, listed three elements: sensations, images, and feelings. Sensations come to us through the senses; images are internal equivalents of sensations (ideas); and feelings are the simplest emotional experiences that accrue to the sensations and images. The sensations are described in terms of their attributes. Expanding on Wundt's quality and intensities for sensations and images, Titchener listed extensity (space), protensity (time), and attensity (clearness or vividness). Like Külpe, Titchener believed it was possible to analyze any conscious mental process, no matter how complex, into these simple states. For this reason, Titchener was able to disregard Wundt's doctrine of creative synthesis since space and time were part of the regular structure of his system. Titchener criticized accessory doctrine such as creative synthesis as psychological "hocus pocus."[31] Similarly, he was able to disregard Wundt's doctrine of apperception, since attensity or attributive clearness was part of the structure.[32] Titchener believed that Wundt's doctrine of apperception, the process through which attention occurs, was a functional and not a structural concept.

In terms of feelings, Titchener also diverged from Wundt. In 1896 Wundt had deserted his simple pleasantness–neutral–unpleasantness dimension for a tridimensional theory of feelings. Titchener retained the simpler approach. Feeling, at least until Titchener's revisions of his system in the 1920s, encompassed simply the qualities of pleasantness or unpleasantness to some quantitative degree from zero to high. Thus, the attributes for the element of feeling were quality (pleasantness or unpleasantness) and intensity (zero through high).

With the elaborations of Wundt's doctrines of creative synthesis and apperception out of the way, Titchener was able to deal with simple perceptions as the direct integration of two or more qualities of some given intensity. Tonal fusions such as musical chords, taste blends such as flavor, and tactual compounds such as wet and oily are of this sort. For Titchener complex perceptions involve simple perceptions with the addition of some spatial or temporal attribute. Thus, musical chords produce melody in some temporal sequence.

Parallel to sensations and perceptions but of internal origin were images and ideas. In general, for every possible sensation and its resultants there was an equivalent image and its resultant ideas. In fact, the two paralleled each other to such a degree that Titchener would collapse idea into sensation and simply call images internal sensations. Once experienced, a sensation or perception could be called up as an image or idea, which is one way in which a context could be formed for a meaning experience.

Following this same arrangement, there was a development of feelings parallel to sensations and images that led to emotions, then to mood (which was an emotion over a longer period of time), and up to temperament (which was an habitual tendency toward mood or emotions).

As with Wundt, it is not possible to detail every aspect of Titchener's system, but it is important to note that Titchener's structural system, as was true of Külpe's system, was able to continue without a seam into the higher mental processes of memory, thought, judgment, and all the other areas that Wundt believed could not be studied experimentally. Since thought was described as the content–experiences that occurred in a given situation (thinking), thought was just as analyzable into simpler states and finally into sensations or images as any perception. The question arises as to whether the "thought" that Titchener and his students described constitute "thinking." Thinking is a function and has a physiological basis. All that Titchener's structural psychology can say about it is the experiences produced. Those experiences *are* thought. Any statement about the underlying process would be inferences about the experiences.

The study of higher mental processes was the reef on which Titchener and Külpe's introspective psychology would founder. As we have seen, Külpe's students found certain components of thought to be unalyzable; Titchener and his students did not. They were able to analyze the thought experiences into their imaginal components. The unanalyzable aspects, Würzburg's *Bewusstseinslagen*, were, to Titchener, the result of Külpe's students mixing meanings with images. The two laboratories were looking at the same experience but seeing different things because they had taken different points of view.[33]

Later Developments

This brief overview of Titchener's system has been that of his *A Textbook of Psychology* of 1910. Titchener's psychology did not remain fixed. During the remaining seventeen years of his life, his systematic views changed considerably.

To some degree, Titchener's decision to collapse image and sensation into two different forms of the same thing (externally aroused versus internally aroused sensations) was a sign of things to come. Around 1918, he dropped the use of the term *elements* in his lectures and started out from his attributive dimensions.[34] After all, if an element is defined in terms of its attributes, then the attributes *are* the element. He was left, then, with "the ultimate 'dimensions' " of psychological subject matter as being quality, intensity, protensity, extensity, and attensity.[35]

We will never completely know the direction Titchener would have taken had he lived another decade. He appears to have been moving toward an experimental phenomenology, dealing with simple experiences as points on a confluence of attributive dimensions.

Boring's obituary of Titchener, published the year Titchener died, closes with the statement that a century may have to pass before it is possible to assess Titchener's place in the history of psychology.[36] From the present perspective of only some fifty years later, the approach to psychology through introspection seems to have closed with Titchener's death. This is not to say that content of consciousness as a source of psychological data has disappeared. That we have progressed beyond Titchener's views anyone with a sense of history would acknowledge, but this inevitable lesson does not detract from the contribution these views represent. Both Wundt and Titchener thought they had set the pattern for psychology. Actually, their work was but a stage in its history and barely survived Titchener's death. In fact, the remarkable aspect is the speed with which the change took place. By 1930 students of Titchener were arguing that the homogeneity among psychologists was much greater than the differences and that, except for a few diehards, a reconciliation among the warring schools was actually taking place. The assimilation of many of Titchener's ideas had begun, particularly those involved in dimensions of experience.

A rigid, contentually subjective view of psychology and an adherence to a conscious mentalism expressed through a search for molecular structures were salient features of Titchener's view of the nature of psychology. This view was modified in later years to a concept that was still molecular, but not unrelievedly so, in which dimensions of experience, not the elements, were the object of study. His insistence that psychology is severely puristic, though characteristic enough, was not vital to it. Search for general laws, or nomotheticism, did reinforce this purism.

In saying that Titchener's system did not long survive him is not to say that his work has not influenced psychology. His insistence on the laboratory as the primary source of information about psychological matters has remained fundamental to the American psychological scene and has since spread all over the world. This is not to say that field studies and case study methods are not used in psychology, but far less frequently than laboratory or otherwise carefully controlled research methods. The fact that every psychology student takes at least one course in experimental methods, typically with laboratory exercises, may be traced to Titchener and his manuals. In that way Titchener put his permanent imprint on the way scientific psychology is taught and practiced.

Another and more subtle influence from Titchener's system is the elementistic structure of psychology. As we will see in Chapter 22, when John B. Watson established his behaviorism, he took over the structural logic of Titchener's system and replaced his mentalistic terminology with behavioral equivalents. To the degree to which behaviorism is still largely elementistic, Titchener's influence survives, though probably not in a way that would have pleased him.

SUMMARY

Titchener was only one of Wundt's students in America, but he did the most to promote the experimental psychology of mind by making use of analytical introspection. Titchener diverged from Wundt in detail, however, although he believed his differences perfected Wundt rather than repudiated him.

Titchener sought to find a place for psychology among the primary sciences, along with physics and biology. To Titchener, psychology was scientific and not applied. Although he held that there were legitimate applications of psychology, he felt they should be carried out by specialists in application rather than by theoretical and experimental psychologists.

Titchener's psychology had strong leanings toward what is commonly called positivism, although his connections to Mach have often been overestimated.

Titchener's early psychological positions emphasized elements and attributes of experience. He later moved toward a dimensional approach to psychological experience.

Of all his contributions, perhaps the most significant was his demand that psychology become a laboratory science in which the laboratory would be the fundamental source of psychology's data. Although his system did not long outlive him, his championing of the laboratory effectively ended the era of philosophical psychology espoused by Brentano and James as a serious challenge to experimental psychology.

NOTES

1. Part of this chapter is drawn from Rand B. Evans, "E. B. Titchener and the Beginnings of American Experimental Psychology," *Revista De Historia De La Psicologia* (Spain), (1984):117–125.
2. J. McKeen Cattell, "The Founding of the Association and of the Hopkins and Clark Laboratories," *Psychological Review, 50* (1943):61–62.
3. E. G. Boring, "Edward Bradford Titchener, 1867–1927," *American Journal of Psychology, 38* (1927):489–506.
4. E. B. Titchener, *Experimental Psychology: A Manual of Laboratory Practice* (New York: Macmillan Co., 1901–1905), I, Pt. II, vii.
5. W. B. Pillsbury, "The Psychology of Edward Bradford Titchener," *Philosophical Review, 37* (1928):95–108.
6. Frank Angell, "Titchener at Leipzig," *Journal of General Psychology, 1* (1927):195–198.
7. W. B. Pillsbury, "The Psychology of Edward Bradford Titchener."
8. E. B. Titchener, *Experimental Psychology.*
9. John B. Watson, Letter to E. B. Titchener, December 14, 1908, Titchener Papers, Cornell University Archives.
10. See Ryan Tweney, "Programmic Research in Experimental Psychology: E. B. Titchener's Laboratory Investigations, 1891–1927" in M. G. Ash and W. R. Woodward, *Psychology in Twentieth-Century Thought and Society* (Cambridge: Cambridge University Press, 1987, pp 35–57).
11. E. G. Boring, "Titchener's Experimentalists," *Journal of the History of the Behavioral Sciences, 3* (1967):316.
12. *Ibid.*, Boring, "The Society of Experimental Psychologists: 1904–1938," *American Journal of Psychology, 51* (1939):410–424; C. James Goodwin, "On the Origins of Titchener's Experimentalists," *Journal of the History of the Behavioral Sciences, 21* (1985):383–389.

13. E. B. Titchener, "Postulates of a Structural Psychology," *Philosophical Review, 7* (1898):449–465; "Structural and Functional Psychology," *Philosophical Review, 8* (1899):290–299.

14. E. B. Titchener, "The Province of Structural Psychology," *Philosophical Review, 7* (1898):449–465.

15. John B. Watson, "Psychology as the Behaviorist Views It," *Psychological Review, 20* (1913):177–179; "Image and Affection in Behavior," *Journal of Philosophy, Psychology and Scientific Methods, 10* (1913):421–423.

16. E. B. Titchener, "On 'Psychology as the Behaviorist Views It,'" *Proceedings of the American Philosophical Society, 53* (1914):1–17.

17. Julian Jaynes, "Edwin Garrigues Boring: 1886–1968," *Journal of the History of the Behavioral Sciences, 5* (1969):102; E. G. Boring, Letter to R. M. Ogden, August 18, 1928, Cornell University Archives.

18. R. B. Evans, "E. B. Titchener and His Lost System," *Journal of the History of the Behavioral Sciences, 8* (1972):169.

19. Edna Heidbreder, *Seven Psychologies* (New York: Appleton–Century–Crofts, 1933), p. 151.

20. For another view, see Kurt Danziger, "The Positivistic Repudiation of Wundt," *Journal of the History of the Behavioral Sciences, 15* (1979):205–230.

21. Ernst Mach, *Die Analyze der Empfindungen und das Verhaeltniss des Physischen zum Psychischen* (Jena: Gustave Fischer, 1885), translated by C. M. Williams and Sydney Waterlow as *The Analysis of Sensations and the Relation of the Physical to the Psychical* (New York: Dover, 1959), pp. 314–315.

22. This section is drawn in part from Rand B. Evans, "The Scientific and Psychological Positions of E. B. Titchener," in Ruth Leys and Rand B. Evans, eds., *Defining American Psychology: The Correspondence Between Adolf Meyer and E. B. Titchener,* (Baltimore: Johns Hopkins University Press, 1990), pp. 1–38. See also Evans, "Titchener's Relativistic View of Observation and Psychological Processes," in Leendert P. Mos, ed., *Annals of Theoretical Psychology, 4* (1986):291–297.

23. Titchener may have set a standard too high even for himself. See Mary Henle, "Did Titchener Commit the Stimulus Error?" *Journal of the History of the Behavioral Sciences, 7* (1971):279–282.

24. E. B. Titchener, *Textbook,* p. 13.

25. Ernst Mach, *The Analysis of Sensations,* trans. C. M. Williams (New York: Dover, 1959; 5th German edition, 1906), p. 51.

26. E. B. Titchener, *Textbook,* p. 14.

27. For a discussion of the background of Titchener's positions on meaning, see Evans, "The Origins of Titchener's Doctrine of Meaning," *Journal of the History of the Behavioral Sciences, 11* (1975):334–341.

28. E. B. Titchener, "The Schema of Introspection," *American Journal of Psychology, 23* (1912):498.

29. E. B. Titchener, *Textbook,* p. 367.

30. See E. B. Titchener, *Thought-Processes;* for a position sympathetic to Külpe, see George Humphrey, *Thinking: An Introduction to Its Experimental Psychology* (New York: John Wiley and Sons, 1963; orig. pub. 1951), pp. 106–131. For an alternate view on Titchener's problems with meaning, see Mary Henle, "Did Titchener Commit the Stimulus Error? The Problem of Meaning in Structural Psychology," *Journal of the History of the Behavioral Sciences, 7* (1971):279–282.

31. E. B. Titchener, "A Note on Wundt's Doctrine of Creative Synthesis," *American Journal of Psychology, 33* (1922):351–360.

32. E. B. Titchener, "The Psychological Concept of Clearness," *Psychological Review 24* (1917):43–61.

33. A discussion of this issue and its significance to modern cognitive psychology may be found in Harry T. Hunt, "A Cognitive Reinterpretation of Classical Introspectionism," in Leendert P. Mos, ed., *Annals of Theoretical Psychology, 4* (1986):245–290.

34. R. B. Evans, "E. B. Titchener and His Lost System," pp. 172–174.

35. *Ibid.,* 172; E. B. Titchener, "The Term Attensity," *American Journal of Psychology, 35* (1924):156.

36. E. G. Boring, "Edward Bradford Titchener."

James Rowland Angell.

Chapter 20

Angell and American Functionalism

*F*unctional psychologies both predate and postdate the arrival of Titchener's structuralism. As we have seen in earlier chapters, functional psychology was concerned with mind in use, with what the mind does for us. Functional psychology is as old as psychology itself. Aristotle was a functional psychologist, as was Descartes. The psychological thought that arose in America in the eighteenth and nineteenth centuries, discussed in Chapter 17, also emphasized mind in use. Faculty psychologies, in their own way, were functional psychologies, since the faculties were the functions of the soul. William James was also functional in his approach. Functional psychologies, owing to their emphasis on the use of mind, lent themselves readily to the practical and to the struggle to get ahead, which made them congenial to the practical American way of looking at things.

FUNCTIONALISM

Functional*isms* as considered in this discussion, are viewed as particular forms of functional psychology, as twentieth-century systems of functional psychology, particularly centered at the University of Chicago and at Columbia University. Functional psychology, then, is the generic form.

Titchener and his structuralists believed that application was technology, not science, and that teleology was unacceptable in a scientific psychology. To characterize functional psychology in terms of utility seemed to them tantamount to criticism. Titchener said that structuralism dealt with the IS of mind, whereas functionalism dealt with the IS FOR. The functionalists also held their discipline to be scientific. They did not view their study of the ways in which consciousness helps the individual to adapt to the environment as any less scientific than biology. In the hands of James Rowland Angell, the Chicago School showed a partiality toward research on learning, perception, and similar processes. It was also interested in animal psychology, physiological psychology, and the psychology of individual differences. Functionalism went far beyond the constraints of Titchener's ''normal, adult, human mind.''

WILLIAM JAMES AS A FUNCTIONAL PSYCHOLOGIST

Functional psychology has many forebears. In his 1898 article contrasting functional psychology with structural psychology Titchener singled out James as a typical functional psychologist.[1] Actually, James was too versatile to be easily labeled. Titchener adopted his terms *structural* and *functional* as well as their differentiation from an article by James that appeared in 1884.[2] James had attached no great importance to the distinction, however, and so, in his *Principles*, James had relegated it to a footnote.[3]

In what sense was James a functional psychologist? In the *Principles*, James assimilated psychology into biology and treated thinking as an instrument in the struggle for life.[4] For James mental processes were activities, and mind was not an entity, but a functional activity of the organism. He emphasized the biological survival value of mind; if consciousness had no value it would not have survived. James saw consciousness as useful because it intervened in the cause–effect sequence, resulting in the spontaneity and productivity of the mind. John Dewey accepted and elaborated on this particular view in his appeal to consciousness as part of the adjustive equipment of the organism, whereas Angell[5] used James's already familiar argument that consciousness is not present when it has no utility.

JOHN DEWEY AS A FUNCTIONALIST

Charles Darwin had helped to prepare the way for functionalism by emphasizing adaptation, activities, and individual differences. He was not a teleologist, however. Such adaptation was merely a process and was not part of some plan of perfection.

Galton and Spencer continued this tradition but added purposiveness to the positions of Darwin, each in his own way, Galton emphasizing individual differences and Spencer, adaptation. Showing its evolutionary heritage, functionalism regarded psychology as the study of how consciousness helps the organism adapt to its environment. Titchener, as we have already seen, criticized this position on the basis that adaptation of the organism to the environment was a biological and not a psychological subject matter.

In the 1890s and early 1900s, in America this view of mind-in-use had already attracted kindred spirits. Such early psychologists as James McKeen Cattell and Robert S. Woodworth at Columbia, James Mark Baldwin at Toronto and later Johns Hopkins, and, in some ways, G. Stanley Hall at Clark made use of the notion. We will consider the Columbia group later in this chapter as an informal school of functionalism; the center of the formal development of functional psychology into functionalism was at Chicago.

Life of Dewey

John Dewey (1859–1952) can be considered the first American functiona*list*.[6] He was born in Burlington, Vermont, in 1859 and entered the University of Vermont at the age of fifteen. He studied philosophy there, which was largely the dominant Scottish Realist philosophy. He also studied the writings of James Marsh, who had earlier been President of the University and who had helped introduce Kantian idealism to America. There he also encountered the evolutionary writings of Thomas Huxley. Dewey graduated in 1879 and taught school for a couple of years. He returned to Vermont and the University of Vermont, where he continued his studies while teaching in a village school. After successfully getting an article accepted in the *Journal of Speculative Philosophy,* Dewey determined to become a philosopher.[7] He enrolled for graduate work at the Johns Hopkins University in Baltimore in 1881 where G. Stanley Hall was just establishing his laboratory. Because Hall was away during Dewey's first semester at Hopkins, Dewey took his courses from George Sylvester Morris (1840–1889), who was then teaching part of each year at Hopkins and part at the University of Michigan. Morris, also a native of Vermont, had studied with Trendelenburg in Germany and was, by the time Dewey met him, an enthusiastic promoter of Hegel's idealism.[8] Dewey fell under Morris's spell. Dewey's dissertation was on Kant, and it was very much in the spirit of George Sylvester Morris.[9] Although Dewey would come under the influence of other thinkers, notably William James, he was fond of saying that Hegel "left a permanent deposit in my thinking."[10]

It was while Dewey was still a graduate student at Johns Hopkins that he wrote an article on the new psychology.[11] His view as expressed in that article is indicative of his functional and teleological tendencies. The new psychology, Dewey wrote,

> emphasizes the teleological element, not in any mechanical or external sense, but regarding life as an organism in which immanent ideas or purposes are realizing themselves throughout the development of experience. . . . We can conclude only by saying that following the logic of life, it attempts to comprehend life.[12]

After receiving his doctorate from Johns Hopkins, Dewey received an appointment in 1884 to the Department of Philosophy of the University of Michigan where he would work until 1894. George Sylvester Morris, then solely at Michigan, was largely responsible for the call. Dewey, following the usual custom, taught psychology as well as philosophy; indeed, in 1886[13] he published a somewhat influential text entitled simply *Psychology,* which contained the philosophical presuppositions characteristic of his time. With the publication of William James's *Principles of Psychology,* however, Dewey changed many of his ideas on psychology. He was particularly influenced by James's notion of the "stream of consciousness." Later editions of Dewey's *Psychology* demonstrate the alteration in his thought.[14] In none of these editions did Dewey consider that psychology could avail itself directly of the experimental method, however.[15] He believed that introspection was the primary source of information about psychological matters. Introspection to Dewey was

> a general power of knowing which the mind has, directed reflectively and intentionally upon a certain set of facts. It is also called internal perception; the observation of the nature and course of ideas as they come and go, corresponding to external perception, or the observation of facts and events before the senses. This method of observation of facts of consciousness must *ultimately* be the sole source of the *material* of psychology.[16]

Dewey's functional leanings are also evident in the title of the second chapter of his *Psychology,* "The Mind and Its Modes of Activity."

The period of Dewey's greatest importance in psychology and his identification with functionalism, however, coincided with his stay at the University of Chicago during the years 1894 to 1904. When he left Chicago for Columbia University in 1905, he no longer worked directly in the field of psychology, although he did utilize psychology in the larger educational and philosophical perspectives that later concerned him.

Dewey and the Reflex Arc

Dewey's paper of 1896 on the reflex arc concept served to introduce the school of functionalism.[17] Just as James before him had attacked psychological atomism by demonstrating that simple ideas have no existential reality in the stream of consciousness, so Dewey found the same doctrine of elementism lurking in the reflex arc. He was searching for a unifying concept for mental life, and he considered the reflex arc, recently borrowed from physiology, a likely possibility. Despite its promise, detailed analysis led him to reject it for this purpose because of its "patchwork" qualities. The reflex arc was not made up of three separate elements—sensation, mediation, and response—but a single, continuous conscious process.[18]

As Dewey saw it, a child's withdrawal of his finger from the flame, often given as the classical example of the reflex arc, does not tell the whole story of what is happening. After an experience of this sort, the visual perception of the flame, previously inviting to the child, is now permanently altered. The stimulus and the response of the burn–withdrawal reflex does not end with the withdrawal. It now serves as the stimulus for another situation that belongs to the same act, instead of being a new occurrence. Every reaction, Dewey argued, is a circuit. That is, adjustment is more than a response to a stimulus: it is a realignment within one's environment. The unitary act completes a circle from sensation through movement to a new sensation that arises out of that movement. Sensation as an "existence" and motion as a response do not account for the psychological facts, which form, not an arc, but a circuit. Dewey argued that reflexes, as well as other forms of behavior, should not be treated as artificial constructs by the abstraction of their sensory and motor phases. It is their significance for adaptation that is crucial. In this way Dewey was making a plea for function as the basis of psychological study.

Here we find two of the fundamental aspects that underlie Chicago functionalism: a holistic rather than an elementistic representation of psychological activity, and an emphasis on consciousness as an adaptive adjustment.

JAMES ROWLAND ANGELL

Without deliberate intention, the functional viewpoint became crystalized as a school. In some measure it came about by answering the critics' attacks of this viewpoint. When Titchener popularized the term *functionalism* by contrasting it with structuralism and criticizing it, James Rowland Angell (1869–1949), a former student of William James and Dewey's younger associate at the University of Chicago, accepted the challenge.[19]

Life of Angell

Angell was born in Burlington, Vermont, in 1869.[20] His father was President of the University of Vermont between 1866 and 1871 and President of the University of Michigan from 1871 to 1909. James R. Angell received his undergraduate education at the University of Michigan between 1886 and 1890, where he studied botany. At Michigan, Angell met John Dewey. Dewey's *Psychology*, which had just recently appeared, was Angell's introduction to psychology. After receiving his bachelor's degree, Angell stayed on at Michigan during 1890–1891, working on a master's degree in philosophy. In 1890, when James's *Principles of Psychology* appeared, Dewey offered a seminar on the new book and Angell took the course. James and the ideas of the *Principles* would influence Angell for the remainder of his career in psychology.

Angell, having decided to go into psychology, went to Harvard to do graduate work during the 1891–1892 school year with William James. After gaining his master's degree at Harvard in 1892, Angell went to Germany for his doctorate. He hoped to work with Wilhelm Wundt, but Wundt's laboratory space was full. Instead, Angell went to Berlin to study with Hermann Ebbinghaus. It is said that Angell, disliking the laboratory work in Ebbinghaus's program, transferred to Halle during the second semester and studied with Benno Erdmann, a philosophical psychologist. He was working on a dissertation on Kant's freedom of the will when he received a call to take an instructorship at the University of Minnesota. Angell, who wanted to marry and needed employment, felt he would not receive a better position even with a doctorate. Thus, he never received his official doctoral degree, but he would receive numerous honorary degrees during his lifetime.

After a year a Minnesota, John Dewey, who had just been appointed Professor of Philosophy at the University of Chicago, brought Angell to Chicago as an Assistant Professor to take charge of the psychology curriculum. In 1904, when psychology became a department independent of philosophy, Angell became its head.

Both Angell and Dewey had been influenced by William James, and it was only natural that they attempted to bring some systematic order to James's unruly psychology. This was important in the mid-1890s because of the threat being posed by Titchener and his highly organized and systematized structural psychology to the ideas of William James and all functionally oriented psychologies. Angell became the most visible opponent of E. B. Titchener's structural psychology during the late 1890s and first decade of this century.

Angell's Functionalist Manifesto

In his paper, "The Province of Functional Psychology," and in his textbook of psychology, Angell attempted to present the functional point of view. The University of Chicago was afterward the major source from which functional psychologists came. It should be emphasized, however, that the Chicago functionalists argued that the heritage of functionalism was so broad that it was, properly speaking, not a school at all, and they expressly stated that it should not be identified with psychology as taught at Chicago. Despite this disclaimer, most psychologists were inclined to consider the Chicago psychologists sufficiently different from other psychologists and sufficiently similar among themselves to warrant classification as adherents to a particular school. In 1906 Angell made a presidential address to the American Psychological Association entitled "The Province of Functional Psychology."[21] He brought together three conceptions of function which he considered acceptable to functional psychologists. (1) Functionalism is concerned with mental operations, the "how" and "why" of consciousness, as contrasted to the "what" of the psychology of mental elements. (2) Mind is a means of mediating between the needs of the organism and the environment. Consciousness, in accordance with the emergency theory of James, is utilitarian, since it serves some end. Because consciousness helps to solve problems, an interest in the applied fields of psychology flows naturally from an interest in it. (3) Functional psychology studies mental processes as a means of adjustment; this in turn implies that the epiphenomenalistic solution, which holds mental activity to be nothing more than a useless byproduct of brain action, is incompatible with functionalism. Angell's article clearly spelled out the functionalist position and in this sense was more important than Dewey's paper, which, though it showed a functionalist spirit in dealing with a particular psychological issue, did not explicate the conceptions of a functional psychology.

In 1904, Angell wrote a textbook entitled *Psychology: An Introductory Study of the Structure and Function of Human Consciousness.*[22] As its subtitle attests, the book was concerned with both the structure and the function of human consciousness. Functional solutions were sufficiently emphasized, however, to make clear what he meant by functional psychology. Angell saw the introspective study of consciousness as the principal method of psychological investigation, but it was not the analytical introspection of Wundt or Titchener. The type of introspection used at Chicago was more like that of James, a phenomenological description of ongoing experience. Angell's approach also differed from that of Titchener because he accepted the objective observation of the individual's actions as a supplement. He even allowed his students to do research on animals, although he required them to "introspect" for the animals, attempting to describe what was going on in their minds. Thus, the study of behavior was explicitly accepted as a method of psychology but was only secondary to the study of mental functions. Angell's functionalism emphasized the mind as a whole, and not as being made up of atomistic parts. He opposed the view that the primary purpose of psychology is to analyze immediate experience into its elements and their attributes.[23] There was room in Angell's psychology for the mentalistic findings of Wundt or Titchener's psychologies, but there was also room for objective methods.

Angell viewed mind as having three primary functions—knowing, feeling, and doing. His functionalism was therefore part of the line of functional psychological thought from Aristotle to James. Angell was influenced not only by James, but also by the Darwinian evolutionary revolution. Angell's functionalism, however, was teleological. It emphasized mind in use. Like James, Angell believed that mind had survival value; if it did not, it would have dropped off in the evolutionary development. To Angell, consciousness was a problem solver, as is clearly demonstrated in Angell's treatment of the lapsed intelligence theory of instincts. Walter Hunter summarizes Angell's theory as follows:

> Consciousness appears (and appeared phylogenetically) when reflexes, instincts, and habits fail to solve the problem which confronts the organism. Consciousness aids in the solution of the problem and then, no problem existing longer at that point, passes on to other points of conflict in the organism's behavior. Where consciousness is not in general a problem-solver, it would have no adaptive value and hence would not have survived as a function of the organism. Not only consciousness in general but consciousness in its various forms has an adaptive function.[24]

Angell believed that instinctive behavior was originally conscious behavior. When an organism encounters a problem that past habits or instincts cannot solve, consciousness comes forth and seeks to resolve the problem. Once solved, if the situation is encountered again and again, the reliance on consciousness become less and less until the action becomes habitual and may no longer be conscious at all. Habits that are deeply ingrained into an organism may be passed on to the next generation by way of instincts.

This idea has its roots far back into Chauncey Wright and William James, and suggests how Angell approached psychological problems. Much of Angell's "lapsed intelligence theory" lost respectability when Lamarckian evolutionary theory evaporated, but every decade or so psychologists who do not know their history rediscover the remainder of the theory.

Angell effectively left the field of psychology in 1911 when he became an administrator at Chicago and, later, President of Yale University. Although he published in psychology only rarely after 1912, he helped its cause through his assistance to Robert M. Yerkes and his primate work at Yale and through his support of the Kinsey sex surveys. After retiring from Yale, he became a top executive of the National Broadcasting Corporation.

Angell graduated many students during his academic career, including John B. Watson, Walter Hunter, and Harvey Carr. Although most of his students eventually moved toward behaviorism, they all strongly influenced the direction psychology was to take over the next fifty years.

HARVEY A. CARR AND LATER CHICAGO FUNCTIONALISM

Harvey Carr (1873–1954) had studied at Chicago with Angell and was appointed to the Department of Psychology there in 1908, when John B. Watson left for Johns Hopkins. When Angell left Chicago, Carr took over as head of the department, a post he held until 1938. During this time he continued the Chicago functionalist tradition and became its primary spokesman.[25] He wrote a text, *Psychology: A Study of Mental Activity,*[26] and a book on space perception,[27] both from the functionalist point of view. During Carr's years at Chicago, about 150 psychologists received their Ph.D.s; their later careers showed the influence of the functionalist spirit.

Carr helped to clarify the meaning of the term *functional,* over which there had been considerable controversy.[28] A charge had been made that the functional psychologists had used *function* inconsistently.[29] It was argued that functional sometimes denoted mental activities such as seeing, hearing, and perceiving; at other times functional served to indicate use or service for some end, as when we speak of the function of a word. The functionalists, it was said, would apply the word *function* to an activity, such as breathing or digestion, and later use it to denote the utility of an activity, as when it is said that oxidation of the blood is a function of breathing. This made it possible to speak of a function of an activity—in other words, of a function of a function—which critics of functionalism saw as an absurd confusion. In replying to this charge, Carr insisted that there is really no discrepancy because at a higher level of interpretation the two meanings are actually the same. The common identity of the two—process and end—is the mathematical meaning of function, as in the expression $y = f(x)$; that is, y is a function of x. When a mathematician says y is a function of x, he or she is merely saying there is a contingent relation between them, but he or she does not specify the precise nature of that relation. Functional psychologists use the term the same way, whether they speak of process or end, act or structure, cause or effect. A contingent relation and a functional relation are synonymous. In this, Carr came very close to contemporary usage. Later, the use of cause and effect, which Carr specifically mentioned as one of these functional relations, led to statements that psychology is the study of functional or contingent relations between antecedent psychological events and their consequents. A considerable number of contemporary psychologists would subscribe to this definition.

Chicago Functionalism brought some order to American functional thought, although it was never as organized or as coherent as Titchener's structuralism. It gave a scientific legitimacy to many of James's ideas and connected them closely with biology. John B. Watson's behaviorism can be seen as a logical extension, with some major revisions, of the Chicago formula.

COLUMBIA FUNCTIONALISM

Clear-cut, self-conscious allegiance to their school of thought did not characterize the functionalists as it did the structuralists. Psychology at Columbia University, represented by James McKeen Cattell, was also sympathetic to a functionalist point of view without being narrowly identified with it. The psychologists at Columbia during the first two decades of this century emphasized mind-in-use, however, and sought experimental means of investigating psychological processes.

JAMES MCKEEN CATTELL

If Columbia Functionalism had a leader, it was J. McKeen Cattell (1860–1944). In the course of an after-dinner speech, Cattell[30] once told the story of his boyhood visit to a phrenologist. After inspecting the bumps of his head, the phrenologist proceeded to describe his characteristics, all but one of which were laudatory. (According to the phrenologist, Cattell suffered from a deficiency in will power!) The eruption of laughter from his friends that greeted his remark seemed to surprise Cattell. In point of fact, many of Cattell's major characteristics centered on this salient trait. Dogged determination, unflagging energy, and resistance to domination by those with what he considered undeserved authority seem to have characterized this American psychologist and scientific statesman.

Cattell's Early Life

James McKeen Cattell, encountered earlier as Wundt's self-appointed first assistant and as a student at Johns Hopkins during G. Stanley Hall's time there, was born in 1860 in Easton, Pennsylvania, where his father was a Professor of Classics and, later, President of Lafayette College.[31] There, in 1880, Cattell took his bachelor's degree. His undergraduate interests were chiefly literary, but these interests changed, and he followed the usual custom of graduate study abroad, going to Göttingen and to Leipzig to study philosophy under Wundt. After a paper in philosophy had won him a fellowship at Johns Hopkins for the years 1882–1883, he returned to the United States, just at the time Hall was organizing his laboratory. In the laboratory Cattell started research on the time taken for various mental activities. This research reinforced his desire to become a psychologist, and so he returned to Leipzig the following year. It was on his return to Leipzig that he announced to Wundt that he would be his assistant.[32]

Indications of his independence and his firm convictions appeared at an early date. Contrary to the usual custom of being assigned a problem by Wundt, Cattell worked on his own problems in reaction time. He also became convinced that the introspective efforts directed toward fractionation of the reaction time into perception, choice, and the like, which were then gospel in Wundt's laboratory, was something he could not carry out and which he doubted others could. The situation reached the point where he did some of his experiments at his lodging rather than in the laboratory, since Wundt would not permit subjects in his laboratory who could not profit from introspection.[33] Though somewhat strained, relations between them never reached a breaking point. Wundt and Cattell did agree on the value of the study of reaction time. In Cattell's eyes it was a valuable tool for the study of the time necessary for mental operation, especially for the investigation of individual differences. As early as 1885,[34] Cattell published a paper on the exposure time necessary before perception of colors, letters, and words was possible. It concluded with a discussion of what he called a matter of "special interest," the individual differences he had obtained. Cattell worked prodigiously during the Leipzig years of 1883 to 1886, publishing nine research papers. Studies on the influences of stimulus intensity on reaction time (1885), the time of word perception (1886), and the association time for various categories (1887) were typical subjects of his research.

After taking his degree at Leipzig in 1886, Cattell divided the next two years between the United States and England. On one side of the Atlantic he taught at Bryn Mawr College and at the University of Pennsylvania, and on the other, he worked in Galton's laboratory in London and lectured at Cambridge.

Cattell found in Galton a kindred spirit—"The greatest man whom I have known," he said.[35] Contrary to the opinion sometimes expressed, his interest in individual differences, as we have seen, had made itself apparent before his contact with Galton. In fact, he began his research into individual differences in America before he went to Leipzig. From the tone of his writings, the most specific reason for his interest in variability was the climate of the times in the United States.

In 1888 Cattell was appointed Professor of Psychology at the University of Pennsylvania. This was the first professorship in psychology in the world. Before Cattell psychologists had been appointed to the Department of Philosophy. With his appointment, the field of psychology had the recognition of its independence from the older discipline. The practice of naming professors of psychology spread rapidly, and before 1900 there were a considerable number of them. Cattell founded a laboratory at Pennsylvania in 1887, but it was not until 1889 that an adequate laboratory was opened.[36] Although not the first in the country, it did have the distinction of being the first to introduce undergraduates to the methods of experimental psychology.

In 1891 Cattell moved to Columbia University as Professor of Psychology and administrative head of the department; he was also charged with the task of administering the work of anthropology.[37] His rapid rise on the American psychological scene is evident. At twenty-eight, he was a professor at the University of Pennsylvania; at thirty-one, the chairman of the Department at Columbia; at thirty-five, President of the American Psychological Association; and at forty, he was elected to the National Academy of Sciences—the first psychologist ever so honored.

Meanwhile, Cattell continued to be active in research. In a paper published in 1890 in *Mind*, the British journal, he coined the term *mental tests*[38] in describing a battery of tests administered to students at the University of Pennsylvania. As distinguished from Alfred Binet's later more complex tasks, these involved elementary operations. The basic tests of this series were dynamometer pressure, rate of movement, sensation areas by means of the two-point threshold, just noticeable differences in weight, reaction time for sound, time for naming colors, bisection of a line, judgment of times, and memory span for letters.

At Columbia, Cattell continued his testing program with largely the same sort of tests. After collecting data from several entering classes, Wissler made an analysis of the results in 1901.[39] Correlations of the individual test scores with academic class standings were found to be inconclusively low, as were the intercorrelations among the scores of the tests themselves. In sharp contrast, academic grades in the various subjects and overall academic standing were substantially correlated with each other. Results with specific sensory-motor tests, likewise showing negligible correlations with other measures, also emerged from Titchener's laboratory at Cornell.[40] It began to appear that the available psychological tests were relatively useless as predictors of ability. Further exploration along the lines suggested by these studies tended to dwindle. Binet's results, which would later dominate, had yet to be appreciated in the university setting.

In the spirit of Galton's earlier work, but with vastly improved methodology, Cattell also carried out studies on the nature and origin of scientific ability, using the method of the order of merit. This method is applicable to any set of stimuli capable of being ranked according to some criterion, such as the relative brightness of shades of gray, the problem he first investigated.[41] It could be and soon was applied to such problems as the relative appeal of pictures or of colors. A number of judges would be asked to arrange the items to be evaluated in order of merit. The average ranking for each item was then calculated and a final rank order obtained.[42]

Cattell applied this method to the relative eminence of American psychologists in 1903.[43] For obvious reasons, the actual names associated with specific ranks were not published immediately; it was not until 1929 that the order of names was released. Rank number one went to William James, and the next five ranks, respectively, to Cattell, Hugo Münsterberg, G. Stanley Hall, J. Mark Baldwin, and Edward Bradford Titchener.

Later Life

In further developing the method of order of merit, Cattell asked men acknowledged to be competent in each of the various scientific fields to rate their colleagues in order. Those emerging at the top of the lists for each science were given a star in the *Biographical Directory of American Men of Science*, a sourcebook that emerged from this work. Through the seventh edition the starred men were asked to select the new men for the directory, a technique not followed in subsequent editions. To this day, the directory in its successive editions is a basic reference book, comparable to a specialized Who's Who. Though originating in a purely scientific study, its practical value has been considerable.

In 1895 Cattell acquired from Alexander Graham Bell the weekly journal *Science*, which had been having financial difficulties. In its publication, Cattell sought and secured the help of leading scientists throughout the country. After overcoming the financial difficulties, *Science* became the leading general scientific publication in the United States and in 1900 was made the official organ of the American Association for the Advancement of Science.

Cattell and other American psychologists, including James,[44] had decided that the *American Journal of Psychology* was functioning primarily as a house organ for the staff of Clark University and some of their associates. Accordingly, in 1894 in collaboration with J. Mark Baldwin, Cattell founded a rival journal, the *Psychological Review*.[45] In his hands this journal grew into an entire series of journals. Editing a weekly and managing journals takes time, and Cattell's personal research productivity began to drop off.

Robert S. Woodworth and Edward L. Thorndike joined him at Columbia not long after his own arrival and were associated with him for many years. Fortunately, the separation of psychologists at the College and Graduate School from those at the Teachers' College, where Thorndike did his work and where Cattell did some of his teaching, had not yet occurred. It was only later that 120th Street, separating the Teachers' College from the main campus, became "the widest street in the world."

During the years Cattell was at Columbia, more "psychologists-to-be" studied at Columbia University than at any other institution in the United States. By and large, Cattell gave his students freedom to advance on their own; he was available for guidance, but he stressed independent work.

Cattell insisted on a similar independence for himself, arguing that a professor's time, if spent within his areas of competence, should not necessarily be devoted solely to the university and its students. He established his home on a hilltop near Garrison forty miles from New York, coming to the university only on certain days of the week. Later he equipped a laboratory and an editorial office in his home, which to some extent freed him from the interruptions of university life.

Cattell's relations with the university administration became strained when he objected that many decisions being left to university administrators were properly matters for faculty decision. He not only raised his voice in pursuit of the aim of faculty participation, but he also helped to found the American Association of University Professors. His most controversial stand was taken during the years of World War I when he wrote a letter to members of Congress protesting the sending of conscientious objectors into combat duty. Though an unpopular and personally disadvantageous position, it was one which he could not in good conscience desist from and so he stood by his position. The president and the trustees, judging his action to be treason, dismissed him from the University. Cattell sued for libel, and the case was settled several years later by his receiving a large annuity. In effect, however, his university career was over.

Many of Cattell's most important activities thereafter continued to be, in the best sense of the word, promotional in character. His numerous presidential addresses were often concerned with the growth and the current status of psychology.[46] He also served as a spokesman for psychology to the other sciences in the United States, as his editorships show. He did not hesitate to criticize and to advise in print universities, philanthropic agencies, the Carnegie Institution, and the National Academy of Sciences. He vigorously defended the growth of applied psychology and psychology as a profession. As early as 1904, he predicted that there would eventually be a profession of psychology as well as a science of psychology.[47] In a similar spirit he organized the Psychological Corporation in 1921 in order to promote the application of psychology.[48] This corporation has grown considerably; it has used its profits to support other research, and it continues to play an important role in professional psychology. Cattell remained active as an editor and senior citizen scientist until his death in 1944.

Cattell was never given to theoretical writing. He was not a systematist but a researcher. He remained in research for some years of his life, thereafter maintaining a respect for research and an ability to criticize it. His interest in individual differences was instrumental in his working for psychology as a profession as well as a science. His bent toward administration and editing places him among that small group of men who gave the beginnings of psychology in the United States its characteristic flavor. His wholehearted devotion to both puristic and utilitarian prescriptions did much to advance both. It also served as a living example that they were not irreconcilable attitudes to hold simultaneously.

ROBERT S. WOODWORTH AND DYNAMIC FUNCTIONALISM

Younger than Cattell, Robert Sessions Woodworth (1869–1962) was also more eclectic. Woodworth, strongly influenced early on by G. Stanley Hall and William James, had been introduced to psychology as an undergraduate at Amherst College by one of the older American philosophical psychologies. After graduating, he discovered William James's *Principles* and was stimulated by James's ideas. He did his graduate work at Harvard beginning in philosophy and worked with both William James and Josiah Royce. His interests, however, turned to psychology. Woodworth's education took a very long time. He worked not only in philosophy and psychology at Harvard, but also in physiology with C. S. Sherrington at Liverpool and with Cattell at Columbia. He joined the faculty at Columbia in 1903 and remained there for most of his career, except for 1912 when he spent a year with Oswald Külpe, who by then had moved from Würzburg to Bonn.[49]

Woodworth's contribution to the functional school is his dynamic psychology. In Woodworth's book, *Dynamic Psychology* (1918), he described psychology as embracing both the older tradition of introspection and the newer one of behavior.[50] The use of the word *dynamic* is misleading, since Woodworth's psychology had little in common with the dynamic psychologies of Freud or other psychoanalysts. It was, in fact, a functionalism dealing with what Woodworth called "the workings of the mind."[51] Edna Heidbreder, who received her degree under Woodworth, described his dynamic psychology, as "a modest, matter-of-fact, unaggressive system."[52] Woodworth was attempting to find a middle ground between the orthodox introspectionist psychologies on one side and the burgeoning behavioral psychologies on the other. Woodworth tells us:

> It is agreed on all sides that psychology studies processes. What the behaviorist observes, and what the introspectionist observes, both come down to process, sequence of events. Structure we observe only in the figurative sense in which a complex process may be said to have structure. We are concerned with antecedents and consequents, cause and effect, stimulus and response, the combination of factors and similar dynamic relations.

> Psychological dynamics is not limited to the study of feeling, emotion, conation and muscular and glandular action. We study also sensations as dependent upon their stimuli, we analyze out the various factors in the perception of depth or distance, we examine the process of learning, and formulate laws of association or recall. The whole subject is permeated with dynamics.[53]

Woodworth's "system" of dynamic psychology was never widely held as a formal position, but it was indicative of the increasing tendency toward eclecticism as a response to the competing claims of orthodox introspectionism and radical behaviorism.

Woodworth's other major contribution to psychology was his *Experimental Psychology*,[54] published in 1938. It included many of the classic methods as did Titchener's manuals, as well as the new methodology involved in human and animal psychology that had emerged since Titchener's volumes were released. That book, with its revision done with Harold Schlosberg in 1954, became the methodological bible of students of psychology from its publication through the 1960s. It played the same role for today's senior psychologists that Titchener's *Experimental Psychology* had played for Woodworth's contemporaries. A notable contribution was Woodworth's popularization of the terms *independent variable* and *dependent variable* in talking about experimental causality.[55]

Another of Woodworth's works, *Contemporary Schools of Psychology*, was one of the first attempts to gain perspectives on the systematic psychologies of the late nineteenth and early twentieth centuries. First published in 1931, it went through three revisions, the last appearing with a co-author, Mary R. Sheehan, in 1964.[56]

EDWARD L. THORNDIKE AND CONNECTIONISM

E. L. Thorndike (1874–1949) was also at Columbia during the first two decades of this century and played a role in what we are calling Columbia Functionalism. Although in the Teachers' College, rather than in the Department of Psychology, Thorndike also proposed a psychology that could be called functionalist. Thorndike's connectionism is so closely identified with the emergence of behavioral psychology, however, that he and his positions will be discussed in Chapter 22.

Columbia had many individuals in psychology who contributed in one way or the other to functional, behavioral, or applied psychology, including Carl Warden (1890–1961) in comparative psychology, and Albert T. Poffenberger (1885–?) and Harry Hollingworth (1880–1956), both in areas of applied psychology.

SUMMARY

By 1930 Harvey Carr said he dared not list functionalists by name lest some he considered to fall within its scope be "rudely shocked."[57] It is probable that a large number of psychologists of the first three decades of the century who thought of themselves simply as "psychologists" (with the exception of the Titchenerians) were closest in spirit to functionalism.[58] This functionalism, however, was much more slanted toward behavior than even Woodworth intended, because, as Chapter 22 will discuss, the latter half of these three decades saw the appearance and eventual domination of behaviorism.

In the clash between the structuralism of Titchener and the functionalisms of Angell and Carr's Chicago and Cattell's Columbia, the American psychologist had a clear-cut choice between different prescriptive patterns. The psychological categories of structuralism were contents, and those of functionalism were activities. Structuralists held fast to the purist prescription, whereas functionalists tended to be more at the utilitarian end. Although many structuralists did quantitative work, they were more likely to observe the qualitative prescription, whereas functionalists tended to be much more quantitative. Structuralism was solidly molecularist, and functionalists were more likely to be molarists. Both structuralism and functionalism made use of contentual subjectivism, but it was functionalism that made the most use of contentual objectivism until the coming of behaviorism, which would, in time, dominate the American psychological scene.

The two schools came to agree on the importance of the experimental method to the investigation of psychological problems. Both the structuralists and the functionalists contributed to the laboratory or at least experimentation as the central approach to the psychological enterprise.

Functionalism arose as an attempt to systemize the often nebulous functional psychology that dominated the American psychological scene in the 1890s. It had as major influences the new biology of the Darwinists, the vestiges of the older American psychology of function, and the rich but sometimes mercurial ideas of William James. Reacting to the real and present danger of Wundt's and Titchenerian elementism, John Dewey and particularly James R. Angell attempted to form the crux of functional psychology into an experimental psychology that had no need of analysis into elements and that dealt with the psychological functions of knowing, feeling, and doing. Chicago functionalism was teleological in its conceptions, viewing consciousness as a problem solver and thus having survival value. Angell made use not only of conscious experience but also of behavioral events as well. In so doing, Angell laid the groundwork for the coming of behaviorism.

Functional psychology also was dominant at Columbia University during the academic lifetime of James McKeen Cattell. Less of a "school" than Chicago functionalism, Cattell and his colleagues such as Robert S. Woodworth influenced legions of Columbia Ph.D's toward an experimental, functional psychology which would blend, almost imperceptibly with later behaviorism.

NOTES

1. E. B. Titchener, "Postulates of a Structural Psychology," *Philosophical Review*, 7 (1898):449–465.
2. W. James, "On Some Omissions of Introspective Psychology," *Mind, 9* (1884):1–26.
3. W. James, *Principles of Psychology*.
4. *Ibid.*, Vol. 1, pp. 6–8, 128–144.

5. James R. Angell, *Psychology, An Introductory Study of the Structure and Function of Human Consciousness* (New York: Henry Holt, 1904).

6. E. G. Boring, "John Dewey: 1859–1952," *American Journal of Psychology, 67* (1953):145–147. Dewey's life and work have been intensively studied. An excellent source of information on Dewey is George Dykhuizen, *The Life and Mind of John Dewey* (Carbondale: Southern Illinois Press 1973).

7. John J. McDermott, "Introduction," *The Philosophy of John Dewey* (New York: G. P. Putnam's Sons, 1973), Vol. 1, pp. xvi–xvii.

8. Neil Coughlan, *Young John Dewey* (Chicago: University of Chicago Press, 1975), pp. 18–36. See also Robert M. Wenley, *The Life and Work of George Sylvester Morris* (New York: Macmillan Co., 1917).

9. *Ibid.*, p. 41.

10. J. J. McDermott, "Introduction," p. xvii.

11. J. Dewey, "The New Psychology," *Andover Review, 2* (1884):278–289.

12. *Ibid.*

13. John Dewey, *Psychology* (New York: Harper and Brothers, 1886).

14. *Ibid.*, 3rd ed., 1891.

15. *Ibid.*, p. 9.

16. *Ibid.*, p. 7.

17. J. Dewey, "The Reflex Arc Concept in Psychology," *Psychological Review, 3* (1896):357–370.

18. *Ibid.*, p. 358.

19. James Angell is sometimes confused with his cousin, Frank Angell. Frank Angell was a student of Wundt who, when he left Cornell for Stanford, was responsible for the call of Titchener to Cornell.

20. The details of Angell's life are taken from W. S. Hunter, "James Rowland Angell, 1869–1949," *American Journal of Psychology, 62* (1949):440.

21. James R. Angell, "The Province of Functional Psychology," *Psychological Review, 14* (1907):61–91.

22. J. R. Angell, *Psychology.*

23. W. Hunter, "James Rowland Angell," p. 446.

24. *Ibid.*, p. 447.

25. H. L. Koch, "Harvey A. Carr: 1873–1954," *Psychological Review, 62* (1955):81–82; W. B. Pillsbury, "Harvey A. Carr: 1873–1954," *American Journal of Psychology, 67* (1955):149–151.

26. Harvey A. Carr, *Psychology: A Study of Mental Activity* (New York: Longmans, Green, 1925).

27. H. A. Carr, *An Introduction to Space Perception* (New York: Longmans, Green, 1935).

28. H. A. Carr, "Functionalism," in C. Murchison, ed., *Psychologies of 1930* (Worcester, Mass.: Clark University Press, 1930), pp. 59–78.

29. Christian A. Ruckmick, "The Use of the Term Function in English Textbooks of Psychology," *American Journal of Psychology, 24* (1913):99–123.

30. R. S. Woodworth, "James McKeen Cattell—in Memoriam: Some Personal Characteristics," *Science, 99* (1944):160–161.

31. R. S. Woodworth, "James McKeen Cattell, 1860–1944," *Psychological Review, 51* (1944):201–209; M. M. Sokal, "The Unpublished Autobiography of James McKeen Cattell," *American Psychologist, 26* (1971):626–635.

32. Cattell's years in Germany and England are shown in Michael M. Sokal, ed., *An Education in Psychology: James McKeen Cattell's Journal and Letters from Germany and England 1880–1888* (Cambridge, Mass.: MIT Press, 1981).

33. J. M. Cattell, "Psychology in America," *Scientific Monthly, 30* (1930):114–126.
34. J. M. Cattell, "The Inertia of the Eye and Brain," *Brain, 8* (1885):295–312.
35. J. M. Cattell, "Psychology in America," p. 116.
36. J. M. Cattell, "Founding."
37. C. Wissler, "The Contribution of James McKeen Cattell to American Anthropology," *Science, 99* (1944):232–233.
38. J. M. Cattell, "Mental Tests and Measurements," *Mind, 15* (1890):373–381.
39. C. Wissler, "The Correlation of Mental and Physical Tests," *Psychological Review Monograph Supplement, 3,* No. 6 (1901).
40. S. E. Sharp, "Individual Psychology: A Study in Psychological Method," *American Journal of Psychology, 10* (1899):328–391.
41. J. M. Cattell, "The Time of Perception as a Measure of Differences in Intensity," *Philosophische Studien, 19* (1902):63–68.
42. An excellent review of Cattell's involvement in anthropometric testing may be found in Michael M. Sokal, "Cattell and the Failure of Anthropometric Testing," in William R. Woodward and Mitchell G. Ash, eds., *The Problematic Science: Psychology in Nineteenth Century Thought* (New York: Praeger, 1982), pp. 322–345.
43. S. S. Visher, "Scientists Starred 1903–1943" in *American Men of Science* (Baltimore: Johns Hopkins University Press, 1947), pp. 141–143.
44. R. B. Perry, *Letters,* Vol. II.
45. R. B. Evans and J. Cohen, "The American Journal of Psychology, *American Journal of Psychology, 100* (1987):321–362.
46. A. T. Poffenberger, ed., *James McKeen Cattell: Man of Science,* I, Psychological Research, II, Addresses and Formal Papers (Lancaster, Pa.: Science Press, 1947).
47. J. M. Cattell, "The Conceptions and Methods of Psychology," *Popular Science Monthly, 46* (1904):176–186, reprinted, in part, "Retrospect: Psychology as a Profession," *Journal of Consulting Psychology, 1* (1937):1–3.
48. A. T. Poffenberger, *James McKeen Cattell,* Vol. 1, p. 498.
49. Robert S. Woodworth, "Autobiography," in C. Murchison, ed., *A History of Psychology in Autobiography.* (Worcester, Mass.: Clark University Press, 1932) Vol. 2, pp. 359–380.
50. R. S. Woodworth, *Dynamic Psychology* (New York: Columbia University Press, 1918), pp. 34–36.
51. R. S. Woodworth, "Dynamic Psychology," in C. Murchison, ed., *Psychologies of 1925* (Worcester Mass.: Clark University Press, 1926), pp. 111–126.
52. E. Heidbreder, *Seven Psychologies,* p. 287.
53. R. S. Woodworth, "Dynamic Psychologies," p. 112.
54. R. S. Woodworth, *Experimental Psychology* (New York: Henry Holt and Co., 1938; 2nd ed., with Harold Schlosberg, 1954).
55. Andrew S. Winston, "R. S. Woodworth and the 'Columbia Bible': How the Psychological Experiment Was Redefined" *American Journal of Psychology,* in Press. *103* (1990).
56. R. S. Woodworth, *Contemporary Schools of Psychology* (New York: Ronald Press, 1931).
57. H. Carr, "Functionalism."
58. Although even Madison Bentley, Titchener's successor at Cornell, in writing on structural psychology in 1925 suggested that the concepts of structure and function were no longer current. Madison Bentley, "The Psychologies Called 'Structural': Historical Derivation," in Murchison, ed., *Psychologies of 1925.*

Alfred Binet.

Chapter 21

Utility in Psychology: The Rise of Applied Psychology

The orthodox psychologies, those psychologies that made use of or at least recognized the value of experimentation in the study of mind, were purist in their prescriptions. Wundt, Titchener, Brentano, James as well as Angell, all sought to understand mental life. Although they differed on the details of how experimentation was possible, they all agreed that, for better or worse, psychology was a scientific discipline. The utility of the knowledge obtained in scientific, experimental psychology was of little concern. The belief, exemplified by Titchener, was that once the scientific facts of mind were understood, the applications would come of themselves.

Because of Titchener's desire to make psychology a fundamental science coequal to physics and biology, he pressed for a model in academic psychology similar to that found in the academic physics and biology of his day. Those fundamental sciences made careful distinction between their pure, theoretical function and the function of utility. Applied physics was not a significant part of the physicist's work. Rather, it was studied as engineering, not only as a different department in the academic structure but also as a different school or college. The same was true of chemistry and biology. Applied chemistry was typically taught as chemical engineering or even home economics, and applied biology as medicine or animal husbandry, or agriculture. Titchener and many early experimental psychologists believed that there should be a separate discipline or disciplines for the applications of psychology, leaving the "pure," experimental psychologist alone to plumb the depths of the mind scientifically, without regard to utility. Educational psychology is an example of an applied psychological discipline that came about in line with this model. Child development was seen as an appropriate study for a department of home economics, psychopathology for psychiatry, and so forth.

In some respects, the development of the functionalist movement, both at Chicago and Columbia, aided in the development of applied psychology. Although Angell at Chicago still emphasized the scientific enterprise, he was not prejudiced against studies that could be considered applied. At Columbia, utility was even more acceptable, as the growth of the testing movement there demonstrates. Even so and even in the functionalist academic circles, during the first decade of this century, a stigma was still attached to the experimental psychologist who "sold out" to strictly applied work.

Groups outside of psychology recognized the applications of psychology quite early in the new discipline's institutional history. Madison Bentley, Titchener's successor at Cornell, coined the pejorative phrase, "the Great Invasions," to describe the overtures by outside groups to get psychologists to apply their discipline.[1] Although we may not accept the prejudicial tone of Bentley's terminology, he was correct in identifying the first overtures to the new, scientific psychology by other academic disciplines, including education, business, and medicine. "With education came the child and came testing, scoring and scaling; . . . with medicine came the clinic, the case-history, and the individual variant; with business came short-cuts to the selection of employees and quick means of manufacture, advertising and sale."[2]

ALFRED BINET AND THE INTELLIGENCE TEST

Although applied psychology would become closely identified with American psychology, it had its beginnings as much in Europe as in the United States. It is always difficult and perhaps relatively useless to claim "firsts," particularly in the applied area. Hermann Ebbinghaus with his completion test was doing applied work. The psychologist turned psychiatrist, Emil Kraepelin, produced applied work. Perhaps the best known of all early applied psychologists, however, was Alfred Binet (1857–1911).

In the early fall of 1904, the French Minister of Public Instruction appointed a committee to recommend what should be done about the education of subnormal children in the schools of Paris. The decision to place them in special schools necessitated the development of some means of identifying them. It was to Alfred Binet, then a man of forty-seven and considered the founder of French experimental psychology, that the Minister of Public Instruction turned for aid in this task.[3] The result was the first widely used intelligence scale.[4] Binet, as we will see, can hardly be cast as an experimental psychologist wooed away from his experimental work by the siren song of education. To obtain a proper appreciation of Binet's contribution, it is necessary to say something about the years of preparation for the task and the status of psychological testing prior to that time.

Life of Binet

Alfred Binet was born in Nice in 1857.[5] He was educated at Paris in law, a subject in which he received his degree in 1878, but when his interests in the sciences and in medicine came to the fore he abandoned law. While still a law student, he had been attracted to the Salpêtrière teaching hospital where the French neurologist J. M. Charcot was the center of attention. Binet's predilection for psychological problems became evident to Charcot, particularly in respect to that burning question of the day, hypnotism. Binet became an enthusiastic and, for a time, uncritical follower of Charcot. He took a doctorate in natural science in 1894 with a thesis on the nervous system of insects, but not a degree in medicine. While still working on his degree, Binet had written a book on hypnosis, published in 1886 with C. Féré,[6] giving a detailed account of its history. Binet had studied hypnosis, using such devices as the dynamometer (a device used to measure strength of grip) and the pneumograph (a device to record breathing rate). These measures were taken in the normal state, in the hypnotic state, and under the effect of various suggestions and compared. As a result of the devastating criticism of his work by members of the Nancy School of hypnotism, Binet forever lost his enthusiasm for the investigation of hypnosis.

Another book by Binet, also appearing in 1886, was concerned with reasoning.[7] This volume was prophetic of his lifelong interest in higher mental processes. However, his sources for the work were a general theory of association, some incidental findings in hypnosis, and his knowledge of logic rather than research data. Meanwhile, events were making him a psychologist, perhaps partly because of these books.

Henri Beaunis (1850–1921), Professor of Physiology on the Faculty of Medicine at Nancy, became the first director of the psychological laboratory founded in 1889 at the Sorbonne.[8] Although located in the Sorbonne, administratively the laboratory was part of the *École Pratique des Hautes Études* rather than the Faculty of Letters. That same year Theodule Ribot, who had previously been in charge of the course in experimental psychology but who had no laboratory, moved from the Sorbonne to the Chair of Experimental and Comparative Psychology at the College of France. In 1892 Binet, who was associated with Beaunis during these years, was asked to be adjunct director. On Beaunis's retirement in 1894, Binet became director of the laboratory, a post he held until his death in 1911 at the age of fifty-four.

Some of Binet's early work stressed the abnormal; he wrote a book on *The Alterations of the Personality*[9] in 1892 and one on *Suggestibility*[10] in 1900. In the same period he carried on studies in tactile sensibility and optical illusions in a fashion similar to that of his German contemporaries. He also studied handwriting, using blind analysis to increase his objectivity, as well as the thinking of chess players. Up to this time Binet was best known for his series of studies on suggestibility—within the tradition of medical psychology. Collaborating with Beaunis, in 1895 he established *L'Annee psychologique,* which became the leading French psychological journal and one of the first journals in Europe to accept publications on the applications of psychology.

In about 1900 Binet began to study thinking by the use of introspection. His previous book on reasoning had been written without the hindrance of research data. Now in his new work, published in 1902, for data he depended on the reports of the thinking of his two daughters, then of high school age.[11]

As happened later with his studies of intelligence, Binet did not find it necessary to work with minute elements of psychic life, and he believed that the psychological problems of thinking could be attacked globally. In fact, it is only in keeping with contemporary usage that this may be called a study of thinking. Actually, Binet referred to it as a study of "intelligence." He asked his daughters to solve problems and then to report to him the steps they took to reach a solution. Often the girls specifically denied the presence of images. In general, these results anticipated and supported the research of the Würzburg School. Like the researchers at Würzburg, Binet found that much thinking could not be reduced to sensory or ideational elements.

Although the girls exhibited similar thinking in regard to matters so far described, they also differed strikingly in their particular ways of thinking and in their personalities. Their father's account devotes considerable attention to these differences. Undoubtedly, this study strengthened Binet's interest in individual differences.

Binet evinced a greater interest in laboratory research than was characteristic of his fellow Frenchmen and wrote a textbook of experimental psychology. Generally, however, his interest in abnormal phenomena was quite in keeping with the tradition of psychology in his country.[12] All this work kept him quite busy, but his claim to greatness rests primarily on his contribution to the measurement of intelligence.

Measurement of Intelligence

In 1905 Binet urged that an accurate diagnosis of intelligence be established if the recommendation of the committee concerning placement of feeble-minded children in special schools was to be carried out adequately.[13]

Binet was sharply critical of medical diagnosis of mental deficiency. Previously, diagnosis of this condition was considered analogous to diagnosis of physical disease. Not surprisingly, errors occurred, since no one invariable sign of mental deficiency was known either then or later. For this purpose, Binet drew attention in copious detail to physicians' diagnostic errors by showing that the same child, when evaluated by different physicians just a few days apart, could carry different diagnoses. Thus it was that the work of the Parisian committee precipitated the development of the Binet Scale and focused Binet's interest on the problem of the diagnosis of the feeble-minded. It did not create his interest in the problem of intelligence.

For many years before the Paris committee of 1904 was established, Binet had had an interest in the measurement of intelligence and individual differences. Since 1887, his principal source of subjects for study had been the schoolchildren in and around Paris on whom he had tried out various tests.[14]

With his collaborator and assistant, Victor Henri (1872–1940), Binet published seven papers on individual differences. The crucial paper on tests appeared in 1896.[15] First, Binet and Henri reviewed the literature, which was already quite extensive. Without confining discussion to the specific tests they reviewed, it will suffice to say that they were presumably familiar with the work of Galton as well perhaps with the contribution of Ebbinghaus on the completion test to be published in 1897. Also available to them was considerable literature on elementary sensory, perceptual, and motor measures. Narrow phases of mental activity, such as sensory acuity, reaction time, attention span, and speed of movement, had been studied during preceding years. Binet and Henri pointed out that too limited and too specialized abilities were being utilized for measuring so complex a matter as intelligence. Moreover, in the study of a problem such as the relation of memory to intelligence, it would be necessary to examine various kinds of memory rather than one kind alone. Several variations of memory must be tapped. Binet and Henri proposed that visual memory of a geometrical design, memory of a sentence, memory of musical notes, memory of color, and memory of digits should all be included as tests of intelligence.

Recognition of the differences in endowments among individuals indicated the need for tests covering a wide scope. For this purpose they urged tests not of elementary functions but of the higher mental processes. Among the ten mental processes they proposed to study were (1) memory, as already noted; (2) images, measured by recalling twelve randomly selected letters exposed to view long enough for two readings at a "natural" rate; and (3) attention, divided into duration (reproduction of the length of a line of a given length shown only once) and scope (the ability to count the total number of strokes of two metronomes set for slightly different speeds with gradual increase of the speeds on successive trials until the subject's limit was reached). The other tests were for measurements of imagination, comprehension, suggestibility, aesthetic appreciation, moral sentiments, strength of will, and motor skill.

During the years between 1897 and 1905 Binet and his collaborators busied themselves with developing new tests, particularly for the higher mental processes. Theodore Simon (1873–1961), a new collaborator, also collected anthropometric measurements.

In 1905 the first intelligence scale appeared as Binet and Simon's joint effort.[16] It consisted of a long series of tests they had given to what was for the time a rather large sample of children. Their guiding concept was that of a scale—a series of tests of increasing difficulty starting with the lowest intellectual level and extending to that of the average level. The scale was avowedly a test to be applied rather than just a means of research, for they encouraged others to use their instrument for measuring intelligence. They urged prospective testers to secure training from them, stressed the need for uniformity of administration, and warned against permitting coaching of the children tested.

In 1908 they revised and improved the scale.[17] The tests were arranged not merely according to level of difficulty, but also according to the age at which presumably normal children could pass them successfully. If on the tryout of a test being evaluated for possible inclusion, it was found that all or nearly all the children six years of age failed, the item was obviously too hard for that age, whereas if practically all eight-year-olds passed it, it was too easy. The only possibility remaining would be to place it at the seven-year level, provided it met the general criterion for placement of a test. The rule was that if 60 to 90 percent of the children at a given age passed a particular test, it was to be considered standard for that age and included in the scale. Thus, the first age scale was launched. In this way children of all levels of intelligence were brought into focus of attention, and the feeble-minded were left merely as a deviant from the normal. A shift away from the relatively specific problem of the detection of feeble-mindedness to the more general problem of the measurement of intelligence at all levels had taken place.

Tabulated below are the tests at both ends of the scale grouped according to the age at which the majority of children succeeded on them:

Age 3 Years

1. Points to nose, eyes, mouth.
2. Repeats sentences of six syllables.
3. Repeats two digits.
4. Enumerates objects in a picture.
5. Gives family name.

Age 4 Years

1. Knows sex.
2. Names certain familiar objects shown to him: key, pocketknife, and a penny.
3. Repeats three digits.
4. Indicates which is the longer of two lines 5 and 6 cm in length.

Age 12 Years

1. Repeats seven digits.
2. Finds in one minute three rhymes for a given word—obedience.
3. Repeats a sentence of twenty-six syllables.
4. Answers problem questions—a common-sense test.
5. Gives interpretation of pictures.

Age 13 Years

1. Draws the design that would be made by cutting a triangular piece from the once-folded edge of a quarto-folded paper.

2. Rearranges in imagination the relationship of two triangles and draws the results as they would appear.

3. Gives differences between pairs of abstract terms, as pride and pretension.[18]

The 1908 scale determined the mental age of the child, regardless of actual chronological age. If the child passed the tests of eleven years, but not those of twelve years, he or she had a mental age of eleven years. Very few children were so obliging as to pass all tests at one level and fail all of them at the next, so inherent difficulties of scoring existed that were not cleared up until the next and last revision.

Binet and Simon applied the scale to feeble-minded children and, on the basis of their results, set limits for three degrees of feeble-mindedness: idiot, two years mental age or below; imbecile, between two and seven years; and moron, above seven years. They recognized that the classification lacked prognostic value, since they were dealing with absolute limits.[19] That is, their definitions did not take into account the actual or chronological age of the child. Hence, with the passage of years as the child continued to grow mentally (although more slowly than the average child), he or she might pass from an idiot to an imbecile to a moron.

After Binet's death William Stern[20] solved this problem by suggesting the use of an intelligence quotient or IQ, to be found by dividing mental age (MA) by actual or chronological age (CA). Since the resulting IQ is a ratio, it removed the difficulty of MAs as an absolute measure being used to define degrees of intelligence, including feeble-mindedness. Hence, a child CA four with an MA of two would have an IQ of 50 (2/4), as would a child eight with a mental age of four (4/8). (The use of a decimal result is eliminated by multiplying by 100.) In the United States Lewis Terman adopted the IQ in his 1916 Stanford Revision of the Binet Scales for which he provided a classification of degrees of intelligence in terms of IQ, not MA. Mental age as an absolute measure was still useful; it was supplemented by the IQ, which placed the individual's intelligence relative to his or her age.

In the United States considerable interest was shown in using the 1908 version of the Binet–Simon Scale, as we will see. However, Ovide J. Decroly and J. Degand performed an early significant study in Belgium.[21] When they tested a group of boys and girls in a private school in Brussels, they found that, on the average, their subjects were one and a half years in advance of the expected standards or norms published by Binet. After a certain amount of understandable confusion, it was realized that the difference was due to the effect of superior social status, since the Belgian children were the sons and daughters of professional men, whereas the Parisian children on whom Binet's norms were based were from poorer sections of the city. This finding opened up the whole problem of the relation of intelligence to social class.

In 1911, the year of Binet's death, the last of his revisions appeared.[22] He had profited from the research done with the test, restandardized the placement of tests, added some new tests, and discarded others, particularly because they were too dependent on school information. He also took care of the difficulties of scoring the 1908 revision by making each test at each year worth a certain fraction of a year of mental age, expressed as months of mental age. Thus, all the tests passed, regardless of the years at which they were placed, could be added together to get the mental age.

Binet had not attempted to analyze intelligence into parts and then devise tests based on this analysis. Rather, he used the combined efforts of a series of promising complex tasks selected as generally relevant to intelligence. Naturally, he had devoted some thought to the nature of intelligence. Throughout the years, he offered, withdrew, and amended a whole series of definitions. We have already seen that he related intelligence to judgment. Probably the most characteristic definition and certainly the definition most commonly associated with his name is that intelligence is a combination of capacities to make adaptations in order to attain a desired end, to maintain a mental set, and to be self-critical.[23]

Evaluation

Speaking generally, Binet advanced objective measurement in psychology. His work and that of others, with his or similar instruments, demonstrated the superiority of objective measurement over clinical diagnosis carried on without such instruments. Binet was not asking the children what they felt or sensed. They were given specific, often behavioral tasks, and either they could do them or they could not. The Binet Scales and the later instruments derived from them were quickly demonstrated to be of practical value in educational, social, and medical settings. Binet also contributed to the more theoretical aspects of psychology by developing a concept of intelligence as a combination of cognitive abilities. In the process of doing so, he distinguished intelligence from the specific sensory and motor abilities with which it had earlier been confused by Galton and others.

One criterion of the greatness of a psychologist is the fruitfulness of his or her contribution in leading to other research. In this regard Binet stands very high. Only one or two other psychologists have stimulated as much research as he did.

WILLIAM STERN AND ANGEWANDTE PSYCHOLOGIE

We have already encountered William Stern (1871–1938) in this chapter in connection with his involvement with the formulation of the intelligence quotient (IQ) for Binet's test. This was only one of Stern's contributions to applied psychology, however, and not necessarily his most important.

Trained at Berlin, working with Hermann Ebbinghaus and Carl Stumpf, Stern accepted a call to the University of Breslau. From the beginning of his career he was interested in the psychology of change, and it was only a short step to individual differences. In 1900 he published *Ueber Psychologie der individuallen Differenzen* (On the Psychology of Individual Differences) in which he declared individual differences to be "the problem of the twentieth century."[24] Stern tells us that aspects of individual differences led him into work in applied psychology.[25] His work on individual differences in memory seemed to have applications to the legal profession, a study that would become the psychology of testimony, a problem still considered in legal psychology. Stern's articles appeared in 1902 as "Zur Psychologie der Aussage," ("On the Psychology of Testimony").[26] The reception of this work motivated Stern to establish a publication, *Beiträge zur Psychologie der Aussage (Contributions to the Psychology of Testimony)*, which appeared between 1903 and 1906. Stern's article in this publication, "Angewandte Psychologie" ("Applied Psychology"), appeared in the 1903 volume of the *Beiträge*.[27] This was Stern's call for a careful, scientifically based psychology, but one concerned with the applications of scientific knowledge to the world at large. He used the word *Psychotechnique* in that publication, which predated the use of the parallel term *Psychotechnics* which is usually believed to have been coined by Hugo Münsterberg in 1914.[28]

In 1906 the Institute of Applied Psychology was founded at Berlin. It was privately established but put at the disposal of the German Psychological Society. Stern was its first director, along with Otto Lippmann, but after he moved to the University of Hamburg Stern relinquished the position to Lippmann. In 1907 Stern founded the *Zeitschrift für angewandte Psychologie, (Journal for Applied Psychology)* which was the first psychological journal devoted to applied work.

Although Stern's most significant work was in child psychology, including intelligence testing, and in his psychological position called personalism, the initial work he did to encourage applied psychology was extremely important to the development of that field, first in Europe and later in America.

THE TESTING MOVEMENT IN AMERICA

The push for applied psychology in America did not begin with the importation of Binet's intelligence test or with Stern's psychology of testimony. As early as 1895, J. McKeen Cattell, then President of the American Psychological Association, had arranged that the Association establish a committee "to consider the feasibility of cooperation among the various psychological laboratories in the collection of mental and physical statistics."[29] The studies initiated by Cattell were primarily anthropometric tests in the tradition of Francis Galton's London laboratory. When the report of the committee was presented in 1897, it was not unanimous. J. Mark Baldwin argued that the senses and motor abilities, though important, were too heavily emphasized in the majority report. He believed that psychological measures of the higher mental processes, such as memory, would be more in line with an initiative of the American Psychological Association than the basically physiological measures proposed by the committee.[30]

As early as Joseph Jastrow's use of anthropometric tests in the Columbian Exposition at Chicago in 1893, Titchener had condemned them as not being psychological.[31] In Titchener's laboratory, one of his students, Stella Sharp, studied the question of mental tests. Sharp compared the elementary sensory and motor measures being promoted by the anthropometrists with the more complex but more psychological tests employed in Europe by Binet and Henri. Sharp concluded that

The theory was provisionally accepted that the complex mental processes, rather than the elementary processes, are those the variations of which give the most important information in regard to the mental characteristics whereby individuals are commonly classed. It is in the complex processes, we assumed, and in those alone, that individual differences are sufficiently great to enable us to differentiate one individual from others of the same class.[32]

Sharp used college students as her subjects and employed tests of memory, mental images, imagination, attention, observation and description, and taste and tendencies. The last, taste and tendencies, was a test about works of art, music, and literature. Her findings for Binet and against Cattell were a significant blow to the anthropometric method. It should be added that Sharp offered a list of improvements on the method of administering the more complex tests of Binet and Henri that would make them methodologically more acceptable but that would make them fairly impractical to administer to masses of subjects. It was damning with faint praise.

Titchener and Sharp were not alone in their criticisms of the anthropometric methods. Clark Wissler (1870–1947) used the newly developed Pearson correlation coefficient to correlate the results of Cattell's anthropometric and psychological tests with the academic performance. A total of 250 freshmen and 35 seniors of Barnard College were used in the study.[33] The results demonstrated that correlations among the various psychological tests were barely above chance. Although the physical tests were shown to correlate among themselves, there was little correlation with the psychological measures. Neither correlated with academic performance reliably or significantly above chance.

These two reports appear to have retarded the growth of the American psychological testing movement, at least in academic settings, for a decade.

In 1910 Guy Montrose Whipple (1876–1941), a student first of G. Stanley Hall at Clark and then in the College of Education at Cornell University (though not in Titchener's Psychology Department), published his landmark two-volume *Manual of Mental and Physical Tests*.[34] Whipple's *Manual* was as significant for psychological testing as Titchener's experimental manuals had been for experimental psychology. The first volume covered the "simpler processes," the anthropometric measures and the sensory and motor capacities. The second volume, the "complex processes," dealt with the more complex tests, emphasizing the higher mental processes. Whipple's *Manual* would remain a staple in the training of psychological testers for twenty years or more.

The reassertion of psychological testing in America came through the appearance of English-language revisions of Simon and Binet's test of intelligence. Its initial application in America was by workers in institutions for subnormal populations, however, rather than in academic settings.[35]

Simon and Binet's Intelligence Test of 1906 was translated into English in 1908 by Henry H. Goddard (1866–1957), the same year Binet produced his "1908 revision."[36] Goddard, a student of G. Stanley Hall, was at the Vineland Training School in New Jersey. He also produced an English version of the 1908 scale in 1910.[37] Goddard is best known for his writings on the feeble-minded, particularly his now controversial Kalikak family study. Goddard's version of Binet's test was immediately popular. Between 1910 and 1914, 20,000 test booklets and 80,000 record blanks of the test were printed and distributed from Goddard's Vineland Laboratory alone.[38] E. B. Huey also published a revision in 1910,[39] and Whipple included a translation of the test and a criticism in the first edition of his *Manual* in 1910, though oddly enough, not in the second edition of 1914. Frederick Kuhlman at Clark University also issued a revision of the test in 1912.[40] The major revision, however, was Lewis Terman's Stanford Binet Revision which appeared in its complete form in 1916.

All five individuals who first promoted the Binet intelligence tests—Goddard, Whipple, Huey, Kuhlman, and Terman—had been students at G. Stanley Hall's Clark University. It is particularly noteworthy since Hall, at the time, did not support psychological tests and even urged Terman against doing his thesis on a testing topic.[41] It should be noted, however, that although these students are usually credited with working with Hall, the individual who ran the day-to-day affairs of the Clark University Psychology Department was not Hall but Edmund C. Sanford. Sanford was a member of the American Psychological Association committee on psychological tests in 1895 and supported the notion of tests. After much soul-searching, Terman shifted from Hall as his major adviser to Sanford.[42]

H. B. Huey introduced Terman to the Binet test after both had graduated from Clark. Terman was not positively impressed by the test when he first encountered it. It was only after he tried it on children that he found it to be useful. "The more I used it the more amazed I was at its accuracy," Terman wrote.[43]

Terman first published his findings on his use of the scale in 1911.[44] He found problems with the scale, however. The two ends of the scale were not accurate; younger children were rated too high whereas older children were rated too low. Still, Terman held that the test made it "possible for the psychologist to submit, after a forty-minute diagnostication, a more reliable and more enlightening estimate of the child's intelligence than most teachers can offer after a year of daily contact in the schoolroom."[45]

Terman and H. G. Childs published an interim revision of the Binet test in 1912.[46] In the meantime, the final version of Binet's test had appeared in 1911. Terman researched on the Binet scales until finally, in 1916, he published *The Measurement of Intelligence,* subtitled *An Explanation of and a Complete Guide for the Use of the Stanford Revision and Extension of the Binet–Simon Intelligence Scale.*[47] Terman's version of the Binet test would be revised in 1937 with Maud A. Merrill and again in 1960 after Terman's death. Terman adopted William Stern's intelligence quotient for generating a single number to stand for intelligence rather than the mental age (MA) alone. It was a significant change in that it allowed intelligence, as represented by IQ, to be correlated by means of the new correlational statistics with other behaviors and traits. It also opened up the Pandora's box of inappropriate uses of IQ as a predictor of future performance. The appearance of the Stanford–Binet scale was a significant step in establishing the psychological test as a diagnostic tool, not only in education but in many other areas as well.

THE INTELLIGENCE TEST GOES TO WAR:
ROBERT M. YERKES

With the entry of the United States into World War I, psychological tests were used on a mass basis for the first time.[48] Robert M. Yerkes (1876–1956) became the head of the military testing service. Most of Yerkes's research had been in comparative psychology, and he is still perhaps best known for his comparative work, particularly his work on chimpanzees. Yerkes was also interested in the concept of intelligence. He had created his own intelligence test in 1915, called the Point Scale. At this time he, Terman, and several other psychologists interested in testing developed the *Army Alpha* and *Army Beta* tests. *Alpha* was developed for individuals who could read and write, whereas *Beta* was for illiterates. In a little over two years, beginning in September 1917, 1,726,966 soldiers were tested.[49] To a much lesser degree, use was also made of a form of Terman's Binet and of Yerkes's Point Scale.[50] During the war, hundreds of young psychologists, experimentalists and those with applied interests alike volunteered or were drafted into military service and served in psychological testing, which was then part of the Sanitary Corps. For many of them, it was their first introduction to applied psychology in general and psychological testing in particular. Applied psychology could not have asked for a more intensive education program for young psychologists than the testing service supplied. One of the volunteers in the Testing Corps, E. G. Boring, had been an instructor at Titchener's Cornell. His comments on the testing experience are representative of how many young experimental psychologists viewed the new field:

> Titchener's in-group at Cornell had appreciated mental testers in much the same way that the Crusaders, gathered around Richard Coeur-de-Lion, appreciated Moslems, but this First World War gave me a respect for the testers. I saw clearly that good, honest, intelligent work in any field merits respect and that testers closely resemble the pure experimentalists in habits of work, in enthusiasm, and in thoroughness.[51]

American academic psychology would never be the same again.

With the war over, Yerkes continued to promote the use of intelligence tests and other kinds of psychological tests in schools and in industry.[52] Although there would be controversy over testing, the 1920s and 1930s saw a rapid expansion of psychological testing of all kinds, particularly intelligence testing.

HUGO MÜNSTERBERG AND THE BEGINNINGS OF
INDUSTRIAL PSYCHOLOGY IN AMERICA

Madison Bentley's second "great invasion" of orthodox psychology came from business. Business and industry rather quickly recognized the possibilities of psychology for the solution of their problems. What Binet was for the testing movement, Hugo Münsterberg (1863–1916) was for industrial psychology in America. In his classic history E. G. Boring claims for Münsterberg the title of "founder" of applied psychology.[53] He was certainly *one* of the founders but must share title with Walter Dill Scott (1869–1955) in America and, as we have seen, William Stern in Europe.

Münsterberg, working and writing from his prestigious position in the psychology program at Harvard, was perhaps the best known psychologist in America after the death of William James and was very influential in promoting many forms of applied psychology. His premature death in 1916 did not allow him to see the result of his work, however. We will emphasize the developments in America.

Life of Münsterberg

Hugo Münsterberg was born in Danzig, which was then in Prussia, in 1863.[54] His father was successful in the lumber business.[55] Münsterberg graduated from the German *Gymnasium* to prepare for a medical career. He enrolled at the University of Leipzig. In his second year, however, he attended the lectures of Wilhelm Wundt. Münsterberg delayed his medical training and received his doctoral degree from Wundt in psychology in 1885. Two years later, he received his medical degree from Heidelberg. Like Wundt's students, Titchener and Külpe, who would come after him, Münsterberg held to a more positivistic position than did Wundt, a fact that led Münsterberg to criticize Wundt in print on several occasions.

Münsterberg became a Dozent at Freiburg in 1887 and established his own laboratory there. His laboratory, funded largely out of his own pocket, quickly came to rank among the best in Europe, rivaling even Wundt's establishment. At the age of twenty-eight he was given the rank of *Extraordentlicher Professor* at Freiburg, which was the equivalent of a tenured associate professor in an American university. The rank guaranteed him a permanent position and salary. Münsterberg's publications gained him recognition not only in Germany, but also in America. Best known was his three-volume *Beiträge zur experimentellen Psychologie* (Contributions to Experimental Psychology) published between 1889 and 1892. A very young E. B. Titchener, still at Leipzig, criticized Münsterberg's work for his misunderstanding of Wundt's ideas and for general superficiality. Titchener's assessment of Münsterberg's book was that "whether the theories of the *Beiträge* stand or fall, their experimental foundation has very little positive worth."[56]

William James welcomed Münsterberg's results, perhaps, as Titchener suggested, because they were anti-Wundtian. James, by then tired of experimental psychology, was looking for a director for the psychological laboratory at Harvard so that he could return to the more comfortable realm of a professor of philosophy. Münsterberg came to Harvard for a trial appointment between 1892 and 1895. He was offered a permanent appointment but went back to Germany for two years, finally accepting for 1897. He would remain at Harvard the rest of his life, dying while lecturing to the students at Radcliffe in 1916.

Münsterberg in America was very different from the experimentalist Münsterberg in Freiburg. His interests in experimental psychology appeared to wane, and he turned to other pursuits such as telepathy, international affairs, and applied psychology. He was also deeply concerned that there be understanding between his German homeland and his adopted country. He worked very hard for international understanding, founding an American Institute in Berlin. When he died at the

height of American anti-German sentiment, his positions and statements supporting Germany only gained him a suspicion in some quarters that he was a German
spy.[57]

Münsterberg and Industrial Psychology

In his early criticism of Münsterberg, E. B. Titchener acknowledged that Münsterberg had a facility for writing. This trait was certainly reflected in the number of
books he produced after coming to America. Even now, a perusal of a second-hand
book store in any large American city will uncover one or two of his books. This
ability to write not only books but also articles and pamphlets, many based on talks
given before a bewildering variety of groups, made him ideal to promote applied
work.

Matthew Hale tells us that, as early as 1891, Münsterberg had devised a set of
mental tests for schoolchildren. Yet in his *Grundzüge,* Münsterberg argued against
broad applications of psychological principles, particularly widespread applications
of psychology to education.[58] Münsterberg was at first cautious. Like Stern, he
wanted an applied psychology to be based on sound experimental and scientific
principles. He was perhaps more cautious than Stern, since even Stern criticized
Münsterberg's *Grundzüge* for "rejecting" the possibility of application on a broad
scale."[59] Later, however, Münsterberg would be heavily criticized for carelessness
and overblown assertions in his applied work. This criticism came not only from
Titchener and his allies, but also from other early applied psychologists such as
Lightner Witmer.[60] Much of Münsterberg's work *was* overblown, particularly his
claims for his clinical work.[61] But the two areas he is best remembered for, his legal
psychology and his industrial psychology, stand on a firmer basis.

Münsterberg's Psychology of Testimony

In 1907 and 1908 Münsterberg published a series of articles in popular magazines,
all related to what we would today call legal psychology. In 1908 these articles were
gathered together and published in book form under the title, *On the Witness
Stand.*[62]

Since the book was made up of popular articles, there was little experimental
support. Clearly, Münsterberg's intent was to promote interest in this applied field
rather than to contribute scholarly research to it. The book was thoroughly attacked by psychologists but widely read by the lay public.[63] In its introduction,
Münsterberg called for an applied psychology but not for the attempt to directly
apply the theories of experimental psychology to applied situations. Münsterberg
called for an independent discipline of applied psychology. He said that "What is
needed is to adjust research to the practical problems themselves and thus, for
instance, when education is in question, to start psychological experiments directly
from educational problems. Applied Psychology will then become an independent
experimental science which stands related to the ordinary experimental psychology as engineering to physics."[64]

Industrial Psychology

Münsterberg's major contribution to applied psychology was his work on industrial psychology. The volume that best represents that work appeared in English in 1913 as *Psychology and Industrial Efficiency*.[65] It had appeared in a slightly different form a few months earlier in German. The subtitle of the German version perhaps expresses more clearly Münsterberg's intent: *A Contribution to Applied Experimental Psychology*.[66] He had written on the topic as early as 1909 in an article for *McClure's Magazine*, "The Market and Psychology."[67] The article argued for an applied psychology and gave particular instances for the steamship and railway companies, whose employees needed to be screened for visual acuity and color-blindness as well as the rapidity and accuracy of their perceptions in order to reduce accidents.

In his introduction to *Psychology and Industrial Efficiency*, Münsterberg states that his aim is "to sketch the outlines of a new science which is to intermediate between the modern laboratory psychology and the problems of economics: the psychological experiment is systematically to be placed at the service of commerce and industry."[68] The articles, though popularly written, outlined the kinds of contributions psychology can make to industry.

Perhaps chastened by the attacks made on him for the broad strokes of his earlier books, Münsterberg adopted a more careful and data-based approach for this work. The result was a series of experiments that made use of what we would now call personnel selection tests.

Münsterberg conducted one set of researches on employees of the New England Telephone Company. The company was concerned because a large percentage of the women hired and trained to be telephone operators were unable to do the job, losing the company large amounts of money in training costs. Münsterberg ran a number of tests on these employees, measuring aspects of "memory, attention, intelligence, exactitude and rapidity."[69] Some were group tests, and others were individually administered. Averages were taken for each individual on the results of all the tests administered. A rank-ordered list was put together, based on these average scores. After three months, the success of the operators in their jobs was compared to their test rankings. Those who were in the lowest ranks on the basis of the tests "in the mean time had either left the company of their own accord or else had been eliminated." Individuals who ranked at the top had been successful, including experienced operators who, unknown to Münsterberg, the company had mixed in with the new employees for their own check of the accuracy of his results. Although the rankings did not correspond perfectly with performance, they were "satisfactory."[70]

Münsterberg did similar work in 1912 for the Boston Elevated Railway Company. Not only did he administer standard mental and physical tests, but he also created what may have been the first simulator of an industrial task, in this case for trolley motormen, to measure their ability to perform in situations analogous to those that would be encountered in a real trolley.[71] Münsterberg was able to establish a formula for accepting and rejecting applicants for the motorman's job on the basis of test scores directed toward their specific job. Although Münsterberg warned that such scores were not absolutely accurate in their predictive value, the correlation appears to have been relatively high. A similar project was carried out for the pilots of oceangoing steamships with similar success.

Psychology and Industrial Efficiency is a landmark book of its type. Along with the works of nonpsychologists such as F. W. Taylor's *The Principles of Scientific Management*[72] and Frank G. Gilbreth's *Motion Study,*[73] both published in 1911, Münsterberg's book helped establish the field of personnel management and has given psychology a legitimate claim to industrial and personnel psychology ever since.

WALTER DILL SCOTT AND BUSINESS PSYCHOLOGY

What Münsterberg was to industrial psychology, Walter Dill Scott (1869–1955) was to advertising and marketing. Scott has been called America's first business psychologist.[74] Born in Illinois, Scott had very little early education. He never received a high school diploma, although he later attended Northwestern University and received his undergraduate degree there. He would be attached to Northwestern in one capacity or another for most of his life. Scott was attracted to psychology and pedagogy. He was introduced to psychology through William James's *Psychology: Briefer Course.* Although he initially believed he had a call to the ministry, he sought to become a missionary after graduating from Northwestern. Finding himself unsuited for the ministry, instead he went to Leipzig and, like Münsterberg, received his Ph.D. from Wilhelm Wundt. In 1900, after graduation, he returned to the United States and went to Northwestern University as Instructor of Psychology and Pedagogy.

In 1901 Thomas Balmer, an advertising agent and early promoter of the scientific approach to advertising, urged Scott to apply his psychological knowledge to the subject of advertising. Balmer had earlier sought out Hugo Münsterberg, Edward L. Thorndike, and others to do the same thing. Each had refused, apparently because the proscription against applied work in academic settings was so great. Scott also refused at first but finally accepted the offer. His first lecture was to the Agate Club in December 1901, and his topic was the psychology of involuntary attention in advertising. John Mahin, also an important figure in the advertising world, seeing the positive response to Scott's talk before the Agate Club, offered to start up a journal, *Mahin's Magazine,* to publish Scott's articles and others in the psychology of advertising if Scott would persevere. Scott agreed.[75] This offer was not as out of place as it might at first seem for a student just out of Wundt's laboratory. Scott's dissertation with Wundt was on the subject of impulse, a topic that dealt with involuntary attention and was rife with potential applications to advertising. This involvement led to the beginning of Scott's lifetime involvement in business psychology.

As Scott himself acknowledged, he was not the first to do experiments in advertising psychology.[76] That title, at least in America, should go to another midwesterner who studied not only with Wundt but also with Ebbinghaus— Harlow Gale (1862–1945).[77] Gale was at the University of Minnesota between

1894 and 1903, a brief and tumultuous academic career. He took over the laboratory left by James Rowland Angell after Angell left for Chicago. Gale was interested in involuntary attention, a topic that would attract Scott some years later. In 1896 Gale carried out experiments on involuntary attention using advertisements as his stimuli. He made use of a form of the order of merit method, apparently before Cattell is credited with inventing it. Gale made use of the concept of suggestion, part of the law of ideomotor action, as an explanation for the unconscious effects of advertising. Gale's studies were published privately in 1900.[78]

Walter Dill Scott, like Gale, had been exposed to Wundtian orthodoxy, but as with so many other of Wundt's American students, Wundtian purism did not survive the trans-Atlantic voyage back to America. They tended to blend aspects of Wundt's psychology together with ideas from their earlier background in American functional psychology—Gale with Ladd at Yale and Scott with William James's *Principles.* Their work moved toward questions of what mind does for us, not what it is. What survived from Wundt was the use of laboratory methods, although not necessarily introspective methods, to explore psychological questions.

In 1903, as a result of his lectures and articles, most of which were published in *Mahin's Magazine,* Scott published his first book on advertising, *The Theory of Advertising.*[79] The book shows Scott's background in the psychology of mind, since it emphasized apperception, association, and other mentalistic concepts applied to the topic. He held, as Harlow Gale had done earlier, that affecting involuntary attention and using suggestion were the primary methods of advertising. In 1908 he published another book on advertising, the *Psychology of Advertising,* also from the same perspective.[80]

Scott's involvement in advertising did not hurt his career in academics, however, although he was careful to promote advertising psychology to the business world but not to attempt to sell the idea to his fellow psychologists. He did not publish on the topic in psychological journals, nor did he give talks at the American Psychological Association on advertising, although he did so for more orthodox psychological topics. This was true even after other psychologists such as Hugo Münsterberg, Robert M. Yerkes, and Edward K. Strong published applied work in mainstream psychological journals.[81] There is evidence, however, that Scott lectured on business and advertising psychology to his students, both at Northwestern and as guest lecturer elsewhere. One such visit was to Carl Seashore's Department of Psychology at the University of Iowa. One student influenced by Scott at that talk was Daniel Starch who would go on to be a major influence in applied psychology.[82]

In 1909 Scott was appointed Professor of Advertising in the School of Commerce at Northwestern, and in 1912 he held a joint position as Professor of Psychology in both the College of Liberal Arts and the School of Commerce. In 1916 Scott took a leave from Northwestern and served as Director of the Bureau of Salesmanship Research at the Carnegie Institute of Technology, commonly called Carnegie Tech, where the Division of Applied Psychology had been formed. He thus became the first Professor of Applied Psychology in America. During World War I, he served as Director of the Committee on Classification of Personnel, and in 1919 he was elected President of the American Psychological Association. After the war he founded the Scott Company, perhaps the first personnel psychology consulting firm in the world. These developments will be considered later in this chapter. In 1920 he became President of Northwestern University, a position he held until his retirement in 1939.[83]

APPLIED PSYCHOLOGY AT COLUMBIA: HOLLINGWORTH AND STRONG

In Chapter 20 we discussed the utilitarian thrust of psychologists in the Department of Psychology at Columbia under the direction of J. McKeen Cattell and at Teachers College, Columbia, where John Dewey and Edward L. Thorndike were active. During the first two decades of this century among the students in these programs were many who would become influential in various aspects of applied psychology. Among them were T. L. Kelley and J. V. Breitwieser in educational psychology, F. L. Wells in clinical psychology, and J. F. Dashiell in legal and social psychology. Two men associated with the program around 1910 were Harry L. Hollingworth (1880–1956) and E. K. Strong, Jr. (1884–1963). They contributed in the 1910s and 1920s to applied psychology, and particularly to the psychology of advertising, a motivational approach. Even at Columbia, openly applied work was still suspect. Much of Hollingworth's early applied activities were done without the knowledge of his colleagues in psychology. Hollingworth received his undergraduate education under one of G. Stanley Hall's former students at the University of Nebraska, leaving in 1907 for graduate work at Columbia in psychology. There Hollingworth worked under James McKeen Cattell and Robert S. Woodworth. He became a tutor at Barnard College, Columbia, in 1909 and was promoted to Instructor in 1910,[84] remaining there until he retired in 1946. In 1910 Hollingworth offered a course in advertising psychology as an extension course. In that year, he also lectured on advertising psychology in association with the Advertising Men's League of New York City.

In the early teens, Hollingworth published two important contributions to applied psychology, *Advertising and Selling: Principles of Appeal and Responses* (1913) and *Advertising: Its Principles and Practice* (1915). *Advertising and Selling* was the first systematic presentation of a behavioral approach to advertising. At Columbia Teachers College, Thorndike was developing his own form of objective psychology, work that would lead to the law of effect and law of exercise. At the same time Woodworth in the Psychology Department at Columbia was developing his dynamic psychology. Both Thorndike and Woodworth were moving away from the mentalism of earlier functionalism and toward other models, behavioral and motivational.

Thorndike's behavioral tendencies appear to have influenced Hollingworth in his first book, and John B. Watson's behaviorism might have been an additional influence. It was at Columbia, in early 1913, that Watson gave the lectures that would become the manifesto of his behaviorism. Both Thorndike and Woodworth appear to have influenced Hollingworth in the development of his own molar behavioral approach in contrast to Watson's more molecular behaviorism. David Kuna suggests that the seeds of Hollingworth's position were already present in his dissertation, *The Inaccuracy of Movement,* in 1909.[85] By 1915, however, Woodworth's dynamic psychology appears to have gained more influence. In his *Advertising: Its Principles and Practices,* Hollingworth appears to move away from his earlier behavioral approach and toward emphasis on the needs, desire, and interests of the consumer. Kuna demonstrates the difference between Hollingworth's behavioral approach of 1913 and his dynamic approach of 1915 by comparing his list of the four main tasks of advertising in the two volumes.

> The former four . . . involved (1) the ad attracting attention, (2) the ad holding the attention, (3) the ad arousing central associations and (4) the ad evoking a response. However, the four tasks presented in 1915 involved (1) tabulation of the fundamental needs of men and women, (2) analysis of the satisfying power of the commodity in terms of the consumer's needs, (3) establishing the association between need and commodity, and (4) making the association dynamic.[86]

E. K. Strong also developed a dynamic approach to advertising. Strong came to Columbia in 1909 after receiving a master's degree at the University of California, Berkeley. He became Hollingworth's assistant at Barnard during 1909–1910 and completed his degree with Hollingworth in 1914. The Advertising Men's League funded a fellowship of which Strong was the first recipient. Strong's dissertation was titled *The Relative Merit of Advertisements*[87] and appears to be the first of its type in American psychology. The acceptance of the topic by Columbia, an obviously business-oriented dissertation in an academic department, was a major breakthrough for applied psychology.

In 1914 Strong became Professor of Psychology at George Peabody College in Nashville, Tennessee, a position he held until 1919. He had been involved with the Committee on Classification of Personnel during the First World War. In 1919 he left Peabody for a position in the Division of Applied Psychology at Carnegie Tech. where he remained four years before finally settling at Stanford University in 1923. Strong continued to write on advertising psychology throughout his life, but the later period was devoted mainly to the measurement of interests.

In the period we are considering, Strong published widely in the psychology of advertising not in esoteric advertising magazines, but in mainstream psychological publications. His "Application of the 'Order of Merit Method' to Advertising" (1911) was published in the *Journal of Philosophy, Psychology and Scientific Methods;* his "Role of Attention in Advertising" (1912) was published in *Psychological Bulletin;* and "The Effect of Size of Advertisements and Frequency of their Presentation" (1914) appeared in *Psychological Review,* just to name a few.[88]

To some degree, Hollingworth did applied work to supplement his income.[89] He appeared, at least in later life, to be embarrassed by his involvement in applied work. For Strong, it was his primary field, not a sideline to his "proper" academic work.

INSTITUTIONALIZATION OF APPLIED PSYCHOLOGY

Between 1910 and 1920 the number of individuals involved in various forms of applied psychology increased dramatically. The applied psychologists had little or no cohesion, however. In 1915 the Economic Psychology Association was formed. Though short-lived (it existed only two years), it was a beginning of the organization of applied psychologists. The organization was founded by J. J. Apatow, a salesman and promoter who had been stimulated by attending Hollingworth's lectures on advertising psychology.[90] It involved not only Hollingworth but also R. S. Woodworth and Hugo Münsterberg as officers. Unfortunately, a controversy over Apatow's budget for the group led to the resignation of the Columbia psychologists and the collapse of the society.[91] It would be a decade later, in 1927, that the International Association of Applied Psychology would be established and 1937 before the American Association for Applied Psychology came into being. The American Psychological Association would not recognize applied psychology as a formal psychological discipline until the reorganization of the Association in 1946.

In 1917 G. Stanley Hall, psychology's professional founder, founded the *Journal of Applied Psychology,* providing a reliable outlet for research on applied topics.[92]

One of the most significant events relating to the professionalization of applied psychology was the establishment of the Division of Applied Psychology at the Carnegie Institute of Technology in 1916. This, the first academic organization dedicated to applying psychology, was directed by Walter Van Dyke Bingham (1880–1952).[93]

Bingham had received his doctorate at Angell's Chicago in 1908, although he had studied earlier with Münsterberg at Harvard. His first academic position after graduating was at Teachers College, Columbia, where he came into contact with E. L. Thorndike. He left Teachers College for Dartmouth in 1910 where he remained until he was called to the Carnegie Institute of Technology as director of the newly established Division of Applied Psychology in 1916. The Division included the Bureau of Mental Tests, the Department of Training of Teachers, the Department of Psychology and Education, and the Bureau of Salesmanship Research. As such, it brought together all the applied disciplines, with the exception of clinical psychology.

As has already been mentioned, Walter Dill Scott was called to Carnegie for a year to direct the Bureau of Salesmanship Research and was given the title of Professor of Applied Psychology. He was the first to receive such a title in an American university. Scott directed the Bureau for two years after which he returned to Northwestern. The name of the Bureau is a little misleading, since the research directed there under Scott was personnel selection and not sales related. One result of this research was the publication of *Aids in the Selection of Salesmen,* one of the first attempts to develop tests for use in business and industry.[94]

Scott was replaced by Guy Montrose Whipple, who had produced the early volumes titled *Manual of Physical and Mental Tests.* He had been at Illinois after leaving Cornell. After World War I, Whipple moved to the Department of Educational Research at Carnegie Tech. E. K. Strong, Jr., became Director of the Bureau of Salesmanship Research. The Division of Applied Psychology at Carnegie Tech was disbanded in 1924 after a change of administrations. The collapse was a setback for applied psychology in academics, but the scattering of the students and staff to other institutions tended to spread applied psychology into more orthodox institutions.

PERSONNEL PSYCHOLOGY AND THE WAR

World War I, as we have already seen, was significant for the development of the intelligence testing movement and personnel testing. We have already seen the beginnings of personnel tests with Münsterberg's *Psychology and Industrial Efficiency*. When the United States entered the war in 1917, Walter Dill Scott and Walter Bingham, impatient with Yerkes's emphasis on intelligence testing, pushed for and got approval for the Committee on Classification of Personnel in the Army. Scott was made director and Bingham the executive secretary. Using the experience at Carnegie, Scott, Bingham, and the Committee developed a complete personnel selection system for the Army.[95]

The measurement of the recruit's intelligence, already described in this chapter, was only the first step in personnel selection. It primarily determined the acceptability or unacceptability for military service. The next step was the classification of personnel in terms of their aptitude for needed jobs in the military effort. The task of Scott and Bingham's committee was to classify and place enlisted men in duties to which they were best suited. By the end of the war the value of personnel selection tests had been demonstrated. The committee developed a trades test, perhaps the first mass use of a personnel selection test. Tests were devised for different trades. The most pressing need was a test for truck drivers and auto mechanics "to determine whether the ammunition and supply trains of the divisions that were about to be sent to France really had the skilled personnel necessary to get the supplies up to the front under battle conditions. By the time that mobilization ceased in November [1918], standardized tests in about eighty of the more important trades were in use."[96]

These tests provided the basis for the modern use of job analysis and personnel selection tests in the military and in business and industry. Personnel psychology had been launched. The years after the war appeared to have great potential for such applications, but there were difficulties ahead.

After the war, Scott left Carnegie and established the Scott Company, which, as noted earlier, was the first consulting firm for personnel selection in industry. The firm, though it lasted only two years, having been a victim of the postwar depression, set the pattern of private personnel consulting firms that came into existence after the Second World War.[97] Although the Scott Company failed, Scott continued to promote personnel psychology. After he became President of Northwestern University in 1920, he was the coauthor of *Personnel Management*, the classic personnel text.[98]

THE PSYCHOLOGICAL CORPORATION

The early period of personnel psychology and, for that matter, all applied psychology closes in 1921 with the founding of the Psychological Corporation. J. McKeen Cattell, who had initiated that committee of the American Psychological Association on physical and mental tests in 1895, was its founder and its first president. The corporation, a nonprofit organization to promote applied work, acted as a "holding company" between psychologists with services to give and corporations with needs for services.[99] Its services would also include the publication of psychological tests, a service for which it would eventually be best known. Almost half the psychologists then in America became stockholders.[100] Even E. B. Titchener joined the corporation, although his intention appears to have been to keep an eye on the applied side.

Cattell resigned as President in 1926 after several years of disappointment in the corporation's operation, but he stayed on in the primarily nominal post of Chairman of the Board. He was replaced as President by Walter V. Bingham who served for four years. Paul Achilles (1890–1976) was appointed Secretary, later rose to General Manager (1931–1942), and finally became President (1942–1946). Achilles played a major role in establishing the corporation as a free-standing organization with divisions devoted to clinical, industrial, marketing and advertising, and a test division. The Psychological Corporation became a major force in the production of tests. It was purchased by a major publishing house in 1970 but still continues as a publisher of tests.

THE BEGINNINGS OF CLINICAL PSYCHOLOGY IN AMERICA

The third of Madison Bentley's "great invasions" of psychology during the first part of this century was from medicine, and the result was the development of clinical psychology. Just as with other forms of applied psychology, clinical psychology encountered considerable resistance. We will treat the history of European thought devoted to abnormal psychology in later chapters, but some mention should be made here of the early developments of clinical psychology in America.

Institutions for the mentally ill and retarded had existed from the early days of the United States. As in Europe, the treatment of these populations was left primarily to medical doctors.[101]

Within academic settings, the first major contribution by a psychologist to clinical populations was in the main educationally oriented and was begun by another of Wilhelm Wundt's American students, Lightner Witmer (1867–1956).[102] Witmer was born in Philadelphia and graduated from the University of Pennsylvania in 1888. While at the university, he worked with J. McKeen Cattell, himself just recently from Leipzig. Although Witmer went to Leipzig and received his doctorate from Wundt, he credited Cattell with more influence on his thinking than anyone else. Returning to America, Witmer became Director of the Laboratory of Psychology at the University of Pennsylvania, replacing Cattell who had gone to Columbia.

Witmer had lectured on children's behavior problems at the University of

Pennsylvania as early as 1894.[103] In 1896 he founded at the University of Pennsylvania a clinic of psychology, the first psychological clinic in America and perhaps the world as an indirect result of those lectures. We are told that the idea of the clinic arose from the case of a child brought to Witmer by a teacher who knew of the lectures. The child could not learn to spell. A second child was brought who had a speech defect. His clinic thus began with an emphasis that would epitomize Witmer's career—diagnostic and remedial work with children with intellectual or educational deficiencies. Witmer's interests remained primarily educational.

Witmer's students included Edwin B. Twitmeyer (1873–1943) who, besides independently discovering the conditioned reflex, specialized in the diagnosis and treatment of speech defects. Morris S. Viteles was also a student of Witmer who became famous for his work in vocational and industrial guidance. Robert A. Brotemarkle, also a student, was a pioneer in the study of personality adjustments in college students. It was Witmer who first popularized the use of the term *clinical psychology.*

Witmer reported his clinical approach in the American Psychological Association (APA) meeting of 1896, outlining the methods he was using and demonstrating the potential of psychological clinics as a service to the community. Even though this was the year after the APA created its committee on mental and physical tests, there was little response to Witmer's presentation.

In 1907 Witmer founded the journal, *Psychological Clinic,* which he edited until 1935 and would become a significant independent outlet for research in clinical psychology, although at first it was little used by mainstream psychologists. He was also responsible for the establishment of a hospital school at the University of Pennsylvania in 1907. Later called the Orthogenic School, it was a place where patients could be treated for extended periods. It was Witmer's intent that the hospital school would train psychological practitioners whom he termed "psychological experts."[104]

Work of the Pennsylvania clinic blended into other applied fields as the testing movement began and grew. Diagnostic tests were a significant contribution of the Pennsylvania clinic. Witmer was little influenced by either the French psychiatry of Janet or the Germanic dynamicism of Freud or Jung. Those influences would come later and would have a greater impact on workers in mental illness than those involved with the subnormal populations dealt with by Witmer.[105]

During the first decade of this century, university clinics were begun at the University of Minnesota, Clark University, and the University of Iowa. The clinic founded by Carl Seashore at the University of Iowa around 1910 was modeled after Witmer's clinic.[106] By 1914 J.E.W. Wallin reported that there were twenty-six such clinics operating in the United States.[107]

Clinics for the Mentally Ill

The clinics discussed thus far were primarily for populations with intellectual or educational defects. Although during the first two decades of this century the mentally ill populations were being treated mainly in private or state-supported institutions, psychologists were beginning to be involved even in these settings. In 1897 William O. Krohn opened a laboratory at the Eastern Hospital for the Insane at Kankakee, Illinois, for the study of insane populations. He remained there until 1899 when he left to study medicine and become a psychiatrist.

Edward Cowles (1837–1919) founded a psychological laboratory at McLean Hospital in 1889. He was a medical man but had studied psychology at Johns Hopkins with G. Stanley Hall and had contributed an article to the first volume of Hall's *American Journal of Psychology* on a clinical topic.[108] Even before 1894, Cowles encouraged the involvement of psychologists working jointly with medical staff. He believed in the relevance of "the new psychology" to the understanding of mental diseases.[109] Both Cowles and his associate at McLean, William Noyes, were charter members of the American Psychological Association. Cowles appointed August Hoch to be psychologist and pathologist at McLean. Hoch was a medical doctor but was sent to Europe to study psychology before taking the position. He appears to have studied briefly with Wundt, Külpe, Marbe, and Kiesow as well as with the psychologist turned psychiatrist, Emil Kraepelin.[110] Hoch did work on the ergograph in clinical situations and published a clinical article in the first volume of the *Psychological Bulletin.*[111]

Shepard Ivory Franz (1874–1933) established his psychological laboratory at McLean in 1904.[112] In 1907 he instituted a routine clinical psychological examination of all new patients at McLean, which probably represents the first instance of routine psychological testing of psychiatric hospital patients.[113] When Franz left for St. Elizabeth's Hospital in Washington, F. L. Wells, who had studied psychology at Columbia, succeeded him and remained there until 1921.

Worcester State Hospital also had close ties with psychologists at G. Stanley Hall's Clark University. Adolph Meyer, the Swiss psychiatrist, was there between 1895 and 1901. He had a firm belief in the association of psychologists with clinical psychology. Meyer, who had been at Kankakee before coming to Worcester, later went to the Phipps Clinic at Johns Hopkins University. There he developed a moderately behavioral position he called psychobiology, which occupied a middle ground between Chicago Functionalism and John B. Watson's behaviorism. Though closely associated with Watson, he did not share all of Watson's behavioral views. Even before Watson declared behaviorism's goals in 1913, Meyer was calling for a psychology and psychopathology of behavior. In 1911, in a paper given at the American Psychological Association, Meyer advocated a psychological study of psychopathology.[114] Still, Meyer as with most psychiatrists of his day was more interested in how psychologists could help teach psychiatrists psychology than in the role psychologists could themselves play in psychopathological settings.

Many psychologists came to believe they had a role in psychopathological settings. In 1909 Hugo Münsterberg published his book, *Psychopathology,* which outlined the role psychologists could play in psychopathology. Although he appears to have been overexpansive as to the curative powers of the psychology of his time, at least he gave the public the notion that psychologists also had something to contribute.

Gradually, psychologists began to become involved in mental hospital settings. Some, like Edwin G. Boring, then a young instructor at Titchener's Cornell who spent the summer of 1912 at St. Elizabeth's hospital working with S. I. Franz on schizophrenia, wanted to find out at first hand what psychopathology was about.[115] Others, like Robert M. Yerkes, had longer term associations and made genuine contributions to the training of psychologists in mental health settings. Yerkes had a half-time position at Boston Psychopathic Hospital between 1913 and 1917, with E. E. Southard overseeing diagnostic tests for clinical populations.[116] Still others, like Grace M. Fernald, who was at the Juvenile Psychopathic Institute at Chicago, were full-time psychological professionals in the clinical setting.

Internships for Psychologists in Mental Health Settings   Boston Psychopathic Hospital established the first internships for psychologists in a mental hospital, primarily for diagnostic testing. They were under the supervision of Yerkes. We have already seen Goddard's involvement at Vineland. Even before he learned about Binet's tests, Goddard had established a genuine laboratory of clinical psychology at Vineland as early as 1906, which involved not only instruction but also research.[117] Goddard made use of internships at Vineland beginning in 1908. Goddard's translation of the Binet intelligence test was of great influence in promoting the use of diagnostic tests in mental institutions, even before the Stanford–Binet was released.

Like Goddard, the psychiatrist William Healy began accepting graduate students in psychology for internships at the Juvenile Psychopathic Institute in Chicago.[118] Healy's Institute had been founded in 1909 and started out with a psychologist on the staff, Grace Fernald. Fernald and later her successor, Augusta F. Bronner, emphasized performance testing and devised many instruments of their own. Healy had introduced a version of the Binet test the same year as Goddard had done at Vineland. In 1927 these tests were published as the *Manual of Individual Tests and Testing.*[119] Other institutions with early internships included Worcester State Hospital, McLean Hospital, the Western State Penitentiary in Pennsylvania, and the New York Institute for Child Guidance.[120] Most psychologists who were involved in clinical settings did so in one form or the other of diagnostic testing. Their involvement was thus tied up with the growth of the testing movement in general.

Attempts at Professionalization of Clinical Psychology

As with all the branches of applied psychology, early attempts at professionalization met with only partial success. In 1915 Guy M. Whipple persuaded the American Psychological Association to go on record "discouraging" the use of mental tests by unqualified individuals, by which he meant nonpsychologists. A niche was beginning to become established in clinical settings for psychologists, and there was danger that other professions or even lay workers might be assigned the job of administering and evaluating psychological tests. In 1917 the APA formed a committee to study qualifications for psychological examiners, and two years later another committee was formed on qualifications for "consulting" psychologists. While this was going on, Harry Hollingworth brought together a group of applied psychologists to form the American Association of Clinical Psychology in 1917. Its members included many of the leaders of psychological testing. The group disbanded in 1919, however, when it appeared that the APA was going to accept clinical psychologists as part of psychology. In 1919 the APA formed the Section of Clinical Psychology, which was originally an informal group instructed to set up program topics on clinical psychology at the annual meeting. By 1921, however, the group had arranged for certification of clinical psychologists. Unfortunately, so few psychologists applied that an APA policy committee decided that certification was not necessary and the APA membership voted to discontinue certification in 1927. The matter of APA certification for clinical psychologists would lapse for many years.[121] The hopes for clinical psychology as a recognized entity with the APA also seemed to wane.

The American Orthopsychiatric Association was founded in 1924. Its ties with child guidance involved a number of psychologists, although it was 1926 before psychologists could become full members. Its publication, the *American Journal of Orthopsychiatry*, became influential in clinical psychology.

In 1930 the Association of Consulting Psychologists was formed. (Actually it was a reorganization and expansion of a group first organized in New York in 1921.)[122] The organization grew out of its dissatisfaction with its representation in the APA. The *Journal of Consulting Psychology* was founded as an outlet for publications in the field.[123] The Association of Consulting Psychologists merged in 1937 with the American Association of Applied Psychology. Similar dissatisfaction led to the formation of the Psychometric Society and of the Society for the Psychological Study of Social Issues, both founded in the 1930s.

After their initial successes in mental institutions prior to World War I, clinical psychology developed slowly in the 1920s and 1930s. In 1918 only fifteen members or 4 percent of the American Psychological Association listed the field of clinical psychology as a research interest, although the full membership was made up primarily of academic psychologists.[124] By 1937 the total number of members expressing interest in clinical psychology had risen to only ninety-nine or 19 percent. In that year, however, the American Psychological Association instituted another membership category of associate, which included individuals outside of academic settings. Of these, 428 or 28 percent were interested in clinical psychology. During the 1920s and 1930s, most psychologists involved in clinical work were employed outside of academic settings, in hospitals, clinics, school, mental institutions, social agencies, homes for the feeble-minded, and similar locations. Clinical psychologists in universities did not represent a significant presence until after the Second World War. One notable exception was the founding at Harvard of the Harvard Psychological Clinic in 1927 by Morton Prince; the purpose of the clinic was to bring together academic and clinical psychology. The clinic was an important source of early research on personality variables. Henry A. Murray took over its direction in the 1930s. Collaborators during the 1930s included such notable psychologists as Donald W. MacKinnon, Saul Rosenzweig, R. Nevitt Sanford, and Robert W. White. In general, however, clinical psychology would have to wait until until the 1940s before playing a significant role in academic settings.[125]

In 1937 psychologists in applied settings, not just clinical psychologists, formed the American Association of Applied Psychology (AAAP), eventually developing four sections—clinical, consulting, industrial and business, and educational.[126] This organization would represent the primary forum for applied psychology until the APA was reorganized in 1945 and a division structure that would include the applied professions was created.

SUMMARY

Applied psychology had its initial beginnings not long after the founding of psychology as an independent academic discipline. At first, it had difficulty being accepted in academic organizations which, by the 1890s, was the primary seat of psychological expertise. Gradually, however, with the growth in the credibility of psychological testing, particularly with the acceptance of the Stanford–Binet test, the various lines of applied work—educational, business and industrial, and clinical—began to develop. Although Madison Bentley described this development in terms of "invasions" by education, business, and medicine, and depicted these groups as luring psychologists away from their proper work, it is clear that in the cases where outside firms approached psychologists, it took very little persuading. Indeed, in most cases, it was psychologists who sought to apply their psychological knowledge.

The influence of applied psychology on American psychology was very significant. Looking across all the applied work we have discussed, we see that they were not working with the introspective analyses of the orthodox psychologies of Wundt, Titchener, James, or even Angell. They were dealing, rather, with behaviors. When Binet tested a child, that child did something. That behavior was either correct or not correct, and so the child could be scaled objectively. The same was true of the early applied work in industry and clinical settings. What gradually became evident was that the utility in psychology was to be found in a study of behavior, not the description of conscious processes. By the beginning of the second decade of this century, that realization appears to have begun dawning on psychologists.

When Titchener reviewed the previous ten years in psychology in his talk at the Symposia organized to celebrate the twentieth anniversary of the founding of Clark University, he saw what perhaps many in his audience had not—that the previous decade had been marked above all with the rise of applied psychology.[127] But even Titchener did not see the implications of the use of behavioral data that went along with it.

NOTES

1. Madison Bentley, "The Nature and Uses of Experiment in Psychology," *American Journal of Psychology, 50* (1937):451.
2. *Ibid.*, pp. 452–453.
3. Binet is so closely identified with the intelligence test that the experimental work on psychophysics, perceptual development, and thought processes that made his early reputation has been eclipsed. Many of these studies have been translated into English and republished in Robert H. Pollack and Margaret W. Brenner, eds., *The Experimental Psychology of Alfred Binet* (New York: Springer Publishing Co., 1969).
4. A. Binet and T. Simon, "Sur la nécessité d'établir un diagnostic scientifique des états inferieurs de l'intelligence," *L'Année Psychologique, 11* (1905):163–190, partial trans. W. Dennis, ed., *Readings in the History of Psychology* (New York: Appleton–Century–Crofts, 1948), pp. 407–411.

5. By far the most authoritative, analytical, and complete biography in any language has been provided by Theta H. Wolf, *Alfred Binet* (Chicago: University of Chicago Press, 1973).

6. A. Binet, *La psychologie du raisonnement* (Paris: Alcan, 1886).

7. William C. Dampier, *A History of Science and its Relation with Philosophy, and Religion,* 4th ed. (London: Cambridge University Press, 1966).

8. Personal communication from P. Fraisse to E. G. Boring, February 5, 1962, through the kindness of E. G. Boring. There has been some confusion about who had priority in founding the first laboratory in France. Presumably this is attributable to the fact that all three independent institutions of higher education were involved in the events of 1889. Ribot moved to the College of France from the Sorbonne, or the College of Letters of the University of Paris. The same year a laboratory was placed in the Sorbonne under the direction of Beaunis in association with Binet, although it was administered by L'Ecole Pratique des Hautes Etudes, still a third educational institution.

9. A. Binet, *Les altérations de la personnalité* (Paris: Alcan, 1892).

10. A. Binet, *La suggestibilité* (Paris: Schleicher, 1900).

11. H. Spencer, *The Principles of Psychology,* 2nd ed. (London: Williams and Norgate, 1870–1872) (1855).

12. A. Binet, *Introduction à la psychologie expérimentale* (Paris: Alcan, 1894). For a convincing demonstration of the breadth and depth of his experimental interests, see R. H. Pollock and Margaret J. Brenner, eds., *The Experimental Psychology of Alfred Binet* (New York: Springer, 1969).

13. A. Binet and T. Simon, *"Sur la nécessité."*

14. A. Binet and N. Vaschide, "La psychologie a l'école primaire," *L'Année Psychologique, 4* (1898):1–14.

15. A. Binet and V. Henri, "La psychologie individuelle," *L'Année Psychologique, 2* (1896):411–465 (Herrnstein and Boring, Excerpt No. 81).

16. A. Binet and T. Simon, "Méthodes nouvelles pour le diagnostic due niveau intellectual des anormaux," *L'Année Psychologique, 11* (1905):191–244.

17. A. Binet and T. Simon, "Le développement de l'intelligence chez les enfants," *L'Année Psychologique, 14* (1908):1–94.

18. Joseph Peterson, *Early Conceptions and Tests of Intelligence* (New York: World Book, 1925).

19. Binet and Simon, *"Le développement."*

20. William Stern, "Die psychologische Methoden der Intelligenz-prüfung." In F. Schumann, ed., *Bericht über den* V. *Kongress für experimentelle Psychologie* (Leipzig: Barth, 1912), pp. 1–102, Chapter 2, translated by G. M. Whipple as *The Psychological Method of Testing Intelligence* (Baltimore: Warwick and York, 1914) (Herrnstein and Boring, Excerpt No. 86).

21. O. Decroly and J. Degand, "La mesure de l'intelligence chez des enfants normaux d'après les testes de Binet et Simon: nouvelle contribution critique," *Archives de Psychologie, 9* (1910):81–108.

22. A. Binet and T. Simon, *A Method of Measuring the Development of the Intelligence of Young Children,* trans. Clara H. Town (Chicago: Chicago Medical Books, 1915) (1911).

23. J. Peterson, *Early Conceptions.*

24. William Stern, *Ueber Psychologie der individuallen Differenzen: Ideen zu einer differentiellen Psychologie* (Leipzig: Barth, 1900); Stern, "William Stern," in Carl Murchison, ed., *History of Psychology in Autobiography* (Worcester, Mass.: Clark University Press, 1930), Vol. 1, p. 347.

25. W. Stern, "William Stern," p. 348.

26. W. Stern, "Zur Psychologie der Aussage," *Zeitschrift für die Gesammelte Strafrecht-swissenschaft* (1902).

27. W. Stern, "Angewandte Psychologie," *Beiträge zur Psychologie der Aussage, 1* (1903):4–45.

28. W. Stern, "William Stern," p. 349.

29. J. McKeen Cattell and Livingston Farrand, "Physical and Mental Measurements of the Students of Columbia University," *Psychological Review, 3* (1896):619.

30. James Mark Baldwin, James McKeen Cattell, and Joseph Jastrow, "Physical and Mental Tests," *Psychological Review, 5* (1898):172–179. This topic is covered in detail in Michael Sokal, "James McKeen Cattell and the Failure of Anthropometric Mental Testing, 1890–1901," in William R. Woodward and Mitchell G. Ash, eds., *The Problematic Science: Psychology in Nineteenth-Century Thought* (New York: Praeger, 1982), pp. 322–345.

31. E. B. Titchener, "Anthropometry and Experimental Psychology," *Philosophical Review, 2* (1893):187–192.

32. Stella Sharp, "Individual Psychology: A Study in Psychological Method," *American Journal of Psychology, 10* (1898–1899):348.

33. Clark Wissler, "The Correlation of Mental and Physical Tests," *Psychological Review, Monograph Supplement, 3*, Whole No. 6 (1901).

34. Guy Montrose Whipple, *Manual of Mental and Physical Tests*, 2 vols. (Baltimore: Warwick and York, 1910; 2nd ed., 1914).

35. J. Peterson, *Early Conceptions*, pp. 109–110. Peterson is an excellent source of detailed information on the development of the Simon–Binet scales and their reception and development in the United States.

36. H. H. Goddard, "The Binet and Simon Tests of Intellectual Capacity," *Training School Bulletin, 5*, No. 10 (1908):3–9.

37. H. H. Goddard, "A Measuring Scale for Intelligence," *The Training School Bulletin, 6* (1910):146–155; "The Binet–Simon Measuring Scale for Intelligence. Revised" *Training School Bulletin, 8* (1911):56–62; "Four Hundred Feeble-Minded Children Classified by the Binet Method," *Journal of Psycho-Asthenics, 15* (1910):17–30.

38. Elizabeth S. Kite, "The Binet–Simon Measuring Scale for Intelligence: What It Is; What It Does; How It Does It; With a Brief Biography of Its Authors, Alfred Binet and Dr. Thomas Simon," Bulletin No. 1 of the Committee on Provision for the Feeble-minded, n.d., ca. 1916, p. 24.

39. E. B. Huey, "The Binet Scale for Measuring Intelligence and Retardation," *Journal of Educational Psychology, 1* (1910):435–444.

40. F. Kuhlman, "A Revision of the Binet–Simon System for Measuring the Intelligence of Children," *Journal of Psycho-Asthenics, Monograph Supplement, 15* (1911): 76–92.

41. J. Peterson, *Early Conceptions*, pp. 225–226.

42. Lewis M. Terman, "Trails to Psychology," in Carl Murchison, ed., *History of Psychology in Autobiography*, Vol. 2 (Worcester: Clark University Press, 1930), p. 318.

43. Kimball Young, "The History of Mental Tests," *Pedagogical Seminary, 31* (1924): 1–48. Cited in Peterson, *Early Conceptions*, p. 226.

44. Lewis M. Terman, "The Binet–Simon Scale of Intelligence; Impressions Gained by Its Application," *Psychological Clinic, 5* (1911):199–206.

45. *Ibid.*, p. 204.

46. L. M. Terman and H. G. Childs, "Tentative Revision and Extension of the Binet–Simon

Measuring Scale of Intelligence," *Journal of Educational Psychology, 3* (1912):61–63, 133–135, 198–200, 277–279.

47. L. M. Terman, *The Measurement of Intelligence,* subtitled *An Explanation of and a Complete Guide for the Use of the Stanford Revision and Extension of the Binet–Simon Intelligence Scale* (New York: Houghton Mifflin Co., 1916).

48. For other aspects of the topic of psychological testing in World War I, see Franz Samelson, "World War I Intelligence Testing and the Development of Psychology," *Journal of the History of the Behavioral Sciences, 13* (1977):274–282.

49. Edwin G. Boring, "Robert Mearns Yerkes (1876–1956)," *Year Book of the American Philosophical Society,* 1956, p. 136.

50. Robert M. Yerkes, J. W. Bridges, and R. W. Hardwick, *A Point Scale for Measuring Mental Ability* (Baltimore: Warwick and York, 1915).

51. E. G. Boring, *Psychologist at Large* (New York: Basic Books, 1961), p. 31.

52. R. M. Yerkes, "Measuring Intelligence for Schools," in P. Sargent, *A Handbook of American Private Schools,* 3rd ed., (Boston: P. Sargent, 1917) pp. 3–9; "How May We Discover the Children Who Need Special Care?" *Mental Hygiene, 1* (1917):252–259; "Mental Tests in Industry," *Transactions of the American Institute of Mining Engineers* (1919):405–416.

53. E. G. Boring, *A History of Experimental Psychology,* 2nd ed. (New York: Appleton–Century–Crofts, 1950), p. 428.

54. Details of Münsterberg's life are taken from Margaret Münsterberg, *Hugo Münsterberg: His Life and Work* (New York: D. Appleton and Co., 1922) and Matthew Hale, Jr., *Human Science and Social Order: Hugo Münsterberg and the Origins of Applied Psychology* (Philadelphia: Temple University Press, 1980).

55. Hale, *Human Science and Social Order,* pp. 19–20.

56. E. B. Titchener, "Dr. Münsterberg and Experimental Psychology," *Mind, 16* (1891):534.

57. E. G. Boring, *History of Experimental Psychology,* p. 428.

58. Hale, *Human Science and Social Order,* p. 108.

59. *Ibid.,* p. 108.

60. Lightner Witmer, "Mental Healing and the Emmanuel Movement," *Psychological Clinic, 2* (January 15, 1909):241.

61. Hugo Münsterberg, *Psychotherapy* (New York: Moffat–Yard, 1909).

62. Hugo Münsterberg, *On the Witness Stand: Essays on Psychology and Crime* (New York: Doubleday, Page and Co., 1909); Münsterberg, *Hugo Münsterberg.* p. 368.

63. Matthew Hale, *Human Science and Social Order*, pp. 156–158.

64. H. Münsterberg, *On the Witness Stand.* pp. 7–9.

65. H. Münsterberg, *Psychology and Industrial Efficiency* (New York: Houghton Mifflin Co., 1913).

66. H. Münsterberg, *Psychologie und Wirtschaftsleben: Ein Beitrag zur angewandten Experimental-Psychologie* (Leipzig: J. A. Barth, 1912).

67. H. Münsterberg, "The Market and Psychology," *McClure's Magazine* (November 1909).

68. H. Münsterberg, *Psychology and Industrial Efficiency,* p. 3.

69. *Ibid.,* p. 101.

70. *Ibid.,* pp. 108–109.

71. *Ibid.,* pp. 66–77.

72. F. W. Taylor. *The Principles of Scientific Management* (New York: Harper, 1911).

73. Frank G. Gilbreth, *Motion Study* (New York, 1911).

74. Jacob Z. Jacobson, *Scott of Northwestern* (Chicago: Louis Mariano, 1951), p. 75.

75. Leonard W. Ferguson, *The Heritage of Industrial Psychology,* Vol. 1 (Hartford, Conn.: Finlay Press, 1962); Jacobson, *Scott of Northwestern,* pp. 70–73.
76. Walter Dill Scott, "The Psychology of Advertising—'Nothing New,' " *Mahin's Magazine, 2* (April 1903):44–45.
77. The best source of information on Gale is David Kuna's unpublished dissertation, *The Psychology of Advertising,* pp. 93–141, University of New Hampshire, 1976.
78. D. Kuna, *Psychology of Advertising,* pp. 95–96, 98–117. Harlow S. Gale, "Psychology of Advertising," in Gale, ed., *Psychological Studies* (Minneapolis: Harlow Gale, 1900).
79. Walter D. Scott, *The Theory of Advertising* (Boston: Small, Maynard and Co., 1903).
80. Scott, *The Psychology of Advertising* (Boston: Small, Maynard and Co., 1908); Kuna, *Psychology of Advertising,* p. 145. A good review of Scott's early researches is found in Kuna, *Psychology of Advertising,* pp. 148–191.
81. Hugo Münsterberg, "The Field of Applied Psychology," *Psychological Bulletin, 6* (1909):49; Robert M. Yerkes, "The Class Experiment in Psychology with Advertisements as Materials," *Journal of Educational Psychology, 3* (1912):1–17; Edward K. Strong, Jr., "Psychological Methods as Applied to Advertising," *Journal of Educational Psychology, 4* (1913):393–404. It should be noted, however, that the *Journal of Educational Psychology* would not have been considered a mainstream psychological journal at the time.
82. Daniel Starch, *Measuring Advertising Readership and Results* (New York: McGraw–Hill, 1966), pp. v–vi, cited in Kuna, *Psychology of Advertising,* p. 209.
83. A number of publications on Scott may be consulted for more details. Besides Jacobson's book and the general history by Ferguson, see Edmund C. Lynch, "Walter Dill Scott: Pioneer in Personnel Management," *Studies in Personnel Management,* No. 20 (Austin, Tex.: Bureau of Business Research, University of Texas, Austin, 1968), pp. 15–23; Edward K. Strong, Jr., "Walter Dill Scott, 1869–1955," *American Journal of Psychology, 68* (1955):682–683; David P. Kuna, "The Psychology of Advertising, 1896–1916," unpublished doctoral dissertation, University of New Hampshire, 1976.
84. There is not yet a detailed treatment of Hollingworth's life and work. His unpublished autobiography, dated 1940, is titled "Years at Columbia" and is in the Hollingworth Papers, Nebraska State Historical Society, Lincoln, Nebraska. This treatment of Hollingworth and Strong is derived primarily from Kuna's dissertation "The Psychology of Advertising 1896–1916, pp. 262–284.
85. D. Kuna, "Psychology of Advertising," p. 290.
86. *Ibid.,* pp. 322–323.
87. E. K. Strong, Jr., *The Relative Merit of Advertisements,* Columbia Contributions to Philosophy and Psychology, Vol. 19, No. 3 (New York: Science Press, 1911).
88. E. K. Strong, "Application of the 'Order of Merit Method' to Advertising," *Journal of Philosophy, Psychology and Scientific Methods, 8* (1911):600–606; "Role of Attention in Advertising," *Psychological Bulletin, 9* (1912):66–67; "The Effect of Size of Advertisements and Frequency of Their Presentation," *Psychological Review, 12* (1914):136–152.
89. A. T. Poffenberger, "Harry Levi Hollingworth: 1880–1956," *American Journal of Psychology, 70* (1957):138; Kuna, "Psychology of Advertising," pp. 266–267.
90. D. Kuna, "Psychology of Advertising." p. 354.
91. Ibid., pp. 355–356.
92. Henryk Misiak and Virginia S. Sexton, *History of Psychology: An Overview* (New York: Grune and Stratton, 1966), p. 192.
93. Walter V. Bingham, "Walter Van Dyke Bingham," in Carl Murchison, ed., *A History*

of Psychology in Autobiography (Worcester, Mass.: Clark University Press, 1953), pp. 1–26.

94. D. Kuna, "Psychology of Advertising," pp. 358–359. For more details, see Ferguson, *The Heritage of Industrial Psychology*, Vol. 5, *Bureau of Salesmanship Research: Walter Dill Scott, Director* (Hartford, Conn.: Finlay Press, 1963), pp. 55–63.

95. Robert M. Yerkes, "Man-power and Military Effectiveness: The Case for Human Engineering," *Journal of Consulting Psychology*, 5 (1941):205. Yerkes leaves out the matter of Scott's disagreement with him. See, however, Ernest R. Hilgard, *Psychology in America: A Historical Survey* (San Diego: Harcourt, Brace, Jovanovich, 1987), pp. 709–710. The involvement of psychologists in applied work during the war was considerable. For more details, see Yerkes, "Psychology and National Service," *Science*, N.S. 46, No. 1179 (1917):101–103; "Psychology in Relation to the War," *Psychological Review*, 25 (1918):85–115; "How Psychology Happened into the War," *New World of Science* (New York: Century Co., 1920), pp. 351–389; Thomas Camfield, "Psychologists at War: The History of American Psychology and the First World War," unpublished doctoral dissertation, University of Texas, 1969.

96. W. V. Bingham, "Measuring a Workman's Skill; the Use of Trade Tests in the Army and Industrial Establishments," quoted in Yerkes, "How Psychology Happened into the War," p. 380.

97. E. R. Hilgard, *Psychology in America*, pp. 711–712.

98. W. D. Scott and R. C. Clothier, *Personnel Management* (Chicago: Shaw, 1923).

99. Michael M. Sokal, "The Origins of the Psychological Corporation," *Journal of the History of the Behavioral Sciences*, 17 (1981):54–67.

100. Paul S. Achilles, "The Role of the Psychological Corporation in Applied Psychology," *American Journal of Psychology* 50 (1937):229–247.

101. There is an enormous literature on this topic, including F. G. Gosling, *Before Freud: Neurasthenia and the American Medical Community, 1870–1910* (Urbana: University of Illinois Press, 1987); Gerald N. Grob, *Mental Institutions in America: Social Policy to 1875* (New York: Free Press, 1973); Grob, *Mental Illness and American Society, 1875–1940.* (Princeton, N.J.: Princeton University Press, 1983); Grob, *The State and the Mentally Ill: A History of Worcester State Hospital in Massachusetts, 1830–1920* (Chapel Hill: University of North Carolina Press, 1966); Franz G. Alexander and Sheldon T. Selesnick, *The History of Psychiatry: An Evaluation of Psychiatric Thought and Practice from Prehistoric Times to the Present* (New York: Harper and Row, 1966); Gregory Zilboorg and G. W. Henry, *A History of Medical Psychology* (New York: W. W. Norton, 1941); John Popplestone and Marian McPherson, "Pioneer Psychology Laboratories in Clinical Settings." In Josef Brozek, ed, *Explorations in the History of Psychology in the United States* (Lewisburg: Bucknell University Press, 1984), pp. 196–272.

102. Biographical details are drawn from Robert I. Watson, "Lightner Witmer: 1867–1956," *American Journal of Psychology*, 69 (1956):680–682.

103. Misiak and Sexton, *History of Psychology*, p. 200.

104. *Ibid.*, p. 201.

105. A review of the case records of Witmer's clinic is discussed in Murray Levine and Julius Wishner, "The Case Records of the Psychological Clinic at the University of Pennsylvania (1896–1961)," *Journal of the History of the Behavioral Sciences*, 13 (1977): 59–66.

106. C. Seashore, *Pioneering in Psychology* (Iowa City: University of Iowa Press, 1942), quoted in R. I. Watson, "A Brief History of Clinical Psychology," in Josef Brozek and Rand B. Evans, eds., *R. I. Watson's Selected Papers on the History of Psychology* (Hanover, N.H.: University Press of New England, 1977), pp. 224–229.

107. J.E.W. Wallin, *The Mental Health of the School Child* (New Haven, Conn.: Yale University Press, 1914).

108. G. Stanley Hall, "Laboratory of the McLean Hospital." *American Journal of Insanity, 51* (1894):358–364; Edward Cowles, "Insistent and Fixed Ideas," *American Journal of Psychology, 1* (1887–1888):222–270.

109. R. I. Watson, "A Brief History of Clinical Psychology," p. 207.

110. *Ibid.,* p. 208.

111. A. A. Hoch, "A Review of Psychological and Physiological Experiments Done in Connection with the Study of Mental Diseases," *Psychological Bulletin, 1* (1904):241–257.

112. S. I. Franz, "Shepard Ivory Franz," in Carl Murchison, ed., *A History of Psychology in Autobiography* (Worcester, Mass.: Clark University Press, 1932), Vol. 2, pp. 89–113.

113. R. I. Watson, "A Brief History of Clinical Psychology," p. 208.

114. Adolf Meyer, "The Value of Psychology in Psychiatry," *Journal of the American Medical Association, 58* (1912):911; reprinted in Alfred Leif, ed., *The Commonsense Psychiatry of Dr. Adolf Meyer* (New York: McGraw–Hill Book Co., 1948), pp. 383–385; See also Meyer, "Objective Psychology or Psychobiology: With Subordination of the Medically Useless Contrast of Mental and Physical," *Journal of the American Medical Association, 65* (1915):860, reprinted in Leif, *Commonsense Psychiatry,* pp. 397–405.

115. E. G. Boring, *Psychologist at Large,* p. 26. The result of Boring's summer was the publication of three articles: "The Course and Character of Learning in Dementia Precox," *Bulletin of the Government Hospital for the Insane, 5* (1913):51–79; "Introspection in Dementia Precox," *American Journal of Psychology, 24* (1913):145–170; *Learning in Dementia Precox* (Princeton, N.J.: Psychological Monographs, 1913), Vol. 15.

116. Ernest R. Hilgard, "Robert Mearns Yerkes (1876–1956)," *Biographical Memoirs, 38* (1965):388.

117. H. Misiak and V. Sexton, *History of Psychology,* p. 203.

118. William Healy and Augusta F. Bronner, "The Child Guidance Clinic: Birth and Growth of an Idea," in L. G. Lowrey, ed., *Orthopsychiatry, 1923–1948: Retrospect and Prospect* (New York: American Orthopsychiatric Association, 1948), pp. 14–49.

119. Augusta F. Bronner, William Healey, Gladys M. Lowe, and Myra E. Shimberg, *A Manual of Individual Mental Tests and Testing* (Boston: Little, Brown, 1927).

120. R. I. Watson, "A Brief History of Clinical Psychology," pp. 210–211.

121. *Ibid.,* p. 210; Samuel W. Fernberger, "The American Psychological Association, 1892–1942," *Psychological Review, 50* (1943):33–60.

122. R. I. Watson, "A Brief History of Clinical Psychology," p. 218.

123. J. P. Symonds, "Ten Years of Journalism in Psychology, 1937–1946: First Decade of the Journal of Consulting Psychology," *Journal of Consulting Psychology, 10* (1946):335–374.

124. R. I. Watson, "A Brief History of Clinical Psychology," p. 211; Fernberger, "The Scientific Interests and Scientific Publications of the Members of the American Psychological Association," *Psychological Bulletin, 35* (1938):261–281.

125. R. I. Watson, "A Brief History of Clinical Psychology," p. 215.

126. E. R. Hilgard, *Psychology in America,* p. 633.

127. E. B. Titchener, "The Past Decade in Psychology," *American Journal of Psychology, 21* (1910):404–421.

John B. Watson.

Chapter · 22

John B. Watson and Behaviorism

During the first decade of this century a number of events occurred that changed the attitude of many psychologists concerning the way psychology had been approached since its establishment as an independent, experimental discipline. One was the controversy over imageless thought between Oswald Külpe and E. B. Titchener. Some psychologists reached the conclusion that if two of the finest experimental laboratories in the world could not determine whether or not there were images in the thought processes by means of introspective analysis, then perhaps there was something wrong with the method of introspection. Even in the minds of psychologists who used introspective methods there was doubt whether it was the sole or even the primary means of obtaining psychological data.

A second influence emerged with the rise of applied psychology. As we saw in the previous chapter, one of the things that much of applied psychology and particularly the testing movement demonstrated was that behavior had a great deal of utility in applied settings. By 1913, although most psychologists would have identified with one or the other of the orthodox psychologies of mind, the commitment was not as deep as it had been a decade before. As early as 1911, even at the meeting of Titchener's own Experimentalists Society, Raymond Dodge, then at Wesleyan but later at Yale, challenged Titchener on introspection.[1] That same year, one of Titchener's early graduates, Walter B. Pillsbury, published an introductory textbook in which he defined psychology as "the science of human behavior." Neither Dodge nor Pillsbury rejected introspection as a legitimate method. They did question, however, its status as the primary source of psychological data.[2] Not everyone would be so moderate.

WATSON'S BEHAVIORIST MANIFESTO

In 1913 an article appeared proposing a new psychology. Written by John Broadus Watson, then only thirty-five years old, it opened as follows:

> Psychology as the behaviorist views it is a purely objective experimental branch of natural science. Its theoretical goal is the prediction and control of behavior. Introspection forms no essential part of its methods, nor is the scientific value of its data dependent upon the readiness with which they lend themselves to interpretation in terms of consciousness.[3]

It was more than a declaration of independence; it was a manifesto against orthodox psychology, stating the intention of behaviorism to occupy the entire field of psychology to the exclusion of introspective psychology. It was not enough that the study of behavior (contentual objectivity) be lifted to status equal with that of consciousness (contentual subjectivity). In Watson's view, behavior was thereafter to be the *only* concern of psychology, and its study was to be the definition of psychology. In Watson's view, in its fifty years as an experimental study psychology had failed to establish itself as a science. To reach its rightful place, he thought, it must discard consciousness and the study of mental states.[4]

Watson sought to exclude from psychology all references to the orthodox modes of experience—mind, consciousness, images, and feelings—anything that could not be demonstrated behaviorally, that is, by the actions of muscles or glands. Much of Watson's work involved attempts at the replacement of the orthodox subject matter of introspective psychology with behavioral equivalents: subvocal speech for thought, discrimination for sensory judgment, and changes in the sex organs for feelings, just to name a few.

Watson held that the introspective method was notoriously unreliable—as exemplified in the imageless thought controversy. As Watson saw it, almost all psychology before him was tarred with the same mentalistic brush and was therefore unscientific. He specified that his quarrel was not only with the structural psychology of Titchener but also with functional psychology, since it also used mentalistic terms and emphases. He was willing to agree that the functionalist emphasis on biological significance was laudable, but he felt that functionalism had still failed to be scientific. In Watson's view, functionalism had slipped into an interactionist position in which mental states were seen as playing some part in the adjustment of the individual. This is nothing more than a relic of philosophy, Watson argued, and the whole issue should and can be ignored by focusing on behavior to the exclusion of all else. He claimed that behaviorism was the only consistent functionalism. The study of functional capacities expressed in behavior is determined relatively easily and directly. References to conscious states in functional terms are not only uncertain, but also trivial and unreal. However, Watson's behavioral "functionalism" lacked the foundation stone of Dewey and Angell's functionalism—holism. Watson was as elementistic as Wundt or Titchener.

One may assume, Watson said, the presence or absence of consciousness as one wishes; it does not affect the problems of behavior one iota.[5] A man has something that may be called consciousness; a psychologist, as a human being, has this something. So, too, does a physicist, as a human being. But what the psychologist shares with the physicist in this regard is no more part of the psychologist's field of research than it is that of the physicist.

In his "Psychologist as the Behaviorist Views It" and his second article "Image and Affection in Behavior," Watson laid out his plan for a behavioral psychology. He recognized no demarcation between humans and the "lower animals." The subject matter of behaviorism was the study of how humans and animals alike adjust to their environment. This adjustment was carried out "by means of hereditary and habit." The descriptive categories were stimulus and response, he said. Watson believed that "In a system of psychology completely worked out, given the stimuli the response can be predicted." His ultimate goal was "to learn general and particular methods by which I may control behavior."

Watson saw the utility of the study of behavior. He believed that "If psychology would follow the plan I suggest, the educator, the physician, the jurist and the business man could utilize our data in a practical way.[6]

Watson's views did not excite a sudden change in psychology. As Franz Samelson has discovered, Watson's initial statements were greeted with little positive reaction and some negative reaction.[7] His position was far more extreme than that of most psychologists, even those who were critical about the reliability and applicability of introspection.

One notable negative response came from E. B. Titchener. In 1914, in a talk before the American Philosophical Society, Titchener evaluated Watson's manifesto. The talk was published as "On 'Psychology as the Behaviorist Views It.' "[8] Titchener attacked Watson on several levels. First, Titchener accused Watson of using not the scientific meaning of "mind" or "consciousness" but the everyday usage of the term. Thus, Titchener concluded that Watson's movement was based on a fundamental misunderstanding of what the science of mind is all about. Titchener also denied Watson's charge that the only lively developments in recent psychology had been in those areas that depended least on introspection such as "experimental pedagogy, the psychology of drugs, the psychology of advertising, legal psychology, the psychology of tests, and psychopathology." In response to Watson's position, Titchener demonstrated that the foundation and development of these movements were due not to behaviorism but to orthodox psychology. He asserted that William Stern's work on legal psychology and Alfred Binet's work on tests, just to name two, were direct outgrowths of these individuals' work in introspective psychology. "I am not here depreciating behaviorism," Titchener says, "but I think there is no justification for behaviorism's depreciation of psychology."

Titchener held that Watson's behaviorism could not replace introspective psychology because the subject matter of behaviorism was fundamentally different from that of introspective psychology. Therefore, in Titchener's terms, it was "logically irrelevant" to introspective psychology. More seriously, Titchener attacked behaviorism's status as a science. Because Watson stated that the goal of behaviorism was to predict and control behavior, Titchener concluded that behaviorism was not a science at all but a technological enterprise, seeking utility rather than the understanding that is the foundation of a science.

According to Titchener, Watson's enterprise was not psychology at all but a form of biology. In fact, many biologists had been doing for years what Watson was now proposing to do in the name of behaviorism. Watson would have psychology give up its independent status as the "science of mind" for a lesser status as part of biology. Watson, Titchener said, was casting away as irrelevant the very aspect that made psychology a discipline—consciousness.

In 1913 Watson stood almost alone in his behavioristic convictions, but by the time he issued his last major publication on behaviorism, seventeen years later,[9] his view had swept through psychology in the United States leaving it, in many respects, a new field.

PAVLOV AND RUSSIAN PHYSIOLOGY

Titchener was correct when he said that Watson's behavioral emphasis was not new. One generation earlier there had been antecedents to Watson's approach in the work of two Russian physiologists, Ivan P. Pavlov and Vladimir M. Bekhterev. In turn, it was a publication by Ivan M. Sechenov, the *Reflexes of the Brain*,[10] which Pavlov acknowledged as the single most important theoretical inspiration for his work on conditioning.[11]

Sechenov

It is generally agreed that Ivan M. Sechenov (1829–1905) founded Russian physiology.[12] After early training in Russia and study abroad with Claude Bernard, DuBois-Reymond, Johannes Müller, and Hermann von Helmholtz, Sechenov returned to teach physiology at the St. Petersburg Military Medical Academy and at various other institutions. He spent his last years as Professor of Physiology at Moscow University.

Early in Sechenov's career, he carried on experimental investigations of the inhibition of reflex movements by the cerebral cortex. This inspired him to show that there was a physiological basis for psychical processes. Thereafter, he tackled the problem of demonstrating that the psyche, rather than being independent of the body, is a function of the brain and central nervous system and is therefore a physiological problem.

Sechenov's thesis was that psychical activity can be explained by reflex activity. With his physiological orientation he tended to emphasize the receptor and motor (muscular) phases of the reflex psychical processes. All physical processes are expressed in motor activity of one sort or another. A few of his characteristic teachings may be mentioned. Sechenov identified reflexes as innate or learned. Learning itself is a process of association. He implies that contiguity is the most important principle in association but that learning is not the primary subject of his investigation. Thinking, Sechenov held, is an inhibited reflex. In thinking we have the receptive phase of the reflex and its transmission, but the end of the reflex, expressed in movement, is absent. In all of this, as Pavlov remarked, Sechenov was developing a theoretical outline.[13] It was Pavlov who took the giant step of submitting his contentions to experimental study.

Pavlov

Ivan Petrovich Pavlov (1849–1936), the son of a village priest, was born in Russia in 1849 and received his early education in a local seminary.[14] In 1870 he entered the natural history section of the University of St. Petersburg, specializing in physiology. After obtaining his degree in 1875, he enrolled as an advanced student in the medical school, not with any thought of a career as a practicing physician, but as further preparation for a research post in physiology. On completion of his thesis, he won a scholarship to Germany, where he worked with prominent physiologists for two years. Nevertheless, it was not until 1890 that he was made Professor of Pharmacology (later physiology) at the St. Petersburg Military Medical Academy and head of the Physiology Department of the Institute of Experimental Medicine. For many years he devoted his research to the processes of digestion. In fact, half his career was taken up with work on digestion, for which he received the Nobel Prize in 1904. Only after the age of fifty did he study what became known as conditioning. This study covered a span of another thirty years.

The specific impetus for the study of conditioning was a phase of his work on the digestive glands, using the dog as the experimental animal. Pavlov's general method was a surgical arrangement so that digestive secretions flowed to the surface of the body for collection and measurement. One aspect of his work was the functioning of saliva in digestion. By operation, a salivary duct could be diverted so that the saliva stimulated by meat in the mouth of the dog flowed through a fistula to the outside of the body where it was collected. Prior to 1900, and before working with the conditioned response, Pavlov had noticed that a dog secreted saliva before the meat was given him. Further observation showed that this occurred not only when the dog saw the meat, but also when it heard the footsteps of the attendant.

The secretory reflex with the innate response of salivation to food on the tongue had now become "conditioned" to the sight of the food or the sound of the attendant's footsteps. Pavlov realized that this happened because this sight or sound had been so often associated with the ingestion of food. This association is by frequency of contiguity, as it would be called in associationist terms. The term *conditioned reflex* was first applied to this phenomenon in 1901.[15]

Pavlov wondered whether he should follow up this new lead into an area that many physiologists would view with disdain, since it was "psychic" in nature. In fact, on hearing of his dilemma, some leading physiologists advised him against embarking on the work. On the other hand, he had the example of Sechenov before him. After a long struggle with himself, he resolved to go ahead and make it a physiological problem by maintaining the role of the external observer with no consideration of introspective findings.[16] This was in 1900 or 1901.

Pavlov absorbed himself in his new task. The basic procedures, with the exception of the selection of the stimulus to bring on salivary flow, had already been standardized through his work on digestion. His already extensive laboratory resources were directed to this new problem. When the Soviet government came to power, his research faculties were expanded. An increasing number of associates and assistants joined him. Over the years, some 200 collaborators worked with him on problems in conditioning.[17]

The basic model for Pavlov's work was the presentation of two kinds of stimuli: one that was "appropriate," "biologically adequate," or "unconditioned"; and another that was "psychic," "conditioned," or "learned."[18] Each reflex has an appropriate (unconditioned) stimulus that brings it on. If food is placed on the tongue, saliva flows; if the finger is pricked, it is jerked back. In his studies, Pavlov tended to depend on the food power leading to the salivary response, though other forms were also used. When a response such as salivation becomes attached to a stimulus that formerly did not arouse it, it is said to be conditioned.

Practically any stimulus, Pavlov found, can act as a conditioning stimulus to produce a conditioned response. The salivation to the sight of the food or the sound of the footsteps of the attendant are stimuli for conditioned responses. The sight of food or the sound of footsteps had come to serve as signals, and they now brought about a response formerly elicited by food in contact with the tongue.

Pavlov originally referred to "psychic reflexes," that is, reflexes aroused not by the adequate stimulus of meat in contact with the tongue but by some other form of stimulation that had been presented along with the meat. He almost immediately dropped this term in favor of "conditioned responses." Over the years, Pavlov preferred to use as conditioned stimuli the sound of a tuning fork, a bell, and a light flash. These were the stimuli that acquired a new reaction, namely, a flow of saliva.

It should be remembered that, like Sechenov, Pavlov saw this work as a problem in physiology, not psychology. Pavlov believed that psychology could never be an independent science and that its position was "completely hopeless."[19] He believed he had completely excluded it from his own work.[20] Still, Pavlov is honored for his insights into a line of research that significantly affected the direction psychology was to take, particularly in America.

Bekhterev

The physiologist, V. M. Bekhterev (1857–1927), was a countryman, a contemporary, and a rival of Pavlov in the opening years of the twentieth century.[21] Independently of Pavlov, he also became interested in the study of conditioning. He, too, worked at the St. Petersburg Military Medical Academy, from which he was graduated. After studying abroad and after holding a Chair in Psychiatry at the University of Kazan, he returned to a Chair in Mental and Nervous Disorders at the Military Medical Academy, where he later had his own research institute. Bekhterev studied conditioning or, as he called it, associative reflexes, through the study of muscular or motor responses.

By motor responses, Bekhterev meant such processes as retracting the finger from an electric shock. The associative reflexes were not the result of any mental process, but they remained reflexes. He became convinced that more complex behaviors could be explained in a similar manner. Habits were seen as the compounding of motor reflexes, and even the thought processes were essentially activities of the speech musculature.

Bekhterev expressed his convictions in a book, *Objective Psychology,* which appeared in Russian in 1907, was translated into German and French in 1913, and into English in 1932, under the title, *General Principles of Human Reflexology.*[22] The change of title reflected the shift to his later preferred term *Reflexology.* It was a plea for a psychology based on the tools and concepts of physiology with no appeal to subjective processes. Psychology expressed in a study of states of consciousness was simply ignored. Objective study would be sufficient for a complete account of human behavior.

AMERICAN COMPARATIVE PSYCHOLOGY

Another source of behaviorism was animal psychology as studied in the United States. In addition, certain currents in psychology in the United States contemporaneous with Watson had influenced him, despite his expressed opposition to them. This was the case with the approaches of Edward L. Thorndike and Jacques Loeb.

Edward L. Thorndike

Edward Lee Thorndike has already been mentioned in Chapter 17 as a student of William James and as one of the psychologists at Columbia University with Cattell.[23] While at Harvard, Thorndike started research with chickens and, lacking more suitable quarters, took advantage of James's generosity and used the basement of his home as a laboratory. When Cattell offered him a fellowship at Columbia, he took it and continued his work with chickens, "the most educated" pair accompanying him in a basket from Cambridge to New York.

Along with two psychologists at Clark University, Thorndike deserves credit for introducing the modern laboratory type of experiment into animal psychology. Pavlov himself acknowledged that the researches in 1898 of E. L. Thorndike were the first experiments in this general research area, but he added that when he began his own work he was unfamiliar with them.[24]

Thorndike's study of the behavior of kittens in a puzzle box is classic.[25] Each series of these boxes, open-slatted affairs, had a different "combination" that, when learned, allowed the hungry kitten to escape from the box and to secure food placed outside it. The kitten's learning tasks involved strings to pull, buttons to turn, and levers to press. At first, the kitten showed excessive activity, clawing all over the box and trying to squeeze through the bars. In this struggle the kitten happened to claw the string or button, and the door opened. In other words, the kitten carried on very actively and randomly until the successful act was hit on. On repeated trials, gradually and one by one, the erroneous, unsuccessful acts were dropped. Ultimately, when the kitten was placed in the puzzle box, he would immediately claw the appropriate button or string and escape from the box.

Thorndike called this process of learning trial and error learning. As the trials succeeded one another, both the number of errors and the time taken to escape decreased. The learning, as expressed in a decrease of errors and time, was gradual. He interpreted the results to mean that practice stamps in correct responses and stamps out incorrect ones.

As a result of his studies, Thorndike formulated two fundamental laws of learning: (1) the law of effect, in which it is stated that any act in a given situation producing satisfaction becomes associated with that situation, so that when the situation recurs, that act is also more likely to recur; and (2) the law of exercise in two complementary parts, the laws of use and of disuse.[26] The law of use states that there is a strengthening of connections with practice, and the law of disuse, that a weakening of connections occurs when practice is discontinued. Research he conducted[27] many years later convinced Thorndike that sheer repetition was unimportant and that reward was much more effective than punishment. The law of exercise is a direct descendant of the old law of association—not the association of ideas, to be sure, but rather a connection between stimulus and response. In fact, Thorndike would later call his psychological position connectionism. The law of effect is of more dubious parentage, but it is at least partially related to the pleasure–pain or hedonistic principle. Here again is an objective approach in that functioning has been inferred from behavior.

Thorndike did not hold that psychology could dispense with consciousness, but he did hope that much of psychology could be objectified. In some ways, Thorndike's influence on modern behavioral psychology is at least as great as that of its touted founder, John B. Watson. To the degree that behavioral methodology is the significant factor that made behaviorism a viable movement, Thorndike deserves at least equal credit with Watson.

Thorndike was not alone in the United States in performing pioneer contentually objective research studies with animals, however. Robert M. Yerkes (1876–1956), under Thorndike's influence, went down the phylogenetic scale to study learning and intelligence in the turtle using a maze.[28] A Clark University student, Willard S. Small (1870–1943), studied learning using rats and a miniature of the Hampton Court maze and firmly established both the maze as a method and the rat as an experimental animal.[29]

Jacques Loeb

Jacques Loeb (1859–1924), a physiologist and one of Watson's teachers, must have had some influence on him, although Watson makes little mention of him except to mention Loeb as one of his three most important teachers at Chicago. Watson's neglect of Loeb may be because of Loeb's failure to reject completely an appeal to the psychic processes. Loeb had revolted against anthropomorphism and sentimentality in interpreting animal activity, but he did not reject consciousness, which he thought to be associative memory or the capacity of the animal to learn from experience.[30] Loeb had announced his theory of tropisms in 1890 and thereafter embarked on mechanistically oriented studies of simple organisms and plants. The classical or narrower theory of tropism conceives of animal behavior as nothing more than a forced movement of a physical-chemical nature. In more general fashion, the theory of tropism has to do with the orientation of the organism in a field of force. According to this view, recourse to such terms as sensation or pleasure is not necessary.

INFLUENCE OF FUNCTIONALISM

Although Watson rejected functionalism as a school, he was at the University of Chicago during its formative years; its emphasis on activity became part of his heritage. From his point of view he had just as much of a quarrel with functionalism as with structuralism. From the present perspective his disagreement with the functionalists was on the grounds that they insisted mental processes were an integral part of psychology. From his point of view they wished merely to study the biological significance of conscious processes rather than to analyze conscious states as did the structuralists,[31] and he found the distinction "unintelligible."[32] In this connection, a case can be made that a good bit of functionalism's conservatism was no more than lip service to the old tradition of psychology as the science of the mind.[33] Much as Watson claimed to reject functionalism, his views shared a fundamental similarity with it; he, too, stressed function and demanded a larger scope of application for psychology. He differed (unpardonably to James Rowland Angell) in that he sought to analyze behavior into its simplest forms, and thus rejected the holistic notion that was the primary basis of Chicago Functionalism.

These years also witnessed other general trends toward contentual objectivity with which Watson was presumably familiar. For example, in 1904 Cattell was so far removed from introspection that he claimed that most of the research done in his laboratory was "nearly as independent of introspection as work in physics or in zoology."[34] Cattell cited studies in which no introspective report was asked—for example, studies of reaction time, accuracy of perception, color preference, fatigue, animal and child behavior studies. At about the same time, certain psychologists were even defining psychology as the study of behavior; witness William McDougall in 1905[35] and again in 1923[36] and Walter Pillsbury, as we have already seen, in 1911. Neither one, however, would exclude introspective data from the field of psychology. This was the step taken most effectively by John B. Watson.

Others, working in the same climate of opinion but independently of Watson, also presented general behavioristic statements, excluding mind and consciousness from psychology. In France, for example, there was Henri Piéron (1881–1964), who had worked with both Pierre Janet and Alfred Binet, and who declared as early as 1907 that psychology could *only* be a science of behavior.[37]

JOHN B. WATSON

Watson carried out one of the most startling scientific coups in American history, although his behavioral revolution did not come all at once.

Early Life

John Broadus Watson (1878–1958) was born in 1878 on a farm near Greenville, South Carolina.[38] He attended Furman University taking an old-fashioned classical curriculum; the only science he elected was chemistry. He remained at Furman through 1900, leaving with a master's degree.

Being more interested in philosophy than in psychology, and knowing of John Dewey's fame, Watson enrolled as a graduate student at the University of Chicago. He found Dewey "incomprehensible," however, and almost immediately lost his enthusiasm for philosophy. Even so he continued to minor in the subject and took a considerable number of philosophy courses. As he himself commented, however, philosophy somehow did not take hold. In these years the Department of Philosophy included courses in psychology, and it was James R. Angell, the functionalist, who awakened his interest in psychology as a career. A second minor, one in neurology, eventuated from his work in the neurological laboratory of H. H. Donaldson, where he made the acquaintance of the white rat. He also took biology and physiology under Jacques Loeb, who wanted Watson to do his dissertation with him. Angell and Donaldson did not consider Loeb quite "safe," so he worked with the two of them instead. His doctoral dissertation made use of both neurological and behavioral techniques in the study of the correlation of the behavior and the growth of medullation in the central nervous system of the white rat. It was to Angell and Donaldson that he dedicated his first book.

Watson graduated in 1903 and was offered an assistantship to work with Angell which he did for a year. At this point he was made an instructor. With his new position he was able to marry Mary Ickes, a Chicago socialite.

Although Watson taught the usual kind of Jamesian psychology in the classroom at Chicago, his major interest was in the studies he was conducting in the animal laboratory he had constructed in the basement. Familiarity with C. Lloyd Morgan's work first stimulated his researches in animal psychology; so also, and even more directly, did the work of Thorndike.[39] At this time he was not aware of the work of either Pavlov or Bekhterev. Watson was a hard worker and produced a considerable number of studies with the white rat, the monkey, and the tern before he left Chicago in 1908 for Johns Hopkins.

At Johns Hopkins Watson received a full professorship in experimental and comparative psychology and the directorship of the laboratory. Watson did his most important work between 1908 and 1920, while at Johns Hopkins.

In 1913 he published his landmark article, "Psychology as the Behaviorist Views It." Behaviorism did not come to Watson suddenly. Actually, Watson said, it was in 1904 that he first broached a behavioristic psychology, presumably in conversation with a colleague at the University of Chicago.[40] He goes on to say that he was told it might work with animals but not with humans. He first publicly expressed his views in 1908 at a colloquium at Yale University. Four years later, at Columbia at Cattell's invitation, Watson gave a series of lectures that included the contents of the crucial article.

In 1914, in his book, *Behavior: An Introduction to Comparative Psychology*, Watson marshaled the available evidence to demonstrate the right of animal psychology to be considered a major specialty.[41] This was an important consideration for Watson. Indeed, in his earliest statement of behaviorism he admitted that part of his motivation for a new psychology was embarrassment about the skepticism he met concerning the value and relevance of animal research to psychology.[42] Animal research contributed very little of value to psychology as long as psychology was considered a study of human experience. What Watson wished to combat was the kind of purist psychology of human experience epitomized by Titchener and his followers. In allowing for an animal psychology, Titchener had to appeal somewhat lamely to the method of analogy.[43] Because an animal shows movements similar to those of a human in similar circumstances, it is possible to reconstruct the animal's consciousness as essentially similar to that of the human under these same circumstances. The observations are then to be interpreted cautiously in terms of human consciousness. Angell used this same sort of procedure at Chicago. Although Angell allowed students to do behavioral research, he always wanted analog "introspections" of their presumed conscious processes. The attention actually paid in Angell's laboratory to this translation into mentalistic terms was not necessarily more than perfunctory, but it was done. Even Watson's first publication bore the subtitle, "the Psychical Development of the White Rat." He began to object strenuously to this attitude. Watson went so far as to describe as "absurd" any interpretation of animal behavior in terms of the information it gives about conscious states.[44]

Conditioning in Watson's Behaviorism

Watson's manifesto of 1913 lacked a major positive characteristic of Watsonian behaviorism—emphasis on the conditioned response as the methodological tool par excellence. Watson had found the German and French translations of Bekhterev and was familiar with the salivary conditioned response studies of Pavlov, but at the time he was writing his article, he was thinking primarily in terms of English associationist principles, not conditioning. However, once he discovered Bekhterev and Pavlov, he immediately assimilated their paradigm into his approach. Watson used the conditioned reflex (with particular emphasis on the value of Bekhterev's motor reflex) as the topic of his presidential address before the American Psychological Association in 1915.[45]

In 1918, through the facilities of the Phipps Clinic in Baltimore, Watson extended his research to young children. Very little experimental work on human infants had been conducted prior to that of Watson and his co-workers. Baby biographies had been maintained, questionnaires used, and tests developed, but the deliberate manipulative introduction of forms of stimulation demanded by experimental study had hardly been attempted.

Setting aside conditioning for later discussion, we will now examine Watson's methods of studying hand preference as illustrative of the other research techniques he used.[46] It is well known that the great majority of adults are right handed. Watson set out to answer the question of whether or not right-handedness is instinctive, applying to young infants a variety of ingenious techniques. He measured the anatomical structure of the arm; the time that the infant would hang suspended from a bar by the right and by the left hand; and the total amount of work an infant does with each hand. The amount of work done was measured by attaching "work adders" (wheels that turn in one direction when there is movement) to both hands; when the child slashed about with his or her hands the wheel revolved, pulling up the cord to which a small weight was attached. After reaching toward an object was established in the infant's behavior repertoire, Watson noted the particular hand extended to secure a peppermint stick. The overall evidence tended to show little or no favoring of the right hand over the left hand. He therefore concluded that right-handedness was not instinctive but a matter of social pressure—a form of conditioning.

Watson's book, *Psychology from the Standpoint of a Behaviorist,* appeared in 1919 and was revised in 1924 and again in 1929.[47] It was essentially an attempt to extend the methods and principles of animal psychology into the human sphere. The value of conditioning as a method of study was extolled.

Later Life

In 1920 Watson's academic career came to an abrupt end as a result of scandal. When divorce proceedings were instituted against him, sensational publicity was the result, and he was asked to resign from the Johns Hopkins faculty. In the same year, he married Rosalie Raynor, with whom he had collaborated on a research study of infants. Although he knew nothing about the world of business, in 1921 he affiliated with the New York City advertising agency of J. Walter Thompson and was highly successful. He was promoted to Vice-President in 1924 and remained with the company until 1936 when he went with William Esty and Company.

Watson maintained his contact with psychology by writing popular articles for *McCall's, Harper's,* and *Collier's* magazines. His book, *Psychological Care of the Infant and Child,* published in 1928, was meant for a general audience.[48] It was almost inevitable that he would write this book. He had a deep-seated enthusiasm for the practical value of psychology in controlling behavior, and his environmentalist position demanded that infancy be seen as an extremely important formative period, for good or for ill. Representative of its contents was the question of whether or not children should live in individual homes or even know their parents, since it was these parents who were the major source of faulty conditioning. Among the advice he gave parents was to avoid creating fears by adverse conditioning, to be alert to the dangers of too much stroking, and to be aware of the pernicious effect of hampering movements. In the terminology of a later time, Watson strongly aligned himself with the regulatory rather than the permissive school of child rearing.

While in New York City, Watson secured a grant for research on the human infant, and the work was carried out by a research associate. For a time, he lectured at the New School for Social Research. These lectures are the basis for his book *Behaviorism,* a statement of his view in a form suitable for popular reading.[49] In retrospect, Watson conceded that the book was too hastily prepared. The revision of this book in 1930 marked, for all practical purposes, his departure from psychology. After that date Watson occupied himself primarily with work in the business world until his retirement in 1946. He died in 1958.

WATSON'S INTERPRETATIONS OF PSYCHOLOGICAL PROBLEMS

In his zeal to remake psychology, Watson attempted to apply the behavioristic approach to a variety of psychological problems. Characteristic are his interpretations of instinct, emotion, thinking, learning and conditioning, and personality. In their study he was guided by the concept of stimulus–response and would limit their study to psychological methods considered acceptable for research.

Behaviorism and Stimulus–Response

Psychology is concerned with the behavior of the whole organism. Physiology, its closest neighbor among the other sciences, is concerned with the functioning of the parts of the body, the organ system, circulation, digestion, and the like.[50] To reduce behavior to its simplest terms, the acts of human behavior always involve a stimulus that brings about a particular response. This stimulus is provided by something in the environment, by movements of the muscles, or by glandular secretions. The response follows on the incidence of the stimulus. If these assumptions are accepted, it follows that the task of psychology is to study the laws of behavior. Thus, when given the stimulus, we may learn to predict the response, or, given the response, we may isolate the effective stimulus.

In terms of a formula, psychology is the science of S–R, where S refers to stimulus and R refers to response. If the stimuli are of a complex character, it is appropriate to speak of the stimulus situation, which is ultimately resolvable into its component parts. Actually, except in the rarest of instances, we are dealing with situations, not with an isolated stimulus. Similarly, responses involve not only the simple responses that are also studied in physiology, such as the knee jerk or eye blink, but also more complex responses, to which the term *act* may be applied. The usual meaning of action is that the organism responds by some movement in space, as in walking, talking, fighting, or eating. Nevertheless, these actions can be reduced to two forms—motor and glandular responses. Responses may be overt, that is, observable; or they may be explicit or nonovert, that is, nonobservable or implicit. A person may show responses while standing apparently immobile; precise measurement would nevertheless show that muscular and glandular changes were taking place.

Besides being either implicit or overt, responses are either learned or unlearned. Specification of the extent and nature of both the unlearned and learned responses is necessary. So, too, is the discovery of the laws of acquisition of the learned responses.

Stimulus–response units, by an extension of their meaning in physiology, are called reflexes. They are not analyzed by the psychologist as minutely as they are by the physiologist. Watson did devote attention to the structures that make behavior possible, but he left to the physiologist the tasks of providing a detailed analysis and unraveling whatever organization takes place within the central nervous system. Brain processes, as such, did not particularly interest him, because of the inaccessibility of the brain, that "mystery box," as he called it.[51] Moreover, earlier psychologists had regarded the brain as the repository for whatever they could not explain in mentalistic terms. Behavior involves the whole body, not the nervous system alone, but the muscles and glands as well. Watson's interest was in somewhat larger segments of behavior, specifically, in what an individual would do in a given situation. For example, with what hand would the infant reach for the peppermint stick, or what would his or her response be to a loud noise?

Although behavior of the whole organism might have been Watson's announced goal, it is now apparent that his approach, problem by problem, was still molecular in character. That is, he was guided by a belief that his behavioral data were to be described in terms of relatively small units. He did not operate at the extreme lower level that he insisted the physiologist did, but he used their units in larger assemblages.

Psychological Methods

Watson championed methodological objectivism. He explicitly states that methods used by the psychologists are: (1) observation, with and without the aid of instruments; (2) the conditioned reflex methods, both secretory and motor; (3) testing; and (4) the verbal report method.[52] Observation is, of course, fundamental and the basis for all other methods. How Watson would use it has been illustrated in his studies of handedness. The conditioned-reflex method is described in a later section. The test methods included use of both those instruments already extant and new ones developed, but their results have been treated as behavior samples to ascertain the general level of behavior and special abilities. Incidentally, intelligence as measured by tests is nothing more than the capability to form new habits according to Watson.

Instinct

Watson's views on instincts were developed in three stages. He started from a more or less conventional acceptance and ended with a sweeping denial of their existence in humans. In his 1914 book on animal psychology, he devoted a considerable number of pages to discussing instinct, noting, however, that it was a much abused word.[53] Nevertheless, he used the term, characterizing it as a series of joined reflexes that unfold as heredity dictates. By 1919, in his *Psychology from the Standpoint of a Behaviorist,* Watson argued that unlearned behavior can be seen only in young infants because this behavior is quickly overlain by habits.[54] His position at this time was that, if we study infants, we can tease out the processes by which the complex learned behavior patterns, loosely called instincts, have developed.

In his *Behaviorism* of 1925 Watson flatly rejected the concept of human instinct.[55] As evidence, he offers a catalogue of the reflex behavior repertoire of the human infant, such as sneezing, crying, smiling, turning the head, arm movements, feeding responses, crawling, walking, and handedness. Because of slight structural differences among infants, there are equally slight but significant differences in how these reflexes are performed. Given the individual differences and the capacity for rapid habit formation, we have the basis for what has erroneously been called inherited characteristics.

Not only did Watson claim there were no instincts, but he went further and said there were no inherited capacities, temperaments, or talents. In so doing, he was taking an extreme environmentalist position. His insistence on the plasticity of human nature was so strong that he wrote:

> Give me a dozen healthy infants, well-formed, and my own specified world to bring them up in and I'll guarantee to take any one at random and train him to become any type of specialist I might select—doctor, lawyer, artist, merchant-chief and, yes, even beggar-man and thief, regardless of his talents, penchants, tendencies, abilities, vocations, and race of his ancestors.[56]

Actually, this extreme environmentalism is not characteristic of the behavioristic emphasis on objective content and methodology and rejection of introspection. Although Watson's stand on instincts was part of his system, it did not follow that it was an integral part of behaviorism. One could be a behaviorist and still reject his interpretation of environmental effect.

Emotion

To Watson, emotions were not matters of experienced states but bodily reactions to specific stimuli.[57] His most famous study was the search for the stimuli that produce emotional responses.[58] Watson described objectively the stimulus situation and the responses that the stimuli brought forth. He stimulated each infant in a variety of ways and narrowed down those that elicited emotional responses to a small number. Watson believed he had found evidence for only three emotions in infants—fear, rage, and love. Fear was produced only by a loud noise (made by striking a steel bar with a hammer) and by loss of support (carried out by allowing the child to drop a few inches or by jerking his blanket). Other situations, such as the presence of furry objects mentioned earlier, or the dark, or a snake, or the thousand and one things of which children are supposedly afraid simply did not at this young age produce fear responses. Watson described the responses of fear as involving startle, a catching of breath followed by rapid breathing, changes in skin color, hand-clutching, puckering of lips and crying, and, if the child was old enough, crawling, walking, or running away.

The only stimulus for rage that Watson found from a wide variety of stimuli was hampering or restricting the infant's movements in one fashion or another, such as holding the head firmly or restraining movements. The behavior exhibited in response to this stimulus was described as stiffening of the body, holding the breath, and slashing movements of arms and legs.

Love, which owing to the restrictions of convention Watson did not investigate as fully as the other two emotions, was produced by stroking of the skin, by gentle rocking, and by patting. Smiling, cooing, and gurgling were the responses to this form of stimulation.

These were the only unlearned emotional responses that Watson could find, although in a more cautious statement than one often associates with him, he said that the presence of others must be left in doubt. All other emotional reactions, he concluded, have to some extent a component of learning, acquired largely through conditioning during early childhood. Just as children acquire their motor skills, walking, skating, or typing, they acquire their fears, loves, and hates.

Watson's findings on emotions stimulated considerable research interest in the emotional development of children, including many studies that attempted to refute his contentions. A considerable amount of evidence has been collected that fails to confirm the existence of the specific emotional responses advanced by Watson.[59]

Thinking

To Watson, the most important kind of implicit sensory-motor behavior occurs when the person stands stock still and, after a lapse of time, comes forth with a solution to some problem, the solution being expressed verbally or by some movement of the body, arms, or legs. The implicit behavior prior to the overt action, of course, would be thinking. To Watson, committed as he was to behavior as his datum, this implicit behavior was genuine and relevant.[60] Thinking, he said, is only *subvocal speech* or muscular habits learned in overt speech that become inaudible as we grow up. After learning to talk by conditioning, thought is nothing more "than talking to ourselves."[61] A bodily response is a word substitute. A person thinks; that is, he or she makes implicit verbal reactions that do not differ in spirit from the overt movements made by a rat in running a maze. Thinking, to be sure, is more implicit and more economical of time and effort, but this difference is one only of degree. If we, for example, attach recording devices to the larynx of the thinker, we get movement that thus becomes explicit.

In a young child who is in the process of learning a language, these quantitative differences in amount of movement are even less great. Often children, and occasionally adults, think aloud. The child will say what she is going to do and then do it. Under the influence of social pressure (conditioning), she learns to give up clear articulation for whispering and finally reaches the stage of inaudible or implicit speech, characteristic of the adult. Watson could not use the most obvious source of evidence, namely, that we are sometimes introspectively aware that we do talk to ourselves while thinking. He could hardly bolster behaviorism with an appeal to introspection![62]

Thought is not merely behavior of the larynx or subvocal talking; it involves the whole body as when we gesture, frown, or nod, or when we carry out any movement that stands for an object or a situation. Watson suggested observing a deaf mute's fingers. During his thinking, muscular movements of the fingers will be found, just as there are movements from the larynx of normal persons. Watson attributed the failure to get consistently positive results from this method to the lack of delicacy of the instruments available. As a matter of fact, use of improved methods has demonstrated that thinking does involve these peripheral muscular factors, but that central or brain processes have also been shown to be present by later research. The judgment of later generations of psychologists is that Watson's theory of thinking as subvocal speech is too schematic and oversimplified.

Learning

Watson's views of learning showed progressive change and expansion. In his 1913 article he conceived of behaviorism as using stimulus–response and habit formation but he made no mention of conditioning.[63] By 1916 in his presidential address he enthusiastically endorsed conditioning.[64] In his *Behavior* of 1919 he described in detail the available research on discriminatory maze and puzzle-box learning.[65] He called Thorndike's law of effect "highly figurative."[66] Evidently, he saw conscious feeling lurking somewhere in this way of formulating the animal's responses. Watson would have substituted recency and frequency for the influence of effect. The successful act, over a series of trials, was that most frequently performed and, by its position within a trial, was also the one that occurred most recently. He argued that, after all, the animal takes the correct path at least once every trial, whereas particular blind alleys are skipped in a given trial. The successful path occurs last and is therefore the most recent. After 1916, Watson emphasized the importance of conditioning. The conditioned reflex became the heir of associationism. He expressed it in contiguous conditioning or a continuation of stimuli accompanying a movement, so that, when this combination recurred, it tended to be followed by the same movement. Watson emphasized repetition while he rejected effect. Consequently, he failed to recognize the importance of reinforcement, a key concept in later conditioning theory.

Watson's application of conditioning principles to learning in general and to thinking and emotion in particular now becomes relevant. Habits are nothing more than complex conditioned responses, such as those involved in playing tennis, in soling shoes, or in exhibiting maternal reactions to children.[67] These habits are integrations of conditioned responses around an activity built up from the available behavior repertoire, starting with innate movements. Movements combine by conditioning into complex acts. Language habits are merely a special case in that, to some extent, they become implicit.

Conditioning is the basis of speech, and speech is the basis of thinking. This bald summary shows why conditioning is important in thinking. Shortly after birth the infant exhibits vocalizations that, after conditioning, are spoken words. The infant's vocalization of "da-da" is attached to the person of the father; through further conditioning it becomes "daddy." With stronger verbal habits, the child no longer has to say aloud the conditioned response of, "father," selectively conditioned from the more primitive, "daddy." Now thinking it alone suffices. Other words and thoughts develop in a similar fashion. Subvocal speech, or thinking, has been developed through conditioning.

The child's fears and other emotional reactions beyond those given to unlearned responses are brought about by conditioning. Watson and Rosalie Rayner demonstrated this contention by building up a conditioned fear in the laboratory.[68] Their single subject, one of the most famous in psychological literature and therefore deserving of specific mention, was Albert B., a healthy, eleven-month-old infant, raised in the hospital where his mother was a wet nurse. The only fear reactions that he showed were to loud sounds. His reaction to anything at all coming chose enough was to reach out toward it and, if possible, to manipulate it. This included animals, such as the white rat. Presented here is the experiment itself, in synoptic form from their laboratory notes, faithful in spirit, but not precise in all details:

(Eleven months, 3 days)

1. Rat introduced. A reached. Just as hand reached, steel bar struck (not visible to A). A jumped violently, fell forward, but did not cry.
2. Again A reached; bar again struck. A jumped violently and whimpered. (One week allowed to lapse so as not to disturb child too seriously.)

(Eleven months, 10 days)

1. Rat presented without sound. Steady fixation, but at first no reaching, then tentative reaching, but withdrawal as rat touched.
2–4. Combined stimulation rat and sound. Started, no crying.
5. Rat alone. Puckered face, whimpered and withdrew.
6–7. Combined stimulation. Started and cried.
8. Rat alone. Turned away, fell over, raised himself and began to crawl away rapidly.

(Eleven months, 15 days)

1. Blocks introduced. Reached readily.
2. Rat alone, whimpered.
3. Rabbit alone. Leaned away, whimpered and then cried.

A conditioned fear had been established. A rat to which Albert had previously shown no fear, now brought forth fear. It can be inferred that such fears could inadvertently build up in a home, so that a child is being conditioned when he is in bed in the dark and hears a loud clap of thunder, producing thereafter a fear of the dark.

This study did more than demonstrate a conditioned emotional reaction. The two research workers went beyond this to show that the conditioned fear transferred to other previously unfeared objects. When the rabbit was introduced, Albert showed fear. Other furry things, a dog, a fur coat, cotton, wool, and a Santa Claus mask, were introduced, to which fear responses were now shown.

If conditioning can produce fears, can conditioning also be used to eliminate them? In another, later study "unconditioning" was compared with other methods as to its efficiency in eliminating fear responses.[69]

Personality

To Watson, with his molecular predispositions, personality was a straightforward summation of activities, neither mysterious nor necessitating concepts other than those used before.[70] All actual and potential reactions, verbal, manual, and visceral, go to make up the personality. Personality is the end product of an individual's habit systems. By habit systems Watson meant general, conveniently large groupings of individual habits that cluster together, constituting a useful way of talking about the various constituents of personality. Habits are formed just as described earlier, but now they are grouped to fit the particular topic. In a particular illustration used by Watson, shoemaking (the man's trade), religious, patriotic, marital, parental, arithmetic, general information, special fear, personal, and recreational habit systems are listed. These, of course, are only a sampling of the habit systems that constitute a personality. In another person, a different classification of habit systems would be used, although some of those listed are of a general character applicable to anyone. Since the cross-section is taken at a point in time, later or earlier cross-sections would show differences because habits are changeable; no individual's personality remains the same throughout life.

In this changeability of personality lies an opportunity for the betterment of humankind. Behaviorism, Watson believed, should stimulate adults to change themselves and especially to be prepared to bring up their children in a scientific way. Will they not "in turn bring up their children in a still more scientific way, until the world finally becomes a place fit for human habitation?"[71]

Overview

Watson's contribution to behavioral psychology, at least in the long run, was the behavioral method rather than his systematic or organizational bravado. The behavioral psychologies that came later and dominated American psychology from the 1930s through the 1960s were tied together primarily by their emphasis on stimulus–response connections and in their treatment of responses as actions that are objectively measurable, whether they be gross muscular acts or electrophysiological responses of the finest sort.

NEOBEHAVIORISMS

Watson's behaviorism was not the only objective psychology of its time, but it remains the classic example of behavioral principles that have come down to the present day. Like Wundt's psychology, it was a starting point for later positions that would disagree with details of the founding system. In addition, there were influences besides Watson on later behavioral developments.

Logical Positivism and Operationism

Just as the positivism of Comte and Mach strongly influenced earlier generations of psychologists, the neobehaviorists were influenced by neopositivism, usually called logical positivism or the positivism of the Vienna Circle, a philosophical position that developed in Vienna earlier in the twentieth century. Rudolf Carnap and Herbert Feigl were major influences in the movement. To logical positivists, for a statement to have meaning for science, it must be expressed in terms of empirical operations. That expression will allow its unambiguous definition, and it can be empirically tested. The emphasis was on the social observability of terminology. Questions about the nature of things were allowable only if they could be empirically observed or measured. The position fitted in very well with the basic approach of behaviorism, which also rejected internal and subjective processes.

In America, operationism was the expression of this same approach. *The Logic of Modern Physics,* a book published by Harvard physicist, Percy W. Bridgeman (1882–1961) in 1927,[72] triggered this interest and acceptance in operational definitions. In physical study he argued that a concept was the same as the corresponding set of operations by which it was found. To illustrate he gave the example of length. What is length? To find out, we perform certain operations. Length is defined in terms of the actions (operations) we go through to observe it. As Bridgeman said, "We mean by any concept nothing more than a set of operations; the concept is synonymous with the corresponding set of operations."[73] Psychology was ready for operationism—so much so that four years before Bridgeman, E. G. Boring, reflecting an already widespread cliché, wrote a paper for a national magazine which pointed out that it could be argued that "intelligence is what intelligence tests test," an operational definition before operationism.[74] On this and other grounds, the climate of opinion was receptive to operationism.

In a 1935 paper, S. S. Stevens called psychologists to adopt "an operational base of psychology."[75] This was followed in 1939 by a book by Carroll C. Pratt that gave the history of operationism and considered its implications for psychology.[76] By 1939 operationism had been seized on avidly, and a flood of articles began to appear. Besides the rigor which this theory introduced into psychologists' research activities, it provided a graceful retreat from the excesses of the "schools" that by this time were embarrassing psychologists.

Operationism is wider than a behavioristic outlook. It can be and is used in situations where conscious experience was traditionally considered to be involved, as in studies of sensation and perception. It can even use mentalistic terms, provided they are operationally defined. In operationism a research situation is arranged, and the observer reports what he sees—the perception is the reaction. The subjective is translated into the objective because it is not a public operation. From the operational reports of one investigation another research worker can go and do likewise, thus verifying or not, as the case may be, that the operations lead to the claimed result. Operationally, in operationism consciousness becomes discriminative behavior. Parallel to operationism is E. C. Tolman's concept of "intervening variable" which will be discussed in the section devoted to Tolman later in this chapter.

Neobehaviorists

Technically, any behavioral approach that came after Watson and his immediate contemporaries may be called neobehaviorism. The neobehaviorists were as diverse as their forebears, but their differences as well as similarities show how American psychology developed during the behavioral era. For this purpose we will discuss this era in terms of three of its major contributors, Clark L. Hull (1884–1952), Edward C. Tolman (1886–1959), and B. F. Skinner (1904–). Skinner may arguably be listed as being in the line of Thorndike. Hull represented the extension of Pavlovian conditioning, and Tolman represented a line with many roots, but most closely representing the behavioral extension of functionalism.

Clark L. Hull   Clark Hull (1884–1952) received his graduate training at Wisconsin and taught there before moving to Yale University as a research professor in 1929. It was during his years at Yale that he carried out his collaborative investigations of learning that made reinforcement central.[77] At Yale, his weekly research seminar became one of the major training grounds for many of those who have taught the present generation of eminent psychologists. Either in connection with the seminar or through other means, Kenneth W. Spence, Neal Miller, John Dollard, Robert Sears, Ernest Hilgard, and O. H. Mowrer were associated with him.

The basic statement of the theory of behavior as proposed by Hull is given in his *Principles of Behavior*[78] published in 1943. It was modified in his *Essentials of Behavior*[79] of 1951 and extended in *A Behavior System*,[80] published the year of his death.

In his autobiography, Hull stated that he

> came to the definite conclusion around 1930 that psychology is a true natural science; that its primary laws are expressible quantitatively by means of a moderate number of ordinary equations; that all the complex behavior of single individuals will ultimately be derivable as second laws from (1) these primary laws together with (2) the

conditions under which behavior occurs; and that all the behavior of groups as a whole, i.e., strictly social behavior as such, may similarly be derived as quantitative laws from the same primary equations.[81]

To implement these aims of objectivity and quantitativity, Hull developed statements about learning in terms of postulates, corollaries, and equations in a hypothetico-deductive framework using carefully defined symbols. A postulate or corollary led to the formulation of empirical predictions for a particular kind of learning situation, such as multidirectional maze learning.

After two preliminary postulates, Hull's third had to do with the key principle of primary reinforcement. To quote:

> Whenever an effector activity (R) is closely associated with a stimulus afferent impulse or trace (s) and the conjunction is closely associated with the rapid diminution in the motivational stimulus (S_p or S_g), there will result an increment to a tendency for that stimulus to evoke that response.[82]

Another of his postulates, which numbered seventeen in all, had to do with habit formation, utilizing the variable of the number of reinforcements. Others concerned primary motivation or drive, stimulus generalization, and experimental extinction.

Hull's theoretical formulations led to many empirically testable propositions and a tremendous amount of research, which it is impossible to summarize here. To some degree, Hull's greatest contribution to behaviorism may be the amount of research, pro and con, that his theoretical formulations stimulated. As with all theorists, his positions were often found wanting, but Hull is one of the best examples of a theoretical psychologist who attempted to state his positions with the kind of precision that would allow their empirical test.[83] At last, however, his theoretical formulations, which had to become so complicated to take account of the various behavioral situations, seemed to break down under their own weight.

Each of Hull's major students carried the behavioral approach beyond him and into different areas of psychology.

Kenneth W. Spence Kenneth Spence (1907–1967) was perhaps Hull's most direct successor in behavior theory and an active and stimulating collaborator during Hull's later career.[84] At first Spence concentrated on discrimination learning; later he turned to the investigation of a theory he had formulated concerning very simple learning.[85] Whereas Hull had attempted to find formulations to cover all behavior, Spence limited his theoretical structures to more tightly definable experimental situations.

Another of Hull's major students, Neal Miller (1909–), also moved away from Hull's attempt to produce a detailed but global theory of behavior. Miller chose a less theoretical and more problem-oriented approach to the study of behavior. This is not to say that Miller was nontheoretical, but his theories were directed to specific problem areas. His work in conflict, displaced aggression, and learned drives are examples of this problem-oriented theoretical approach.[86] He extended behavior theory into social learning, imitation, and even personality and psychotherapy, with a fruitful collaborator, John Dollard.[87]

Edward C. Tolman   Edward Tolman (1886–1961) is more difficult to place in the behavioral framework, although his significance to the development of behavioristic psychology is undoubted. Is he a neobehaviorist or is he one of Watson's contemporaries, such as Hunter? Because his contribution to behavioral psychology involves developments that came onto the scene after Watson's early work, we are classifying Tolman as a neobehaviorist.

Tolman was devoted to research on learning that was more or less independent of the prevailing schools of thought of his time. But his behaviorism, his molarism, and his purposiveness outweigh his contributions to the cognitive theory of learning, which has variously been described as involving sign–Gestalts, sign–significances, or expectancies. According to Tolman's autobiographical statement, in his work he stressed not learning, but a formulation of these other concepts. He did so in a fashion that was much less militant and strident than that of the earlier generation of behaviorists. In many respects, Tolman could be considered as much of a neofunctionalist as a neobehaviorist, although as one gets further away from the first generation of behaviorists and functionalists, the difference between these two positions begins to blur. He showed the influences of a number of lines of thought, including the purposivistic psychology of William McDougall and the molaristic approach both of Chicago Functionalism and Gestalt psychology.[88]

Tolman did his graduate work at Harvard, and in the main, his training had been in the Titchenerian vein. His encounter with Watson's *Behaviorism* in Robert M. Yerkes's course in comparative psychology was both a stimulus and a relief, for he had already been troubled about the inadequacies of introspection. He took his degree in 1915, and in 1918 he moved to the University of California at Berkeley where he remained. On arriving at Berkeley, his choice of a new course to teach was comparative psychology, and he soon embarked on research in learning in rats. He concluded that Watson's notions of stimulus and response were oversimplified, and, influenced by his exposure to Gestalt psychology (he had spent some time in Giessen with Kurt Koffka, one of the leaders of Gestalt psychology), he began to develop his particular views of psychology. Since he conceived of psychology as dealing with something larger than muscle contractions—with behavior as behavior, as he stated it—it was not surprising that he borrowed from his philosophy professor at Harvard, R. B. Perry, the notion that purpose and cognition, though essential to understanding behavior, can still be basically descriptive. While at Harvard Tolman was also influenced by William McDougall's *Social Psychology* and other works that represented McDougall's particular brand of purposive, functional psychology.

These influences as well as logical positivism led Tolman to develop his own view of behavior. In 1932 he published his *Purposive Behavior in Animals and Men.*[89] He used the term *purposive* in a descriptive rather than a teleological way. More specifically, he saw purpose as an urge to get to or away from a type of goal object, shown by persistence and the tendency to use the shortest route. By taking this position, he was calling attention to such matters as the readily observable fact that if, upon reaching the food box, the rat finds no food, he will try other ways of finding it. A series of trials, not a single trial, shows that blind alleys are eliminated and that the shortest possible route is finally adopted. The animal is learning a route to a goal, the means to an end. For Tolman "learning the maze" is decisive evidence of goal seeking. This definitely was not a teleological use of the term. In contrast to molecular behavior, which had to do with the underlying physiological activity, Tolman emphasized the molar behavior of humans and animals acting in respect to ends.

Tolman employed the concept of "intervening variables" in dealing with behavioral explanation. As early as 1936 Tolman had mentioned "operational behaviorism" as representing his view.[90] His views on operationism paralleled those of S. S. Stevens. The central theme of Tolman's paper was the functional and mathematical dependencies of "intervening variables" on the other variables. He then pointed out the necessity of using an operational means of specifying these intervening variables. Discussion of intervening variables in his presidential address before the American Psychological Association, published in 1938,[91] gave his position the wider audience his earlier paper had lacked. Thereafter, the concept of intervening variables was integrated with operationism in a way that made the two central to theoretical endeavors of the time. In 1948 Kenneth MacCorquodale and Paul E. Meehl[92] published an extremely significant paper that attempted (and, as later events showed, in some measure succeeded) in bringing order into this confusion of terms. They made the distinction between hypothetical constructs which involve hypothesizing a process or event that is not itself observable (such as events within the nervous system), and intervening variables that do not involve such hypothetization but abstract the empirical relationships without surplus meaning being involved.

Tolman is the best representative of the neobehaviorist position. He shared the widely held opinion that "grandiose" systems, such as his own, are at least temporarily out of step with the present. Although his title for his article in the Koch volumes is the "Principle of Purposive Behavior," the article itself is devoted almost exclusively to specifying his position on learning. Other than his skeptical comment just mentioned, he makes no mention of behaviorism as a system. The structure of his system is stated in terms of independent variables (past and present), intervening variables (demand variables such as means to an end readiness, expectation, and cognitive variables such as perceptions of objects and recognition of previously perceived places), and dependent variables. His intervening variables, he cheerfully admits, share in the surplus meaning of the hypothetical constructs as the term is used by MacCorquodale and Meehl.

Tolman's purposive behaviorism was at odds with the straight-line associationism of Watson's behaviorism and with Thorndike's connectionism. During the 1940s, he was the primary alternative to Hull's form of behaviorism.

B. F. Skinner and Radical Behaviorism

Burrus Frederick Skinner (1904–) more than any other behaviorist may be seen as the founder of a school of behavioral psychology.[93] His form of behaviorism has continued to be more militant than the other forms we have discussed. His behaviorism attempts to be a descriptive discipline, avoiding theories of behavior. Having once accepted intervening variables,[94] even this form of hypothesis was rejected in his *Science and Human Behavior* of 1953.[95] Skinner is thus the representative in the twentieth century of Francis Bacon's approach to scientific inquiry. The variables we have available for scientific analysis, Skinner tells us, are operations performed on the organism from without, such as water deprivation, and a kind of behavior, say, drinking. The inner condition "thirst" (what would be called a hypothetical construct) is useless in trying to control behavior because we cannot manipulate it as we can the operation from without, that is, the water deprivation. Skinner would entirely do away with all such intermediaries.[96] Since theories depend on these intermediaries, it is quite logical that he would also dispense with theories. Psychology as a field, he holds, is still inadequate for theorizing, and we must collect much more data. The nearest approach to a theory he tolerates is the assumption that order is to be found in behavioral data. Needless to say, Skinner rejects the hypothetico-deductive theoretical approach accepted by Tolman, Hull, and their intellectual successors. An understanding of behavior is not to be found in comparing theoretical constructs with data, but in meticulous description of the antecedent conditions and the behavioral results.[97]

Skinner and his followers have emphasized the technique of collecting large amounts of data on a small number of subjects. The analysis of the behavior of individuals is preferable to the averaging of the data gathered on multitudes. The use of statistical analyses, he believes, tends to lose the very events one is attempting to study.

Skinner's behaviorism seeks functional relationships between stimuli, broadly defined, and behaviors. The technique employed to discover these antecedent-consequent relationships is operant conditioning, or instrumental conditioning. The relationship of Skinnerian instrumental conditioning to Thorndike's methodology employed in his "trial and error learning" experiments is similar in spirit but quite different in detail.

Skinner's use of reinforcement schedules is perhaps his greatest single contribution to behavioral psychology. The different schedules are precisely defined environmental histories. The degree to which they lead to different behavioral outcomes, both in modes of responding and in resistance to extinction, is essential to the descriptive, functional relationships that underlay Skinner's entire behavioral position.

Skinner's emphasis on the relationship between individuals' environmental history and their consequent behaviors led Skinner far afield from the pigeon box. The fact that behaviors can be shaped—that is, elaborate conditioned behaviors may be constructed by reinforcing parts of the behavior—places Skinner in the class of elementistic behaviorists, reminiscent of John B. Watson. Such behavioral shaping has applied consequences. Skinner developed a system during World War II in which pigeons were trained to keep a target in the center of a cross-hair guidance system. Mounted in gliders, these birds would have been the equivalent of modern guidance computers. Once locked in on a target, they would manipulate the glider by pecking one side or the other of the target until the glider, armed with an explosive, crashed onto the target. The technique was never put into effect.[98] The same technique has been used in the training of animals to do tricks and entertain.[99] More seriously, reinforcement techniques originated by Skinner and his students have found wide application in present-day psychology. Programmed learning has been widely used in educational situations.[100]

Another application of operant techniques has been in clinical psychology in the form of behavior modification and behavior therapy. Such techniques have been used for simple problems such as hiccoughs and nervous tics to use in catatonic schizophrenics and autistic children.

In some respects, Skinner and his followers have realized John B. Watson's hopes in effecting not only prediction but also control of behavior. Like Watson, Skinner has promoted behavioral psychology as an essential component in remaking society. Skinner's novel *Walden Two* represents his idea of what society might be like with the concerted application of Skinnerian behaviorism.[101] Skinner, however, seems to recognize the problem that Watson ignored, that is, who controls the controller. Skinner admits that a science of behavior has the potential of being misused. He contends, however, that the best defense against its misuse is "to make all behavioral processes as familiar as possible. Let everyone know what is possible, what can be used against them."[102]

Karl S. Lashley and Physiological Psychology

Karl Lashley (1890–1958) studied with Watson at Johns Hopkins, although he received his doctorate with H. S. Jennings in zoology in 1914.[103] He worked with the psychiatrist Adolf Meyer there as well. Although his major degree work was in biology, he worked more with Watson than with his major professor. After graduation, he decided that psychology was the career of choice. He stayed on after graduation with a scholarship and worked with Watson between 1915 and 1917. It was during this time that Lashley came into contact with Shepard Ivory Franz (1874–1933), then at St. Elizabeth's Hospital in Washington. In 1917, Lashley published two papers with Franz on the effects of brain damage on learning in the rat,[104] which are exemplary of his own later work.

The way for Lashley's work was prepared by S. I. Franz.[105] Around 1900, Franz had combined the method of studying animal learning with that of the surgical extirpation of brain tissue which he used in a series of studies. Typical was his study "Variations in the Distribution of the Motor Centres" published in 1915.[106] In the study, he attacked the most firmly established "fact" of localization, Frisch and Hitzig's localization of motor functions. His results showed considerable lack of precision to cerebral localization. Lashley's findings were seen as hardly more than negative, however; no more general significance was attached to them.

Research Lashley performed, first with Franz at St. Elizabeth's Hospital, then at the University of Minnesota, and finally under the auspices of the Behavior Research Fund in Chicago, led to his appointment at the University of Chicago and in 1935 to a call to Harvard.[107]

What research led to his rapid academic rise, to say nothing of the presidency of the American Psychological Association and membership in the National Academy of Science before he was forty years of age? His seminal work concerned the effect of differential extirpation of the rat's cerebral cortex on intelligence (defined here as learning ability). Lashley saw behavior as a biological problem and felt that biological methods, including surgery, were appropriate in its study. To appreciate the significance of this problem, it is necessary to refer to the neurophysiological interpretation of learning which was then current. At that time, learning in the nervous system was seen as a matter of isolated neurons and synaptic resistances forming reflex paths with detailed localization of function in the cerebral cortex. The accepted rough model of the brain's function was that of the electrical switchboard. Changes at the synapses in a network of neurons had come to be the physiological equivalent of what started at the psychological level as association of ideas. It was still a strongly molecular point of view.

Begun about 1920, Lashley's research culminated in his 1929 publication, *Brain Mechanisms and Intelligence.*[108] In it, he reported overwhelming evidence for much less localization of function in the cortex than had heretofore been accepted, and he further demonstrated that large lesions affect learning more than small lesions. For these results, he supplied a conceptual framework involving "equipotentiality" and "mass action." Equipotentiality is the capacity of the intact portion of the brain to continue to carry out the function previously served by it and the extirpated part of the functional area. Mass action, though indicating a functioning of an area as a whole, serves as a reminder that there can still be proportional reduction of efficiency in complex functions. The reduction is in proportion to the extent of the injury. Considerable evidence for modes of organization rather than isolated, single, specific pathways and reactions was found in a series of experiments. In short, at the physiological level Lashley rejected the simple stimulus–response connectionism of Watson and Thorndike.[109]

A widespread misconception of the significance of Lashley's results arose partly because of the way Lashley presented them. He was interpreted as saying that what happens in the nervous system is guided by mass action, that when any area of the cortex is removed, another area can carry out its functions. What, under this interpretation, is left for physiological psychology to do? Based on a general acquaintance with his findings, an antiphysiological trend set in, and psychologists lost interest in physiological research, even coming to see the nervous system as irrelevant to psychology. "Behavior theorists," to use a loose but sufficiently apt term, could trace part of their skepticism concerning physiology directly back to Lashley's work.

This loose interpretation of Lashley's results has ignored what a more careful examination would have shown. Lashley was not denying localization. What he was saying was that localization was both less precise than and different from what previously had been conceived—and considerably more complicated. In some cases equipotentiality held; in others it did not. Mass action was not always a factor. Mass action and equipotentiality are more evident in complex problems and less so in simple ones, which leaves plenty of scope for physiological-psychological research.

Disappointment with the results of Lashley's experiments and Lashley's own argument that psychologists should stay away from neurologizing[110] had actually retarded development of physiological research within psychology. The understanding of an alternative to simple stimulus–response networks had to await Donald Hebb.

Donald O. Hebb and Cell Assembly Theory   Donald Hebb (1904–1985) probably did more than any other individual to reestablish modern physiological psychology as a part of behavior theory. Hebb, a Canadian born in Nova Scotia, received his bachelor's degree at Dalhousie. He taught in public school until 1929 when he entered McGill University part time, receiving his master's degree there in 1932. At McGill he worked with two of Pavlov's students, Boris B. Babkin and Leonid Andreyev.[111]

Hebb's conditioning work led to an offer from Robert M. Yerkes of Yale, which he declined, going instead to Chicago to study with Karl Lashley. When Lashley went to Harvard in 1935, Hebb went with him, completing his doctorate under Lashley there in 1936. His dissertation dealt with the discrimination of size and brightness by rats reared in total darkness.[112]

Hebb worked with Lashley an additional year after his dissertation. In 1937 he returned to Canada as fellow of the Neurological Institute in Montreal where he worked with brain surgeon Wilder G. Penfield (1891–1976). This experience would influence much of Hebb's later life and research. The problem of intelligence and brain damage which had dominated Lashley's work was now being investigated by Penfield and his staff, but this time with humans.[113] After a short stint at Queens University in Ontario, Hebb spent the years 1942–1947 at the Yerkes Laboratories of Primate Biology in Orange Park, Florida. It was at Yerkes's laboratory that Hebb noticed the emotional response elicited by chimpanzees on seeing a clay model of a chimpanzee's head. Their response could be elicited by any detached body member such as a hand. Their response also extended to humans, since they reacted to a mannequin hand. This emotional response increased with age. This study and other experiences dealing with the personalities of the chimps led Hebb away from the "hard-boiled" view of behavior theorists who rejected the concept that animals were "mentalistic."[114] Many years later he would write on this subject in an article titled "The Social Significance of Animal Studies."[115]

Hebb continued to deal with the problem of human intelligence and brain action. It was in 1944 that he adopted the position that would come to be known as the cell assembly theory. Hebb tells us:

> I found out that Rafael Lorente de Nó had recently shown: (1) that reentrant or closed circuits were to be found throughout the brain, which thus was no longer to be seen as a through-transmission, sensorimotor mechanism, but as one capable of a purely internal activity also, as a possible basis of thought; and (2) that one neuron by itself may not be able to excite a second neuron at the synapse, but can do so if supported by simultaneous action from another neuron. (That is, two presynaptic neurons can be effective when one is not, which, in principle, offers an explanation of the selective effect of attention, when some activity that is going on in the cortex provides such support for one sensory input but not for another.) The first idea offered a solution for my earlier problem, What is a concept?—namely, that it is a group of cortical neurons exciting and reexciting each other. The second idea was a fascinating one, for attention and set had been a complete mystery up to that time . . . and now I had a possible solution.[116]

Hebb was now looking at thought "as a sequence of brain events, each excited jointly by the preceding event and by the sensory stimulation of the moment. The schema implied that thought must be disrupted in a strange environment with unfamiliar contingencies: *A* being accompanied by *C* instead of the usual B."[117] It was then that Hebb thought back to the chimpanzees at Yerkes's laboratory and their fear reactions to dismembered organs. He concluded that "emotional disturbance is a disruption of thought due to a conflict with environmental events or to a lack of usual sensory support."[118] This notion would become part of Hebb's cell assembly theory.

In 1947 Hebb returned to Canada with a professorship at McGill. At that time, most behavior theorists ignored physiology. Hebb later assessed the situation in the late 1940s as follows: "Positivism and the black box were the style, Hull avoiding and Tolman and Skinner denouncing any involvement with the brain. Apart from Lashley's lab, only Frank Beach's and Harry Harlow's that I knew of did much physiologically."[119]

Hebb detailed his theory in his influential book, *The Organization of Behavior* (1949).[120] Cell assembly theory provided a theoretical structure for research, not only in physiological psychology but in behavioral psychology as well. For this reason, Hebb is included as one of the primary postwar behavior theorists. His theory went beyond only one area, however, and did much to stimulate research in a number of areas.

Two concepts are important in Hebb's theory: cell assemblies themselves and phase sequences. A cell assembly is a group of neurons clustered together functionally because of a past history of being stimulated together. Their main characteristic is that they are capable of acting together for a time as a closed system. They may have been produced through some sensory event, or they may have been aroused by some previously existing assembly. One cell assembly may activate another assembly. Patterns of these mutual activations represent central facilitation, which is Hebb's nucleus for the function of attention.

Cell assemblies that are activated at the same time may become organized into "phase sequences," which are a sequence of cell assembly functions. Taking the child as his subject, Hebb tells us that when a baby hears footsteps

> an assembly is excited; while this is still active, he sees a face and feels hands picking him up, which excites other assemblies—so that "footsteps-assembly" becomes connected with "face assembly" and the "being-picked-up assembly." After this has happened, when the baby hears footsteps only, *all three* assemblies are excited; the baby then has something like a perception of a mother's face and the contact of her hands before she has come in sight—but since the sensory stimulations have not taken place, this is ideation or imagery, not perception.[121]

Hebb pointed away from the straight-line connectionistic approach, which explained behavior as a simple stimulus–response chain. Associationists for centuries, including their modern counterparts in behavior theory such as John B. Watson and E. L. Thorndike, held the serial model or connectionist approach. Hebb stated that "Neural transmission is not simply linear, but apparently always involves some closed or recurrent circuits; and a single impulse cannot ordinarily cross a synapse—two or more must act simultaneously, and two or more afferent fibers must, therefore, be active in order to excite a third to which they lead."[122] The reflex arc is not a simple loop but one that may have many loops built into it, some of which may be recurrent or reverberatory and others of which are simply closed. He also opposed the notion that the nervous system was a passive transmitter of sensory information from receptors. He based his opposition on the idea that the central nervous system may be activated without external stimulation.

These are broad notions, even though they are explicated in terms of physiological structures and processes. In spirit it is in line with other explanatory attempts using hypothetical nervous processes, such as William James's physiological explanation for the stream of thought.[123] Like James's notion, Hebb's cell assembly theory excited a considerable interest in physiological processes underlying mental and behavioral events. As we will see, Hebb was also a stimulus in the coalescence of cognitive psychology.

SUMMARY

With the rise of behaviorism, the prescription of both methodological and contentual objectivism came to dominate the psychological scene. This is not to say that the study of sensation, perception, and its allied topics disappeared with the appearance of Watson's behaviorism or even the neobehaviorists. Even these traditional topics came to be studied in a different way, however. Nonetheless, introspection, both in the elaborate form used by Titchener and in the more restricted form used by the functionalists, began to fade. By the late 1930s such studies involved more objective methodology such as discrimination tasks and threshold tasks. Even sensory and perceptual psychology became more quantitative and far less qualitative.

The behaviorisms and neobehaviorisms differed among themselves just as much as the orthodox introspectionist psychologies had done. There were as many behaviorisms as there were behaviorists. What they shared, however, was an attempt to use objectifiable concepts and to make the acceptable psychological terms empirically definable and measurable.

NOTES

1. Raymond Dodge published his paper as "The Theory and Limitations of Introspection," *American Journal of Psychology, 23* (1912):214–229.
2. Walter B. Pillsbury, *Essentials of Psychology* (New York: Macmillan Co., 1911).
3. J. B. Watson, "Psychology as a Behaviorist Views It," *Psychological Review, 20* (1913):158–177 (Herrnstein and Boring, Excerpt No. 94).
4. *Ibid.*
5. *Ibid.*
6. *Ibid.*
7. Franz Samelson, "The Struggle for Scientific Authority: The Reception of Watson's Behaviorism 1913–1920," *Journal of the History of the Behavioral Sciences, 17* (1981):399–425. For developments in the 1920s, see Samelson, "Organizing for the Kingdom of Behavior: Academic Battles and Organizational Policies in the Twenties," *Journal of the History of the Behavioral Sciences, 21* (1984):33–47.

8. E. B. Titchener, "On 'Psychology as the Behaviorist Views It'," *Proceedings of the American Philosophical Society, 53,* No. 213 (1914):1–17.

9. J. B. Watson, *Behaviorism,* 2nd ed. (New York: W. W. Norton, 1930).

10. I. M. Sechenov, "Refleksy golovnogo mozga," translated as "Reflexes of the Brain," by A. A. Sobkov, in I. M. Sechenov, *Selected Works* (Moscow and Leningrad: Gozmedizdat, 1935), pp. 264–322 (1863) (Herrnstein and Boring, Excerpt No. 63).

11. I. P. Pavlov, *Selected Works,* ed. K. S. Kostoyants, trans. S. Belsky (Moscow: Foreign Languages Publishing House, 1955) (1873–1936).

12. I. M. Sechenov, *Selected Works.*

13. I. P. Pavlov, *Selected Works.*

14. I. P. Pavlov, "Autobiography," *Selected Works,* pp. 41–44 (undated); B. P. Babkin, *Pavlov, a Biography* (Chicago: University of Chicago Press, 1949).

15. I. P. Pavlov, *Lectures on Conditioned Reflexes,* 3rd ed., trans. W. H. Gantt (New York: International Publishers, 1928) (1904).

16. *Ibid.*

17. I. P. Frolov, *Pavlov and His School* (London: Kegan Paul Trench, Trubner, 1937).

18. I. P. Pavlov, *Selected Works,* pp. 76–80 (Herrnstein and Boring, Excerpt No. 101).

19. *Lectures,* p. 219.

20. *Ibid.*

21. A. L. Schniermann, "Bekhterev's Reflexological School," in C. Murchison, ed., *Psychologies of 1930* (Worcester, Mass.: Clark University Press, 1930), pp. 221–242.

22. V. M. Bekhterev, *General Principles of Human Reflexology,* trans. 4th Russian ed. (New York: International Publishers, 1932) (1907).

23. E. L. Thorndike, "Edward Lee Thorndike," in C. Murchison, ed., *A History of Psychology in Autobiography* (Worcester, Mass.: Clark University Press, 1936), Vol. 3, pp. 263–270; Geraldine M. Joncich, *The Sane Positivist: A Biography of Edward L. Thorndike* (Middletown, Conn.: Wesleyan University Press, 1968).

24. I. P. Pavlov, *Lectures on Conditioned Reflexes.*

25. E. L. Thorndike, "Animal Intelligence: An Experimental Study of the Associative Processes in Animals," *Psychological Review Monograph Supplement, 2,* No. 4 (1898) (Herrnstein and Boring, Excerpt No. 97).

26. E. L. Thorndike, *The Elements of Psychology* (New York: Seiler, 1905), p. 203.

27. E. L. Thorndike, *The Fundamentals of Learning* (New York: Teachers College, 1932); E. L. Thorndike, *The Psychology of Wants, Interests, and Attitudes* (New York: Appleton, 1935). An excellent collection of Thorndike's papers is his *Selected Writings from a Connectionist's Psychology* (New York: Appleton–Century–Crofts, 1949).

28. R. M. Yerkes, "The Formation of Habits in the Turtle," *Popular Science Monthly, 58* (1901):519–525 (Herrnstein and Boring, Excerpt No. 98).

29. W. S. Small, "Experimental Study of the Mental Processes of the Rat, II," *American Journal of Psychology, 12* (1901):206–232 (Herrnstein and Boring, Excerpt No. 99).

30. J. Loeb, *Einleitung* in *die vergleichende Gehirnphysiologie und vergleichende Psychologie mit besonderer Berucksichtigung der wirbellosen Thiere* (Leipzig: Barth, 1899) (English trans. 1900) (Herrnstein and Boring, Excerpt No. 89).

31. J. B. Watson, *Behavior: An Introduction to Comparative Psychology* (New York: Henry Holt, 1914), p. 8.

32. *Ibid.*

33. G. Bergmann, "The Contribution of John B. Watson," *Psychological Review, 63* (1956):265–276.

34. J. M. Cattell, "The Conception and Methods of Psychology," *Popular Science Monthly, 66* (1904):175–186.
35. W. McDougall, *Physiological Psychology* (New York: Macmillan Co., 1905).
36. W. McDougall, Outline of Psychology (London: Methuen & Co., 1923), pp. 43–120.
37. Paul Fraisse, "French Origins of the Psychology of Behavior: The Contribution of Henri Piéron," *Journal of the History of the Behavioral Sciences, 6* (1970):111–119.
38. J. B. Watson, "John B. Watson," in C. Murchison, ed., *A History of Psychology in Autobiography* (Worcester, Mass.: Clark University Press, 1936), Vol. 3, pp. 271–281; R. S. Woodworth, "John Broadus Watson: 1878–1958," *American Journal of Psychology, 72* (1959):301–310. An excellent biography of Watson is Kerry W. Buckley, *Mechanical Man: John Broadus Watson and the Beginnings of Behaviorism* (New York: Guilford Press, 1989).
39. J. B. Watson, *Psychology from the Standpoint of a Behaviorist*, 3rd ed. rev. (Philadelphia: Lippincott, 1929), preface.
40. *Ibid.*
41. J. B. Watson, *Behavior.*
42. J. B. Watson, "Psychology as a Behaviorist Views It."
43. E. B. Titchener, *A Textbook of Psychology* (New York: Macmillan Co., 1909).
44. Watson, *Behavior*, p. 3.
45. J. B. Watson, "The Place of the Conditioned-Reflex in Psychology," *Psychological Review, 23* (1916):89–117.
46. J. B. Watson, *Behaviorism.*
47. J. B. Watson, *Psychology from the Standpoint of a Behaviorist* (Philadelphia: Lippincott, 1919).
48. J. B. Watson, *Psychological Care of Infant and Child* (New York: W. W. Norton, 1928).
49. J. B. Watson, *Behaviorism.*
50. *Ibid.;* Watson, *Psychology* (1929).
51. J. B. Watson, *Behaviorism*, p. 49.
52. J. B. Watson, *Psychology* (1929).
53. J. B. Watson, *Behavior.*
54. J. B. Watson, *Psychology* (1919).
55. J. B. Watson, *Behaviorism.*
56. *Ibid.*, p. 104.
57. *Ibid.*
58. J. B. Watson and J.J.B. Morgan, "Emotional Reactions and Psychological Experimentation," *American Journal of Psychology, 28* (1917):163–174.
59. M. Sherman, "The Differentiation of Emotional Responses in Infants," *Journal of Comparative Psychology, 7* (1927):265–284, 335–351.
60. J. B. Watson, *Behaviorism; Psychology* (1929).
61. J. B. Watson, *Psychology* (1929), p. 238.
62. M. F. Washburn, "Introspection as an Objective Method," *Psychological Review, 29* (1922):89–112.
63. J. B. Watson, *Psychology as the Behaviorist Views It.*
64. J. B. Watson, "Place of Conditioned-Reflex."
65. J. B. Watson, *Behavior.*
66. *Ibid.*, p. 256.
67. J. B. Watson, *Behaviorism.*
68. J. B. Watson and R. Rayner, "Conditioned Emotional Reactions," *Journal of Experimental Psychology, 3* (1920):1–14.

69. J. B. Watson, *Behaviorism.*
70. *Ibid.*
71. *Ibid.,* p. 304.
72. P. W. Bridgeman, *The Logic of Modern Physics* (New York: Macmillan Co., 1927).
73. *Ibid.,* p. 36.
74. E. G. Boring, "Intelligence as the Tests Test It," *New Republic, 34* (1923):35–36.
75. S. S. Stevens, "The Operational Basis of Psychology," *American Journal of Psychology, 47* (1935):323–330.
76. C. C. Pratt, *The Logic of Modern Psychology* (New York: Macmillan Co., 1939).
77. Clark L. Hull, "C. L. Hull," in Boring et al., eds., *A History of Psychology in Autobiography* (New York: Appleton–Century–Crofts,), Vol. 4, pp. 143–162.
78. Clark Hull, *Principles of Behavior: An Introduction to Behavior Theory* (New York: Appleton–Century–Crofts, 1943).
79. C. Hull, *Essentials of Behavior* (New Haven, Conn.: Yale University Press, 1951).
80. C. Hull, *A Behavior System: An Introduction to Behavior Theory Concerning the Individual Organism* (New Haven, Conn.: Yale University Press, 1952).
81. E. G. Boring et al., *A History of Psychology in Autobiography,* Vol. 4, p. 155.
82. C. Hull, *A Behavior System,* pp. 5–6.
83. An excellent collection of Hull's papers is Abram Amsel and Michael E. Rashotte, eds., *Mechanisms of Adaptive Behavior: Clark L. Hull's Theoretical Papers, with Commentary* (New York: Columbia University Press, 1984).
84. Howard H. Kendler, "Kenneth W. Spence: 1907–1967," *Psychological Review, 74* (1967):335–341.
85. Kenneth Spence, *Behavior Theory and Conditioning* (New Haven, Conn.: Yale University Press, 1956); *Behavior Theory and Learning: Selected Papers* (Englewood Cliffs, N.J.: Prentice–Hall, 1960); H. W. Kendler and J. T. Spence, eds., *Essays in Neobehaviorism: A Memorial Volume to Kenneth W. Spence* (New York: Appleton–Century–Crofts, 1971). For an excellent review of the Hull–Spence approach, see F. A. Logan, "The Hull–Spence Approach," in Sigmund Koch, ed., *Psychology: A Study of A Science,* Vol. 2, *General Systematic Formulations, Learning and Special Processes* (New York: McGraw–Hill, 1959), pp. 293–358.
86. Neal E. Miller, "Liberalization of Basic S–R Concepts: Extensions to Conflict Behavior, Motivation and Social Learning, in Koch, ed., *Psychology: A Study of a Science,* Vol. 2, pp. 196–292; "Experimental Studies in Conflict," in J. McV. Hunt, ed., *Personality and the Behavior Disorders* (New York: Ronald Press, 1944); "Theory and Experiment Relating Psychoanalytic Displacement to Stimulus–Response Generalization," *Journal of Abnormal and Social Psychology, 43* (1948):155–178; "Learnable Drives and Rewards," in S. S. Stevens, ed., *Handbook of Experimental Psychology* (New York: John Wiley and Sons, 1951), pp. 435–472.
87. Neal E. Miller and John Dollard, *Social Learning and Imitation* (New Haven, Conn.: Yale University Press, 1941); Dollard and Miller, *Personality and Psychotherapy* (New York: McGraw–Hill, 1950).
88. E. C. Tolman, "Edward Chace Tolman," in Boring et al., eds., *A History of Psychology in Autobiography,* Vol. 4, pp. 323–339.
89. E. C. Tolman, *Purposive Behavior in Animals and Men* (New York: Century Book Co., 1932).
90. E. C. Tolman, "Operational Behaviorism and Current Trends in Psychology," *Proceedings of the 25th Anniversary Celebration of the Inauguration of Graduate Studies at the University of Southern California* (Los Angeles: University of Southern California Press, 1936), pp. 89–103.

91. E. C. Tolman, "The Determiners of Behavior at a Choice Point," *Psychological Review, 45* (1938):1–41.

92. K. MacCorquodale and P. E. Meehl, "On a Distinction Between Hypothetical Constructs and Intervening Variables," *Psychological Review, 60* (1948):95–157.

93. Skinner has given us excellent and exhaustive accounts of his life. See B. F. Skinner, *Particulars of My Life* (New York: Alfred A. Knopf, 1976); *The Shaping of a Behaviorist* (New York: Alfred A. Knopf, 1979); *A Matter of Consequences* (New York: Alfred A. Knopf, 1983).

94. B. F. Skinner, *The Behavior of Organisms: An Experimental Analysis* (New York: Appleton–Century–Crofts, 1938).

95. B. F. Skinner, *Science and Human Behavior* (New York: Macmillan Co., 1953).

96. B. F. Skinner, "Behaviorism at Fifty," *Science, 140* (1963):951–958; also in Trenton Wann, ed., *Behaviorism and Phenomenology: Contrasting Bases for Modern Psychology* (Chicago: University of Chicago Press, 1964), pp. 79–108.

97. B. F. Skinner, *Contingencies of Reinforcement: A Theoretical Analysis* (New York: Appleton–Century–Crofts, 1969).

98. B. F. Skinner, "Pigeons in a Pelican," *American Psychologist, 15* (1960):28–37.

99. K. Breland and M. Breland, *Animal Behavior* (New York: Macmillan Co., 1966).

100. B. F. Skinner, "Teaching Machines," *Science, 128* (1958):969–977; F. S. Keller and J. G. Sherman, *PSI: The Keller Plan Handbook* (Menlo Park, Calif.: Benjamin, 1974). Skinner did not originate teaching machines, however. See Ludy Benjamin, "A History of Teaching Machines," *American Psychologist, 43* (1988):703–712.

101. B. F. Skinner, *Walden Two* (New York: Macmillan Co., 1948).

102. B. F. Skinner, in Richard I. Evans, *The Making of Psychology* (New York: Alfred A. Knopf, 1967), p. 90.

103. D. O. Hebb, "Karl Spencer Lashley: 1890–1958," *American Journal of Psychology, 72* (1959):142–150.

104. S. I. Franz and K. S. Lashley, "The Retention of Habits by the Rat After Removal of the Frontal Portion of the Cerebrum," *Psychobiology, 1* (1917):3–18; "The Effects of Cerebral Destruction upon Habit-formation and Retention in the Albino Rat," *Psychobiology, 1* (1917):71–139.

105. S. I. Franz, "Shepard Ivory Franz," in C. Murchison, ed., *A History of Psychology in Autobiography* (Worcester, Mass.: Clark University Press, 1932), Vol. 2, pp. 89–113.

106. S. I. Franz, "Variations in the Distribution of the Motor Centres," *Psychological Monographs,* no. 19 (1915):81.

107. D. O. Hebb, "Karl Spencer Lashley."

108. K. S. Lashley, *Brain Mechanisms and Intelligence: A Quantitative Study of Injuries to the Brain* (Chicago: University of Chicago Press, 1929).

109. For an understandable but generally ignored article by Lashley on this topic, see Lashley, "The Problem of Serial Order in Behavior," in Lloyd A. Jeffress, ed., *Cerebral Mechanisms in Behavior: The Hixon Symposium* (New York: John Wiley and Sons, 1951), pp. 112–136.

110. Karl Lashley, "Basic Neural Mechanisms in Behavior," *Psychological Review, 73* (1930):1–37.

111. E. R. Hilgard, *Psychology in America: A Historical Survey* (New York: Harcourt Brace Jovanovich, 1987), p. 437.

112. D. O. Hebb, "The Innate Organization of Visual Activity: I. Perception of Figures by Rats Reared in Total Darkness," *Journal of Genetic Psychology, 51* (1937):101–126; "The Innate Organization of Visual Activity: II. Transfer of Response in the Discrimination of Brightness and Size by Rats Reared in Total Darkness," *Journal of Comparative Psychology, 24* (1937):277–299.

113. D. O. Hebb, "D. O. Hebb," p. 290; "Intelligence in Man After Large Removals of Cerebral Tissue: Report of Four Left Frontal Lobe Cases," *Journal of Genetic Psychology, 21* (1939):73–87; "Intelligence in Man after Large Removals of Cerebral Tissue: Defects following Right Temporal Lobectomy," *Journal of Genetic Psychology, 21* (1939):437–446; Hebb and Penfield, "Human Behavior After Extensive Bilateral Removal from the Frontal Lobes," *Archives of Neurology and Psychiatry* (Chicago), *44* (1040):421–438.

114. D. O. Hebb, "D.O. Hebb," pp. 294–295.

115. D. O. Hebb and W. R. Thompson, "The Social Significance of Animal Studies," in Gardner Lindzey, ed., *Handbook of Social Psychology,* (Cambridge, Mass.: Addison–Wesley, 1968), Vol. 2, pp. 532–561.

116. D. O. Hebb, "D. O. Hebb," p. 295.

117. *Ibid.,* p. 296.

118. *Ibid.*

119. *Ibid.,* p. 299.

120. D. O. Hebb, *The Organization of Behavior* (New York: John Wiley and Sons, 1949).

121. D. O. Hebb, *Textbook of Psychology,* 3rd ed. (Philadelphia: W. B. Saunders, 1972), p. 67.

122. *Ibid.*

123. William James, *Principles of Psychology* (New York: Holt, 1890), Vol. 1, pp. 224–290.

Max Wertheimer. The device that looks like a wheel in this rare photograph is a form of tachistoscope used in the early Gestalt experiments.

Chapter
23

Wertheimer, Koffka, and Köhler: Gestalt Psychology

In 1910, so the story goes, a young German psychologist named Max Wertheimer was traveling by train from Vienna to the Rhineland on his vacation.[1] During this journey an idea came to him for a research study that was to result in the founding of Gestalt psychology. Gone were his plans for a vacation. At Frankfurt, he left the train, bought a toy zoetrope, and took it to his hotel room to verify, in a preliminary way, the insight that had just come to him. The zoetrope is a device that allows successive still pictures to be exposed at a constant rate of speed so that movement is perceived. Before the advent of motion pictures, a later development of the same principle, zoetropes were relatively common as children's toys. Wertheimer did not have to use the zoetrope in his formal experiment; the University of Frankfurt placed at his disposal a tachistoscope, a device for regulating the length of time during which a visual stimulus, such as a nonsense syllable or a figure drawing, is exposed. It may also be used to present successive stimuli, separated by short and precisely regulated intervals of time.

What was this epoch-making experiment? It was a problem in the perception of apparent motion, that is, the perception of movement when no movement has actually taken place.[2] Two lines were exposed in two different places on the face of the tachistoscope. Each exposure lasted a very short time and was separated from the next exposure by varying lengths of time. If there was too long a time between exposures, the subject would see the lines successively. If the time was too short, the subject would see the lines simultaneously. When the interval of time between the exposures was at an optimal length, the subject saw, not two lines successively or simultaneously, but one line moving from one place to another. The visual experience was that of a single line that moved, despite the fact that actually there were two successively exposed stationary lines separated by an interval of time. Variations—such as exposing a vertical line followed by a horizontal line, causing the observer to see a line swinging around through ninety degrees—gave the same result. Wertheimer called this apparent movement the phi phenomenon. Sometimes an observer reported movement alone, with no line seen; this he called pure phi.[3] Although the name was new, the phenomenon itself had been known for years. This seemingly trivial verification of what was already known was to a launch a new movement in psychology.

Wundt's view of psychology will illustrate what Wertheimer and others would try to combat through this and similar studies. To Wundt, as we have seen earlier, various elementary experiences were available for compounding—quality, intensity, pleasantness–unpleasantness, tension–relaxation, and excitement–depression. When these experiences are compounded by association, ideas and perceptions are formed. Wundt had been aware that these compounds had characteristics as a whole, not readily explained by their parts. His solution, however, depended on creative synthesis. Wertheimer's study arose from dissatisfaction with this elementistic and associationistic position, which left many characteristics of percepts unexplained by their supposedly ultimate components.

ANTECEDENTS OF GESTALT PSYCHOLOGY

Some of the perplexities of configuration had already been elucidated, and explanations had been attempted before Wertheimer appeared in Frankfurt.

In *The Analysis of Sensations*,[4] Ernst Mach showed that changes in spatial orientation—such as first viewing a square from one of its sides and then shifting to a corner; or first hearing a series of sounds at one tempo and then hearing them at a faster or slower tempo—did not bring about a radical change in the experience of the overall configuration. Despite wide variation in viewing conditions, a table remains a table, no matter how viewed. Look at a table from one corner with its edge at eye level. Although the retinal image is a complex quadrilateral, you see a rectangle oriented obliquely in space. Mach went on to speak of sensations of space–form and sensations of time–form as kinds of experience in themselves. The circle may change size or color without changing its space–form of circularity.

Christian von Ehrenfels (1859–1932) at the University of Graz in Austria further developed Mach's conception of sensations of space–form. He noted that in the visual field certain visual characteristics, such as roundness, angularity, and slenderness, are ignored when we deal with sensations.[5] Their occurrence seems to be due to something beyond single sensations. If individual stimuli are changed in the same proportion, these particular characteristics of slenderness, angularity, and roundness are still present. Among the other phenomena he considered was the effect of transposing a melody. A melody made up of one series of notes is still heard as the same melody when played in a different key. Von Ehrenfels labeled as *Gestaltqualität* or form quality that aspect of perception characterized by the transposition of melodies and proportionate changes in roundness, angularity, and slenderness. These perceptions were based on something more than the sum of the individual lines, and on something over and above the tones. Von Ehrenfels treated the form quality as another element (although not a sensation), so that if there were nine notes and a *Gestaltqualität* there would be ten elements in all—nine sensory and one nonsensory. A variant explanatory principle offered accounted for the phenomenon with "relations between elements." Ehrenfels and the Austrian School of *Gestaltqualität* that developed at Graz held that form qualities were constructed out of sensory data, and, since the elements were the ultimate facts of consciousness, they continued an old tradition rather than beginning a new one.

Other relevant work outside what was to become the Gestalt tradition went on more or less simultaneously with that of Wertheimer. Friedrich Schumann (1863–1940), G. E. Müller's assistant and collaborator in the invention of the memory drum, was Wertheimer's host in Frankfurt. In studies of visual shape and size perception, Schumann had already found that analysis of sensory elements was of no help in explaining the results.[6]

Gestalt psychology was influenced by the growing influence in Europe of phenomenological observation. From the observations on color made in the early nineteenth century, a phenomenological trend had continued to develop close to the mainstream of psychology, although the dominant tradition did not accept it. Since phenomenology involved the study of immediate experience, its conclusions were thought to follow directly from the experience. Ewald Hering's studies of color and space, for example, essentially demonstrated experimentally the presence of some color phenomenon or visual perception. However, Hering did not feel the need to go beyond this demonstration to arrive at quantitative values for his findings.[7]

Before Wertheimer's time, phenomenology had received increased support and interest because of the work of Edmund Husserl (1889–1938), Professor of Philosophy at the University of Göttingen, mentioned earlier as a student of Franz Brentano. Husserl had accepted Brentano's distinction between psychology's contentual area, the act of "seeing" color, and physics' contentual concern of the color object itself, which was an underpinning to Brentano's view of intentionality. After a period of positive interest in phenomenology as applied to psychology,[8] Husserl disavowed psychology, especially that of the Wundtian variety, and turned to what would be his major life's work: establishing a new approach to philosophy based on a description of immediate experience with all its biases, which included keeping the scientific-psychological aspect at the lowest possible level.[9] In this process the realm of consciousness is sharply separated from the material, physical world. The material, though not denied existence, is said to be irrelevant to the task. Phenomenologically, consciousness is a unique realm that is not dependent on physical processes. It is paramountly a medium of access to whatever exists. This kind of subjective experience is used to synthesize a meaningful universe. This is the task of pure phenomenology as Husserl saw it. In contrast to Wundtian introspection, phenomenology does not search for presumed elements but examines meaning, forbidden to Wundtians because it was a source of stimulus error. For the phenomenologist, elements do not exist, and stimulus error is not an error but the very core of what they investigate.

Edgar Rubin (1886–1951),[10] a Danish phenomenologist and a contemporary of Wertheimer, emphasized the distinction between the figure—the substantial appearance of objects—and the ground—the general homogeneous environment in which the object exists. Perception, he argued, is selective. Not all stimuli are perceived with the same clarity and distinctness. Those perceived with greater clarity form the figure; the remainder provide the ground. The house against the sky, the word or picture on the white page, the recognized face against the rest of the faces in the photograph—all have this relation of figure and ground. Wertheimer went beyond his predecessors by submitting these convictions to experimental study. From these experiments, Wertheimer found a new understanding of these perplexing phenomena and integrated the results into a new way of looking at psychological phenomena.

EARLY LIFE OF MAX WERTHEIMER

Max Wertheimer (1880–1943) was born in Prague; his father had directed and taught in a commercial school.[11] After attending a local Gymnasium, Wertheimer studied law at the university for two and a half years but shifted to the study of philosophy. He attended, among others, the lectures of von Ehrenfels. At Berlin, he continued to study philosophy and psychology. He studied under both Schumann and Carl Stumpf; Stumpf was a friend of William James and a specialist in the psychology of music. From Berlin, Wertheimer went to Würzburg, where in 1904 he received his degree summa cum laude. He had worked at Würzburg under Oswald Külpe at a time when the Würzburg School was carrying on research in thought processes, the imageless thought studies. Their revolt was not against elementism as such but against the constraints Wundt put on the elements.

One of Wertheimer's early research interests, in keeping with his interest in law, was in the association experiment used to detect knowledge that subjects wished to keep secret. He published on this research in 1905 and in later years.[12] The years 1904 to 1910, before Wertheimer's arrival in Frankfurt, are not well documented, but some of his activities in Prague, Vienna, and Berlin concerned psychological matters.

FRANKFURT, PHI PHENOMENON, KÖHLER, AND KOFFKA

On his arrival in Frankfurt in 1910, after trying out his hypothesis with the toy stroboscope, Wertheimer sought out his old teacher Schumann, who had just arrived at the University of Frankfurt. It was Schumann who placed a tachistoscope at his disposal. Wertheimer's first subject was Wolfgang Köhler (1887–1967), and his second, Kurt Koffka (1886–1941). These two men would be junior only to Wertheimer in their pioneering contributions to Gestalt psychology in the years to come. Koffka and Köhler had taken their degrees at Berlin in 1908 and 1909, respectively, and were the new assistants in the Psychological Institute at Frankfurt.[13] They had already done some research in psychology, Köhler on hearing and Koffka on imagery and thought. These three were intially brought together by their discontent with Wundtian elementism. As good subjects should be, Köhler and Koffka were kept ignorant of the purpose of the experiment until after its completion. Sometime in 1911, Wertheimer called them in to explain the experiment.[14] From then on their lives and work were intricately interwoven.

Wertheimer's paper, "Experimental Studies of the Perception of Movement," appeared in 1912.[15] This single study stimulated over a hundred papers on apparent movement in the next thirty years.[16] By and large, Wertheimer's findings were substantiated. Reverberations from his study extended into other psychological fields, particularly those dealing with memory, thinking, and action.

Several explanations of apparent movement were already current.[17] The traditional view of discrete elements was that each stimulus gives rise to its own sensation, and, on the basis of past experience, our perceptions of them are integrated. To be more specific, Wundt attributed apparent movement to the kinesthetic sensations produced by the movement of the eyes.[18] Arranging the experimental setting with suitable pairs of lines so as to require two simultaneous movements in opposite directions, Wertheimer early ruled out Wundt's theory. Phi phenomenon still occurred. The eyes could hardly move in both directions at the same time, and Wundt's explanation fell to the ground.

THE PHI PHENOMENON AND GESTALT

Wertheimer argued that the apparent movement generated in his experiment had no counterpart in the sensory elements. Local sensory stimulation could not be responsible for the actually perceived phenomenon. He could not fit this fact into existing theories of perception. A general reevaluation of the basic nature of perception seemed necessary to him. Whatever it was that Wertheimer explained to Köhler and Koffka in 1911 about his experiment on phi phenomenon, it was not the full-blown Gestalt theory.[19] Without doubt, however, what was said seemed to them to challenge the established order. Wertheimer was aware by then that the *Gestaltqualität* interpretation was not sufficient and said so in his paper, but a more complete statement had to await later work. Two papers devoted to theoretical statements published by Wertheimer in 1922[20] and 1925[21] will serve to explain Gestalt psychology in a preliminary way.

In the phi phenomenon, Wertheimer wrote, the subjects perceived a whole, or Gestalt, not the isolated elements. Von Ehrenfels and the members of the Graz School had been on the right track in raising an important problem, but in depending on a summation principle, they had been wrong.[22] What takes place in each part depends on the whole. This is true of all perceptual experience. In our perception of objects, certain characteristics cannot be attributed to a single sensation. This Gestalt, or whole, is a "given" of perception, not something unstructured. The Gestalt is in itself primary and inherent in the process of sensory reception. Wertheimer agreed with William James that the elementists had found the secondary products of analysis. What was important was not the mosaic but a dynamic field in which the parts interact through the receptive process. Perception shows a totality, a whole, a configuration, an articulated structure; it is the task of psychology to account for this, not by explaining it away, but by exploring its characteristics as a structure. Gestalt psychology restored the "thing–language," as Egon Brunswik phrased it many years later, to its place in the psychology of immediate experience.[23] For psychology to advance, "a procedure 'from above' is required, not a procedure 'from below upward' ";[24] understanding of whole properties must precede consideration of the significance of the "parts." A Gestalt is primary to the parts and is not merely their sum. It now becomes relevant to quote Wertheimer's formal definition of Gestalt: "There are wholes, the behavior of which is not determined by that of their individual elements, but where the part-processes are themselves determined by the intrinsic nature of the whole."[25] He was announcing that Gestalt psychology is committed to the molar prescription as the basis for both its research and, as we will see in a moment, its protest against the psychology of the day.

Sometimes the words *configuration, structure,* and *whole* are used as English translations for Gestalt, but the untranslated term is preferable, since none of these words captures its complete meaning. Two meanings of the German word *Gestalt* must be specified. On one hand, there is Gestalt as object. A Gestalt is an entity that in itself has form, such as a chair or table. On the other hand, Gestalt is the property of things—their squareness or triangularity. Gestalt, then, is both the object and the form characteristics of that object.

The emphasis on wholes has sometimes led to a misunderstanding about the Gestalt theorists' precise attitude toward parts in the psychological field and toward the process of analysis. The Gestalt position does not demand, for example, that the entire visual field be organized into a single pattern. We need do no more than use our eyes to see that it is not. Certain aggregates within this field are Gestalten.

The Gestalt psychologists do use analysis; their objection is not to analysis as such, but only to analysis of sensational elements that have no existence as bits of experience. If there is analysis into genuine parts, then this is not only permissible, but also demanded.

Analysis is exemplified by the various laws of Gestalten. In one sense, each law is a statement of analysis, as is the distinction made between figure and ground. The parts, however, are derived from their meaningfulness in the total context, not from sensory elements. Attitudinal analysis is also possible. By adopting a particular attitude, an observer may select some parts of the Gestalt and suppress others. This happens in reversible perspective, as in a line drawing capable of being seen two ways, permitting the observer to switch from one view to the other. In this kind of analysis there is a change in the organization of the field, so that the impression one receives is different depending on how one perceives it.

GESTALT AS A PSYCHOLOGY OF PROTEST

Not only a Gestalt theory, but also a Gestalt movement developed, and these three men zealously propagandized for the Gestalt molar point of view in the years to come. In furthering this aim, Köhler and Koffka were much more ready than Wertheimer to systematize their thinking and put it into print.

Gestalt psychology developed in Germany at the same time that behaviorism made its appearance in the United States. Both were psychologies of protest.[26] Unlike the behaviorists, however, Gestalt psychologists did not question the existence of consciousness; they only doubted the reality of the elements of which other psychologists said consciousness was constituted. Wertheimer summarized these mistaken beliefs in the "bundle hypothesis" and the "association hypothesis."[27] Sensory elements do not form a bundle, he said, and association does not serve as a means of binding them together, because there is not a summative relationship, as the psychologists they were attacking claimed. Gestalt psychology was very much a revolution against the established order in psychology. In its early years, the exposure of the inadequacies of the entrenched position in psychology was almost as important to Gestalt psychologists as their positive contributions. They aspired to nothing less than a complete revision of psychology, but from the figure down rather than the ground up.

WERTHEIMER AND THE PRINCIPLES OF ORGANIZATION

Wertheimer lectured at Frankfurt, where he was Dozent, from 1912 until 1916 when he went to Berlin. In 1922 he became an Assistant Professor at Berlin, and in 1929 he became Professor at Frankfurt, where he was given Schumann's old chair. Relevant publications by Wertheimer were slow in coming. During the First World War years, he collaborated on research in the development of binaural listening devices for use in submarines and harbor defense installations; these devices were not particularly relevant to Gestalt psychology.

Wertheimer's influence on the thinking of other psychologists was considerable, although, as E. B. Newman remarks, it is hard to evaluate.[28] His students learned about Gestalt psychology mostly from his lectures and his inimitable conversations. At Berlin and Frankfurt, colleagues and students carried out research theses on a variety of studies.

Much of what was contained in Wertheimer's lectures during these years did not see print until after the war. A paper on creative thinking that appeared in 1920 (as well as a paper on thinking that appeared as early as 1912), in some respects anticipated his major work in this field, which did not appear for more than twenty years.[29]

In 1923 an important paper on perceptual grouping appeared.[30] In this paper Wertheimer attempted to show that we perceive objects just as directly as we see motion in the phi phenomenon—that is, not as clusters of sensations but as unified wholes. The principles of organization of Gestalten that Wertheimer formulated had specific reference to perception, that is, they dealt with how Gestalten was organized. He preferred to use simple visual phenomena—such as dots, lines, or figures made of a few lines—or simple auditory stimuli—individual musical notes, for example—to avoid being charged with confusing the issue with common objects whose sheer meaningfulness would suggest organization.

Wertheimer presented various principles, including the following. First, there is the principle of proximity—other things being equal, the parts of a figure that are parts closest together are perceived together. (See, for instance, Figure 23.1.) The lines that are closest together seem to belong together, and those farther apart appear to be separate. This demonstration works not only for lines but also for sounds in temporal order. Second, there is the principle of similarity. In Figure 23.2 we see dots of equal distance but of similar or different appearance. Note that, with all other things being equal, the dots that are similar seem to belong to each other.

Figure–ground as a Gestalt law of organization was borrowed from the work of Edgar Rubin. The perceptual field tends to be divided into two parts, a foreground and a background. The line patterns in Figures 23.1 and 23.2 tend to organize themselves in that way. Rubin's famous figure of the philosopher's cup (Figure 23.3) is the classic demonstration of figure–ground organization. What you see is determined by whether the cup or the two faces constitute the figure. When one is figure, the other is ground.

Still another principle of organization is that of closure. Closure is the tendency to complete a figure, no matter what the sensory modality. Visual forms are included, of course. For example, if a figure is drawn with incomplete lines or small gaps (as are many cartoons and sketches), the perceiver completes it, typically disregarding or not "seeing" its incompleteness. Closure is essentially a special instance of the most general of configurational laws, that of Prägnanz. This law states that "Psychological organization will always be as good as the controlling circumstances permit."[31] Besides closure, the law of Prägnanz embraces factors of proximity and similarity as well as symmetry and regularity.[32]

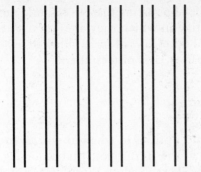

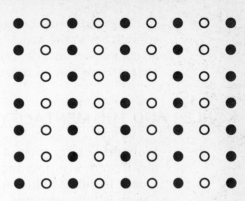

Figure 23.1 Demonstration of the Gestalt Law of Proximity. Note that the lines tend to organize vertically since the lines are closer to each other vertically than horizontally.

Figure 23.2 Demonstration of the Gestalt Law of Similarity. Note that the dots tend to organize vertically.

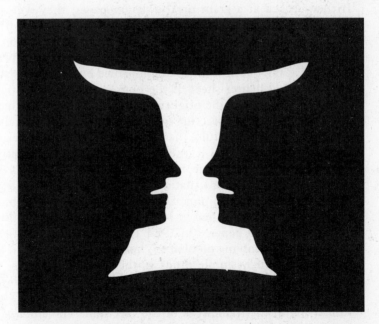

Figure 23.3 Rubin's goblet/faces figure-ground illusion. [*Source:* E. B. Boring, Herbert Sidney Langfeld, and Harry Porter Weld, *Psychology: A Factual Textbook* (New York: John Wiley & Sons, Inc., 1935), p. 290. (Original source: Edgar Rubin, Visuell wahrgenommene Figuren, Copenhagen: Gyldendalske Boghandel, 1921.)]

The Gestalt psychologists were demonstrating that we respond not to isolated stimuli, but to the nature of the setting in which they are found. A considerable amount of work developing these and other laws of form followed. By 1933, Harry Helson[33] was able to isolate 114 separate laws of Gestalten.

KÖHLER AND THE MENTALITY OF APES

Wolfgang Köhler remained at Frankfurt until 1913 when he was given an opportunity to work with apes and chickens at the Anthropoid Station of Tenerife in the Canary Islands.[34] Köhler arrived there shortly before World War I broke out. The Canary Islands were quickly seized by the British, who, not knowing what to do with this German scientist, left Köhler there for the duration of the war. The climate was beastly, but Köhler made the most of his experience by conducting some Gestalt experiments that would become classics.

One of Köhler's experiments with chicks performed during these years, though simple, clearly shows what the Gestalt psychologists were trying to demonstrate.[35] Two shades of gray paper on which grain was scattered were exposed. Hens were trained to take grains from one of these papers, the darker shade of gray. If they pecked at a grain on the darker paper, they were permitted to swallow it; if they pecked at a grain on the lighter paper, they were driven away. Eventually, after hundreds of trials, they learned to peck only at grain on the darker paper. The crucial series of trials was now begun. The darker gray paper of the learning trials was used again, but now it was accompanied by a sheet of a still darker gray instead of the original lighter sheet. If the hens pecked on the original gray, they would be responding to specific brightness; if they pecked at what now was the darker paper, they would be reacting to a total situation or Gestalt, that is, to a relation of lighter–darker. As a rule, the hens pecked at the darker gray, not the particular one on which they had learned to peck. This was a relative response in which "darker of two" was the cue, not the specific gray. The hens reacted not to a specific element in the learning situation but to the pattern or Gestalt.

Kohler's work on chimpanzees at Tenerife resulted in his classic book, *Mentality of Apes*, first published in 1917 and later translated into English,[36] along with another important paper,[37] in 1927. His task was to investigate the intelligence of chimpanzees in solving problems. The studies took place in and around their cages and involved such simple props as the bars of the cages, which blocked direct access, bananas for them to secure, sticks to be used to draw in the bananas from outside the cage, and boxes on which to climb. One study involved a stick which Köhler hid in the framework of the cage roof. The chimpanzees were allowed to watch Köhler while he hid the stick. Afterward, the animals were taken to their living dormitory for the night. The next morning they were brought back to the cage, and one of them found that there was a bunch of bananas outside the cage. The animal was already familiar with using a stick to draw them in. As Köhler put it, he looked around as a man would in seeking a tool, but he did not find what he was looking for. After some seconds, his eyes went to the place where the stick had been hidden the night before. The stick was not in sight, but he immediately climbed up to where it was hidden, brought it down, and used it to draw in the bananas.

Another study involved a banana, placed at the level of the cage ceiling, and a box, from which, if moved under the banana, the chimpanzee could jump up to secure the banana. Almost all the chimps solved the problem of moving the box to the correct spot under the banana, climbing up on the box, and jumping to get the banana.

Contrast their behavior with that of a relatively stupid chimpanzee. He had been present many times while the others were learning to use the box as a tool to reach the banana. These other chimpanzees even tried to show him how to use it, but he imitated only parts of their behavior. He would move the box but, as often as not, away from the food. He would then climb on the box and jump, but not under the banana, and, after climbing off the box, he would then jump up under the banana. He never formed the Gestalt; for him there were two separate groups: climb–box–jump and jump–under–fruit. He did not relate the parts of the activity to the essential structure of the total situation.

Köhler interpreted these and similar results as evidence of insight—the seeing of relations.[38] These Gestalten occurred in the process of solving problems. The animals' activity formed a continuous whole in which everything fell into place. There was continuity, a direction toward a goal, and closure. The insightful solutions they displayed are interpreted as making closure of the gap in the animals' psychological field. Capacity for perception of relations varied in different animals and thus became an indication of intelligence.

KÖHLER AND PHYSICAL GESTALTEN

In 1920 Köhler left Tenerife for a Germany in the throes of economic and social reconstruction. He managed to secure only temporary academic appointments for a year or so. Formal recognition of Gestalt psychology by the academic world, however, came in 1922 when Köhler was appointed to a chair and the directorship of the laboratory at the University of Berlin. He occupied this post until 1935. Presumably the publication of a book two years before, whose translated title is *Static and Stationary Physical Gestalts*,[39] was in part responsible for this major appointment.

To evaluate its significance, it is necessary to return to Wertheimer's original experiment.[40] Wertheimer postulated brain action as a configural total process to account for phi. These processes must be essentially similar for apparent and for true motion, since they are experienced as identical. If two phenomena are perceived as identical, one must assume that they have corresponding brain processes. If the nervous system were organized so that it consisted of interlocking elements, it simply could not account for phi. There must be some correspondence between the patterning of the psychological experience and the underlying brain process. The nervous system has unitary properties, its parts being included in the larger units or Gestalten. Wertheimer suggested that the seen movement was a consequence of a physiological shortcut. With precisely the right temporal interval, "physiological cross processes" took place. These were modes of functional interconnection in larger patterns rather than in points on the cortex. The physiological processes had whole properties themselves, which were essentially the same in phi as in real motion.

Köhler generalized this point of view in his book of 1920,[41] *Die physischen Gestalten.* A theory that physical systems possess Gestalt properties was the consequence, and this theory made it possible for Köhler to offer a transition from psychological to physical systems. The brain process and the perceived object correspond in that they are both Gestalten. In relating the mental and physical, Köhler advanced the thesis that the form of the mental event is the same as the form of the physical.[42] This is the principle of isomorphism; there is a formal correspondence between the brain processes and the experienced consciousness. This correspondence is not the relation of the object to its mirror image; it is topological. These two, the physical process and the experience, are different spatially. There is a formal correspondence but not a literal identity between the phenomenal experience and the brain pattern. In framing a psychophysical isomorphism, Köhler drew not only on Wertheimer's formulation for perceived movement already cited,[43] but also on Hering's anticipation of isomorphism in visual phenomena[44] and G. E. Müller's use of the principle in formulating what he considered fundamental psychophysical axioms.[45] In his statement of isomorphism Köhler offered his particular solution to the age-old mind–body problem; isomorphism was his way of integrating the mind with the rest of the world.

Isomorphism was but a phase of a much more ambitious undertaking by Köhler.[46] He was intent on nothing short of demonstrating that biology, chemistry, physics, and even astronomy also involved Gestalten. It should be mentioned that Köhler had studied physics under Max Planck, whose work in the quantum theory influenced him considerably. Köhler's attempt at model building was a heroic effort, the effect of which is difficult to assess. Certainly it was meant to be more than an analogy, and in the contemporary period of psychology, Köhler had success in applying it to further psychological investigation.

KOFFKA AND THE GROWTH OF THE MIND

Kurt Koffka left Frankfurt in 1911 for a long period of service at the University of Giessen (1911–1927), which was interrupted by visits to universities in the United States.[47] During these years he wrote the *Growth of the Mind: An Introduction to Child Psychology,* which was first published in English in 1924 and is based on a work in German that had appeared three years before.[48] Koffka made use of a developmental concept in his account, stressing what he called the convergence theory.

To place convergence theory in its proper setting, it is necessary to say something more about the phenomenological strain in Gestalt psychology. Phenomenology tended to go hand in glove with more sympathetic acceptance of nativism, as distinguished from empiricism. According to Gestalt theory, one does not need to learn to see structures in the sense that the properties of the psychological field are used to explain the events taking place within that field. It is sometimes charged that Gestalt psychology is nativistic because it believes that movement in space is perceived as itself. This position is closer to that of Ewald Hering, the nativist, than to that of Helmholtz, the empiricist. Gestalt psychologists were not nativistic in the meaning of holding a belief in innate ideas or innate tendencies or in the notion of organic predisposition due to inheritance of brain structures. To the Gestalt psychologists, the dynamics of the psychological field are products of nervous processes. Their belief that the nervous system operates in a certain way and obeys certain laws is not "nativistic." Gestalt psychologists actively denied an adherence to either nativism or empiricism. In fact, they do not accept the nativism–empiricism dichotomy at all; rather, they adhere to a principle of invariant dynamics. Invariant dynamics are natural principles that operate independently of genetics and experience. Mary Henle explains the principle as follows:

> What is it that organisms share with inorganic nature? General principles (like conservation of energy), forces, elementary processes such as electric currents. Thus electric currents occur in the brains of organisms as well as in streaks of lightning. Since they are found throughout nature, they must be independent of the genetic equipment of any species or any individual. Surely, nobody would maintain that electric or chemical processes corresponding to perception are inherited.[49]

What evolution contributes is a limitation of possibilities by the structure of the nerve processes themselves. Koffka thought the misapplication of the term *nativist* to Gestalt might have arisen because Gestalt psychology denies that learning is an establishment of a specific connection between neurons.[50] He attributed this view to the empiricists, hence admitting that he was antiempirical, but only in this sense. Köhler, argued that there is a third kind of process, neither learned (empirical) nor inherited (nativist)—neither chromosomal nor dependent on evolution—but, instead, owing to the invariant nature of physical-chemical processes that occur in living and nonliving organisms, such as electrical currents and chemical reactions.[51] These invariant processes are equally unaffected by learning and heredity. They give rise to the general principles of action in matter, which include the relation of the organism to space.

Koffka submitted the concepts of reflex and instinct to Gestalt analysis. Consistent with the Gestalt principle of the priority of the whole over the parts, he saw reflexes as derived from instincts rather than the reverse. To illustrate his handling of instinct, Koffka held that one of its most conspicuous characteristics is its tendency to require the individual to work toward attaining some goal. This, in turn, brings closure in a temporal Gestalt.

Although Wertheimer had done earlier work in learning, Koffka's book served to emphasize in a detailed fashion that the learning process is clearly within the sphere of Gestalt psychology. The laws of organization in perception were seen as applicable to learning problems. Köhler's work on chimpanzees illuminated the point. Koffka used his results to challenge the theory of trial and error learning, offering "insight" as a replacement to account for the learning process. The trial and error hypothesis assumes that, in learning, a large number of random movements are made, the correct responses are gradually learned, and the incorrect ones are eliminated. A variety of explanations have been offered as to why this takes place, but at this time, the differentiation between those responses learned and those eliminated was attributed to the respective pleasure and pain that accompanied them.

To Koffka, learning was not a gradual mechanical process but involved the same principles as perceptual Gestalten. Koffka rejected trial and error as a principle for learning, pointing out that the customary puzzle boxes and mazes were apparatuses that forced the animals to trial and error because no other approach was possible under these circumstances. The artifacts of such studies, as well as of those in sensation, were seen as results of the laboratory procedure. To be sure, an obstacle between the animal and the goal must be provided, but it should be of such a nature as to permit intelligent, insightful behavior, if the animal is capable of it. This was the case with Köhler's procedures. The causative relations were open to the animals' observation, and insight resulted. Insight takes the place of practice or repetition as the crux of learning, in the Gestalt description of learning. Practice does have some effect. After the Gestalt has been assimilated, practice makes its execution easier, as is the case when a musician grasps the Gestalt of a composition and with the aid of practice proceeds to play it better.

GESTALT PSYCHOLOGY COMES TO AMERICA

With the rise of Hitler to power in Germany, nearly all the leaders of Gestalt psychology emigrated to America, although the movement did not entirely disappear from Germany. Under Hitler, psychology as a whole became a minor subject in the German academic hierarchy.

Before the migration, psychologists in the United States were not unfamiliar with the Gestalt psychologists' work. They had read their publications, and several visits by leading Gestalt psychologists had been made. In 1922, in the *Psychological Bulletin*, Koffka wrote the introductory statement of the Gestalt position for American psychologists.[52] As the medium for his presentation he used the study of perception, a field in which he was now specializing. Although admirable in many respects, unfortunately his article created the misapprehension among psychologists that Gestalt psychology was little more than a theory of perception—a view not entirely dissipated to this very day. Koffka and Köhler made several visits during the 1920s and early 1930s. Koffka was the first to settle in the United States, in 1927 becoming a Professor at Smith College where he remained until his death in 1941. He worked principally on color vision in relation to perceptual organization. Köhler's book, *Gestalt Psychology,* appeared in 1929.[53] In 1934 he lectured at Harvard, returned to Germany, and in 1935, in view of his open defiance of the Nazi regime, decided to emigrate permanently.[54] He became Professor of Psychology at Swarthmore College, where he remained until his retirement. Between them, Köhler and Koffka carried on more of the polemics for Gestalt psychology in the United States than did Wertheimer.

In 1933 Wertheimer and his family left Germany and came to the United States. In 1934, he became a part of the "University in Exile" of the Graduate School of the New School for Social Research in New York City. This affiliation would continue until his death in 1943.

Other psychologists more peripherally related to Gestalt psychology also came to the United States. One of these was Kurt Lewin, who had taken his degree at the University of Berlin after World War I. He arrived in 1933 and did important work related to Gestalt psychology. There was also Kurt Goldstein, the neurologist, who was affiliated with Gestalt psychology in Germany. When he came to the United States in 1935, Goldstein continued to make use of Gestalt concepts in his clinical work.

The reception of Gestalt psychology in the United States was mixed, and it made relatively slow progress. Behaviorism was riding the crest of a wave, and the language barrier stood in the way. A philosophical substratum was seen as lurking in the background of Gestalt thinking. The Gestalt critique of introspective elementism left many American psychologists somewhat baffled. Titchenerian structuralism had passed its peak some years before, and functionalism was asking and answering questions that, in part at least, made people think that the Gestaltists were insisting on fighting over a dead issue. Instead of arguing that they were wrong, some American psychologists said they were correct but either left it at that or added that they were unoriginal.

The Gestalt movement soon had a new opponent—behaviorism, with its elementistic and reductionist tendencies. Gestalt psychologists accepted the study of behavior as legitimate but insisted that the approach to it should be molar, not molecular. Their isomorphic view was opposed to the point-by-point correspondence of the S–R formula. This controversy was accentuated by the disagreement over the validity of introspection, even though this was not the same sort of introspection as that of Wundt or Titchener. Behavior composed of reflexes and conditioned responses was considered to be open to the same criticisms that had been made of Wundt and Titchener's brick and mortar psychology.

American psychologists who were sympathetic to Gestalt theory seldom went so far as to become complete adherents. Seeing it as valuable, they assimilated it more generally into an eclectic pattern where it served as a needed corrective to a more atomistic approach. In fact, criticism had been published even before the Gestalists had arrived in the United States. Harry Helson, a sympathetic critic, had pinpointed what was to be a major criticism, then and later.[55] He argued that Gestaltists had followed the advice of Goethe to a friend on how to solve problems; they had changed the problem into a postulate. He said that the Gestalt psychologists treated the issue of organization in mental life not as a question to be wrestled with, but as a ''given'' of nature. This is close to solving a problem by denying its existence.

Wertheimer's years in the United States, 1933 to 1943, were busy ones, but not as quantitatively productive as might have been wished. Burdened as he was with adapting to a new environment and struggling with a foreign language, Wertheimer suffered increasing exhaustion.[56] He continued trying little informal experiments, communicating them to his friends and at meetings of psychologists, but not recording them in published form.

Wertheimer did not live by psychology alone. He devoted time and energy to social issues, logic, and ethics. At the New School for Social Research he was a member of a heterogeneous group of social scientists, which facilitated the spread of his interests beyond psychology. He saw the Gestalt point of view as extending into other scientific areas where it could help in the understanding of their complex problems. Wertheimer felt deeply the social issues of his time and wrote eloquently and incisively on matters such as the meaning of freedom.[57]

One characteristic of the then current work in anthropology which caused him considerable distress was the doctrine of culture relativism, which he combatted vigorously. He discussed ethics in relation to this principle of relativity and pleaded that studies of ethnology, sociology, and cultural history were not enough.[58] The conditions of evaluation themselves needed study, he said. This would lead to psychological studies, some of which would use Gestalt concepts. Another of his papers concerned the question of truth.[59] Science and logic have applied the proposition that truth is correspondent to the object, but difficulty has arisen because it is possible to define an object by one of its parts, making this statement true to the part but false to the whole. For example, a man who hires another to steal something for him, when asked if he stole, replies, ''No.'' Although he is telling the truth to the question (which is only a part), he is lying in relation to the whole situation. This error is an instance of a piecemeal view of reality. From this point of departure Wertheimer goes into logistics, the study of relational networks, in which the Gestalt part–whole problem is considered. This paper leads directly to his remaining major contribution to Gestalt psychology, a posthumously published book on thinking.

WERTHEIMER AND PRODUCTIVE THINKING

The investigation of thinking had been an implicit and explicit interest for Wertheimer for many years. His interest in the problem of thinking went back to at least 1912, for it was in that year—in which he also published his historic paper on perception—that he first published on this topic. Since Gestalt psychology is sometimes described as if it contributed only to perceptual problems, it is fitting to emphasize that Wertheimer's interest in thinking was contemporaneous with his interest in perception. His study of thinking culminated in the book *Productive Thinking,* [60] which he prepared for publication after his arrival in the United States. As Wertheimer interpreted it, the main factor in productive or creative thinking is grasping the structure of the situation—the Gestalt. Productive thinking serves to relate the problem at hand, whatever it may be, to the tasks and goals and to the total situation. Analyzed are not the parts but part–whole relationships.

It would be impossible to capture the characteristic flavor of Wertheimer's presentation without direct lengthy quotations quite beyond our present scope. A summary, no matter how adequate on the surface, is to some extent false to the original. Characteristically, Wertheimer gave not a polished presentation leading step by step to the solution, but the raw protocol of both productive and unproductive thinking using a great variety of materials in the process-geometrical figures, numerical manipulations, physical principles, and social situations. Productive thinking has its fumbling and false starts, just as unproductive thinking; but in productive thinking there is a return to the theme without undue delay, a sense of direction, and an ability to isolate essential features. In productive thinking, the given material is seen in a new light, and what was obscure before becomes obvious. Consider Wertheimer's example of the task of computing the sum of the numbers in an ascending arithmetical series, that is, $1 + 2 + 3 + 4 + 5 + 6 + 7 + 8 + 9 + 10$. If, instead of laboriously adding, as the problem seems to call for, the individual sees that, from the two ends of the series going toward the middle the terms increase and decrease at the same rate, a new approach is suggested. It will be noted that the middle pair is 5 and 6, on one side of which the numbers increase and on the other side decrease by one, giving pairs $4 + 7$, $3 + 8$, $2 + 9$, and $1 + 10$. Each pair equals 11. There are five pairs of 11 each; therefore, the answer is 55. There is a re-centering; a regrouping has taken place so that a new figure–group organization emerges. Instead of a single progressive series → it is seen as two series meeting in the center → ←. There has been a reorganization of the field. Once the principle of reorganization has been grasped, the recognition of the particular steps necessary for the solution to the problem can be found.

In productive thinking, habitual ways of using familiar concepts must often be overcome in order to solve problems in a novel fashion. Especially fascinating in this regard is Wertheimer's account of the thinking that culminated in the theory of relativity. His account was derived from the many hours he spent with Einstein himself in reviewing, decisive step by decisive step, the thinking Einstein had done in formulating his theory. In this recounting, each step seemed to emerge because it was required for the solution. This new theory had the difficulty of going against the strong Gestalt of the traditional Newtonian system of physics. To produce his general transformation formula, Einstein had to transform his thinking at each stage against the weight of this well-articulated structure.

Wertheimer also showed the relevance of the Gestalt principle to teaching. It became the basis for criticism of the emphasis on repetition and routine practice, which had derived its rationale from the associationist theory of learning. Inculcation of rules and principles by rote memory is rarely productive, Wertheimer held; more often than not, the student's response is a blind repetition of arbitrarily learned materials. This lack of productivity is demonstrated, Wertheimer believed, by the student's inability to solve a variation of the original problem. When teachers arrange their problems so that the whole is available to the student, insight is more likely to occur.

SUMMARY

Max Wertheimer saw an old problem in a new way and thereby founded a new approach to psychology based on a consistent adherence to a molar attitude. He was joined in this enterprise by two other psychologists, Wolfgang Köhler and Kurt Koffka, but it was he who first saw the problem. It was Wertheimer who grasped the significance of spontaneous groupings in sensory fields, as Köhler[61] said, and it was Wertheimer who was the "first founder," as Koffka[62] called him.

Wertheimer never wrote a complete, systematic statement of Gestalt psychology. He probably had no desire to do so, any more than he wished to engage in the endless polemics concerning the value of Gestalt psychology. It was not that he did not care; he did care, but these were tasks for someone of a different temperament. He had a restless, inquiring approach to many aspects of life and psychology, and he was prodigal with his carelessly tossed-off insights. His spontaneity and brilliance resulted in his productive contribution to psychology. Paradoxically, he was compulsively careful about gathering and analyzing data. He would publish his results only if the data were crystal clear and the experiment unequivocal. This prodigality and brilliance helped his students to learn more from him than others who depended on the written word for their knowledge of his work.

As a school and movement in psychology, Gestalt psychology was characterized by a pattern of prescriptive adherences. Molarism was salient and so, to a somewhat lesser degree, was centralism, an emphasis on what goes on within the organism. Both isomorphism and convergence are instances of centralism and illustrate how Gestalt psychology relates central to peripheral factors. They shared in common with psychologists other than behaviorists an emphasis on conscious mentalism and contentual subjectivism. They also shared nomothetic adherence.

NOTES

1. E. B. Newman, "Max Wertheimer: 1880–1943," *American Journal of Psychology, 57* (1944):428–435; W. Köhler, "Max Wertheimer: 1880–1943," *Psychological Review, 51* (1944):143–146. Wertheimer's son Michael, also a psychologist, says that the story is apocryphal. It was apparently told even during Wertheimer's lifetime, however. Anyway, it makes for a good story.

2. M. Wertheimer, "Experimentelle Studien über das Sehen von Bewegung," *Zeitschrift für Psychologie, 61* (1912):161–265.

3. *Ibid.*

4. E. Mach, *The Analysis of Sensations* (La Salle, Ill.: Open Court Publishing Co., 1914) (1886).

5. C. von Ehrenfels, "Ueber Gestaltqualitäten," *Vierteljahrsschrift für Wissenschaftliche Philosophe, 14* (1890):249–292.

6. E. G. Boring, *Sensation and Perception in the History of Experimental Psychology* (New York: Appleton–Century–Crofts, 1942), pp. 247–248.

7. L. M. Hurvich, "Hering and the Scientific Establishment," *American Psychologist, 24* (1969):497–514.

8. E. Husserl, *Philosophie der Arithmetik,* Vol. 1, *Logische Studien und psychologische Untersuchungen* (Halle: Pfeffer, 1891).

9. E. Husserl, *Ideas: General Introduction to Pure Phenomenology,* trans. W.R.B. Gibson (New York: Macmillan Co., 1952) (1913); E. Husserl, *Phenomenology and the Crisis of Philosophy: Philosophy as Rigorous Science* (1911), and *Philosophy and the Crisis of European Man* (1936–1954), trans. Q. Lauer (New York: Harper, 1965).

10. E. Rubin, *Synsoplevede Figurer* (Copenhagen: Gyldendal, 1915); *Experimenta Psychologica: Collected Scientific Papers in German, English & French* (Copenhagen: Ejnar Munksgaard, 1949).

11. The major sources for biographical details are Newman, "Max Wertheimer," and Köhler, "Max Wertheimer."

12. M. Wertheimer, "Experimentelle Untersuchungen zur Tatbestands-diagnostik," *Archiv für die Gesamte Psychologie, 6* (1905):59–131.

13. C. Murchison, ed., *The Psychological Register* (Worcester, Mass.: Clark University Press, 1929), Vol. 2.

14. K. Koffka, *Principles of Gestalt Psychology* (New York: Harcourt, Brace, 1935).

15. M. Wertheimer, "Experimentelle Studien über das Sehen von Bewegung."

16. E. G. Boring, *Sensation and Perception.*

17. *Ibid.*

18. G. W. Hartmann, *Gestalt Psychology: A Survey of Facts and Principles* (New York: Ronald Press, 1935), p. 5.

19. B. Petermann, *The Gestalt Theory and the Problem of Configuration* (New York: Harcourt, Brace, 1932).

20. M. Wertheimer, "Untersuchungen zur Lehre von der Gestalt," *Psychologische Forschung, 1* (1922):47–58. Abridged trans. in W. D. Ellis, ed., *A Sourcebook of Gestalt Psychology* (New York: Harcourt, Brace, 1938), pp. 12–16.

21. M. Wertheimer, "Ueber Gestalttheorie," *Philosophische Zeitschrift für Forschung und Aussprache, 1* (1925):39–60 (trans. in *Social Research, 11* [1944]:79–99).

22. *Ibid.*

23. E. Brunswik, "The Conceptual Framework of Psychology," in O. Neurath et al., eds., *International Encyclopaedia of Unified Science* (Chicago: University of Chicago Press, 1955), pp. 655–760.

24. M. Wertheimer, "Untersuchungen zur Lehre von der Gestalt," p. 55.

25. M. Wertheimer, "Ueber Gestalttheorie," p. 43.

26. E. B. Newman, "Max Wertheimer."

27. M. Wertheimer, "Untersuchungen zur Lehre von der Gestalt," p. 49.

28. E. B. Newman, "Max Wertheimer."

29. M. Wertheimer, *Ueber Schlussprozesse im produktiven Denken* (Berlin: De Gruyter, 1920).

30. M. Wertheimer, "Untersuchungen zur Lehre von der Gestalt," *Psychologische Forschung, 4* (1923):301–350. Abridged trans. in D. C. Beardsall and M(ichael) Wertheimer, eds., *Readings in Perception* (Princeton, N.J.: D. Van Nostrand Co., 1958), pp. 115–135 (Herrnstein and Boring, Excerpt No. 43).

31. K. Koffka, *Principles of Gestalt Psychology,* p. 110.

32. *Ibid.*

33. H. Helson, "The Fundamental Propositions of Gestalt Psychology," *Psychological Review, 40* (1933):13–32.

34. Mary Henle, "Wolfgang Köhler (1887–1967)," *Yearbook American Philosophical Society* (1968):139–145.

35. W. Köhler, "Optische Untersuchungen am Chimpanse und am Haushuhn," *Abhandlungen Preussische Akademie der Wissenschafen* (Physische-Mathematische Klasse) (1915), nr. 3.

36. W. Köhler, *The Mentality of Apes* (New York: Harcourt, Brace, 1927).

37. W. Köhler, "Intelligence of Apes," in C. Murchison, ed., *Psychologies of 1925* (Worcester, Mass.: Clark University Press, 1927), pp. 145–161.

38. W. Köhler, "Intelligenzprüfung an Anthropoiden," *Abhandlungen Preussiche Akademie der Wissenschaften* (Physische-Mathematische Klasse) (1917), nr. 1 (Herrnstein and Boring, Excerpt No. 102).

39. W. Köhler, *Die physischen Gestalten in Ruhe und im stationaren Zustand* (Erlangen: Weltkreisverlag, 1920).

40. M. Wertheimer, "Experimentelle Studien Ueber das Sehen von Bewegung" (Herrnstein and Boring, Excerpt No. 55).

41. W. Köhler, *Die physischen Gestalten.*

42. *Ibid.,* pp. 189–193. (Herrnstein and Boring, Excerpt No. 56).

43. M. Wertheimer, "Experimentelle Studien ueber das Sehen von Bewegung."

44. E. Hering, *Zur Lehre vom Lichtsinne* (Vienna: Gerolds Sohn, 1878), pp. 74–80 (1872–1874).

45. G. E. Müller, "Zur Psychophysik der Gesichtsempfindungen," *Zeitschrift für Psychologie, 10* (1896):1–82 (Herrnstein and Boring, Excerpt No. 54).

46. K. Köhler, *Die physischen Gestalten.*

47. M. Harrower, "Kurt Koffka: 1886–1941," *American Journal of Psychology, 55* (1942):278–281.

48. K. Koffka, *The Growth of the Mind: An Introduction to Child Psychology,* 2nd ed. (London: Routledge and Kegan Paul, 1929) (1921).

49. Mary Henle, "Gestalt Psychology in America," in Henle, *1879 and All That* (New York: Columbia University Press, 1986) p. 123.

50. K. Koffka, *The Growth of the Mind.*

51. W. Köhler, "The Mind–Body Problem" in S. Hook, ed., *Dimensions of Mind* (New York: New York University Press, 1960), pp. 3–23.

52. K. Koffka, "Perception: An Introduction to the Gestalt–Theorie," *Psychological Bulletin, 19* (1922):531–585.

53. W. Köhler, *Gestalt Psychology* (New York: Liveright, 1929).

54. Mary Henle, "One Man Against the Nazis—Wolfgang Köhler," in Henle, *1879 and All That,* pp. 225–237.

55. H. Helson, "The Psychology of Gestalt," *American Journal of Psychology, 36* (1925):342–370.

56. K. Köhler, "Max Wertheimer."

57. M. Wertheimer, "A Story of Three Days," in R. N. Anshen, ed., *Freedom: Its Meaning* (New York: Harcourt, Brace, 1940), pp. 555–569; Mary Henle, "A Tribute to Max Wertheimer: Three Stories of Three Days," in Henle, *1879 and All That,* pp. 241–253.

58. M. Wertheimer, "Some Problems in the Theory of Ethics," *Social Research, 1* (1935):353–367.

59. M. Wertheimer, "On Truth," *Social Research, 1* (1934):135–146.

60. M. Wertheimer, *Productive Thinking,* ed. Michael Wertheimer, enlarged ed. (New York: Harper and Row, 1959).

61. W. Köhler, *Gestalt Psychology,* 2nd ed. (New York: Mentor Books, 1947), p. 85 (1929).

62. K. Koffka, *Principles,* p. 18.

Sigmund Freud, 1909.

Chapter 24

Freud and
Psychoanalysis

While modern psychology was developing in academe, other important contributions were taking place in a quite different setting. Far removed from the psychological laboratory, Sigmund Freud was developing another approach to psychology through the study of personality disturbances revealed through clinical observation. He was learning that behind the conscious and rational person there was another phase of human nature, expressed through the dark, emotion-ridden unconscious motivations of his patients. He used the techniques of the clinical method rather than the controls of the experimental method. After a long period of isolation, he gained a few supporters. Two of these supporters went on to develop their own views, which are both important and significantly different from those of Freud. Consequently, after discussing psychoanalysis as expressed through the life, work, and theoretical system of Sigmund Freud in this chapter, attention will be devoted to Alfred Adler (1870–1937) and his individual psychology and to Carl Gustav Jung (1875–1961) and his analytical psychology in the next.

THE HERITAGE OF FREUD

To understand some of the individuals and intellectual influences that affected Freud, it is necessary to start not in Austria but in France. From the beginning of the nineteenth century, the French psychological tradition had centered on psychopathological problems. Pierre Janet, one of France's leading psychologists toward the end of the century, was to affirm that the development of "pathological" psychology was most characteristic of France.[1] The French were both utilitarian and idiographic in outlook in contrast to the Germans, who leaned toward purism and nomotheticism. Even psychologists who had their degrees in philosophy or in one of the sciences were apt to be influenced by these traditions. There were two discriminable groups of psychologists in France at the time—the physician–psychologist, interested in abnormal mental phenomena and their treatment, and the academic-medical psychologist who paid some attention to the more conventional aspect of psychology, including its teaching, but who was also drawn into consideration of the same phenomena that interested his medical counterparts. Jean-Martin Charcot (1825–1893) and Hippolyte Bernheim (1840–1919) represent the first group, and Théodule Ribot (1839–1916) and Pierre Janet (1859–1947), the second. Alfred Binet, as befits the greatest French psychologist of his time, shared in this tradition but also created one of his own. He has already been treated in Chapter 21.

PINEL AND THE TREATMENT OF THE INSANE

Near the beginning of the nineteenth century, France became the first country to begin developing adequate care for the insane and the feeble-minded. This achievement may have stemmed in part from the development of French mechanistic philosophy that came to view human behavior as a product of brain action. It is only a short step to treating human misbehavior also as a product of brain action and thus beyond the will of the affected individual. The treatment of mental illness was thus a treatment of nervous diseases, which explains why most of the individuals who dealt with such issues in the nineteenth century were neurologists. If the mechanistic position was correct, then it was improper to keep the insane in the inhuman conditions then current. Their treatment as subhumans was based in part on the premise that they were willingly possessed by the devil or that they were throwbacks to an earlier, animalistic state.

Philippe Pinel (1745–1826) was one who made such a moral argument for the humane treatment of the insane. Pinel was one of France's leading physicians at the turn of the nineteenth century.[2] In 1792 he was appointed superintendent of the asylum at Bicêtre. In the wake of the French Revolution he made his own particular application of the "Rights of Man" to the miserable patients in his charge, who heretofore had been kept in chains and treated as wild beasts, even to the point of being placed on exhibit to those who paid a small fee. After a personal plea before the Revolutionary Convention, Pinel was permitted to dispense with the chains. He treated his patients humanely and placed them under the care of reasonably competent physicians. His book on mental diseases was a powerful plea for more humane treatment of the insane.[3] Instead of accepting the view then current that the insane were wicked and in the grip of demoniacal possession, Pinel was convinced that brain dysfunction was related to severe psychological disorders. Pinel was succeeded in his work by Jean Etienne Esquirol (1771–1840), who worked assiduously at establishing properly run asylums. He also wrote a monumental work on mental diseases, one that was more rational and descriptive than the barren speculations of most of his predecessors.[4]

Jean Itard (1775–1838), a contemporary of Pinel and Esquirol, was a pioneer in the systematic study of mental deficiency.[5] A teacher of the deaf, he was consulted about the "wild boy of Aveyron" in 1798. The year before, in a woods in the Department of Aveyron, hunters had found a so-called wild boy. He was brought to Itard to see if he could be trained to live in civilization, a topic of more than usual interest in that period as a consequence of the then prevalent theories of the "noble savage." Itard worked long and arduously but could not in any way restore the child to normality. Through much effort, the boy learned a few habits more in keeping with his new environment, but he was still unable to take care of himself. Finally, it dawned on Itard that the boy was an idiot or an imbecile. He abandoned further work with the child as hopeless, since he shared in the common belief that idiots or imbeciles were but brutes incapable of any sort of training. His assistant, Edouard Seguin (1812–1880), continued to work with the boy after Itard had given up because he appreciated that the gains made, slight though they were, caused the child to be both happier and better adjusted to society. Afterward, Sequin devoted his career to attempts to train feeble-minded children and eventually was put in charge of a school for the feeble-minded. This was the first institution of its kind; its establishment marks the beginning of training schools for the mentally retarded.

HYPNOSIS

Another source of medical psychology in France was an interest in hypnotic phenomena. The history of phenomena of what came to be called hypnotism is at least as old as temple medicine in ancient Greece. Its modern phase begins with the work of Franz Anton Mesmer (1734–1815).[6] After attracting considerable notoriety in Vienna through use of his so-called animal magnetism in treating all sorts of patients, Mesmer was ordered to leave the city. He settled in Paris during the 1780s, where his remarkable cures, especially of what we would now call hysterical patients, made him well known. He thought of animal magnetism as an invisible fluid whose magnetic power he communicated to his patients by making his hands pass over their bodies, after which he assured them that they were cured. When physicians called Mesmer an impostor, the French government appointed the first of several commissions to investigate his powers. One of its members was Benjamin Franklin. The general conclusions of this and later commissions was that Mesmer effected many cures but was mistaken in attributing to animal magnetism what was actually due to some as yet unknown physiological cause. Whatever else may have been taking place, magnetism as known in physics had nothing to do with these phenomena. The reports, generally unfavorable, were widely disseminated. As a result of this unfavorable publicity, Mesmer lost his practice and retired.

For some time after the French Revolution, Mesmerism, as it was by then called, led a checkered career, kept alive by a few who used it with little or no understanding of what they were doing. Meanwhile, most physicians derided it as quackery.

In 1843 James Braid (c. 1795–1860) in England named the various phenomena "hypnotism."[7] He believed that hypnotism caused a change to take place in the nervous system as the result of psychological instigation. Braid described hypnotism as induced sleep and considered hypnosis nothing more than a convenient and quick means of throwing the nervous system into a state useful for treating certain disorders.[8] He showed that hypnotism could be produced by focusing the eyes on an inanimate object, a procedure that helped to remove it from the realm of the uncanny. His lack of exaggeration, his caution, and his modest admission of lack of understanding impressed other medical men. The fact that he first expressed his interest in the topic by publicly attacking the mesmerists probably gave him a respectability that the earlier workers had lacked. His work became known in France in the middle of the nineteenth century through a Dr. Azam, a surgeon of Bordeaux. Azam saw its advantage in surgical operations and proceeded to use it in this way. He was followed by others. Hypnosis did not attain national prominence, however, until the work of Charcot.

Jean-Martin Charcot

Jean-Martin Charcot (1825–1893), a physician, was appointed Professor of Pathological Anatomy at the University of Paris in 1860.[9] Two years later, he was appointed a senior physician to the Salpétrière, a hospital for mental disorders, where he established a neurological clinic. He is often called the father of neurology because of his ability to relate clinical signs present in the functioning of his patients to the normal and morbid anatomy of the nervous system, a correlation that is precisely the basis of neurology today. He carried on important studies of such diseases as multiple sclerosis and spinal paralysis and worked with problems of the localization of lesions in the brain and spinal cord. He was also famous as a teacher, for he was skilled in communicating his knowledge of diagnosis and anatomy to his pupils through case conferences. His fame was international, and students came to him from all over Europe. In 1885–1886, Sigmund Freud worked under Charcot, learning enough from him to refer to him later as "my master."[10]

Charcot was already a well-established teacher and researcher when he acquired his interest in hypnosis. In 1875 Charles Richet (1850–1935) had judged the phenomenon of hypnosis to be undoubtedly genuine. Accepting this statement of a respected colleague, Charcot launched into a period of intense clinical investigation and made his case conferences famous by demonstrating the many phenomena that can be induced by hypnosis. He began to center his attention on patients showing symptoms of hysteria.

What are some of the symptoms of hysteria? Somnambulism (sleep walking), fugues (running away without awareness of doing so), multiple personalities, and convulsive attacks are all included whenever organic causes can be ruled out, as are contractures, paralyses, vomiting, deafness, blindness, loss of speech, and anaesthesia of parts of the body.[11] To add to the complexity, the symptoms even change from day to day, with one day a patient complaining of vomiting and the next day of headache. Mesmer and the mesmerists must have treated a large number of individuals who later would have been in this category. Hysteria is the great simulator of other diseases, such as tumors, intestinal obstructions, lesions of the bones and muscles, as well as organically based blindness and deafness.

Charcot soon compared the phenomenon of hypnosis to artificial hysteria. The patients of Salpétrière, whom he found to be amenable to hypnosis and especially to very deep phases of hypnosis, were already diagnosed as hysterics. He soon discovered that the symptoms of the hysteric patient could be modified by hypnosis, and hypnosis came to be the preferred method of treatment for this category of patients. Thus, he moved against established medical opinion, which still regarded hypnosis as somewhere between a theatrical stunt and sheer charlatanism.

At Salpétrière under Charcot's leadership it was believed that the hypnotic phenomenon arose from hysteria in that only a person with an hysterical makeup could be brought to hypnotic sleep. Based on studying various degrees of the depth of hypnosis, Charcot asserted the existence of three main progressive stages in the depth of hypnosis: lethargy (drowsiness), catalepsy (isolated suggestions can be accepted and acted on, since there is no interference by other ideas), and somnambulism (ability to carry out complicated activities with no recollection afterward).[12]

Charcot's interest in producing deep hypnosis arose from his desire to be absolutely certain of being able to distinguish between true hysteria and the simulation of these conditions. Hysteria and malingering are not easy to differentiate, and Charcot was satisfied only with placing his patients under deep hypnosis in order to be sure faking was eliminated.

Meanwhile, in Nancy Liebéault and Bernheim were developing another approach to hypnosis.

Liebéault and Bernheim

A country doctor, Ambroise-Auguste Liebéault (1823–1904),[13] had been using hypnosis in his practice without fee with all peasants who would agree to its use, whereas they had to pay for other forms of treatment. Knowing a bargain when they saw one, the peasants flocked to him. It was not until he happened to treat a former patient of the neurologist Hyppolyte Bernheim (1840–1919) that his work received the attention that would ultimately place it in the history of psychology and medicine. This patient, who suffered from sciatica, had not responded to Bernheim's treatment, but he did to Liebéault's hypnosis. The already well-known Bernheim was impressed. He became a pupil of Liebéault in 1882, and a few years later he wrote a text that made him the leader of the Nancy School.[14]

Together, Liebéault and Bernheim had founded the clinic at Nancy, which was presently to rival Paris as another center for work in hypnotism. These workers, seeing no essential difference between spontaneous and induced sleep,[15] used the suggestion of sleep as the basis for the production of hypnosis. Essentially, the Nancy School's method of treatment was based on suggestion which meant that the patient under hypnosis would uncritically accept new attitudes and beliefs and would then behave in accordance with these new ideas. During hypnosis, the two doctors would tell their patients that they would feel well or that their symptoms would disappear. In a fair number of instances, the effect appeared to be permanent.

The Nancy and Paris clinics became ideological rivals. At Nancy it was taught that hypnosis, at least the mild form of it that was customarily used there, could be induced in nearly all subjects and that it was essentially a passive-receptive state brought about by suggestion. On the other hand, Charcot regarded hypnosis as a pathological state of the organism. At Nancy they challenged the identification of hypnosis with hysteria, arguing that the very stages that Charcot found were the result of specific suggestions. Later findings have tended to support Bernheim and Liebéault rather than Charcot.

Workers at Nancy and at Salpétrière, far apart as they might have thought themselves at the time, were both laboring with similar groups of patients—the neurotics. No longer was interest in abnormal mental phenomena to be confined to the severely disturbed on the wards of mental hospitals. These men had isolated the neuroses from other mental diseases and in doing so had discovered them.

Théodule Ribot

Théodule Ribot (1839–1916) had perhaps the greatest breadth of interests and certainly was the most well read of the French psychologists of his time. He served as the psychological educator of his countrymen. In 1870[16] and 1879[17] he published books that interpreted English associationism and German experimentalism to his colleagues. In general, French psychologists tended to be skeptical about the value of German experimental psychology and to make only sparing use of associationism. As a medical psychologist in the French tradition, Ribot also systematically explored what was known about the pathological aspects of affective life. He wrote books about diseases of the will, memory, and personality, regarding these abnormalities as products of faulty brain functioning. In discussions of diseases of personality and in his presentation of cases, Ribot stressed dissociation, the splitting of the bonds of consciousness. He also reintroduced evolutionary thinking into French psychology. In 1875 he founded and edited the Revue Philosophique, which was to publish a fair amount of psychological material.

Ribot was appointed Professor of Experimental Psychology in 1889 at the College of France. He was not, however, an experimental psychologist in the sense of having a laboratory. In his strategic position he was to have as students many of the next generation of academically oriented French psychologists.

PIERRE JANET

Pierre Janet (1859–1947) studied philosophy and psychology in the Faculty of Letters and then went on to the Faculty of Medicine at the University of Paris.[18] Before completing his medical training, he accepted a teaching post in philosophy at a Lycee outside of Paris. At this time he was only twenty-two years old. Eager to advance his career, he became interested in a patient named Leonie, already known to the medical profession for exhibiting both hypnotic and clairvoyant phenomena. After making a careful study of this intriguing combination, he reported that it seemed she could be hypnotized from a distance. Through this case study Janet came into contact with Charcot.

Shortly afterward Janet returned to Paris to study again in both the Faculties of Letters and Medicine, and in 1889 he received his doctorate in letters with a thesis on the psychology of automatic activities.[19] The following year Charcot invited him to become director of the psychological laboratory of Salpétrière, where he tried to bring some order and system into the classification of hysteria and, in turn, to the conceptions of academic psychology. This study became the thesis for his doctorate in medicine, a degree he received in 1892.[20] After teaching at the Sorbonne from 1895 to 1902, Janet succeeded Ribot in the chair in the College of France, which he held until his retirement. He visited the United States in 1906 to lecture at Harvard University Medical School. The lectures were published in English as *The Major Symptoms of Hysteria*, the book for which he is best known in the United States.[21] During all these years, in addition to carrying out his academic duties, he was also a busy practicing physician, specializing in mental diseases. He died in 1947.

Janet himself clearly differentiated his work from that carried on at Salpétrière. The work under Charcot was primarily neurological, so that paralyses, contractures, and disturbances of the senses were emphasized. In contrast, Janet saw hysteria as a mental disease, which chiefly consisted of an exaggerated suggestibility. He therefore emphasized mental phenomena—particularly impairments of memory and the presence of fixed ideas. This appeal to fixed ideas was based on the fact that hysterical patients had somehow fastened on the idea that they were paralyzed or had lost sensitivity. These symptoms were not readily resolved and, hence, were referred to as fixed ideas. Thus, Janet was closer to Bernheim in his interpretation than to Charcot, for both Janet and Bernheim saw many of the phenomena of hypnosis and of hysteria as products of suggestion. This resemblance becomes evident when one stops to consider that the behavioral phenomena are similar. The only difference seems to be that under hypnosis we know how the behavioral phenomena were instilled; that is, we know their origin, whereas in hysteria we do not.

Psychic energy and its diminution or depletion was a guiding concept of Janet.[22] Feelings of pressure experienced by the patient and consequent feelings of effort served to individuate this diminution of functioning quite apart from behaviors considered as symptomatic of psychic energy. Janet held that we do not know the nature of the energy, but we can study its manifestations. Individuals differ in quantity of energy available to them from both hereditary and environmental origins.[23] Janet cited fatigue, malnutrition, disease, pernicious experience, and inadequate education as the environmental sources responsible for lessened energy. Neuroses are fundamentally due to conditions of low mental tension—an inability to mobilize enough energy to meet the exigencies of life. There was a weakness in these hysterical patients. Illustrative of how weakness came to be postulated is the frequent triviality of the precipitating situation. At age twenty a man found himself near a heavy object as it fell from a window, breaking glass with a sound as of a gun shot. The man became dumb for two months, and twenty-six years later the slightest unexpected noise would still strike him dumb for several months at a time.[24] An even more famous case was observed in Boston, where a young woman, upon being kissed unexpectedly, developed symptoms that kept Morton Prince, an American psychologist, busy for years.[25]

To Janet, personality was a matter of integration. Within the normal individual, this integration of tendencies and ideas is relatively stable. In the hysterical individual this unity is lacking, and in extreme cases a lack of integration may extend to the point of splitting the personality into alternating personalities, most often two but sometimes more. In these extreme cases a failure of conscious control has taken place. There is, said Janet, a narrowing of the field of consciousness open to the individual. In the contraction of consciousness, the hysterical symptoms are manifested without the individual being consciously aware of them. A rhythmic movement of the arm evokes in the patient no sense that he or she is doing it; the patient looks at it as something alien. The arm is carrying out the movement without the patient's volition. The paralyzed leg is an alien "stump," as some of Janet's patients called it, attached to the body but not part of the person. If double personalities develop, the primary personality may not be aware of the thoughts, feelings, and experiences of the secondary personality. When a fugue occurs, a person may travel, eat in restaurants, answer questions, and generally behave in a fashion that attracts no attention, yet, on "awakening," he will not know where he is, how he got there, or what he did in the interval of the weeks or months during which he lived in the fugue state.

Janet believed that the dissociative split of consciousness originated in a mental or physical shock. He often found that the patient's history showed either a long-maintained or a continued series of conflicts. Essentially, hysteria is a contraction of consciousness owing to the exhaustion of the higher functions.[26] Overall, the dynamic factor is conversion symbolism, the "driving back" of that which is unacceptable in consciousness. The patient tries to get rid of thoughts that are painful or in opposition to moral feelings; he struggles to drive them out of consciousness. When he succeeds in making these experiences unconscious, his symptoms develop with the contraction of consciousness. As a result of clinical investigation, Janet came close to a conception of unconsciousness as a dynamic process. He had spoken of automatic activities as early as 1889 in his doctoral thesis and had discussed the unconscious, but impartial critics see in this usage hardly more than a figure of speech.

As for treatment itself, Janet found that under hypnosis these forgotten experiences can often be recalled to the patient. Moreover, the symptoms, the origin of which is unknown, can be traced back to their source and, after hypnotic suggestions, will even disappear (although other symptoms might turn up to take their place).

As might be anticipated, these views created a strained relationship between Janet and Sigmund Freud, whose formulations were similar. Freud saw Janet as working in a similar area but at a superficial level. In turn, Janet claimed that psychoanalysis originated from his and Charcot's work.[27] As an eclectic in psychotherapy, Janet considered psychoanalysis one among many forms of treatment. Specifically, it served to bring about dissociation of traumatic memories.

The French psychopathologists saw their patients as sick individuals in need of care. They were interested in them as individuals as well as in what they could learn about them. An impersonal attitude, natural to study of the generalized human mind, was in the process of being supplemented by an interest in the welfare of the individual. Janet[28] made this point explicit in a paper describing his approach to investigating the individual's unique characteristics. The French psychologists of the nineteenth and early twentieth centuries advanced the understanding of the clinical method in psychology to a point where Freud and others could carry through the next stage. It seems clear that both utilitarian and idiographic prescriptions were being fostered. Moreover, hesitant steps were being made toward accepting the value of unconscious mentalism, irrationalism, developmentalism, and dynamicism, that is, factors making for change in the individual.

THE UNCONSCIOUS BEFORE FREUD

In an effort to glorify Freud, some enthusiastic disciples write as if his genius came into the world unaided by an intellectual-cultural heritage. They interpret psychology before Freud as concerned exclusively with conscious experience, while the world waited for Freud to discover the unconscious. Nothing could be further from the truth.[29]

The influence of unconscious psychological phenomena has been a theme throughout the ages, from Plato's sleeping beast through Augustine's limitless room of memory to Aquinas's inability to view the soul apart from awareness of its acts. We can leave aside Descartes, Spinoza, Leibniz, and the others who considered unconscious phenomena in some detail and move directly to the nineteenth century. Fechner with his iceberg analogy of the mind had the greatest influence on Freud. As Fechner stated, the mind is mostly below the surface of awareness and is moved more by powerful hidden currents than by the winds of awareness. Fechner also introduced a topographical distinction between the sleeping and waking states. Sleep differs from the waking state, not only in intensity of mental function, but also in the activities of different stages. Others immediately preceding Freud seriously considered unconscious psychological phenomena, though, perhaps, without any direct influence on him. Helmholtz, for example, utilized unconscious inference; Ebbinghaus wrote his dissertation on Hartmann's philosophy of the unconscious; and even Wundt had to have been aware of unconscious phenomena in order to deny them a place in psychology. Those who came before Freud attached varying degrees of significance to unconscious functioning. Some dismissed unconscious psychological phenomena as curiosities, to be mentioned but then ignored. Others attached a fair amount of meaning, or even importance, to manifestations of unconscious functioning. None of them, however, grasped the crucial importance of unconscious motivation or found a way to study it. Freud found a use for the unconscious. He thought that its exploration might help to explain otherwise inexplicable phenomena, and he saw that thoughts and feelings beyond awareness played a role in directing behavior. Moreover, he found a means of studying these unconscious processes.

OTHER INTELLECTUAL INFLUENCES ON FREUD

Among familiar aspects of the intellectual atmosphere that Freud absorbed in developing psychoanalysis were the Helmholtzian view of mechanistic determinism, the Darwinian ideas of development, the French psychopathological view of dissociation, and the Galtonian-Wundtian-Kraepelinian view of association. Factors outside the main psychological tradition were also influential, particularly the writing of Johann Wolfgang von Goethe (1749–1832), to which aspects of libido theory are traceable.[30] Freud acknowledged that Darwin's theories and Goethe's famous essay on nature influenced his choice of a medical profession.[31] Many strands of the past affected Freud's thinking. His genius lay in creating a dynamic interpretation of unconscious motivation.

THE DEVELOPMENT OF PSYCHOANALYSIS THROUGH THE LIFE OF FREUD

The sheer wealth of material available about the life of Sigmund Freud (1856–1939) makes it possible to relate rather closely his personal experiences to the development of his ideas.[32] This is especially pertinent to Freudian conceptions regarding sex, since it is easy to be skeptical of his views unless it can be shown that their sources were not his own biases and preconceptions, but experiences with his patients. Experience with some of his first patients suggested aspects of what emerged as the free association method and helped him construct some of his major theoretical concepts.

Early Life

Sigmund Freud was born in 1856 in Freiburg, a town in what is now Czechoslovakia but was then a part of the Austro-Hungarian Empire. His father was a wool merchant, and the family background was lower middle class. When Sigmund was four years of age, his family moved to Vienna, where he was to live and work for nearly eighty years.

Freud's high intellectual capacity was recognized early, and the family soon realized that he was destined to be its scholar. Homely but revealing evidence of this recognition is the fact that his study–bedroom was the only one equipped with an oil lamp; the rooms of the other members of the household had only candles. A year earlier than usual he entered the Gymnasium, from which he was graduated with distinction at the age of seventeen. Reading and studying seem to have filled the greater part of his life during these years. Then and later he read widely. He was interested in problems of social reform and, perhaps somewhat surprisingly, in military history. He had a considerable gift for languages and in maturity knew four or five quite thoroughly.

As for his choice of a career, the only professions open to a Viennese Jew in the 1870s were law and medicine. Freud turned to medicine, not because of any direct or compelling attraction to it, but because he felt it might give him an opportunity to work on those problems of science that interested him. As was not too uncommon in his time, he took eight years, several more than necessary, to complete the medical curriculum. His penchant for sampling other fields not directly required for his training delayed his graduation until 1881.

This love of wide study led Freud to take several nonobligatory courses in philosophy with Franz Brentano. As a consequence, Freud was thoroughly familiar with Aristotle. The precise relation of this intellectual excursion to his later thinking is still an obscurity in Freud's intellectual development. Among his other teachers was the German physiologist Ernst Brücke (1819–1892), mentioned before in connection with the pact sworn against vitalism. It was from Brücke that Freud learned to see the human being as a dynamic system following the laws of nature.

During these years, Freud had somewhat vaguely considered following a medical teaching career. When he concluded that an academic career was not open to him, he turned to medical practice. Unfortunately, he had rather neglected the clinical phases of medical training. Realizing he would need more experience, he worked in a variety of clinics and hospitals. He devoted considerably more time to neurology and speech psychopathology than was customary. He carried on research in a variety of problems. Then and later he was a prodigiously hard worker. It is worth noting that his very first research endeavor involved sex—in this case an attempt to determine the precise structure of the testes of a species of eel. The results were inconclusive; in this endeavor, the future discoverer of the castration complex was unsuccessful.

Freud did a considerable amount of microscopic work in Brücke's physiological institute. It was here that he discovered the analgesic power of cocaine, and he just missed becoming the first physician to apply it in eye operations, which turned out to be by far its most useful application in medicine. Freud also became a very competent neurologist and actually coined the term *agnosia,* which is still used in neurological clinics. Indeed, he maintained a part-time practice in this specialty until almost the end of the nineteenth century.

Freud now had an even more compelling reason for going into practice: he had met and fallen in love with Martha Bernays. The courtship was a stormy one on his side; he exhibited violence, jealousy, and moodiness to a much greater degree than was characteristic of him either before or afterward.

With Freud's tremendously long work hours, he saw relatively little of either his wife or his children. His wife did not accompany him on his vacations. He had discovered she could not keep up with his rapid traveling pace, and it seems never to have occurred to him to slow his pace down. To Freud, the place of women was in the home. His social recreations were card games with old cronies and visits to his mother, who lived to an advanced age.

Freud and Breuer

One friendship that developed during these years was to be very important for both Freud and psychoanalysis. He became friends with Josef Breuer (1842–1925), a highly successful, sophisticated, and urbane practitioner whom Freud admired immensely. Breuer became for Freud what today we would call, using Freudian terminology, a father figure. Breuer also helped him in a material way, lending him money and offering him advice, both practical and medical. Naturally, this included discussion of the cases handled by Breuer. One case, that of "Anna O" which Freud first heard about in 1882, was of crucial significance.

In December 1880 Breuer began to treat Fraulein Anna O., a girl of twenty-one who had developed a whole host of symptoms. Hers seemed a classical case of hysteria—paralysis of the limbs, anesthesias, disturbances of sight and speech, nausea, and confusion. The illness had first appeared while she was caring for her severely ill father. She was compelled by her own illness to abandon nursing him. The events during her nursing made a deep impression on her, but when Breuer first saw her, she could not remember them. Anna got into the habit of relating to Breuer the disagreeable events of the day. This provided a release for her pent-up emotions or, as it came to be called, a catharsis. By talking about her problems she experienced relief and on occasion even the disappearance of a particular symptom. For example, during a period when she could not drink water, despite an intense thirst, she told Breuer that the same thing had occurred for a time when she was a girl. She now remembered that at that time she had seen the much-disliked dog of her governess drinking from a glass. She told Breuer this story in disgust and anger. Afterward, she found she could drink water again without trouble, and there was no recurrence of this particular difficulty.

She referred to her sessions with Breuer as the "talking cure" and as "chimney sweeping." Breuer discovered that she was relieved of her symptoms if she was placed under hypnosis and induced to express her dominant feelings and emotions at the moment. It also turned out that what was unconscious to her, except under hypnosis, was some thought or impulse that she found repugnant. Symptoms replaced these thoughts or impulses. When she lived through the traumatic scenes again, without the inhibition of the associated feelings, Breuer found that the symptoms in question were reduced in severity or even disappeared. Up to this time her emotions could not be expressed in a normal way, so the emotions associated with these events had expressed themselves in symptoms. Breuer was so interested in her case that he began to devote more and more of his evenings to working with her. He apparently saw Anna for hours at a time every day for more than a year.

He became so engrossed in working with her that his wife was at first bored and later jealous. Unknowingly, Breuer had developed what in later psychoanalytic perspective would be called a countertransference. When he finally realized what was happening, he stopped treating the girl. Anna herself had developed a positive transference: she had transferred to him, as she conceived him to be, the loves and hates she had felt for her father. The evening that Breuer told Anna of his decision to stop seeing her, he was called to her home to find her excited and in the throes of hysterical childbirth, which he terminated by hypnosis.[33] This incident was too much for Breuer, who fled to Venice with his wife for a second honeymoon. Freud was very interested in this particular case, finding it exciting and, unlike Breuer, not at all threatening.

Charcot and Hysteria

In 1885 Freud was granted a small stipend to go to France to work under Charcot. Charcot's influence on Freud as a result of this visit was expressed in theoretical and procedural influences. Heretofore he had held what might be called an organic point of view; after working under Charcot he became much more interested in the functional aspects of mental disorder.

A casual incident that occurred at about this time is of importance. In the course of an informal conversation one evening, Charcot insisted that the origin of the difficulties of a particular patient, the wife of an impotent man, had a sexual basis.[34] The gist of this incident was repeated for Freud on several occasions with other physicians, but always it was mentioned casually and in passing. Freud began to wonder why the medical literature had not followed up this lead in a more systematic and serious fashion. Remembering this incident, he was thereafter on the alert for any indication of sexual factors in the etiology of his patients. His knowledge of Anna O. must also have sensitized him to this particular connection.

Freud also learned Charcot's methods, particularly his use of hypnosis in the study of hysteria. Hysteria was a condition not at all well understood. At that time the very symptoms of hysteria made it faintly unrespectable. Many physicians still interpreted it as a confusing mixture of stimulation, an overwrought imagination, and a wandering womb. Greek medicine had considered hysteria a condition due to movement of the womb, and in fact, the word comes from the same root as hysterectomy. With this etiology, it was popularly and professionally supposed that hysteria was a condition limited to women. While working with Charcot, however, Freud observed instances of male hysteria. On his return to Vienna he insisted on lecturing on this topic. To put it mildly, his views, especially those on the reality of male hysteria, were not well received. He was publicly challenged to find a male with the symptoms Charcot claimed for hysteria. Without going into further details, it is easy to see why Freud thereafter disliked the members of organized medicine in Vienna and why they, in turn, regarded him as an unconventional medical practitioner.

Freud's Use of Hypnosis

In his practice, Freud had been using electrotherapy. This method is not the same as electric shock therapy as used today; it consisted of the application of a painful electric shock directly to the afflicted organ, such as the arm. (It was later demonstrated that in those cases where it was successful, the result was due to suggestion rather than the shock.)

Disappointed in the results of electrotherapy, Freud turned to hypnosis, a technique that was still held in disrepute. Its use in his practice hardly added to his professional standing, but his interest was prompted by the power of hypnosis–concentration to bring forgotten thoughts to the surface. As Breuer and Charcot had demonstrated, this was important for the understanding of hysteria.

Freud modified hypnosis in the direction of Breuer's cathartic method of release of emotions. Gradually, however, he eliminated the hypnotic trance until he arrived at the technique of merely having the patient lie on a couch, touching her forehead, and telling her to start talking. One day one of Freud's patients threw her arms around him. Unlike Breuer's panic over a display of affection, Freud saw this action as a matter of considerable scientific interest. Dimly at first, but with gradually increasing clarity, he began to realize that somehow effective work with the neurotic depended on a personal relationship between the physician and his patient.

The Method of Free Association

During these years Freud would customarily question his patients rapidly and in considerable detail and would interject other comments freely as they occurred to him. One of his patients, Fraulein Elizabeth, sharply reproved him for interrupting her flowing thoughts. He saw the validity of her reproof and, gradually, the method of free association emerged. Basic to this concept is a thoroughgoing belief in causality—that all matters, dreams, and thoughts, no matter how trivial, incongruous, and inconsequential, actually had some cause. One of his favorite authors, Ludwig Borne, had also discussed the value of allowing one's mind to wander. This author had written an essay with the striking title "The Art of Becoming an Original Writer in Three Days." As quoted by Ernest Jones, it concludes as follows:

> Here follows the practical prescription I promised. Take a few sheets of paper and for three days in succession write down, without any falsification or hypocrisy, everything that comes into your head. Write what you think of yourself, of your women, of the Turkish War, of Goethe, of the Fonk criminal case, of the Last Judgement, of those senior to you in authority—and when the three days are over you will be amazed at what novel and startling thoughts have welled up in you. This is the art of becoming an original writer in three days.[35]

The method of free association that Freud used thereafter consisted essentially of instructing his patients that the basic rule they were to follow was to say whatever came to mind, allowing no selection and no rearrangement whatsoever. This letting one's mind go, akin to daydreaming aloud, sounds relatively easy to do. His patients often found it unexpectedly difficult, since either there would be blanks, or, violating the rule, they would struggle to rearrange the flow of their thoughts. Freud soon realized that these unexpected difficulties were significant signs that material meaningful to the patient was close to the surface. He became alerted to the fact that when his patients experienced difficulties in associating, something of significance seemed to be occurring. From this finding arose his insistence that they must follow the basic rule, and the analysis progressed when they did so.

Other aspects of the psychoanalytic method developed during these years. Freud recognized his patients' remarkable unwillingness to disclose painful memories, a mechanism that he called resistance. Freud saw a connection between resistance and repression. Repression causes memory gaps or amnesias; the forces that produce repression also produce resistance.

The following example of free association illustrates a purposeful failure of memory, the Freudian significance of which is discussed a little later in this chapter.[36] It is atypical only in that it occurred during a conversation rather than in the course of the analysis of the patient. An acquaintance, in conversation with Freud, stumbled over a Latin quotation and omitted the word *aliquis*. Knowing of Freud's contentions on this matter, this acquaintance challenged him to find the reason why he had forgotten the word. Freud accepted the challenge. He gave the young man the usual instructions about free associations; the young man responded with what he himself considered to be the faintly ridiculous idea of dividing the word into two parts, *a liquis*. The gist of the succession of free associations thereafter was as follows: "reliques–liquidation–liquidity–fluid–an article entitled, What St. Augustine Said Concerning Women,'–St. Januarius and his Blood Miracle." (Freud—"Didn't St. Januarius and St. Augustine have something to do with the calendar?") "Yes, and as for St. Januarius a phial of his blood liquified on the date of a certain holiday, and if it doesn't take place the people get excited. A French general occupying the town once demanded the miracle take place forthwith." Young man hesitates. (Freud—"Why do you hesitate?") "Something too intimate to tell, comes to mind." What was too intimate to mention had to do with the menstrual cycle. As the acquaintance admitted, he was hoping for a miracle: an intimate female friend of his had missed her period.

Although Freud altered his method of approach during these years, he did not vary the aims of his procedures. His principal endeavor was to bring to the surface of the patient's consciousness the traumatic event that was the presumed pathological starting point. Even when this point was achieved and the trauma revealed, Freud continued further back in time. The memories that these patients were able to produce inexorably went further and further into childhood, as if the patients were somehow attracted to this period of life. The importance that Freud attached to childhood will be brought out later in a more systematic discussion of the psychoanalytic theory.

Importance of Sexual Factors

Freud found that a remarkable number of his patients' repressed memories centered on sexual matters. This finding, of course, came long before the importance of sexual factors in psychoanalysis became a matter of common knowledge, and it could not be attributed to his patients' knowledge that sexual disclosures were expected of them. After trying the method of direct inquiry into these sexual matters, Freud realized that this approach impeded treatment. He therefore resumed his passive position in treatment but maintained vigilance to detect the appearance of sexual material.

In the late 1880s and early 1890s, Freud tried to interest Breuer in publishing material on his patient Anna O. and others treated by Freud. From Freud's point of view, Breuer was inexplicably reluctant. Eventually, however, they prepared and published in 1895 the *Studies on Hysteria*, from which it has become customary to date the advent of psychoanalysis.[37] It included a joint paper, previously published, and five case histories, among them those of Anna O. and Elizabeth. Although *Studies on Hysteria* received a few reviews, mostly unfavorable, it created little stir. Only 626 copies were sold in the next thirteen years, for which each author received in royalty a sum equivalent to about $170. Between 1895 and 1897, bitterness developed between Freud and Breuer, creating a breach that was never healed. Thereafter they went their separate ways.

In 1896 Freud delivered a paper on the etiology of hysteria before a psychiatric and neurological society in Vienna. In it he referred specifically to his conviction that at the basis of every case of hysteria will be found a premature sexual experience early in childhood. He had become convinced that all his patients had experienced something resembling seduction when they were children; most often the adult seducer was an older relative, often the father. It was this trauma that produced the symptoms. One point that convinced him of the validity of his interpretation was his patients' extreme reluctance to give a detailed description of that scene and the feeling of unreality that pervaded it. It was as if, unlike other forgotten material, they really did not remember the experience. This convinced him they were not malingering, because they seemed to protest that, although the reported incident was the truth, they felt somehow it could not have happened. A short time after he gave this paper, he came to the conclusion that in most, but not all, instances these childhood seductions had never actually occurred.

A lesser man might have hidden his mistake and tried to forget it. A less clinically acute individual might have "bravely" confessed his error and turned to other more profitable matters. Freud did neither. Instead, he went beyond his mistake and asked why their fantasies took the particular form they did. His patients were not lying; they believed their fantasies. Was not the very fact that their fantasies took sexual form evidence that there was a sexual tinge to their thinking, and was he not right to emphasize the sexual basis of their difficulty, even though the situations they had described had never actually taken place? Despite the temporary setback, this mistake was later to be seen as an advance. Armed with this new insight, Freud was now ready to explore the whole range of sexuality. In recent years, some question has arisen over whether Freud was perhaps correct in his original judgment after all. The answer remains unclear.[38]

Self-Analysis

For some time Freud had been aware that he needed to explore his own personality. It was immediately obvious that the method of free association would be impossible for him. He could not assume the attitude of the patient, give uncritically his flow of free association, and at the same time take on the role of the analyst alertly listening to the material. In earlier years some of his patients had spontaneously brought him their dreams for analysis, and he had already done some work with dream interpretation. Consequently, dream interpretation suggested itself to him as a means of self-analysis.

This self-analysis was important to Freud; he needed it, since he was quite neurotic. In the course of his self-analysis, his neurosis, with its frustrations, insecurities, intensities, impracticalities, uncertainties, and vulnerability to threat, gave way to that more integrated, assured, persevering person whom his disciples were to know.

The Interpretation of Dreams

Freud's self-analysis and the writing of *The Interpretation of Dreams*, both of which were completed in the summer of 1899, went hand in hand.[39] This book is, by general consensus, Freud's most important single work. The procedure he followed was to record his dream on waking and then free associate to the material of the dream. He found that his dreams contained material touched off by events of the day that had not been completely worked through to some satisfactory solution. In dreaming, the problem would be taken up again. Dreams, he found, represent a disguised effort to bring about a solution. He referred to this wishful aspect of the dream as wish-fulfillment. A person dreams of drinking before waking up thirsty. A medical student, wishing to continue sleeping after being called, dreams he is already at the hospital. Dreams have meaning, and deep-seated desires can be investigated by dream analysis, although dream analysis, it must be emphasized, is but an extension of free association and not a substitute for it.

Freud drew a distinction between the manifest and the latent content of the dream. The manifest content is the dream taken at its face value, whereas the latent content is the meaning behind it. The task of interpretation is to go from manifest to latent content. This is a complex task, and only some of Freud's dream symbols can be illustrated. Freud saw dreams of falling as circumlocutions for giving way to erotic temptations; dreams of flying signified longing for sexual accomplishment. Certain images in dreams stand for or symbolize objects and desires from the patient's world in a relatively constant fashion. The more common symbols in dreams tend to repeat themselves from patient to patient—for example, money for feces; journey for death; a king for a father; a tree, a steeple, a sword, or a snake for the penis; a box, a book, or a purse for the vagina; or a pair of sisters for the breasts. Common symbols, Freud warned, are not to be interpreted without knowledge of the particular patient's unconscious conflicts; the symbols have usual but not invariable meanings.

In spite of the fact that the book devoted to so-called symptomatic acts was not published until 1904, the subject was of concern to Freud during these earlier years. The theme of this book, *The Psychopathology of Everyday Life,* was the interference with conscious functioning by the unconscious process.[40] An example is the one already presented of the young man who could not remember a crucial word when he worried about the possible pregnancy of his sweetheart. Freud supplied a wealth of illustration drawn from many areas to emphasize the unconscious significance of common errors: forgetting names; making mistakes in speech, reading, and writing (the famous Freudian slip); forgetting intentions; "chance" activities; "clumsy" actions; and the like. Such acts, he found, reveal unconscious desires.

The fact that "chance" acts, mannerisms, and slips of the tongue have unconscious motives opened another route to the understanding of the patient for Freud. Again he had evidence that no act is uncaused. Analysis of actions, along with dream analysis, became subsidiary to free association as a method of psychoanalysis. With these developments we come to the end of both a century and the formative and, in many ways, the most important period of Freud's life.

EMERGENCE FROM ISOLATION AND LATER LIFE

In the years 1901 through 1906, Freud began to emerge from the isolation that had surrounded him. As the period began, he was forty-five years of age, his practice was increasing, and in 1902 a weekly discussion group was founded for those interested in learning his conception of *psychoanalysis,* the term he applied to his approach. Not only were these men young, but they were also relatively obscure and just at the beginning of their careers. Alfred Adler, to be discussed in the next chapter, worked with him during these years. Carl Gustav Jung, who first came to see him in 1907, had already established himself as a promising and potentially important young psychiatrist in Zurich. Unlike most of the others who lived in Vienna, Jung visited Freud and then returned to his practice in Switzerland. For the next five years they were closely associated, and Freud began to feel that Jung was his spiritual son and the heir to psychoanalysis. It was during these years that Jung suggested to Freud that prospective psychoanalysts should themselves be analyzed, a procedure Freud adopted.[41] Otto Rank (1884–1939) also joined Freud in Vienna as a disciple at about the same time. A. A. Brill (1874–1948), his American translator, and Ernest Jones (1879–1958), his biographer, were both in touch with him in 1908.

During these years, Freud published prolifically, including the highly important volume, *Three Essays on the Theory of Sexuality.*[42] Just as the interpretation of dreams had made him ridiculous in the eyes of many of his contemporaries, this new volume made him appear prurient as well, for he argued that all children are born with sexual drives. Despite the notoriety that his views were now receiving,

other more perceptive individuals showed some appreciation of what he was attempting to do.

The first official recognition of Freud's work on an international scale came in
1909 when, on the invitation from G. Stanley Hall, Freud was invited to lecture
at a conference at Clark University in celebration of the university's twentieth
anniversary.[43] Though appreciative, Freud was not too attracted to Hall and spoke
of him as having "a touch of king-maker about him," which was a rather perceptive
remark.[44] Freud attended the meeting, however, as did many other psychologists,
Titchener, Cattell, and James, to name just a few. Jung accompanied Freud and also
gave lectures at the celebration. Troubled by a bladder infection and affected by
the roughness of some aspects of American life, Freud did not consider the trip an
unqualified success and thus maintained an uncomplimentary view of the United
States. Although the papers Freud gave were subsequently published in the *American Journal of Psychology* and were covered in numerous newspapers and magazines in the United States, it probably was somewhat of a blow to him that he did
not receive the public attention he had expected. Still, the visit was important for
him, for his recognition not only in America but in Europe as well. Since the
American Journal of Psychology was widely read in Europe, Freud's introduction
to many European psychologists was through his articles published there.[45]

Two years later, in 1911, came the break with Alfred Adler, one of his earliest
associates. Aside from differences of personality, the issue was whether or not
Adler's ideas could be incorporated into psychoanalysis. Adler held that the individual has a tendency to compensate for a feeling of inferiority. In this and other
respects, Adler was focusing on aspects of behavior that demanded consideration
of the social environment. At this time Freud could not see how it could be
explained in terms of his theoretical position. Differences of opinion between Adler
and Freud were aired through the discussion group that by now was called the
Vienna Psychoanalytic Society. Both Freud and Adler eventually came to realize
that their differences were irreconcilable, and Adler and some of the other members
resigned from the Society. Acrimony seems to have existed on both sides, which
Adler expressed by forming his own separate group. Freud himself was relieved by
this final break with Adler because, rightly or wrongly, he had come to consider
him unreliable and recalcitrant.

This was not the case with the break that came with Carl Jung. In Freud's view,
very relevant to the issue over which they ultimately separated was the general
religious and moral climate of Switzerland. Jung and other Swiss psychoanalysts
had for some time shown a tendency to minimize the theoretical importance of the
sexual basis of psychoanalytic theory. When they did so they found that their
relations with both their patients and the general public improved considerably.
In May 1911 Jung told Freud that he regarded "libido" to be a term expressing
general, not sexual, tension. After a trip to New York Jung wrote Freud on how
successful he had been in making psychoanalysis acceptable by leaving out matters
of sex!

On Freud's part, he saw this disagreement not merely as one about the theoretical importance of sex in psychoanalysis, important though it undoubtedly was. To

a great extent, his distress arose from a conviction that Jung's reason for minimizing sex was an intellectually dishonest one. Freud believed that Jung was catering to popular opinion by omitting the sexual factor. Then and later, there was some suggestion that Jung believed Freud's Jewish background had something to do with his overemphasis of sex. This hurt Freud deeply.

In 1914 Jung formally severed his connection with Freudian psychoanalysis by resigning his position as President of the International Association of Psychoanalysis. As Freud put it, they took leave of one another without feeling a need for further meetings.[46] The break was difficult on both sides, but it was inevitable and final. The Jungian side of the story will be taken up in the next chapter.

World War I interrupted Freud's work to some extent but brought no personal tragedy, unusual hardships, or limitations except in number of patients, food restrictions, and reduced income. His own interests were moving into the more theoretical channels of "metapsychology," as he called it. Metapsychology was a term coined by analogy with Aristotelian metaphysics—going beyond psychology. What he meant by it was accounting for a mental process in terms of its dynamic significant, topographical features, and economic significance. He aimed to arrive at a general theoretical structure that would guide psychoanalysts in collecting and meaningfully organizing clinical data. These contributions will form a major part of the systematic account of psychoanalysis given later. During his remaining years Freud was occupied with a great variety of writings. He continued to make clinical contributions, but much of his time was taken up by metapsychology and the contributions of psychoanalysis to biology, anthropology, sociology, religion, art, and literature. The standard English edition of his works, from *The Interpretation of Dreams*[47] of 1900 through the posthumously published *An Outline of Psychoanalysis*,[48] fills twenty-four volumes.

From 1919 until his death in 1939 Freud was at the pinnacle of his fame. In the years immediately following the war, of course, Europe was in chaos. Both the International Association of Psychoanalysis and the newly organized publishing house founded in Vienna in 1919 were in a precarious state.

One of Freud's most faithful and hard-working assistants in these administrative ventures was Otto Rank, who had been one of Freud's protegés. Under Freud's urging he had taken a nonmedical university degree preparatory to further theoretical work in psychoanalysis. He had a special flair for the interpretation of myths, legends, and dreams. Rank's book, *The Trauma of Birth* (1923),[49] dealt with birth trauma as a source of anxiety. At first, Rank saw this conception as falling within the framework of conventional psychoanalysis, but other psychoanalysts did not accept his reinterpretation of other Freudian contentions in terms of this theme— weaning as anxiety provoking because it was a separation from the mother, and the male sexual urge as a desire to return into the mother's body. Many heated arguments began. Because of his fondness for Rank, Freud tried to reconcile his views with Rank's as well as with those of Rank's opponents. The attempt was doomed to failure since Rank viewed it as rejection by Freud. Meanwhile Rank had developed an increasingly severe emotional disturbance. After several trips to the United States, he finally settled there. His break with Freud was final and complete.

In 1923 the first symptom of cancer of the jaw, from which Freud eventually died, had developed. A series of operations was necessary, and he had to wear a prosthesis that so greatly interfered with his voice that he could hardly be understood. In all, he had thirty-three operations. During these years his daughter Anna was his nurse. He had to reduce the number of patients he saw and take longer summer vacations. He had many financial worries during this period, created by the publishing house as well as the public's ambivalent attitude toward him. Abuse from the medical profession continued. On the other hand, he became a world figure, becoming acquainted with and, in some instances, close friends with prominent individuals, such as Thomas Mann and H. G. Wells. Meanwhile, the International Asssociation was going through a certain amount of controversy. One of the most important sources of contention was the question of the practice of psychoanalysis by individuals without medical training. The American Psychoanalytic Association, which had been formed under medical leadership, was vehemently opposed to so-called lay analysis. Associations in other countries were divided in opinion but were generally favorable to the practice of psychoanalysis by individuals who had the requisite training but no medical degree. Freud's book, *The Question of Lay Analysis* (1926),[50] unequivocally supported the position that a medical degree was not necessary in order to practice psychoanalysis, a position from which he never wavered.[51]

In the 1930s Adolf Hiter came into power in Germany. As early as May 1933, the Nazis made a bonfire of Freud's books in Berlin. By 1934 all Jewish psychoanalysts in Germany who could escape had done so. Freud's friends urged him to leave Vienna, but he insisted stubbornly that he would remain. In March 1938 the Nazis invaded Austria. The Nazis had actually taken over Vienna, and storm troopers had broken into his home before he was finally persuaded to leave. The Nazis held him in Vienna until his stock of unsold books could be brought back from Switzerland for public burning. The Nazis were persuaded to release Freud partly through the intervention of W. C. Bullitt, then U.S. Ambassador to France. Freud's arrival in London created a sensation that was given considerable space in the press. During this time his physical health was failing rapidly, but he was still very alert mentally. He continued to work almost up until the end. He finished his book *Moses and Monotheism* in 1938,[52] and died on September 23, 1939.

THEORY OF PERSONALITY

Freud's work yielded a method of investigation, an approach to psychotherapy, and a theory of personality that were major aspects of his metapsychology.[53] His clinical method of investigation has already been discussed. It should be added that for verification of findings, at first he depended mainly on the same relationships occurring repeatedly among his patients. Later, those trained in psychoanalysis added to this store of clinically verified findings. It might not unjustly be called validation by consensus of "informed" opinion. The difficulty that this description creates, however, is a strong tendency to disregard the findings of others not trained in psychoanalysis. Freud's approaches to psychotherapy, particularly his method of free association and dream analysis, have already been presented in some detail.

Any summary of Freud's metapsychology is apt to give the impression that it was static—a fixed system, frozen into the form in which it is encountered. This is misleading because, to Freud, it was a loosely integrated group of theories that evolved through the years with momentarily important points discarded by the wayside. With Freud, as with others, theoretical formulations outlived their usefulness. They are vehicles to be used in part of one's journey but are eventually to be given up when no longer cogent. This same evolution continued after Freud. What follows is an attempt to give a classic picture of psychoanalysis as Freud saw it. By the same token, it cannot be a complete view of contemporary psychoanalysis. An effort is made to present only the orthodox Freudian position, differentiated from the steadily increasing number of neo-Freudians who would assimilate Freud into a larger—typically a social—framework of non-Freudian origin.

The Dynamics of Structure of Personality

To Freud, personality was essentially a dynamic concept in which mental life was an interplay of reciprocally urging and checking forces.[54] Consequently, it is necessary to examine the nature of these forces and the structures through which their interplay takes place. That is, there needs to be concern with the dynamics and structures of personality. One form of specification of dynamics can be seen by examining Freud's theory of instincts.

Theory of Instincts

In accordance with the deterministic and positivistic philosophy of his era, Freud employed the theory of finite energy as the power behind this reciprocal interplay of forces. He maintained that the physiological energy of the human organism, by virtue of Helmholtz's principle of the conservation of energy, may be transformed into energy for psychological activity. Psychic energy and its psychological manifestation, instinct, together emerge as the basic unit in the dynamics of personality structure. It is a quantum of psychic energy, which functions on transformed physiological energy, linking a body's need to a psychological wish. A number of separate bodily needs exist, each of which gives rise to erotic wishes. These may be identified by referring to the erogenous zones of mouth, anus, and sex organs as centers for different wishes. Taken together, these insticts are the sum total of psychic energy. An instinct has four functional characteristics: (1) impetus, the motor element in the amount of force that it represents; (2) aim, the satisfaction obtained by abolishing the condition of stimulation; (3) object, that through which the aim can be achieved; and (4) source, the somatic process in a body part that eventuates a stimulus.[55]

Freud appealed to the concepts of instinct and energy to give his views on sex a scientific footing and to provide a means of describing their interrelationships meaningfully. This formulation occurred shortly after the turn of the century.

About two decades later, Freud faced another problem. The war years forced him to direct his attention to aggressive behavior and to the subsidiary problem of understanding it in relation to sex. The theory of the death instinct was the consequence. At this point he held that in representing bodily demands, the instincts follow two aims—the life instinct (Eros) and the death instinct (Thanatos).[56] Under these two headings, Freud assumed a multitude of instincts, although he never identified all of them specifically nor did he derive their total number. The life instinct operates for human survival and racial propagation, and includes such categories as hunger, sex, and thirst. The form of energy for the manifestations of the life instinct is called libido. The death instinct of Freudian theory, impelling one toward death, is analogous to the catabolic, the breaking-down, processes of the body and is therefore opposed to the anabolic, or building, processes of the life instinct. The death instinct, which has the aim of reducing living things to inorganic matter,[57] is systematically less important and, following Fenichel,[58] will be dispensed with in the account to follow. But aggression is utilized within the framework of libido theory. Aggression is an innate, independent, instinctual disposition.[59]

The Id, Ego, and Superego

Originally, Freud conceived of the personality structure in terms of the unconscious, the conscious, and the preconscious (that which is capable of consciousness without special effort). This original focus on conscious and unconscious phenomena was brought about by Freud's concern with hysteria and hypnosis. In hypnosis, for example, there is a clear distinction between what the subject is aware of in the waking state and what he or she can report in the hypnotic state. The distinction between consciousness and unconsciousness was sufficient at this point to account for the phenomena theoretically. Later, however, Freud preferred to use the unconscious descriptively as a quality of experience.[60] In the psychoanalytic hour, with the shifting panorama of free association, terms like *conscious* and *unconscious* are too bald to be used for behavior that is the result of interacting, supporting, or canceling forces. Identification is difficult when only these results are open to observation. Consequently, in the interest of a greater dynamic emphasis, Freud modified his conceptual scheme.

The structural components of the personality are the inherent system of the id and its derivatives, the ego and the superego.[61] The ego and the superego derive their energy from libido, the primary psychic energy reservoir of the id. Consequently, the libido is not only the basic force for personality dynamics, but also the source of organization of the personality structure. Each of these structures must now be examined in detail, and attention must be paid to their interrelationship in the fully developed personality. The course of development of the three structures is reserved for presentation in terms of psychosexual stages.

The id is unconscious[62] and is the oldest of the personality structures.[63] It contains everything that is inherited, present at birth, or fixed in the constitution.[64] It includes the source of the instinctual energy, the libido, which demands discharge.[65]

The libido is expressed in the id through the principle of tension reduction—the pleasure principle—by which the id operates. A physiological tension occurs in an area of bodily need and is then translated into a psychological wish, the aim of which is to reduce tension. The id obeys the pleasure principle[66] in the seeking of pleasure and the avoidance of pain without any other consideration to modify or direct it.[67] The goal of the id is the satisfaction of needs, regardless of considerations of danger or preservation of life.[68] In the words of the musical comedy song of some years ago, "It wants what it wants when it wants it." There is no consideration of decorum, morals, or modesty.[69]

The id does not have a direct relation with the external world.[70] Everything we know about the id relates to the ego.[71] Since it is unconscious, it can be known only through the ego, which is conscious. Consequently, while still considering the id, it is necessary to deal briefly with this ego function. The id is known through its intrusions into the consciousness of the ego. Dreams, for example, are an externalization of this internal process in which the id tendencies are partially released during the relaxation of the ego in sleep.[72] Examination of dreams is one way of gaining some dim and frightening knowledge of id sources.[73] According to Freud, the dreams of even the most straight-laced person contain amoral elements, illustrative of the functioning of the id.

The ego includes the conscious portion of the personality structure. The processes of the ego alone are conscious.[74] More strictly, the ego includes the preconscious as well, that is, that which is capable of becoming conscious voluntarily.[75] The ego is formed by the individual's experience.[76]

In contradistinction to the id, which is guided by the pleasure principle, the ego follows the reality principle.[77] In guiding activities, the ego takes into account the external world and its realities. The ego is the organization interpolated between sensory and perceptual processes and motor activity, of which the individual is aware as his or her "I."[78]

The instincts of the id press for satisfaction; the ego modifies and channels these drives.[79] Since all libido was originally id, the ego arises from a modification of the id.[80] Once it does so, the ego serves as an intermediary between the id and the external world. Here its constructive function is to interpose intellectual activity, which calculates ways and considers alternatives, before allowing the demands of instinct to be accomplished.[81] As an approximation, the ego represents reason, whereas the id represents the untamed passions. Of course, when the passions are represented in consciousness, it is also through the ego.[82] If one were to draw on the previous history of psychology for an illustration, Plato's fable of the charioteer would come to mind. The ego is in control of voluntary movement and is aware of external events.[83] It stores up experiences in memory; it adapts, it leans, it avoids. Thus, it has relation to both the id and the external world.

In summary, ego refers to both awareness of self and the carrying on of executive functions. In following the reality principle, the ego mediates between the imperative pressures from the id, the structures of the superego (described in a moment), and the demands of external reality.

Despite what was just said about ego and consciousness, a portion of the ego is unconsciousness.[84] This unconscious portion results from repression. Materials once conscious, but unacceptable to the ego, are pushed back into the unconscious.[85] Because of its origin, we call this portion of the ego the repressed. In eliminating unwelcome impulses from consciousness,[86] repression is a flight mechanism.[87] That which is repressed has an "upward driving force," that is, an impulsion or drive to break through into consciousness again.[88] The ego, under the influence of external reality, controls its entrance into consciousness, and an interplay of reciprocally checking and urging forces develops in which libido must be expended. Repression requires a continuous expenditure of effort.[89]

By definition, anxiety is something "felt."[90] As an affective state it is experienced by the ego and serves it as a danger signal. The id cannot be afraid; it cannot estimate danger, for it knows nothing of the external world. There are three kinds of anxiety.[91] Reality anxiety occurs in the face of the dangers from the external world which are too great to cope with; normal or moral anxiety (guilt) in the face of superego restrictions; and neurotic anxiety in the face of the demands of the id. Anxiety, no matter what its particular form, serves as a signal of danger.[92]

The ego, operating through the reality principle, is capable of investigating energy in either an inanimate object, some "favorite" possession, or another person. This energy attachment Freud called cathexis, the sum of psychic energy with which an object is invested.[93] This attachment of energy is analogous to an electric charge.[94] When libido of the ego is invested in an object (including persons), it becomes object–libido.[95] This process of investment transforms ego–libido into object–libido.[96] The reverse also takes place. Object–libido can return to ego–libido. Moreover, libido is mobile[97] and can pass from one object to another.

A form of cathexis is operating within the structure per se in the process of ego–id interaction.[98] In checking the id, the ego must automatically expend a great amount of energy. This checking force is anticathexis and is the princple that maintains repression.[99]

The so-called ego defense mechanisms need elucidation.[100] Each ego makes use of various characteristic ways of defending itself against anxiety. Since there are a large number of defense mechanisms, the fact that each individual has a characteristic pattern of them, with some stronger than others, allows for a considerable variety in personality structures. Repression, just described, is one of the major ego defense mechanisms. Not only repression but also fixation, projection, introjection, and others serve the same function. Just as repression, they demand the expenditure of libido to keep anxiety from appearing. They maintain "peace and quiet," but in a manner analogous to a garrison keeping an otherwise unruly population in check. At best they maintain a stalemate; at worst they express themselves in the eruptions of neurotic or psychotic symptoms.

An important ego function that does not require this continual expenditure of energy is sublimation. This is the most successful of the various mechanisms in that it allows the discharge of energy to bring about a cessation of impulses without the continued defensive function of the other mechanisms. Sublimations are the socially approved ways of discharging libido without anxiety; they express libido with aims other than sexual gratification. Illustrations may be drawn from the various stages of psychosexual development. A child's oral pleasures may be sublimated by pleasures in speaking, and he may go on to a career as a politician or professor. Interest in anal matters may be sublimated by work in the arts; phallic interests may be sublimated by nature study. Many forms of sublimation, however, would not show the obvious relations just sketched. In fact, sublimation takes on protean forms with law, order, social progress, interaction, and achievement as areas of manifestation.

The superego, the third of the personality structures, serves as the vehicle for the conscience.[101] It develops out of the ego, arising as an aftermath of the Oedipus Complex, a facet of development discussed later. It is organized in much the same manner as the ego and deals with the ego as a strict father would toward his child.[102] The tension this engenders is guilt,[103] which was defined earlier as moral anxiety. The superego serves the special function within the ego of demanding restriction and rejection,[104] and it therefore follows that repression is the work of the superego.[105] Although in conflict in many situations, the superego and ego may function harmoniously. In fact, only when there is a conflict can we distinguish between them.[106] When this happens, the superego serves as a pressure on the ego. It makes the child feel guilty, just as his parents had made him feel guilty. In a more general fashion, the superego expresses the child's moral imperatives, ideals, and the like. It serves to control those sexual and aggressive impulses that would otherwise endanger social stability.

Such are the dynamics and structures of personality as Freud and his followers viewed them.

Stages of Psychosexual Development

Freud conceptualizes psychoanalytic personality development as a progression through a series of psychosexual stages.[107] These stages are determined by changes in areas of libidinal localization expressed in changing modes of pleasure findings. They are characterized by differences in object–relations, the structural organization of personality, and the appearance of various behavior mechanisms, that is, the ego defense mechanisms. Freud's original notion about psychosexual stages was developed to explain the appearance of sexuality in infancy and childhood and the underlying structure of sexual perversions. One of Freud's senior collaborators, Karl Abraham (1877–1925),[108] contributed a great deal to the elaboration of the theory of psychosexual stages, especially to its extension to explain character structure in the adult on the basis of the child's experiences in the various stages. Because Freud subsequently accepted this work, in this sense it is orthodoxly Freudian.

In the progression from birth to adolescence, there are the oral, anal, phallic, and genital psychosexual stages (with the later two stages separated by the so-called latency period). Although the stages overlap and characteristics of an earlier stage are not entirely absent before the appearance of later stages, erotic pleasures tend to be localized successively in the particular erogenous zones corresponding to the stages.

The Oral Stage The oral stage extends from birth to some time in the second year. In the early oral phase, the mode of pleasure finding is most concretely expressed in sucking and in swallowing or, more figuratively, in incorporating, that is, symbolically making objects part of oneself. Sensations of the lips, mouth, tongue, and cheeks are exciting in and by themselves. Freud points to the prevalence of thumbsucking without the reward of food as an illustration of pleasure of and for itself.[109] Sucking is pleasurable and is thus a manifestation of libido. The infant's general mouth-centeredness is also illustrative. "He puts everything in his mouth," says the mother.

At birth the infant makes no distinction between world and ego. Libidinal energy is entirely narcissistic; it is directed toward himself but without awareness that there is a separation of self and world. For example, the mother's breast and body are not distinguished from his own body. The distinction between the infant's self and the environment comes with the diversion of libido from id to ego functions. According to Anna Freud, this distinction comes about because his needs are not met immediately. If he could always summon up the breast immediately, there would be no occasion to develop any awareness of "self" and "other" from this experience. But his needs are met only after a delay; the mother, by the very nature of things, fails to respond instantaneously. The inevitable delays in ministering to his wants force a recognition on his part that there is a world "out there" that is not part of "him," from which he is separate. Self and social awareness develop hand in hand, when the world and ego begin to be distinguished from each other.[110]

The mother is the first object of the infant's libido, that is, ego–libido becomes object–libido as invested in the mother. In nonpsychoanalytic terminology, the child is bonding, beginning to form a positive attachment; he is learning in an infantile way to "love" his mother. Some id has been transformed, whereas the remainder is unchanged.[111] Out of the id, present from birth, the ego begins with awareness of the world.

In attempting to control id impulses, the ego supplements the pleasure principle, previously the only regulating principle, with the reality principle, which requires the individual to take into consideration conditions imposed by the outer world.[112] The first signs of the reality principle operating in infants may be nondramatic and hardly noticeable, but they exist. For example, there are the barest beginnings of tolerating delays in having his needs met when the infant does not cry continually because of hunger pangs. After a signal cry, he may be quiet for a few seconds. As the mother describes it, "Johnny isn't as impatient as he used to be." This toleration is the beginning of conforming to the reality principle.

If the mother is gentle and adroit, the infant's little world is pleasant; if the mother is rough and clumsy, the world is bad, not in any clear-cut, thought-out way but in a nonverbal "feeling." This last observation goes a long way toward accounting for the fact that difficulties of adjustment can occur in homes that look ideal to an adult. The world of the infant is very small and does not take into account the income of the family, the amount of land surrounding the house, the number of servants, or any other indices so obvious to adult eyes. His world is his interaction with his mother.

Incorporation is important in this oral phase. From incorporation or nonincorporation comes the development of two important personality mechanisms, that is, characteristic ways in which the infant (and later the adult) operates. These mechanisms are introjection and projection.[113]

The late-oral or oral-sadistic phase begins at about the age when the eruption of teeth occurs. The modes of pleasure finding shift. Biting dominates, whereas devouring and destroying are more figurative expressions. The situation is intensified by the process of weaning, which usually occurs at this time. The child is in pain and is frustrated, and ambivalence makes its appearance. No longer is there unalloyed positive attachment to the mother. The object-relation with the mother, heretofore only loving, is complicated by the appearance of feelings of hatred, so that both positive and negative feelings are concurrently present. How these problems of weaning affect the infant depends in considerable measure on whether or not weaning is either too abrupt or too early. In either case, trouble of adjustment is to be expected. Anxiety will inevitably appear, but it will be intensified if this source of frustration is not introduced slowly and gradually. Each child fixates, that is, invests some libido in oral matters, but the amount is determined by the extent of oral gratification.[114] Undue frustration or too much gratification can produce too great a fixation, possibly resulting in less than optimal adjustment later.

The oral stage ends sometime in the second year of life, but oral activities continue to be sources of satisfaction, in varying degrees, from individual to individual.[115] Too great or too little gratification may result in an oral character, with oral preoccupations forming a disproportionate part of day-to-day interests—excessive eating, drinking, kissing, and smoking. There will be not only these excessive mouth habits, but also more symbolic manifestations of orality in attitudes of dependence or assurance. An infant overgratified in the oral stage may in adulthood be sanguinely optimistic that everything will turn out all right, whereas lack of gratification may contribute to the formation of a pessimistic individual, who is passively dependent on others for his feelings of esteem. Frustrations in the late oral stage can result in a host of ambivalent adult attitudes, friendly–hostile, aggressive–submissive, and so on, along with a tendency to exaggerate and swing from one extreme of these attitudes to the other. A tendency toward "biting" remarks is also characteristic.

The Anal Stage   The area of libidinal localization is shifted to the anal region sometime during the second year of life, giving rise to the anal stage. Before examining this phenomenon, look for a moment at the situation as the infant might. There is nothing about the odor, texture, or appearance of the feces that is inherently unpleasant. The infant has no innate repulsion. He has created it, and the mother seems to prize it, since she is pleased when he has a movement and concerned when he does not. According to Freudian thinking, the infant "perceives" defecation as the giving of a gift. What happens to his gift? The mother flushes it down the toilet! Often he acts out his puzzlement about this strange behavior by toilet play, throwing toys in the toilet, only to retrieve them again.

There are two phases to the anal stage—the expelling and the retaining phases. In other words, pleasure is obtained first from the sheer act of expelling and later from the feeling of retaining a full lower intestine. The more figurative or symbolic pleasures of the first phase are expressed in rejecting or destroying, whereas the pleasures of the later phase are expressed in controlling or possessing. Extending over both phases is a sadistic overlay. Anal behavior used to hurt someone else may be manifest in the more symbolic pleasures associated with both phases. The infant may take pleasure in using expulsiveness as a means of defying the parents, or he may withhold excretion as a means of defiance. Parents may not necessarily agree with the Freudian interpretation, but they will certainly agree that the toilet training period is typically one of struggle and the infant seems to be doing just what has been described.

The child's ego, equipped with self-awareness by the oral stage, extends its prowess in the anal stage away from passive functions toward actively directing his own behavior according to his changing environment. In short, the ego begins to take on executive functions; it is becoming the doer. The infant no longer must induce others to do for him but begins to do for himself. He learns to keep clean, to walk, and to talk. With these accomplishments, he can begin to manipulate his environment. In learning to talk, he can let his wants be known more efficiently. Speech is also important in ego development; through it he learns to handle himself as well as to communicate with others. He now self-communicates. Language is such a wonderful tool that in psychoanalytic thinking it assumes a magical and symbolic significance to the child. An illustration from children somewhat older than the age under consideration is particularly apt. "Sticks and stones may break my bones, but names may never hurt me!" This chant is learned by children for its reassurance value. They have to be reassured that names will, in fact, not hurt them. Parents will attest that on occasion they do have to tell their children at this age that being called a "garbage pail" does not make them one!

Not only is mastery of motility taking place, but judgment on the part of the ego is beginning to develop as well. Partly dependent on the growth of speech, judgment is shown through reality testing. The infant tries out everything, in the process of which his behavior would make most mothers modify the old saying to read—"Fools (and little children) rush in where angels fear to tread." However immature his judgment may be, the child certainly is exercising it.

Difficulties of adjustment experienced during the anal stage may also leave their mark on the adult personality in the form of the so-called anal character. According to Freud[116] the triad of characteristics that are associated with the anal character is orderliness, parsimoniousness, and obstinacy. In this context, orderliness refers to scrupulousness in keeping everything just so—socks placed away by color, the desk blotter in its precise place—and finickiness about cleanliness. Parsimoniousness refers to "tightness" with money and other things such as speech. Obstinacy refers to immobility even to the point of defiance and irritability. Scrooge, the character in Dickens's *Christmas Carol*, and his present-day comic strip descendants exemplify the anal character. These characteristics are generalized extensions of earlier compliance with the parents' wishes regarding excretion. "Cleanliness," "tightness," and "immovability" suffice to show the rationale of this extension.

The Phallic Stage   Libidinal interests are shifted to the genital zone at about the end of the third or the beginning of the fourth year. Genital interests have been present before this age—erections have occurred and masturbation is not unknown—but the interests are now intensified. Part of this intensification is maturational in character, because physical changes are taking place. This is referred to as the phallic stage. Interests center on the sex organs themselves with touching, looking at, and exhibiting genitals, rather than heterosexual behavior which is characteristic of the genital stage yet to come. Sexual fantasies appear, and, in general, a high value is placed on the sex organs as such. An important consequence of the phallic stage is that boys become more masculine and girls more feminine. (As a result, it will no longer be possible here to use "he" generically for both boys and girls. The sexes must now be distinguished, psychoanalytically speaking.)

An event of tremendous importance takes place during the years of the phallic stage—the formation and, under normal circumstances, the dissolution of the Oedipus Complex. Hence, it is both logical and convenient to discuss it at this point. However, unless attention is directed to it, an historical inaccuracy could be perpetrated. The theory of the Oedipus Complex was one of Freud's own unique contributions, dating from the period around the turn of the century, not the later years when the theory of psychosexual stages was formulated.

The high valuation of the sex organs characteristic of the phallic stage is significant in the emergence of the Oedipus Complex, which, as might be expected, takes a different course for boys and girls. Its operation in boys will be considered first.

The legend of Oedipus is best known from Sophocles' trilogy of plays. The essentials of the plot revolve around Oedipus killing his father and marrying his mother. Freud turned to this legend for the name, Oedipus Complex, to describe the symbolic playing out of this same drama in the life of every boy. By the very nature of things, the boy will fall in love with his mother and direct death wishes toward his father.

With the coming of phallic interests, the boy develops feelings and behavior directed toward the mother that, commensurate with his age and physical state, are sexual in nature. In fumbling childish ways he shows his sexual feelings. His mother rebuffs these advances.[117] The boy also sees the father as having privileges with the mother from which the child is barred. For example, when the father is away, the boy may have the privilege of sleeping in the mother's bed, but when the father returns, this is not permitted. He becomes jealous, and strong hostile feelings toward the father develop. But mother–son incest is prohibited in almost all cultures, bringing into play a powerful taboo reinforced by the father's authority over the boy. The boy is a rival to an all-powerful father, and he also has feelings against which all society sets its face. Small wonder that he develops anxiety and fears the loss of both his parents' love. Massive anxiety, therefore, makes its appearance. As if this were not enough, he has a more specific anxiety about his sex organ, on which he places a high value. This is castration anxiety, a fear from implied or actual threat to the organ that some parents employ. The boy's learning of the anatomical lack in girls may reinforce his belief in the reality of castration. The cumulative pressures of these anxieties are so great that he represses his desires for the mother, replacing them with tender affection, whereas his feelings of hostility toward the father are replaced by identification. The Oedipus Complex is "smashed," but its effects are still there. It has not disappeared but is under the control, sometimes shaky, of maintained repression.

In the girl the Oedipus Complex takes a different course, because she, unlike the boy, must give up her original pre-Oedipal object choice of the mother and redirect libido toward the father.[118] Moreover, the castration anxiety of the boy is impossible for her since the lack that this implies is already a fact. She notices this lack, and "penis envy" develops. She has fantasies that this castration has happened as a punishment, and she wishes to regain it through the father. This drives her into the Oedipus situation in which the loss may be repaired again in fantasy by having a child through the father. She "loves" the father and therefore "hates" the mother, her rival, whom she also blames for her castration. As a means of solving this problem, the girl learns to identify with the mother. The already existing ambivalence toward the mother aids in this displacement of love to the father. In this way the girl is prepared for the Oedipus shift, events driving her into it, rather than destroying it, as was the case with the boy. Because of the way it was formed, there is less drive for the girl to overcome it as abruptly as does the boy. In fact, the Oedipal situation remains in effect with the girl for a longer period and is continued more or less indefinitely.

One may ask why this stirring drama which takes place in both boys and girls is not so clearly remembered that it becomes common knowledge of our individual past. The answer, psychoanalytically speaking, is simple. We have repressed our knowledge, and, although it is still operative unconsciously, we cannot consciously recall it.[119]

For both the boy and the girl the aftermath of the Oedipal situation is the formation of the superego.[120] The superego is the heir of the Oedipus Complex in that it arises after the complex has been repressed.[121] Parental influence is again paramount.[122] The child identifies with parental views on manners and morals, or rather with their idealized and purified views. He makes both their approving and disapproving attitudes his own. These demands are often exacting, beyond his childish capacities of accomplishment. Consequently, he is plagued with feelings of guilt; he has measured himself with this idealized view and falls short.

In adult life, an individual showing the disproportionate effects of the phallic stage would have continuing castration anxiety or penis envy. The male phallic character gives the impression of being a devil-may-care, masculine, assured person.[123] Intense vanity, exhibitionism, sensitiveness, and a tendency to maintain the offensive are characteristic. At least fitting the stereotype of the phallic character would be the motorcycle fan, the professional wrestler, and the like. A girl driven by her envy would use her physical charms or other capabilities to overcome the male in any way she could. Actually, both male and female phallic characters are dependent, narcissistic, and unable to have mature heterosexual relations. Sexual conquests are precisely that, and not means of relating to other individuals.

With the formation of the superego, the last major constituent of the topographical organization of personality has come into being. The interrelationships among id, ego, superego, and environment are taking on their final form. Earlier in this account, consideration was given to the dynamics and structure of personality. If a strictly developmental sequence of presentation had seemed desirable, that discussion could have been interpolated at this point with relatively little modification.

The Latency Period   The latency period extends over the years five to ten with no new area of libidinal localization making an appearance. It was originally considered a period of sexual quiescence. However, sexual interests are still very much present, but sublimation and other mechanisms are operative, producing a relatively quiet period. Social feelings are extended to individuals outside the family circle at this age. The opinion of their peers looms very large to children in this period.

The Genital Stage   At about the age of ten, the genital stage is introduced by the prepubertal phase preparatory to physical maturity. During the next two or three years or so, there is a sharp increase in the sheer amount of libido available. As sketched by Anna Freud, regression occurs; libido is redirected to infantile love objects; Oedipal fantasies reappear; aggressive impulses are intensified; habits of cleanliness may be lost; immodesty and cruelty may be apparent.[124] There are no new elements, but rather a revival of tendencies from infancy is evidenced. A general disruption of id, ego, and superego relationships occurs. When the id is in the ascendancy, means of pregenital gratification predominate; when the ego is the stronger, anxiety results. Criminal attacks that make the headlines of our newspapers, although more often involving a youngster a year or two older, frequently involve what is essentially a failure to hold id impulses in check.

The arrival of bodily sexual maturity or puberty tends to be accompanied by a dropping away of the sloppy and violent behavior characteristic of the earlier phase, and greater refinement and even fussiness may appear. Sexual interests again extend beyond family figures. The boy or girl may behave as if a stranger in his own family, with uneasiness over displays of affection. "Crushes" on persons who are parent substitutes may be of high intensity but short duration, and are quickly forgotten. In general, the disruption of the earlier genital phase gives way to the beginnings of some approximation of the genital character of adulthood.

The normal, genital character of adulthood is one of nonneurotic sexual adjustment with extensive use of sublimation as a constructive means of ego adjustment.[125] Nevertheless, all adults show some effects of the other previous psychosexual stages. Oral, anal, and phallic characters, despite their deviation, are within the normal range of adjustment. In fact, the dividing line between them and the genital character is a matter of degree. In a sense the genital character is an ideal imperfectly achieved by most adults.

The psychoanalytic theory of psychosexual development places considerable stress on the formative decisiveness of the early years of life. More space has been devoted here to the first five or six years of life than to the rest of the first fourteen years through adolescence, and adulthood has received hardly more than a footnote. This proportion of space is in keeping with psychoanalytic emphasis.[126] Adulthood is an elaboration of the events in infancy and childhood.

SUMMARY

A unique pattern of prescriptive emphases is found in psychoanalysis. Idiographicism predominates over nomotheticism. Unconscious mentalism, dynamicism, developmentalism, and irrationalism are intertwined salient factors. Shared with some of the other views of psychology discussed in previous chapters are centralism, contentual subjectivism, and determinism. It is not surprising that psychoanalysis is not completely integrated with the rest of psychology even to this day, despite today's broader acceptance and utilization of the very prescriptions considered central to psychoanalysis. This greater rapprochement was a development to come in the generations after Freud.

In considerable measure, psychoanalysis has been seen to emerge from Freud's experience with patients. His was a clinical method of both investigation and verification. Through free associations, actions, and dream analyses he found individual interpretive clues that he then related to other presumably congruent findings from the same sources, either from the same or other patients. Consistency of the data, either within a case or from one case to later cases, led to increased confidence and ultimately to certainty about them. Conspicuous by its absence was the control that would have been given by experiment or some other method of studying exceptions to his generalizations. His emphasis on sex—extended sex as it were, with ramifications into all areas of human behavior and experience—is at the same time indicative of the emphasis he placed on the instinctual character of the human drives to action. Freud attached crucial importance to childhood development. The decisive imprint of childhood on our adult behavior was not only expressed through a psychogenetic emphasis, but was also to be played out in a manner that followed a remorseless, biologically genetic pattern. Similarly, he emphasized the dark, primordial forces of the id, which had the ego at its mercy.

All these foci were to be questioned, modified, or amplified in varying degrees by Freud's followers and critics. The use of methods other than the clinical, emphasis on forms of motivation other than the sexual, greater emphasis on experience after childhood, increased emphasis on the social at the expense of the instinctual factors, and recognition of a greater autonomy of conscious control by the ego—all were to come in the period after his death. Psychoanalysis as a means of investigation, as a method of treatment, and as a theory of personality continued after Freud. The book will return to these themes in the next chapter.

NOTES

1. P. Janet, *The Major Symptoms of Hysteria,* 2nd ed. (New York: Macmillan Co., 1920).
2. W. Riese, *The Legacy of Philippe Pinel: An Inquiry into Thought on Mental Alienation* (New York: Springer, 1969).
3. P. Pinel, *Traité médico-philosophique sur l'aliénation mentale* (Paris: Richard, Caille and Revier, 1801).

4. J. E. Esquirol, *Des maladies mentales* (Paris: Baillière, 1838).

5. R. Pintner, *Intelligence Testing: Methods and Results* (New York: Holt, 1923).

6. H. F. Ellenberger, *The Discovery of the Unconscious: The History and Evolution of Dynamic Psychiatry* (New York: Basic Books, 1970).

7. *Ibid.*, p. 112.

8. J. Braid, *Neurypnology; or, The Rationale of Nervous Sleep; Considered in Relation with Animal Magnetism* (London: Churchill, 1843) (Reprinted 1899).

9. G. Guillain, *J. M. Charcot 1825–1893: His Life—His Work,* trans. P. Bailey (New York: Hoeber, 1960).

10. S. Freud, "The History of the Psychoanalytic Movement," in A. A. Brill, ed., *The Basic Writings of Sigmund Freud* (New York: Random House, 1938), p. 943 (1912).

11. P. Janet, *Major Symptoms.*

12. J. M. Charcot, *Clinical Lectures on Diseases of the Nervous System,* trans. T. Savill (London: New Sydenham Society, 1889), III.

13. G. Zilboorg and G. W. Henry, *A History of Medical Psychology* (New York: W. W. Norton, 1941), pp. 357–378.

14. H. Bernheim, *Hypnosis and Suggestion in Psychotherapy: A Treatise on the Nature and Uses of Hypnosis,* 2nd ed., trans. C. A. Herter (New Hyde Park, N.Y.: University Books, 1964) (1884–1886).

15. A. A. Liébeault, *Du sommeil et des états analogues, considérés sur tout au point de vue de l'action de la morale sur le physique* (Paris: Masson, 1866).

16. T. A. Ribot, *English Psychology* (London: King, 1873) (1870).

17. T. A. Ribot, *German Psychology of To-day* (New York: Scribner's, 1886) (1879).

18. P. Janet, "Pierre Janet," in C. Murchison, ed., *History of Psychology in Autobiography* (Worcester, Mass.: Clark University Press, 1930), Vol. 1, pp. 123–133; W. S. Taylor, "Pierre Janet, 1859–1947," *American Journal of Psychology,* 60 (1947):637–645.

19. P. Janet, *L'automatisme psychologique* (Paris: Alcan, 1889).

20. P. Janet, *L'état mental des hystériques* (Paris: Rueff, 1892).

21. P. Janet, *The Major Symptoms of Hysteria* (New York: Macmillan Co., 1907).

22. P. Janet, *L'analyse psychologique (Psychology analysis),* in English, in C. Murchison, ed., *Psychologies of 1930* (Worcester, Mass.: Clark University Press, 1930), pp. 369–373.

23. W. S. Taylor, "Pierre Janet."

24. P. Janet, *Major Symptoms.*

25. M. Prince, *The Dissociation of a Personality* (New York: Longmans, Green, 1905).

26. Janet, *L'analyse psychologique.*

27. P. Janet, *Psychological Healing: A Historical and Clinical Study,* 2 vols., trans. E. and C. Paul (London: Allen and Unwin, 1925).

28. P. Janet, *L'analyse psychologique.*

29. For discussion of this problem and, indeed, practically all aspects of Freudian thinking, see Ellenberger, *The Discovery of the Unconscious.*

30. S. Rosenzweig, "The Cultural Matrix of the Unconscious," *American Psychologist,* 11 (1956):561–562.

31. S. Freud, "An Autobiographical Study" in J. Strachey, ed., *The Standard Edition of the Complete Psychological Works of Sigmund Freud* (London: Hogarth, 1959), Vol. XX, pp. 7–70 (1925). Frank Sulloway's interesting treatment of Freud is appropriately titled *Freud, Biologist of the Mind: Beyond the Psychoanalytic Legend* (New York: Basic Books, 1979).

32. Albrecht, *The New Psychology in America.* There is no lack of biographical work on Freud. Sulloway has been mentioned already. Another excellent recent biography is

Ronald W. Clark, *Freud: The Man and the Cause* (New York: Random House, 1980). The classic treatment of Freud is Ernest Jones, *The Life and Work of Sigmund Freud* (New York: Basic Books, 1953), 3 vols. A much smaller, more personal work is Hanns Sachs, *Freud: Master and Friend* (Cambridge, Mass.: Harvard University Press, 1944). The most recent treatment by Peter Gay *Freud: A Life for Our Time* (New York: Norton, 1988) was not read in time to be used in this chapter. This does not begin to list the totality of the literature, however.

33. Anna O.'s real name was Bertha Pappenheim. She never married, was very devout, and went on to a career in social work. She became so distinguished in her field that Germany issued a postage stamp in her honor in 1954. What has been reported in the text is the "received opinion" as given by Breuer, Jones, and Freud. H. F. Ellenberger, however, has unearthed new evidence reported in "The Story of 'Anna O': A critical Review with New Data," *Journal of the History of the Behavioral Sciences, 8* (1972):267–279, which casts considerable doubt that there was either catharsis or a cure.

34. S. Freud, "The History of the Psychoanalytic Movement," in A. A. Brill, ed., *The Basic Writings of Sigmund Freud* (New York: Random House, 1938), pp. 933–977 (1914).

35. E. Jones, *The Life and Works of Sigmund Freud,* Vol. I, p. 246.

36. S. Freud, "Psychopathology of Everyday Life," in Brill, ed., *The Basic Writings of Sigmund Freud,* pp. 35–178 (1904).

37. J. Breuer and S. Freud, *Studies on Hysteria* (London: Hogarth, 1955) (1895).

38. Jeffrey M. Masson, *The Assault on Truth: Freud's Suppression of the Seduction Theory* (New York: Farrar, Straus and Giroux, 1984). A revision of the revisionist view is found in Frank Cioffi's review, "The Cradle of Neurosis," *Times Literary Supplement,* July 6, 1984, pp. 743–744.

39. S. Freud, *The Interpretation of Dreams* (London: Hogarth, 1953) (1900).

40. S. Freud, *Psychopathology of Everyday Life.*

41. M. Fordham, *The Objective Psyche* (New York: Humanities Press, 1960).

42. S. Freud, *Three Essays on the Theory of Sexuality* (London: Hogarth, 1953) (1905).

43. Rand B. Evans and William A. Koelsch, "Psychoanalysis Arrives in America: The 1909 Psychology Conference at Clark University," *American Psychologist, 40* (1985):942–948.

44. S. Freud, "Autobiographical Study," p. 51.

45. S. Freud, "The Origin and Development of Psychoanalysis," *American Journal of Psychology, 21* (1910):181–218.

46. S. Freud, "The History of the Psychoanalytic Movement."

47. S. Freud, *The Interpretation of Dreams.*

48. S. Freud, *An Outline of Psychoanalysis* (New York: W. W. Norton, 1949) (1939).

49. O. Rank, *The Trauma of Birth* (New York: Harcourt, Brace, 1929) (1923).

50. S. Freud, *The Question of Lay Analysis* (New York: W. W. Norton, 1950) (1926).

51. For an interesting parallel between Freud's attitude toward lay analysis and that of the phrenologist, Gall, see Karl M. Dallenbach, "Phrenology Versus Psychoanalysis," *American Journal of Psychology, 69* (1956):511–525.

52. S. Freud, *Moses and Monotheism* (New York: Alfred A. Knopf, 1939).

53. N. Fodor and F. Gaynor, *Freud: Dictionary of Psychoanalysis* (New York: Philosophical Library, 1950). This reference is a convenient source to find citations of the definitions of some of the crucial characteristics of psychoanalysis.

54. S. Freud, "Psychogenic Visual Disturbances According to Psychoanalytic Conceptions," *Collected Papers* (London: Hogarth, 1924), Vol. II, pp. 105–112 (1910).

55. S. Freud, "Instincts and Their Vicissitudes," *Collected Papers,* Vol. IV, pp. 60–83 (1915); S. Freud, *The Ego and the Id* (London: Hogarth, 1947) (1923).
56. S. Freud, *Beyond the Pleasure Principle* (New York: Boni and Liveright, 1922) (1920).
57. S. Freud, *An Outline of Psychoanalysis,* Chapter 2.
58. O. Fenichel, *The Psychoanalytic Theory of Neuroses* (New York: W. W. Norton, 1945).
59. S. Freud, *Civilization and Its Discontents* (London: Liveright, 1930), Chapter 6 (1929).
60. S. Freud, *An Outline of Psychoanalysis.*
61. *Ibid.*
62. S. Freud, *The Question of Lay Analysis,* Chapter 2.
63. S. Freud, *An Outline of Psychoanalysis,* Chapter 2.
64. *Ibid.*
65. S. Freud, *New Introductory Lectures on Psychoanalysis* (New York: W. W. Norton, 1935), Chapter 3 (1932).
66. S. Freud, *An Outline of Psychoanalysis,* Chapter 8.
67. S. Freud, *Beyond the Pleasure Principle,* Chapter 1.
68. S. Freud, *An Outline of Psychoanalysis.*
69. S. Freud, *New Introductory Lectures on Psychoanalysis,* Lecture 2.
70. S. Freud, *An Outline of Psychoanalysis,* Chapter 8.
71. *Ibid.,* Chapter 2.
72. S. Freud, "Metaphysical Supplement to the Theory of Dreams," *Collected Papers,* Vol. IV, pp. 137–151.
73. S. Freud, *An Outline of Psychoanalysis,* Chapter 2.
74. S. Freud, *The Question of Lay Analysis,* Chapter 2.
75. S. Freud, *Moses and Monotheism,* Part III, Sec. 1.
76. S. Freud, *An Outline of Psychoanalysis,* Chapter 1.
77. S. Freud, *The Question of Lay Analysis,* Chapter 3.
78. *Ibid.,* Chapter 2.
79. *Ibid.,* Chapter 3.
80. S. Freud, *An Outline of Psychoanalysis,* Chapter 1.
81. *Ibid.,* Chapter 8.
82. S. Freud, *New Introductory Lectures on Psychoanalysis,* Lecture 3.
83. S. Freud, *An Outline of Psychoanalysis,* Chapter 1.
84. S. Freud, *New Introductory Lectures on Psychoanalysis,* Lecture 1.
85. S. Freud, *An Outline of Psychoanalysis,* Chapter 4.
86. S. Freud, "Repression," *Collected Papers,* Vol. IV, pp. 84–97 (1915).
87. S. Freud, *The Problem of Anxiety* (New York: W. W. Norton, 1936), Chapter 10 (1926).
88. S. Freud, *New Introductory Lectures on Psychoanalysis,* Lecture 3.
89. S. Freud, *The Problem of Anxiety,* Chapter 10.
90. *Ibid.,* Chapter 8.
91. S. Freud, *New Introductory Lectures on Psychoanalysis,* Lecture 3.
92. S. Freud, *An Outline of Psychoanalysis,* Chapter 1.
93. S. Freud, *Wit and Its Relation to the Unconscious* (New York: Moffat, 1916), Chapter 5 (1905).
94. S. Freud, *An Outline of Psychoanalysis,* Chapter 2.
95. S. Freud, *Three Essays on the Theory of Sexuality.*
96. S. Freud, *New Introductory Lectures on Psychoanalysis,* Lecture 4.
97. S. Freud, *An Outline of Psychoanalysis,* Chapter 2.

98. *Ibid.,* Chapter 6.
99. S. Freud, "The Unconscious," *Collected Papers,* Vol. IV, pp. 98–136 (1915).
100. A. Freud, *The Ego and the Mechanisms of Defense* (London: Hogarth, 1937).
101. Freud, *An Outline of Psychoanalysis,* Chapter 5.
102. *Ibid.*
103. Freud, *New Introductory Lectures on Psychoanalysis,* Lecture 3.
104. *Ibid.*
105. *Ibid.*
106. Freud, *The Problem of Anxiety,* Chapter 3.
107. The general outline of what follows is dependent on Freud, *An Outline of Psychoanalysis,* but some of the details are derived from other sources. For example, Freud originally described only one oral phase, but this and other stages were elaborated and, as Freud accepted them, these elaborations are presented.
108. K. Abraham, *Selected Papers on Psychoanalysis* (London: Hogarth, 1927).
109. S. Freud, *Three Essays on the Theory of Sexuality.*
110. A. Freud, "Some Remarks on Infant Observation," in Ruth S. Eissler et al., eds., *Psychoanalytic Studies of the Child* (New York: International, 1947), Vol. II, pp. 11–30.
111. S. Freud, *An Outline of Psychoanalysis,* Chapter 4.
112. S. Freud, *The Question of Lay Analysis,* Chapter 3.
113. G. S. Blum, *Psychoanalytic Theories of Personality* (New York: McGraw–Hill, 1953), pp. 46–47 (reprinted by permission).
114. O. Fenichel, *The Psychoanalytic Theory of Neuroses.*
115. *Ibid.*
116. S. Freud, *New Introductory Lectures on Psychoanalysis,* Lecture 6.
117. R. L. Munroe, *Schools of Psychoanalytic Thought* (New York: Dryden Press, 1955).
118. *Ibid.*
119. S. Freud, *New Introductory Lectures on Psychoanalysis,* Lecture 3.
120. *Ibid.*
121. S. Freud, *An Outline of Psychoanalysis,* Chapter 8.
122. *Ibid.,* Chapter 1.
123. O. Fenichel, *The Psychoanalytic Theory of Neuroses.*
124. S. Freud, *Ego and Mechanisms of Defense.*
125. O. Fenichel, *The Psychoanalytic Theory of Neuroses.*
126. S. Freud, *Moses and Monotheism,* Part III, Sec. II.

Top: Alfred Adler. *Bottom:* Carl G. Jung.

Chapter 25

Adler, Jung, and the Third-Generation Dynamic Psychologists

*F*reud "invented" psychoanalysis and appears to have wanted it to remain theoretically monolithic, but it was not to be that way. We have already discussed the breaks between Freud and two of his most brilliant followers, Alfred Adler (1870–1937) and Carl Jung (1875–1961). This chapter will deal with the development of their positions and those of the generation of dynamic psychologists and psychoanalysts.

ALFRED ADLER

Although Alfred Adler disagreed with Freud on many issues, he came from a similar, clinical tradition. Consequently, the approach to psychology that emerged from his interaction with his patients shows much closer kinship with that of Freud than with anything encountered earlier.

Life and Earlier Views of Adler

Alfred Adler was born in 1870 in a suburb of Vienna, the second son of a relatively well-to-do grain merchant.[1] Although his early years had many attractive features, having been spent in the open country, in comfortable circumstances, and with a love of music shared by all his family, Alfred believed he had had an unhappy childhood. The "villain of the piece" was his model elder brother, whose achievements he never felt he could equal. This brother was his mother's favorite; Alfred was his father's. Alfred suffered from rickets and was watched over with the greatest solicitude. The running and jumping at which his brother excelled, therefore, caused Alfred unhappiness, and he apparently felt himself to be undersized and ugly. Nevertheless, he was a friendly, outgoing child. Adler reports that his decision to become a physician was made at the age of five when he was recovering from an illness that he learned had been almost fatal. He later interpreted this life goal as a means of ending his childlike distress at the fear of death, expecting more from this choice than it could accomplish. More than one facet of Adler's later psychological views may be found in these memories of childhood.

Adler attended the University of Vienna and received his medical degree in 1895. Two years after graduation, he married Raissa Tinofejewna, a wealthy Russian girl who had come to Vienna to study. She was an emancipated, outspoken woman whose greatest interest was in the social betterment of her homeland. Her independence of thinking and her liberalism forced a considerable contrast to the domestic ideal of Viennese men of Adler's class. That they had their difficult times there is no doubt, but in later years even though their respective fundamental convictions remained unchanged, a mellowness seems to have marked their life together.

Throughout Adler's years in Vienna, the cafe, so much part of the life of that city, was also part of his life. He met his friends and students there, thoroughly enjoying the informality, the jokes, the wine, the food, and the animated conversation. Adler loved people and was charming, friendly, and informal. In turn, many individuals from all walks of life were attracted to him. Socialistic in his political views for a time, he insisted that his psychological views had nothing to do with politics. His political position, however, was but a specific manifestation of a dedication to social betterment, a purpose on which he acted all of his life.[2] Adler was familiar with Freud's *The Interpretation of Dreams*, which he believed to be an important contribution to the understanding of human nature. The occasion of his first association with Freud and his precise status in relation to him is a matter of interpretation and uncertainty, as an examination of even a portion of the literature demonstrates.[3] To put it bluntly, the Freudians claim he was a disciple who sought and received membership in the Freudian group. The Adlerians see their relationship as one of equals joining forces at the invitation of Freud. At any rate, Adler became a leading member of the group, and Freud named him as his successor as President of the Vienna Psychoanalytic Society and as coeditor of *Zentralblatt für Psychoanalyse.*

In 1907 Adler published his views on organ inferiority and compensation.[4] As an ophthalmologist and then as a general practitioner, he had recognized that disease afflicts inferior organs, a point already well known. In his monograph Adler went on to indicate that this inferiority must be considered relative to the person's environment. Disease is a result not only of organ inferiority, but also of external demands on the organ. Moreover, an outcome other than disease may occur to a person with an inferior organ in a particular environment. One outcome may be to overcompensate for this inferiority through that particular organ. History and literature, Adler points out, are filled with instances where an individual's compensation for a weakness went beyond this level to overcompensation. Demosthenes, the stutterer who overcame his handicap and became a great orator, is illustrative. Similarly, Nietzsche, afflicted with a physical infirmity, took up the pen, instead of the sword, and wrote a philosophy of power.

In 1910 Adler went on to explore more fully the notion of overcompensation.[5] He recognized that organ inferiority led to subjective feelings of inferiority, a concept not used in his earlier paper. Often children who have inferior organs and inadequate development manifest it in weakness and clumsiness (as Adler himself showed in childhood), which give rise to feelings of inferiority.

This interest signaled a shift of emphasis from biology and disease to psychology and the subjective state of the person. For feelings of inferiority, individuals may overcompensate by excessive striving in the area of the felt weakness or some other area, or, instead of striving in either fashion, may become submissive. More specifically, Adler introduced the concept of masculine protest—the striving to be strong and powerful in compensation for a feeling of being unmanly. Freud had already defined compensation in terms of inadequate sexual developments leading to a need to compensate for this deficiency. Adler was using it to bring a social emphasis to bear on sex. Freud accepted the masculine protest but used it in reference to castration fear and penis envy. Although Freud used these findings to indicate the omnipresence of sex, Adler used them to point up the individual's interaction with the world, particularly the social world. In women, the masculine protest occurred because in our social world they are made to feel inferior in many ways. Men also show the same protest. In their case it is directed against the assumption that men have to be superior, that they have to live up to this demand despite feelings of inadequacy.[6]

This social emphasis was clearly present as early as 1905.[7] In an account for the general public of Freud's *Three Essays on the Theory of Sexuality*, Adler asked the question, "What purpose is served when nature equips the infant with sexuality?" His answer was that the passion for satisfaction it engenders forces the infant to enter relations with the outer world, a very precise foreshadowing of his emphasis on the social aspect of sexuality.

To return to the theme of organ inferiority, Adler realized as his thinking developed that, regardless of the presence or absence of organ inferiority, this inferiority feeling is a universal fact with children because they are small and dependent on adults. Big, strong people, adults, try to control the child's every movement. Neurotic tendencies develop when children employ manifestations of this inferiority feeling to excuse them from doing what they are capable of. When this continues into later life, inferiority feeling becomes the Inferiority Complex. The individual may overcompensate or use inferiority as an excuse to give up striving. Inferiority per se, however, is not a sign of abnormality. It is a fact of normal development which occurs when the individual combats feelings of inferiority by striving to be superior. Aggression then arises not from felt superiority but from felt inferiority. At this stage of his thinking, Adler said, everyone has a drive toward a superiority in order to overcome feelings of inferiority. As will be seen, this view also changed.

At the time, Freud saw this work of Adler as a contribution to ego psychology and compensation, a valuable, though peripheral, clue to the neuroses. The charge that Adler's approach is superficial in that it is an "ego" psychology alone (as differentiated from a psychology of id, superego, and ego) is still the basic argument of the Freudian psychoanalyst against Adlerian psychology. At the time under discussion, however, Adler's views were not seen as a separate system. Only when it was realized that Adler was making compensation central, rather than peripheral, was there a parting of the ways. The two put up with one another for some time. Finally, Adler rebelled against Freud's demand that Jung censor Adler's publications in Freud's *Zentralblatt*. At this junction Freud wrote the proprietors of the *Zentralblatt* demanding that they withdraw either his name or Adler's from the title page. Several meetings of the Vienna Psychoanalytic Society were devoted to a consideration of Adler's views.[8] Since Freud and several others of those present argued that it was impossible to reconcile Adler's views with psychoanalysis, Adler and a group of his followers withdrew. At this time they called themselves the Society for Free Psychoanalytic Research, but shortly thereafter they began to refer to their work as "individual psychology." Contrary to the frequently expressed opinion, this change in title was not made in order to stress individuality of personality.[9] Nor does it mean that the individual moves alone, barred from effective relation with his or her fellows. In fact, this is the diametric opposite of Adler's position: only within a social matrix do the partial processes of the individual achieve meaning.

Adler later spoke of what he called Freud's mythology of sex and regarded psychoanalysis as founded on the selfishness of a pampered child, containing within it an attack on moral law itself. In general, Adler objected to the pansexualism of psychoanalysis as expressed in Freud's libido theory. Adler also believed, as we have already seen in connection with the "masculine protest" and the sexuality of infants, that the phenomena with which Freud dealt were capable of a nonsexual interpretation. For example, the Oedipus Complex, if it arises at all, comes about from the dependency of the pampered child on his mother. Sexual feelings exist, to be sure, just as hunger and thirst do, but these biological factors come into psychological prominence only to the extent that they come into the striving for superiority. Adler did not deny the reality of unconscious motivation, although he was inclined to stress ego functions to a greater degree than Freud. He also found dream interpretation useful, although he saw the dream as a vicarious solution to a problem of the individual, a means of planning for the future. The dream had an emotion-producing function, expressed by Adler's reference to dreams as the factory of emotions.

In 1911 a German philosopher, Hans Vaihinger, published a book, *The Psychology of "As If,"* which almost immediately influenced Adler's thinking.[10] Vaihinger advanced the idea that the individual lives by fictional goals that actually have no counterpart in reality. He said that we create the fiction that the universe is an orderly determined affair, and, by acting as if it were so, even though the universe may really be chaos, in a sense we make it orderly. We create a God when we act as if He existed. Although these goals may be falsifications of experience, we act as if they were real. Hence, they affect our thinking and behavior.

Adler applied this notion to his more specifically psychological problems, especially the issue of purpose and causality.[11] It will be recalled that Freud established causality as a fundamental principle and laid great stress on constitutional factors and childhood experiences as determiners of personality. Adler found in these conceptions of Vaihinger a means of rebutting this rigid determinism. The individual, Adler said, is motivated more by future expectations than by past experiences. People behave as if motivated by a goal. These goals are part of a teleological design, although they are fictions; they permit us to guide our behavior in line with our expectations. The goal toward which we strive explains our behavior. The goals we "see" determine what we will do. Not that we are aware of these goals; as a matter of fact, we are largely unaware of them—they are goals that we do not understand. The hidden goals are the essential content of unconsciousness.[12] Adler called one aspect of the fictional goal the guiding self-ideal.[13] It was by means of his unifying principles that the individual found superiority, an enforcement of safeguarding of self-esteem. The neurotic tries to enforce self-esteem by being a "real man."

During World War I Adler served as a physician in the Austrian Army. Afterward, through the intercession of a leading Viennese citizen interested in education, he was given the opportunity to organize child-guidance clinics in the Vienna school system. His point of view had expanded to the point where it was applicable to teacher–child as well as parent–child relationships and to normal as well as problem children. His influence on teachers, then and later, was very strong. Unlike Freud, he never insisted on long, drawn-out training for practitioners, and many of the more successful and prominent individual psychologists have come from the ranks of teachers who combined his teachings with educational practices. It is perhaps appropriate to add that for the rest of his life Adler carried out much of his teaching through public lectures and institutes to which teachers and anyone else who was interested were invited.

In the 1920s Adler's fame spread. In Vienna many students and admirers surrounded him, and he spent much time with them. Lecture tours took him to various countries. In 1926 he made his first trip to the United States, where he was warmly received by the teachers who had attended his European conferences. He made several half-year visits thereafter. In 1927 he was appointed lecturer at Columbia University, and in 1932 he was made Professor of Medical Psychology at Long Island College of Medicine, a connection that continued until his death. In 1934 Adler decided to make the United States his permanent home. The following year he founded the *International Journal of Individual Psychology*, which was short-lived. In the spring of 1937 he embarked on a strenuous lecture tour of Europe, which sometimes called for appearances in two towns in one day. After completing the continental portion of this tour, he had a fatal heart attack while walking the streets of gray, granite Aberdeen.

Adler was a prolific writer who addressed a large number of books to the general public. Since his writings were based on his lecture series, they lack the systematic coherence arrived at only by selection and rearrangement, a task H. L. and R. R. Ansbacher have carried out admirably.[14]

Mature Systematic Position

Adler's systematic views may be sketched against the setting of his earlier conceptualizations of inferiority feeling, fictional goal, and family situation, but in a larger and changed perspective. To Adler, the individual person exists in a context of social relations.[15] Everyone has an innate urge to adapt positively to the social environment. This innate capacity for friendly and loving responses, called "Social Interest," is the most important facet of our striving. Instead of all people being driven by inferiority feelings to strive toward superiority, as Adler had stated earlier, Social Interest was more basic, permitting normal individuals to move toward participation and integration according to their mature view. Neurotics suffer from these feelings of inferiority and have a drive to superiority, but normal persons do not. Normal persons, though inferior because by the very nature of things they must be incomplete, show a willingness as well as an ability to participate that is basic to Social Interest. There are three major social ties, which set for each person three major problems: occupation, social contact with one's fellow beings, and love and marriage. Failure in any or all of these tasks is a failure as a human being. If we fail to adjust to these problems or direct our life to escaping these tasks, we are potentially neurotic or delinquent. A complete refusal to accept these tasks is a psychosis.

In a variety of other ways, Adler emphasized the social factors that help shape the personality. One expression of Adlerian interest in social factors is his emphasis on the importance of the child's position in the family in relation to that of other children.[16] The sibling relationships of a given child may lead to certain characteristic experiences. Some of the more prominent characteristics are as follows. The "only child" is most often spoiled by the parents, although occasionally hated by them; he tends to dominate the mother and father, be hyperintellectual and overmature for his age, and show considerable adroitness in getting along with adults. The "second born" not only dethrones the first born but often ends up dominating him as well as his parents; he often tends to be somewhat more competitive as well. The youngest child in the family enjoys the doubtful privilege of never being displaced, that is, of being "little" and "helpless" forever; as a consequence, he often learns to get his way through stealth and guile.

The characteristic way in which a person's individuality is expressed in its environment Adler calls "style of life."[17] The individual's life style, as it is more commonly called, is an effort to reach his or her goals. These styles of life are generalized ways of coping with the problems the individual faces, which are unique for each individual. Everyone has a style of life, but no two are alike. The goals of security, unity, and oneness are the same, but the routes to them are different. "Acting out of character" is an everyday phrase that shows recognition of the style of life. In every expression of the personality, the individual shows a unity, a consistency, which is the style of life.[18]

In identifying the life style, Adler found it highly useful to ask his subjects to recount their first memories. His own early memory of his illness at five years of age and his decision to become a doctor in order to ward off fear of death is illustrative of what he was seeking to find. He checked this particular conviction by asking a sample of doctors for their first childhood memory and found that they most often reported something involving recovery from a serious illness or a death in the family. Conversely, he asked children in families where there had been a death what they thought they wanted to be when they grew up—and the answers most often given were ''doctor'' or ''nurse.''[19]

A faulty style of life may arise from three major sources in childhood experiences—inferiorities, neglect, and pampering. Children with infirmities may be handicapped by considering themselves failures. With the aid of understanding parents or by appropriate psychotherapy, they may compensate for these inferiorities and actually transform them into strengths. Pampering may produce a child without social feeling who is self-centered and expects society to conform to his wishes; this results in a clash between the child and society. Neglect in childhood may lead to a style of life in which revenge against society is sought. Pampering or neglecting the child usually results in the individual lacking confidence to meet the demands of life.

The decision to compensate is dependent on individual courage, in addition to parents or psychotherapy and quite apart from these external sources. These particular sources may lead to compensation, or they may not, depending on the child's interpretation of them and courage in facing them. He or she may creatively choose either to compensate or to remain a failure. Adler pointed out that people are not merely the creation of the environmental forces to which they are exposed; there is a creative power in individuals.[20] They fashion their own unity; they direct their drives and decide their goals. It is interesting to observe that neglect, pampering, and organic inferiority were all present in Adler's own personality and could have led to inferiority feelings and neuroses. Yet they did not. Adler's forms of compensation, both personally to solve these problems and socially to develop his systematic approach, show his own creative solution.

Adlerian Psychotherapy

Patients come to the therapist because their life style is incapable of solving their life situation, their particular difficulty being a way of evading conflicts. The fundamental mistake that patients make is to draw false conclusions about the world from their early social relations. The goal of psychotherapy is to cut through this erroneous life style and suggest a new one.

Patients cannot change their style of life until they gain understanding.[21] They gain that understanding when their Inferiority Complex is traced to its origin in early childhood maladjustments. More specifically, Adler recommended that the following methods be used: (1) to study the family constellation; (2) to infer from the earliest childhood recollection some of the aspects of the style of life ideal; and (3) to investigate and interpret dreams to see in what particular way, guided by the style of life ideal, the person allowed emotions to interfere with his or her particular style of life.

Needless to say, Adler did not follow the techniques of Freudian therapy. He used a much more conversational face-to-face situation than Freud would have countenanced. He was sympathetic and encouraging in attitude, appealing to his patients' social interest, while at the same time trying to aid them to find a solution through their own efforts. Encouragement was by no means an incidental attitudinal matter—its use was an essential aspect of his therapy. Exaggerated inferiority feeling leading to an Inferiority Complex is, in another sense, discouragement arising from maladjustments and deficiencies. Hence, encouragement is important.

There was a characteristic "openness" to Adler's therapy. His clinics with children were conducted before any and all interested individuals who wished to attend—parents, teachers, anyone. Children were questioned directly as if they were contemporaries, although in the simplest of language. On first meeting the child, it was also characteristic of Adler to try to make swift insightful decisions about the child's problem. Seeing a very discouraged child whom he judged had a passionate desire to shine, Adler promptly sat down on a step lower than that of the child. On first seeing a boy with a strong temper, Adler asked what he liked to do. He received the reply, "Play football." Adler said, "It's fine barging into the other boys, isn't it?" On meeting a child noted for showing off in class, Adler drew himself up on tiptoes as high as he could, and sank slowly back and said, "I am making myself bigger than I am, just as you do, but there are other ways of doing this than by upsetting the class."

Overview

Adler shared with Freudian psychoanalysis an adherence to idiographicism, dynamicism, and developmentalism but placed less emphasis on unconscious mentalism and irrationalism. He continued sharing with the rest of nonbehavioristic psychology, as did psychoanalysis in general, an adherence to centralism and contentual subjectivism, but he deviated from both on the issue of determinism. Adler rejected the exclusive influence of what came to be called hard determinism, that is, external objective causation. Instead, he added self-determinism, a form of teleological causation.

Adler directed his thinking toward the social sciences and away from biology and medicine. The heart of his teaching was social interest, although, in a restricted sense, his theory was biological in its view of the individual as inherently a being with social interests. Nevertheless, Adler directed his thinking to the exploration of how the social environment influenced the individual's development and personality.

Freud had found the family and society necessary for the vicissitudes of the libido to unfold, but can hardly be said to have elaborated the influence of specific experiences arising in the family or in society. In contradistinction, Adler made the social setting fundamental. At first he stressed organ inferiority, but in time he emphasized the attitude persons adopted toward their defect, and finally he arrived at a view in which positive Social Interest was basic. Adler's influence on other psychologists will be considered later in this chapter.

CARL GUSTAV JUNG

Another former colleague of Freud, Carl Jung, made contributions of such magnitude and originality as to demand detailed consideration here.

Life of Jung

Carl Gustav Jung was born in 1875 in the Swiss village of Kesswil, located on Lake Constance, and grew up at Basel, a university town, where he received his early schooling.[22] The family background was scholarly: one grandfather had been a Professor of Anatomy and Internal Medicine at Basel, the other a grammarian, and his father a philologist and pastor in the Swiss Reformed Church. Jung's youthful interests were in philosophy and ancient history. He would have liked to become an archaeologist, an early expression of his continued desire to explore the roots of human thinking in the historical past.[23] Another current of interest, reflected in his dreams during his student years, led him to the study of the natural sciences. The difficult choice of a profession was limited by the fact that the University of Basel offered no curriculum in archaeology, and Jung was not financially able to study elsewhere. He decided to combine his humanistic and scientific interests in the study of medicine, and he received his medical degree at Basel in 1900. After a year or two of clinical experience, he went to Paris for a semester to study psychology with Pierre Janet. In 1903 he married Emma Rauschenbach who, over the years, did much collaborative work with him.

Jung's first clinical appointment was to the Psychiatric Clinic of the University of Zurich and its hospital, known as Burgholzi. In 1898 both had come under the leadership of Eugen Bleuler (1857–1939), the best known psychiatrist in Switzerland in his day. Bleuler's particular interest was in the psychopathology of dementia praecox on which he was to publish a monumental work. He coined the term *schizophrenia* to signalize the revolutionary reformulation he made. Bleuler argued that, contrary to the previously held view, so-called dementia praecox was a group of psychiatric reactions, not a single formal disease. Patients so designated were not incurable; mental deterioration did not inevitably occur; and the patients did not lack an affective or feeling life.

In 1900 Jung was appointed Bleuler's assistant and, in 1905, Lecturer in Psychiatry at the university. At the same time he was advanced to physician of the clinic, a position he occupied until 1909.

Jung's first publication, in 1902, was a clinical study of an adolescent girl who, in somnambulistic states, performed as a medium.[24] It clearly bore the impress of Janet, under whom Jung had worked during the year of its publication.[25]

Word Association

Beginning in 1903, Jung devoted considerable attention to experiments in word association.[26] The immediate inspiration for his work was a review by the Swiss psychologist, Edouard Claparède (1873–1940). Jung stressed the affective determinants as differentiated from the studies of Galton, Cattell, and others who emphasized cognitive aspects.[27] He investigated the emotional preoccupations of his patients and of normal persons through their responses to a specially prepared list of 100 words. To each of these words subjects were instructed to respond with the first word that came to mind. Typical words were "head," "green," "water," "sing," "dead," and "ship." The time it took to respond to a word was noted by means of a stopwatch. With some of his subjects a measure of breathing rate was also taken through use of a pneumograph strapped to the chest, while changes in the electroconductivity of the skin caused by sweating were measured by a psychogalvanometer attached to the palm of the hand. If a word produced a long reaction time, an irregularity in breathing, and the onset of sweating, an emotional response connected either with the stimulus word or with the reply seemed indicated. Sometimes the individual is aware of matters brought to light by responses but has chosen to keep them secret, as exemplified in this method's later, relatively widespread use in lie and crime detection. Actually, Jung applied it in precisely this fashion on the occasion of a theft at one of the hospitals. As "complex indicators" he used the names of objects in a stolen purse, such as "key" or "mirror," which to an innocent person would seem quite neutral in content.

To Jung, use of the method to detect unconscious problems was much more important systematically. In such instances, the subject's response to a word with signs of emotion but no knowledge of its significance—that is, he was unconscious of its meaning—was still an emotional indicator. Jung asserted that when this happened, a "complex" had been touched.

To Jung, complexes were psychic fragments that had been split off owing to traumatic influences or certain incompatible tendencies. From the association experiments, Jung concluded that complexes interfere with the intentions of the will and disturb the conscious performance; they produce disturbances of memory and blockages in the flow of association; they appear and disappear according to their own laws; they can temporarily obsess consciousness, or influence speech and action in an unconscious way.[28] Clearly, at this time Jung was dealing with the concept of repression, that is, the disturbing effect of pain-producing thoughts when they are repressed into the unconscious. He saw how these repressed contents tended to erupt into consciousness, interfering with the normal processes of associative thought.

Relations with Freud

On reading Freud's *The Interpretation of Dreams* soon after its publication, Jung was greatly interested, seeing in it an exposition of the concept of repression from a point of view different from his own, namely, its effect in the formation of dreams. In many ways, Freud's understanding of the complex agreed with Jung's independent observations. Encouraged by Bleuler, Jung began to apply Freud's theories to his patients at Burgholzi. This resulted in his monograph *The Psychology of Dementia Praecox*, published in 1907.[29] His application of psychoanalytic principles to the psychotic was highly original. His clinical findings led him to compare the contaminated, disintegrated associations of the dementia praecox patient with those of the neurotic patient's dream life, and he attributed to repression the inadequate and "flat" feeling tone that the dementia praecox patient manifested. He applied his own technique of controlled association to these patients and related the two kinds of findings.

In 1906 Freud and Jung began correspondence, and in 1907 Jung made the journey to Vienna to meet Freud. From this meeting developed a strong friendship, based on mutual liking and respect, but it lasted only a few years.

Until 1913, Jung worked closely with Freud, serving as an editor of a yearbook sponsored by Bleuler and Freud and, in 1911, as first President of the International Psychoanalytic Society. It was also in 1911 that Jung expressed to Freud his doubts about the essentially sexual nature of libido. In 1912 Jung's book, *The Psychology of the Unconscious*,[30] and a series of lectures given at Fordham University, entitled *The Theory of Psychoanalysis*,[31] brought their differences about libido into sharp focus. Although Freud broadened his views later, at this time he conceived of libido as narrowly sexual in nature. Although Jung recognized the importance of sexuality, he did not give it a central position in his theoretical approach. He understood libido, rather, as psychic energy that could communicate itself on different levels of intensity or value to any field of activity: power, hunger, hatred, sexuality, or religion. It was not itself a specific instinct.[32] Sexuality was but one of its manifestations. Libido expressed itself in nutrient terms in infancy, in play and social interaction in the years following, and in heterosexual form only after puberty. Jung did not deny a possible relationship between nutritive and sexual traits. In fact, libido freed itself from nutritional traits only with difficulty, and some individuals never do break the association. The libido, in its progression from nutritional to sexual zones, retains the nutritive traits so abundantly demonstrated by Freudian study. Jung's libido includes the whole range of drives and is all-embracing, being closer in spirit to Plato's Eros or Schopenhauer's will-to-live than to Freud's more restricted meaning. Instead of stressing psychological trauma, Jung saw it merely as the patient's device to bring his or her difficulty into focus. The patient's past experiences were important to Jung primarily in their usefulness in delineating a pattern to better understand the patient's present needs.

Jung and Freud were closely associated between 1909 and 1913, during which time they traveled together to the United States to lecture on behalf of the psychoanalytic movement. Even then, however, Jung could not fully accept what he considered Freud's "dogmatic" view on sexuality. He noted in his autobiography that he alone logically pursued the two problems that interested Freud most: the problem of "archaic vestiges" and that of sexuality.[33] Jung saw the value of sexuality—and this played an essential part in his psychology—as an expression of psychic wholeness. But his main concern was to investigate, over and above its personal significance and biological function, its spiritual aspect and its meaning in myth and religion. Freud saw Jung's divergence as an attempt to desexualize psychoanalysis and thus negate his own efforts. Consequently, a rift developed between the two. In 1914 Jung officially severed his connection with Freudian psychoanalysis by resigning the presidency and, a little later, by giving up his membership in the Society. Jung retained his admiration for Freud and, on several later occasions, explicitly acknowledged the importance of his work. Thereafter Jung applied the term *analytic psychology* to his own theories.[34]

Extraversion and Introversion

Jung first presented his views on extraversion and introversion at the International Psychoanalytic Congress at Munich in 1913,[35] although he had been thinking about these concepts in his years of practical medical work.[36] He was struck with the fact that among the many individual differences in human psychology, there also existed these "typical" distinctions. He described the two types in one of his best known works, "Psychological Types."[37] Individuals who habitually derive their motivations from inner necessity and are preoccupied with the inner life, Jung called introverts. Individuals who habitually derive their motivation from external factors, including social relations, he called extraverts. Later, he used these two types to explain the differences between Freud and Adler.[38] He interpreted Freud's view as that of an extravert, based on a relation with a sexual object, whereas he saw Adler's view as that of an introvert, since it was based on the subjective side, the individual, and the will to power. Jung admitted an even more personal reason for his interest. He elaborated his type theory in an attempt to understand better what brought about his own break with Freud. The essential point of the type theory is that it holds the germ of Jung's recognition that every psychological phenomenon contains implicitly the seeds of its opposite, and that for an understanding of the individual's complete nature it is necessary to determine both the overtly expressed and the latent tendencies.

Later Life

To follow this trend of thinking, Jung realized he would have to devote more time to research into the unconscious. Therefore, in 1913 he gave up his university appointment in order to work independently without the restrictions of academic tradition. He could then devote his attention to the significance of myths, legends, and cultural history for the unconscious life of the individual.[39] This interest became most prominently expressed in his contention that, in addition to the individual unconscious, there is a collective unconscious, which expressed through the individual the deeper images and experiences shared by all humankind.

Jung's interest in this problem led him to make field expeditions to study the mental processes of primitive peoples, first in North Africa in 1921, later among the Pueblo Indians of Arizona and New Mexico, and, in 1926, in Africa where he studied the natives of Kenya. Jung also carried on collaborative work with the aid of specialists in philology, mythology, Chinese philosophy, and poetry. An astonishing array of books was the result. Not only did he study medieval alchemical texts, but he also wrote commentaries on Chinese and Tibetan historical documents that had recently become available through translation into German. He also considered modern mystical writings and reported on the phenomenon of occultism.

The results of some of these studies may at first appear puzzling to the present-day reader accustomed to a logical exposition of factual material. Consider a book originally appearing in 1944 and published in English in an expanded form in 1953, which bears the title, *Psychology and Alchemy.*[40] Its editors for the English edition assure us that it is of such major importance as to rank with *The Psychology of the Unconscious* and "Psychological Types." Along with the text, it contains 270 illustrations drawn from prints, beginning with one depicting "the Creator as Ruler of the threefold and fourfold universe"—from a manuscript of 1652—through the allegory of the psychic union of opposites circa 1550, to the phoenix as a symbol of resurrection from a 1702 manuscript. He regarded the symbols which he found in the works of alchemy as a projection of psychic contents into matter. The decoding of these symbols served as a parallel or model for understanding the psychic processes through analysis. He noted that alchemists who were aware of the spiritual aspect of their work stated that "our gold is not the common gold," indicating that their search was more than an attempt to turn base metals into gold. For many of those who worked with it, alchemy was a symbolic way to understand nature—to find the philosopher's stone. Alchemy, to use Jung's term, was an "under-current" to the Christianity that ruled on the surface.[41] He went on to suggest that alchemy was related to Christianity as the dream was to consciousness. In this framework, he discusses alchemical symbolism in the book by drawing on material from several hundred dreams.

In another book, Jung argued that the religious impulse is a fundamental human instinct.[42] Take away their gods, and human beings will find others, whether it be by deifying leaders of the state or by the obsessive charging of such things as money or work with godlike qualities. Only with the recognition of good and evil within us can we come to a true understanding of self and have a chance to solve the crises of the present-day world.

Jung resumed academic lecturing in 1933, when he also became Professor at the Federal Polytechnical University in Zurich. He remained there until 1942, when he gave up this post for reasons of health. In 1944 Jung was named Professor of Medical Psychology at Basel, a position especially created for him. He held this appointment only a year or so. On relinquishing it, he also gave up medical practice. In 1948 a Jungian training center, the C. G. Jung Institute, was founded in Zurich through the initiative and funds of various persons and institutions who wished to further his work. Honorary degrees and other academic and professional honors came to him from all over the world from the 1930s through the 1950s. In 1961 he died at his home in Kusnacht, near Zurich.

Systematic Views on Psychology

Jung considered his systematic position to be growing and changing, and therefore tentative and incomplete.[43] Some of the earlier steps have already been mentioned: how he defined complex, his formulation of libido and its development, his general conception of introversion–extraversion, and his emphasis on the importance of the collective unconscious. These earlier conceptualizations must now be integrated into a larger perspective, involving his mature views on introversion–extraversion, the personal and collective unconscious, the polarities and antitheses, the conscious ego, and the self.

Type Theory Introversion and extraversion, defined by Jung as attitudes or directions of outlook and interest, are considered collectively in Jungian theory as the direction of libido. In the introvert, there is a turning inward of libido toward the self. In the extravert, libido is directed outside the self to objects and relationships with objects. An introvert is reflective, thoughtful, and tends to be self-assertive; outside influences meet resistance, expressed by the individual wanting his or her own way. An extravert adapts quickly to the environment, pays attention to objects; the extravert's shyness is minimal.

As Jung is sometimes labeled a "type" theorist, the Jungian concept of the average person needs clarification before we can proceed to further ramifications of the theory. In the earlier stage of his theorizing, Jung stated that average people form an even more extensive group numerically than do the introverts and extraverts. Although later he would not make this claim, then he saw such a person as influenced more or less equally from within as from without.[44] Even here, however, the introverted and extraverted attitudes, which should be complementary, tended to function in opposition. Jung warned against a rigid dependence on types: "Every individual is an exception to the rule."[45] The individual shows not only conformity but also uniqueness.

Without altering the essential meaning of extraversion and introversion based on direction of libido, Jung later went on to treat them as categories superordinate to the four functions, which may be thought of as four possible ways of viewing or dealing with any specific situation. Jung identified the functions as thinking, feeling, sensation, and intuition. He selected these functions as basic because they are not further reducible, that is, thinking is different from feeling and cannot be reduced to it, any more than any one of the other functions can be reduced to another. Each of the four functions may be carried on through either an introverted or an extraverted attitude, depending on the direction in which the libido is turned.

A theory of two types had given way to a theory of two classes and four types.[46] Feeling imparts value in the subjective sense of rejection or acceptance. Thinking is conceptual and apperceptive, telling us what a thing is. Sensation transmits a physical stimulus to conscious perception. Intuition transmits perception in an unconscious way (as when having a hunch). Sensation and intuition are the perceiving functions, and thinking and feeling the rational or judging functions. To consider thinking as telling us what a thing is causes no particular trouble. At first glance, however, feeling as a judging function seems to be contradictory. For it to make sense requires an unusual separation—but one demanded in Jungian theory—the separation of feeling from emotion and mood. Mood and emotion are not matters of function, but of sensitiveness, which actually is unsettling of judgment. To Jung, feeling has a judging function; it gives a positive or negative value to a thing and consequently is not an aspect of emotion. Indeed, any function can lead to, but is always distinct from, an emotion. From Jung's point of view, emotion is the result of being hit in a blind spot, a consequence of the individual being touched in an unconscious, usually "defended" area. It is an affect and may be characterized by a measurable physiological reaction.

Only one of the perceiving functions and only one of the judging functions can be dominant at the same time. Either sensation or intuition, thinking or feeling, can be dominant, but not both. Persons either tend to observe consciously what is going on about them, or they unconsciously perceive the details and respond with an awareness that is a synthesis of what they have "seen." They experience this as an intuitive impression or "hunch." Similarly, either thinking or feeling is dominant, for persons either approach something with the objectivity that comes from a neutral logical approach, or they weigh it and give it a subjective value. Since it is already established that either introversion or extraversion can be dominant, but not both, it follows that eight possible combined types emerge up to this point. There may be an extravert (1) with intuition and feeling, (2) with intuition and thinking, (3) with sensation and feeling, and (4) with sensation and thinking. The introvert would show the same four combinations among these variables. It may be well to give examples. A person who is an introverted, thinking, intuitive "type," like Jung himself, with the consequent combination of abstraction and hunch, may be a creative scientist whose brilliant excursions must be checked and elaborated by others plodding behind. On the other hand, intuition and feeling in a setting of extraversion might produce a visionary prophet, burning with zeal to lead others but distrustful of logic.

In terms of degree of dominance, an individual may be called an introvert when there are more occasions that this aspect dominates than the extravert. On some occasions the introvert will manifest the unconscious attitude, thought sporadically and without finesse, as when an "introvert" in a burst of enthusiasm over something that interests him considerably, say a coin collection, will chatter on and behave as an extravert might, but with no realization that his captive audience is bored.[47] To consider introversion–extraversion alone utilizes only a portion of Jungian theory. One must specify the presence of both one of the perceiving functions and one of the judging functions and then determine whether the perceiving or thinking function dominates the other. Only through this procedure will all the ramifications of Jungian-type theory be employed.

Each person manifests these attitudes and functions in varying degrees but tends to emphasize in one or another of the combinations an habitual attitude and particular functions. Few individuals achieve the harmonious adjustment of attitude and functions. Usually, the predominance mentioned earlier will take place rather than the ideal harmonious development.

At a given moment, although mutually exclusive aspects cannot be operative, nonhabitual, nondominant, latent functions nevertheless appear in relation to a given experience.[48] A type, in the sense just discussed, applies to the conscious psyche. A response always implies a choice, and the response not chosen remains unconscious as a potential rather than an actual way of dealing with the situation. This idea is borne out in the analysis of dreams, through which Jung was able to find evidence that a conscious type of introvert with intuition and feeling dominant will be extraverted with sensation and thinking dominant in his unconscious. The more the individual consciously develops his or her natural inclination toward one or the other attitude and function, the greater is the unconscious libidinal charge of its opposite. This contrast between the conscious and unconscious facets of an individual's personality runs as a theme through all that follows. It is Jung's conception of the complementary relationship between conscious and unconscious that must now be examined.

The Ego, Persona, and the Unconscious   The ego, at the center of consciousness, possesses a high degree of continuity and identity, having, as it does, an awareness of "I."[49] The individual often regards the ego as the center of his personality, although, as we will see, Jung held that this is not the case.

The persona, a term derived from the masks worn in ancient Greek plays, refers to a similar mask figuratively worn by the individual in society, that is, the expected social role he or she plays that covers the private personality existing behind this facade. The individual adopts to some extent the characteristics expected in his role—a businessman is energetic, an artist otherworldly, and so on. The persona is the outer layer of the personality, serving as mediator between the exterior world and the other aspects of personality, including the ego and the other, even deeper unconscious layers.

The unconscious includes both individual factors in the personal unconscious and dispositions inherited from one's ancestors in the collective unconscious.[50] The personal unconscious is derived from several sources. Forgotten experiences may become unconscious; repression occurs in our more or less deliberate withdrawal of attention, and subliminal perception occurs without the individual's awareness, leaving traces that are to be found in the unconscious. Instead of removing the child's nature, animal-like acquisitiveness, aggressiveness, and lustfulness, education pushes these tendencies back into the personal unconscious, where they live on. Even more important than any of these sources is the fact that the personal unconscious serves to reflect one-sided development, the attitudes and functions neglected in the conscious being active in this area in accordance with the principle of unconscious development of opposites.[51]

The collective unconscious, which is more or less common to all individuals, is the product of generations past, the deposit of the experiences to which our ancestors were exposed. It contains the wisdom of the ages in which a person's innate potential lies and which emerges from time to time in the form of "new" ideas and various creative expressions. Jung attached great importance to the collective unconscious; elucidation of its secrets points the way to the individual's future and relates that individual to the development of all humankind.

The collective unconscious consists of the sum of the instincts and their correlates, the archetypes.[52] These are archaic vestiges or primitive modes of functioning that carry a charge of energy and that may be manifested through their ability to organize images and ideas.[53] "Archetypes are typical modes of apprehension," says Jung, "and whenever we meet with uniform and regularly recurring modes of apprehension we are dealing with an archetype, no matter whether its mythological character is recognized or not."[54] The archetypes themselves are unconscious and should not be confused with their conscious representations in images and ideas,[55] since they are but possibilities of ideas.[56] They are the "a priori determinants" of all psychological experiences.[57] Archetypes are inherited with the structure of the brain, of which they represent the psychic, that is, nonmaterial, aspect.[58] Despite the contrary opinion sometimes expressed, it would seem that Jung was talking not about the inheritance of archetypes as acquired characters but about the inheritance of potentialities or predispositions.

These archetypes are rooted in people and predispose them to react the same way as did their ancestors to experiences common to humankind over all parts of the world, "primitive and "civilized" alike. Even more important than the sheer frequency of these everrepeated experiences is their attachment to significant, emotion-laden events—birth, death, marriage, transitional stages of life such as adolescence, and awe-inspiring experiences. An example of this last category is the course of the sun and the change from day to night, impressed on the mind of every human being from time immemorial.[59] What is found in the archetypes is not a scientific explanation but an expression in terms of a worldwide analogy. The conglomerate basic tale that Jung found is that of a god–hero born from the sea, who mounts the chariot of the sun; in the West a great mother awaits him, by whom he is devoured as evening comes; in the belly of a dragon he travels the midnight sea and after a combat slays the dragon of the night and is born again.

Though almost entirely submerged during the waking stage of normal adults, archetypal images tend to emerge in dreams, in adult fantasies, in children, in the delusions of the insane—in whom the individual ego has been overwhelmed by the collective unconscious—and in myths and fairy stories found throughout the world.

It is from these sources that Jung sought his evidence. For example, a dream image that had been reported among his patients would be isolated, and the patient would be encouraged to elaborate on it until a more complete image was formed.

Jung's general argument for the reality of the existence of archetypes rests on finding that highly complex and detailed representations of them, similar down to the smallest detail, may appear in all parts of the world and at different points in time. In addition, the fact that archetypal images are produced by patients who have no conscious knowledge of their existence or significance attests to their universality. In *Psychology and Alchemy,* for example, Jung argued that he had presented evidence demonstrating the existence of the archetypes in humans. He found his evidence in the parallels between dream symbols and the symbols of the medieval alchemist. A concrete example which Jung himself gave may help us understand this concept.[60] Around 1906 Jung observed a paranoid patient who had grandiose ideas and active hallucinations. One day Jung saw him gazing at the sun through the window, making at the same time a curious movement of his head from side to side. He told Jung he wanted to show him something—if one looks at the sun with eyes half shut one can see the sun's phallus and by moving the head from side to side one sees the sun's phallus likewise move from side to side. The patient added that this was the origin of the wind. At this time, Jung considered it a bizarre incident and nothing more. In 1910 Jung came across the so-called Paris magic-papyrus of the Mithraic cult of many, many centuries ago, which had only recently been deciphered, and he found it contained an account of a vision that the sun had a tube by the movement of which one could tell the prevailing wind. Still later, he found that in medieval art, the tube of the sun was depicted as a sort of hose pipe by which the immaculate conception reaches Mary in the form of a dove. Jung believed that these widely scattered images, separated by centuries of time and thousands of miles of space, were evidence of the working of a collective unconscious.

Jung would not accept the contention that the collective unconscious was a consequence of nothing more than diffusion, a common conception of cultural anthropology, which holds that the scattering of a myth (or any other cultural product for that matter) from a central source occurs by cultural contact with neighboring peoples. Instead, Jung insisted that myth and ritual appeared in similar form the world over because people, no matter where they happen to be, are endowed with certain innate tendencies that result in their thinking and symbolizing in the same manner. Jung attributes this similarity to the collective unconscious. Archetypal images appear in many forms—as persons, supernatural figures, geometrical shapes, numbers. Behind this diversity of form, the archetypes themselves are limited in number.[61] There is the mother archetype, embodying nourishment, and the father archetype, symbolizing strength. All preexisting mothers with their protective nourishing influences combine to form an image; fathers signify strength and authority. Jung finds the mother archetype in the Chinese yin, and the father archetype is exhibited in yang.[62] Archetypes are not always expressed as something readily recognizable as "mother," but there are many more distant associations as with "earth," the warming hearth, the protecting cave, or even the milk-giving cow. So, too, the father archetype is glimpsed in rivers, winds, storms, battles, bulls, and all things that are moving and dynamic.

In contrasting his views with those of Freud and Adler, Jung claimed that his theory was "based on the principle of opposites, and possibly pluralistic, since it recognizes a multiplicity of relatively autonomous psychic complexes."[63] A self-regulative function is expressed by these opposites; the libido flows between opposite poles as between the positive and negative poles of an electric circuit.[64]

The Total Personality   The psyche, or total personality, is constructed in terms of complementary opposites. It is already apparent that, in his system, Jung recognized several pairs of polarities or opposing forces. When libido flows into introversion, it is withdrawn from extraversion. Similarly, libido directed toward certain functions is withdrawn from the others. The same principle of complementarity holds in the relation of the conscious to the unconscious. Psychic energy is constant; only its distribution is variable.[65] Several other complementary opposites drawn from the theory of the archetypes must be indicated.

The shadow, or darker self, is unrecognized and disowned; the inferior, animal-like part of the personality is rejected by the ego, but it is, nevertheless, present and active, though unconscious. As an archetype, it is Mr. Hyde to our Dr. Jekyll, wanting to do everything that we will not permit ourselves to do. When the shadow dominates, as it sometimes does, we speak with more truth than we know in saying, "I was not myself." In archetypical collective fashion, the shadow is expressed by the image of a demon or a witch. The man without awareness of his shadow, statistically a very common occurrence, is the man who believes he is actually only what he knows about himself, and is thereby not a complete individual. He usually projects his shadow to individuals in the outside world, and this becomes evident when he reacts with inappropriate affect to someone who expresses views or values that he consciously rejects. Thus, unreasonable predilections against certain types of persons—xenophobia, racial prejudice—may be partially understood as evidence of the projected shadow. Only by recognizing that not all the evil is outside the individual himself can a person withdraw the projections and attend to that aspect of the problem that is a part of his own shadow personality.

Jung held that, at a psychological level, masculine or feminine characteristics are exhibited by the opposite sex. Under certain circumstances, homosexuality may be an extreme manifestation of this condition. The personality structure of the man contains elements of repressed femininity, whereas the woman is largely unconscious of her masculine tendencies. These contrasexual elements in the man are referred to as a feminine archetype, the anima; those in the woman are said to be a masculine archetype, the animus.[66] Characteristically, the man experiences unconscious feminine attitudes expressed through the anima, whereas the woman experiences unconscious masculine attitudes expressed through the animus. A man first makes a relationship with a woman through the projection of his anima, and a woman with a man through her animus. In both sexes, trouble is to be expected in heterosexual relationships if the archetypal image of the opposite sex is too disparate from the love object on whom it is projected. Discrepancies between real and ideal must be compromised if adequate adjustment is to take place.

The self is to be differentiated from the ego, since the ego is mostly conscious. The self is the central archetype, the archetype of order and the totality of the personality.[67] It embraces not only the conscious, but also the unconscious psyche and is therefore a personality that we also are. There is little hope of our ever being able to reach even approximate consciousness of the self, since however much we make conscious there will always exist an indeterminate and indeterminable amount of unconscious material that belongs to the totality of the self.[68]

The self as an archetype is expressed in human striving to reach psychological unity. For a healthy or integrated personality each of the elements must be permitted to reach its fullest development, and differentiation is therefore necessary. This developmental process is referred to as individuation or an urge toward self-realization.[69] It does not call for the self to take the place of the ego; if the ego becomes identified with the self it becomes inflated into a sort of pseudo-superman. If the reverse occurs, and the self becomes all important with a resultant diminution of the ego, the individual will have a very low opinion of himself, becoming depressed or even psychotic. Both ego and self must preserve their intrinsic qualities. The appropriate adjustment occurs when the self acts compensatorily to the ego-consciousness. A continuing dialogue between the two is healthy, not unhealthy, and makes for self-realization. Nevertheless, the self, the midpoint of personality, is the means whereby its various parts are unified. It acts as a balance point for stability and equilibrium.

Jung's Psychotherapy

Jung's approach to treatment emerged from his theoretical position. The purpose of psychotherapy, he said, is to help the patient become a whole person.[70] It is necessary to aid in releasing the hidden potentialities that are being stifled and to integrate them with the already more active and dominant aspects of the personality. A person's religious striving must also be recognized and made a part of the integrated harmony between various polarities and systems, separating him from his self. This last point is especially pertinent with older patients. In a complete orientation of consciousness, all the functions should cooperate with one another.[71] Instead of conflict, cooperation between the conscious and the unconscious is sought as a goal of therapy. More specifically, the conscious ego must come to terms with the unconscious components of its personality.[72] For example, there must be a realization that the shadow is present and active. In selected cases the therapist interprets the meanings of archetypes, the deep universals, to the patient. Instead of stressing the sexual etiology of the individual with the intent of uncovering the conflicts of childhood, Jung found it more useful to stress an analysis of the immediate conflicts in all their various ramifications.

Overview

In common with Freud and Adler, Jung shared an adherence to idiographicism and developmentalism and, with Freud, the depth of unconscious mentalism. Centralism and contentual subjectivism also characterized his position.

Central to Jung's view of development was his emphasis on goals that guide or direct human destiny. The individual is determined by the past under the principle of causality, and is also determined by the future (teleology).[73] A person is guided not only by individual and racial history, but by aims and aspirations as well. Jung's approach is functionally oriented toward the present and future. In this respect, he stands in contrast to the Freudians' exclusive dependence on hard determinism.

NEO-FREUDIANS

The so-called neo-Freudians differ from modern psychoanalysts in the major Freudian tradition in two ways. First, although accepting many Freudian tenets, they decisively reject other salient features of Freudian thinking. Second, they put much more emphasis on the influence of social factors on personality development.

Karen Horney (1885–1952) was most explicit on points of agreement and disagreement.[74] She accepted the doctrine of unconscious motivation, strict determinism, the pervasive influence of emotion on formation of attitudes and behavior, and the concepts of conflict and repression. On the other hand, she considered that libido theory was unsubstantiated. She held that needs grow not out of instinct but out of a child's need to cope. For Horney, the Oedipus Complex is not a biological imperative, but stems from describable conditions in the family environment. She rejected penis envy, and she saw the phenomenon subsumed under this rubric as being aroused in women by the superior status given to masculine qualities in our culture.

Another neo-Freudian, Erich Fromm (1900–1980) sees the human being as primarily a social creature whose major characteristic is precisely an independence from instincts.[75] Although influenced by Freudian thinking concerning psychosexual stages, he deals with character structure in the context of social factors.

Some psychologists have contributed to the theory of psychoanalysis and so interpret it in a fashion that would bring out its relation to the general, nonanalytic psychology. The papers of David Rapaport[76] (1911–1960) are outstanding in their effort to make psychoanalysis a complete and unified theory of individual and social behavior coextensive with psychology. Robert R. Holt and George S. Klein have worked toward the same end.[77]

Erik H. Erikson (1902–), another prominent psychologist–psychoanalyst, has attempted to integrate psychoanalysis with psychology and anthropology with special success in the field of child development. In general, however, psychology has taken from psychoanalysis the concepts that have served its purpose in specific research settings or theoretical positions and has left the overall system pretty much alone. In most respects, Freudian psychoanalysis remains apart from the main body of psychological science. Its origin in the treatment of adult neurotics, its investigatory method of free association, its insistence on the primacy of unconscious sexual factors, its development of its own terminology, and its derivation of most of its personnel from the ranks of physicians show how its separation came about and how it is maintained.

Collectively, psychoanalysts resist any move toward integration with the rest of psychology. It may be protested at this point that Rapaport, Klein, Holt, and the other psychologists whose contributions toward rapprochement we just considered surely show movement in this direction. But what about most psychoanalysts, physicians within medical settings and their affiliated training institutes and those in private practice? It is not that they oppose a rapprochement. Actually, they are indifferent and perhaps are hardly aware that an attempt is being made in this direction.

The sheer wealth of supporting data of case after case convinced Freud and his followers of the validity of their contentions. Become psychoanalysts, they say to critics, and you, too, will be convinced. In reply, the nonpsychoanalytic psychologist is apt to ask that they go beyond this piling up of positive instances and apply the method of experiment much more frequently than they did in the past. Admittedly, this task is a difficult one, but it is necessary before psychoanalysis becomes an integral part of the mainstream of psychology.

As various surveys show, there has been no lack of attempts at experimental verification of psychoanalytic propositions as well as an extensive literature examining the extent to which psychoanalysis meets the canons of the scientific method. These critics include E. R. Hilgard,[78] Robert R. Sears, and B. F. Skinner. Others, writing with more of a psychoanalytic allegiance, such as Merton Gill, Lawrence Kubie, and Heinz Hartmann,[79] have emphasized the relation of theory to method in an attempt at reconciliation. John Dollard and Neal E. Miller have made a valiant in-depth attempt to integrate Hull's learning theory and some aspects of psychoanalysis.[80]

Some psychologists contend that almost all the research studies of psychoanalysis are at fault because in most instances they do not measure what they purport to measure. Even when the results obtained support psychoanalytic contentions, it is not clear that it is any more than an analogous relationship.[81]

NEO-ADLERIANS

Alfred Adler anticipated the psychological temper of the present day in emphasizing the influence of social factors on personality and development. To be more specific, it will be remembered that Adler emphasized ego functions, denied the primacy of the sexual drive, insisted that attention be given to the individual unity of each person, wanted psychology to look at the individual from an ethical point of view, and counseled a more active role in psychotherapy. One of the more general reasons why psychologists have been responsive to Adlerian thinking is its strong functional character. In these emphases, Adler was prophetic of much current thinking, not only among Adlerians but also among neo-Freudians and many other psychologists. As time passed Freud's followers moved closer and closer to these views of Adler, without surrendering their more specifically Freudian tenets.

Although her evaluation may be more than usually colored by personal feelings, Alexandra, Adler's daughter, claims that the theory of individual psychotherapy has changed relatively little.[82] She therefore looks to and writes about applications in psychotherapy, such as its use in conjunction with drugs.

For all these reasons, present-day psychologists have become more interested in Adlerian formulations since his death. Several formally organized groups can be found, particularly in New York, Chicago, and Los Angeles.

Although systematic, controlled research is not entirely absent, particularly on various facets of the psychological influence of sibling position, without question a greater research orientation, other than clinical, is still very much needed. In general, however, the overall estimation of psychoanalysis has decreased, owing largely to the lack of experimental verification of theoretical positions.

NEO-JUNGIANS

The number of individuals interested in analytical psychology has increased considerably since Jung's death in 1961. Jung's books are popular, and commentary in magazines and newspapers keeps his name before the public. There are three formal institutes devoted to Jung's teachings—in Zurich, London, and New York—but many smaller institutes can be found in major cities throughout America. In 1955 the first Jungian journal was founded in London, the *Journal of Analytic Psychology.* In 1958 the first international congress was held in Zurich. Jung has had great influence on scholars in diversified fields. Individuals as varied as theologian Paul Tillich, historian Arnold Toynbee, novelist Philop Wylie, critic Lewis Mumford, and anthropologist Paul Radin acknowledge their intellectual debt to Jung and his views.

Yet, the reaction from academic psychology has been largely one of silence. Relevant articles, even in criticism, are almost nonexistent. Only one eminent psychologist, Henry A. Murray, has acknowledged a debt to Jung, but he takes pains to point out that he is not a Jungian. How can we account for this lack of identification? Aside from research of Jung's earlier and admittedly less theoretically important work in word association and introversion–extraversion, almost no research has been conducted in the major psychological tradition. Some Jungians' conceptions have been adapted to others' frameworks, such as complex and introversion–extraversion, but they are out of their Jungian context. Essentially, the validity that Jung sought and that the neo-Jungians continue to seek is one of mutual corroboration among psychology, archaeological, anthropological, and mythological material. Instances of cross-comparison are sought and woven into an intricate tapestry. Hardly any way for research, as most psychologists understand the term, has yet been found. Until this can be accomplished, Jungian thinking will stand apart. In recent years, however, a few chairs in analytical psychology in psychological departments have been created. Only the future will elucidate the relationship between Jungian psychology and mainstream psychological thought.

NOTES

1. P. Bottome, *Alfred Adler, A Biography* (New York: G. P. Putnam's Sons, 1939).
2. H. L. Ansbacher and R. R. Ansbacher, eds., *Superiority and Social Interest: A Collection of Later Writings by Alfred Adler* (Evanston, Ill.: Northwestern University Press, 1964) (1928–1937). Editorial introduction.
3. C. Furtmüller, in Ansbacher and Ansbacher, eds., *Superiority and Social Interest;* A. H. Maslow, "Was Adler a Disciple of Freud? (A Note)," *Journal of Individual Psychology, 18* (1962):125; H. L. Ansbacher, "Was Adler a Disciple of Freud? (A Reply)," *Journal of Individual Psychology, 18* (1962):126–135; E. Federn, "Was Adler a Disciple of Freud? (A Freudian View)," *Journal of Individual Psychology, 19* (1963):80–82.
4. H. L. Ansbacher and R. R. Ansbacher, eds., *The Individual Psychology of Alfred Adler: A Systematic Presentation in Selections from His Writings* (New York: Basic Books, 1965), pp. 23–35 (1907–1937).
5. *Ibid.,* pp. 45–52 (1910).
6. R. Dreikurs, *Fundamentals of Adlerian Psychology* (Philadelphia: Chilton Book Co., 1950).
7. A. Adler, "Die sexuelle problem in der Erziehung," *Die neue Gesellschaft, 1* (1905):360–362.
8. K. M. Colby, "On the Disagreement between Freud and Adler," *American Imago, 2* (1951):229–238.
9. Dreikurs, *Fundamentals of Adlerian Psychology.*
10. H. Vaihinger, *The Psychology of "As If"* (New York: Harcourt, Brace, 1925) (1911). (Sections excerpted in Ansbacher and Ansbacher, *Individual Psychology,* pp. 77–87.)
11. A. Adler, *The Neurotic Constitution* (New York: Moffat–Yard, 1917).
12. H. L. Ansbacher and R. R. Ansbacher, *Individual Psychology.*
13. A. Adler, *The Neurotic Constitution.*
14. H. L. Ansbacher and R. R. Ansbacher, *Individual Psychology;* Ansbacher and Ansbacher, *Superiority and Social Interest.*
15. A. Adler, *What Life Should Mean to You* (New York: Blue Ribbon Books, 1937); H. L. Ansbacher, "The Structure of Individual Psychology," in B. B. Wolman and E. Nagel, eds., *Scientific Psychology: Principles and Approaches* (New York: Basic Books, 1965), pp. 340–364.
16. *Ibid.*
17. A. Adler, *The Science of Living,* H. L. Ansbacher, ed. (Garden City, N.Y.: Doubleday and Co., 1969); H. L. Ansbacher, "Life Style: A Historical and Systematic Review," *Journal of Individual Psychology, 23* (1967):191–212.
18. A. Adler, *What Life Should Mean to You.*
19. H. Orgler, *Alfred Adler: The Man and His Work: Triumph over the Inferiority Complex* (London: Daniel, 1939).
20. H. L. Ansbacher and R. R. Ansbacher, *Individual Psychology.*
21. A. Adler, "Individual Psychology," in C. Murchison, ed., *Psychologies of 1930,* pp. 395–405.
22. J. Jacobi, *The Psychology of C. G. Jung,* rev. ed. (New Haven, Conn.: Yale University

Press, 1951); F. Fordham, *An Introduction to Jung's Psychology* (London: Penguin Books, 1953).

23. C. G. Jung, *Memories, Dreams, Reflections* (New York: Pantheon Books, 1961), p. 84.
24. C. G. Jung, "On the Psychology and Pathology of So-Called Occult Phenomena," *Psychiatric Studies* (New York: Pantheon Books, 1957).
25. Fordham, *An Introduction to Jung's Psychology.*
26. R. A. Clark, "Jung and Freud: A Chapter in Psychoanalytic History," *American Journal of Psychotherapy, 9* (1955):605–611.
27. C. G. Jung, *Studies in Word Association* (New York: Moffat–Yard, 1919).
28. C. G. Jung, "Psychological Factors in Human Behavior," *The Structure and Dynamics of Psyche* (New York: Pantheon Books, 1960), p. 121.
29. C. G. Jung, *The Psychology of Dementia Praecox,* trans. A. A. Bill (New York: Mental and Nervous Disease Publishing, 1908).
30. C. G. Jung, "The Psychology of the Unconscious," *Two Essays on Analytical Psychology* (New York: Pantheon Books, 1953).
31. C. G. Jung, "The Theory of Psychoanalysis," *Freud and Psychoanalysis* (New York: Pantheon Books, 1961).
32. C. G. Jung, "The Concept of Libido," *Symbols of Transformation* (New York: Pantheon Books, 1956), p. 137.
33. C. G. Jung, *Memories, Dreams, Reflections,* p. 168.
34. C. G. Jung, "The Theory of Psychoanalysis."
35. C. G. Jung, "Psychological Types," *Contributions to Analytical Psychology* (London: Kegan Paul, 1928).
36. *Ibid.*
37. *Ibid.*
38. *Ibid.*
39. R. A. Clark, "Jung and Freud."
40. C. G. Jung, *Psychology and Alchemy* (New York: Pantheon Books, 1953).
41. *Ibid.,* p. 23.
42. C. G. Jung, *The Undiscovered Self* (Boston: Little, Brown, 1957).
43. J. Jacobi, *The Psychology of C. G. Jung,* foreword.
44. C. G. Jung, "Psychological Types."
45. *Ibid.,* p. 303.
46. H. Gray and J. B. Wheelwright, "Jung's Psychological Types, Including the Four Functions," *Journal of General Psychology, 33* (1945):265–284.
47. F. Fordham, *An Introduction to Jung's Psychology.*
48. H. Gray and J. B. Wheelwright, "Jung's Psychological Types."
49. Jung, "Psychological Types."
50. C. G. Jung, "The Conscious Mind, the Unconscious and the Individuation," *Archetypes and the Collective Unconscious* (New York: Pantheon Books, 1959), Pt. 1.
51. Blum, *Psychoanalytic Theories of Personality.*
52. C. G. Jung, "Instinct and the Unconscious," *The Structure and Dynamics of the Psyche* (New York: Pantheon Books, 1960), p. 138.
53. C. G. Jung, "On the Nature of the Psyche."
54. *Ibid.;* Jung, "Instinct and the Unconscious," pp. 137–138.
55. *Ibid.*
56. C. G. Jung, "Mind and the Earth," *Contributions to Analytical Psychology* (London: Kegan Paul, 1928), p. 110.
57. C. G. Jung, "Instinct and the Unconscious," p. 133.
58. C. G. Jung, "Psychological Types."
59. C. G. Jung, "Mind and the Earth."

60. *Ibid.*
61. C. G. Jung, "Instinct and the Unconscious."
62. C. G. Jung, "Mind and the Earth."
63. C. G. Jung, "Introduction to Kranefeldt's Secret Ways of the Mind," *Freud and Psycho-analysis* (New York: Pantheon Books, 1961), p. 329.
64. C. G. Jung, "The Psychology of the Unconscious."
65. C. G. Jung, *Modern Man in Search of a Soul* (New York: Harcourt, Brace, 1933).
66. C. G. Jung, "Mind and the Earth."
67. C. G. Jung, *Memories, Dreams, Reflections,* p. 386.
68. C. G. Jung, "The Relations Between the Ego and the Unconscious," *Two Essays on Analytical Psychology,* p. 175.
69. C. G. Jung, "On the Nature of the Psyche."
70. C. G. Jung, *Psychology and Alchemy.*
71. C. G. Jung, *Contributions to Analytical Psychology.*
72. C. G. Jung, "On the Nature of the Psyche."
73. C. G. Jung, *Analytical Psychology* (New York: Moffat–Yard, 1916).
74. Karen Horney, *New Ways in Psychoanalysis* (New York: W. W. Norton, 1939); Horney, *The Neurotic Personality of Our Time* (New York: W. W. Norton, 1937).
75. Erich Fromm, *Man for Himself, An Inquiry into the Psychology of Ethics* (New York: Rinehart and Co., 1947); Fromm, *The Sane Society* (New York: Rinehart and Co., 1955); R. I. Evans, *Dialogue with Erich Fromm* (New York: Harper and Row, 1966).
76. M. M. Gill, ed., *The Collected Papers of David Rapaport* (New York: Basic Books, 1967); David Rapaport, "The Structure of Psychoanalytic Theory: A Systematizing Attempt," in Sigmund Koch, ed., *Psychology: A Study of a Science,* (New York: McGraw-Hill, 1959) Vol. III, pp. 55–183.
77. R. R. Holt, "Ego Autonomy Re-evaluated," *International Journal of Psychoanalysis, 46* (1965):151–167; G. S. Klein, "Consciousness in Psychoanalytic Theory: Some Implications for Current Research in Perception," *Journal of American Psychoanalytic Association, 8* (1959):5–34.
78. E. R. Hilgard, "Impulsive Versus Realistic Thinking: An Examination of the Distinction Between Primary and Secondary Processes in Thought," *Psychological Bulletin, 59* (1962):477–488; R. R. Sears, "Survey of Objective Studies of Psychoanalytic Concepts," *Social Science Research Council Bulletin, 51* (1943); B. F. Skinner, "Critique of Psychoanalytic Concepts and Theories," *Scientific Monthly, 79* (1954):302–307.
79. M. M. Gill, "The Present State of Psychoanalytic Theory," *Journal of Abnormal Social Psychology, 58* (1959):1–8; L. S. Kubie, "Psychoanalysis and Scientific Method," *Journal of Nervous and Mental Disorders, 131* (1960):495–512; H. Hartmann, "Psychoanalysis as a Scientific Theory," in S. Hook, ed., *Psychoanalysis, Scientific Method and Philosophy* (New York: Grove, 1959), pp. 3–37.
80. J. Dollard and N. E. Miller, *Personality and Psychotherapy* (New York: McGraw–Hill, 1950).
81. There is no dearth of critical analyses of Freudian psychoanalysis. See R. L. Munroe, *Schools of Psychoanalytic Thought: An Exposition, Critique and Attempt at Integration* (New York: Dryden Press, 1955); G. S. Blum, *Psychoanalytic Theories of Personality* (New York: McGraw–Hill, 1953); Seymore Fisher and Roger Greenberg, *The Scientific Credibility of Freud's Theory and Therapy,* 2nd ed. (New York: Columbia University Press, 1985; B. A. Farrell, *The Standing of Psychoanalysis* (Oxford: Oxford University Press, 1981; Paul Kline, *Fact and Fantasy in Freudian Therapy,* 2nd ed. (London: Methuen, 1981), just to name a few.
82. Alexandria Adler, "Adlerian Psychotherapy and Recent Trends," *Journal of Individual Psychology, 19* (1963):55–60.

Wilhelm Dilthey.

Chapter 26

European Psychologies of the Twentieth Century

With the exception of the major mainstream psychological schools, we have not discussed other movements in twentieth-century European psychology. Although two world wars would take their toll of continental psychology, events important to the history of psychology were taking place. Despite hopes that psychology would become a science with a universally agreed-on content, national differences are still so important that it is necessary to order discussion to national-linguistic boundaries. Therefore, this chapter examines German, French, Russian, and British psychology of the recent past, and the next chapter discusses recent events in the United States. This division still neglects other important developments in many other nations around the world, but space limitations forbid more detailed treatment.[1]

GERMAN PSYCHOLOGY

To examine one potent intellectual force in post-Wundtian German psychology,[2] it is necessary to return to a contemporary of Wundt, Wilhelm Dilthey (1833–1911).[3]

Dilthey and Psychology as a Cultural Science

Although he was an important and popular Professor of Philosophy at the University of Berlin, Dilthey's posthumous influence was even greater. In considerable measure this was because his views were in accord with the pervasive background of German Romanticism, widespread in Germany but with relatively little influence beyond. His views gained momentum during the rise of experimental psychology in Germany but commanded a dominant position in Germany after Wundt's death.

Dilthey drew on the philosopher Wilhelm Windelband's (1849–1915) distinction between the natural sciences *(Naturwissenschaften)* and cultural sciences *(Geisteswissenschaften).* This distinction led to a spirited and widespread conflict over whether to conceive of psychology as an empirical, natural science or as a cultural science.[4] Dilthey argued that empirical psychology was inadequate in its study of the elements of consciousness. Instead, the total structure of the mind must be understood. Dilthey and his supporters referred to this "structure" in a new sense that was diametrically opposed to the structure of Wundt and Titchener. The search for elements, in Dilthey's view, is a pseudostudy in an attempt to develop a natural science and should be replaced. As he put it, the proper task is not the study of the bricks and mortar but of the overall architecture of the completed structure which shows how it relates to the parts. Disclosure of development in order to understand the dynamics of the mind is yet another task. Dilthey thus opposed considering psychology as a natural science. He held that the natural sciences explain and that psychology has no need for explanations, since the mind acts as a unit. What is needed is not to explain details but to understand the mind as a whole. Nevertheless, there is a cultural science of psychology. This psychology, *Verstehende-psychologie* in his terminology, is a descriptive or understanding endeavor, not an explanatory science.[5]

Dilthey's early attacks on psychology were met by spirited rebuttals, such as that of his former pupil, Hermann Ebbinghaus, who argued that Dilthey's views were directed against antiquated representatives of empirical molecular psychology, such as Herbart, rather than the contemporary views of psychology.[6] By and large, however, experimental psychologists at the turn of the century, and for perhaps two decades thereafter, merely shrugged their shoulders and went on with their work.

Only in later years did Dilthey's views become a threat to experimental psychology. Philosophers more and more were influenced by Dilthey's antagonism to experimental psychology. Psychology, academically speaking, was still in the philosophical faculty, which was usually within the division of the humanities. Decisions about new appointments and the direction psychology was to take therefore rested with those who were suspicious of experimental methods.[7] A decline in the power and prestige of psychology as a natural science became evident. Wundt's explanatory psychology, indeed any scientific psychology, began to lose ground in Germany, and with this decline there was an increase in the influence of a psychology in agreement with Dilthey's position.

Leipzig After Wundt

It is now fitting to return in time to Leipzig after Wundt's retirement. In 1917 Felix E. Krueger (1874–1948) succeeded Wundt to the chair of the Psychological Institute at Leipzig. Disregarding certain nuances of difference, he established what has been called *Ganzheitspsychologie,* totality psychology, holistic psychology, as well as the Leipzig Gestalt School.[8] German psychologists had always referred to Gestalt psychology in terms of its original university setting. Thus, the work of Wertheimer, Koffka, and Köhler became known as the Berlin Gestalt School. The Leipzig Gestalt School accepted the integrated whole or Gestalt concept, but it owed perhaps as much or more to the oldest of Gestalt schools, that at Graz where Christian von Ehrenfels had done his work on *Gestaltqualität* before that of Wertheimer. They were also influenced by Dilthey's concepts of totality and structure. Krueger and his associates at Leipzig accused the Berlin School of limiting itself to cognitive processes and consequently of neglecting the all-embracing totality of the life of feeling. Moreover, Krueger's school placed considerably more emphasis than the Berlin School on understanding the psychological phenomena of the mind in the light of its development, and insisted that the scope of psychology be broadened to include social and cultural factors.[9]

Although Dilthey had denied that experimental psychology would be a natural science, as indicated before he did accept the notion that psychology of personality could be classificatory and descriptive provided it was molar in nature. He sketched rationalistically derived insights from this view in terms of broad areas of human activity.

Eduard Spranger (1882–1963), a student of Dilthey and a philosopher at the University of Berlin, adopted this point of view. Spranger first published in 1913 on personality types expressed in attitudes or values.[10] He differentiated types of men according to the attitude that predominated in the individual. These attitudes, which are expressed as aims, are the economic, the theoretical, the aesthetic, the religious, the social, and the political. The economic man aims at the political and utilitarian; the theoretical man aims at cognition; the aesthetic man, the artistic values of life; the religious man, the spiritual values of life; the social man, the rights of other individuals; and the political man, power. These are ideal types and do not occur in pure form. Instead, there is a mixture with varying degrees of strength in the individual. Whereas Spranger was content to present his theory in a rationalistic, impressionalistic, insightful fashion, Gordon Allport in the United States saw it as the starting point for empirical investigation and developed a test of values.[11]

The schools at Berlin and Leipzig would dominate German psychology until the collapse of German academic psychology during the Second World War.

World War II and German Psychology

The influence of World War II on psychology cannot be confined to the dates between the declaration of war and the signing of a cease-fire agreement. It extended through most of the 1930s, beginning with Adolf Hitler's rise to power, encompassing the 1938–1945 war years, and the effects of the decimation of Germany during the war, which lasted throughout the 1940s. Metzger estimates that Germany lost 40 percent of its psychologists as a result of the Nazi rise to power.[12] Jewish psychologists were forced to retire or to leave their positions. Those who could leave Germany did so. Other, non-Jewish psychologists who opposed the Nazis were either forced out or left on their own, seeing that academic psychology was coming to an end in Germany.

The scholarly journals ceased publication. A bibliography of German literature prepared after the war by Albert Wellek tells the story.[13] By 1943–1944, except for Swiss publications in German, there were no psychological articles, and the handful of books published were propaganda glorifying the ideal type, the Nazi. It took years for the flow of publications to resume.

Only in recent years has German academic psychology recovered from the circumstances prevailing before and during the war.[14] The number of professional chairs is still small. This is not to say that psychology did not exist during the Nazi era. In fact, aspects of German psychology, particularly those devoted to industrial psychology and other applied disciplines, have been said to have flourished during the Nazi era.[15] The "schools," organized systems of psychology, and academic, theoretical psychology were largely lost to Germany during that era.

Postwar Psychology

With the division of Germany after the war into the Federal Republic of Germany on the west and the German Democratic Republic on the east, the two Germanies developed differently. Many German psychologists who left Germany before and during the Nazi era returned, largely to the Federal Republic. Having spent years in America, they came back with more behaviorally oriented psychological positions than had existed before the war. On the other hand, psychology in the German Democratic Republic has seen the heavy influence of Soviet psychology.[16]

In more recent times, German psychology has begun to reestablish its own national flavor. Ludwig J. Pongratz describes these years as "a period marked by a decline of the uncritical dependence on psychologies abroad, by a flourishing of home-grown ideas."[17] The study of cognition and clinical and social psychology has dominated the psychology of the Germanies.[18]

After the war, younger representatives of the Leipzig Gestalt School, such as Albert Wellek,[19] continued that tradition. While upholding the school's emphasis on totality, Wellek emphasized its relation to stratification theory just discussed. In so doing he stressed the breadth of the humanistic emphasis, and he considered that, although experimentation has a place, it is a relatively limited one.

In the more rigorous Berlin Gestalt tradition, the senior representative for three decades or more had been Wolfgang Metzger (1899–1973) of Münster. His 1968 statement of the current status of Gestalt psychology was a highly systematic, orthodox treatise on the subject.[20] His own research is best represented by his volume on visual perception.[21]

The stress on learning problems, so obvious in the United States, has not developed equivalently in Germany.[22] On the other hand, in contrast to the United States, the Germans have shown considerably more research interest in problems of the will, aesthetics, graphology, and expressive movements in general. Some research in perceptual problems is carried on, especially that cast in the phenomenological mold.

In the last few years a spirit of greater empiricism, accompanied by the continuing strong influence of philosophy, has been developing in German psychology. This spirit is vividly expressed in the twelve-volume summary of psychology, *Handbuch der Psychologie,* which was originally under the editorial auspices of Philipp Lersch of Munich and Friedrich Sander and Hans Thomae of Bonn,[23] but now also involves a large and representative sample of German psychologists.

FRENCH PSYCHOLOGY

The University of Paris, intricately affiliated with the Sorbonne, the Collège de France, and the École pratique des hautes études, dominated psychology in France to an extent almost inconceivable in the United States, which has perhaps ten universities of at least roughly the same degree of excellence.[24] In relatively recent years the University of Paris has been renamed Université de René Descartes.

Henri Piéron

Henri Piéron (1881–1964) was the dominant figure in French psychology for over fifty years—from 1911, when he succeeded Binet as head of the Sorbonne psychology laboratory and assumed editorship of *L'Année Psychologue,* until his death in 1964. Pieron had been trained in philosophy and physiology but believed he was influenced primarily by physiology.[25]

As mentioned briefly in the chapter on behaviorism, Piéron had insisted that behavior or conduct was the only proper subject of psychological investigation some years before John B. Watson's pronouncements on the matter. Piéron emphasized the physiological substratum. This did not mean he would have abandoned psychology and become a physiologist. Both the total reaction (psychology) and the partial reactions (physiology) of the organism are essential. His books exercised considerable influence. One, on the senses, with emphasis on sense physiology, is a standard reference.[26] Piéron's interest and contributions extended over all of French psychology. He was active in fostering psychotechnology[27] which embraced the industrial and school psychology of personnel selection and vocation guidance, in animal psychology,[28] including work with insects, and in psychophysics.[29]

French Compendia

Georges Dumas (1866–1946) was the editorial catalyst who twice integrated the state of French psychological science into multiple-volumed series, first in the 1923–1924 *Traité de psychologie*[30] and again in the 1930–1941 *Noveau traité de psychologie.*[31] Some research and theories originating in other than French-speaking locales were included, but only a miniscule percentage of them. Another French series, edited by Paul Fraisse and Jean Piaget,[32] began to appear in 1963, and, like the American and German series, aimed to summarize and evaluate research and theory. Some of the volumes have been translated into English.

Michotte and French-Speaking Belgian Psychology

In certain respects, Albert Michotte (1881–1965), who taught at Louvain from 1905 to 1956, was to Belgian psychology what Piéron was to the French.[33] Of almost identical life spans, both published over a sixty-year period and both they and their universities dominated psychology in their respective countries. They parted company, however, in their research interests and their attitudes toward psychological problems.

Michotte had worked a half year under Wundt at Leipzig and another half year with Külpe at Würzburg, while teaching experimental psychology at Louvain the other half years. His Würzburg background led to his occupation, before World War I, in problems of volition, using Külpe's approach of systematic experimental introspection. However, the evidence which Wundt, Titchener, and others amassed during this period on the inadequacy of the method led him to abandon his approach. After the war, he turned to problems of perception of movement and rhythm, with introspective reports being limited to the presence or absence of the phenomena in question.

Michotte's studies on the perception of causality, spurred by his interest in Gestalt principles, attracted greatest international interest. Michotte took up the Humean problem of the conditions that prompt us to believe a sequence of events is causally connected. The action used was simple but effective—one thing seems to hit another and thereby "cause" it to move. A rotating disk behind a slit, with appropriately painted stripes, allowed systematic variation of time, position, and velocity. Phenomenological overtones are apparent in this conception that his work showed the fundamental structures of the phenomenal world being linked with identifiable conditions of stimulation. He contended that "causality," "reality," and "permanence" (i.e., of the world) are at least preshadowed at the level of perception. These studies culminated in a book first published in French in 1946 and translated into English as *The Perception of Causality.* [34]

Piaget and French-Speaking Swiss Psychology

Swiss-French psychology was initiated by Théodore Flournoy (1854–1920), who studied with Wundt.[35] In 1893 he opened a laboratory at Geneva, the first to be attached to a Faculty of Science. One of his students was his cousin, Edouard Claparède (1873–1940),[36] and together, in 1901, they founded the *Archives de Psychologie.* Claparède established the Jean Jacques Rousseau Institute for the study of the school child in 1912 and a little later was given a professorship at Geneva. The Rousseau Institute is best known for its association with Jean Piaget, however.

The greatest of all Swiss psychologists, Jean Piaget (1896–1980), became interested in natural history while still very young. (His first paper was published in a local scientific journal when he was ten years of age.)[37] Before he was twenty-three, he had worked with mollusks and their classification, maintained copious notebooks, studied philosophy and science, had a religious crisis, published a novel, and obtained a doctorate in science. In 1918 he went to Germany to study psychology and psychiatry. Afterward he studied at the Sorbonne, where he became acquainted with Simon, Binet's collaborator in the intelligence test that bears their names. He worked in Simon's laboratory school, ostensibly on the standardization of Cyril Burt's tests for reasoning, but he was actually exploring the reasons for each particular child's failures by exposing them to verbal tasks involving concrete relations of cause and effect. Submission of a psychological article (his third) to Claparède for publication in the *Archives* resulted in a call to be the Director of Studies at the Institute Jean Jacques Rousseau. So in 1921 he moved to Geneva, where he became Professor of Psychology, Director of the Psychological Section of the Institute of Education, Director of the Center for Genetic Epistemology, and editor of the *Archives de Psychologie.*

Piaget is the author of perhaps sixty books and a proportionate number of monographs and articles, an enormous productivity that is difficult to summarize in a short space.

The first of two broad phases of his work centered on the development of the cognitive abilities of the child.[38] Piaget followed the conversational method first used in Simon's school, proceeding in a clinical-genetic fashion that would liberate the child's thinking to enable him to show not just what he does, but what he would do if given the opportunity. The mass of information Piaget has revealed about cognitive development—how the child forms concepts of space, time, number, reasoning, and causality—is extremely revealing. His blithe, seemingly unpremeditated, excursions into the child's intellectual development do show an overall plan to study the stages by which a particular form of cognitive process is individuated from experience, how it changes with further experience and yet is still related to previous stages.

Piaget's studies of child psychology, especially the earlier works, were considered quantitatively unsound and based on far too few subjects by American standards. Many of his pronouncements on child experience and behavior served as a challenge for more careful research by others. His statements were often found to be, not so much wrong, as much too sharply demarcated as to the age ranges involved.

In his later years, Piaget devoted attention to a second major phase: work in so-called genetic epistemology,[39] which is an attempt to integrate psychology and epistemological philosophy, with the central theme being the study of the way in which the individual constructs his knowledge during his development. Related problems of the philolsophy of science, such as application of the techniques of symbolic logic to thought structures, have also received his attention.[40]

When Piéron died in 1964, he was succeeded at the Sorbonne and as editor of *L' Année Psychologue* by Paul Fraisse whose research centered on experimental psychology of the perception of time and rhythm.[41] Another successor to Piéron was Alfred Fessard, Professor and Director of the Laboratory of General Neurophysiology of the College of France and (loosely translated) co-editor of *L' Année Psychologue.* In the tradition of Piéron, Fessard continued work on the neuropsychological bases of memory and learning, centering on brain potentials.[42]

RUSSIAN AND SOVIET PSYCHOLOGY

Russian psychology[43] also had its Wundtian—G. I. Chelpanov[44] (1862–1936), who had received his training at Leipzig. He served as Director of the Psychological Institute of Moscow, which was founded in 1911, and he founded the first Russian psychological journal. The Wundtian tradition was considered idealistic and hence anathema to the victors of the 1917 Revolution, to which Chelpanov made adjustment in various Marxian-oriented publications in the 1920s.

An assistant to Chelpanov, Konstantin N. Kornilov (1879–1957) remained at Moscow University, weathering several changes in the ideological climate. In the 1920s, he developed a psychology in line with dialectical materialism, which he called reactology.[45] Following Marx, he said that social existence determines consciousness. Psychic life cannot be reduced to simple mechanistic motion. Hence, reactology was not confined to mere behavior but centered on the subjective content of reactions. This view, dominant for a time, had a rapid demise. In the early 1930s, the Communist cell of Moscow University reached the conclusion that reactology was too passive for the activism of Lenin, Marx, and Engels. Although reactology disappeared with hardly a trace, Kornilov did not. He returned to educational psychology, moving to the Institute of Pedagogy. As early as 1927, he published a textbook based on dialectic materialism, compiled over the years in collaboration with others, and he wrote a series of textbooks and continued as a senior Soviet psychologist until his death in 1957.[46]

Research on conflict or disorganization of human behavior was carried out during the 1920s by A. R. Luria, who used hand movements and associative responses into which conflict situations were interjected. Under hypnosis, for example, a subject would be instructed to think of some "indecent" word as the response. The book containing the results of this research was translated into English in the early 1930s and established its author as the senior Soviet psychologist in American eyes.[47]

Another psychologist who became rather well known at the same time was L. S. Vygotsky (1896–1934), who published an article about his test of concept formation in the United States in 1934, the year of his death.[48] His more general and theoretical statement concerning the relation of thought and speech to intellectual development was published posthumously. Many years later it was translated into English.[49] This general line of research was used particularly with the genesis of thought and speech in children. Psychological development is social in nature, and language development is crucial to it. Practical application in education with the handicapped eventuated.

During this period the Pavlovian tradition as a field of physiology was still very active, expressed, for example, in the work of Konstantin M. Bykov (1886–1959).[50] Psychologists, however, were not involved in this research because it was still considered the province of physiologists.

In the 1930s, political pressures were very strong. Luria, for example, criticized Western or bourgeois psychology as primitively biological or idealist.[51] In 1936 a decree of the Central Committee condemned mental testing, which then largely disappeared. In the early 1940s military efforts were paramount.[52]

As a discipline, psychology was officially called to task in 1950 for not paying sufficient attention to Pavlov's work.[53] Previously, Pavlov's work had been considered to lie in the area of the physiology of higher nervous activity. Research was carried out in biology faculties and very definitely was outside psychology. An adjustment in the thinking of psychologists occurred so rapidly that within two years Soviet psychologists held a Pavlovian session of their own. Theoretical control, which was so strong in the 1950s and 1960s, did not materially interfere with the empirical advances in Soviet psychology.[54] In fact, it is a mistake to consider Soviet psychology nothing more than Pavlovian. Based on the number of papers delivered at the National Congress between 1959 and 1963, psychological research more than doubled in that period.[55] The 1963 papers were almost equally divided between "applied educational research" and "basic research." In turn, the basic research could be subdivided into three approximately equally important areas: engineering and information theory, traditional experimental, and comparative psychology.

In recent years, we have not lacked English translations. The *Annual Review of Psychology* publishes periodic assessments.

The cognitive processes expressed in developmental terms, language usage, the thought processes, and information processing were the concerns of Alexi N. Leontiev,[56] his country's spokesman at international congresses, professor and head of the department of Moscow University, and recipient of the Lenin Prize for Science.

Outside of the Soviet Union the mistaken impression has arisen that Soviet psychology is still dominated by Pavlovian thinking. In spite of frequent introductory remarks praising Pavlov in practically any kind of psychological publication, the reported research content ranges over almost as wide an area as in contemporary publications in the United States, despite differences in emphases.

In many respects a "new" Soviet psychology can be dated from 1971 when the USSR Academy of Sciences announced its plan to establish a new Research Institute of Psychology.[57] The central task of the new institute was to emphasize research on basic research in general experimental psychology, relating neurophysiological bases of mental functions, and to provide theoretical foundations for applied psychology, particularly industrial and engineering psychology. Interest in social psychology has also been rising among Soviet psychologists.[58]

BRITISH PSYCHOLOGY

As we have seen earlier, experimental psychology was slow to become established in British universities. During the early decades of this century, laboratories were just beginning to be founded; chairs (i.e., professorships) in psychology, so important as sources of academic power, were yet to be established.[59] The first of these was the chair founded at Manchester in 1919 and held by Tom H. Pear. Charles Spearman held the Grote Chair of Mind and Logic at University College, London, until 1928; Cambridge had its first chair in 1931, but Oxford was not to establish one until 1946. The first occupant of this chair was George Humphrey[60] (1889–1966), an Oxford man and a Canadian, who had taught in both his native country and the United States.

The British Psychological Society, founded in 1901, still had fewer than 100 members in 1918 (although this was due in part to restrictive requirements for membership).[61] At the outbreak of World War II, the total lecturing staff in psychology at British universities numbered only about thirty.[62] As a consequence, work by physiologists and statisticians loomed large in these years. Names such as Hughlings Jackson, Charles Sherrington, Henry Head, and Charles E. Spearman come to mind as representative of the period, and of these only Spearman was a psychologist. This is reflected in the account to follow.

British Physiological Psychology

Charles Sherrington   The long life of Sir Charles Sherrington[63] (1857–1952), Nobel prize laureate in physiology, covered much of the period that saw the emergence of modern psychology. First at Liverpool (1895–1913) and then at Oxford (1913–1935), he not only carried on distinguished work in neurophysiology, but he also lent his prestige and facilities to the developing field of psychology. He did much to establish the bases of our knowledge of neural functioning. His major work, *The Integrative Action of the Nervous System,*[64] first appeared in 1906 and was reprinted in 1947. In this work, the reflex was examined, not as it functions in isolation, but as the unit of functional integration in which it came under control of high levels of neural action. His task was to work out the mechanisms involved in this integration. The discovery of reciprocal innervation led him to work out many of the details of excitation and inhibition, particularly showing that inhibition, too, is an activity. In his Liverpool laboratory, psychologists served as researchers and lecturers, as did Robert S. Woodworth and Cyril Burt.

Henry Head   Henry Head (1861–1940), a disciple of Hughlings Jackson and Sherrington's friend and contemporary, did for sensation what Sherrington had done for reflex action. He also worked directly with psychologists—not only with W.H.R. Rivers, mentioned shortly, but years later with F. C. Bartlett. In 1905 and 1908 Head,[65] with W.H.R. Rivers (1864–1922), ethnologist and early teacher of experimental psychology at Cambridge, published research on the cutaneous sensitivity of injured nerves and found that a dissolution, in Jackson's meaning of the term, occurred. Head did this by cutting nerves in his arm and studying the loss and then return of sensibility. On the basis of these and other observations, he postulated three levels of sensibility—"deep" sensibility, responsive to extremes of heat, cold, and pain; "protopathic" sensibility, widely dispersed and only coarsely discriminating; and "epicritic"[66] sensibility, accurate and discriminating for all forms of cutaneous stimulation.

Head's other major line of research concerned speech disorders and culminated in *Aphasia and Kindred Disorders of Speech*,[67] which appeared in 1926. One facet of the work was his concept of vigilance, which accounted for the level of efficient alertness that keeps automatic actions under control.[68] Lowered vigilance occurs when neural disorders or debilitating disease cause loss of this controlling function. For example, a sick child loses vigilance when he wets the bed, which was previously prevented because of control by a spinal reflex. Head did not develop this concept in any detail, but he did stimulate considerable research by others later.

Edgar D. Adrian   The tradition of physiological work intertwined with psychological aspects did not cease with the passing of Sherrington and Head. It was continued by Edgar D. Adrian (1889–1977), who worked on the refractory period of the nerve fiber and, more generally, as the title of one of his major works indicates, *The Mechanism of Nervous Action*.[69] Lord Adrian took advantage of the availability of vacuum tubes to amplify the small electrical charges that corresponded to individual nerve impulse passage. It led to his conclusion that no radical differences exist in the nature of the nerve impulses in either different kinds of sense organs or different parts of the brain.

Quantitative Psychology

British psychologists have made a major contribution in the area of quantitative psychology, particularly centered on the question of human intelligence.

Fisher and Statistical Methods   R. A. Fisher (1890–1962), a Cambridge mathematician, did his major research through an agricultural research station. He was sharply critical of the work of Karl Pearson and the psychologists who used his statistical procedures, since they were based on an assumption of infinitely large samples. In research in the field, he argued, small samples are the rule. He proceeded to supply means of calculating exact sample distributions. In 1922 he published a paper that provided a rigorous statistic for measurement,[70] and in 1925 he published the first edition of *Statistical Methods for Research Workers*,[71] which by 1963 had appeared in thirteen editions.

Although Fisher's procedures had many ramifications, probably the most characteristic and widely known is the null hypothesis: one sets out to test the logical contradiction of the hypothesis being tested. The null hypothesis, then, is that there is no difference greater than chance. If the null hypothesis can be disproven, then a difference has been demonstrated.

The work of Fisher and other British statisticians came into common use in psychology relatively slowly because it originated in agriculture and called for difficult and even seemingly paradoxical mathematics. Wide application of small sample statistics, both in Britain and in the United States, was essentially a post-World War II phenomena.

Spearman and "G"   After a considerable period of reading and reflection while serving in the military service, Charles E. Spearman (1863–1945) decided at the age of thirty-six that psychology was the field he wished to pursue.[72] At the beginning of this century, he turned to Leipzig and obtained a degree with Wundt, Krueger, and Wirth. Although he admired Wundt as a person, he did not have the same feeling toward his work, which he characterized as being too centered in sensation. He spent the several years that followed his degree in casual but intensive postdoctoral work with Külpe, G. E. Müller, and various physiologists. In 1907 he accepted an appointment at the University College, London, and in 1911 was made professor, a position he held until 1931.

Spearman saw his major task as nothing less than finding the fundamental laws of psychology.[73] Although he was familiar with the doctrine of association and its claim to establishing such laws, he was not satisfied with their formulations. He believed that the associationists had ignored the mental power of knowing relations and generating items of knowledge not known before. Old relations in new situations, he believed, can bring about the generalizing of new plans of behavior. In point of time, his theory came after some earlier work he had done in statistics, supplying it with a theoretical substratum. Inspired in part by Galton's work, he published two seminal papers in 1904.[74] In the first of these papers, he provided a necessary safeguard for the correlational analysis of mental traits by showing the need to take into account and make allowance for the measurements' degree of reliability. This precaution had previously been unappreciated. In the second paper, he concluded from a statistical study of intercorrelations of test scores of a heterogeneous group of schoolchildren that all intellectual tasks use a single capacity—general intelligence or "G"—as well as whatever capacities are specific to each test involved. This was the famous two-factor theory of intelligence, which would be the center of vigorous study, pro and con, for many years to come.

Central to Spearman's factor theory was what he termed the hierarchy of the specific intelligences, that is, a systematic interrelation of the correlation coefficients "such as to allow the table of correlations to be arranged with the highest values in one corner and with the other values regularly decreasing in both horizontal and vertical directions."[75]

The Abilities of Man, published in 1927, contains the most comprehensive account of the work Spearman and his associates had done, along with a vigorous criticism of what he called "rival doctrines."[76] After demonstrating to his satisfaction that "G" and "s" exist, he proceeded to relate them to response speed, attention, perseveration, conation, and the like. It was on the basis of its scope, as he saw it, that he was led to write an article in which G is offered as a school to end schools. He claims that application of the general theory of two factors isolates the factors, whereas use of the subtheories explains them.[77] In England, the history of factor analysis can be told in terms of the reaction of others to his proposals and findings.

Factor Analysis[78]   While serving as Wilde Reader in mental philosophy at Oxford, William Brown (1881–1952) took the position that, although Spearman's studies of factor analysis were an epoch-making advance, he nevertheless disagreed with his interpretation of the significance of the hierarchical order in matrices of correlation coefficients. He was joined in this critique by Godfrey H. Thomson (1881–1955), who collaborated with him in the second and third editions of the *Essentials of Mental Measurement.*[79] The gist of their argument was that the hierarchical order could be produced by random overlap of group of factors without any general factor being present. Thomson, located at Edinburgh University from 1925 on, continued this effort in a very successful general and remarkably nonpartisan statement of factor analysis, *The Factorial Analysis of Human Ability.*[80] He was also concerned with the development of intelligence tests, evaluation of the educational significance of intelligence, and a general furtherance of educational psychology.[81]

Burt and the Inheritability of Intelligence   Sir Cyril Burt (1883–1971), Spearman's successor at the University College, London, came to the post in 1931 with the most varied background of interests and experience of any British psychologist since Galton himself.[82] He had been William McDougall's student at Oxford. McDougall, aware of Spearman's interest in the work of the then still living Galton, encouraged him to work in standardizing tests. A period at Würzburg followed, which, in turn, was followed by a period at Liverpool with Sherrington. At Liverpool, Burt taught medical students and continued his research on tests. His experiences during the next twenty years in one way or another involved work with mental tests and statistical procedures. He served as a clinical psychologist in the first official British child-guidance clinic. During World War I, he was employed by the National Institute of Industrial Psychology. Only after this varied experience was he appointed to the chair at the University College, a post he held for twenty years. His research was similarly varied, but true to the statistical tradition, his most important work was *The Factors of the Mind*, [83] published in 1941. He took the position that all factor methods are either approximations or linear transformations of the same set of theoretical values. Consequently, reconciliation among the methods is possible. Burt was also a strong advocate of the overwhelming importance of heredity on intelligence.

Burt's major studies on intelligence in twins raised either together or separately were influential in psychology for many years in emphasizing the hereditary influence on intelligence. Only after his death was it discovered that much, if not most, of the data for the studies were bogus.[84] His reputation has thus fallen to a low ebb, which is unfortunate since his contributions outside of the twin studies appear to have been legitimate. The revelation of Burt's perfidies was tragic.

British Cognitive Psychology

Frederic C. Bartlett Beginning in 1931, and for many years thereafter, the Chair of Psychology at Cambridge University was held by Sir Frederic C. Bartlett[85] (1886–1969). Directing one of the very few British advanced graduate programs, Bartlett exercised tremendous administrative and educational influence. For about a quarter of a century he edited the *British Journal of Psychology.* In his laboratory were trained many of the present holders of chairs in British universities.

As for personal research, one of Bartlett's main studies, *Remembering*, significantly bore the subtitle *A Study in Experimental and Social Psychology.* [86] He tells us that early in his career he became dissatisfied with the use of nonsense syllables on various grounds. These stimuli are still meaningful, their use creates an artificial situation, and, on the response side, their use ignores the influence of a subjective attitude toward the material. Consequently, for his research he used material from everyday life. Following up on some of Head's physiological theorizing concerning postural change, Bartlett and some of his students after him insisted that past experiences were not replicated but gave rise to a personal schema, a model of ourselves which consequently changes but with which we meet subsequent experiences.[87] In the 1940s two of his students, R. C. Oldfield and O. L. Zangwill,[88] summarized not only the results of Bartlett's schema approach, but also Head's earlier position.

In view of Bartlett's importance in shaping the thinking of British psychology (other than in the statistical area), it might be well to pause and examine the other major intellectual influences at work. James Ward had died as recently as 1925, and his evolutionary views and conception of the mind as active were still part of the thinking of most British psychologists. Another potent influence was William McDougall. Long after his departure for the United States in 1920, he influenced British psychology, particularly through his *Social Psychology*, which was reprinted twenty-four times between its first appearance in 1908 and McDougall's death in 1938.[89] Both "instinct" and "sentiment," as he promulgated them, were concepts much used by British psychologists. Psychology defined as the science of mental life was still entirely acceptable. All psychologists accepted the existence of a conscious sense as central. Cognition and will were still favorite subjects of research.

James Drever and Scottish Psychology   James Drever, Sr. (1873–1950), for many years represented Scottish (as differentiated from British) psychology.[90] Trained at Edinburgh (and later London), he represented psychology at the only one of four Scottish universities at which the subject was then on an equal footing with the other arts subjects. Financial circumstances had required that he spend many years teaching school. This experience, coupled with the pioneering reforms in Scottish education, including the requirement that all teachers receive training in psychology (this innovation as early as 1905), brought him an appointment in education and, in a few years, a laboratory in educational psychology. His interests were considerably broader than this seems to imply, however; he did much work in general psychology, on instinct, for example.[91] After World War I, Drever transferred to the Psychology Department, and in 1931 he was made Professor of Psychology, the third such chair in the British Isles. While continuing his other interests, he added juvenile delinquency and the psychology of the deaf.[92]

Psychoanalysis in Britain

On his return from Canada just before World War I, Ernest Jones[93] (1879–1958), a Welshman, whom we have already encountered as Freud's biographer, introduced psychoanalysis to London. In later years he became Britain's principal national and international spokesman on psychoanalytic matters.[94] Two other world leaders of child psychoanalysis, Melanie Klein[95] (1882–1960) and Anna Freud,[96] practiced and taught in London for many years. There would be little quarrel with the statement that they more than any others brought the psychoanalytic study of the child from its position of relative obscurity during Sigmund Freud's lifetime to a point where it is now equal to adult psychoanalysis.

In British psychology the major general development after World War II was probably the increased number of graduate students and the opening of several new universities in various parts of England.[97] Wider latitude for individualized programs, rather than following the traditions of "Oxbridge," seems apparent. A new generation of psychologists occupies the forty or so chairs. Leadership is not as concentrated in a few individuals as it had been.[98]

SUMMARY

A major contribution of European psychology to the United States is the migration of Europeans to the United States, which supplied the first generation of both psychoanalysts and Gestalt psychologists. Other imports that have traveled well are certain seminal theories: Wundtian, Freudian, Jungian, and Pavlovian, in the past, and, most recently, theories based on Piaget's work. European scholars are frequent U.S. visitors, and there has been an increased flow in recent decades from the United States in the other direction.

The research interests which contemporary European psychologists follow and the prescriptive attitudes they adhere to almost defy brief summary. A few outstanding aspects of research interests and some major manifestations of prescriptive adherence may be sketched.

The battle of the schools, so obviously compelling in the United States, hardly influenced European psychology, with the exception of psychoanalysts and Gestalt psychologists. Somewhat comparable ideological differences were found in the arguments between Europeans supporting psychology as an explanatory science and those who saw it as a descriptive, holistic venture.

Ties with acknowledged philosophical assumptions are characteristic of continental psychology. This relation is particularly true in Germany and France, but overwhelmingly so in the Soviet Union where compatibility with Marxism remains the essential characteristic.

European psychologists did not take a militant stance on objectivity of method and content that characterized neobehaviorism in the United States. Consequently, they were less preoccupied with these issues.

The Germans showed a reserve about elementistic reduction and so tended to be molar in attitude. They showed an even stronger reservation concerning methodological objectivism. Insistence on more exactly controlled research has made some inroads, especially through the work of the younger people trained at least partly in the United States.

NOTES

1. For coverage of over forty national psychologies, see Virginia S. Sexton and Henryk Misiak, eds., *Psychology Around the World* (Monterey, Calif.: Brooks/Cole Publishing Co., 1976).
2. Ludwig J. Pongratz, "Germany," in Sexton and Misiak, eds., *Psychology Around the World,* pp. 154–188.
3. W. Dilthey, *Gessammelte Schriften,* eds. H. Mehl et al., 12 vols. (Stuttgart: Teubner, 1914–1958), variously reprinted.
4. W. Dilthey, "Einleitung in die Geisteswissenschaften," in *Gesammelte Schriften* (1883), Vol. 1.
5. W. Dilthey, "Ideen über eine beschreibende und zergliedernde Psychologie," *Sitzungberichte Akademie der Wissenschaften in Berlin, 2* (1894):1309–1407. Reprinted in *Gesammelte Schriften,* Vol. 5, pp. 139–240.
6. H. Ebbinghaus, "Ueber erklärende und beschreibende Psychologie," *Zeitschrift für Psychologie, 9* (1896):161–205.
7. W. Metzger, "The Historical Background for National Trends in Psychology: German Psychology," *Journal of the History of the Behavioral Sciences, 1* (1965):109–115.

8. F. Krueger, *Ueber Entwicklungspsychologie, ihre sachliche und geschidliche Notwendigkeit* (Leipzig: Engelmann, 1915); F. Krueger, *Zur Philosophie und Psychologie der Ganzheit: Schriften aus den Jahren 1819–1940,* ed. E. Heuss (Berlin: Springer–Verlag, 1953); F. Sander, "Structure, Totality of Experience, and Gestalt," in Carl Murchison, ed., *Psychologies of 1930* (Worcester, Mass.: Clark University Press, 1930), pp. 188–204.

9. In 1938 the Nazis forced Krueger to leave his chair at Leipzig. He was replaced briefly by P. Lersch and in 1941 by Volkelt, who had been a student of Wundt and Krueger. After World War II, he was succeeded by W. Fischel. See Ludwig J. Pongratz, "Germany," in Sexton and Misiak, eds., *Psychology Around the World.*

10. E. Spranger, *Lebensformen* (Tübingen: Niemeyer, 1913); E. Spranger, *Types of Men: The Psychology and Ethics of Personality,* trans. 5th ed. (Berlin: Springer–Verlag, 1967) (1921).

11. P. E. Vernon and G. W. Allport, "A Test for Personal Values," *Journal of Abnormal and Social Psychology, 26* (1931–1932):231–248.

12. W. Metzger, "The Historical Background for National Trends."

13. A. Wellek, ed., *Gesamtverzeichnis der deutschsprachigen psychologischen Literatur der Jahre 1942 bis 1960* (Göttingen: Verlag für Psychologie, 1965).

14. W. Metzger, "The Historical Background for National Trends."

15. L. Pongratz, "Germany," in Sexton and Misiak, eds., *Psychology Around the World,* pp. 163–164. Ulfried Geuter deals with this issue in detail in his book, *Die Professionalisierung der deutschen Psychologie im Nationalsozialismus* (Frankfurt am Main: Shurkamp, 1984).

16. W. F. Angermeier, "Psychology in East Germany," *American Psychologist, 19* (1964):846.

17. L. Pongratz, "Germany," in Sexton and Misiak, eds., *Psychology Around the World,* p. 166.

18. See *ibid.,* pp. 166–178, for a summary of the work done in Germany up to the mid-1970s.

19. A. Wellek, *Ganzheits Psychologie und Strukturtheorie,* 2nd ed. (Bern: Francke, 1969) (1955).

20. W. Metzger, *Psychologie: Die Entwicklung ihrer Grundannahmen seit der Einfhrung des Experiment,* 4th ed. (Darmstadt: Steinkopff, 1968) (1954).

21. W. Metzger, *Gesetze des Sehens,* 2nd ed. (Frankfurt am Main: Kramer, 1953) (1936).

22. W. Metzger, "The Historical Background for National Trends."

23. P. Lersch et al., eds., *Handbuch der Psychologie,* 12 vols. (Göttingen: Verlag für Psychologie, 1959–1967).

24. Michel Huteau and Pierre Roubertoux, "France," in Sexton and Misiak, eds., *Psychology Around the World,* pp. 131–153.

25. H. Piéron, "Henri Piéron," in E. G. Boring et al., *A History of Psychology in Autobiography* (Worcester, Mass.: Clark University Press, 1952), Vol. IV, pp. 257–278.

26. H. Piéron, *Aux Sources de la conaissance: La sensation, guide de vie,* 3rd ed. (Paris: Librarie Gallimard, 1955) (1945); H. Piéron, *The Sensations, Their Functions, Processes, and Mechanisms* (New Haven, Conn.: Yale University Press, 1952).

27. H. Piéron et al., *Methodologie psychotechnique: Traité de psychologie appliquée* (Paris: Presses Universitaires de France, 1951).

28. H. Piéron "Psychologiezoologique," in G. Dumas, ed., *Noveau traité de psychologue* (Paris: Alcan, 1941), Vol. 8, no. 1, pp. 1–255.

29. H. Piéron, "Les echelles subjectives. Peuvent-elles fournir la base d'une nouvelle loi psychophysique?" *L'Année Psychologique, 59* (1959):1–34.

30. G. Dumas, ed., *Traité de psychologie,* 2 vols. (Paris: Alcan, 1923–1924).

31. G. Dumas, ed., *Nouveau traité de psychologie,* 8 vols., (Paris: Alcan, 1930–1941).

32. P. Fraisse and J. Piaget, eds., *Traité de psychologie experimentale,* 9 vols. (Paris: Presses Universitaires de France, 1963–1967).

33. A. Michotte, "Albert Michotte van den Berck," in Boring et al., eds., *A History of Psychology in Autobiography,* Vol. IV, pp. 213–236.

34. A. Michotte, *The Perception of Causality,* 2nd ed. (New York: Basic Books, 1963) (1946).

35. H. F. Ellenberger, "The Scope of Swiss Psychology," in Henry P. David and Helmut von Bracken, eds., *Perspectives in Personality Theory,* (New York: Basic Books, 1957), pp. 44–64.

36. E. Claparède, "Edouard Claparède," in C. Murchison, ed., *A History of Psychology in Autobiography* (Worcester, Mass.: Clark University Press, 1930), Vol. 1, pp. 63–97.

37. J. Piaget, "Jean Piaget," in Boring et al., eds., *A History of Psychology in Autobiography,* Vol. IV, pp. 237–256.

38. J. Piaget, *The Language and Thought of the Child* (New York: Harcourt, Brace, 1928); J. Piaget, *The Child's Conception of Physical Causality* (New York: Harcourt, Brace, 1930).

39. J. Piaget, *The Grasp of Consciousness: Action and Concept in the Young Child,* trans. Susan Wedgwood (Cambridge, Mass.: Harvard University Press, 1976) (1974).

40. J. H. Flavell, *The Developmental Psychology of Jean Piaget* (Princeton, N.J.: Van Nostrand, 1963).

41. P. Fraisse, *Les structures rhythmiques: Études psychologique* (Louvain: Publications Universitaires de Louvain, 1956); P. Fraisse, *The Psychology of Time,* trans. Jennifer Leith (New York: Harper and Row, 1963).

42. A. Fessard, "Mechanisms of Nervous Integration and Conscious Experience," in J. F. Delafresnaye, ed., *Brain Mechanism and Consciousness* (Oxford: Blackwell, 1954), pp. 200–236.

43. Josef Brozek and Levy Rahmani, "Soviet Russia," in Sexton and Misiak, eds., *Psychology Around the World,* pp. 370–388.

44. G. I. Chelpanov *(Psychology and Marxism)* (Moscow: Russki Knizhnik, 1924); G. I. Chelpanov *(Objective Psychology in Russia and America)* (Moscow: Dunov, 1925); see Alex Kozulin, "Georg Chelpanov and the Establishment of the Moscow Institute of Psychology," *Journal of the History of the Behavioral Sciences, 21* (1985): 23–32.

45. K. N. Kornilov, "Psychology in the Light of Dialectic Materialism," in C. Murchison, ed., *Psychologies of 1930* (Worcester, Mass.: Clark University Press, 1930), pp. 243–278; G. Razran, "K. N. Kornilov, Theoretical and Experimental Psychologist," *Science, 128* (1958):74–75.

46. K. N. Kornilov *(A Textbook of Psychology in the Light of Dialectic Materialism),* 5th ed. (Moscow: Giz, 1931) (1927).

47. A. R. Luria, *The Nature of Human Conflict,* trans. W. Horsley Gantt (New York: Liveright, 1932).

48. L. S. Vygotsky, "Thought in Schizophrenia," *Archives of Neurology and Psychiatry* (Chicago), *31* (1934):1063–1077.

49. L. S. Vygotsky, *Thought and Language*, trans. E. Hanfmann and G. Vakar (Cambridge, Mass.: MIT Press, 1962) (1934).

50. K. M. Bykov, *The Cerebral Cortex and the Internal Organs*, ed. and trans. from 3rd Russian ed. by W. Horsley Gantt (New York: Chemical Publishing, 1957).

51. A. R. Luria, "The Crisis in Bourgeois Psychology," *Psikhologia*, 1–2, (1932):63–88.

52. R. A. Bauer, ed., *Some Views on Soviet Psychology* (Washington, D.C.: American Psychological Association, 1962).

53. L. Rahmani, *Soviet Psychology: Philosophical, Theoretical and Experimental Issues* (New York: International Universities Press, 1973).

54. G. Razran, "Soviet Psychology and Psychophysiology," *Behavioral Science, 4* (1959):35–48.

55. G. Razran, "Growth, Scope and Direction of Current Soviet Psychology: The 1963 All-Union Congress," *American Review of Psychology, 15* (1964):342–347.

56. A. N. Leontiev *(The Origin and Initial Development of Language)* (Moscow: Akadimya Nauk, USSR, 1963).

57. Josef Brozek and and L. Mecacci, "New Soviet Research Institute of Psychology: A Milestone in the Development of Psychology in the USSR," *American Psychologist, 29* (1974):475–478.

58. Brozek and Rahmani, "Soviet Russia," in Sexton and Misiak, eds., *Psychology Around the World*, pp. 380–381.

59. See L. S. Hearnshaw, *A Short History of British Psychology: 1840–1940* (New York: Barnes and Noble, 1964).

60. G. Humphrey, "Five Years in the Oxford Chair," *British Journal of Psychology, 44* (1953):381–383.

61. Beatrice Edgell, "The British Psychological Society," *British Journal of Psychology, 37* (1947):113–132.

62. L. S. Hearnshaw, *A Short History of British Psychology*, p. 208.

63. John C. Eccles and William C. Gibson, *Sherrington: His Life and Thought* (Berlin: Springer–Verlag, 1979); R. Granit, *Charles Scott Sherrington: An Appraisal* (London: Nelson, 1966); Judith P. Swazey, *Reflexes and Motor Integration: Sherrington's Concept of Integrative Action* (Cambridge, Mass.: Harvard University Press, 1969).

64. C. Sherrington, *The Integrative Action of the Nervous System* (New Haven, Conn.: Yale University Press, 1947) (1906).

65. H. Head, W.H.R. Rivers, and J. Sherren, "The Afferent Nervous System from a New Aspect," *Brain, 28* (1908):323–450.

66. H. Head, *Studies in Neurology* (London: Frowde, Hodder and Stoughton, 1920), Vol. 1.

67. H. Head, *Aphasia and Kindred Disorders of Speech*, 2 vols. (Cambridge: Cambridge University Press, 1926).

68. *Ibid.*, Vol. 1, pp. 479–487.

69. E. D. Adrian, *The Mechanisms of Nervous Action: The Activity of the Sense Organs* (Oxford: Clarendon Press, 1932).

70. R. Q. Fisher, "The Goodness of Fit of Regression Formulae and the Distribution of Regression Coefficients," *Journal of Royal Statistical Society* 85 (1922):597–612.

71. R. A. Fisher, *Statistical Methods for Research Workers*, 13th ed. (New York: Hafner, 1963) (1925).

72. C. E. Spearman, "C. Spearman," in Murchison, ed., *A History of Psychology in Autobiography*, Vol. 1, pp. 299–233.

73. *Ibid.*

74. C. E. Spearman, "The Proof and Measurement of Association Between Two Things," *American Journal of Psychology, 15* (1904):201–293; C. E. Spearman, "General Intelligence, Objectively Determined and Measured," *American Journal of Psychology, 15* (1904):201–293.

75. C. E. Spearman, "General Intelligence," p. 231.

76. C. E. Spearman, *The Abilities of Man: Their Nature and Measurement* (New York: Macmillan Co., 1927).

77. C. E. Spearman, "G and After—A School to End Schools," in Murchison, ed., *Psychologies of 1930*, pp. 339–366.

78. For an indictment of the factor analysis approach to the study of intelligence, see Stephen Jay Gould, *The Mismeasure of Man* (New York: W. W. Norton, 1981), pp. 235–320.

79. W. Brown and G. H. Thomson, *The Essentials of Mental Measurement*, 3rd ed. (Cambridge: Cambridge University Press, 1925) (1911).

80. G. H. Thomson, *The Factorial Analysis of Human Ability*, 4th ed. (London: University of London Press, 1950).

81. G. H. Thomson, "The Trend of National Intelligence," *Eugenics Review, 38* (1946):9–18.

82. C. Burt, "Cyril Burt," in Boring et al., eds., *A History of Psychology in Autobiography*, Vol. IV, pp. 53–73.

83. C. Burt, *The Factors of the Mind: An Introduction to Factor Analysis in Psychology* (New York: Macmillan Co., 1941).

84. L. S. Hearnshaw, *Cyril Burt: Psychologist* (Ithaca, N.Y.: Cornell University Press, 1979); L. J. Kamin, *The Science and Politics of IQ* (Potomac, Md.: Erlbaum, 1974); H. J. Eysenck and L. Kamin, *The Intelligence Controversy* (New York: John Wiley, 1981); Gould, *The Mismeasure of Man*, pp. 235–237.

85. F. C. Bartlett, "Frederic Charles Bartlett," in C. Murchison, ed., *A History of Psychology in Autobiography*, Vol. III, pp. 39–52.

86. F. C. Bartlett, *Remembering: A Study in Experimental and Social Psychology* (New York: Macmillan Co., 1932).

87. *Ibid.*, pp. 199–201.

88. R. C. Oldfield and O. L. Zangwill, "Head's Concept of the Schema and Its Application in Contemporary British Psychology. 1, 2, 3, 4," *British Journal of Psychology, 32, 33,* (1941–1943, 1942–1943):267–286, 58–64, 113–129, 143–149.

89. L. S. Hearnshaw, *A Short History of British Psychology*, p. 212.

90. J. Drever, "James Drever," in Murchison, ed., *A History of Psychology in Autobiography*, Vol. II, pp. 17–34.

91. J. Drever, *Instinct in Man: A Contribution to the Psychology of Education*, 2nd ed. (London: Cambridge University Press, 1921) (1917):J. Drever, "The Classification of the Instincts," *British Journal of Psychology, 14* (1924):248–255.

92. J. Drever and M. Collins, *Performance Tests of Intelligence: A Series of Nonlinguistic Tests for Deaf and Normal Children* (Edinburgh: Oliver and Boyd, 1936).

93. E. Jones, *Free Associations: Memories of a Psychoanalyst* (New York: Basic Books, 1959).

94. E. Jones, *Papers on Psycho-analysis*, 5th ed. (London: Ballière, Tindall and Cox, 1948) (1912, reprinted 1961).

95. M. Klein, *Contributions to Psychoanalysis, 1921–1945* (London: Hogarth Press, 1948).

96. A. Freud, *The Ego and the Mechanisms of Defense* (New York: International Universities Press, 1946) (1935); A. Freud, *The Psycho-analytical Treatment of Children* (London: Imago, 1946).

97. C. Monchaux and G. H. Keir, "British Psychology 1945–1957," *Acta Psychologica* (Amst.), *18* (1961):120–180.

98. For recent British psychology, see Brian M. Foss, "United Kingdom," in Sexton and Misiak, eds., *Psychology Around the World*, pp. 428–444. For Irish psychology, see Peter J.R. Dempsey, "Ireland," in Sexton and Misiak, eds., *Psychology Around the World*, pp. 212–218.

L. L. Thurstone.

Chapter 27

Psychology in the United States Since World War II

Unfortunately, this chapter cannot be as inclusive as its title would suggest. The worldwide explosion of psychology which has occurred since World War II has been nowhere so evident as in the United States. It would take an entire book just to summarize the developments, as in fact it has.[1] This period of rapid growth has also been a period of disorganization in the field. The definition of psychology, difficult enough to make in the 1930s, is even more difficult today. The era of schools of psychology came to an end in the late 1930s to mid-1940s. Behaviorism, Gestalt psychology, psychoanalysis, and forms of functional psychology were still in evidence, but the attempt to find one all-inclusive, global psychological position was largely deserted in favor of intensive theories on a smaller aspect of the field, such as specific behavior theories and models of even smaller subsets of the subject matter.

The postwar period has witnessed a dramatic development in areas that previously had been on the fringes of the psychological field: clinical psychology, personality theory, social psychology, and developmental psychology. Clinical psychology emerged after the war as the most highly funded aspect of psychology by various agencies of the federal government, and most of that funding was for training programs to produce clinical psychologists. This was due primarily to the Veterans Administration's need to staff its expanded hospital facilities owing to the war casualties. The other applied disciplines such as industrial psychology, engineering psychology, and psychological testing also received a large boost after the war. The study of social, personality, and developmental factors, which had begun to develop even before the war, came into its own afterward. The most immediate effect of these developments was that the experimental psychology of sensation and perception was displaced to the lowest position in the modern history of the field and began actively competing with learning as the dominant subject matter of academic psychology. The period since the war also saw behaviorism rise to its acme in the early 1960s and then begin to share its once largely unchallenged position as *the* American psychology with modern cognitive psychology.

ADVANCES IN QUANTITATIVE METHODS

Before dealing with these major trends, we would do well to consider an advance in American experimental psychology that greatly influenced how experimentation was conducted in the postwar period: experimental design.

Statistical methods had been used since the early development of experimental psychology, beginning with descriptive statistics such as mean, mode, and probable error (PE) and mean variation (MV). A major step came with the introduction of inferential statistics, begun in Britain with "Student's" t by R. A. Fisher. The use of "z" tests and "t" tests became more widespread in the reporting of psychological research in the prewar period. Major steps in the development of multivariate statistics can be dated from Spearman's publication of his application of Pearson's product moment correlation coefficient to psychological problems in 1904[2] and 1908[3] with "Student's" solution of a small-sample problem for the correlation coefficient. In the 1910s and 1920s, multiple regression statistics developed.[4] It was in the late 1930s, however, that correlations were taken beyond the $p = q = 2$ case, and multivariate analyses began to be more commonly used.[5] One aid in the advance of multivariate statistics was the development of relatively fast calculators and, after the war, of computers.

With the analyses went the study of experiment designs that would take advantage of advanced analyses such as analysis of variance and factor analysis. The most important "core" course in any graduate program became the course in experimental design. In some programs in the postwar period it would be the only required course. With such designs the way in which experimentation took place in psychology changed radically from the 1940s on, from simple comparisons of two group designs to elaborate multitreatment and multiple-group designs.

THURSTONE AND FACTOR ANALYSIS

To a considerable extent, factor analytic research in the United States was derived from earlier work in Great Britain on statistical analysis as outlined in Chapter 26. In this area of research, at least one individual in the United States reached the stature of Spearman, Thomson, and Burt: L. L. Thurstone (1887–1955).

Thurstone[6] took a degree in electrical engineering at Cornell, worked as an assistant to Thomas Edison, and taught engineering before he turned to graduate work in psychology in 1914, studying both at Chicago and the Carnegie Institute of Technology.[7] He had done so, he tells us, to pursue an interest he had developed in studying learning as a scientific problem. Somewhere along the line, however, his interest shifted to factor analysis and psychometrics.

After teaching at Carnegie Institute of Technology for seven years and carrying out some research in Washington, Thurstone returned to the University of Chicago, where his interests in factor analysis came to the fore. Instead of repeating Spearman's question about the presence or absence of a general factor, he asked how many factors must be postulated in order to account for a matrix of correlations. Consequently, he saw no reason to call one factor more general than another. In this setting, the G of Spearman came to be seen as a "second-order" factor emerging in correlational study only after the first-order multiple factors. It was the multiple factors obtained, not G, which he considered in order to account for the obtained correlations. By and large, however, his results are not so much in opposition to those of Spearman as an extension of his work. His principal publication was *The Vectors of Mind*, published in 1935.[8] As he continued to work with this approach, it became more and more complex and the data collected became more and more extensive. As a consequence, the earlier book was rewritten in a more extended form to appear in 1947 with the new title, *Multiple-Factor Analysis*.[9]

Thurstone was a prime mover in the founding of the Psychometric Society in the establishment of its journal, *Psychometrika*. *Psychometrika* was extremely influential in the promotion of advanced statistical methods and designs in psychology and education and remains a primary source of such material. Factor analysis and allied multivariate techniques, as we have seen, would become a mainstay of the newer social science developments in psychology.

ALLPORT, MURRAY, AND ROGERS: THE STUDY OF PERSONALITY

Personality was and is an amorphous field, to which it is hard to set boundaries or even say precisely what it includes. But in the 1930s Gordon W. Allport and a program of in-depth research by Henry A. Murray helped bring order and clarity to the field in the attempted integration of its various widely scattered aspects.

Gordon W. Allport   Gordon Allport (1887–1967) was graduated from Harvard in 1919.[10] He had come to college with an already formed conviction that guidance of conduct would be for him what could be described as "diffusive sympathetic affections." It is significant in this connection that his first faculty appointment at Harvard in 1924 was as instructor in social ethics. For the intervening years, except for a short digression to Robert College of Istanbul and to Dartmouth, he was in the Psychology Department at Harvard (and later, after its reorganization and split, the Department of Social Relations).

Allport found that, within psychology, his social interests best related to the question of personality and how it should be studied. With remarkable consistency, he maintained this focus throughout his career, from his doctoral dissertation on traits of personality in relation to social diagnosis and his first article on the topic of personality and character. "Trait" and "Organization" and "Development" had characterized his approach; the individual's characteristics cannot be divorced from the pattern they form because both develop over time. It was his *Personality: A Psychological Interpretation* (1937) which established the modern concept of personality as an area of investigation.[11] Later works, extending in time beyond 1945, followed the same path. His work is eclectic in the finest sense of that term. If he did not succeed in integrating the diverse strands of personality, it was not for lack of ability or devotion to the task, but because the field was still too fragmented during his lifetime.

Henry A. Murray   Henry Murray (1893–1988) arrived at Harvard in 1926 by a series of idiosyncratic intellectual experiences that perhaps ideally fitted him for the work he carried on.[12] After graduating from Harvard in 1915 there followed medical school, a surgical internship, years of biochemical research, a short but important relationship with Carl Jung, and then the Harvard appointment.

In 1938 Murray published his *Explorations in Personality,*[13] which recounts the work he carried out with his clinical staff of highly talented associates, including Erik H. Erikson, Donald W. MacKinnon, Saul Rosenzweig, and Robert W. White. They used an in-depth approach in a multipronged simultaneous attack on as many aspects of personality as their resources afforded. Harvard undergraduate subjects were assessed by several investigators, each working independently and each using a particular technique. The data from all sources on a specific individual were interpreted by one investigator before the assembled group of investigators who criticized his efforts. Discussion continued until a consensus was obtained. This procedure was used for all forty subjects. These results, in turn, were subjected to a synthetical interpretation based not only on Freud's system, but also on the contributions of such diverse theorists as Jung, McDougall, Adler, and Lewin. From this work came a conceptual system for assessing a personality in terms of his motives (needs) and the environmental forces bearing on him (press). It was from the results of this study that much of Murray's later work emerged.

The major vehicle for Murray's research was the Thematic Apperception Technique,[14] a projective device in which subjects told stories in response to pictures that were mostly perceptually clear in detail but permitted wide interpretation of what was happening and would happen afterward. Individual personality portraits emerged from the kinds of stories told, for example, from the various themes emphasized.

The other major projective technique, the Rorschach Test, was brought to the

United States by the psychiatrist David Levy (1892–1977) in the early 1920s after he had studied with Rorschach. His student, Samuel J. Beck[15] (1896–1980), became a leading figure in developing the technique for clinical use. Later, Wayne Holtzman expanded and developed this technique to its highest point.[16]

During the 1960s, enthusiasm for projective devices as measures of personality waned. This was due to the sharply critical conclusions that emerged from rigorous study, despite protests from protagonists that many of the studies were inappropriate. Nonetheless, the technique remains a standard part of the clinical repertoire.

Carl Rogers and Psychotherapy   During the 1940s and 1950s, Carl R. Rogers[17] was occupied with developing an approach to counseling and therapy and later with quantitative research on the effect of psychotherapy.[18] After some years a theory of personality and interpersonal relations emerged from this work which stressed the role of self-concept in self-actualization.[19] Rogers became convinced that his patients must change their self-structures by themselves if improvement was to occur.

The patients' self-concepts regulated their behavior and their views of psychological environmental reality. Their views were distorted; if they changed their concept of self, environmental distortions might disappear or be modified. The result of this position was Rogerian therapy or client-centered therapy.[20]

The innovations and developments in personality theory that occurred in the 1930s and 1940s apparently declined somewhat in the 1950s. Nevitt Sanford recalled:

> In the early 1950s a reaction set in. To me it seemed sudden, though it probably had been building for some time. By 1955, surely, the reaction was plain. True enough, the outpouring of personality research continued, and courses were still taught. . . . But much of the life had been drained from the great movement of the 1930s and 1940s. Most (if not all) of the theorists discussed by these authors had done their great work in the decades before.[21]

MURPHY AND LEWIN AND SOCIAL PSYCHOLOGY

Like personality, the notion of social psychology has been around for a long time. In "The Historical Background of Modern Social Psychology," Gordon Allport cites sources going back to the eighteenth century.[22] For most of its history, however, social psychology has been an armchair discipline, evolving from an individual retiring to his study to spin out a system for which empirical illustrations were then selected. It is true, however, that perhaps the first experimental social psychological study published was that by N. Triplett in 1898.[23] The study dealt with physical performance in competitive as compared to noncompetitive situations. It is also an early sports psychology study. At the time, however, no one apparently realized that Triplett's study represented a new approach in psychological research.

By 1910 only two significant books had appeared on the topic. One depended on the instinct concept and was McDougall's *Introduction to Social Psychology*, which enjoyed considerable popularity in England and in America. The other, published the same year by E. A. Ross, approached the problem from the point of view of sociology. This early disciplinary split raised the question, still unresolved, as to whether social psychology is a subdiscipline of psychology or of sociology. Courses under the rubric "social psychology" still appear in both departments. Ross's *Social Psychology: An Outline and Source Book*[24] is as often cited as the initiator of social psychology as McDougall's. Ross was a sociologist, not a psychologist, and he cited the earlier sociological literature whereas McDougall cited the earlier psychological literature. The two traditions have continued to the present day, with sociologists primarily citing sociologists and psychologists primarily citing psychologists.

Although there was little activity in the production of books on social psychology in the teens (only two are found in Allport's list for the period), the 1920s showed growth in the topic, with fourteen books appearing. Among those books was Floyd Allport's *Social Psychology*, which appeared in 1924. In some respects, social psychology as a subject matter in psychology programs owes much to Allport's textbook. It became a standard textbook for many years, giving legitimacy to the subject matter. It was more acceptable in American college classrooms than was McDougall's book because it was more in line with the behavioral tendencies of the period and avoided instincts and other concepts that had lost favor with the new behavioral positivism. It was in the 1930s, however, that social psychology as an experimental discipline really got started. Certainly, a major influence on the growth of experimental social psychology was the appearance of Gardner and Lois Barclay Murphy's *Experimental Social Psychology* in 1931.[25]

Gardner and Lois Murphy   Gardner Murphy received graduate training at Harvard and Columbia, where he took his Ph.D. in 1923.[26] He was associated with Columbia until 1940, when he moved to the College of the City of New York. Although he published in the history of psychology,[27] it was his work in social psychology that marked his Columbia days.

Lois Barclay Murphy (1902–) was coauthor of the first edition of the book and was a close collaborator with Gardner Murphy. She graduated from Vassar in 1923 with a bachelor's degree and, after marrying Murphy in 1926, attended Teachers College, Columbia, where she received her Ph.D. in child psychology.

The title of the Murphys' book tells it all: *Experimental Social Psychology.*[28] Gardner Murphy's prior decision to make social psychology his specialization, his teaching responsibilities, and his share in the overall graduate program at Columbia directed him toward this area. He came to the field with an already firmly established eclecticism, which included the conviction that findings from both the biological and the social sciences were important to social psychology. It became a challenge to him to utilize comprehensively both the social and the biological research literature.

Personality development, which Murphy was convinced was an integral aspect of social psychology, became an increasing concern and an area in which he was also a pioneer. The subtitle of his major work in personality, "A Biosocial Approach to Origins and Structure," is indicative of the consistency of Murphy's viewpoint on social psychology.[29]

Kurt Lewin Kurt Lewin's (1890–1947) earlier views are closely identified with Gestalt, particularly as it was applied to psychological development in the child. His later work, after he came to the United States, extended Gestalt field theory into social psychological matters.[30]

After leaving Germany in the 1930s, Lewin taught for a while at the University of Iowa where he completed many of his studies of child development. His last position was as Director of the Research Center for Group Dynamics at the Massachusetts Institute of Technology. In all his research, he made use of a form of field theory, calling his particular approach, topological Psychology.[31] It was only a short step from talking about cognitive fields to talking about social fields and thus group dynamics. This aspect of his work can best be seen in the posthumous compilation of his writings by Dorwin Cartwright, *Field Theory in Social Science.* [32]

Lewin characterized field theory as "a method of analyzing causal relations and of building scientific constructs." The psychological field is always contemporaneous. If past experiences are still effective, they are part of that field. The psychological task is to identify the general variables that determine behavior at a given moment. In the life space (the psychological as differentiated from the physical environment) of the individual, the various psychological phenomena are interdependent. According to many social psychologists, Lewin made a conceptually illuminating success of applying his method and these concepts to such problems as "intention," "frustration," "regression," "resistance," and "conflict." The very nature of the problems listed also emphasized that field theory extends far beyond the boundaries of social psychology.

Lewin is sometimes called the father of experimental social psychology. That is an arguable point, but it is clear that he has had a profound influence on the field. Lewin's students and colleagues at Berlin, at Iowa, and at MIT dominated the first generation of experimental social psychologists in the United States.

Two studies in particular should be mentioned. The first is Tamara Dembo's study on anger done under Lewin's direction while he was still at Berlin. That study demonstrated that when subjects were frustrated in their ability to take direct action toward gaining their goals they sometimes sought roundabout methods of gaining their goals, although they often gave up entirely. The relation to the Gestalt detour problem is obvious. At Iowa, Lewin extended the problem to determine the behavioral effects of frustration and how they could be produced. Children were put in "normal" goal-seeking situations and in "frustrating" ones. Erik Wright at the Iowa station carried out this procedure but added a social setting, whereas Barker, Dembo, and Lewin observed their children individually. The study showed that children facing frustration in a group setting tend to regress in their behavior. The number of aggressive reactions also rose significantly. The result of the experiments were summarized as follows: "Frustration as it operated in these experiments resulted in an average regression in the level of intellectual functioning, in increased unhappiness, restlessness, and destructiveness, in increased ultra-group unity and in increased out-group aggression. The amounts of increase in negative emotionality were positively related to strength of frustration."[33] Another significant study was conducted to show the relationship between aggressive behavior in groups of children organized in authoritarian, democratic, and laissez-faire groups.[34]

After Lewin's untimely death, the Research Center for Group Dynamics moved to the University of Michigan and continued in the directions set by Lewin. His influence continued to shape the field through his students long after his death.

Theodore Newcomb   In some respects, Gardner Murphy and Kurt Lewin's lines of influence lead to the University of Michigan, although they did not come together there. Theodore Newcomb (1903–1984) represents Gardner Murphy's line. Although Newcomb did his doctoral work with Goodwin Watson at Teachers College, Columbia, he worked closely with Gardner Murphy. Newcomb held several academic appointments after receiving his degree. First he was at Lehigh, next at Western Reserve, and then at Bennington College, where he stayed between 1934 and 1941. It was at Bennington College that Newcomb conducted his famous studies on the changes of social attitudes of Bennington students. These researches were published in 1943 as *Personality and Social Change.* During the Bennington years, Newcomb collaborated in the revision of Murphy's *Social Psychology,* the book appearing in 1937.

In 1941 Newcomb left Bennington for the University of Michigan, although his appointment was in sociology, not in psychology. There he attempted to bring the sociological and psychological tracks of social psychology together. With the outbreak of the war, Newcomb left for Washington and government service, to return to Michigan in 1945. On his return, Newcomb headed up an interdisciplinary doctoral program in social psychology. He was himself appointed Professor of Sociology and Psychology. The program would last twenty years, disbanding in 1967; the sociological and psychological groups found their approaches too disparate for successful integration.

Newcomb's work on attitudes demonstrated that such topics of social psychology could be studied experimentally. He helped legitimize attitude research and other areas using similar self-report methodology. His textbook, *Social Psychology* (1950), continued his efforts to bring the social psychological aspects of psychology and sociology together. In many respects, the failure of that attempt may have been responsible for much of the sterility in social psychology encountered in the 1970s.

Other attempts at interdisciplinary cooperation were attempted. One, at the Institute of Human Relations at Yale University, also functioned for about twenty years. It was even more ambitious than the Michigan program, attempting complete integration of teaching and research in all the human disciplines. James Rowland Angell, once leader of Chicago Functionalism, was then President of Yale and was influential in the creation of the institute. Participants from psychology included Raymond Dodge, Clark Hull, and Robert Yerkes. Among the anthropologists was John Dollard, whose work with Neil Miller has already been discussed in the chapter on behaviorism. The institute was successful in integrating talents from a number of different areas and emphasizing eclectic approaches; it investigated individual problems rather than attempting global integrations or systematic summary. The book *Frustration and Aggression* by John Dollard, L. W. Doob, Neal Miller, O. H. Mowrer, and Robert Sears (1939) is a good example of the institute's intent.[35]

Yet another attempt at integration was the Department of Social Relations at Harvard which existed between 1946 and 1970. Like the others, the institute attempted to be multidisciplinary. Psychologist Gordon Allport participated as did sociologist Talcott Parsons and anthropologist Clyde Kluckhohn.[36] In addition, although psychologists, as at Yale, participated in the institute, there was also an established and independently operating Department of Psychology that was much more involved in traditional experimental psychology than in social research.

These interdisciplinary attempts are mentioned because they point up one of the difficulties of social psychology: to find a comfortable home in departments of psychology. Social psychology has always had the problem of a self-identity, perhaps stemming from its Doppelganger relationship with sociological social psychology. Moreover, social psychology, unlike cognition or learning or other academic subtopics of psychology, does not have an independent subject matter. It began in studying the social aspects of traditional psychological subject matters. This has sometimes led social psychologists to jump from one subject matter to another, often neglecting to build any sort of systematic underpinning for their research.

Contributions of Social Psychological Research

Much of the best early research in social psychology was in the area of group dynamics. This very general term includes topics as diverse as leadership, propaganda, and morale. Much of it was stimulated by the problems and experiences of the war.[37]

Attitude change was a particularly significant problem to come out of the war. Newcomb's study of the attitude changes of students at Bennington is a good example of this kind of research, although it was conducted before the war. During World War II, a great deal of interest was generated in attitude change as a technique in propaganda, that is, how to effect changes in attitudes. Examples ranged from an interest in how to convince Americans to eat unpopular parts of animals such as the pancreas and sweetbreads to ways to reduce bigotry. Carl Hovland summarized much of this research conducted during the war years.[38]

Leadership and small-group dynamics also became a popular topic of study after the war. What holds groups together and forces them apart was significant not only to wartime situations but also to peacetime pursuits. J.R.P. French's article "The Disruption and Cohesion of Groups," published in 1941, is an example of this kind of research.[39] By the 1950s works like Cartwright and Zander's *Group Dynamics: Research and Theory*[40] did much to legitimize the field. A textbook that also became classic and helped popularize small-group social psychological research in field settings was Muzafer and Carolyn Sherif's *An Outline of Social Psychology*, first published in 1948.[41] In the 1950s and early 1960s, small-group research stimulated by such books as these was a rich and active part of social psychology.

In the 1940s and 1950s social psychology continued to expand its field, involving social perception and self-perception. The ideas of Kurt Lewin and of other Gestalt psychologists had considerable influence here. Fritz Heider, who had received his doctorate from Kurt Koffka in Germany and who had been associated with Kurt Lewin in America, was highly influential in a number of areas involving social psychology. His balance theory for person perception, published in 1946,[42] was a seminal source for Leon Festinger's classic work on cognitive dissonance theory.[43] Fritz Heider's book *The Psychology of Interpersonal Relations*[44] appeared in 1958 and was also influential in promoting the development of what Jones and Davis would call attribution theory.[45]

In the 1960s and 1970s problems seemed to fragment in social psychology. Although the subject remained popular and legions of doctoral students were being produced, the field seemed to stagnate, as appears to have been true of much of social science in and out of psychology. In terms of social psychology, a lack of cohesion was evident in both method and subject matter. The subject matter of social psychology was the whole field of psychology and at the same time nothing that it could call its own. The appearance that it was conducting trivial research and was faddish, jumping from one "hot" topic to another but doing little to lay down a coherent foundation for the discipline, became and remains a point of criticism against social psychology. Social psychology seemed to lose some credibility in the 1960s and 1970s. In recent years, however, it has shown signs of finding a role for itself again, particularly in the form of applied social psychology, but it still awaits the kind of synthesis that is necessary for a coherent self-identity.[46]

INDUSTRIAL/ORGANIZATIONAL PSYCHOLOGY

Parallel to the development of social psychology, but largely independent of it, has been the development of industrial and organizational psychology. We have already discussed the pioneering work by Münsterberg, Scott, Bingham, and their contemporaries in Chapter 21. Something should now be said about the development of the field in postwar America.

Morris S. Viteles

If there is a single work that can be called the seed that led to the professionalization of industrial psychology it was Morris S. Viteles' *Industrial Psychology* published in 1932.[47] Viteles investigated how the job and the worker could best be fitted together. His approach is typical of the way in which the industrial psychologist has worked since, drawing together methods and techniques from a variety of subject matters, including social psychology but not dependent on any one discipline.

The Hawthorne Studies

Equally significant to the rise of industrial psychology are a group of studies conducted in the mid-1920s called the Hawthorne Studies. C. E. Snow, an electrical engineer at MIT, originally started the experiments as straightforward engineering studies. They began simply enough with an investigation of how the level of illumination in the workplace influenced the workers' productivity. A work area was set up where illumination could be carefully controlled. A group of workers were selected to be subjects and were aware they were subjects. The researchers found that when illumination increased productivity increased. Conversely, they also found that when illumination was decreased productivity increased. Only gradually did the researchers realize that it did not matter what they did to the workers; as long as they did something, the productivity would increase. What motivated the workers was the feeling of being studied or being the objects of interest, not the level of illumination. When the workers felt that they were being treated as important, external manipulations had little effect on their efficiency. Ever since, this result has been called the Hawthorne Effect.

Western Electric conducted the formal studies motivated by these early findings between 1927 and 1932. The findings have been treated in detail elsewhere.[48]

Influence of the War

World War II, just as World War I, required a massive application of personnel testing and job analyses and selection devices. Not only that, but human–machine relationships became more important, since warfare had become far more technical and the machines of war were only as good as the individuals who controlled them. Out of this effort grew the present-day disciplines called engineering psychology in psychology departments and human factors engineering in engineering departments. It also led to the postwar establishment of programs in industrial psychology, not only in departments of psychology but also in management programs in the newly developing schools of business. Much of this work was carried out in Lewin's Research Center for Group Dynamics at MIT. After Lewin's death and the center relocated to Michigan, it continued to be influential in research topics which today we call industrial and managerial psychology.

Gradually, after the war, courses in topics of engineering psychology and industrial/organizational psychology began appearing around the country. The Doppelganger of industrial/organizational psychology, being found in both management and psychology departments, has been a continuing problem for psychology. In the same way, the duplication of engineering psychology in departments of psychology and human factors engineering in engineering departments has posed problems. At present, psychology appears to be losing ground to these other disciplines, largely because of the salary differential between psychology departments which are usually in liberal arts colleges and management and engineering departments which are generally in more heavily funded colleges. At present, the resolution is not clear.

DEVELOPMENTAL PSYCHOLOGY

Developmental psychology is hardly a postwar subject matter in psychology. Psychological ideas of development have been around as long as any other area of psychology. The child-study movement initiated by G. Stanley Hall and carried on by others dated from the earliest days of modern academic psychology. John B. Watson's studies on children, including the ''Albert'' study, have been discussed. A. P. Weiss, the behaviorist at Ohio State, has done studies of new-born children. We have seen Kurt Lewin working at the Iowa Child Welfare Research Station in the 1930s. In addition, there were a number of longitudinal studies, the most famous of which was conducted by Lewis M. Terman at Stanford beginning in the early 1920s. As a field of its own, however, developmental psychology is really a postwar creation. Developmental psychology's formulation into an identifiable field of its own has been retarded for the same reason as social psychology has. Development cuts across all the other fields of psychology, including social psychology, and a self-identity was more difficult than in other areas. There is sensory-motor development, cognitive development, emotional development, social development, and so forth, all subsets of developmental psychology.

Influence of Piaget   Perhaps the greatest influence on postwar developmental psychology was Jean Piaget (1896–1980). (We have already discussed aspects of Piaget's thought in Chapter 26.) Piaget had been making contributions to child psychology since the 1920s. Several of his books were available in English not long after they appeared in French.[49] After an initial and brief period of interest in the late 1920s, American psychologists seemed to lose interest in Piaget's ideas. It was a time when Arnold Gesell's work on maturation norms in children held center stage in developmental psychology. To some degree, the strong environmentalistic slant which psychology had taken with the victory of behaviorism made Piaget's ideas seem ''mentalistic'' and thus old fashioned. Piaget's use of only a few subjects in his experiments rankled the ''dust bowl empiricists'' of the 1930s. Gesell referred to Piaget positively but described his method as ''essentially clinical, utilizing a naturalistic form of experimentation.''[50]

Between 1932 and 1950 Piaget's work was largely ignored in America. Then in 1950, his *Psychology and Intelligence* appeared in English.[51] Jerome Bruner at Harvard, one of the leaders in establishing cognitive psychology in the 1950s, played a significant role in popularizing Piaget in American psychology. This was appropriate since Piaget's notions would influence not only developmental psychology but also cognitive science.

Influence of Psychoanalysis   Psychoanalysis also had its effects on developmental psychology after the war. Erik Erikson (1902–), a psychiatrist trained by Anna Freud, went to Berkeley in 1939 to work in the Berkeley Growth Studies. There he worked on child-rearing practices.[52] The result of his work was his theory of stages of psychosocial development. His stage theory was based on the Freudian concept of ego and considered society's influence on the developing personality. Erikson's stage theory was not limited to children but covered adulthood as well.

The literature in developmental psychology is far too extensive for us to attempt an overview here. Since the 1950s, developmental psychology has found a solid and apparently permanent place for itself in psychology. It seems to have overcome the problem of self-identity that has continued to plague social psychology. The early emphasis on the child may have contributed to this self-identity. Because most psychological studies had to do with adults, the subjects of child development made their study a subject matter unto itself.[53]

CLINICAL PSYCHOLOGY

As with the other social science aspects of psychology, clinical psychology grew rapidly after World War II. The expansion actually began during the war with the need for psychotherapists outstripping supply. This led in part to the acceptance of psychologists in a therapeutic role as well as their earlier primarily assessment role.[54]

The Veterans Administration and the U.S. Public Health Service heavily supported training programs after the war and well into the 1960s. For many years the primary institutional employers of clinical psychologists were veterans hospitals and mental health clinics.

This new role for clinical psychologists made it necessary to define their relationship with psychology. In 1947 David Shakow chaired a committee that issued as its report "Recommended Graduate Training Program in Clinical Psychology."[55] This report became the basis of the scientist/practitioner model of clinical psychology in which clinical psychologists were expected to be trained as psychologists first and to gain general competence in their field rather than merely be trained in clinical skills. Also known as the "Boulder Model,"[56] the approach in modified form is still the most widely held training model for clinical psychology.

Theoretical Influences

After World War II a number of influences came to bear on clinical psychology as therapeutic psychology. The wave of Freudian and neo-Freudians had an initially major impact on psychologists after the war. The work of Karen Horney and Henry Stack Sullivan led to a strong following among American clinical psychologists. Carl Rogers' client-centered therapy became a major competitor for therapeutic practice in the 1950s and 1960s.[57]

As a result of Hans Eysenck's criticism of the effectiveness of psychotherapy, many orthodox psychoanalysts lost their confidence. In 1952 Eysenck, after followup studies of a number of individuals treated by psychoanalysis, reported "an inverse correlation between recovery and psychotherapy; the more psychotherapy, the smaller the recovery rate."[58] This judgment was controversial and was itself criticized.[59] Still, Eysenck brought up the issue of measuring the outcome of therapeutic treatment in a way that it could not be disregarded, although Rogers' therapy had long emphasized the monitoring of therapy sessions, usually by tape recordings, and measurement of the effects of therapy. As with psychoanalysis, however, the effects of Rogerian therapy were not always measurable, and the "measures," where possible, were often very subjective.

By the mid-1960s, a more objective form of therapy came on the psychological scene: behavior therapy. The degree to which Eysenck's criticism contributed to its rise is uncertain, but it certainly did not hurt the cause of behavior therapy. In the late 1960s, and early 1970s there was a wave of "pop" therapies. The issues of a new popular publication, *Psychology Today*, were filled with all manner of unusual therapies. To some degree, these often outlandish new therapies only contributed to the questions many had about the value of "mentalistic" therapies.

Although behavior therapy did not push the "humanistic" and "mentalistic" therapies immediately from the national psychological scene, in many universities it became the primary and sometimes the only form of therapy considered acceptable. By the early 1970s orthodox psychoanalytic influence in psychotherapy had been largely displaced by behavioral therapy, at least in academic settings.

Another blow against orthodox psychoanalysis was the development of drugs that helped control at least the symptoms of many forms of mental illness. Tranquilizers, mood enhancers, and even antipsychotic drugs brought about a major change in the institutionalization of mentally ill patients. Although these developments affected psychiatry more than psychology, they still had their effect.

Behavioral therapies, whether Skinnerian, Pavlovian, or other in origin, had the advantage of being able to demonstrate a therapeutic outcome. They were useful not only for simple problems such as nervous tics but also for severe problems such as autism. Another form of behavior therapy made use of biofeedback techniques, a physiological basis for an individual's control of bodily processes.

Partly in response to this "mechanization" of psychotherapy, the early 1960s also saw the beginnings of humanist-existential-phenomenological psychology. Gilgen traces the beginning of the movement to 1958 with the publication of the book, *Existence: A New Dimension in Psychiatry and Psychology* by Rollo May, Ernest Angel, and Henri F. Ellenberger.[60] Within this approach, many include the ideas of Carl Rogers as well. His approach could certainly be called humanistic. It is within this context that Fritz Perls introduced his Gestalt therapy, which, though phenomenologically based, has nothing to do with Gestalt psychology. Many other therapies arose during the late 1960s and early 1970s such as Viktor Frankl's logotherapy and George Kelley's personal construct theory. It was during this period that Rogerian group therapies came into vogue along with sensitivity training and "T groups." We still stand too close to these movements to see through the dust raised by so many different approaches.[61] Certainly, orthodox psychoanalysis has become less influential and behavioral therapies have risen in prominence. Whether humanistic and phenomenalistic therapies prove to have lasting influence or to be simply fads, as many "pop" therapies have, is a question for the future.

THE REEMERGENCE OF COGNITIVE PSYCHOLOGY

Perhaps the largest single change in American psychological orientation since World War II has been the rise of cognitive psychology. There is no one source for its development. The founding of the movement is often dated with the appearance of Ulrich Neisser's *Cognitive Psychology* in 1967.[62] We would agree that Neisser's book, as a textbook and as a coherent resource, was a major spark for the movement, but a case could also be made for the date 1955 and a symposium on cognition held at the University of Colorado. That symposium, published in 1957 as *Contemporary Approaches to Cognition,*[63] included contributions by J. S. Bruner, Egon Brunswik, Leon Festinger, Fritz Heider, Karl F. Muenzinger, C. E. Osgood, and David Rapaport. The introduction to the book announced that in recent years "psychologists have felt free, as well as stimulated, to attack perhaps less precise but certainly far more interesting and significant problems of human behavior." The major contributors presented observations, either empirical or theoretical, from their own professional perspective on the study of cognition. What makes the book so prophetic is that cognition had ceased to be defined simply as "knowing" and spilled over into a wide variety of meanings, a situation that has since plagued cognitive psychologists in their attempt to define the discipline.

Perhaps the best candidate for an origin date for the movement is 1956 with the appearance of *A Study of Thinking* by Jerome Bruner, Jacqueline Goodnow, and George A. Austin.[64] Bruner uses that date himself.[65] The book was a product of the Harvard Cognition Project, founded by Bruner and conducted in the Laboratory of Social Relations at Harvard beginning in 1952. In their introduction to this volume, the authors defined cognitive processes as "the means whereby organisms achieve, retain, and transform information."[66] They saw the revival of interest in the higher mental processes as follows:

> Partly, it has resulted from a recognition of the complex processes that mediate between the classical "stimuli" and "responses" out of which stimulus–response learning theories hoped to fashion a psychology that would by-pass anything smacking of the "mental." The impeccable peripheralism of such theories could not last long. As "S–R" theories came to be modified to take into account the subtle events that may occur between the input of a physical stimulus and the emission of an observable response, the old image of the "stimulus–response bond" began to dissolve, its place being taken by a mediation model. As Edward Tolman so felicitously put it some years ago, in place of a telephone switchboard connecting stimuli and responses it might be more profitable to think of a map room where stimuli were sorted out and arranged before every response occurred, and one might do well to have a closer look at these intervening "cognitive maps."[67]

The authors might have also credited D. O. Hebb with his hypothetical neurology of intervening processes with its closed loops and cell assemblies.

A second development the authors credited came directly from the war effort. It was information theory which arose from communications research. Just as with stimulus–response psychology, the

> inputs and outputs of a communication system, it soon became apparent, could not be dealt with exclusively in terms of the nature of these inputs and outputs alone nor even in terms of such internal characteristics as channel capacity and noise. The coding and recoding of inputs—how incoming signals are sorted and organized—turns out to be the important secret of the black box that lie athwart the communication channel.[68]

It was from this background of communications research that information processing theory originated. In 1948 Norbert Wiener at MIT coined the word *cybernetics* in his book *Cybernetics: Or Control and Communication in the Animal and the Machine.* The notion of feedback mechanisms was particularly influential in the later cognitive science. Also in 1948 Claude Shannon at Bell Telephone Laboratories approached the topic of the measurement of information processing in his article, "A Mathematical Model of Communication."[69] It was Shannon who coined the word *bit,* a contraction for "binary digit" as the simplest unit of information transfer.[70] It would be the information processing approach in

Shannon and in Wiener's ideas rather than the measurement of information transfer that would be influential in cognitive psychology. Shannon's flow charts, the labeled boxes with arrows, have become a fixture of modern cognitive psychological modeling.

Another contribution of the wartime research on communications and other highly elaborate processes was the development of computers. The study of computers, "thinking machines," would provide a model for many future researchers in cognition. George A. Miller, co-founder with Bruner of the Center for Cognitive Studies at Harvard, dates the beginning of cognitive science to September 11, 1956, when the Second Symposium on Information Theory was held at MIT. The symposium began with Newell and Simon's paper, "the Logic Theory Machine," and ended with Noam Chomsky's paper on the topic of syntactic structures.[71] Both would play major roles in the development of modern cognitive science.

A third source of cognitive psychology, according to Bruner, Goodnow, and Austin, was the "New Look" perception theories of the early 1950s. This approach to perception made use of personality theory and ego psychology as illustrated by Anna Freud's *The Ego and the Mechanisms of Defense* and Gordon Allport's *Personality.*[72]

A fourth influence, one that Bruner et al., do not mention, was that of Gestalt psychology. Gestalt psychology had been doing research on the higher mental processes throughout the rise of behavioral psychology. The Gestalt psychologists and their students had been doing a great deal of what was being rediscovered in the 1950s and 1960s as cognitive psychology. This work has already been reviewed in the chapter on Gestalt. Behaviorists, however, had come to reject any such research as "Gestalt phenomena," as though Gestalt psychology were studying some other organisms than everyone else. Gestalt influence on the new cognitive psychology was often indirect, through Gestalt influences on Tolman or Heider.

Ulrich Neisser, whose *Cognitive Psychology* was a masterful summary of the then current literature and an attempt to group it under a consistent point of view, played a major role in focusing the field and making it understandable. In devising his survey, Neisser drew on all the traditions just mentioned. He gives what is still perhaps the best definition of cognitive psychology:

> the term "cognition" refers to all the processes by which the sensory input is transformed, reduced, elaborated, stored, recovered, and used. It is concerned with these processes even when they operate in the absence of relevant stimulation, as in images and hallucinations. Such terms as sensation, perception, imagery, retention, recall, problem-solving, and thinking, among many others, refer to hypothetical stages or aspects of cognition.[73]

Neisser recognized that this definition gave the impression that cognitive psychology studied everything a human might possibly do. At the same time he argued that cognitive psychology approaches the subject matter from a particular point of view. He differentiates the cognitive point of view from the dynamic as follows:

> Dynamic psychology, which begins with motives rather than with sensory input, is a case in point. Instead of asking how a man's actions and experiences result from what he saw, remembered, or believed, the dynamic psychologist asks how they follow from the subject's goals, needs, or instincts. Both questions can be asked about any activity,

whether it be normal or abnormal, spontaneous or induced, overt or covert, waking or dreaming. Asked why I did a certain thing, I may answer in dynamic terms, "Because I wanted . . . ," or, from the cognitive point of view, "Because it seemed to me."[74]

This does not mean that motivation is ignored in cognitive psychology. It is not, but it is treated as a separate operation that may influence cognitive processes but is not basic to these processes.

Neisser also discriminates among cognitive psychology and behavioral psychology and physiology, although he does not challenge the validity or value of each of these positions own approaches to the subject matter. "The basic reason for studying cognitive processes has become as clear as the reason for studying anything else," Neisser tells us: "because they are there. . . . Cognitive processes surely exist, so it can hardly be unscientific to study them."[75]

A major step forward in legitimizing cognitive psychology as a field was the establishment at Harvard in 1960 of the Center for Cognitive Studies.[76] It was founded through the efforts of Jerome Bruner and George A. Miller. Miller was the author of a 1956 paper, "The Magical Number Seven Plus or Minus Two: Some Limits on Our Capacity for Processing Information," which can be termed a seminal document of the new psychology of cognition.[77] The Center for Cognitive Studies would be a focus for some dozen years of the most significant contributors to cognitive psychology. It became the model for centers of its type around the world today.[78]

Another major contributor to cognitive psychology was Noam Chomsky. Through his linguistic theory, Chomsky played an important role in reestablishing the study of verbal behavior as something other than the simplistic behavioral representation of it as primarily learned behavior. In a book review of Skinner's *Verbal Behavior*, Chomsky sounded an early volley in the cognitive movement.[79] His theories and researches are too complicated to consider in this brief overview, but suffice it to say that his *Current Issues in Linguistic Theory* (1964) and his *Language and the Mind* (1968), along with his other publications and those of his students, helped revitalize the field of language study and with it to establish another branch of cognitive psychology.[80]

We stand too close to see whither cognitive psychology is going. It appears to be fragmenting as is so much of current psychology, but that may be because the straightforward concept of a cognitive psychology espoused by Neisser has been overcomplicated by researchers trying to stretch the term *cognitive* to fit whatever they happen to be interested in at the moment. It is possible that as the term begins to encompass everything it will end up encompassing nothing. Much of the answer will come when cognitive psychology's place in the overall rubric of cognitive science is settled.

SUMMARY

This chapter can do little more than present a thumbnail sketch of developments in American psychology and that, an incomplete one. Psychology in America exploded after World War II, altering the entire flavor of the psychological enterprise. Most of the developments were present before the war but received new unction in the 1940s and 1950s. Certainly the most significant change in American psychology has been the rise of cognitive psychology. The cognitive "revolution" may be as significant for the 1990s as the behavioral revolution initiated by John B. Watson was for the 1930s.

An important thing to note about the postwar psychologies is the degree to which they overlap with each other and share influences that themselves overlap. Whether one talks about clinical, developmental, social, industrial, personality, or cognitive psychology, all have been influenced in one way or another by psychoanalysis and by phenomenology (particularly Gestalt or Lewinian psychology). It is also important to note the degree to which the more successful developments have also involved disciplines outside of psychology such as social anthropology, engineering, or neurophysiology.

Present-day psychology is still trying to find its way. With the apparent loss by psychology to other disciplines of comparative psychology, much of engineering psychology and industrial psychology, and the neurological aspects of physiological psychology, there is justifiable concern as to what psychology will be like in another decade. Much will depend on how successful cognitive psychology is in defining itself and in preventing itself from stagnating. The primary threat to psychology's core is neuroscience. Recent introductory neuroscience texts parallel almost entirely the subject matter of introductory psychology texts but from the neurological perspective. One can only speculate about the possibility of being on the verge of a major reorganization of the old academic disciplines in which psychology could be split among neuroscience, cognitive science, and social science. Only time will tell.

NOTES

1. Albert R. Gilgen, *American Psychology Since World War II: A Profile of the Discipline* (Westport, Conn.: Greenwood Press, 1982).
2. C. Spearman, "The Proof and Measurement of Association Between Two Things," *American Journal of Psychology, 15* (1904):72–101.
3. "Student," "Probable Error of a Correlation Coefficient," *Biometrika, 6* (1908):302–310.
4. A history of this topic may be found in R. C. Bose, "Early History of Multivariate Statistical Analysis," in P. R. Krishnaiah, ed., *Multivariate Analysis—IV* (Amsterdam: North-Holland, 1977); see also Richard J. Harris, "Multivariate Statistics: When Will Experimental Psychology Catch Up?" in Sigmund Koch and David Leary, eds., *A Century of Psychology as Science* (New York: McGraw–Hill, 1985), pp. 678–697.
5. For instance, S. N. Roy, "P-statistics or Some Generalizations in Analysis of Variance Appropriate to Multivariate Problems," *Sankhya, 4* (1939):381–396.
6. Dael Wolfle, "Louis Leon Thurstone: 1887–1955," *American Journal of Psychology, 69* (1956):131–134.
7. L. L. Thurstone, "L.L. Thurstone," in E. G. Boring et al., eds., *A History of Psychology in Autobiography* (Worcester, Mass.: Clark University Press, 1952), Vol. 4, pp. 295–321.

8. L. L. Thurstone, *The Vectors of Mind: Multiple-Factor Analysis for the Isolation of Primary Traits* (Chicago: University of Chicago Press, 1935).

9. Thurstone, *Multiple-Factor Analysis: A Development and Expansion of the Vectors of Mind* (Chicago: University of Chicago Press, 1947).

10. G. W. Allport, "Gordon W. Allport," in E. G. Boring and G. Lindzey, eds., *A History of Psychology in Autobiography* (New York: Appleton–Century–Crofts, 1967), Vol. 5, pp. 3–25.

11. G. W. Allport, *Personality: A Psychological Interpretation* (New York: Henry Holt Co., 1937).

12. H. A. Murray, "Henry A. Murray," in Boring and Lindzey, eds., *A History of Psychology in Autobiography,* Vol. 5, pp. 285–310.

13. H. A. Murray, *Explorations in Personality: A Clinical and Experimental Study of Fifty Men of College Age* (New York: Oxford University Press, 1938).

14. C. D. Morgan and H. A. Murray, "A Method for Investigating Fantasies: The Thematic Apperception Test," *Archives of Neurology and Psychiatry, 34* (1935):289–306.

15. S. J. Beck et al., *Rorschach's Test:* I. *Basic Processes,* 3rd ed., II. *A Variety of Personality Pictures,* III. *Advances in Interpretation* (New York: Grune and Stratton, 1945, 1948, 1961).

16. W. H. Holtzman, J. S. Thorpe, J. D. Swartz, and E. W. Herron, *Inkblot Perception and Personality: Holtzman Inkblot Technique* (Austin: University of Texas Press, 1961).

17. C. R. Rogers, "Carl R. Rogers," in Boring and Lindzey, eds., *A History of Psychology in Autobiography,* Vol. 5, 341–384.

18. C. R. Rogers, *Client-Centered Therapy: Its Current Practice, Implications and Theory* (Boston: Houghton Mifflin, 1951).

19. C. R. Rogers, "A Theory of Therapy, Personality and Interpersonal Relationships, as Developed in the Client-Centered Framework," in S. Koch, ed., *Psychology: A Study of a Science,* Vol. 3, *Formulations of the Person and the Social Context* (New York: McGraw–Hill, 1959), pp. 184–256.

20. Carl R. Rogers, "In Retrospect: Forty-Six Years," *American Psychologist, 29* (1974):116; *Client-Centered Therapy: Its Current Practice, Implications, and Theory* (Boston: Houghton Mifflin, 1951).

21. Nevitt Sanford, "What Have We Learned About Personality?" in Koch and Leary, eds., *A Century of Psychology as Science,* p. 497.

22. Gordon Allport, "The Historical Background of Modern Social Psychology," in Gardner Lindzey, ed., *Handbook of Social Psychology,* Vol. I, *Theory and Method* (Reading, Mass.: Addison–Wesley, 1954), pp. 3–56.

23. N. Triplett, "The Dynamogenic Factors in Pacemaking and Competition," *American Journal of Psychology, 9* (1898):507–533.

24. E. A. Ross, *Social Psychology: An Outline and Source Book* (New York: Macmillan Co., 1908).

25. Gardner Murphy and Lois Barclay Murphy, *Experimental Social Psychology* (New York: Harper and Bros., 1931).

26. G. Murphy, "Gardner Murphy," in Boring and Lindzey, eds., *A History of Psychology in Autobiography,* Vol. 5, pp. 255–282.

27. G. Murphy, *Historical Introduction to Modern Psychology* (New York: Harcourt, Brace, 1929).

28. The book appeared in its second edition as G. Murphy, L. B. Murphy, and T. M. Newcomb, *Experimental Social Psychology: An Interpretation of Research upon the Socialization of the Individual* (New York: Harper and Brothers, 1937).

29. G. Murphy, *Personality: A Biosocial Approach to Origins and Structure* (New York: Harper and Brothers, 1947).

30. A. J. Marrow, *The Practical Theorist: The Life and Work of Kurt Lewin* (New York: Basic Books, 1969).

31. K. Lewin, *Principles of Topological Psychology* (New York: McGraw–Hill, 1936).

32. K. Lewin, *Field Theory in Social Science: Selected Theoretical Papers,* D. Cartwright ed., (New York: Harper and Brothers, 1951).

33. R. Barker, T. Dembo, and K. Lewin, "Frustration and Regression: An Experiment with Young Children," *University of Iowa Studies in Child Welfare, 18,* No. 386 (1941).

34. K. Lewin, R. Lippitt, and R. White, "Patterns of Aggressive Behavior in Experimentally Created Social Climates," *Journal of Social Psychology, 10* (1939):271–299.

35. John Dollard, L. W. Doob, Neal E. Miller, O. H. Mower, and Robert Sears, *Frustration and Aggression* (New Haven, Conn.: Yale University Press, 1939).

36. See E. R. Hilgard, *Psychology in America: A Historical Survey* (New York: Harcourt Brace Jovanovich, 1987), pp. 599–602 for more details on the institute.

37. Daniel Katz, "Studies in Social Psychology in World War II," *Psychological Bulletin, 48* (1951):412–419.

38. C. I. Hovland, A. A. Lumsdaine, and F.D. Sheffield, *Experiments in Mass Communication* (Studies in Social Psychology in World War II, Vol. 3) (Princeton, N.J.: Princeton University Press, 1949).

39. J.R.P. French, Jr., "The Disruption and Cohesion of Groups," *Journal of Abnormal and Social Psychology, 36* (1941):361–377.

40. Dorwin Cartwright and Alvin Zander, *Group Dynamics: Research and Theory* (Evanston, Ill.: Row, Peterson and Co., 1953).

41. Muzafer Sherif and Carolyn W. Sherif, *An Outline of Social Psychology* (New York: Harper and Bros., 1948).

42. F. Heider, "Attitudes and Cognitive Organization," *Journal of Psychology, 21* (1946):107–112.

43. Leon Festinger, *A Theory of Cognitive Dissonance* (Evanston, Ill.: Row, Peterson and Co., 1957).

44. F. Heider, *The Psychology of Interpersonal Relations* (New York: John Wiley and Sons, 1958).

45. E. E. Jones and K. E. Davis, "From Acts to Dispositions: The Attribution Process in Person Perception," in L. Berkowitz, ed., *Advances in Experimental Social Psychology,* Vol. 2 (New York: Academic Press, 1965).

46. Daniel Katz, "Social Psychology: Progress and Prospects," *American Behavioral Scientist, 21* No. 5 (1978):627–795.

47. Morris Viteles, *Industrial Psychology* (New York: W. W. Norton, 1932).

48. E. Mayo, "The Western Electric Experiment," *Human Factor, 6* (1933):1–2; *The Human Problems of an Industrial Civilization* (New York: Macmillan Co., 1933); F. J. Roethlisberger and W. J. Dickson, *Management and The Worker* (Cambridge, Mass.: Harvard University Press, 1939).

49. Jean Piaget, *The Language and Thought of the Child,* trans. M. Warden (New York: Harcourt, Brace, 1926); *Judgment and Reasoning in the Child,* trans. M. Warden (New York: Harcourt, Brace, 1928).

50. Arnold Gesell, "The Individual in Infancy," in Carl Murchison, ed., *Foundations of Experimental Psychology* (Worcester, Mass.: Clark University Press).

51. Jean Piaget, *The Psychology of Intelligence* (New York: Harcourt, Brace, 1950).

52. Erik Erikson, *Childhood and Society* (New York: W. W. Norton, 1950).

53. For an excellent review of the recent history of developmental psychology, see Hilgard, *Psychology in America,* pp. 524–571.

54. S. L. Garfield, "Psychotherapy: A 40-Year Appraisal," *American Psychologist, 36* (1981):175–176.

55. Gilgen, *American Psychology,* pp. 177–178.

56. Victor C. Raimy, *Training in Clinical Psychology* (New York: Prentice–Hall, 1950); Gilgen, *American Psychology,* p. 178.

57. Rogers puts his therapy in perspective in "A Theory of Therapy, Personality and Interpersonal Relationships as Developed in the Client-Centered Framework," in Sigmund Koch, ed., *Psychology: A Study of a Science* (New York: McGraw–Hill, 1959), Vol. 3, pp. 184–256.

58. Hans J. Eysenck, "The Effects of Psychotherapy: An Evaluation," *Journal of Consulting Psychology, 16* (1952):322.

59. Hans Strupp, "The Outcome Problem in Psychotherapy Revisited," *Psychotherapy, 1* (1963):1–13.

60. Gilgen, *American Psychology,* pp. 187–188; Rollo May, Ernest Angel, and Henri F. Ellenberger, *Existence: A New Dimension in Psychiatry and Psychology* (New York: Basic Books, 1958).

61. Gilgen, *American Psychology,* pp. 185–190.

62. Ulrich Neisser, *Cognitive Psychology* (New York: Appleton–Century–Crofts, 1966).

63. J. S. Bruner, E. Brunswik, L. Festinger, F. Heider, K.F. Muenzinger, C. E. Osgood, and D. Rapaport, *Contemporary Approaches to Cognition* (Cambridge, Mass.: Harvard University Press, 1957).

64. Jerome Bruner, J. J. Goodnow, and G. A. Austin, *A Study of Thinking* (New York: John Wiley and Sons, 1956).

65. Jerome Bruner, *In Search of Mind: Essays in Autobiography* (New York: Harper and Row, 1983), p. 120.

66. *Ibid.,* p. vii.

67. *Ibid.*

68. *Ibid.,* vii–viii.

69. Claude Shannon, "A Mathematical Model of Communication," *Bell System Technical Journal, 27* (1948):623–656.

70. Claude Shannon and W. Weaver, *The Mathematical Theory of Communication* (Urbana: University of Illinois Press, 1949).

71. Bruner, *In Search of Mind,* pp. 121–122.

72. *Ibid.,* p. viii.; Anna Freud, *The Ego and Mechanisms of Defense* (New York: International Universities Press, 1937); Gordon Allport, *Personality: A Psychological Interpretation* (New York: Holt, 1937).

73. Neisser, *Cognitive Psychology,* p. 4.

74. *Ibid.,* p. 4.

75. *Ibid.,* p. 5.

76. Jerome Bruner, *In Search of Mind,* p. 64.

77. George Miller, "The Magical Number Seven, Plus Or Minus Two: Some Limits on Our Capacity for Processing Information," *Psychological Review, 63* (1956):81–97.

78. Bruner, *In Search of Mind,* pp. 122–126.

79. Noam Chomsky, "A Review of B. F. Skinner's *Verbal Behavior,*" *Language, 35* (1959):26–58.

80. Chomsky, *Current Issues in Linguistic Theory* (The Hague: Mouton, 1964); *Language and Mind* (New York: Harcourt Brace Jovanovich, 1968).

Name Index

Note: Page numbers in roman type are for individuals mentioned in the text; page numbers in italics are for authors listed in notes. Editors of volumes are not indexed.

Subject Index